JUVENILE JUSTICE

JUVENILE JUSTICE

POLICIES, PROGRAMS, AND PRACTICES

FOURTH EDITION

ROBERT W. TAYLOR, PH.D.
The University of Texas at Dallas

ERIC J. FRITSCH, PH.D.
University of North Texas—Denton

JUVENILE JUSTICE: POLICIES, PROGRAMS, AND PRACTICES, FOURTH EDITION

Published by McGraw-Hill Education, 2 Penn Plaza, New York, NY 10121. Copyright ©2015 by McGraw-Hill Education. All rights reserved. Printed in the United States of America. Previous editions © 2011, 2007, and 2002. No part of this publication may be reproduced or distributed in any form or by any means, or stored in a database or retrieval system, without the prior written consent of The McGraw-Hill Companies, Inc., including, but not limited to, in any network or other electronic storage or transmission, or broadcast for distance learning.

Some ancillaries, including electronic and print components, may not be available to customers outside the United States.

This book is printed on acid-free paper.

1 2 3 4 5 6 7 8 9 0 DOW/DOW 1 0 9 8 7 6 5 4

ISBN 978-0-07-802656-0
MHID 0-07-802656-3

Senior Vice President, Products & Markets: *Kurt L. Strand*
Vice President, General Manager, Products & Markets: *Michael Ryan*
Vice President, Content Production & Technology Services: *Kimberly Meriwether David*
Managing Editor: *Penina Braffman*
Developmental Editor: *Nicole Bridge*
Brand Coordinator: *Adina Lonn*
Associate Marketing Manager: *Alexandra Schultz*
Director, Content Production: *Terri Schiesl*
Content Project Manager: *Mary Jane Lampe*
Buyer: *Jennifer Pickel*
Cover Designer: *Studio Montage, St. Louis, MO*
Cover Images: *Gang tattoos: Aaron Roeth Photography; Juvenile in handcuffs: Ingram Publishing; Gang women: Aaron Roeth Photography; Teen boy sitting on sidewalk: Design Pics/Don Hammond; People in alley: Brand X Pictures*
Compositor: *Laserwords Private Limited*
Typeface: *9.5/12 New Aster*
Printer: *R. R. Donnelley*

All credits appearing on page or at the end of the book are considered to be an extension of the copyright page.

Library of Congress Cataloging-in-Publication Data
Taylor, Robert W.
    Juvenile justice : policies, programs, and practices / Robert Taylor, Ph.D., The University of Texas at Dallas, Eric J. Fritsch, Ph.D.,The University of Texas at Dallas—Fourth edition.
        pages. cm.
    Summary: "Juvenile Justice: Policies, Programs and Practices provides a student-friendly introduction to the juvenile justice system. Practical application is emphasized through features that focus on policies, programs, practices and careers. The text reviews the current legal atmosphere of juvenile justice and current events that have impacted the field. "-- Provided by publisher.
    ISBN-978-0-07-802656-0 (hardback)
    1. Juvenile justice, Administration of—United States.   I. Fritsch, Eric J.   II. Title.
HV9104.T39 2011
364.360973—dc23

2014004796

The Internet addresses listed in the text were accurate at the time of publication. The inclusion of a Web site does not indicate an endorsement by the authors or McGraw-Hill, and McGraw-Hill does not guarantee the accuracy of the information presented at these sites.

www.mhhe.com

Dedication

In memory of Dr. Tory J. Caeti,
a founding author of this textbook and a great friend,
whose tragic death in 2006 left an immeasurable void in our lives.
We miss ya' Tory !

ROBERT W. TAYLOR

and

ERIC J. FRITSCH

ROBERT W. TAYLOR is professor and director of the Justice Administration and Leadership Program in the Department of Criminology at the University of Texas at Dallas. Prior to assuming this position, he was the founding director of the Caruth Police Institute. The Institute was established through a $9.5 million grant from the Communities Foundation of North Texas in January 2008, and is located within the Dallas Police Department as a part of the University of North Texas at Dallas. For nearly 15 years, Dr. Taylor was professor and chair of the Department of Criminal Justice at the University of North Texas at Denton. He has an extensive background in academic and professional criminal justice, having served as a sworn police officer and major crimes detective (in Portland, Oregon) and as an active consultant to various U.S. and international criminal justice agencies. He has authored or coauthored over one hundred and fifty articles, books, and manuscripts focusing on police administration, contemporary police problems, international and domestic terrorism, human and drug trafficking, computer fraud, and criminal justice policy and has been the recipient of nearly $15 million in external funding. Dr. Taylor was awarded the *University of North Texas Regent's Lecture Award for 2003* for his work in the Middle East, and in 2008, the Academy of Criminal Justice Sciences presented Dr. Taylor with the *O.W. Wilson Award* "in recognition of his outstanding contribution to police education, research and practice." He is an active member of the Academy of Criminal Justice Sciences and the American Society of Criminology.

ERIC J. FRITSCH is professor and chair of the Department of Criminal Justice at the University of North Texas in Denton, Texas. He has authored and coauthored several books, journal articles, book chapters, and technical reports. Many of his publications focus on juvenile justice, in particular juvenile violence. He is the founding editor of *Youth Violence and Juvenile Justice: An Interdisciplinary Journal*. His areas of interest include juvenile justice and delinquency, gangs, criminological theory, law enforcement, criminal procedure, research methods, and organizational assessment. Prior to attending graduate school, he was a police officer and a substance abuse counselor.

Brief Contents

CONTENTS

PART TWO
Theories of Juvenile Delinquency 87

CHAPTER FOUR
Choice, Deterrence, Biological, and Psychological Theories 89

CHAPTER FIVE
Social Structure, Social Process, and Social Reaction Theories 115

Contents

The Juvenile Court 243

Juveniles in the Criminal Justice System 265

CHAPTER FOURTEEN

Special Populations 393

CHAPTER FIFTEEN

Future Directions in Juvenile Justice 427

The Fourth Edition

Juvenile Justice: Policies, Programs, and Practices takes a detailed look at the juvenile justice system with a student-friendly focus. With an emphasis on practical application, this text provides comprehensive insight into how the juvenile justice system operates in the United States. The focus of this text is on presenting examples of programs, policies, and current practices in the juvenile justice system to highlight and emphasize the key concepts presented. Numerous changes have been made to the juvenile justice system over the past 25 years in response to issues of juvenile crime and problems in dealing effectively with serious habitual juvenile offenders. This text reviews these laws and discusses changes to the juvenile justice system and its operation that have occurred recently. Regardless of your stance on these issues and what should be done with juvenile offenders, a solid working knowledge of the juvenile justice system is important to understanding the broader issues of juvenile justice in the United States.

Juvenile Justice is designed to serve as a text in introductory courses on juvenile justice. This text is not just for students interested in pursuing a career in juvenile justice, however. It is also for students who simply want to learn more about this important social institution. A major theme of this book is that much of what the public "knows" about juvenile justice in the United States is myth—that is, either wrong or significantly misunderstood. Consequently, in addition to presenting current, accurate information about juvenile justice in the United States and generally accepted interpretation of historical and modern development, this book "sets the record straight" in areas where, we believe, many people are being misled.

In addition to updating the text throughout with the latest available statistics and research, including updated box items, figures, tables, and photos, this edition also features expanded discussion of some of today's most pressing issues in juvenile justice.

- Chapter 3, "Juvenile Crime, Criminals, and Victims," examines data discussion about the Violent Crime index reaching a historic low, exactly the opposite of what experts projected would happen at the turn of the millennium. The chapter also includes the analysis surrounding the paradox that while crime has been decreasing among juveniles, delinquency caseloads in our court systems have more than doubled. There is new discussion of the Monitoring the Future Program self-report survey at the University of Michigan and how it questions teens about social and ethical issues.

- Chapter 6, "Delinquency Prevention and Intervention," includes an updated Focus on Programs: the Office of Juvenile Justice and Delinquency Prevention.

- Chapter 7, "Police and Juveniles," includes a new Focus on Programs about youth outreach programs. A new Myth or Fact asks readers to consider police involvement with juvenile matters beyond arrests. New Internet Activities send students to the Dallas, Texas, PAL website to explore programs for youth and send them to the national D.A.R.E. website.

- Chapter 8, "Juvenile Law and Procedure," includes a new map, "Megan's Law: Juvenile Sex Offender Registration."

- Chapter 10, "Juveniles in the Criminal Justice System," features a new discussion of the Eighth Amendment's cruel and unusual punishment clause as it relates to juvenile justice.

- Chapter 11, "Community-Based Corrections for Juveniles," includes a new discussion about executive agencies that administer probation and a new figure, "Case Processing Overview".

- Chapter 12, "Institutional Corrections for Juveniles," has been dramatically updated to include a new discussion about public preference of rehabilitation for juvenile offenders, discussion of the Sandy Hook elementary shootings, and an examination of the presence of sexual victimization of juveniles at state-run, local, and private facilities. New features include Focus on Practice: "Arts Programs for Juvenile Offenders," and Focus on Programs, "California Works to Dismantle Its State Juvenile Justice Agency."

- Chapter 14, "Special Populations," features a new Focus on Practice: "Bullying: The *Other* School Violence," a new Focus on Policy: "Zero Tolerance," and a new Focus on Practice: "Synthetic Drugs: A New Threat for Teens." The chapter includes a new figure, "Easy Access to the Census of Juveniles in Residential Placement," and a new key term: *synthetic marijuana—K2* or *"spice."*
- Chapter 15, "Future Directions in Juvenile Justice," includes a new discussion on the recent influences on the punitive model of juvenile justice including BARJ, the economic downturn, and political agendas. There is a new section on the decentralization of state juvenile justice systems and a new discussion of intervention strategies and the economic strains that the intervention model poses. The chapter also includes a new Myth or Fact about juvenile recidivism.

Organization

This book is divided into 15 chapters organized into five parts. Part 1, "Juvenile Justice and Delinquency in the United States," introduces students to the juvenile justice system as well as juvenile crime and victims, risk and protective factors, and the history of the juvenile justice system. Part 2, "Theories of Juvenile Delinquency," focuses on explanations of juvenile delinquency as well as efforts to prevent it. Part 3, "Policing Juveniles, the Law, and the Courts," is dedicated to the role and function of the police and courts in the juvenile justice system with special attention paid to juvenile law and juveniles in the adult justice system. Part 4, "Juvenile Corrections," introduces students to the corrections system, institutions, detention centers, community corrections, and release of offenders back into the community. Part 5, "Issues in Juvenile Delinquency," is dedicated to some of the most pressing challenges facing the juvenile justice system today: gangs, violent offenders, sex offenders, the exploitation of children, and more.

Pedagogical Aids

Working together, the authors and editor have developed a learning system designed to help students get the most out of their juvenile justice course. The learning system within this text as a whole is without peer in juvenile justice textbooks. In addition to the changes already mentioned, redesigned and carefully updated tables and figures highlight and amplify the text coverage. And chapter outlines, objectives, reviews, marginal definitions, and an end-of-book glossary all help students master the material. Other innovative learning tools include:

FOCUS ON POLICY, PRACTICE, AND PROGRAMS. These boxes appear throughout the text and are used to provide in-depth information on, and examples of, policies, practices, and programs in the juvenile justice system.

CAREERS IN JUVENILE JUSTICE. These boxes focus on career options in the juvenile justice field and highlight the many options available to students interested in pursuing a career in juvenile justice.

JJ ONLINE. These inserts enable students to explore chapter topics on the Net in a directed fashion.

FYI. These sidebars present eye-opening additional information to retain students' interest and keep them thinking about what they are reading.

MYTH VS. FACT. These inserts debunk common misconceptions about the juvenile justice system and alert students to the need to question what they see in the media.

We are especially excited about our comprehensive end-of-chapter review sections. In these sections, we provide every kind of review and study tool students could need:

- *Summary by Chapter Objectives*—a terrific study tool, because it is organized into sections that mirror the chapter-opening objectives exactly.
- *Key Terms*—a comprehensive list of the terms defined in the chapter, complete with page references to make it easy for students to go back and review further.
- *Review Questions*—study questions that allow students to test their knowledge and prepare for exams.
- *Hands-On Activities*—unique experiential exercises that enable students to broaden their understanding of chapter material by taking it to the next level.
- *Internet Exercises*—still more Internet-based exercises for today's Internet-oriented learner.
- *Critical Thinking Exercises*—these exercises challenge students to think about and apply chapter concepts.

Supplements Package

As a full-service publisher of quality educational products, McGraw-Hill does much more than just sell textbooks. The company creates and publishes an extensive array of print, video, and digital supplements for students and instructors. This edition of *Juvenile Justice* is accompanied by a comprehensive supplements package:

FOR THE STUDENT

- The Online Learning Center contains flashcards that can be used to master vocabulary, quizzes with feedback that students can use to study for exams, and more. Please go to www.mhhe.com/taylorjj4e.

FOR THE INSTRUCTOR

Password-protected instructor resources can be found at www.mhhe.com/taylorjj4e and include the following:

- Instructor's Manual/Testbank—detailed chapter outlines, key terms, overviews, lecture notes, and a complete testbank
- Computerized Testbank—easy-to-use computerized testing program for both Windows and Macintosh computers
- PowerPoint Slides—complete, chapter-by-chapter slide shows featuring text, art, figures, and tables
- Online Learning Center—password-protected access to downloadable state supplements and other important instructor support materials and additional resources.

Please ask your publisher's representative for access information.

Acknowledgments

The authors and editors would like to thank the following reviewers for their valuable contributions to the revision of *Juvenile Justice*. Thanks to each of you for lending us your time and professionalism in helping make this a better book.

Rhonda Allen
California State University–Chico
Sonya Brown
Tarrant County College
Darrel K. Mills
Pima Community College
Jeffrey B. Shouldice
Kalamazoo Valley Community College

In closing we would like to acknowledge the support we received from the McGraw-Hill staff: Our developmental editor Nicole Bridge, our managing editor Penina Braffman, our project manager Mary Jane Lampe, our designer Margarite Reynolds, and the rest of the team. Lastly, we would like to give a special thanks to Dr. Taylor's assistant, Ms. Jennifer Davis-Lamm, for all her hard work, help and assistance.

THE JUVENILE JUSTICE SYSTEM

CHAPTER ONE

Chapter Outline

Chapter Objectives

After completing this chapter, you should be able to:

1. Describe the jurisdiction of the juvenile court.

2. Explain what is meant by delinquency.

3. Explain what is meant by status offenses.

4. Compare the ways in which the various states define a juvenile.

5. Identify and define the unique terms used in the juvenile justice system.

6. Outline the three major steps in the juvenile justice process.

7. Describe the five decision points in the juvenile justice process.

8. Compare and contrast the juvenile and criminal justice systems.

Origins of the Juvenile Justice System

Before the establishment of the **juvenile justice system,** courts and judges treated juveniles as adults and, in many instances, juvenile offenders received the same punishment as adults. There was only one system of justice in the United States, and all offenders were processed through it without regard to age. Under common law doctrine, the legal system the American colonists brought from England, a juvenile age seven or older could receive the same punishment as an adult. Juveniles were housed in prisons with adults and sometimes received the death penalty; however, evidence shows that the most severe punishments were rarely given to juveniles.[1] The establishment of separate institutions to confine juvenile offenders separately from adults occurred in the early 1800s. In 1899, the first juvenile court was founded in Cook County, Illinois.

Why should there be a separate system of justice for juvenile offenders? Those who were concerned about the treatment of juveniles in the adult system argued that because juveniles are less mature than adults and cannot develop the same level of intent as adults, they should be handled differently. In fact, because of their immaturity, it was believed that some juveniles could more easily be rehabilitated.

Based on assumptions that juveniles are less mature than adults, incapable of the same level of intent as adults, and more easily rehabilitated, a separate system of justice was developed in the late 1800s to deal exclusively with juveniles. This system is known as the juvenile justice system. Eventually, every state developed a separate juvenile justice system with its own set of courts and institutions.

The juvenile justice system is comprised of those agencies whose primary duty is to manage juvenile offenders. Today, most major police departments have officers whose sole responsibility is to deal with juvenile delinquency. In fact, because of recent school shooting incidents, many departments have officers regularly assigned to local elementary and secondary schools in their communities. In addition, every state has juvenile courts with their own judges, probation departments, and prosecutors. Furthermore, every state has separate places such as detention centers and institutions in order to confine juveniles apart from adults.

The juvenile justice system was founded on the belief of **parents patriae,** roughly translated into "state as parent." The state, acting through a juvenile court judge, can act in the role of parent for the juvenile when parents are deemed incapable or unwilling to control their children. Therefore, the juvenile justice system was designed to do whatever is in the best interest of the juvenile, just as a parent should. The juvenile justice system has evolved significantly from its origins, which will be discussed in later chapters.

This chapter describes the juvenile justice system. Definitions of a juvenile and the types of cases confronting the juvenile justice system are given. The definitions of terms used exclusively in the juvenile justice system, a brief overview of the major steps in the juvenile justice process, and an explanation of how juveniles are typically processed will be provided. The similarities and differences between the adult and juvenile justice systems are also discussed.

1.1 SELF-CHECK

What assumptions led to the establishment of a separate system of justice for juvenile offenders?

juvenile justice system The system of agencies that is designed to handle juvenile offenders.

parents patriae A legal doctrine in which the state plays the role of a parent.

jurisdiction The authority granted by law to hear a case.

Juvenile Court Jurisdiction

Jurisdiction is the authority granted by law to hear a case. State law, in what is commonly referred to as a juvenile or family code, specifies the jurisdiction of the juvenile court. The concept of jurisdiction involves the answers to two questions:

1. For what acts committed by juveniles does the juvenile court have jurisdiction?
2. What age does an individual have to be in order to be under juvenile court jurisdiction?

DEFINING DELINQUENCY

Juvenile **delinquency** is any behavior that is prohibited by the juvenile law of a state. The juvenile court has jurisdiction over all acts of delinquency. Each state's legislature defines delinquency in that particular state. However, delinquency generally consists of two categories. The first category of delinquency is any act committed by a juvenile that would be defined as a crime if committed by an adult. Therefore, an act of delinquency in juvenile court is the same as a crime in adult court. Offenses such as theft, burglary, assault, and robbery are acts of delinquency, just as they are adult crimes. Even without knowing these definitions, when people think of delinquency, they usually think of acts committed by juveniles that would be considered crimes if committed by adults. The second category of delinquency includes acts known as **status offenses.** A status offense would not be considered a crime if committed by an adult but would be considered an act of delinquency if committed by a juvenile. Status offenses include running away from home, skipping school (truancy), violating curfew, incorrigibility or ungovernability (not obeying one's parents), illegal purchase of alcohol, smoking tobacco, and underage drinking.

Typical juvenile court in the United States. *How is the picture of a juvenile court similar to or different from pictures you have seen of adult courts? How does the picture differ from your original perception of what a juvenile court looks like?*

About one-half of all the states classify status offenders as delinquents. The other states have established categories that distinguish juvenile delinquents from status offenders. These states classify status offenders as:

- CHINS or CINS—children in need of supervision
- PINS—persons in need of supervision
- JINS—juveniles in need of supervision
- MINS—minors in need of supervision

Two reasons for separating juvenile delinquents from status offenders are to remove the stigma of being classified as a juvenile delinquent from status offenders and to demonstrate that these juveniles have special problems and needs, but are not criminal in nature.

The term *juvenile delinquency* describes acts that range from truancy to murder. With such a range of acts considered delinquent by law, almost all juveniles might be classified as delinquents at one time or another, because many young people have committed at least one act of delinquency. Although almost all juveniles commit delinquent acts, most are not processed in the juvenile justice system for these offenses because they are never taken into custody for their actions.

Frequently, the juvenile court has jurisdiction over several matters in addition to juvenile delinquency, including child abuse and neglect cases, adoption, termination of parental rights, child custody, and child support. Some states separate these matters into family courts, child welfare courts, and probate courts. The focus of this book, however, is on the court's role in matters of delinquency.

DEFINING A JUVENILE

Just as each state has defined delinquency, each state has defined the term juvenile. As far as the law is concerned, the only difference between a juvenile and an adult is age. Similarly, age is the only difference between a delinquent and

delinquency Any behavior that is prohibited by the juvenile law of a state.

status offense An act of delinquency committed by a juvenile that would not be considered a crime if committed by an adult

Running away is a status offense. *What role do you think the juvenile justice system (including police, courts, and corrections) should play in dealing with runaways?*

a criminal. Therefore, if an individual is within a certain age range, he or she is classified as a **juvenile** and subject to juvenile court jurisdiction. Each state's legislature determines the minimum and maximum age at which a person is considered a juvenile. If an individual is above the maximum age, he or she is considered an adult and is processed in the **criminal justice system.**

Although it varies by state, the most common maximum age of a juvenile is 17. Therefore, in states that classify 17 as the **maximum age of juvenile court jurisdiction,** a 17-year-old who commits an offense is processed in juvenile court, while an 18-year-old who commits the same offense is processed in adult court. Figure 1.1 shows the maximum age of juvenile court jurisdiction by state. As shown, most states do define the maximum age of juvenile court jurisdiction as age 17. However, the maximum age of juvenile court jurisdiction

juvenile An individual who falls within a specified age range and is subject to the jurisdiction of the juvenile court.

criminal justice system The system of agencies that is designed to manage adult offenders.

maximum age of juvenile court jurisdiction The upper age limit for which the juvenile court may hear a case.

FIGURE 1.1	Maximum Age of Juvenile Court Jurisdiction by State
AGE	STATES
15	New York, North Carolina
16	Georgia, Louisiana, Massachusetts, Michigan, Missouri, New Hampshire, South Carolina, Texas, Wisconsin
17	Alabama, Alaska, Arizona, Arkansas, California, Colorado, Connecticut, Delaware, District of Columbia, Florida, Hawaii, Idaho, Illinois Indiana, Iowa, Kansas, Kentucky, Maine, Maryland, Minnesota, Mississippi, Montana, Nebraska, Nevada, New Jersey, New Mexico, North Dakota, Ohio, Oklahoma, Oregon, Pennsylvania, Rhode Island, South Dakota, Tennessee, Utah, Vermont, Virginia, Washington, West Virginia, Wyoming

Source: OJJDP Statistical Briefing Book. Online. Available: http://www.ojjdp.gov/ojstatbb/structure_process/qa4101.asp?qaDate=2011. Released on December 17, 2012.

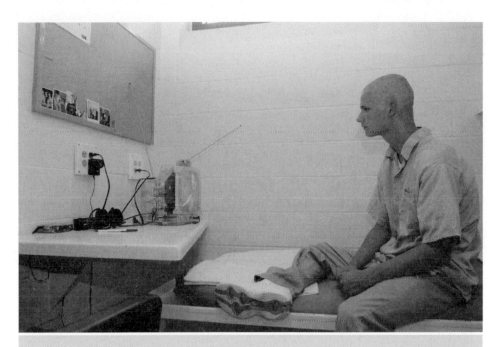

The juvenile court has jurisdiction over acts of delinquency. *What factors do you think lead youth to commit delinquent acts? What can be done to prevent delinquency?*

in two states (New York and North Carolina) is 15. In these states, when individuals 15 years of age or younger commit an offense, they are processed in the juvenile justice system, while those 16 years of age or older are processed in the criminal justice system. In 10 other states, the maximum age of juvenile court jurisdiction is set at 16.

As far as state and federal law and processing in the justice system are concerned, there is not a universally agreed upon age as to when a person stops being a juvenile and becomes an adult. One can easily see that, as far as justice system processing is concerned, there is no magic age at which an individual becomes a mature adult, capable of making adult decisions. In Texas, a 17-year-old who commits an offense is handled in adult court because the maximum age of juvenile court jurisdiction in Texas is 16. On the other hand, if the same juvenile travels to California and commits the same offense while still 17 years of age, the individual would be handled in juvenile court because the maximum age of juvenile court jurisdiction in California is 17.

Every state has a maximum age of juvenile court jurisdiction, but not every state has a specified **minimum age of juvenile court jurisdiction** (see Figure 1.2). Individuals who are younger than the minimum age of juvenile court jurisdiction are believed to lack the ability to develop intent and to know right from wrong. Therefore, these individuals cannot be processed in the juvenile justice system, regardless of the act they commit. Under common law doctrine, individuals under age 7 were presumed to be unable to develop intent and therefore could not be prosecuted and punished for their actions. States that do set a minimum age of juvenile court jurisdiction usually set the age between 6 and 10.[2] For example, the minimum age of juvenile court jurisdiction in New York, Massachusetts,

Myth	Fact
The term juvenile is defined the same way in each state.	How the term juvenile is defined varies from state to state. Source: OJJDP Statistical Briefing Book. Online. Available: http://www.ojjdp.gov/ojstatbb/structure_process/qa4101.asp?qaDate=2011. Released on December 17, 2012.

minimum age of juvenile court jurisdiction The lower age limit for which the juvenile court may hear a case

FIGURE 1.2	Minimum Age of Juvenile Court Jurisdiction by State
AGE	**STATE**
6	North Carolina
7	Maryland, Massachusetts, New York
8	Arizona
10	Arkansas, Colorado, Kansas, Louisiana, Minnesota, Mississippi, Pennsylvania, South Dakota, Texas, Vermont, Wisconsin
No minimum age specified	Alabama, Alaska, California, Connecticut, Delaware, District of Columbia, Florida, Georgia, Hawaii, Idaho, Illinois, Indiana, Iowa, Kentucky, Maine, Michigan, Missouri, Montana, Nebraska, Nevada, New Hampshire, New Jersey, New Mexico, North Dakota, Ohio, Oklahoma, Oregon, Rhode Island, South Carolina, Tennessee, Utah, Virginia, Washington, West Virginia, Wyoming

Source: OJJDP Statistical Briefing Book. Online. Available: http://www.ojjdp.gov/ojstatbb/structure_process/qa4101.asp?qaDate=2011. Released on December 17, 2012.

and Maryland is 7, while the minimum age is 10 in states such as Colorado and Texas. North Carolina has the lowest minimum age of juvenile court jurisdiction (6 years of age).

In those states that set a minimum age of juvenile court jurisdiction, individuals who are younger than the minimum age are not subject to juvenile court jurisdiction. They cannot be processed in juvenile court regardless of the offense committed and cannot be held liable for their actions. For example, the minimum age of juvenile court jurisdiction in Colorado is 10 years. In Colorado, an individual younger than that age cannot formulate intent and therefore, cannot be processed in the juvenile justice system if he or she commits an offense. Therefore, if a 9-year-old committed murder, the juvenile justice system would not have jurisdiction over the case. The juvenile would not be incarcerated for the action but would be released to the custody of his or her parents. If the parents are deemed unfit, the Department of Human Services could remove the child from the parents' home and place the child in a foster home, but the juvenile court could not confine the individual for the action.

1.2 SELF-CHECK

1. What is a status offender?
2. What is the most common maximum age of juvenile court jurisdiction?

The Language of Juvenile Justice

One of the goals of the juvenile justice system, when it separated from the criminal justice system, was the rehabilitation of juvenile offenders. Because the stigma attached to juveniles who were labeled as criminals interfered with the rehabilitation process, the juvenile justice system needed to be distanced as much as possible from the criminal justice system. In order to accomplish this, a different set of terms is used in the juvenile justice system. Each term has a companion term in the adult system. For example, delinquent acts in the juvenile justice system essentially mean the same as crimes in the criminal justice system. Similarly, the term *delinquent* essentially means the same as criminal. Figure 1.3 gives a list of defined terms used in the juvenile justice system and the companion terms used in the criminal justice system.

1.3 SELF-CHECK

Why was a separate set of terms established for use in the juvenile justice system?

FIGURE 1.3	Comparison of Terms Used in the Juvenile Justice System and in the Criminal Justice System

JUVENILE JUSTICE SYSTEM TERM	CRIMINAL JUSTICE SYSTEM TERM
Adjudicated delinquent—Found to have engaged in delinquent conduct	Conviction
Adjudication hearing—A hearing to determine whether there is evidence beyond a reasonable doubt to support the allegations against the juvenile	Trial
Aftercare—Supervision of a juvenile after release from an institution	Parole
Commitment—Decision by a juvenile court judge to send the adjudicated juvenile to an institution	Sentence to prison
Delinquent act—A behavior committed by a juvenile that would have been a crime if committed by an adult	Crime
Delinquent—A juvenile who has been adjudicated of a delinquent act in juvenile court	Criminal
Detention—Short-term secure confinement of a juvenile for the protection of the juvenile or for the protection of society	Confinement in jail
Detention center—A facility designed for short-term secure confinement of a juvenile prior to court disposition or execution of a court order	Jail
Disposition—The sanction imposed on a juvenile who has been adjudicated in juvenile court	Sentence
Disposition hearing—A hearing held after a juvenile has been adjudicated	Sentencing hearing
Institution—A facility designed for long-term secure confinement of a juvenile after adjudication (also referred to as a training school)	Prison
Petition—A document that states the allegations against a juvenile and requests a juvenile court to adjudicate the juvenile	Indictment
Taken into custody—The action on the part of a police officer to obtain custody of a juvenile accused of committing a delinquent act	Arrest

Overview of the Juvenile Justice System

The ways juveniles are processed in the juvenile justice system vary greatly among states and even within the same state. Each state has its own juvenile code that specifies the laws and procedures of the system in that state. However, because of local practice and tradition, the processing of juvenile offenders varies from state to state and even from county to county. Therefore, it is difficult to describe precisely how juveniles are processed through the juvenile justice system. With these variations in mind, an overview of the major steps in the juvenile justice system follows. Figure 1.4 provides a graphical display of the major steps in the juvenile justice system.

LAW ENFORCEMENT AND OTHER REFERRAL SOURCES

A juvenile enters the formal juvenile justice system by being referred to juvenile court. Two main sources of referrals to juvenile court are:

1. law enforcement agencies
2. others such as parents, victims, schools, and probation officers

Law enforcement agencies refer the vast majority of cases alleging that a juvenile has committed a delinquent act. Not every juvenile that a law enforcement agency takes into custody is referred to juvenile court for further action. When a law enforcement officer takes a juvenile into custody, the officer frequently

JUVENILE JUSTICE ONLINE

Juvenile Arrests 2009
Go to **www.ojjdp.gov/pubs/236477.pdf**
What conclusions can be drawn about trends in juvenile arrests?

FIGURE 1.4   **The Juvenile Justice System**

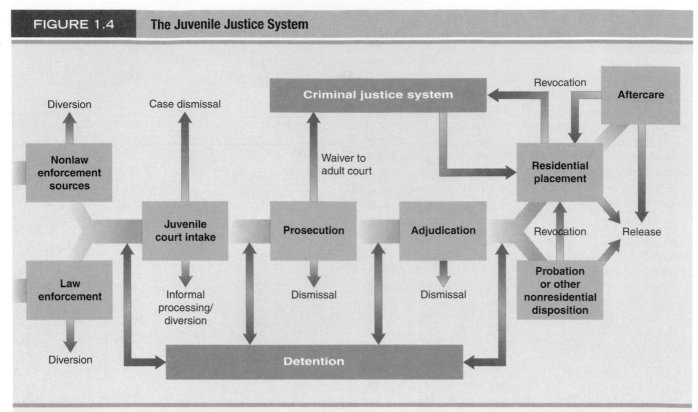

Source: This figure is adapted from Howard N. Snyder and Melissa Sickmund, *Juvenile Offenders and Victims, 2006 National Report*, Pittsburgh, PA: National Center for Juvenile Justice, 2006.

1.9 Million Arrests

Law enforcement agencies in the United States made 1.9 million arrests of persons under age 18 in 2009.

SOURCE: Charles Puzzanchera and Benjamin Adams. Juvenile Arrests 2009. Washington DC: Office of Juvenile Justice and Delinquency Prevention. 2011.

diversion A procedure by which a juvenile is removed from the juvenile justice process and provided with treatment services.

intake The procedure by which juvenile court staff decide whether to process the case further in court, handle the case informally, or dismiss the case.

decides whether to send the case further into the juvenile justice system or to divert the case out of the system—many times into **diversion** programs. An officer makes the decision after speaking with the victim, the juvenile, and the parents. In 2009, about 22 percent of all juveniles taken into custody by police officers were handled within law enforcement agencies. In some of those cases, juveniles were placed in a diversion program in order to receive some services. The remaining juveniles taken into custody were referred to juvenile court for further action in the case.[3]

JUVENILE COURT

The process in juvenile court involves three distinct procedures: intake, prosecution, and adjudication. Each step in the juvenile court process is briefly described in this section.

JUVENILE COURT INTAKE After a case has been referred to juvenile court, it is sent to **intake.** Intake is usually the responsibility of the juvenile probation department or the prosecutor's office. At this point in the juvenile court process, an important decision is made. The decision usually involves three alternatives:

1. dismiss the case against the juvenile and release the individual to his or her parents
2. handle the matter informally
3. refer the case further into the juvenile justice system for formal intervention by the court[4]

Cases that are dismissed at intake usually involve minor offenses or first-time offenders. They often lack enough evidence to support the allegations against the juvenile. In 2009, 19 percent of all delinquency cases were dismissed at intake.[5]

An additional 27 percent of all cases referred to juvenile court are handled informally at intake, with juveniles agreeing to some sort of voluntary sanction.[6] In many instances, the juvenile agrees to complete certain requirements (determined by juvenile court personnel) in exchange for having the case handled informally and not processed further in the system. The juvenile is typically required to pay **victim restitution,** complete a drug counseling program, perform **community service,** attend school, or some other related requirement. If the juvenile completes the requirements, then nothing further occurs with the case (that is, the case is dismissed). This process is sometimes called **informal probation.**[7] However, if the juvenile does not complete the requirements, then the case can be sent to juvenile court for further processing within the juvenile justice system.

When juveniles are processed further in the system, an intake officer decides whether the juvenile should be placed in detention or released to the community. Most juveniles are not held in a detention center prior to adjudication; however, a juvenile is likely to be detained (1) if he or she is determined to be a threat to the community; (2) if he or she will be in danger if returned to the community; or (3) if he or she is a flight risk and may not appear at the adjudication hearing.[8] In 2009, juveniles were detained in one of every five cases.[9]

Law enforcement is the most common referral source to juvenile court. *What factors do you think impact an officer's decision to take youth into custody and refer them to juvenile court?*

Schools serve as referral sources to juvenile court. *What offenses that occur in school are most likely to be referred to juvenile court?*

victim restitution A sanction by which a juvenile offender pays the victim for the harm done.

community service A sanction requiring a juvenile offender to perform a predetermined number of hours of volunteer work.

informal probation A process by which a juvenile agrees to meet certain requirements in exchange for dismissing a case.

Juvenile court adjudication is a major step in the juvenile court process. *What decisions are made during adjudication?*

waiver to adult court The process through which a juvenile court relinquishes jurisdiction over the juvenile offender and the case is processed in adult court.

adjudication Decision by a juvenile court judge that a juvenile committed the delinquent act.

PROSECUTION Once an intake officer decides to process the juvenile further in the system, a prosecutor receives the case. The prosecutor decides whether to file a petition in juvenile court. The petition states the allegations against the juvenile and asks the juvenile court to adjudicate the juvenile as delinquent. If the prosecutor chooses not to file a petition in the case, the case is dismissed at that time. A prosecutor may also have the option to waive the juvenile to the criminal justice system for prosecution. This process is known as **waiver to adult court,** certification, or transfer, and involves a juvenile court's relinquishing its jurisdiction over the offender and allowing a juvenile to be sent to adult court for prosecution. Once waived to adult court, the juvenile is treated as an adult and if convicted may be eligible for the same punishments as adults, excluding the death penalty. In addition, juveniles are not eligible to receive life without the possibility of parole for nonhomicidal offenses. The prosecutor is usually the individual who starts the process of waiving a juvenile to adult court.

ADJUDICATION If a prosecutor files a petition against a juvenile alleging delinquent conduct, then the next step in the process is **adjudication.** In 2009, juvenile courts in the United States handled approximately 1.5 million cases in which a juvenile was charged with a delinquent offense that would have been a crime if committed by an adult.[10] From 1985 through 1997, the number of delinquency cases climbed steadily (63 percent increase) and from 1997 through 2009, the delinquency caseload dropped 20 percent. However, juvenile courts handled 30 percent more cases in 2009 than in 1985.[11] Adjudication hearings are held in juvenile court to determine if the juvenile committed the offense. They are the trial stage of the juvenile justice process. Usually, a

CAREERS IN JUVENILE JUSTICE

Juvenile Court Referee

Juvenile court judges must tend to a large volume of cases on a daily basis. In order to assist with the workload, referees are frequently appointed by the juvenile court judge to assist with the duties of the court. Referees are sometimes called commissioners or masters. For example, they are called referees in Michigan, masters in Delaware, and commissioners in Missouri.

The local governing body over the juvenile court typically approves of the use of referees in their jurisdiction. Referees are usually attorneys (but not always) and are appointed by the juvenile court judge. The position is full-time in most jurisdictions.

The duties of a referee vary from jurisdiction to jurisdiction, but the primary responsibility of the referee is usually to hear cases and tend to preadjudication hearings

such as detention hearings and arraignments. The referee also presides over adjudication hearings involving less serious cases so that the juvenile court judge can focus on more serious felony offenses. Referees are typically prohibited from conducting waiver hearings or jury trials. In some jurisdictions, they are prohibited from hearing any cases that involve felony offenses or may lead to the institutionalization of the juvenile.

Critical Thinking

Research the juvenile court structure and process in your own state and find out whether only attorneys are allowed to become referees. What other professional backgrounds might prepare an individual to become a referee?

judge determines if a juvenile committed an offense, but in some states, juries are occasionally used in juvenile court.

DISPOSITION

After a juvenile has been deemed delinquent, a juvenile court judge will provide a disposition in the case. The disposition frequently involves probation or residential placement.

PROBATION OR OTHER NONRESIDENTIAL DISPOSITIONS

The most common disposition in juvenile court is probation. **Probation** allows a juvenile to remain in the community as long as he or she abides by certain conditions of probation. Many times, probation orders require a juvenile to attend counseling programs (for example, drug counseling), to perform community service, and to pay victim restitution. The probation term is usually for a specified period of time (for example, one year). If the juvenile successfully abides by the conditions of probation for the specified period of time, then the case is completed and no further action in the case is warranted. However, if the juvenile does not abide by the conditions of probation, the probationary sentence can be revoked and the juvenile may be placed in a residential facility.

The prosecutor represents the state in cases against juveniles. *What decisions are made by the prosecutor?*

RESIDENTIAL PLACEMENT

Another disposition involves residential placement, which means a juvenile is sent to an institution, camp, ranch, or group home. The placement may be for a specified period of time, or it may be indeterminate. In 2009, 27 percent of the juveniles adjudicated delinquent were placed in a residential facility.[12] The facility may be a ranch-type environment or an institution-like environment and may be publicly or privately operated. Once a juvenile is released from a residential placement, the juvenile is often required to serve a period of aftercare. The juvenile continues to be under the supervision of the juvenile corrections department, but if the juvenile does not follow the terms of release from the residential facility, then the juvenile may have his or her aftercare revoked and be recommitted to the facility.

There are two circumstances in which a juvenile in a residential placement may be sent to the criminal justice system for confinement:

1. If the offender commits a crime while in the facility and is old enough to be classified as an adult in the state, then the individual may be sent to prison if convicted in the criminal justice system for the offense. For example, if an 18-year-old is confined in an institution and murders another person in the institution, then the individual will probably be sent to the criminal justice system for processing and incarcerated in prison since the individual is now an adult under state law (that is, age 18).

2. The individual may be sent to the criminal justice system if the individual is subject to blended sentencing. Blended sentencing involves the imposition of juvenile and/or correctional sanctions for serious and violent juvenile offenders who have been processed in the juvenile or adult court. (Blended sentencing will be discussed in detail in Chapter 10.)

1.4 SELF-CHECK

What is the most common disposition in juvenile court?

JUVENILE JUSTICE ONLINE

Juveniles in Residential Placement, 2010
Go to **www.ojjdp.gov/pubs/241060.pdf**
Read the report and write a two-page summary. In the summary, be sure to include comments on what you found most interesting about the report.

probation A disposition imposed by the court allowing the adjudicated offender to remain in the community as long as the offender abides by certain conditions.

Comparison of Juvenile and Criminal Justice Systems

There are many similarities and differences between the juvenile justice system and the criminal justice system, but not all apply to each state or jurisdiction because of the variations in the juvenile justice system mentioned previously.

Figure 1.5 illustrates the basic similarities and differences between the juvenile and criminal justice systems. The first column, entitled "Juvenile Justice System," lists the characteristics that are unique in the juvenile justice system. These are the characteristics of the juvenile justice system that differ from those of the criminal justice system. The second column, "Common Ground," displays the characteristics similar in both the juvenile and the criminal justice systems. The third column, "Criminal Justice System," lists characteristics unique to the adult criminal justice system. These are features of the criminal justice system that do not exist in the juvenile justice system.

The figure is also divided into eight categories. The similarities and differences between the juvenile and criminal justice systems are presented for each category.

Myth / Fact

Myth

The juvenile and criminal justice systems are the same, only the ages of the offenders differ.

Fact

There are numerous differences between the juvenile and criminal justice systems.

Source: Howard N. Snyder, and Melissa Sickmund. *Juvenile Offenders and Victims: 1999 National Report*. Washington, DC: Office of Juvenile Justice and Delinquency Prevention, 1999.

1.5 SELF-CHECK

Do the similarities and differences between the juvenile justice system and criminal justice system apply to every jurisdiction?

Juveniles are sometimes placed in halfway houses prior to or after institutionalization. *How does the picture of this halfway house differ from your original perception of residential placement facilities for juveniles?*

FIGURE 1.5	Comparison of the Juvenile Justice and the Criminal Justice Systems	
JUVENILE JUSTICE SYSTEM	**COMMON GROUND**	**CRIMINAL JUSTICE SYSTEM**
OPERATING ASSUMPTIONS		
• Youth behavior is malleable. • Rehabilitation is usually a viable goal. • Youth are in families and not independent.	• Community protection is a primary goal. • Law violators must be held accountable. • Constitutional rights apply.	• Sanctions should be proportional to the offense. • General deterrence works. • Rehabilitation is not a primary goal.
PREVENTION		
• Many specific delinquency prevention activities (e.g., school, church, recreation) are used. • Prevention is intended to change individual behavior and is often focused on reducing risk factors and increasing protective factors in the individual, family, and community.	• Educational approaches are taken to specific behaviors (e.g. drunk driving and drug use).	• Prevention activities are generalized and are aimed at deterrence (e.g., Crime Watch).
LAW ENFORCEMENT		
• Specialized "juvenile" units are used. • Some additional behaviors are prohibited (truancy, running away, curfew violations). • Some limitations are placed on public access to information. • A significant number of youth are diverted away from the juvenile justice system, often into alternative programs.	• Jurisdiction involves the full range of criminal behavior. • Constitutional and procedural safeguards exist. • Both reactive and proactive approaches (targeted at offense types, neighborhoods, etc.) are used. • Community policing strategies are employed.	• Open public access to all information is required. • Law enforcement exercises discretion to divert offenders out of the criminal justice system.
INTAKE—PROSECUTION		
• In many instances, juvenile court intake, not the prosecutor, decides what cases to file. • The decision to file a petition for court action is based on both social and legal factors. • A significant portion of cases are diverted from formal case processing. • Intake or the prosecutor diverts cases from formal processing to services operated by the juvenile court, prosecutor's office, or outside agencies.	• Probable cause must be established. • The prosecutor acts on behalf of the State.	• Plea bargaining is common. • The prosecution decision is based largely on legal facts. • Prosecution is valuable in building history for subsequent offenses. • Prosecution exercises discretion to withhold charges or divert offenders out of the criminal justice system.
DETENTION—JAIL/LOCKUP		
• Juveniles may be detained for their own protection or the community's protection. • Juveniles may not be confined with adults unless there is "sight and sound separation."	• Accused offenders may be held in custody to ensure their appearance in court. • Detention alternatives of home or electronic detention are used.	• Accused individuals have the right to apply for bond/bail release.
ADJUDICATION—CONVICTION		
• Juvenile court proceedings are "quasi-civil" (not criminal) and may be confidential. • If guilt is established, the youth is adjudicated delinquent regardless of offense. • Right to jury trial is not afforded in all states.	• Standard of "proof beyond a reasonable doubt" is required. • Rights to be represented by an attorney, to confront witnesses, and to remain silent are afforded. • Appeals to a higher court are allowed. • Experimentation with specialized courts (i.e., drug courts, gun courts) is under way.	• Defendants have a constitutional right to a jury trial. • Guilt must be established on individual offenses charged for conviction. • All proceedings are open.

JUVENILE JUSTICE SYSTEM	COMMON GROUND	CRIMINAL JUSTICE SYSTEM
DISPOSITION—SENTENCING		
• Disposition decisions are based on individual and social factors, offense severity, and youth's offense history. • Dispositional philosophy includes a significant rehabilitation component. • Many dispositional alternatives are operated by the juvenile court. • Dispositions cover a wide range of community-based and residential services. • Disposition orders may be directed to people other than the offender (e.g., parents). • Disposition may be indeterminate, based on progress demonstrated by the youth.	• Decisions are influenced by current offense, offending history, and social factors. • Decisions hold offenders accountable. • Decisions may give consideration to victims (e.g., restitution and "no contact" orders). • Decisions may not be cruel or unusual.	• Sentencing decisions are bound primarily by the severity of the current offense and by the offender's criminal record. • Sentencing philosophy is based largely on proportionality and punishment. • Sentence is often determinate, based largely on offense.
AFTERCARE—PAROLE		
• Function combines surveillance and reintegration activities (e.g., family, school, work).	• The behavior of individuals released from correctional settings is monitored. • Violation of conditions can result in reincarceration.	• Function is primarily surveillance and reporting to monitor illicit behavior.

Source: Howard N. Snyder and Melissa Sickmund. *Juvenile Offenders and Victims: 1999 National Report.* Washington, DC: Office of Juvenile Justice and Delinquency Prevention, 1999.

1. Describe the jurisdiction of the juvenile court

The juvenile court has jurisdiction over acts of delinquency, which describe any behavior a juvenile commits that would be a crime if committed by an adult. In addition, delinquency typically includes status offenses. A status offense is any act committed by a juvenile that would not be considered a crime if committed by an adult. Each state defines the age range of the term juvenile, but typically it is a person under age 18.

2. Explain what is meant by delinquency

Delinquency is any behavior that is prohibited by the juvenile law of the state.

3. Explain what is meant by status offenses

A status offense is an act committed by a juvenile that would not be considered a crime if committed by an adult, such as running away from home, truancy, violating curfew, and underage drinking.

4. Compare the ways in which the various states define a juvenile

Each state legislature determines the minimum and maximum ages at which a person is defined as a juvenile. The most common maximum age of a juvenile is 17, while some states set the maximum age at 15 or 16. Not every state has a specified minimum age of juvenile court jurisdiction. Some states do not set a minimum age, but those that do usually set the age between ages 6 and 10.

5. Identify and define the unique terms used in the juvenile justice system

Adjudicated delinquent or found to have engaged in delinquent conduct—Decision by a juvenile court judge that a juvenile committed the delinquent act (same as conviction in criminal justice system).

Adjudication hearing—A hearing to determine whether there is evidence beyond a reasonable doubt to support the allegations against a juvenile (same as trial in criminal justice system).

Aftercare—Supervision of a juvenile after release from an institution (same as parole in criminal justice system).

Commitment—Decision by a juvenile court judge to send an adjudicated juvenile to an institution (same as sentence to prison in criminal justice system).

Delinquent—A juvenile who has been adjudicated of a delinquent act in juvenile court (same as criminal in criminal justice system).

Delinquent act—An act committed by a juvenile that would have been a crime if committed by an adult (same as crime in the criminal justice system).

Detention—Short-term secure confinement of a juvenile for the protection of the juvenile or protection of society (same as confinement in jail in criminal justice system).

Detention center—A facility designed for short-term secure confinement of a juvenile prior to court disposition or execution of a court order (same as jail in criminal justice system).

Disposition—The sanction imposed on a juvenile who has been adjudicated in juvenile court (same as sentence in criminal justice system).

Disposition hearing—A hearing held after a juvenile has been adjudicated delinquent to determine what sanction should be imposed on the juvenile (same as sentencing hearing in criminal justice system).

Institution—A facility designed for long-term secure confinement of a juvenile after adjudication; also referred to as a training school (same as prison in criminal justice system).

Petition—A document that states the allegations against a juvenile and requests the juvenile court to adjudicate the juvenile (same as indictment in criminal justice system).

Taken into custody—The action on the part of a police officer to obtain custody of a juvenile accused of committing a delinquent act (same as arrest in criminal justice system).

6. Outline the three major steps in the juvenile justice process

The three major steps in the juvenile justice process are referral, juvenile court (which involves three different procedures: intake, prosecution, and adjudication), and disposition.

7. Describe the five decision points in the juvenile justice process

At the referral stage, the major decision is whether to send the case to juvenile court or to handle the matter in some other manner. At the intake stage, two major decisions are made: (a) whether the case should be dismissed, handled informally, or adjudicated, and (b) whether a juvenile should be placed in detention or released to the community.

At the prosecution stage, the major decision taken is whether to file a petition in juvenile court. At that stage, the prosecutor also decides whether to initiate proceedings to waive a juvenile to adult court. At the adjudication stage, an adjudication hearing is held to determine if the juvenile committed the offense alleged.

The major decision at the disposition stage is to determine the sanction that will be imposed on the offender.

8. Compare and contrast the juvenile and criminal justice systems

There are numerous similarities and differences between the juvenile and criminal justice systems. For example, both systems require the standard of "proof beyond a reasonable doubt" and both frequently use probation. However, traditionally, rehabilitation has been seen as a viable goal in the juvenile justice system, but it is not a primary goal in the criminal justice system.

KEY TERMS

juvenile justice system, p. 4
parents patriae, p. 4
jurisdiction, p. 4
delinquency, p. 5
status offense, p. 5
juvenile, p. 6
criminal justice system, p. 6
maximum age of juvenile court jurisdiction, p. 6
minimum age of juvenile court jurisdiction, p. 7
diversion, p. 10
intake, p. 10
victim restitution, p. 11
community service, p. 11
informal probation, p. 11
waiver to adult court, p. 12
adjudication, p. 12
probation, p. 13

REVIEW QUESTIONS

1. What is considered the founding concept of the juvenile justice system? Explain its origin and significance.
2. What two categories of acts are classified as delinquent in many states?
3. What is a juvenile?
4. What is the maximum age of juvenile court jurisdiction in most states?
5. What is the minimum age of juvenile court jurisdiction in most states?
6. Who usually refers juveniles to a juvenile court?
7. What terms are used exclusively in the juvenile justice system? Define each.
8. What are the three major steps in the juvenile justice process?
9. What major decision(s) is made at each step in the juvenile justice process?
10. Which types of cases are commonly dismissed at intake? Why?
11. List the similarities and differences between the juvenile and the criminal justice systems.

HANDS-ON ACTIVITIES

1. **Define Who Is a Juvenile** Go to the library and find out how your state defines a juvenile. This information is part of the juvenile laws for your state. You may also use the Internet. Document the section number of the law that defines a juvenile in your state.
   a. What are the minimum and maximum ages of juvenile court jurisdiction in your state?
   b. How does the law in your state compare with laws in other states?
   c. Using your knowledge of your community or recent news reports from TV or the local newspaper, do you think the age requirements in your state protect the community and juveniles adequately? Give examples and explain your position on the topic.

2. **Test Average Understanding of the System** Develop a quiz for your family and friends. On a sheet of paper, list the 13 juvenile justice terms discussed in this chapter on the right side of the paper. On the left side of the paper, put the corresponding criminal justice system terms in mixed-up order. Give the quiz to five people who are not in your class. Tabulate their results. What is the level of understanding of the people who took the quiz?

1. Go to **www.ojjdp.gov** Review the website and answer the following questions: What role does the Office of Juvenile Justice and Delinquency Prevention play in the operation of the juvenile justice system?

2. Go to **www.cdcr.ca.gov/Reports_Research/docs/research/ CYLOS2010.pdf** California Department of Corrections and Rehabilitation, Division of Juvenile Justice, Research and Statistics Web page. Review and write a one-page report of the document entitled "Length of Stay of Division of Juvenile Justice Youth."

1. **Define Juvenile Court Jurisdiction** You have recently been appointed by your state legislature to review the current juvenile law in your state. One of the responsibilities you have is to recommend a change to the minimum and maximum ages of juvenile court jurisdiction in your state. Currently the maximum age of juvenile court jurisdiction is age 16. Therefore, a person who commits an offense at age 16 is a juvenile while a 17-year-old is an adult. The minimum age of juvenile court jurisdiction is 12. Therefore, a person who commits an offense when 11 years old cannot be handled by the juvenile court system. You have studied the age minimums and maximums in all states and reviewed the statistics for juvenile adjudication.

    a. What would you recommend to the state legislature as the new minimum and maximum ages of juvenile court jurisdiction?

    b. What factors led you to raise or lower the current maximum age of juvenile court jurisdiction?

    c. What factors led you to raise or lower the current minimum age of juvenile court jurisdiction?

2. **Decide on Possible Adjudication** You are an intake officer with the local juvenile probation department.

One evening the police bring to you a juvenile named Jeremy Williams who has been accused of assault. The assault arose out of a confrontation between Jeremy and his ex-girlfriend's current boyfriend. According to the police, the boyfriend confronted Jeremy at a local mall and started to threaten Jeremy if he did not stop harassing his ex-girlfriend. Jeremy shoved the boyfriend who tripped and fell down a flight of stairs. The fall led to minor injuries to the boyfriend. Jeremy has never been taken into custody before and is a good student at school. He appears to be remorseful for his actions and is polite and courteous to you during the intake process. All indications are that Jeremy is a "good kid" but got caught up in a bad situation.

    a. What would you decide to do with the case? Would you dismiss the case, handle the matter informally, or refer the case for adjudication?

    b. What factors influenced your decision? State law allows you to place in detention any juvenile who has been arrested for assault. Would you place Jeremy in the detention center or release him to his parents?

    c. Why did you make the decision you did?

1.1 Self-Check

What assumptions led to the establishment of a separate system of justice for juvenile offenders? The assumptions are that juveniles are less mature than adults, incapable of the same level of intent as adults, and more easily rehabilitated. This led to the basic theory that the juvenile justice system should be more rehabilitative than punitive, and this affects the ways in which juvenile offenders are managed at almost every step of the process.

1.2 Self-Check

1. What is a status offender?
A status offender is a juvenile who commits status offenses, a category of delinquent acts that are illegal only when committed by juveniles. Status offenders

include truants, runaways, and underage smokers and drinkers.

2. What is the most common maximum age of juvenile court jurisdiction?

The most common maximum age is 17, although the range among the 50 states is from 15 to 17.

1.3 Self-Check

Why was a separate set of terms established for use in the juvenile justice system?

Since the original goal of the juvenile justice system was to rehabilitate, rather than punish, offenders, a separate set of terms was devised to further distance the two systems from one another. The purpose is to aid rehabilitation by not labeling the process in criminal terms. Therefore, in the juvenile justice system an offender is not a criminal, his or her adjudication is not a trial, and so on.

1.4 Self-Check

What is the most common disposition in juvenile court?

Probation, which allows the juvenile to remain in the community as long as he or she abides by the terms of probation. Probation requires that the juvenile avoid breaking the law; it can also require counseling programs (such as drug counseling), community service, or payment of victim restitution.

1.5 Self-Check

Do the similarities and differences between the juvenile justice system and criminal justice system apply to every jurisdiction?

Not necessarily. For example, some jurisdictions do not allow juveniles who are taken into custody to be photographed and fingerprinted; in the past, all jurisdictions followed this rule. This is one example of how, gradually, the line between adult and juvenile is appearing to blur.

HISTORY OF THE JUVENILE JUSTICE SYSTEM

CHAPTER TWO

Chapter Outline

The Changing Shape of the Juvenile Justice System

Historical Treatment of Juveniles

Juvenile Justice under the English Common Law

Juvenile Justice in Colonial America

Children During the Industrial Revolution

Early American Juvenile Institutions

Houses of Refuge

The Development of *Parens Patriae* and Reform Schools

Early Juvenile Justice in the United States

Juvenile Justice During the Victorian Era

The Traditional Model of Juvenile Justice (1900s–1960s)

The Due Process Model of Juvenile Justice (1960s–1980s)

The Punitive Model of Juvenile Justice (1980s–Present)

The Shifting Assumptions of Juvenile Justice in the United States

Cyclical Changes in Juvenile Justice: History Repeating Itself

The Cycles of Change

Chapter Objectives

After completing this chapter, you should be able to:

1. Describe how juvenile offenders were treated by the law throughout history.

2. Identify the early institutions of juvenile justice.

3. Explain the forces behind the creation of the juvenile justice system in the United States.

4. Outline the three major historical periods in juvenile justice.

5. Identify assumptions of the traditional model of juvenile justice.

6. Identify assumptions of the due process model of juvenile justice.

7. Identify assumptions of the punitive model of juvenile justice.

8. Describe how changing assumptions affect the juvenile justice system.

The Changing Shape of the Juvenile Justice System

The juvenile court system in the United States has been in existence since 1899. However, over the past century, the juvenile justice system has been marked by many shifts in thinking concerning how to treat juveniles. The juvenile justice system of today is remarkably different in scope, purpose, and operation than the early founders of the system ever envisioned. The reasons behind these shifts are often debated and have led some people in certain academic and legal circles to call for the abolition of the juvenile justice system.

Unlike the criminal justice system, a separate juvenile justice system is not constitutionally guaranteed. States are free to abolish their separate systems of juvenile justice at any time and simply put juveniles into regular criminal court. Nonetheless, it is unlikely that juvenile justice is going to be abolished any time soon.

The juvenile justice system is a network of interrelated social service and criminal justice agencies designed and operated for the treatment and care of children. Although a complex system, the juvenile justice system is much easier to change than the criminal justice system. Recently, many states have adopted a more accountable and punitive juvenile justice system.

Throughout this chapter, we discuss the various **assumptions** and views of theorists, legal scholars, politicians, and practitioners of juvenile justice in the United States. Assumptions are ideas and beliefs that are the foundation for theories, programs, and policies. Assumptions about the causes of juvenile delinquency, about how best to deal with delinquency, and about the operation of the juvenile justice system have been fundamental factors in shaping the system over the past 100 years. Changes in assumptions have dramatically altered how the juvenile justice system in the United States operates. Scholars may argue about the reasons behind these changes, but they are generally in agreement about the changes themselves and when they occurred.

2.1 SELF-CHECK

Do you understand what an assumption is and what role assumptions play in the development of juvenile justice?

Historical Treatment of Juveniles

Before the 20th, juveniles were essentially **chattel,** or property, in the eyes of society and the courts around the world. Juveniles could be bought, sold, and treated like any other property with the owner being the person in total control of the child. Many common social practices of the time treated children, by today's standards, dreadfully. Not given a separate status in the eyes of the criminal court, a juvenile was treated the same as an adult in the criminal justice system and subject to the same penalties, including death. Juveniles, once convicted of a crime, were sent to the same prisons as adults.

Even though juvenile offenders were subjected to the same punishments as adults, the criminal justice system tended to take a more paternalistic approach to handling these cases, and many times the punishments for juveniles were reduced or never imposed.[1] Children did not receive special protections in the criminal justice system, nor were they allocated special privileges in other segments of society, either. This view of children is still common in many societies around the world today. There are horror stories of children as young as 7 being put to death.

JUVENILE JUSTICE UNDER THE ENGLISH COMMON LAW

Under English common law, a juvenile accused of a crime was usually treated no differently than an adult offender. Juveniles could be given a variety of corporal punishments, banishment, and the death penalty for their offenses. In

assumptions Ideas and beliefs that serve as the foundation for theories, programs, and policies. In juvenile justice, these assumptions consist of what people believe about the causes of juvenile delinquency, what we should do about juvenile delinquency, and how the juvenile justice system should function.

chattel The legal term for property. In the past, juveniles were viewed as property in the eyes of the law.

terms of criminal responsibility, any child over the age of 7 was accountable for any criminal acts that child committed. Age 7 was established in early Roman laws, adopted by the English common law, and eventually brought into the American system of justice.

A system of **orphanages, workhouses, training schools, and apprenticeships** developed in England in the 1600s to deal with unwanted, abandoned, and orphaned children. These institutions and their operation are perhaps best described in many of the writings of Charles Dickens, especially *Oliver Twist*. Children were brought into the adult world through **involuntary servitude** and apprenticeships. The focus of these systems was to train juveniles in trades so that they could contribute to society. Many of these practices were brought to the United States by the colonists and continued well into the 20th century.

The only similarity between the juvenile justice system of English common law and the one in operation today in the United States is that there were and still are a variety of public and private institutions, organizations, religious groups, and others who deal with wayward and delinquent children. Oftentimes, intractable, difficult children are dealt with through such organizations, and this practice continues today.

JUVENILE JUSTICE IN COLONIAL AMERICA

During the colonial era in the United States, children were viewed in much the same way as in England. Although explanations vary, many scholars believe that a parent's bond to a child was low due to high infant mortality rates. The family was the primary caregiver and the primary supervisor of children. In addition, parents were free to sell their children into slavery; they could care for and discipline their children as they saw fit. The move away from viewing children as chattel to viewing them as those in need of protection had its origins in Europe's Renaissance period (14th through 17th centuries) amidst a variety of educational and religious reforms. As a result, the criminal justice system and other social institutions began to view children as not being fully developed or capable of exercising free will. Thus, a variety of new social welfare programs were initiated to educate, reform, and instill morality in children and adolescents.

Prior to the development of a formalized juvenile justice system, an informal network of the youth's family, community members, and religious officials served as control mechanisms. Juvenile delinquency was viewed as a private matter with the family being the ultimate arbiter and punisher in such cases. The church played a prominent role in such matters in colonial America. The punishments were meted out at the church, in schools, and in the home—and were often quite severe and embarrassing.

CHILDREN DURING THE INDUSTRIAL REVOLUTION

Once the Industrial Revolution of the 18th and 19th centuries took hold, new issues in the treatment of children emerged. Despite the social reform programs started during the Renaissance period (such as social welfare and training schools), as more people moved into urban areas and as more industry was developed in these urban areas, wayward children were being trained to occupy a place in the industrial development. During this period of the Industrial Revolution, children worked long hours alongside adults in factories. However, many reform groups began to question how children were being treated in the new industrial society that was spreading across cities throughout the world. Early child labor laws and programs designed to alleviate the ills of urbanization were precursors to the current juvenile justice system. The puritanical ideal which centered on the idea that the best way to cure juvenile delinquency was to remove the juvenile from the corrupting influence of the city and poverty

orphanages, workhouses, training schools, and apprenticeships An informal system of public and private institutions that were designed to take in wayward children. Their goal was to take care of children whose parents were unable or unwilling to fulfill their responsibilities. These institutions attempted to raise children to become productive members of society.

involuntary servitude The practice of selling children into service to a business person or wealthy person. In exchange for the money, parents would essentially give up all rights to their children.

Urban poverty, misery, and crowding intensified during the Industrial Revolution. Children's rights and juvenile justice proponents advocated moving troubled youths to the countryside as a means of rehabilitation. *Do you think effecting a change in environment brings about rehabilitation? Why or why not?*

2.2 SELF-CHECK

1. How were children treated prior to the development of separate institutions for wayward juveniles?

2. What programs and facilities were initiated under English common law for juveniles?

3. What issues in the treatment of children were problematic during the Industrial Revolution?

still pervades juvenile corrections in many forms today. The progressive idea that all children could be saved, combined with puritanical ideologies, led to innovative programs and facilities long before the creation of the juvenile court system in the United States.

Early American Juvenile Institutions

The concept of rehabilitation has its roots in 16th and 17th-century puritan America. The **Puritans** believed that through hard work and intense prayer a person became closer to God. These ideas were reflected in early American penal institutions as well as in the earliest juvenile institutions.

The first American penal institution to address juvenile issues specifically was the **Walnut Street Jail** in Philadelphia, Pennsylvania. The facility was the first real attempt to segregate and classify offenders based on such characteristics as age and gender.

During the early post-colonial period in the United States, several policy initiatives designed to deal with juveniles were enacted. Many of these initiatives changed child labor practices and the treatment of children in orphanages and workhouses.

One clear theme in most academic writings about the history of juvenile justice is that the Industrial Revolution led to many of the institutions that were developed in the United States. As the lower-class and immigrant population moved into the cities, the city itself was viewed as partially responsible for wayward children. As a result, many institutions were created for juveniles, typically far out in the country. The idea that country living and

Puritans A religious group in early America who believed that through hard work, religion, and education a person could get closer to God. These ideals served as the foundation of early institutions of juvenile justice in the United States.

Walnut Street Jail The first jail in the United States that separated inmates and sought to reform their behavior rather than just punishing them. Opened in 1790 in Philadelphia, Pennsylvania, it was also the first correctional facility to separate women and children from adult male inmates.

A variety of social institutions were created in England and in the United States to deal with wayward children prior to the inception of a juvenile justice system. *What type of institutions still exist today that are reminiscent of these early ones?*

traditional agrarian values could cure juvenile delinquents is still today the tenet of numerous juvenile correctional ranches, camps, and outdoor programs. Anthony Platt argues that the reforms and corrective measures were simply a means to control the poor and retrain them to work in the industrial factories.[2] Indeed, as the Industrial Revolution wore on, more and more training and industrial schools for juveniles appeared.

HOUSES OF REFUGE

Initially, the reforms for juveniles began in the urban areas of New York City, Philadelphia, and Boston. In 1823, the Society for the Prevention of Pauperism focused on the plight of the horde of "dirty, foul-mouthed children who thronged the city streets and subsisted on picking pockets and other crimes." The Society advocated the construction of a new facility designed to deal with the different problems and issues facing children.[3]

Houses of refuge were created in New York, Pennsylvania, and Massachusetts and were designed to take in all children who were neglected, abused, or delinquent. Founders believed in an ideal way of life and that juveniles could be saved through hard work and religion. These ideas were embraced in the houses of refuge where juveniles would be protected from weak and immoral parents, the crime of street life, and, most importantly, from their own wicked temptations. At the center of the teachings in these houses was the strong belief that humans are inherently evil and must be taught to be good. In these early institutions, the notion that the state was sometimes in a better position than the family to raise a child, and had a duty to do so whenever it was in the best interest of the child, began to take root. By the end of the 19th century, the belief that we could accurately diagnose the reasons for delinquency,

traditional agrarian values The ideas and beliefs shared by those who worked the land and espoused Puritan or Quaker values. The idea was that the city was a source of many juveniles' "evil ways," and the best way to change these youths was to remove them from the city and place them in remote rural locations.

houses of refuge Early institutions specifically designed for juveniles in the United States. These facilities would take in and care for dependent, neglected, and delinquent children.

GOAL, in Walnut Street PHILADELPHIA.

The first institution to separate juveniles from adults was the Walnut Street Jail in Philadelphia. *What are some of the reasons why it is important to separate juveniles from adults in the criminal justice system?*

combined with the notion that the state could and should intervene in the lives of children, resulted in the formation of the first juvenile court in the United States.

THE DEVELOPMENT OF *PARENS PATRIAE* AND REFORM SCHOOLS

The idea that the state could incarcerate juveniles on the basis of their status as delinquent, dependent, or neglected was fundamental to the houses of refuge. The concepts of *parens patriae* (see complete definition in Chapter 1) and **in loco parentis** served as the legal foundation for such interventions. The constitutionality of these concepts would be tested in Pennsylvania by a father whose daughter was committed to a house of refuge (see Focus on Policy). Following the legal acceptance of *parens patriae* in the **Ex Parte Crouse** case, a multitude of new facilities designed specifically for juveniles began to spring up around the nation. During the mid-1800s, reform schools were opened which purported to provide a more stable environment where wayward juveniles were educated through strict discipline and religious principles. The Lyman School for Boys was the first reform school in the United States and was opened in Westboro, Massachusetts, in 1847. A reform school for girls was soon to follow in Lancaster, Massachusetts, in 1855.[4] In addition, the concept of probation for criminal offenses began to take hold in Massachusetts during this time (a complete review of juvenile probation is included in Chapter 11). These early institutions and legal proceedings firmly established the foundation of a separate juvenile system in the United States. The reforms were very innovative and, as

in loco parentis The legal concept of allowing the state to "act in place of the parents." This gives the state the legal right to take away parental custody of children when it is in the best interests of the child.

Ex Parte Crouse The first court case in the United States that declared the concept of *parens patriae* constitutional.

FOCUS ON POLICY

THE LEGITIMIZATION OF *PARENS PATRIAE* IN *EX PARTE CROUSE*

The first documented case where the concept of *parens patriae* was questioned in a legal setting in the United States occurred in the 1838 case of *Ex Parte Crouse*.

In this case, a father attempted to free his daughter from the Philadelphia house of refuge following her commitment there. A petition had been filed by Crouse's mother to have her committed because she was poor and lacked supervision. Her father challenged the commitment, arguing that her commitment without a trial was unconstitutional. The case was brought to the Pennsylvania Supreme Court and challenged the right of the state to take into custody children who had not committed crime and also challenged the right of the state to commit a child without a trial by jury. The court ruled that the practice of *parens patriae* was constitutional and a legitimate state function. The court stated, "The right of parental control is a natural, but not an inalienable one." As such, the court found that when the natural parent was not prepared for the task of parenting or unworthy of it, *parens patriae* allowed for the state to take the place of the parents (*in loco parentis*).

In essence, the state was not punishing the child, but saving him or her. In addition, the court gave legitimacy to the various houses of refuge that were springing up all over the United States. It stated, "the House of Refuge is not a prison, but a school, where reformation, not punishment, is the end." Finally, the court also legitimized the idea that children were not guaranteed the same rights as adults in the United States. In short, they could be deprived of constitutional guarantees given to adults in the course of the state's exercising its rights under *parens patriae*. This case preceded the formation of the first juvenile court in the United States by some 60 years.

The importance of the *Crouse* decision is that it is the first case which lays the legal foundation for what will eventually become the modern juvenile justice system. The Pennsylvania Supreme Court legitimized the ability of the state to take custody of a child, legitimized the purposes of the houses of refuge, and also legitimized the idea that children were different from adults in the eyes of the law.

Critical Thinking

What implications do you think *Ex Parte Crouse* has for parental and juveniles' rights in court and status in society?

---

time passed and reform schools became more common, a **grassroots movement** would question their goals and operational practices and those of the houses of refuge.

Early Juvenile Justice in the United States

As a call for reform and the emerging juvenile justice system continued into the late 1800s and early 1900s, a progressive reform movement was taking hold which would be responsible for a variety of social programs and grassroots public policy initiatives. The members of this group primarily consisted of prominent women who became known as the **child savers.** Activists such as Jane Addams and Julia Lathrop of the Settlement House Movement and the National Congress of Mothers lobbied and were successful in convincing key politicians of the utility of a separate system of juvenile justice. In addition to criminal justice reform, the targets for their reforms included child labor practices, child abuse, runaways, homeless children, and newly immigrated children. Scholars have argued about the reasons behind the creation of the juvenile justice system in the United States. Some believe that the system was formed out of a feeling of benevolence, as espoused by Progressive Era "child savers,"[5] while others claim that it was simply a mechanism designed to control the nefarious effects of the Industrial Revolution such as poverty, urban

2.3 SELF-CHECK

1. What religious group's values were used in the development of juvenile justice in the United States?

2. What are houses of refuge and what role did they play in the early juvenile justice system?

3. What two legal concepts serve as the foundation for the juvenile justice system?

grassroots movement A movement that starts with the general public and not in the political arena.

child savers The group of progressive reformers who, in the late 1800s and early 1900s, were responsible for the creation of the juvenile justice system in the United States.

The child savers were a group of progressive activists, mostly women, who were responsible for the creation of a separate system of juvenile justice. Shown above are Jane Addams (middle) and Julia Lathrop (left). *Why do you think women were so active in this area?*

decay, and crime.[6] Some conclude that the children were never "saved" and that the juvenile justice movement was a coercive and conservative influence backed by big business in order to control and train the poor to be workers in a newly industrialized society.[7]

Frederick L. Faust and Paul J. Brantingham conclude that the conditions of urban decay and the harsh treatment of juveniles by the criminal justice system combined with positivistic notions about the nature of crime to promote a religious-humanistic criminological view of delinquency.[8] This view, traditional American values of wholesome care, and the legal doctrine of *parens patriae* merged to undergird the formation of a socialized juvenile court. The influences of the Industrial Revolution, an end to post–Civil War Reconstruction, and Victorian thinking about poverty and crime combined to form the early juvenile justice system in America. All of these factors contributed to the emergence of the juvenile justice system as a separate system of justice, which is, in essence, an ongoing experiment.

JUVENILE JUSTICE DURING THE VICTORIAN ERA

The most cited assumptions of the proponents of the early juvenile justice system centered on the need to provide juvenile offenders with more individual attention than the criminal justice system of the time could provide. The early juvenile justice system was founded on the belief that the state could and should act *in loco parentis* under the doctrine of *parens patriae*. Instead of an adversarial contest whose fundamental purpose was to determine facts, assess blame, and punish the guilty, the juvenile justice system of the late 19th century was to be more of an *inquisitorial system* whose purpose was to determine cause, diagnose illness, and prescribe treatment. The emerging juvenile justice system reflected the belief of the late-1800s-and-early-1900s Victorian Era that science had progressed to such a degree that it was possible to diagnose juveniles accurately and effectively to treat and cure them.

Juvenile delinquency was one of many ills the progressive movement sought to eradicate. The early juvenile system was thus viewed as progressive, state-of-the-art, and the morally right thing to do. The system was not intervening in the lives of juveniles for society's good, but for the juvenile's good. Not only was the system thought to be a cure for the ills that plagued the urban centers of America, it was thought to be righteous and indeed took on a church-like quality.

Some, however, question the motives of *parens patriae* and conclude that the state was not a benevolent parent; it simply enforced a moralistic code through warehousing, punishing, and proselytizing. Platt notes that the crimes designated specifically for the new juvenile court (begging, sexual crimes, frequenting vice establishments, loitering, staying out all night) were all crimes associated with the urban poor.[9] He argues that the bias established against the poor remained in the juvenile justice system: Poor children were sent to

2.4 SELF-CHECK

1. Who were the child savers, and what role did they play in the development of the juvenile justice system?

2. What are the differing opinions given as to why the juvenile justice system was created in the United States?

The first formal juvenile court was opened in Cook County, Illinois, in 1899. The opening of the court marked the creation of a separate system of justice for juveniles in the United States. *Do you think we need a separate court for juveniles accused of delinquency? Why or why not?*

reformatories while the middle- and upper-class children were sent home. Regardless of the specific reasons for its creation, the juvenile justice system became part of the United States legal system with the passage of the Illinois Juvenile Court Act of 1899.

The Traditional Model of Juvenile Justice (1900s–1960s)

The notion of juvenile justice was beginning to take hold in several states in the late part of the 19th century. Children were tried separately in Suffolk County, Massachusetts, in 1870, and the practice was adopted statewide in 1872. New York developed a similar statute in 1892, followed by Indiana and Rhode Island. In 1893, Pennsylvania enacted legislation that prohibited children under age 16 from being incarcerated with adults.[10] The law also required that juveniles be tried separately from adults and that separate records be kept.

These practices were consolidated and solidified by the **Illinois Juvenile Court Act of 1899** (see Focus on Policy). This act was the first legislation in the United States to specifically provide for a separate system of juvenile justice and to delineate many of the assumptions and practices of the new system, which we refer to as the traditional model of juvenile justice. The role of the juvenile court was fundamentally different from criminal courts in the United States. Further, juvenile court officials were given wide discretion in order to be able to treat juveniles who came under their jurisdiction.[11]

Myth   Fact

Myth: Juveniles have always had the same rights in delinquency proceedings as adults have had in criminal proceedings.

Fact: Several U.S. Supreme Court decisions in the 1960s and 1970s granted juveniles fundamental due process rights. Prior to these decisions, juveniles could be incarcerated for long periods of time without basic rights, such as the right to an attorney, notice of the charges, and full and fair hearing. Today still, juveniles are not granted the right to a jury trial in many delinquency proceedings.

Illinois Juvenile Court Act of 1899 The law that established the first separate juvenile court in the United States.

FOCUS ON POLICY

THE ILLINOIS JUVENILE COURT ACT OF 1899

The first official separate juvenile court was established in Cook County, Illinois, in 1899. The Illinois Juvenile Court Act of 1899 specifically outlined the types of cases the court had jurisdiction over and separated the juvenile justice system from the adult criminal justice system. Following passage of this act, similar legislation was enacted in states across the nation so that by the mid-1920s, juvenile courts were operational in almost every state. Specifically, the act established:

- The age at which a juvenile becomes an adult (16 in this act; varying ages were adopted in other states, and age limits changed over time in several states as well).
- The definitions of dependent, neglected, and delinquent children, which broadened the jurisdiction of the court in juvenile matters.
- The establishment of a separate courtroom, different procedures, and a separate record for juvenile cases involving dependent, neglected, or delinquent children.
- The specification of placement for juveniles determined to be dependent, neglected, or delinquent.

- The right of the court to continue to supervise children who have been adjudicated delinquent even after placement.
- The recognition that the juvenile court is not a criminal court, but a civil court, emphasizing the rehabilitation and treatment of children. This led to different roles on the part of court participants including judges, attorneys, and probation workers.
- The development of probation programs and authorization of probation officers to assist the court in juvenile cases.
- The statutory concept of *parens patriae* by describing the ability of the court to place juveniles outside the home and determine what is best for the child.

Overall, the Illinois Juvenile Court Act of 1899 gave legislative authorization to the principles of juvenile justice which were already established in the United States. It also created a separate court to hear and handle matters involving juveniles. The dual role of adjudicating juvenile offenses and dealing with juveniles who needed protection was given to the court through this act. The passage of this act is regarded as the official beginning of juvenile justice in the United States.

CRITICAL THINKING

Do you think there could be problems associated with having a separate court system for juveniles? Explain why or why not.

Many writings reflect the belief that everyone in the United States supported the progressives' drive for the creation of the juvenile court. In reality, the entire concept of the juvenile justice system has always had its detractors. Simply because most states had passed juvenile court statutes by the mid-1920s doesn't mean that there were separate systems of juvenile justice in operation. In fact, several research studies about the juvenile justice system prior to the due process revolution of the 1960s argued that the system was far from its paternalistic and benevolent ideal.[12]

An examination of the early juvenile justice system revealed that, for the most part, there was a wide gap between what was intended by progressive reformers and the actual system operation.[13] Indeed, some legal scholars began to argue that the juvenile court was nothing more than a junior criminal court where juveniles were denied basic due process rights.[14] These arguments combined with several high-profile cases led the higher courts to examine the operation and administration of the juvenile justice system more closely. Prior to the U.S. Supreme Court's addressing the problems of juvenile justice in the 1960s, some states were already in the process of changing their laws to include some basic due process rights in juvenile court.[15] The issues and problems within the juvenile justice system were already on the social and political agendas long before the U.S. Supreme Court made its famous rulings in the 1960s.

Anthony Platt summarizes his alternative view of the juvenile court movement and the child savers into three themes:

- First, he argues, delinquents were seen as "needing firm control and restraint" if they were to be rehabilitated. Thus, the child savers were not benevolent and were in fact recommending increased imprisonment as a means of removing children from corrupting influences.
- Platt notes that the determining factors considered in deciding whether to remove a child from his or her home were fraught with middle-class or upper-class bias and were exclusively used to evaluate the competency of the lower-class home. "The child savers set such high standards of family propriety that almost any parent could be accused of not fulfilling his or her 'proper function.'"
- Finally, he argues that the child savers blurred the distinction between dependent and delinquent children. As such, due process was lost for criminal children and all children were now viewed as dependent. Anyone who disputed the intentions of the juvenile court or argued that due process must remain a part of the process was labeled uninformed and impeding the worthy goals of the juvenile system.[16]

> ## 2.5 SELF-CHECK
>
> 1. What was the Illinois Juvenile Court Act of 1899? Why is this act so important?
> 2. What is Platt's alternative view of the juvenile court and the child savers?

Eventually, however, the criticisms of the juvenile court began to outnumber the accolades, and the juvenile justice system would be a substantial target of the due process movement during the turbulent decade of the 1960s.

The Due Process Model of Juvenile Justice (1960s–1980s)

From its inception, the early juvenile court was subject to criticism that largely centered on the practicality, constitutionality, and lack of punishment in the juvenile court. For decades, the juvenile justice system experienced criticism from the general public, scholars, and the judicial system. This culminated in several U.S. Supreme Court decisions which fundamentally altered the functioning of the system (all of the important U.S. Supreme Court cases on juvenile justice during this period are discussed fully in Chapter 8). These criticisms stemmed from the inability of the juvenile justice system to fulfill its intended mission of rehabilitating juveniles. There were many abuses of discretion, which led the U.S. Supreme Court to eventually conclude that juveniles received the "worst of both worlds." In other words, the child received neither fair treatment in the courts nor rehabilitation in the juvenile correctional system.

People began to realize that the conflicting goals of juvenile justice (best interest of the child versus the best interests of society) made the process indistinguishable from a criminal trial in that the end result was punishment, deterrence, and incapacitation. The due process changes in juvenile justice in the 1960s–1980s moved away from the idea that a child was property—neither the parents' property nor the state's property. Now a child was recognized as a person with associated rights and protections other than just the right to be saved. This shift also resulted in a reduction in individualized justice.

Criticisms of the juvenile justice system and the due process revolution resulted in reforms in both substantive and procedural justice. Procedurally, a juvenile court now had to provide due process. Although the U.S. Supreme Court stopped short of abolishing the separate system of juvenile justice, its nature was nonetheless altered. Substantively, a juvenile court would now

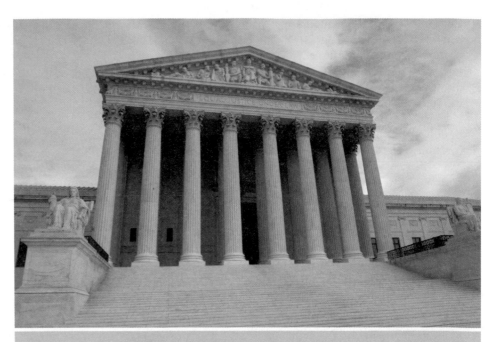

The Supreme Court headed by Chief Justice Earl Warren was responsible for a variety of changes to the criminal and juvenile justice systems in the United States during the 1960s. *Do you think juveniles accused of delinquency deserve all of the rights expressed in the Constitution as adults facing criminal charges? Which rights would you exclude and why?*

CAREERS IN JUVENILE JUSTICE

Juvenile Defense Attorney

Prior to the due process revolution of the 1960s, defense attorneys were not a regular part of the juvenile justice process. Once fundamental due process became part of the juvenile justice system, the role of defense attorneys in juvenile court became much more prominent. Indeed, juvenile justice is a specialty in many states and is recognized by the American Bar Association.

The primary job of the juvenile defense attorney is to serve as the legal advocate for a juvenile accused of a delinquent act. Similar to a lawyer in an adult criminal proceeding, the juvenile defense lawyer prepares the case for the juvenile and represents him or her at all critical stages of the proceedings. This can include detention hearings, adjudication hearings, disposition hearings, and plea negotiations. In addition to knowing all of the rules regarding criminal court procedure, the juvenile defense lawyer has to know juvenile justice procedure in his or her state. Juvenile law varies from state to state and some states require certification in juvenile and family law before an attorney can represent a juvenile. Many states and counties operate separate public defender offices for juveniles, and others have juvenile designees within a central public defender's office.

Juvenile defense attorneys have an integral role in the process beyond legal representation. Juvenile court proceedings are much less formal than adult proceedings, and the actors in the court (judge, prosecutor, probation officer, and defense attorney) frequently work together as a team to determine what is best for the juvenile. This is what separates adult justice from juvenile justice in the courtroom. As part of this role, defense attorneys help to ensure that a juvenile is complying with orders from the court and following some type of treatment plan. They serve as the advocate for the juvenile throughout the court process and while under sanction as well.

To become a juvenile defense attorney you must have a law degree and pass the bar exam within your state. Many jurisdictions require additional training in juvenile law prior to being able to represent juveniles in juvenile court.

Critical Thinking

Go to **www.njdc.info** and find links on the National Juvenile Defender Center site. Read about juvenile defense attorneys' tasks and responsibilities and use this information to write a short report listing the main qualifications for the job.

handle only more serious crimes, as status offenses were slowly deinstitutionalized.[17] Most of the original assumptions of juvenile justice survived the due process revolution. Only two were markedly changed:

1. The juvenile justice system did not need the broad discretion originally envisioned by the founders.
2. Due process was important and helped treatment.

The changes in the assumptions resulted from recognized abuses within the system itself and not an abandonment of the original goals of juvenile justice. In subsequent years, criticism would take a different form, specifically that juvenile offenders were slipping through the cracks and that they were not as innocent as the system was treating them.

The Punitive Model of Juvenile Justice (1980s–Present)

The most salient criticism of the juvenile justice system that led to the punitive model of juvenile justice was that the system was ineffective in dealing with the issues of violent crime and repeat offenders.[18] Although various studies indicate that the number of juveniles who commit violent offenses and/or who recidivate is small, these offenders are of great concern to the public, media, and politicians.

The inability of juvenile justice system personnel to deal with these offenders resulted in a wave of "get tough" legislation that began in the 1970s and continues today. Previous minor tinkering with juvenile justice policy gave way in several states to broad, comprehensive rewriting of juvenile and family codes. These new codes are rooted in assumptions that are markedly different from those of the founders of the juvenile justice system. The agenda of deinstitutionalization, diversion, and reform has been openly questioned and criticized.[19] According to one writer, "What was once a small system seeking to ameliorate the social condition of the neglected, abused, and delinquent youths has become an institution that often vacillates from one extreme to another."[20] By the late 1970s, lawmakers began responding to calls for stricter legislation, and many state politicians began to de-emphasize rehabilitation in favor of punishment, justice, accountability, and public protection.[21]

Under the punitive model of juvenile justice, the function of the system has shifted to assessing the level of harm to society from the actions of a juvenile and imposing the appropriate level of punishment to deter the juvenile from future delinquency. This change in the system's function is particularly evident in the expansion of the **determinate sentence** law in Texas following enactment of House Bill 327 in 1996. This law is now applicable to 23 offenses, up from the original 6 offenses, for which a juvenile may receive up to a 40-year sentence, depending on the offense committed. Juveniles can receive these sentences in juvenile court from a juvenile court judge. A juvenile offender serves his or her sentence at the Texas Youth Commission until age 17, at which point a review hearing is held. A juvenile court judge can send the youth back to the Youth Commission until age 19 or to the prison system to serve the rest of the sentence. As a result, the number of waivers to adult court in Texas have recently declined. As evidenced in Texas, the goal of the juvenile justice system has shifted from providing protection and treatment for the juvenile offenders to meting out a punishment that fits the crime.

The current trend to increase the punitive nature of the juvenile justice system reflects certain societal factors. Four important forces that helped to bring

determinate sentence A sentence that has a fixed number of years to serve that is associated with more punitive goals than rehabilitative ones. The indeterminate sentence is a hallmark of the juvenile justice system. The idea was that in order to rehabilitate juveniles, you could not specify the amount of time it would take to cure them.

FOCUS ON PRACTICE

TEEN WHO KILLED TEACHER SENTENCED TO 28 YEARS IN PRISON

WEST PALM BEACH, Florida (CNN)—Nathaniel Brazill, the 14-year-old boy convicted in May for the murder of his middle school teacher, was sentenced to 28 years in prison Friday in a Florida courtroom. Palm Beach County Circuit Court Judge Richard Wennet also ordered Brazill to serve two years house arrest. Brazill could have been sentenced to life in prison for shooting teacher Barry Grunow in the head on the final day of classes of the 2000 school year.

After the sentencing, Brazill's mother, Polly Powell, said she thought the sentence was fair, but that she would fight to try to have him freed sooner. "I know now my son will be coming home one day," she said.

Brazill's father, Nathaniel Brazill Sr., said his family would appeal. "A 28-year sentence is a lot less than we expected; we can live with it, but it's not over," he said.

On Thursday, Brazill testified that he did not mean to hurt Grunow and that he wished he could go back and change what happened. He said that he was sorry for what he did to Grunow's family and to his community.

"Mr. Grunow was a great man and a great teacher and I'm sorry I took him away from you," Brazill said. He said he often thought about how Grunow's children would feel when they are his age.

Brazill was convicted of second-degree murder for the May 26, 2000, shooting death of Grunow, a popular 35-year-old language arts teacher at Lake Worth Community Middle School. That verdict was a lesser charge than the first-degree murder sought by the prosecution, which would have carried a mandatory sentence of life in prison without the possibility of parole. The law Brazill was sentenced under is called the 10–20–Life law, enacted in 1999. On Thursday, Brazill's mother broke down in tears on the stand and asked the judge for mercy. Grunow's mother and brother asked for the maximum sentence against Brazill. The voice of Grunow's widow, Pam, broke as she made her statement.

"Nathaniel has consequences to face and everyone must consider the cause," she said. "Why does a young person make such a sad choice? Then maybe tomorrow, another woman's husband, another little boy's daddy, and another great teacher won't be sacrificed in an angry, crazy moment."

A number of Grunow's friends and fellow teachers testified about what a good father he was and the influence he had on his students. One teacher showed the court a quilt made of drawings, poems and writings her students made in memory of Grunow. She read several of the students' writings, including one that said "he was the best teacher who has ever lived and I am glad to have known him."

Last month, Wennet ruled Brazill can be sentenced as an adult under Florida's strict gun-use law. Defense attorney Robert Udell had argued before Judge Wennet that Brazill, who was 13 at the time of the shooting, was too young to face such a harsh sentence. "It tells you all you need to know about the United States of America in the year 2001, doesn't it?" Udell said after Wennet ruled against him. "We've lost our soul."

Under that law, anyone convicted of carrying a gun during a crime faces 10 years in prison. Those who fire a gun during a crime face a mandatory 20 years in prison, and those who fire a gun, harming or killing someone during a crime face 25 years to life with no parole and no time deducted for good behavior.

During trial, the teen testified about how he pulled the .25-caliber handgun out of his bag and pointed it at Grunow because the teacher would not let him speak to two girls in his class. Brazill said he cocked the pistol because he wanted Grunow to take him seriously, but that he didn't intentionally pull the trigger. He said he thought the safety was on.

Prosecutors argued that Brazill brought the gun to school because he was angry about being suspended by another teacher for throwing water balloons. They said he was also upset because he was failing Grunow's class.

At one point while on the stand, Brazill clutched the handgun used in the shooting, showed jurors how he cocked the weapon and put a bullet in the chamber. Brazill showed little emotion during his testimony, but shed tears when asked if Grunow took him seriously "after you shot him."

"What did Mr. Grunow do when he fell to the ground?" asked Assistant State Attorney Marc Shiner. After a long pause and with tears welling up in his eyes, Brazill said, "What do you think he did?"

Udell, the boy's attorney, pleaded with jurors to consider Brazill's age while deliberating. "Any of you who have dealt with 13-year-olds, or have one, know that they get stupid on us."

Source: "Teen Who Killed Teacher Sentenced to 28 Years in Prison," CNN, July 27, 2001. © 2001 Cable News Network LP, LLLP.

about this model can be identified. There are several that deserve mention, so this list is by no means complete.

1. Whether there has actually been a substantial increase in juvenile violent crime is not as important as the *belief* that such increases have occurred. Perception, paranoia, and politicking often drive policymaking, not empirical facts.

2. The recognition of and research on serious habitual juvenile offenders resulted in calls for changes in several traditional precepts of the juvenile system, most notably information sharing, record keeping, and increased incarcerative ability.

3. Increasing rates of drug use and gang membership among juveniles created a crisis situation in many jurisdictions. Criminal justice systems across the country developed a siege mentality concerning gangs and drugs. An increase in female involvement in delinquency and gangs was coupled with a general perception that juveniles had become the most dangerous and least trusted segment of the population.

4. Perhaps the most prominent force for change was the due process revolution of the 1960s. In society, rights come with responsibilities, and the more the juvenile justice system takes on an adult character, the more juvenile offenders are seen as slipping through the cracks on technicalities.

Underlying all these problems is the fact that the juvenile justice system *has not been able* to fulfill its intended mission of rehabilitating juveniles. The goals and objectives of this new punitive model of the juvenile justice system are delineated and embraced in the **Balanced Juvenile Justice and Crime Prevention Act of 1996** outlined in Figure 2.1. This federal law has been mirrored in several states as they have changed the fundamental purposes of their juvenile justice systems.

2.7 SELF-CHECK

1. What fundamental changes to juvenile justice in the United States were made by the Balanced Juvenile Justice and Crime Prevention Act of 1996?

2. What are the reasons why the juvenile justice system has become more punitive?

The Shifting Assumptions of Juvenile Justice in the United States

Created to deal with the special problems juvenile offenders posed, the juvenile justice system was founded on several assumptions that policymakers believed at the time the various statutes were enacted. As noted earlier, the juvenile justice system is not a constitutional guarantee; the various states are free to alter or eliminate it at their discretion. This is what leads to substantial variation in both substantive and procedural justice across the juvenile system. The initial founding of the juvenile justice system was haphazard and decentralized, and this nebulous policymaking continues today. States have historically been the principal sources of innovation in juvenile justice policy.[22] National trends indicate that juvenile justice systems are growing more formal, restrictive, and punitive. Indeed, policy shifts in the juvenile justice system are more about changing assumptions than they are about actual practice, empirical study, or philosophic reasoning. Figure 2.2 is a comparison of eight assumptions the juvenile justice system has held over its short history.

In order to understand the issues facing juvenile justice today, one must recognize how the assumptions underlying the system have shifted and changed. As shown in Figure 2.2, the assumptions have been fundamentally altered since the creation of the juvenile justice system. The most basic belief in the traditional model was the idea that juveniles as a group do not possess the same

Balanced Juvenile Justice and Crime Prevention Act of 1996 A law passed by Congress that embraces the punitive and accountability assumptions advocated in the late 1970s and 1980s and continue into today. This act is reflective of the fundamental changes in assumptions about juveniles and juvenile justice.

FIGURE 2.1	The Balanced Juvenile Justice and Crime Prevention Act of 1996

In 1996, a bill was enacted by Congress that fundamentally altered the purpose of juvenile justice in the United States. This new law represented the culmination of years of tinkering with the juvenile justice system in the United States and reflected the new mission and operational philosophy of juvenile justice in this country. This law reflects the new assumptions of juvenile justice that currently exist in the United States.

Sec. 2. Findings

1. Violent juvenile crime is increasing both in frequency and severity.
2. The system of criminal justice for juveniles has not kept up with the changing nature of juvenile crime. Many acts of juvenile delinquency can be appropriately handled under existing court procedures, but adequate response to the increasingly violent criminal acts of the more serious juvenile offenders demands major procedural changes to ensure prompt and effective criminal prosecutions and punishment.
3. Penalties imposed under the current juvenile justice system also have failed to keep pace with and deter violent juvenile crime.
4. To deter violent juvenile crime and protect innocent Americans, prosecutors must be empowered to prosecute particularly serious juvenile offenders as adults.
5. Drugs and gun-related crime threaten the life and well-being of American youth and the future of the nation.
6. The number of American youths killing with, and killed by, firearms has increased.
7. To deter the use of firearms in the commission of crime and to protect the law-abiding public, there must be swift disposition of gun-related offenses in our courts, and there must be the certain prospect of punishment for those who commit such crimes.
8. Drug use and addiction among American youth have increased, and only with a comprehensive strategy of deterrence through education and sure punishment, in tandem with provision of treatment for addicted youth, can American youth grow into productive and responsible citizens and parents.
9. Gangs have spread nationwide, inhabit cities large and small, and have growing juvenile membership.
10. The use of illegal drugs supports the drug trafficking industry and the often violent crime associated with the drug trade.
11. Drug courts effectively address drug-related crime by offering intensive treatment to nonviolent, drug-addicted offenders who seek to become drug free.
12. The responsiveness of community-based organizations to local community values and concerns allow such organizations to effectively create and implement youth development programs.
13. The problems facing troubled youth demand a cooperative effort involving parents, schools, local government, law enforcement, juvenile and family courts, and community based organizations.
14. A lack of youth programs providing meaningful and positive after-school activities for at-risk youth contributes to the proliferation of violent juvenile crime, including gangrelated violence and drug trafficking, and the overall hopelessness among the nation's youth.
15. Although parents have responsibility for the social, moral, emotional, physical, and cognitive development of their children, social and demographic changes in recent decades have had a significant effect on family life and youth development, increasing the need for programs to strengthen families and help parents meet the social, moral, emotional, physical, and cognitive needs of their children.

Source: 104th Congress; 2nd Session in the House of Representatives as introduced in the House, 1996 H.R. 3445; 104 H.R. 3445

mens rea or criminal intent as adults. This assumption has changed radically in the past few decades due to the shift in thinking that juvenile crime is no less serious than adult crime. All persons must be held accountable for their criminal behavior and therefore responsible for their actions.

The second assumption in Figure 2.2, according to traditional and due process models, is that juveniles are not as intellectually, socially, or morally developed as adults. As Martin L. Forst notes, "underlying the reforms was the assumption that minors were not fully developed, either physically or mentally, and needed to complete their intellectual, social, and moral maturation before being expected to bear the responsibilities of adulthood."[23] In one respect, this still holds true today, although the age at which a juvenile can be held accountable has dropped. Evidence for this can be seen in younger ages at which juveniles can be certified to adult court.[24] However, in another sense, the new punitive legislation is really saying, "it doesn't matter." The current assumption is that the offense, not the offender, dictates the role of the justice system in a juvenile's development. The move from offender-based to offense-based goals essentially treats all juvenile offenders similarly. Today, in the punitive model, the criteria for sentencing and placement are based on the offense committed, prior offenses, and the evidence at hand. Psychological assessments of development, pre-sentence investigations of socioeconomic and family conditions, and direct testimony on a juvenile's character are naturally less valid criteria in an offense-based juvenile system.

The third assumption of the traditional model of juvenile justice is based on the positivistic notion (see Chapter 4 for more complete discussion of the positivistic school) that the causes of delinquency came from the broader social environment—the neighborhood, the family, and specific child-rearing

mens rea Literally translated means "guilty mind." In the juvenile justice system it was traditionally assumed that juveniles could not form the same level of intent to commit a crime that adults could.

FIGURE 2.2	The Historical Assumptions of Juvenile Justice		
ASSUMPTIONS	TRADITIONAL MODEL (1899–1960s)	DUE PROCESS MODEL (1960s–1980s)	PUNITIVE MODEL (1980s–PRESENT)
1. Juvenile's culpability	Diminished; juveniles are not capable of forming the same *mens rea* as adults	Recognized that the system viewed juveniles as less culpable, but net result of process was criminal culpability	Certain juveniles, especially violent or multiple offenders, are just as culpable as adults
2. View of juvenile's development	Juveniles are not as intellectually, socially, or morally developed as adults	Juveniles are not as intellectually, socially, or morally developed as adults	Unimportant with regard to juvenile justice system processing
3. Causes of delinquency	The broader social environment— the neighborhood, poverty, urban decay, the family, and child rearing practices	Belief in positivism withstood judicial modifications; the causes of delinquency are essentially unimportant as long as juveniles are treated fairly in the system	In general, delinquency is a matter of a juvenile choosing to commit a crime for which he or she must be held accountable
4. Role of the state	The state could and should act in *loco parentis,* and in the best interests of the child	To act *in loco parentis* and in the best interests of the child while providing fundamental fairness and due process	To act *in loco parentis* for the best interests of society. The more serious the crime committed, the more society needs protection
5. Role of due process	Unimportant; hinders rather than promotes treatment	Heightened due to the need to protect juveniles from abuses in the system; due process does not conflict with treatment goals	To ensure processing is formalized and uniform
6. Level of discretion	Broad and widespread, necessary to take into account the various causes and cures for delinquency	Discretion to treat and intervene; unchanged as long as the process meets constitutional standards	The level of discretion is inversely related to the seriousness of the crime committed. Discretion in dealing with serious or violent juveniles is strictly limited if not eliminated
7. Records	Once the juvenile is rehabilitated, he or she deserves a second chance. Records held to strict confidentiality standards	Assumes that a juvenile is still not convicted of a crime and recognizes the risk of labeling a juvenile a criminal	The lack of record keeping hinders coordination of the system which results in juveniles slipping through the cracks. Records are essential to holding the youth accountable and protecting society
8. Goals of the system	Prevention of future delinquency through treatment and rehabilitation	Prevention of future delinquency, rehabilitation, and protection of a juvenile's rights	Prevention of future delinquency through punishment, incapacitation, deterrence, and holding juveniles accountable

practices, for example. The idea that the causes of delinquency were external to the individual led to the belief that delinquency was an illness brought on by the social diseases of poverty, parental neglect, ignorance, and urban decay. Since the causes of delinquency were beyond the control of the juvenile, rehabilitation rather than punishment was appropriate. The chief assumption on which the rehabilitative model was built was that scientific knowledge had reached a point where we could not only diagnose a juvenile's "illness," but intervene and treat it as well. The social reformers responsible for juvenile justice drew two important ideas from positivistic criminology: (a) A broad range of people— the persistently poor, the uneducated, the criminal, the new immigrants—were considered to be basically similar and were all suffering from the same complex of knowable and treatable biological and social ailments; and (b) most offenders could be helped by accurate diagnosis and prompt intervention with available treatment techniques (usually some form of education).[25] Under a punitive model of juvenile justice, however, it is assumed that juveniles commit delinquent acts because they have made a rational choice to do so. With a shift from an offender-based to an offense-based system, the reason a juvenile engages in delinquency is secondary to the offense the juvenile committed.

The fourth assumption of the traditional model of juvenile justice was that the legal concept of *parens patriae* meant that the state could and should act *in loco parentis*. The early juvenile justice system advocates believed that intervention was in the best interests of the child and, therefore, that it was not only the state's right but duty to intervene. Indeed, the philosophy of the juvenile court was that the wayward child was to be taken in hand by the state, and the state was to act not as an enemy but as a protector. Today, the interventions are still occurring, but for the protection of society. The punitive model of juvenile justice assumes that the role of the state is to act in the best interest of society, not the best interest of the child. Justifying intervention on the basis of community protection gives further support to the idea that the causes, diagnosis, prescribed treatment, and rehabilitation of juveniles are not as important under a punitive model of juvenile justice as is incapacitating the child so that no further harm to society results.

The structure of the juvenile court, assumptions about the causes of delinquency and how to treat them, and the role of the state led to the fifth assumption: that due process is not important in the juvenile justice system and would, in fact, hinder treatment. The perception was that the only rights a child had were rights to shelter, protection, and proper guardianship. If the role of the state was to act in the best interests of the child under the concept of *parens patriae*, then providing a child due process was unnecessary. However, with the perception that juveniles many times receive "the worst of both worlds," the U.S. Supreme Court accorded juveniles certain procedural rights where none had been before. The changes in juvenile justice in recent years have led some to question whether or not juveniles are now entitled to the full panoply of rights accorded adults in criminal processing, including the right to a jury trial. Barry C. Feld, in writing about changes to Minnesota's juvenile code, stated, "viewed as a whole, the revisions eliminate almost all remaining distinctions between juvenile and adult criminal proceedings."[26] Under the punitive model of juvenile justice, it is assumed that the role of due process is to ensure that processing in the system is fair and uniform. Uniformity in sentencing, release decisions, and diversions are now emphasized.

The absence of due process in juvenile justice was essentially founded on and related to the use of a medical model and led to the sixth assumption of the traditional model of juvenile justice: the juvenile justice system, by definition, needs broad discretion to be able to take into account the various causes of delinquency and associated varying treatment. The juvenile court was designed to function as a social clinic which would meet the needs of the child. The belief was that the special types of evidence, psychological testimony, and socio-demographic information that were to be essential to the traditional model of juvenile justice required a more liberal and informal proceeding, allowing juvenile court personnel to exercise broad discretion. Changes in state and federal statutes severely limit the exercise of discretion by juvenile justice officials. As illustrated in the Focus on Policy, **the Juvenile Justice and Delinquency Prevention Act of 1974 (JJDP)** limited the discretion of the juvenile justice system in dealing with status offenders. Legislative enactments that limit who is eligible for informal sanction, prescribe sentence lengths, and exclude certain juveniles from alternative treatments tell judges how to treat juveniles. The discretion that had remained essentially intact after the due process revolution is now eliminated in many states, along with the elimination of any semblance of a medical

The Juvenile Justice and Delinquency Prevention Act of 1974 (JJDP) The law that limits the discretion of the juvenile justice system in dealing with status offenders. JJDP introduces more uniformity and fairness into the system.

Myth	Fact
Offenders cannot be rehabilitated; instead they commit more and more crimes. No program can change them.	Research indicates that intervention programs reduce overall recidivism not only among juvenile offenders, but also among serious offenders. For example, a study of 200 programs showed an overall 12 percent decrease in recidivism for these juvenile offenders.
	Source: *Effective Intervention for Serious Juvenile Offenders*, Office of Juvenile Justice and Delinquency Prevention, May 1, 2000.

FOCUS ON POLICY

THE JUVENILE JUSTICE AND DELINQUENCY PREVENTION ACT

Horror stories about the treatment of juveniles in the juvenile justice system combined with compelling statistics on confinement of status offenders provided the impetus for Congress to enact the Juvenile Justice and Delinquency Prevention (JJDP) Act of 1974. Passage of the JJDP Act was aided by the strong consensus of three groups assembled, in part, to examine the juvenile justice system: (1) the President's Commission on Law Enforcement and the Administration of Justice; (2) the National Council on Crime and Delinquency (NCCD); and (3) the National Advisory Commission on Criminal Justice Standards and Goals.

The President's Commission was the first to recommend that "serious consideration . . . should be given to complete elimination of the (juvenile) court's power over children for noncriminal conduct." In 1966, at the request of the President's Commission, NCCD surveyed state and local correctional agencies and institutions across the United States. The survey documented extensive use of detention facilities to confine juveniles accused of noncriminal conduct. In 1974, the National Advisory Commission on Criminal Justice Standards and Goals observed that at least 50 percent of detention populations were "status offenders" who had committed no crime and who were often held under deplorable conditions. The JJDP Act currently focuses on four primary system reform mandates:

1. **Deinstitutionalization of Status Offenders** The Deinstitutionalization of Status Offenders (DSO) mandate provides, as a general rule, that no status offender (a juvenile who has committed an act that would not be a crime if committed by an adult) or nonoffender may be held in secure detention or confinement.

2. **Sight and Sound Separation** The separation mandate provides that juveniles shall not be detained or confined in a secure institution in which they have contact with incarcerated adults. This requires complete separation such that there is no sight or sound contact with adult offenders in the facility.

3. **Jail and Lockup Removal** The jail and lockup removal mandate establishes, as a general rule, that all juveniles who may be subject to the original jurisdiction of the juvenile court cannot be held in jails and law enforcement lockups in which adults may be detained or confined. There are three exceptions to this rule:

   a) A six-hour hold exception for accused delinquent offenders, for the limited purposes of identification, processing, interrogation, transfer to a juvenile facility or court, or to detain pending release to parents. The exception does not apply to status offenders, nonoffenders, or adjudicated delinquents. Sight and sound separation from adults during the six hours is required.

   b) The statute and regulation provide a "rural exception" for jails and lockups located outside a Standard Metropolitan Statistical Area (SMSA). Facilities outside an SMSA may hold an accused delinquent for up to 24 hours, excluding weekends and holidays, while awaiting an initial court appearance.

   c) A final regulatory exception concerns juveniles under the jurisdiction of a criminal court for a felony offense. It applies only after such jurisdiction has been invoked through the official filing of criminal felony charges in a direct file situation, or after a juvenile has been officially waived to criminal court through a judicial waiver process.

4. **Disproportionate Minority Confinement** The Disproportionate Minority Confinement (DMC) mandate requires States to address efforts to reduce the number of minority youth in secure facilities where the proportion of minority youth in confinement exceeds the proportion such groups represent in the general population.

In addition to the mandates, the JJDP Act created the Office of Juvenile Justice and Delinquency Prevention (OJJDP). OJJDP is the primary federal agency charged with juvenile justice issues and research.

CRITICAL THINKING

Choose one of the mandates listed above and explain why it represents significant change in the system. (You will need to research juvenile justice practices in your state prior to this enactment.)

Source: Excerpted from Kathleen Kositzky, Crank. *The JJDP Act Mandates: Rationale and Summary. OJJDP Fact Sheet #22.* January 1995.

JUVENILE JUSTICE
ONLINE

Visit OJJDP's website at **www.ojjdp.
gov/ojstatbb/default.asp** The website
includes the Statistical Briefing Book,
which allows you to easily find comprehensive statistical information on juvenile
offending, victimization of juveniles, and
involvement of youth in the juvenile justice system. Pick a topic of interest to you
and describe its current statistical trends

model of juvenile justice. The assumption under the punitive model of juvenile justice is that discretion led to juveniles falling through the cracks, and the only way to ensure accountability is to eliminate as much discretion as possible.

The seventh assumption of the traditional model of juvenile justice assumes that juvenile records should be held to strict confidentiality standards. The role of a juvenile's delinquent history and use of a record in adult court and other areas of society have received considerable attention in recent years. The idea that a violent juvenile offender got a clean slate upon reaching the age of majority evoked a visceral response from the victims of juvenile offenders, the media, the general public, and politicians alike. The punitive laws concerning juvenile records and information sharing served to solidify and validate the perceptions that the system was too soft. Research has found that most workers in the juvenile justice system believe that records are regularly used and/or remembered by judges, thus invalidating many of the confidentiality and sealing provisions of many states. In one respect, the revisions of state codes which lessen the restrictions on record use are simply legitimizing what occurs regularly on an informal basis. Regardless, lessening confidentiality restrictions and increasing the system's ability to create and maintain juvenile records reflect a changing assumption from the traditional model of juvenile justice. Under the punitive model of juvenile justice, it is assumed that the lack of record keeping hinders the coordination of the system which results in juveniles slipping through the cracks. Therefore, records are essential to holding youth accountable and protecting society.

Finally, the goals of the system are what flow from the assumptions detailed above. Assumptions about juveniles, their delinquency, and what to do about them led to the eighth assumption of the traditional model of juvenile justice: the goal of the system was treatment and rehabilitation. Hence, it was assumed that the mission, objectives, and effectiveness of the juvenile justice system were based on rehabilitation. The due process model left these assumptions intact, changing only the process by which these goals would be reached. Legislation that has been enacted around the country since the 1980s is based on the punitive model assumptions and changes the fundamental goals of the system, and therefore alters the system's operation. The prime example of this is the Balanced Juvenile Justice and Crime Prevention Act of 1996 detailed in Figure 2.1 on page 38. The new goals speak of community protection, retribution, restitution, and punishment. While many still espouse the goal of rehabilitation, it is either secondary or must be done in concert with the new goals of the system.

In essence, we had a court with a mission of child saving and a correctional system with a mission of warehousing juveniles. This doomed the effectiveness of the system from its inception. The new goals of many juvenile justice systems have increased the debate concerning the outright abolition of the system, because the distinctions between a juvenile justice system based on the punitive model and the adult justice system are definitely blurred.

2.8 SELF-CHECK

1. What are the differences between the traditional, due process, and punitive models regarding a juvenile's culpability and development and the causes of delinquency?

2. What are the differences between the traditional, due process, and punitive models regarding the role of the state, the role of due process, and record keeping in juvenile justice?

3. What are the differences between the traditional, due process, and punitive models regarding the level of discretion needed in juvenile justice and the ultimate goals of juvenile justice?

Cyclical Changes in Juvenile Justice: History Repeating Itself

The fundamental assumptions about juveniles, juvenile delinquency, and how to deal with the problem have changed dramatically over the history of the juvenile justice system. It is currently in vogue to get tough on juvenile crime, and it is relatively easy to change policies as there are no constitutional rules governing the nature of the juvenile justice system. The current trend in juvenile justice rests on the perception that juvenile crime is increasing, that juvenile criminals are just as dangerous if not more so than adults, and that the system is not doing an adequate job of protecting the public from these juvenile predators. We do not care any longer how intellectually, socially, or morally developed a juvenile is when facing certain criminal charges. We have shifted from an offender-based to an offense-based system where rehabilitation is taking a back seat to public protection. Perhaps the greatest philosophical change concerns the disposition of juveniles. The current practices assume that punishment and accountability are, in fact, rehabilitative. Regardless of the merits of this idea, it is a marked move from the original founders' assumptions. The changing goals of the juvenile justice system are more a reflection of our changing attitudes toward juvenile crime itself than a concern with flaws in the original goals.

THE CYCLES OF CHANGE

The cyclical pattern of rehabilitation and punishment in juvenile justice policies is generated by factors constant since its founding:[27]

- Juveniles are in a high-crime group
- They receive less punishment than adults who commit similar crimes
- The public tends to believe it is in the midst of a juvenile crime wave[28]

These beliefs foster the punitive assumptions that have been previously outlined and result in pressure to increase punishment for juvenile offenders. There may come a time when the only two choices are to punish harshly or to do nothing at all. Whether the juvenile justice system is successful can be a matter of interpretation. However, the mere fact that the system handles a large number of juveniles, the vast majority of whom will not come into contact with the system again, is perhaps reason enough to consider the system a qualified success. Thomas Bernard claims that we are destined to have cyclical changes in the juvenile justice system until the philosophic context of the cycle is broken and we treat the broad social conditions which create delinquents in the first place. His belief is that an as-yet-undiscovered juvenile justice policy, or "silver bullet," will transform juveniles into a low-crime-rate group.[29]

In the past few decades the juvenile crime rate fluctuated substantially, peaking in the early 1990s. This peak, however, has been followed by a decrease in crime, especially violent crime. As a result, the frequent calls for increased juvenile accountability and punishment have subsided as well. Indeed, the "problem" of juvenile crime is not a high-profile issue as it once was. With crime at record lows, the prophecies of a "new wave" of juvenile "superpredators" did not come to fruition. Nonetheless, many juvenile justice systems were fundamentally altered in the decades of the 1980s and 1990s. Why did juvenile crime decrease and why are we less concerned with juvenile crime? The answer may lie in the nature of the cycles or, alternatively, in the numerous punitive policy changes that occurred over the past few decades. Perhaps another cycle will manifest itself over the next 20 years.

2.9 SELF-CHECK

1. What changes in juvenile justice have resulted from shifts in assumptions in the last few decades?

2. What is meant by the cyclical pattern of juvenile justice? Between what philosophies does juvenile justice cycle?

SUMMARY BY CHAPTER OBJECTIVES

1. Describe how juvenile offenders were treated by the law throughout history

Throughout history, there was no separate designation given to youths in the courts or other societal institutions. Prior to the 1800s, juveniles were essentially chattel in the eyes of society and the courts. A juvenile was treated the same as an adult in the criminal justice system and subject to the same penalties as an adult, including death. Children charged with a crime were tried the same as an adult and if convicted were sent to the same prisons as adults. Children did not receive special protections in the criminal justice system, nor were they allocated special privileges in other segments of society.

2. Identify the early institutions of juvenile justice

Early juvenile justice institutions included a variety of orphanages, training schools, workhouses, and correctional institutions. Each of these had varying goals to some degree; however, each was designed to deal with wayward children in some way, shape, or form. These agencies were in place and already fully established prior to the creation of the juvenile justice system.

3. Explain the forces behind the creation of the juvenile justice system in the United States

Reform groups began to question how children were being treated during the Industrial Revolution. Early child labor laws and programs designed to cure the ills of urbanization were precursors to the juvenile justice system. A new puritanical ideal developed that centered on the idea that the best way to "cure" juvenile delinquency was to remove the juvenile from the corrupting influence of the city and poverty. The progressive ideology that all children could be saved, combined with puritanical ideas about how to save juveniles, eventually led to a number of innovative programs and facilities long before the creation of the juvenile court in the United States.

4. Outline the three major historical periods in juvenile justice

The traditional period of juvenile justice existed from the early 1900s to the mid-1960s. During this period, the traditional assumptions about what to do about juveniles centered on the idea that juveniles were not as responsible as adults for their crimes and that the juvenile justice system would act as a doctor designed to cure juveniles of their delinquency. The due process period began in the 1960s and ran through the 1980s. During this era, most of what was assumed to be true about juveniles and what to do about them still held true. However, the realization that the juvenile justice system was doing little in the way of rehabilitation began to take hold. Although the assumptions didn't change, the way in which the system operated did. Finally, the punitive era in juvenile justice began in the 1980s when the violent juvenile crime rate skyrocketed and people began to think that juveniles were getting away with serious crimes with little, if any, accountability. As a result, the assumptions regarding both juveniles and what to do about juvenile crime changed and were reflected in new juvenile laws.

5. Identify assumptions of the traditional model of juvenile justice

The traditional model assumes that juveniles are not capable of forming the same *mens rea* as adults because they are not as intellectually, socially, or morally developed as adults. The causes of delinquency were assumed to come from the broader social environment—the neighborhood, poverty, urban decay, the family, and child rearing practices, etc. As such, the juvenile justice system should work for prevention of future delinquency through treatment and rehabilitation. In order to carry out this role, the system required broad and widespread discretion which was necessary to take into account the various causes and cures for delinquency.

6. Identify assumptions of the due process model of juvenile justice

The due process model assumes that the system viewed juveniles as less culpable, but the net result of the process was criminal culpability. The causes of delinquency and its treatment were unchallenged, but the method in going about determining whether or not a juvenile was delinquent changed substantially. The due process model assumes that adhering to legal due process is more important in the juvenile system due to the need to protect juveniles from abuses in the system and that due process does not conflict with treatment goals.

7. Identify assumptions of the punitive model of juvenile justice

Finally, the punitive model represents a fundamental shift away from many of the assumptions of the traditional model of juvenile justice. The punitive model believes that certain juveniles, especially violent or multiple offenders, are just as culpable as adults. The reasons that a juvenile becomes delinquent are not as important as the offense the juvenile committed. In general, delinquency is a matter of a juvenile's choosing to commit a crime for which he or she must be held accountable. Rather than looking out for the best interest of the juvenile, the punitive model holds that the best interests of society can outweigh the need to treat a juvenile. Finally, the punitive model holds that rehabilitation does not work and the prevention of future delinquency should be through punishment, incapacitation, deterrence, and holding juveniles accountable.

8. Describe how changing assumptions affect the juvenile justice system

The new assumptions of juvenile justice rest on the fundamental belief that juvenile crime is increasing, that juvenile criminals are just as dangerous as (if not more dangerous) than adults, and the system is not doing an adequate job of protecting the public from these juvenile predators. We do not care any longer how intellectually, socially, or morally developed a juvenile is when facing certain criminal charges. This is a reflection of the shift from an *offender*-based to an *offense*-based juvenile system. Rehabilitation is taking a back seat to public protection. We now assume that punishment and accountability *are* rehabilitative. The changing goals of the juvenile justice system are more a function of our changing assumptions about the nature of juvenile crime itself than problems regarding the original goals.

KEY TERMS

assumptions, p. 24
chattel, p. 24
orphanages, workhouses, training schools, and apprenticeships, p. 25
involuntary servitude, p. 25
Puritans, p. 26
Walnut Street Jail, p. 26

traditional agrarian values, p. 27
houses of refuge, p. 27
in loco parentis, p. 28
Ex Parte Crouse, p. 28
grassroots movement, p. 29
child savers, p. 29

Illinois Juvenile Court Act of 1899, p. 31
determinate sentence, p. 35
Balanced Juvenile Justice and Crime Prevention Act of 1996, p. 37
mens rea, p. 38

The Juvenile Justice and Delinquency Prevention Act of 1974 (JJDP), p. 40

REVIEW QUESTIONS

1. What are assumptions and what three areas of assumptions are most important for understanding the shifts in juvenile justice policy over the past 100 years?

2. How were juveniles treated by the criminal justice system prior to the creation of a separate system of juvenile justice?

3. What was the earliest age at which juveniles could be held accountable in the Roman and English common law systems?

4. What early institutions were developed in England to deal with wayward children?

5. What religious philosophy served as the foundation for the early systems of juvenile justice in the

United States? What practices were central to this philosophy?

6. What were the houses of refuge? What was their purpose?

7. Define the legal concepts of *parens patriae* and *in loco parentis*. What role do these concepts play in juvenile justice?

8. What is the legal importance of the *Ex Parte Crouse* case?

9. What is the difference between how the traditional model views a juvenile's culpability and how the punitive model views it?

10. What are the differences between what the traditional model and the punitive model assume causes juvenile delinquency?

11. What are the differences concerning how the juvenile justice system should operate according to the traditional and the punitive models?

12. What was the primary change in juvenile justice that occurred during the due process period?

HANDS-ON ACTIVITIES

1. **Find Your State Statutes** Visit a library with a law section that has the most recent statutes for your state. Many of these statutes are now available on-line. Find your state's statutes relating to juvenile justice. Many state juvenile justice statutes contain what is commonly referred to as a purpose clause where the legislators outline the purposes of the juvenile justice system in their state. What statements are made in your state's juvenile statutes relating to the purpose of the juvenile justice system? Which period of juvenile justice does your state most conform with: traditional, due process, or punitive?

2. **Researching Different Points of View** Contact someone currently working in the juvenile justice system: a juvenile court judge, a juvenile officer with the police, a juvenile probation officer, a juvenile correctional officer, a juvenile parole officer, etc. Ask them what they think the purpose of juvenile justice should be as well as what operational philosophy currently exists in their agency. Are they more traditional or punitive?

INTERNET ACTIVITIES

1. Visit the website of the Nobel Peace Prize and read the biography of Jane Addams at **nobelprize.org/peace/laureates/1931/addams-bio.html.** Were you aware that she had won this prestigious award?

2. Go to **supreme.courttv.findlaw.com/supreme_court/justices/** and find links to sites related to the Earl

Warren Court and Justice Fortas. After reviewing the information available, decide whether some elements of the due process revolution are being weakened by the current punitive model of juvenile justice.

CRITICAL THINKING EXERCISES

1. **Prepare a Presentation** Assume you are presenting a paper to a group of people who know nothing about juvenile justice in America. During the course of your presentation, you outline the original purposes of the juvenile justice system in the United States and the associated assumptions of the founders of the juvenile justice system. Someone from your audience asks, "which of the original assumptions are still in place in juvenile justice?" How would you answer this question?

2. **Apply Historical Knowledge** Robert, a 15-year-old juvenile, has been accused of committing the offense of shoplifting. Based on the information and assumptions of each of the three historical periods, what would likely be the outcome of this case in the traditional, due process, and punitive eras? What would people from each of the eras conclude caused Robert to become a delinquent? What would people from each of the eras assume about what to do to cure Robert's delinquency?

2.1 Self-Check

Do you understand what an assumption is and what role assumptions play in the development of juvenile justice?

An assumption is an idea or belief that serves as the foundation for theories, programs, and policies. The main assumptions of juvenile justice are contained in the traditional model, the due process model, and the punitive model, all of which are covered in detail in Figure 2.2 on page 39.

2.2 Self-Check

1. How were children treated prior to the development of separate institutions for wayward juveniles?

Prior to that time, children were tried, sentenced, and punished in ways similar to the treatment of adult criminals. If incarcerated, they were imprisoned with adult men and women; if banished, they received sentences comparable to those of adults.

2. What programs and facilities were initiated under English common law for juveniles?

England managed its orphaned and abandoned children through a large system of public and private orphanages, workhouses, training schools, and apprenticeship programs, as well as involuntary servitude when the child entered adulthood. These systems were largely exploitative, as children often worked long hours for no pay and lived in miserable conditions.

3. What issues in the treatment of children were problematic during the Industrial Revolution?

Many people were concerned about excessive child labor, since factories would employ children for long hours with little pay. Reform groups began pressing for early child labor laws and other programs that would cure the negative effects that urban life and industrialization would have on children. This approach foreshadowed the creation of a juvenile justice system.

2.3 Self-Check

1. What religious group's values were used in the development of juvenile justice in the United States?

The values used to develop juvenile justice in the United States, particularly the belief that hard work and intense prayer brought a person closer to God, were rooted in the Puritan faith.

2. What are houses of refuge and what role did they play in the early juvenile justice system?

Houses of refuge were first created by reformers seeking to house and reeducate orphaned or wayward juveniles into a productive way of life. They were designed to take in all children who were deemed by the state as being in need of greater supervision than their parents would or could provide. Sometimes, therefore, they housed children against the will of one or both parents.

3. What two legal concepts serve as the foundation for the juvenile justice system?

The two concepts are *parens patriae*, which gives the state the right to intervene in the lives of people for their best interests, and *in loco parentis*, which means that the state can "act in place of the parents." *In loco parentis* serves as the legal right of the state to take away parental custody of children when it is in the best interest of the child.

2.4 Self-Check

1. Who were the child savers, and what role did they play in the development of the juvenile justice system?

The child savers were prominent women who were social activists on behalf of better treatment for children. People such as Jane Addams and Julia Lathrop, as well as the National Council of Mothers, lobbied successfully for a separate juvenile justice system.

2. What are the differing opinions given as to why the juvenile justice system was created in the United States?

Some believed that it was out of the benevolent efforts of the child savers, and others believed that it was a reaction to the increased delinquency and desolation caused by the Industrial Revolution. Still others conclude that the system never intended to "save" children, but rather exploited them and molded them into submissive workers.

2.5 Self-Check

1. What was the Illinois Juvenile Court Act of 1899? Why was this act so important?

This act established the first official and separate juvenile court in the United States, thus setting a precedent for other states to do the same. By the 1920s, several states had passed similar statutes.

2. What is Platt's alternative view of the juvenile court and the child savers?

In 1969, Platt summarized three themes: (1) The child savers were not benevolent, because they imprisoned children for long periods of time under the pretext of protecting them from corrupting influences; (2) the ideal home setting was gauged by idealized middle- or upper class standards that would be difficult for anyone to maintain; and (3) the child savers blurred the line between dependent and delinquent children, so any criminal child lost the right to due process and anybody who argued this point was treated as uninformed.

2.6 Self-Check

What changes to the juvenile justice system happened during the due process era?

The key change was that juveniles were recognized as individuals in their own right, and no longer as chattel that belonged to either parents or the state. This meant the following things: (1) The juvenile court process was similar to an adult trial and, as such, juveniles have some fundamental rights; (2) the juvenile justice system was found to not need the broad discretion that was originally assumed to be necessary; and (3) due process was found to help, rather than hinder, the treatment of juveniles.

2.7 Self-Check

1. What fundamental changes to juvenile justice in the United States were made by the Balanced Juvenile Justice and Crime Prevention Act of 1996?

This act stated that the juvenile justice system still had not been able to solve the growing problems of juvenile crime, in particular serious juvenile crime. Therefore, it advocated a new, more punitive model. The concepts of this act have been adopted by several states into their own laws, as they changed the purpose of their juvenile justice system to reflect a more punitive approach.

2. What are the reasons why the juvenile justice system has become more punitive?

There are several reasons, four of which are: (1) The public perceives an uncontrollable increase in violent juvenile crime, and this paranoia affects policy; (2) effective deterrence of criminals requires information sharing, record keeping, and increased sentence limits; (3) increased rates of drug use and gang membership created crises in certain jurisdictions; and (4) a reaction to the due process revolution, which seemed to let juvenile offenders "slip through the cracks" after committing serious crimes.

2.8 Self-Check

1. What are the differences between the traditional, due process, and punitive models regarding a juvenile's culpability and development and the causes of delinquency?

According to the traditional model, juveniles have diminished culpability and are not as mentally or socially developed as adults; the causes for delinquency lie in the broader social environment. According to the due process model, juveniles are recognized by the system as less culpable but treated as criminally culpable, and are not as mentally or socially developed as adults; the causes for delinquency lie in the broader social environment, but are essentially unimportant as long as juveniles are treated fairly within the system. According to the punitive model, violent or repeat juvenile offenders have full culpability, and their mental or social development is irrelevant; the causes for delinquency lie within the juvenile's exercise of free will.

2. What are the differences between the traditional, due process, and punitive models regarding the role of the state, the role of due process, and record keeping in juvenile justice?

According to the traditional model, the role of the state is that it can and should act *in loco parentis* for the best interests of the child, due process is unimportant and can hinder treatment, and record keeping should be held to strict confidentiality. According to the due process model, the role of the state is that it can and should act *in loco parentis* for the best interests of the child while providing due process and fairness, due process is highly important to protect juveniles from abuses within the system and can help treatment, and record keeping should be held to strict confidentiality to avoid labeling a juvenile a criminal. According to the punitive model, the role of the state is that it can and should act *in loco parentis* for the best interests of society, due process is necessary to ensure that processing is uniform, and record keeping needs to be thorough and readily available to prevent future crime.

3. What are the differences between the traditional, due process, and punitive models regarding the level of discretion needed in juvenile justice and the ultimate goals of juvenile justice?

According to the traditional model, the role of discretion is broad and widespread to consider the various causes and cures for delinquency; the ultimate goal is the prevention of future delinquency through treatment and rehabilitation. According to the due process model, the role of discretion is to treat and intervene; the ultimate goal is the prevention of future delinquency, rehabilitation, and protection of a juvenile's rights. According to the punitive model, the role of discretion is limited or eliminated when dealing with serious or violent offenders; the ultimate goal is the prevention of future delinquency through punishment and incapacitation.

2.9 Self-Check

1. What changes in juvenile justice have resulted from shifts in assumptions in the last few decades

As before, the changes resulted from a belief that the old system was not working. New changes include increased juvenile culpability, enhanced sentencing for the serious or violent offender, and an emphasis on protecting society by incapacitating serious or violent offenders.

2. What is meant by the cyclical pattern of juvenile justice? Between what philosophies does juvenile justice cycle?

It means that juvenile justice swings back and forth periodically from a rehabilitative model to a punitive one. An example of a rehabilitative model is the due process model, and an example of a punitive one is the punitive model. One could make the argument that the traditional model was stated to be rehabilitative, but was actually punitive.

JUVENILE CRIME, CRIMINALS, AND VICTIMS

Chapter Outline

Chapter Objectives

After completing this chapter, you should be able to:

1. Identify three main ways that juvenile crime is measured in the United States.

2. Analyze the strengths and weaknesses of victimization surveys and self-reports for juvenile crime.

3. Demonstrate an understanding of juvenile crime and victimization in the United States.

4. Describe the concepts of risk factor and protective factor.

5. List the various risk and protective factors and explain how these relate to juvenile delinquency.

Issues in the Measurement of Juvenile Crime

The fear of juvenile crime reached new heights in the past couple of decades. This fear remains high despite falling juvenile crime rates over the past 10 years. Despite the media's sharp focus on high-profile juvenile cases, the nature and extent of juvenile delinquency in the United States remain elusive for several reasons:

- First, measuring total crime in the United States is extremely difficult; singling out juvenile crime presents its own set of unique problems.
- Second, the juvenile justice system is decentralized; each jurisdiction maintains separate records and collects information differently.
- Third, record keeping in the juvenile justice system is still subject to **confidentiality and sealing restrictions** in many locations. Therefore, accurate records concerning juveniles who commit delinquent acts are difficult, sometimes impossible, to obtain.
- Fourth, there are many options available for juveniles who come into contact with the system. Since there are innumerable placements, diversionary programs, and facilities, the true extent of juvenile delinquency is subject to debate and various interpretations.
- Finally, the statistics that are collected are oftentimes dated due to lags in collection and processing.

Despite these complicating factors, there are mechanisms in place to measure juvenile delinquency. Each method has its strengths and weaknesses, and each presents different issues in both measurement and interpretation. Theories, laws, programs, and initiatives in juvenile justice are developed by policy-makers and researchers using the results of these attempts to accurately measure juvenile crime. Therefore, it is crucial to understand how juvenile crime is measured and what these measurements reveal about the nature and extent of juvenile delinquency.

In this chapter, we will explore the ways in which juvenile crime is measured and the extent of juvenile crime and victimization in the United States. We will also examine some of the **correlates** of juvenile delinquency, those variables that predict who will and who will not become delinquent.

You may note that throughout this chapter, some of the statistics appear to be dated. However, these are the most current statistics available at the time of this writing. You should think about how this delay might affect thinking about juvenile crime and how it affects policymaking as well.

What causes a juvenile to become delinquent? Some theorists argue that television,[1] music (such as rap, metal, or rock),[2] or the occult can cause a person to become delinquent. Others have argued that social, familial, economic, and political variables are responsible for delinquency and violence. These issues are explored in greater depth in Chapters 4 and 5.

Research on delinquency and juvenile offenders has led to a variety of conclusions about what causes, and what correlates with, juvenile crime. Since research on the correlates of juvenile crime is extensive, often contradictory, and confusing, it can only be stated that there are many variables constituting **risk factors** in juvenile offending. However, there are also many **protective factors** that keep people from committing delinquent acts. Thus, there is no one answer to the question of what causes juvenile delinquency. This lack of a definitive answer ultimately leads to confusion over how best to deal with juvenile delinquency.

3.1 SELF-CHECK

What factors help explain the elusive nature of juvenile delinquency in the United States?

confidentiality and sealing restrictions Laws that keep juvenile records confidential and prevent them from being read.

correlates Variables that are related to each other. Correlates should not be interpreted to imply causation.

risk factors Variables that research has found to be correlated with juvenile delinquency.

protective factors Variables that research has found to protect or insulate a juvenile from becoming a delinquent.

Measuring the Extent of Juvenile Crime

The question of how much juvenile crime exists is typically answered through three main methods of gathering crime statistics: **official records**, **victimization surveys**, and **self-report surveys**. Each method has its own strengths and weaknesses; each method collects data differently; and each method typically results in different estimates of how much juvenile crime exists. As a result, it is always important to determine the method by which crime data was collected before attempting any interpretation. In addition to measuring the extent of juvenile crime in the United States, each of these methods is used to provide insight into trends of juvenile offending patterns. Since many measures of crime are not juvenile-specific, it is important to understand what these measures do and do not tell us about crime that is specifically "juvenile."

OFFICIAL RECORDS AND MEASURES

"Official" statistics and measures are data collected by city, county, state, or federal governmental agencies. The primary storage agency for juvenile records is typically the juvenile probation agency. While the juvenile court is the heart of the juvenile justice system, the juvenile probation department is an arm of the juvenile court.

Typically, each county has its own juvenile probation agency and its own system of record keeping. In many states there is a centralized juvenile probation administration or other youth bureau. However, only recently have many states begun to develop central depositories for juvenile records. As confidentiality and other restrictions on obtaining juvenile records have eased, it is likely that more centralized records on juvenile offenders will be established.

Although probation agencies usually house the greatest amount of information on juvenile offenders, typically these records are not used to estimate or count the number of juvenile crimes outside of the county or state itself. Official records of juvenile crime are based almost exclusively on police records and counts of crimes.

LAW ENFORCEMENT STATISTICS The most comprehensive official measure of crime in the United States is the **Uniform Crime Reports (UCR)**, compiled annually by the Federal Bureau of Investigation (FBI). The UCR is a summary measure of a variety of offenses based on official police reports. The types of crimes counted by the UCR are expanded upon below. The UCR is a simple count of the number of crimes reported to police. The UCR is divided into two parts: **Part I Offenses:** the most serious crimes (also known as "the index crimes") and **Part II Offenses:** less serious crimes. Included in Part II offenses are three status offenses—runaway, curfew, and truancy—that involve only juveniles; these give the exact number of juvenile status offenses handled by police. In 2004, police arrested or took into limited custody over 400,000 youth due to status offenses.

The UCR collects data from police agencies throughout the United States that count the number of crimes reported for each category of offense and send those statistics to the FBI. The Bureau then counts the number of crimes committed each year throughout the United States as well as the number of arrests. From the arrest data, estimates are made of how many juvenile offender arrests the police have made.

In 2010, law enforcement agencies made an estimated 1.6 million arrests of juveniles. Juvenile offenders accounted for about 14 percent of all arrests for violent crimes, and about 22 percent of all property crimes that year.

The juvenile crime rate for 2010, which is the last year for which data is available as of April 2013, is one of the lowest in decades. During the late 1980s,

official records Statistics and data collected by law enforcement agencies, courts, and correctional institutions.

victimization surveys Survey research conducted with victims or potential victims of crime.

self-report surveys Survey research conducted with offenders or potential offenders.

Uniform Crime Reports (UCR) Statistical report compiled by the FBI from law enforcement agencies across the country. The report is broken into two main categories of offenses: Part I and Part II offenses.

Part I Offenses Also known as the index crimes. The counts of the most serious crimes in the UCR (felonies) including murder, rape, robbery, aggravated assault.

Part II Offenses The less serious crimes counted in the UCR, mainly misdemeanors.

Criminal records are recorded and maintained by several agencies.
Why is it so important to have official measures of crime?

there was a sizeable growth in violent crime arrests for juveniles that actually peaked in 1994. Since that time, the numbers have declined—falling nearly 55 percent. Though there was a slight uptick in arrest rates for juveniles in 2005 and 2006 (due to higher rates of juvenile arrests for murder and robbery), the **Violent Crime Index** numbers have dropped nearly 12 percent since that time, reaching a historic low. (See Figure 3.1A.)

It is worth noting that as a result of the high rates of juvenile crime between about 1987 and 1994, there were dire predictions from a number of academicians, researchers, and politicians about a new wave of juvenile violence and juvenile "superpredators" that were thought to be coming at the turn of the millennium. However, in spite of the fact that the overall juvenile population in the United States has steadily increased since then, juvenile crime has continued to decrease. Why? Why did the statistics do the exact opposite of what experts predicted?

Between 1994 and 2010, Violent Crime Index arrest rates (which include murder, forcible rape, robbery, and aggravated assault) declined for all age groups, but declines among juveniles were much more substantial. Rates dropped about 54 percent for 15- to 17-year-olds, but

| FIGURE 3.1A | **Juvenile Arrest Rates for Violent Crime Index Offenses, 1980–2010** |

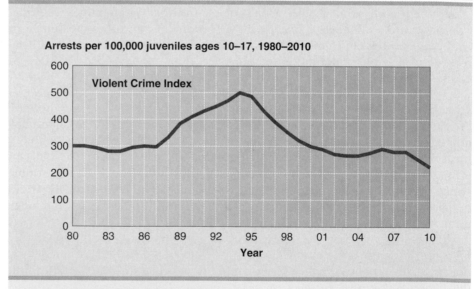

Arrests per 100,000 juveniles ages 10–17, 1980–2010

Note: Rates are arrests of persons ages 10–17 per 100,000 persons ages 10–17 in the resident population. The Violent Crime Index includes the offenses of murder and non-negligent manslaughter, forcible rape, robbery, and aggravated assault.

- The juvenile Violent Crime Index arrest rate increased in 2005 and 2006, and then declined through 2010 to its lowest level since at least 1980. The rate in 2010 was 24 percent below its 1980 level and 55 percent below the peak year of 1994.
- In 2010, there were 225 arrests for Violent Crime Index offenses for every 100,000 youth between 10 and 17 years of age.
- If each of these arrests involved a different juvenile (which is unlikely), then no more than 1 in every 445 persons ages 10–17 was arrested for a Violent Crime Index offense in 2010, or less than one-fourth of 1 percent of all juveniles ages 10 to 17 living in the United States.

Adapted from Puzzanchera, C. and Adams, B. (2012). *Juvenile Arrests 2009.* Washington, DC: Office of Juvenile Justice and Delinquency Prevention.

Violent Crime Index The violent crimes included in the Part I Offenses—murder, rape, robbery, and aggravated assault.

FIGURE 3.1B	Juvenile Arrest Rates for Property Crime Index Offenses, 1980–2010

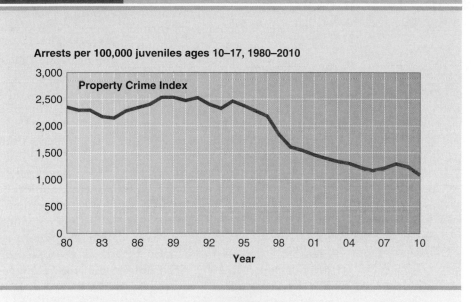

Arrests per 100,000 juveniles ages 10–17, 1980–2010

Note: Rates are arrests of persons ages 10–17 per 100,000 persons ages 10–17 in the resident population. The Property Crime Index includes the offenses of burglary, larceny-theft, motor vehicle theft, and arson.

- The juvenile arrest rate for property crimes in 2010 was at its lowest point since at least 1980.
- After years of relative stability, the juvenile Property Crime Index arrest rate began a decline in the mid-1990s that continued annually until reaching a then-historic low in 2006, down 54 percent from its 1988 peak.
- This nearly two-decade decline was followed by a 10 percent increase over the next two years, and then a 15 percent decline since 2008. As a result, juveniles were far less likely to be arrested for property crimes in 2010 than they were 30 years earlier.
- In 2010, for every 100,000 youth in the United States ages 10 to 17, there were 1,084 arrests of juveniles for Property Crime Index offenses.

Adapted from Puzzanchera, C. and Adams, B. (2012). *Juvenile Arrests 2009*. Washington, D.C.: Office of Juvenile Justice and Delinquency Prevention.

only about 38 percent for adults ages 18 to 24; 35 percent for 25- to 29-year-olds; and 37 percent for 30- to 39-year-olds.

The **Property Crime Index** has continued its decline since the mid-1990s, despite a minor increase of about 10 percent in 2007 and 2008. This index includes burglary, larceny-theft, motor-vehicle theft, and arson. As of 2010, Property Crime Index arrests were at their lowest level since 1980. (See Figure 3.1B.)

Status offenses—which include truancy, runaways, and curfew/loitering violations—were once reported as Part II offenses, but are trending out of the UCR's statistical picture. Truancy has not been part of the reported UCR statistics in recent years, and runaway arrests are no longer counted as of 2010. However, arrest rates for curfew and loitering violations dropped about 53 percent between 1996 and 2010.

Statistics for all of the crimes committed by juveniles seem to be on a downward trend, but it's interesting to consider that while crime has been decreasing among juveniles in the past few decades, delinquency caseloads in our court systems have more than doubled for person, drug, and public order offenses. Perhaps this is because once juveniles are taken into custody, there are many more options for dealing with them. As our options for punitive or rehabilitative measures have grown, so too have the numbers for formally processed cases.

Property Crime Index The property crimes included in the Part I Offenses: burglary, motor vehicle theft, larceny-theft, and arson.

Myth | Fact

Myth	Fact
Juveniles are responsible for most crimes in the United States.	According to arrest data, in 2011 juveniles were involved in just under 12 percent of arrests made in this country. Juveniles were involved in about 13 percent of violent crime arrests and just over 20 percent of property crime arrests. Source: *Crime in the United States, 2011.* Online. Available http://www.fbi.gov/about-us/cjis/ucr/crime-in-the-u.s/2011/crime-in-the-u.s.-2011/tables/table-38. March 26, 2013.

In the past, as few as 50 percent of juveniles taken into police custody were formally referred to juvenile court; about 40 percent of those cases were handled within the police department, and juveniles were routinely released. Today, the percentage of formally processed cases is around 70 percent; only around 22 percent of juvenile offenders were dealt with solely by the arresting police department.

JUVENILE COURT STATISTICS The **Office of Juvenile Justice and Delinquency Prevention** collects data from state and local agencies. The Office collects both **automated case-level data** and **aggregate data** from juvenile courts around the country. It is important to note that these statistics are *estimates* and should not be viewed as a comprehensive count of court activity. Nonetheless, the information provides another method to determine how much juvenile delinquency there is. Figure 3.2 depicts the delinquency cases processed by juvenile courts in 2009. According to the research, juvenile courts processed almost 1.5 million delinquency cases that year.[3]

However, it is not surprising that many arrested juveniles are not formally referred to juvenile court. The **funnel effect** (which is also present in the adult criminal justice system) is much more pronounced in the juvenile justice system. There, the funnel effect operates in part because of the perception that many youths deserve a second chance. Several other factors are operative: it is unlikely that the juveniles referred to the court have had prior contact with law enforcement or may have committed a serious offense that merited greater attention. Figure 3.3 shows that once a juvenile reaches the juvenile court system, there are many exit points that further narrow the total number of juveniles formally processed.

JUVENILE CORRECTIONAL STATISTICS Another official measure of delinquency in the United States is based on correctional statistics: the tabulated number of juveniles committed to public and private facilities. These counts accurately indicate how many juveniles have been incarcerated for delinquency. Figure 3.4 shows the total number of juveniles incarcerated in both public and private facilities in the United States in 2010. The funneling effect is apparent in this figure as well. It is also worth noting that juveniles who commit crimes classified in the Violent Crime Index are more likely to be incarcerated than those who commit crimes classified in the Property Crime Index or those who commit status offenses. This indicates that, in the juvenile justice system, incarceration is used mostly for the most serious offenses. To wit, status offenses accounted for just 4 percent of incarcerated juvenile offenders.

STRENGTHS AND PROBLEMS WITH OFFICIAL RECORDS AND MEASURES The chief strength of official records is that they are reliable counts of juveniles who have been arrested, processed, and incarcerated by the juvenile and/or the criminal justice system. A substantial number of cases are dismissed or are handled informally. In addition, a large number of juveniles are diverted once they reach juvenile court. Summary counts, based on actual cases, also give a clear idea of the workload the system must handle. The most comprehensive data available on juvenile crime and juvenile case processing is found in official

Office of Juvenile Justice and Delinquency Prevention (OJJDP) A component of the U.S. Department of Justice, Office of Justice Programs. Primary federal agency responsible for addressing the issues of juvenile crime and delinquency and the problem of missing and exploited children.

automated case-level data Data collected by agencies at the individual case level containing details on the offender, victim, disposition, and other relevant items.

aggregate data Data collected by agencies on how many crimes or dispositions they process. No individual-level data is collected, only summary statistics and counts.

funnel effect Way in which the number of cases processed through the juvenile justice system decrease at each successive step.

FIGURE 3.2 — Delinquency cases disposed by most serious offense, 2009

In 2009, juvenile courts in the United States handled an estimated 1.5 million delinquency cases that involved juveniles charged with criminal law violations. Now consider this: between 1985 and 1997, the number of delinquency cases climbed 63 percent, and then from 1997 through 2009, it dropped 20 percent. As you can see in the chart below, those numbers continue to decrease. Why, then, do you think that juvenile courts handled 30 percent more cases in 2009 than in 1985?

MOST SERIOUS OFFENSE	NUMBER OF CASES	10 YEAR 2000–2009	5 YEAR 2005–2009	1 YEAR 2008–2009
Total delinquency	1,504,100	−12%	−11%	−8%
Person offenses	365,700	−8	−16	−9
Criminal homicide	1,300	−10	−4	−9
Forcible rape	4,000	−5	−11	−8
Robbery	29,500	35	16	−9
Aggravated assault	45,500	−18	−17	−8
Simple assault	243,900	−10	−18	−8
Other violent sex offenses	13,200	3	−17	−7
Other person offenses	28,300	−11	−20	−14
Property offenses	567,100	−19	−8	−8
Burglary	99,500	−15	−3	−8
Larceny–theft	273,300	−15	−1	−3
Motor vehicle theft	19,500	−49	−38	−16
Arson	6,800	−26	−19	−13
Vandalism	92,200	−10	−10	−12
Trespassing	46,800	−16	−13	13
Stolen property offenses	15,300	−40	−22	−15
Other property offenses	13,800	−49	−35	−19
Drug law violations	167,100	−10	−10	−6
Public order offenses	404,200	−5	−13	−9
Obstruction of justice	197,400	−9	−7	−4
Disorderly conduct	109,800	7	−18	−12
Weapons offenses	32,800	−2	−23	−16
Liquor law violations	18,800	−4	−6	−12
Nonviolent sex offenses	11,200	−17	−14	−3
Other public order offenses	34,200	−12	−20	−14

Source: Crystal Knoll and Melissa Sickmund, 2012. *Delinquency Cases in Juvenile Court, 2009* Washington, D.C.: U.S. Department of Justice, Office of Juvenile Justice and Delinquency Prevention.

statistics. They present the national picture of juvenile crime and allow for comparison among jurisdictions and geographical areas of the country. Trends in arrests and processing can be seen which may ultimately affect policymaking decisions. Court and correctional statistics are excellent measures of the number of cases processed and the population in juvenile correctional facilities. However, they are limited by the fact that many juvenile dispositions occur outside formal processing, and very few juvenile offenders are ever sent to a secure correctional facility (and therefore are not entered in correctional numbers). Nonetheless, official statistics, which are used as the primary measures of crime and offending patterns in the United States, allow researchers to see trends in arrests, court filings, and incarceration.

There are, however, several problems and weaknesses related to official statistics, in particular those in the UCR. The UCR depends on accurate counts from law enforcement agencies around the country. Yet, not all law enforcement agencies report to the UCR. Sometimes, the counts reported by law enforcement agencies are inaccurate. The UCR numbers also underestimate the

FIGURE 3.3	Juvenile Court Processing of Delinquency Cases, 2009

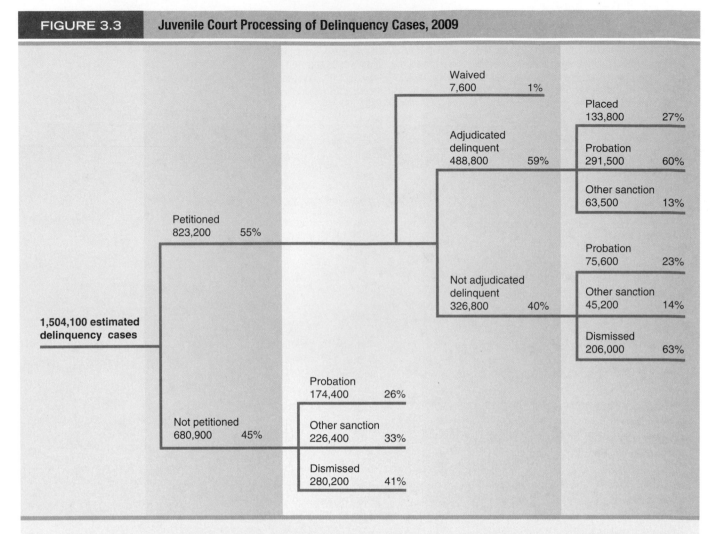

Source: Crystal Knoll and Melissa Sickmund, 2012. *Delinquency Cases in Juvenile Court, 2009* Washington, D.C.: U.S. Department of Justice, Office of Juvenile Justice and Delinquency Prevention.

total amount of crime in the United States. This is referred to as the **dark figure of crime**. The UCR underestimates crime for several reasons:

- First, not all crimes are reported to police. In some cases, a crime may require the police to initiate action rather than respond to a report. Certain crimes such as prostitution and drug dealing are referred to as **victimless crimes** because both parties "consent." This is especially true for juvenile status offenses such as violation of curfew, truancy, and running away. Without police action there is no case to report.
- Second, even when people are willing to make a report, they frequently do not, either because they want to handle it informally or because the juvenile is a friend or relative.
- Third, the UCR uses a **hierarchy rule** when multiple crimes occur during one incident. In other words, when someone commits several crimes during the same criminal incident, only the most serious crime is reported to the UCR. This especially affects juvenile crime counts because juveniles frequently commit crimes in groups and commit multiple offenses during one incident.
- Fourth, the UCR may also underestimate juvenile crime because of the broad discretion and variety of dispositional options within the juvenile justice system. Many juvenile offenders are handled informally by police,

dark figure of crime The phrase used to describe the number of crimes committed but undiscovered or unreported.

victimless crimes Crimes in which the victim is often a willing participant, for example, in crimes of prostitution and drug use.

hierarchy rule Rule used in collecting data for the UCR that states only the most serious crime in any one criminal event will be counted. For example, if a person kidnaps, rapes, and then murders another person, the crime is counted as one murder.

FIGURE 3.4	Juveniles in Placement Facilities by Offense, 2010			
COUNT	DETAINED	COMMITTED	DIVERSION	TOTAL
Person Offenses: Criminal homicide	436	474	14	924
Person Offenses: Sexual assault	758	3,797	83	4,638
Person Offenses: Robbery	2,076	4,813	107	6,996
Person Offenses: Aggravated assault	1,925	4,050	122	6,097
Person Offenses: Simple assault	1,497	3,778	167	5,442
Person Offenses: Other person	604	1,232	74	1,910
Property Offenses: Burglary	1,879	5,247	120	7,246
Property Offenses: Theft	1,012	2,677	70	3,759
Property Offenses: Auto theft	585	1,853	31	2,469
Property Offenses: Arson	114	413	6	533
Property Offenses: Other property	846	2,107	76	3,029
Drug Offenses: Drug trafficking	291	720	23	1,034
Drug Offenses: Other drug	1,017	2,846	83	3,946
Public Order Offenses: Weapons	967	1,979	67	3,013
Public Order Offenses: Other public order	1,443	3,520	135	5,098
Technical violations	4,630	6,640	322	11,592
Status offenses	499	2,281	235	3,015
Total	20,579	48,427	1,735	70,741

Source: Melissa Sickmund, T.J. Sladky, Wei Kang, and C. Puzzanchera, 2011. *Easy Access to the Census of Juveniles in Residential Placement.* Washington, D.C.: U.S. Department of Justice, Office of Juvenile Justice and Delinquency Prevention.

schools, or other authorities. There are also numerous diversionary placements for a juvenile in place of arrest. In the case of informal disposition or diversion, the incident will go undocumented or unreported.

Although more serious crimes are more accurately reflected, less serious Part II Offenses are more a measure of police activity than of actual juvenile crime. As noted in Figure 3.2, the increase in police attention to lower priority crimes and status offenses might have led to a decrease in more serious juvenile crime.

Victimization surveys document that only about half of violent victimizations are reported to police,[4] and that—shockingly—only about one third of victimizations experienced by juveniles are reported to authorities.[5] Research on juvenile victimization has shown that juveniles are less likely to report attempted and completed violent crime regardless of the location of the incident, the presence of a weapon, the degree of injury, the age of the perpetrator, or the relationship between victim and perpetrator.[6]

The percentage of crimes reported to police does increase with the victim's age (see Figure 3.5). However, these statistics are still telling in that they point out that only a small percentage of crimes perpetrated against juveniles is reported to police or other authorities. Research also shows that most offenses against juveniles ages 8 to 15 were committed by another juvenile.[7]

A newer system of data collection attempts to solve many of the problems with official statistics: the **National Incident-Based Reporting System (NIBRS)** collects information in much greater detail than do UCR summary reports and other census data. NIBRS seeks to gather data on the crime itself by dividing offenses into more than 40 indexes; by differentiating between completed and attempted crime; and by collecting specific information about both victims and offenders. However, NIBRS has not yet been widely adopted; it remains an optional program for law enforcement agencies. Participation in the NIBRS program has grown steadily, however, and the benefits of this type of reporting promise to increase the accuracy and validity of criminal justice statistics in general, and juvenile crime in particular.

National Incident-Based Reporting System (NIBRS) Data collection system implemented to collect individual-level data on offenders, victims, and crime from police departments. It is designed to address many of the problems with the UCR.

| FIGURE 3.5 | Violent Victimization Reported to Police by Age of Victims, 2010 |

Violent victimizations not reported to the police and the most important reason they went unreported, by victim characteristics, 2006–2010

| | | | MOST IMPORTANT REASON VICTIMIZATIONS WENT UNREPORTED | | | | |
VICTIM CHARACTERISTIC	AVERAGE ANNUAL NUMBER NOT REPORTED[A]	PERCENT NOT REPORTED	DEALT WITH IN ANOTHER WAY/ PERSONAL MATTER	NOT IMPORTANT ENOUGH TO VICTIM TO REPORT	POLICE WOULD NOT OR COULD NOT HELP	FEAR OF REPRISAL OR GETTING OFFENDER IN TROUBLE	OTHER REASON OR NOT ONE MOST IMPORTANT REASON
Age							
12–17	844,300	68%	42%	22%	10%	12%	14%
18–34	1,379,600	51	30	18	16	16	21
35–64	1,100,300	47	34	15	20	12	18
65 or older	58,000	46	19	21	33	9	18

Source: Lynn M. Langton, C. Krebs and Hope Smile-McDonald, 2012. *Victimizations Not Report to Police, 2006-2010*. Washington, D.C.: U.S. Department of Justice, Bureau of Justice Statistics.

VICTIMIZATION STATISTICS AND MEASURES

Another way juvenile crime is measured is through victimization surveys. For this type of research, people are randomly selected throughout the country to be surveyed about any criminal victimizations they have experienced over the last 6 to 12 months. The statistics gathered from this sampling are then used to generate estimates of the amount of crime that occurs in the United States. The largest and most well-known victimization survey, conducted by the Bureau of Justice Statistics and the U.S. Census Bureau, is the **National Crime Victimization Survey (NCVS)**. This survey provides different data than that in the UCR. While the UCR collects and reports summary crime statistics (counts), the NCVS reports data on criminal incidents (cases). The NCVS provides a better picture of the dark figure of crime—underestimated crime—than the UCR. The NCVS consistently shows that official statistics underestimate the total amount of crime in the United States.

A better measure of juvenile crime comes from data taken from self-reported victimization at schools. Many self-report surveys discussed below include measures of victimization which are likely to be more accurate pictures of the true extent of both juvenile victimization and crimes committed at school.

STRENGTHS AND WEAKNESSES WITH VICTIMIZATION STATISTICS AND MEASURES Victimization studies do capture the dark figure of crime. They also tend to show a more realistic picture of the total number of crimes committed annually. In addition, if a survey is conducted with juveniles in a school setting, it is probably a very accurate measure of juvenile victimization.

The main drawback in the measurement of juvenile crime is that the primary measures of victimization surveys are sent to homes, asking that the head of household complete the survey. It is, therefore, unlikely that a juvenile would be involved in filling out the survey. Many juveniles do not tell their parents about the victimizations they experience at school or out in the community. This makes it unlikely that the head of household knows the true extent of victimization affecting children who live in the house. Furthermore—as previously discussed—we know that only about 3 percent of victimizations experienced by those ages 12 to 19 are reported to police.[8] It can therefore be safely concluded that victimization studies under-represent juvenile crime.

Further, for victimization studies to be accurate measures of juvenile crime, the victim must know the identity of the victimizer. For most of the crimes reported in the NCVS, the offender is unknown. Even if the offender were known, the victim might not be able to assess the age of the offender accurately enough to identify him or her as a juvenile.

National Crime Victimization Survey (NCVS) A national survey of households on the subject of victimization, conducted by the Bureau of Justice Statistics.

Juveniles taken into custody by police are not always referred to juvenile court. *What factors may contribute to a juvenile's not being referred to juvenile court?*

SELF-REPORT STATISTICS AND MEASURES

Self-report statistics are gathered from surveys of youths who volunteer information about their criminal and drug histories. Of the three methods of measurement (official records and victimization statistics are the other two methods), self-report surveys of juveniles are the most numerous and most diverse. In fact, these are the only research projects specifically targeted at juveniles. Since self-report surveys ask juveniles a battery of questions concerning their past, these probably give the most accurate picture of juvenile crime currently available.

An example of a self-report surveys include the Monitoring the Future program, based at the University of Michigan and funded by the National Institutes of Health and the National Institute on Drug Abuse. This survey asks 8th, 10th, and 12th graders about delinquent behavior, drug use, victimization, and other social and ethical issues, and it also sends follow-up surveys to a random sample from graduating classes. Another self-report survey is the Centers for Disease Control and Prevention's Youth Risk Behavior Survey, which measures a range of behaviors that contribute to violence (such as fighting or carrying weapons), as well as a swath of other behaviors relevant to public health.

Another notable self-report research endeavor is the combination of three coordinated surveys that began in 1986, including the **Denver Youth Survey**, the **Pittsburgh Youth Survey**, and the **Rochester Youth Survey**. These were longitudinal projects, where the same youth were surveyed annually over a span of years. Each team worked together to ensure that certain core measures were uniform across the sites, including self-reported delinquency and drug use; community and neighborhood characteristics; youth, family, and peer variables; and arrest and judicial processing histories.[9] These programs, collectively titled The Causes and Correlates of Delinquency

Denver Youth Survey, Pittsburgh Youth Study, and Rochester Youth Survey Three interrelated studies designed to assess the level and correlates of juvenile crime.

Research Projects, are described in Focus on Programs. Some of the findings from these studies are discussed in the section on risk factors and correlates that follows.

STRENGTHS AND WEAKNESSES WITH SELF-REPORT STATISTICS AND MEASURES Self-report surveys measure offenses not known to the police and the number of times an individual commits offenses. Self-report data has shown that individuals commit many more offenses than those for which they are arrested. A juvenile may commit as many as 100 assaults before being formally arrested. Self-reports allow researchers to probe juveniles' backgrounds and reasons they may have for committing delinquent acts. The data in self-reports also allows an examination of trends in juvenile offending and juvenile risk-taking behavior. This method gives a detailed picture of juvenile crime and offenses.

One criticism commonly leveled at self-report research on delinquency is that the data gained may not be perfectly accurate. Problems such as inaccurate memory, exaggeration, confusion over definitions, and outright lying are frequently cited. However, research reveals that self-report data is highly correlated with official records and other sources of data.[10] This correlation tends to disprove criticisms regarding accuracy and reliability.

Another problem with self-report research involves the population the researchers choose to survey. Because several of the most comprehensive youth surveys are typically taken in a school setting, some researchers have observed that certain types of youths are excluded from the surveys, such as chronic truants and serious habitual delinquents (who may be incarcerated).[11]

Other problems with self-report research are raised by the questionnaires. Some questionnaires focus on nonserious offenses and exclude more serious offenses. In addition, there are frequently problems with offense definitions in some questionnaires. Many people do not understand what is and what is not a crime or what does and does not constitute certain criminal behavior. For example, many people confuse "robbery" and "burglary." It is also difficult to be specific in these types of questionnaires. For example, a frequently asked question concerns theft. The question asked cannot contain complexities of law about theft: that the value of the property stolen determines whether the theft is a misdemeanor or a felony; or that stealing certain items (such as a car) may be part of a separate category in the penal code of an individual state. Finally, the responses from which the juveniles choose can be misleading. Typical response choices include "often," "sometimes," "occasionally," and "never." These choices of response obviously can cause confusion and misinterpretation.[12]

COMPARISON OF THE THREE METHODS

There are several notable differences between self-report data and official statistics. Self-report data show that nearly all juveniles break the law at one time or another. However, only a small percentage of juveniles go on to become **serious or habitual delinquents**. Self-reports show less impact of gender, race, and social class on juvenile offending than official statistics show. The best measure of juvenile crime and juvenile offending patterns comes from self-reports and probably the least useful comes from victimization surveys. Because each of the measures has certain strengths and weaknesses, these should be taken into account when making any conclusions about the true nature and extent of juvenile crime in the United States (see Figure 3.6).

serious or habitual delinquents Juveniles who persist in delinquency. Research has shown that a small number of habitual delinquents commit a disproportionate amount of crime.

THE CAUSES AND CORRELATES OF DELINQUENCY RESEARCH PROJECTS

The following programs are somewhat legendary within criminology annals, combining self-report surveys with in-depth interviews of the juvenile, plus family members and teachers. Official records were also referenced. Ultimately, the information that emerged from the projects—which started in 1986—painted a picture of how youth develop within the context of family, peers, and community and how that development might influence delinquency.

The Denver Youth Survey

The Denver Youth Survey was based on a random sample of households in high-risk neighborhoods in Denver, Colorado. The survey respondents were 1,527 children and youth (806 boys and 721 girls) who were 7, 9, 11, 13, or 15 years old in 1987 and lived in one of the 20,000 households randomly selected. Interviews with the youth and one caregiver were conducted annually from 1988 until 1992; the process them resumed in 1995 through 1999. The retention rate was very high, with about 93 percent completion in the first phase and 80 percent for the second.

The Pittsburgh Youth Study

The Pittsburgh Youth Study began with a random sample of boys in the first, fourth, and seventh grades from the Pittsburgh, Pennsylvania, public school system. Information from the initial screening was used to select the 30 percent with the most disruptive behavior. This group of boys, together with a random selection from the remaining 70 percent of the population, made up the sample for the study. There were approximately 500 boys at each grade level, for a total of 1,517 boys. Each child and his primary caregiver were interviewed at six-month intervals for the first five years of the study; teacher ratings of each student were also obtained. The middle samples, consisting of fourth graders, were discontinued after seven assessments. The youngest samples and oldest samples were interviewed annually through their 20s. The study was also successful in retaining participants, with upwards of 80 percent per assessment.

The Rochester Youth Study

The Rochester Youth Development Study sample consists of 1,000 students (729 boys and 271 girls) who were in the seventh and eighth grades of the Rochester, New York, public schools during the spring semester of the 1988 school year. Males were oversampled because they are more likely to engage in delinquent behavior than females. Students from high-crime areas were oversampled based on the assumption that they are at greater risk for offending. Members of the sample and one of their parents were interviewed at six-month intervals from 1988 to 1992 and at annual intervals from 1994 to 1996. In spring of 1997, 846 of the initial 1,000 subjects were re-interviewed (an 85 percent retention rate). The Rochester Youth Study recently procured additional funding to study the eldest biological children of the original sample in order to determine transmission of antisocial behavior across generations.

CRITICAL THINKING

Based on what you know about how the surveys were conducted, what correlates for delinquency do you think they might have found?

Source: Browning, Katharine, David Huizinga, Rolf Loeber and Terence P. Thornberry. 1999. *Causes and Correlates of Delinquency Programs, OJJDP Fact Sheet #100*. Washington, DC: OJJDP.

Trends in Juvenile Crime and Statistics

After reading this section, you might be wondering why we experienced sharp rises in juvenile crime during the 1980s and early 1990s followed by substantial declines to the lowest levels in decades since the mid-1990s. You are not alone. Juvenile justice scholars and practitioners alike have been debating the same questions over the past 20 years, and a variety of explanations and potential causal factors have been proffered to explain the statistics. Several potential explanations focus on the changing nature of juveniles and our culture, while others focus on changes in system dynamics and how we now process juveniles. Regardless, it is an interesting issue.

FIGURE 3.6	**Strengths and Weaknesses of the Three Measures of Juvenile Crime**	
	STRENGTHS	**WEAKNESSES**
Official Statistics	• Accurate and reliable assessment of formal juvenile offender processing • Allows for trend analysis and comparisons over time • Good measure of police activity in juvenile justice • Allows for comparisons to be made among different jurisdictions	• Some agencies do not report and most numbers are estimates • Excludes all juveniles who were processed informally • Most juveniles do not report crimes to the police • Many juvenile offenders are handled informally by police and courts • Specific problems with how the UCR is collected • Underestimates juvenile crime • Poor measure of status offending victimless crimes involving juveniles
Victimization Surveys	• Tracks the dark figure of crime • When conducted with juveniles at schools, probably the best measure of juvenile victimizations and school crime	• Most victims do not know if they were victimized by a juvenile • Primary measure of victimization sent to households and not juveniles themselves • Most juveniles do not reveal victimizations to police, officials, or parents
Self-Report Surveys	• Most accurate measure of juvenile crime and offending • Assesses victimless crimes and status offenses • Juveniles themselves fill out the survey • Gives insight into motivation, demographics, and correlates of juvenile crime • Only measure that can estimate the total picture of juvenile crime • Data can be cross-checked with other official data	• Memory, exaggeration, and lying by juveniles filling out survey • Surveys can exclude certain juveniles such as chronic offenders • Manner in which the questions are asked can bias survey • Juveniles can misinterpret survey questions

Juvenile crime rates, especially violent crime rates, increased substantially during the late 1980s and early 1990s. Why? Some advocates believed that juveniles had changed through a variety of societal causes and cultural reasons. There were more single-parent families; it was thought that the American nuclear family had disintegrated; it was also noted that extended families were increasingly being spread out across the nation. The transient nature of our society had also increased substantially with people moving more frequently and at greater distances. The role of gangs and the pop culture that grew from the gang phenomena of the 1980s was also faulted. Increasingly, society placed labels on this generation of youth, calling them the "lost generation" or "generation X" to denote a cohort of juveniles who felt no remorse, were solely interested in themselves, and were highly materialistic and uncaring. Additionally, the availability of guns, pornography, descriptions of graphic violence, and other lewd and violent imagery increased substantially as our society embraced thousands of channels on cable and satellite, and the Internet made its way into the American household. These and other revelations led some to conclude that as the juvenile population increased into the next millennium, we were certain to see a new breed of juvenile offender, a juvenile superpredator (the term coined by criminologist John Diulio) who would come to ravage American society as youths would become more aggressive, more violent, and increasingly less susceptible to treatment.

However, a funny thing happened on the way to the new juvenile crime wave—statistics showed substantial decreases in crime beginning in 1994. This occurred during a substantial rise in the juvenile population in the United States. These decreases have led to the lowest rates of juvenile crime in over 30 years. What happened? Why have all the predictions failed and why are juveniles now showing more civilized behavior? Let us explore some of the potential reasons for this while noting that this list is not exhaustive, nor is it intended to be taken as the "real" reasons why juvenile crime dropped; it is informed speculation.

- **The punitive juvenile justice explanation.** Vast changes to the juvenile justice system in the United States occurred in the 1980s and 1990s that made the system more punitive and less confidential. Proponents of those changes would argue that such a shift led to the reductions (see Chapter 2 for a discussion of these changes). Juveniles are now subject to longer sentences, increased use of waiver or certification to adult court, fewer restrictions on the confidentiality of their records (some states use juvenile records in three-strikes cases), and more formal processing. Punitive juvenile justice proponents would contend that these changes have resulted in the worst kids getting more time and as a result, there is a concomitant decrease in juvenile crime. In short, the message was sent that a real deterrent now exists in the juvenile justice system, and an incapacitative effect has been achieved.
- **The society has changed its values explanation.** Some would argue that the impetus behind many of the problems during the spike in juvenile crime has evaporated. Gangs, drugs, violence, and guns have all received such bad press and attention in the school system that kids aren't as infatuated with them anymore. Proponents of intervention and education programs would point out that DARE, GREAT, and other interventions (while maligned in academic literature) have had an effect. Indeed, there is now a much greater focus on violence prevention in schools and there are many more programmatic efforts to reduce the problems associated with juvenile delinquency in schools and the community.
- **The community policing / community justice explanation.** Many community policing advocates (discussed in Chapter 7) would note that the embracement of community policing and community justice models have led to an increase in the involvement of positive influences with juveniles. In short, these institutions and philosophies have taken the place of the absent parents in the homes. The need to fill the void left by single-parent homes

During the four week GREAT program, students are taught by individual police officers in the classroom on the topics of gangs, school violence, communication, and how to peacefully resolve conflicts with other students. *Do you think that using a police officer in the classroom is a cost-effective venture?*

and lack of supervision was addressed over time and now these models have become surrogate parents. Although proponents of these models would state that these models address the root causes of juvenile delinquency, the empirical evidence demonstrating their effectiveness is either lacking (especially in the case of community policing) or still in its early stages.

- **The regression to the mean explanation.** The fact that the spike witnessed between 1985 and 1994 was so great and so high leads some to conclude that the drop between 1994 and 2003 was simply a regression to the mean. That is, spikes are just that—a spike that is usually followed by a similar drop that returns the trend line to the original mean. Translation: all of the factors that led to the spike, in particular, the war on drugs and the gang problem, could not be sustained over time and the rates of juvenile crime simply regressed to where they started.

- **Increased capacity to deal with juvenile offenders—the incapacitation effect.** One outgrowth of the increased focus on juvenile crime in the 1990s was the increase in the correctional budgets of youth authorities and juvenile correctional systems across the country. As such, the bed space available for juveniles increased substantially as well. New correctional facilities had to be opened to accommodate all of the juveniles under correctional supervision. The fact that formal processing of juvenile delinquents increased from 40 to nearly 80 percent is indicative of the shift in police thinking, but it is also a shift because of the increased number of beds in placements. If you take off the streets a substantially higher proportion of the kids who commit serious delinquency, you cannot help but come out with an incapacitation effect, resulting in lower crime rates. If this is true, then we have to wonder what will happen to the adult crime rate when these kids grow up and are released from secure placement.

Like most things in life, the explanation is never a singular one, nor is it easy to diagram and understand. The reasons for the drop in juvenile crime are numerous and complex. Simply put, we will likely never be able to distinguish which factor had the greatest impact on reducing juvenile crime. Further, when the next spike does arrive, what will be the factors that drive it? An examination of the history of juvenile crime reveals that spikes in the juvenile crime rate are periodic. The pundits of past cycles are as confused as we are in attempting to determine the causes for the peaks and valleys of the juvenile crime rate.

School crime has received a great deal of media attention following several high-profile shootings at schools in the United States. *Why are crimes committed by and against juveniles likely to occur in school?*

Juvenile Victimization Rates and Trends

Determining the level of juvenile victimization is as difficult as determining the amount of juvenile crime in this country. Juveniles represent a small proportion of the total amount of crime committed in the United States; they are much more likely to be the victims. Research conducted in the Denver Youth Survey revealed several interesting facts:

- Over a five-year period (1987–91), 85 to 87 percent of juveniles were victims of violent offenses or theft. About 25 percent of the youths were victims of serious violent offenses.
- Two-thirds of the youths were chronic multiple victims, meaning they were victims of more than one crime, or offense, during one year.

- Most youths were both victims and perpetrators of crime.
- The best predictors of victimization were delinquent behavior of the victim's friends; the victim's own delinquent behavior, especially injury-inflicting offenses; being male; and frequency of alcohol use.[13]

The increase in violent crime in the late 1980s was accompanied by an increase in the number of juvenile victims of violent crimes. Over the past decades, though, the number of serious violent victimizations involving juveniles has fallen from those peak numbers (see Figure 3.7). Although there has been a slight increase in the past few years, victimizations are far below what they were in the mid-1990s. Figure 3.7 shows the number of juvenile victims of homicide over a 24-year period. Homicides in which a juvenile was the victim increased 66 percent between 1985 and 1995. This figure also shows the rate of serious violent victimizations (aggravated assault, rape, robbery, and homicide) of juveniles over the same period of time.

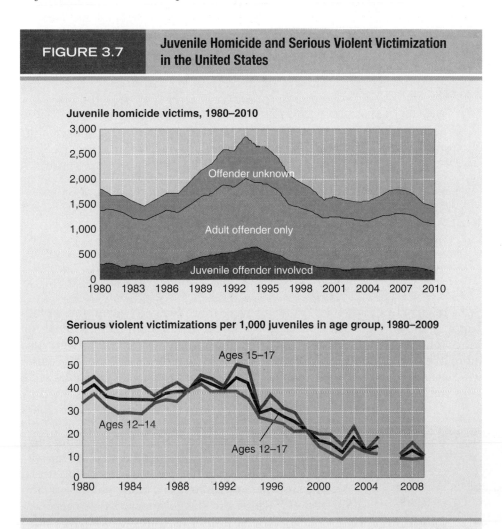

| FIGURE 3.7 | Juvenile Homicide and Serious Violent Victimization in the United States |

Juvenile homicide victims, 1980–2010

Serious violent victimizations per 1,000 juveniles in age group, 1980–2009

- Homicides of juveniles peaked in 1993 at about 2,840. The number of juvenile homicide victims in 2010 was 49 percent below the 1993 peak and near the level of the mid-1980s. Juveniles represented about 10 percent of all murder victims in 2010.
- The rate of serious violent victimization for youth ages 12–17 in 2009 was about one-quarter the rate in 1993.

Source: Office of Juvenile Justice and Delinquency Prevention Briefing Book. Online at: http://www.ojjdp.gov/ojstatbb/victims/index.html. Retrieved January 15, 2014.

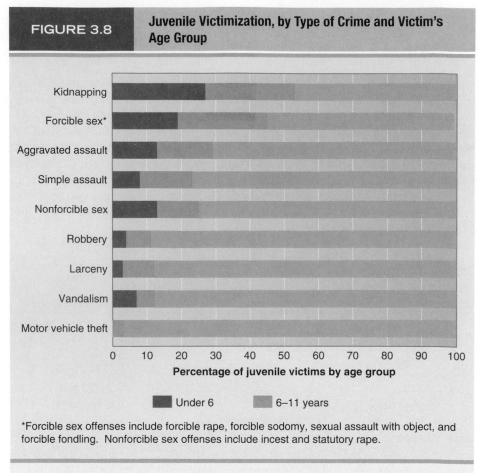

| FIGURE 3.8 | Juvenile Victimization, by Type of Crime and Victim's Age Group |

*Forcible sex offenses include forcible rape, forcible sodomy, sexual assault with object, and forcible fondling. Nonforcible sex offenses include incest and statutory rape.

Source: Finkelhor, David and Annie Shattuck. 2012. *Characteristics of Crimes Against Juveniles*. Durham, New Hampshire: Crimes Against Children Research Center, University of New Hampshire. Online. Available at http://www.unh.edu/ccrc/pdf/CV26_Revised%20Characteristics%20of%20Crimes%20against%20Juveniles_5-2-12.pdf. March 19, 2013.

As reflected in Figure 3.8, preteens were more likely to be victims of kidnapping and forcible sex than older children, and sexual assaults make up nearly one-third of all pre-teen victimizations.[14] Younger juveniles were also more likely to be victims of more violent crime than older juveniles. Juveniles were also more likely to be the victims of property crime than adults were (149 victims per 1,000 versus 129 victims per 1,000 for adults).[15] According to recent data, juveniles ages 12 to 17 were 25 times more likely than adults to be the victim of a non-fatal violent crime. Compared with adults, these youth were twice as likely to be robbery or aggravated assault victims, 2.5 times as likely to experience a rape or sexual assault, and three times as likely to be victims of simple assault.[16] These are staggering statistics, especially considering that most crimes committed against juveniles go unreported.

Many crimes committed by and against juveniles occur at school. Recent, high-profile crimes at schools—including bullying incidents and school shootings—have focused attention on the nature and prevention of school violence. For example, in 2010, students ages 12 to 18 were victims of an estimated 228,700 serious violent crimes; nearly two of every five

Myth

Most crimes committed against juveniles are reported to police.

Fact

Only a small percentage of crimes against juveniles are ever reported.

Source: David Finkelhor and Richard Ormrod. 2000. *Reporting Crimes against Juveniles*. Washington, DC: Office of Juvenile Justice and Delinquency Prevention.

of these incidents took place at or on the way to school.[17] Thefts remain the most common reported victimization in schools, accounting for nearly 60 percent of offenses.[18]

Risk and Protective Factors in Juvenile Delinquency

"What's wrong with kids today?" is a question that has been asked by adults for many generations. In the United States, the answer has often typically been a simplistic one: rock and roll, rap, and punk music; pornography; the Internet; television violence; violent video games; media coverage of crime; and the glorification of crime and violence in movies.

The fact is that juveniles have always been crime-prone. Due to the fact that juveniles commit crimes and other acts of delinquency for a variety of reasons, juvenile crime should be considered *multivariate* in nature. In other words there is no single variable, such as television or music, that causes a juvenile to commit crime.

Because there are many variables involved in the formation of a delinquent, an area of research has emerged that is focusing on risk and protective factors. To understand the thrust of this research, it is necessary to understand first the difference between a **causal factor** and a risk factor. A causal factor is a variable that *causes* a juvenile to be delinquent. A risk factor is a variable that, by its presence or absence, is correlated with the youth's becoming delinquent. A juvenile who possesses several risk factors will not necessarily become a delinquent. However, the presence of these factors does mean that a youth is at greater risk of becoming delinquent.

In contrast, a protective factor is a variable or characteristic that correlates with *not* committing delinquent acts. Another way to think about risk and protective factors is that risk factors put a juvenile in greater danger of becoming delinquent while protective factors insulate a juvenile from becoming delinquent. Risk factors do not necessarily cause delinquency; protective factors do not prevent delinquency. Statistics show, however, that the presence or absence of a risk or protective factor is related to delinquency.

An **at-risk youth** may be defined in several ways. Boys Town in Omaha, Nebraska, a facility that has been dedicated to the rescue of troubled boys for many years, has this definition: any youth who is in danger of placement outside of the home; has had negative contact with law enforcement, schools, churches, or other agencies; or who has been impacted directly by substance abuse, sexual promiscuity, physical abuse.[19] The model that Boys Town bases its intervention plan on is its definition of an at-risk youth, along with several risk factors identified through observation of the youths who come into contact with the program at Boys Town.

Caution must be used when interpreting and examining risk factors just as in analyzing other data related to delinquency. We are not able to say that certain factors cause or prevent delinquency. The interaction between risk factors and a juvenile's mind and perceptions is practically impossible to determine. For every juvenile at risk who becomes a delinquent, there is one who does not. One thing is certain, there is no single factor that either causes or prevents delinquency.[20]

A multitude of sources discuss risk and protective factors.[21] Risk and protective factors are best understood as being interrelated. Figure 3.9 depicts a **conceptual model** of the factors and the ways in which they lead to behaviors and outcomes. In general, the risk and protective factors can be categorized into six areas: **biology and genetics, personality, family, social environment, ecological environment, and educational environment.** The model recognizes that there

causal factor A factor that is said to cause another factor or outcome.

at-risk youth A youth who is in danger of becoming a delinquent.

conceptual model A model designed to show the interrelation of several different components.

biology and genetics A set of hereditary factors correlated with juvenile delinquency.

personality A set of factors focusing on psychological makeup and attitudes correlated with juvenile delinquency.

family A set of factors focusing on parents, siblings, extended family members, and the inner workings of the family, correlated with juvenile delinquency.

social environment A set of factors focusing on the juvenile's peers, social class, and activities and interests correlated with juvenile delinquency.

ecological environment A set of factors focusing on the community and neighborhood correlated with juvenile delinquency.

educational environment A set of factors focusing on the juvenile's school, attitude toward education, and academic behavior and performance, correlated with juvenile delinquency.

FIGURE 3.9	Conceptual Diagram of Risk and Protective Factors

Biology and genetics → Family → Personality → Social environment → Ecological environment → Educational environment

Behavior and lifestyle

Outcomes and opportunities

Author's conception of the role risk and protective factors play in behavior, lifestyle, outcomes, and opportunities.

are various worlds in which juveniles live. These worlds—family, social, ecological, and school—can determine what types of behaviors and lifestyles juveniles will develop. Although the six categories interact and influence each other, the degree to which each influences the other is the subject of debate. However, research has shown that risk and protective factors are predictive of who will and who will not become delinquent. The interaction of risk and protective factors is different for each juvenile. There is no pattern or number of risk factors that determines who will and who will not become delinquent. In short, the model should be viewed as *predictive* and not *causal*.

BIOLOGY AND GENETICS

The notion that delinquents are "born" instead of "made" has always received a great deal of attention. Unfortunately, much of the research conducted in this area has been haphazard and inconclusive. Nonetheless, researchers have some interesting findings and they are still researching biological and genetic explanations for delinquency (see Figure 3.10). For example, low **IQ** has been found to be related to delinquency independently of socioeconomic status,

FIGURE 3.10	Biological and Genetic Risk and Protective Factors

RISK FACTORS	PROTECTIVE FACTORS
• Male	• Female
• Second or later-born in large family	• First-born
• Children of substance abusers	• No congenital defects
• Mother used drugs or alcohol during pregnancy	• No family history of chemical dependence
• Acquired physical handicap	• No acquired handicaps
• Low IQ	• High IQ
• Congenital defect	
• Chronic pain	
RACE AND ETHNICITY	
• Lack of cultural enrichment at home	• Ethnic group is family-centered
• Racial or ethnic group are "new immigrants"	• Ethnic group offers identity and role definition
• Racial or ethnic group values criminal behavior	• Ethnicity is valued by juvenile
	• Ethnic group values conventional social norms

IQ Intelligence Quotient. Standardized test score used for measuring intelligence.

ethnicity, neighborhood, and impulsivity.[22] Yet how we develop IQ, socially or genetically, is still not determined.

Another area of contention has been the connection between race and crime. One line of research found that there were no differences between African-American and Caucasian boys at 6 years, but differences gradually developed, with the prevalence of serious delinquency at age 16, reaching 27 percent for African-American boys and 19 percent for Caucasian boys.[23] As the incidence of delinquency increased, so did the average frequency of serious offending. It rose more rapidly for African-American than for Caucasian boys. With regard to the onset of offending among the boys involved in serious delinquency, 51 percent of African-American boys and 28 percent of Caucasian boys had committed serious delinquent acts by age 15.[24]

Gender is a genetic risk factor that is clearly a predictor of delinquency. Boys are more involved in more serious forms of delinquency than girls. However, in recent years there has been a marked increase in female involvement in delinquent acts. From 1997 through 2006, arrests of juvenile females decreased at a rate that was less than male arrest in most offense categories, and in some categories female arrests increased while male arrests decreased. In 2006, 29 percent of juvenile arrests involved females. This is due mainly to spikes in the number of assaults, both simple and aggravated, committed by females. In 2006, the female rate for aggravated assault was up a staggering 94 percent, and simple assault arrests nearly quadrupled.[25]

In general, the most powerful predictors of individual violent criminality are age and gender. Boys in late adolescence and young men are much more likely to be serious high-rate offenders than girls or older men.[26] Many studies confirm that males are more violent, are more prone to bullying and violent behavior at school, and are arrested for more violent offenses than females.

FAMILY

A large body of research has assessed many family characteristics and found that parental criminality, child maltreatment, and poor family practices, such as those outlined in Figure 3.11, are related to delinquency and drug use.[27]

FIGURE 3.11	Family Risk and Protective Factors

RISK FACTORS	PROTECTIVE FACTORS
• Parent has drug or alcohol problem or is currently in treatment	• No family history of chemical dependence
• Parental rejection	• Much attention from mother during first year
• Low presence of parents as social resources/parental absence	• Juvenile views parent(s) as accessible resources for advice and support
• Low parental monitoring, discipline, and supervision	• Parent(s) monitor where juvenile is and with whom juvenile will interact
• Juvenile does not spend much time at home	• Juvenile goes out for "fun and recreation" three or fewer nights per week
• Mother pregnant again before youth was 2 years old	• Four or fewer children with next child being born at least two years later
• Low parental standards/favorable attitudes and involvement in crime	• Parent(s) have standards for appropriate conduct
• Poor communication in family	• Has frequent, in-depth conversations with parent(s)
• Perceives a lack of consistent care, support, and understanding	• Family life provides high levels of love and support
• Easy access to guns at home	• Juvenile does not have easy access to guns at home
• Low involvement with parents	• Positive parent-child relationship
• Low attachment to parent	• Family values are shared/coherent
• Poor parenting/family distress and low stability	• Familial direction and power
• Lack of support from extended family	• Extended family is active in child's life/informal network of kin/supportive and available for counsel
• Family members arrested or incarcerated	
• Mother away working when child is home (latchkey child)	• Parental guidance, discipline, rule enforcement
• Friends engage in problem behavior	• Mother has steady employment but is home when child returns from school
• History of illiteracy in family	• Family values education/other family members attending college
• Older sibling left household or is a runaway	
• Low religiosity in family	
• Family history of antisocial or high-risk behavior	
• Physical abuse by parent or family member/domestic violence	

Other strong risk factors include absence of parental supervision, parental rejection, and lack of parental involvement with the juvenile.[28] Medium- and lesser-strength predictors include parental marriage status and relations, parental criminality, parental discipline, parental health, and parental absence.[29]

One particularly interesting research finding is that a small number of families produce a disproportionate number of delinquent children.[30] While this suggests that the family can be a strong risk factor, it is more difficult to define what it is about the family that leads to delinquency in children. The presence of a delinquent sibling also increases the likelihood that other children in the family will become delinquent. When breaking down certain family factors, several interesting findings include that:

- The presence of a father reduces the chances of a delinquent son.
- First-born children are less likely to be delinquent.
- The larger the family size, the more likely it is that a child in the family will be delinquent.

The reasons for the existence of these factors are subject to interpretation. However, they are interesting correlates.

A large study of previous research on families found that there was an impact from a **broken home** on delinquency, but the effects were minimal.[31] The study also found that the correlation between a broken home and delinquency was greater in minor forms of delinquency. Another body of research does suggest that youths who are not closely bonded with their parents are more likely to be delinquent.[32] Some research also finds that the family structure is moderately related to delinquent behavior.[33]

Of the family risk factors examined by the study, poor supervision was the variable that best explained delinquency, increasing the risk of delinquency for the oldest youths in the sample and increasing the risk somewhat less for the younger samples. Poor parent-child communication and physical punishment by the mother also increased the risk of delinquency.[34] Although several studies found a weak relationship between a broken home and delinquency, one study did find that increasing numbers of "family disruptions" (separations, divorces) led to increasing levels of delinquency.[35]

The Rochester Youth Study examined the quality of parent/child relationships to determine the impact of factors in the family "process," such as attachment, involvement, and supervision on delinquency. Researchers found that:

- Attachment and involvement were both significantly related to delinquency. Children more attached to and involved with their parents were less involved in delinquency.
- The relationship between family process factors and delinquency is circular; poor parenting increased the probability of delinquent behavior, and delinquent behavior further weakened the relationship between parent and child.
- The impact of family variables appeared to fade as adolescents became older and more independent from their parents.[36]

As noted in Figure 3.11, factors in children's lives such as weak emotional bonds with family, lack of parental supervision and communication, and parents' inconsistency of punishment and avoidance of discipline all relate to delinquency. High levels of delinquency and drug use by a juvenile, in turn, are related to poor levels of family attachment and poor parenting behaviors.

A link has also been found between childhood victimization and delinquent behavior. Greater risk exists for violent offending when a child has been physically abused or neglected. Such a child is more likely to begin violent offending earlier and to be more involved in such offending than children who have not been abused or neglected.[37] Research has shown that, in general, abused or neglected children are likely candidates for delinquency and adult criminality;

broken home Home that is plagued by a variety of serious problems such as abuse or neglect; a correlate of juvenile delinquency.

the relationship of mistreatment to subsequent drug or alcohol abuse, specifically, is less clear. The study found that mistreatment during childhood is a significant predictor of adult arrests for alcohol and/or drug-related offenses. Contrary to expectations, however, juvenile arrests for these offenses were not significantly related to early victimization.

The overall effect of family on delinquency is difficult to assess definitively. Depending on the measurements used, the types of crimes examined, and the juveniles studied, the results of the research in this area are conclusive, but the effects are weak. This could mean that the research is not specifying the relationship between family and delinquency correctly. It could also mean that the relationship is there, but its overall role in delinquency is not as strong as we might think. One argument that supports a relationship is that the criminal justice system treats juveniles from broken homes differently from those who have come from intact households. When parents are present in what seems to be a "normal" home, school officials and the police are more likely to handle delinquency problems informally. Thus, the ultimate effect of the family is difficult to assess.

PERSONALITY

Most research is still in its infancy in the area of personality characteristics and their relationship to youths' being at risk. The biggest problem with research conducted in this area is the way in which concepts are defined and measured. Different studies have varying definitions of many of the concepts listed in Figure 3.12. Nonetheless, there is some consistency about which personality characteristics are common to delinquents and which protective factors are common to nondelinquents. Many correctional and counseling programs seek

FIGURE 3.12	Personality Risk and Protective Factors
RISK FACTORS	**PROTECTIVE FACTORS**
• More likely to feel under stress "most" or "all" of the time	• Good coping skills
• Lack of conformity and/or rebellious	• Responsible
• Shyness, especially when combined with hostility	• Good social skills
• Dependent	• Independent thinking
• Several emotional problems: depression/anxiety	• Sense of well-being
• Impulsivity	• Internal locus of control
• Alienation and rebelliousness	• Good communication skills
• Low self-esteem	• Reasonably high self-esteem
• Low positive view of the future	• Positive view of the future
• Low prosocial values	• Values helping other people
• Low global concern	• Concerned about social problems
• Low ability to show empathy	• Cares about people's feelings
• Unhealthy attitude toward drug use	• Healthy attitude toward drug use
• Lack of discipline	• Values sexual restraint
• Sexually promiscuous attitude	• Good assertiveness skills
• Low resistance to peer influences	• Strong belief in religion
• Lack of religious beliefs	• Achievement via independence
• More likely to place high importance on self-serving (hedonistic) values	• Good planning skills
	• Good decision-making skills
	• Good friendship-making skills
• Stubbornness prior to age 12, then defiance and avoidance of authority	• Disapproves of and perceives as harmful alcohol, drugs, and tobacco
• Suicidal actions/thoughts/statements	• Good verbal skills
• Antisocial personality	
• Favorable attitudes toward problem behaviors	
• Easy and frequent lying	
• Learning disabled	

to reduce the characteristics listed as risk factors and increase those listed as protective factors. Research shows that characteristics such as hyperactivity, restlessness, risk-taking behavior, and aggressiveness are predictors of future delinquency and drug use. The lists in Figure 3.12 highlight the personality characteristics of typical delinquent and nondelinquent juveniles.

SOCIAL ENVIRONMENT

The social environment of juveniles has been defined and described in many different ways in various studies. In the context of factors contributing to or preventing delinquency, social environment is described as juveniles' peers, social class, and activities and interests. These variables define young people's social world as much as their social world defines them and their behavior.[38] The effects of peers, social class, and activities and interests on juvenile delinquency have been well researched (see Figure 3.13).

It is only recently that research has uncovered that the presence of delinquent peers has a greater influence on later violence in adolescence than on early development. Associating with delinquent peers is strongly and consistently related to delinquency, in part because delinquent peers provide positive reinforcement to delinquent behavior. The opposite is also true: having **peers** who disapprove of delinquency is a protective factor.[39]

The idea that **social class** influences delinquency has been hotly contested. One theory is that poverty predicts delinquency. However, findings from self-report research show that youths from all backgrounds participate equally in delinquency. Nevertheless, one study found that "structural" position, such as social class and community of residence, had important effects on delinquency.

peers Classmates, friends, and associates.

social class The socioeconomic level of a juvenile's family, typically defined as underclass, lower class, working class, middle class, upper-middle class, upper class, etc.

FIGURE 3.13	Social Environment Risk and Protective Factors

RISK FACTORS	PROTECTIVE FACTORS
PEERS	
• Friends engage in problem behavior • Peers in the juvenile/criminal justice system • Reported use of drugs and alcohol by friends/peers in drug treatment • Peers in frequent trouble at school • Rejection by school peers • Easy access to guns through peers • Peers with adolescent pregnancies • Peers with sexually transmitted diseases	• Positive peer influence—friends behave responsibly • Peers do not engage in delinquency • Drug-free peer group • Peers value education and achievement • Strong positive peer bonding • Peers do not possess or use guns
SOCIAL CLASS	
• Underclass backgrounds • Economic hardship • Stressful life events • Persistent high level of poverty	• Upper to upper-middle class
ACTIVITIES AND INTERESTS	
• Most free time is unstructured • Activities revolve around hanging out or doing nothing • Little interest or time spent in religious activities	• Most free time is structured • Involved in music: juvenile spends one hour or more per week in music training or practice • Involved in extracurricular school activities: juvenile spends one hour or more per week in school sports, clubs, or organizations • Involved in religion: juvenile spends one hour or more per week attending programs or services

Children from underclass backgrounds (those where there is persistent, high-level poverty) were more involved in delinquency, especially serious delinquency. Another line of research disputes the findings that social class is involved in delinquency and claims that these youths are only subjected to greater criminal justice system scrutiny.[40] If we look at self-reports, social class is not that strong a predictor of delinquency; if we look at official statistics, it is.

Finally, several theories examine a juvenile's involvement in conventional and nonconventional activities. An old saying expresses this theory: "Idle hands are the devil's workshop." In short, the greater the amount of time juveniles are involved in extracurricular activities, the less time they have to be delinquent. The fact that involvement in conventional activities can serve as a protective factor and that lack of involvement can be a predictor of delinquency serves as the basis for delinquency prevention initiatives such as police athletic leagues and midnight basketball.

ECOLOGICAL ENVIRONMENT

Another world that a juvenile lives in is the neighborhood and its surrounding community. The number of juveniles engaging in delinquency in a particular area is strongly correlated to community crime rates and vice versa. Research reveals that small areas within large cities typically have disproportionately high levels of violence and crime and that juveniles living in these areas tend to be more involved in crime and violence as well.[41] Areas with high poverty rates, those where there is easy access to drugs and firearms, those where neighborhood adults are involved in crime, and those that are socially disorganized have all been found to be risk factors in delinquency (see Figure 3.14).[42]

The community a juvenile grows up in can have a significant impact on delinquency. *How can the effects of living in a "bad neighborhood" be counteracted?*

EDUCATION

There are three broad areas related to education and listed in Figure 3.15 that are either risk or protective factors related to juvenile delinquency: the school itself, the juvenile's attitude toward education, and the juvenile's behavior and performance at school.

The school itself is related to delinquency: the overall level of delinquency at the school, the truancy rates, and the number of students dropping out. The physical environment of the school and its atmosphere can be predictive of delinquent conduct. However, this does not mean that delinquency and drug use do not occur at "better" schools. As noted previously, recent research on school violence found that school violence transcends social class and surroundings.[43]

The research also shows the relationship of other factors in the educational environment. Juveniles who fail academically, who have weak or no ties to their school, who have made frequent school transitions, and who have dropped out are more likely to use drugs and persist in delinquent conduct. Juveniles who are not committed to school have higher rates of street crime, and those who commit street crimes have less commitment to school. School performance, whether measured by reading achievement or teacher-rated reading performance, and "retention" in grade (being held back) also relate to delinquency as either risk or protective factors.[44]

FIGURE 3.14	Biological and Genetic Risk and Protective Factors

RISK FACTORS	PROTECTIVE FACTORS
• Lack of community resources for activities and sports • Extreme economic and social deprivation • Easy availability of firearms • Easy availability of drugs • Neighborhood with high crime rate • Segregation and heterogeneity of community • Concentrated poverty • Community laws and norms favorable to drug use, firearms, and crime • High unemployment rate • Level of drug gang status, recruiting, and power • Low neighborhood attachment and community disorganization • Schools with high failure rate/dropout rate • Social dislocation/transitions and mobility • Media portrayal of violence in community	• Good level of community resources to occupy juvenile's time • Strong neighborhood cohesion • Significant adults do not "overvalue" the importance of guns • Juvenile has access to nonparent adults for advice and support • Juvenile has frequent, in-depth conversations with nonparent adults • Interacts with adults in extracurricular or community activities on a regular basis • Access to special services such as social services or counseling • Informal network of neighbors available for emotional support and counsel • Adults working with children of substance-abusing youth and who understand their vulnerability • Strong church in community • Adults who can have close, rewarding relationships with substance-abusing youths through dance, music, sports, etc. • Strong schools tied in with community

FIGURE 3.15	Educational Risk and Protective Factors

RISK FACTORS	PROTECTIVE FACTORS
SCHOOL ITSELF	
• School climate is not perceived as positive • Schools with high failure rate/dropout rate • Segregation in school and community • Low parental involvement in school • School has high rates of absenteeism • School has high rates of truancy • School has high rates of transiency • School has high rates of delinquency	• Positive school climate • School actively seeks to enroll students in college • School is achievement oriented • Parents are involved in helping students succeed in school • Trustworthy role models/staff worthy of trust • Juvenile does not have easy access to guns at school • Access to special services (mental health, remedial classes) • Counsel available from teachers, guidance counselors
JUVENILE'S ATTITUDE TOWARD SCHOOL AND EDUCATION	
• Low commitment to school • Desire to drop out: wants to quit school before completing high school • Low achievement/motivation • Low educational aspiration • Low positive view of the future	• Juvenile is highly bonded to school environment • Juvenile aspires to pursue post–high school education (e.g., trade school, college) • Motivation to do well in school • Juvenile views success through education • Strong school bonding
JUVENILE'S BEHAVIOR AND PERFORMANCE IN SCHOOL	
• Early and persistent antisocial behavior/elementary school disciplinary problems • Low standardized test scores • Poor performance in school • Low homework completion or attention • School absenteeism: skipped school two or more days "in the last month" • Drops out of school	• Juvenile's time in school is highly structured through involvement in multiple extracurricular activities • High scores on standardized tests • School performance is above average • Reports doing six hours or more of homework per week • Attends regularly • Completes high school

One recent study examined the relationship between educational factors and delinquency and drug use and found that:

- Weak school commitment and poor school performance were associated with increased involvement in delinquency and drug use.
- School success was associated with resilience. Those youths who avoided delinquency and drug use, even though they were high-risk juveniles, were more attached to school and teachers and had better performance scores than those high-risk juveniles who were involved in delinquency and drug use.
- Involvement in delinquency reduced commitment to school; involvement in drug use increased the chances of dropping out of school.[45]

Another study found that dropping out of high school had an effect on delinquency even when age, employment, and marriage were considered. In other words, juveniles who dropped out were more likely to be arrested even when they got older, got a job, or got married. Higher education has been found to be a protective factor against delinquency.

BEHAVIOR AND LIFESTYLE

Juveniles who possess risk factors tend to engage in different behaviors than juveniles who possess protective factors. The Research on the Causes and Correlates of Delinquency,[46] examining behavior as a whole, found that the boys generally developed disruptive and delinquent behavior in an orderly, progressive fashion, with less serious problem behaviors preceding more serious problem behaviors. Pittsburgh Youth Study researchers identified three developmental pathways in which progressively more serious problem behaviors are displayed. The pathways, representing conceptually similar groupings of behaviors, are:

- **Authority Conflict** Youth on this pathway exhibit stubbornness prior to age 12, then move on to defiance and avoidance of authority.
- **Covert** This pathway includes minor covert acts, such as lying, followed by property damage and moderately serious delinquency, then by serious delinquency.
- **Overt** This pathway includes minor aggression followed by fighting and violence.[47]

This progression to more serious delinquency leads to a certain **lifestyle** that the juvenile adopts. The word "lifestyle" denotes an organized pattern of interrelated behaviors.[48] When lifestyle is considered, it is a way of looking at the whole juvenile and not just at groups of risk factors. Once a juvenile has adopted a particular lifestyle—student, achiever, gang member, delinquent—that lifestyle is reinforcing and leads to subsequent risky or protective behavior. In short, the range of behaviors involved in a lifestyle is a broad view of the full scope of juvenile behavior rather than a narrow consideration of any one or several risk factors.

Interestingly, many of the risk and protective factors involved in a lifestyle also relate to the odds of becoming the *victim* of a crime. Juveniles who adopt a risky lifestyle also put themselves at greater risk of being victims of assault, robbery, rape, and murder. Although this theory of victim-precipitation or victim-facilitation has come under scrutiny in recent years, the likelihood that a criminal lifestyle substantially increases the odds of becoming a victim cannot be dismissed. The areas, or behaviors, that define the lifestyle of at-risk and not-at-risk juveniles are listed in Figure 3.16.

lifestyle Pattern of individual behaviors, attitudes, and outcomes.

FIGURE 3.16	Risk and Protective Factors in Behavior and Lifestyle

RISK FACTORS	PROTECTIVE FACTORS
DRUGS AND ALCOHOL	
• Frequent alcohol use: has used alcohol six or more times "in the last 30 days" • Binge drinking: has had five or more drinks in a row, once or more "in the last two weeks" • Daily cigarette use: smokes one or more cigarettes per day • Frequent chewing tobacco use: has used 20 or more times "in the last 12 months" • Frequent use of illicit drugs: has used marijuana, cocaine or crack, PCP, LSD, amphetamines, heroin, or other narcotics six or more times "in the last 12 months" • Driving and drinking: has driven after drinking two or more times "in the last year" • Riding and drinking: has ridden with a driver who has been drinking two or more times "in the last year"	• No early experimentation with alcohol or marijuana • Does not binge drink • Does not experiment with hard drugs • Does not use tobacco • Does not ride with anyone who has been drinking
CRIMINAL JUSTICE SYSTEM	
• Chronic truancy • Runaway problems • Police trouble: got into trouble with the police two or more times "in the last 12 months" • Theft: stole something from a store two or more times "in the last 12 months" • Weapon use: used knife, gun, or other weapon "to get something from a person," two or more times "in the last 12 months" • Early age of initiation (related to behaviors previously listed)	• No contacts with criminal justice system

RISK FACTORS	PROTECTIVE FACTORS
SOCIAL BEHAVIOR	
• Early and persistent antisocial behavior • Low involvement in four key areas (music, school co-curricular activities, community organizations, and church/synagogue) • More likely to spend two or more hours per day alone at home without an adult • Violence and aggression • Lying • Cheating • Stealing • More likely to frequently attend parties where peers drink • Vandalism: destroyed property "just for fun," two or more times "in the last 12 months" • Group fighting: took part in a fight between two groups or gangs two or more times "in the last 12 months" • Non-use of seat belt: does not use seat belt "all" or "most" of the time • Sensation-seeking behavior • Minor covert acts (such as lying) followed by property damage and moderately serious delinquency, then serious delinquency • Gang membership • Gun possession	• Achieves independently • High involvement in four key areas • Spends time at home, goes out for fun and recreation three or fewer nights per week

RISK FACTORS	PROTECTIVE FACTORS
SEXUALITY	
• Sexually active: has had sexual intercourse two or more times • Non-use of contraceptives: is sexually active and self or partner does not always use contraceptives • Sexual acting out	• Does not engage in sexual intercourse until an adult • Does not have multiple sexual partners during adolescence
PHYSICAL AND HEALTH CONDITION	
• Poor diet/malnutrition • Does not exercise • Early health problems • Does not see doctor on a regular basis • Bulimia: vomits on purpose after eating once a week or more	• Good balanced diet • Exercises regularly • Good physical health • Regular checkups for medical problems

DRUGS AND ALCOHOL Although drug use has been correlated with many adverse consequences and outcomes, the still unanswered question about drug use is whether drug use or delinquency comes first. Drug use has been found to be a risk factor in a variety of delinquent and violent behaviors. In addition, drug use is a risk factor in becoming a victim of violent behavior at school. A recent study found that among juvenile arrestees, 60 percent of males and 46 percent of females tested positive for drug use upon admission.[49] A study of around 1,800 detained juveniles in Cook County, Illinois, showed that about 85 percent used marijuana within the past six months and 22 percent used cocaine within the last six months.[50] Another major study of frequent drug-abusing juveniles conducted by the National Institute on Drug Abuse (NIDA) had some striking findings, of the 611 juveniles who were studied:

- 95 percent used marijuana three or more times a week.
- 64 percent used cocaine daily.
- These juveniles reportedly committed 429,136 criminal acts during the 12-month period before being interviewed—an average of 702 offenses per subject.
- The majority (60 percent) of the crimes committed were drug transactions of some type.
- Over the same time period, these 611 youths also committed 18,477 serious felonies, including 6,269 robberies and 721 assaults.
- 88 percent reported carrying a weapon most or all of the time.[51]

CONTACT WITH THE SYSTEM It is not unusual for juveniles to have contact with the police. This contact does not mean that they go on to become serious delinquents or to get involved in drug abuse. However, the early initiation of the juvenile into criminal or drug-using behavior, accompanied by early serious contact with the criminal justice system, is one of the most predictive risk factors associated with delinquency. The Denver Youth Survey findings suggest that many high-risk juveniles are

Researchers continue to study factors that help protect juveniles from delinquency and those that tend to put juveniles at risk. *What do you think are the most protective or risky of the factors discussed thus far?*

JUVENILE JUSTICE
ONLINE

Analyze Data
Go to an academic library and research
the primary sources of data on juvenile
crime. Or, visit the FBI's Web page at
http://www.fbi.gov/stats-services/
crimestats and examine their statistics
on juvenile crime. Or, visit the *Statistical Briefing Book* at OJJDP's Web site
at **http://www.ojjdp.gov/ojstatbb/
default.asp** and examine their statistics
on juvenile crime. What trends do you
find to be the most interesting and which
do you find to be the most troublesome?

arrested and have contact with the juvenile justice system. For many youths,
arrest and juvenile justice system processing did not have the desired effect
of deterring future delinquent involvement. When the delinquent behavior
in the year following arrest for first-time arrestees was compared to that of
a matched control group, the majority—about 75 percent for status offense
arrests and 92 percent for serious offense arrests—of first-time arrestees displayed similar or higher levels of delinquency.[52]

SOCIAL BEHAVIOR How juveniles behave in society and how they interact
with others is also a risk factor. Those who lie, cheat, and steal are obviously
more at risk than those who don't. Antisocial and aggressive behavior found in
young children is also a risk factor for future delinquency and drug use.

Many youths who join gangs, regardless of the reasons, are substantially
more at risk for becoming arrested or becoming a victim of crime. Research
has found that those youth who remain in gangs for a long time have extraordinarily high rates of delinquency. Of the most stable members, 64 percent
commit street crimes and 88 percent commit other serious offenses.[53] The
Rochester Youth Study found a strong relationship between gang membership
and delinquent behavior, particularly serious and violent delinquency. In addition, the study found that:

- Although they represented only one-third of the Rochester sample, gang
  members accounted for 86 percent of serious delinquent acts, 69 percent of
  violent delinquent acts, and 70 percent of drug sales.
- Gang members had higher rates of violent offenses at the time they were
  active gang members than either before they belonged to the gang or after
  they left the gang. This suggests that the norms and group dynamics of the
  gang facilitated delinquent and violent behavior.
- Gang membership had a strong impact on the incidence of violent behavior,
  even when other risk factors such as poverty, prior involvement in violence,
  and association with delinquent peers were constant. This indicates that the
  high rates of violence by gang members were not simply the result of the
  accumulation of risk in their backgrounds.[54]

In addition to gang membership, data from the Rochester Study found that
by ninth and tenth grades, about 7 percent of boys own illegal guns; most carry
them on a regular basis. Seventy-four percent of the illegal gun owners commit
street crimes, 24 percent commit gun crimes, and 41 percent use drugs.[55]

OTHER BEHAVIORS Behaviors related to sexual practices, health, and safety
are also risk factors that can predict delinquency and drug use. Delinquents, as
a group, tend to be sexually promiscuous and to take poor care of themselves
in the areas of diet and health care. They also tend to engage in unsafe conduct.
A series of surveys concerning juvenile risk behaviors were conducted every
other year beginning in 1991 and show those trends in risk-taking behavior that
have improved (carrying a weapon, having multiple sexual partners); those that
have worsened (using tobacco, cocaine, and steroids); and those that have not
changed substantially (use of drugs and alcohol on school property, enrollment
in physical activity).

CUMULATIVE EFFECTS OF RISK FACTORS

It is not any one risk or protective factor that determines delinquency. Instead,
the **cumulative effect** of risk or nonrisk behavior, background, and attitude
is more important. The cumulative effects of risk factors on serious delinquency were examined using a risk score based on 12 key variables. This analysis showed that the probability of delinquency increased as the number of risk

cumulative effect The total result of
combined risk factors.

factors increased.[56] When the number of risk factors exceeded the number of protective factors, the juvenile's chance of having a delinquency-free adolescence was very small. The chances of a juvenile's having a successful adolescence did not become high until the number of protective factors far exceeded the number of risk factors.[57] The best predictors of success were having conventional friends, having a stable family and good parental monitoring, having positive expectations for the future, and not having delinquent peers.[58]

OUTCOMES AND OPPORTUNITIES

Engaging in risky behaviors or lifestyles typically leads to certain **outcomes and opportunities** or the lack of them. Conversely, avoiding risky behaviors and adopting a certain lifestyle typically leads to other outcomes and opportunities. For those juveniles already involved in risky behavior, serious and negative outcomes may be likely—teenage pregnancy, school failure, trouble with the criminal justice system, unemployability, poor self-concept, and chemical dependency.[59]

Adolescent pregnancy, one result of engaging in risky behavior, is tied to other kinds of delinquent behavior. Males who used drugs frequently were much more likely to become teenage fathers than were low drug users (70 percent of high-frequency drug users versus 24 percent of nonusers or low users). Similarly, juveniles who reported a high frequency of delinquent conduct were much more likely to become teenage fathers than were the non- or low-rate delinquents (47 percent versus 23 percent).[60]

Once a youth adopts a certain lifestyle, that lifestyle tends to either open or restrict access to opportunities. The more successful and protective factors youths have, the more opportunities for advancement they are likely to enjoy. It is also true that the adoption of a delinquent lifestyle, even at an early age, blocks or restricts access to opportunities.

outcomes and opportunities The consequences of a person's particular lifestyle; low-risk lifestyles lead to different outcomes and opportunities than high-risk lifestyles.

CAREERS IN JUVENILE JUSTICE

Crime Analyst/Crime Statistician/Crime Researcher

Many local criminal justice agencies employ crime analysts, criminal statisticians, and crime researchers. Their primary responsibilities are managing the volume of data that agencies collect. In addition, they also produce reports for agency heads, government officials, and members of the community. The role of this personnel has become greater in recent years because of the explosion of information-gathering capabilities generated by faster, more powerful computers. Crime analysts in police departments serve a vital role. They typically prepare crime bulletins for the officers. These are based on their analysis of the crime data collected by their agency. They are also responsible for identifying and recognizing patterns in the data as well as crime trends that deserve additional attention. Many times crime analysts can predict where crimes will occur based on their analysis of the data. In addition, the crime analyst serves to disseminate information for the entire department.

Researchers and statisticians employed at the federal, state, and local levels are usually responsible for preparing reports on crime trends and analyzing crime data for government officials and the public. In addition, they are frequently called on to assess the effectiveness of programs and initiatives designed to reduce crime or to prevent delinquency.

The federal government employs thousands of people responsible for data collection, data coding, and data analysis. The heads of these agencies typically have at least a master's degree or a doctorate in criminal justice, statistics, sociology, or other related fields. Many entry-level positions may require a bachelor's degree or less. Excellent computer skills, however, are necessary for all research-related careers.

Critical Thinking

What do you think is the most helpful background a person can have to become a crime researcher? Explain why. Give ideas of alternative backgrounds.

It is wise to be wary of claims that any one thing causes delinquency and that some other single factor prevents it. Nonetheless, it is possible to adopt policies and create programs designed to deal with risk factors and promote protective factors.

The relationship of risk and protective factors to delinquency is a continuing object of research, and the factors discussed in this chapter have typically been found through research to relate to delinquent and violent conduct. However, the relationship between factors and the presence or absence of delinquency is not always as strong as one might expect. Several variables and other characteristics affect the strength of the relationship between a given risk or protective factor and delinquency. Nonetheless, risk and protective factors do offer a partial explanation for delinquency. For this reason, identified risk and protective factors have found their place in programmatic interventions and initiatives designed to reduce juvenile delinquency and violence.

3.4 SELF-CHECK

What is the difference between a causal factor and a risk factor?

1. Identify three main ways that juvenile crime is measured in the United States

Official statistics and measures are any data collected by city, county, state, or federal governmental agencies. There are three main sources for official statistics of juvenile crime: police records, court records, and correctional records. The most comprehensive official record measure of crime in the United States is the Uniform Crime Reports (UCR), compiled annually by the Federal Bureau of Investigation (FBI).

Another way juvenile crime is measured is through victimization surveys. The largest and most well-known victimization survey is conducted by the Bureau of Justice Statistics and the U.S. Census Bureau. This National Crime Victimization Survey (NCVS) provides different data from what is collected in the UCR. Self-report statistics are gathered from surveys of youth who volunteer information about their criminal and drug histories.

In a self-report survey, a juvenile is asked a battery of questions concerning past activities. Since 1975, the National Institute of Drug Abuse has conducted an annual survey of high school seniors called Monitoring the Future: A Continuing Study of the Lifestyles and Values of Youth, or Monitoring the Future (MTF). Another self-report survey of juveniles comprises three coordinated projects: the Denver Youth Survey, the Pittsburgh Youth Study, and the Rochester Youth Development Study.

2. Analyze the strengths and weaknesses of victimization surveys and self-reports for juvenile crime

The chief strength of official records is that they are very reliable counts of juveniles who have been arrested, processed, and incarcerated by the juvenile and criminal justice system. Official statistics are also the most comprehensive measure of juvenile crime available. They show trends in arrests and processing which may ultimately affect policymaking decisions. Court and correctional statistics are excellent measures of the number of cases processed and the population in juvenile correctional facilities. There are, however, several problems with official statistics, in particular the UCR: (1) not all law enforcement agencies report to the UCR; (2) the counts reported by law enforcement agencies may not be accurate; and (3) the UCR underestimates the total amount of crime in the United States.

The chief strength of victimization studies is that they can show unreported crimes and may show a more realistic picture of the total number of crimes committed annually. In addition, in a school setting, it is probably an accurate measure of juvenile victimization. However, a chief drawback is that the primary measures of victimization in the United States are sent to households asking that the head of household complete the survey. It is, therefore, unlikely for a juvenile to be involved in filling out the survey.

Strengths of self-reporting include the measurement of offenses not known to the police and the number of times an individual commits offenses. Self-reports also allow researchers to probe into juveniles' backgrounds and the reasons they may have had for committing delinquent acts. Self-reports also allow for an examination of trends of juvenile offending and juvenile risk-taking behavior. In short, this method is undoubtedly the most accurate picture of juvenile crime and offending currently available.

Several weaknesses also exist. One of the most common criticisms is that data gained from the juveniles may not be accurate because of inaccurate memory, exaggeration, confusion over definitions, and outright lying. Another problem involves the population the researchers are surveying. As some researchers have observed, certain types of youths are excluded from the surveys—chronic truants and serious habitual delinquents (who may be incarcerated). Other problems with self-report research concern the questionnaires themselves.

3. Demonstrate an understanding of juvenile crime and victimization in the United States

The level of juvenile crime and victimization has been relatively constant in recent years. There was a dramatic increase in juvenile violent crime which began in the late 1980s and peaked in the middle 1990s; recently, the level has dropped below 1989 levels. Most juvenile crimes in the United States involve property offenses. Most juvenile victims of crime are victimized by another juvenile, usually at school. The level of juvenile violent victimization virtually mirrors the trends in juvenile violent offending behavior. Perceptions of the extent of juvenile crime and victimization probably depend on which methods of measuring crime are used.

4. Describe the concepts of risk factor and protective factor

The difference between a causal factor and a risk factor is an important one. A causal factor is a variable that *causes* a juvenile to be delinquent. A risk factor is a variable that, by its presence or absence, is correlated with the youth's becoming delinquent. In other words, juveniles' possession of several risk factors does not mean that they will become delinquent. It simply means that they are at greater risk of becoming delinquent. In contrast, a protective factor is a variable or characteristic that correlates with *not* committing delinquent acts. Another way to think about risk and protective factors is to understand that risk factors put a juvenile in greater danger of becoming delinquent; protective factors insulate a juvenile from becoming delinquent. Neither risk nor protective factors cause or prevent delinquency, but statistics show that the presence or absence of a risk or protective factor is related to delinquency.

5. List the various risk and protective factors and explain how these relate to juvenile delinquency

There are six categories of risk and protective factors: biology and genetics, personality, family, social environment, ecological environment, and educational environment. Some biological and genetic factors are related to delinquency. Gender is a risk factor in juvenile crime; being male substantially increases the risk of delinquency. Although several other factors have been found to be related, their impact is difficult to assess and explain. Race is related to delinquency to the extent that a particular racial group may value either criminal or conventional behavior, or to the extent that a juvenile lacks cultural enrichment at home. A multitude of family variables relate to juvenile delinquency. Generally, the presence of a strong,

involved family tends to keep juveniles free of delinquent behavior. A lack of family support, the presence of family members who have criminal histories, and poor parenting practices tend to increase the odds that a juvenile will be delinquent. A juvenile's personality is also a predictor of delinquency—juveniles with poor attitudes toward life, who have antisocial personalities, and who are impulsive tend to be more delinquent than juveniles who feel good about themselves, who have positive values, and who have good social skills.

Influences from the social environment such as peers, social class, and activities and interests have all been found to relate to delinquency. The effect of these factors has been disputed, especially the effect of social class. Juveniles' peers and how they spend their time are both risk factors. The neighborhood where a juvenile lives can have an effect on delinquency when the neighborhood has high crime rates.

Three areas of education can affect juvenile delinquency: the school itself, the juvenile's attitude toward education, and the juvenile's performance in school. Education is strongly correlated with delinquency.

Behavior and lifestyle have been shown to be related to delinquency. Juveniles with a risky lifestyle are more likely to engage in delinquency and to get arrested. Juveniles who adopt a protected lifestyle are far less likely to be delinquent.

KEY TERMS

confidentiality and sealing restrictions, p. 52
correlates, p. 52
risk factors, p. 52
protective factors, p. 52
official records, p. 53
victimization surveys, p. 53
self-report surveys, p. 53
Uniform Crime Reports (UCR), p. 53
Part I Offenses, p. 53
Part II Offenses, p. 53
Violent Crime Index, p. 54
Property Crime Index, p. 55

Office of Juvenile Justice and Delinquency Prevention (OJJDP), p. 56
automated case-level data, p. 56
aggregate data, p. 56
funnel effect, p. 56
dark figure of crime, p. 58
victimless crimes, p. 58
hierarchy rule, p. 58
National Incident-Based Reporting System (NIBRS), p. 59

National Crime Victimization Survey (NCVS), p. 60
Denver Youth Survey, Pittsburgh Youth Study, and Rochester Youth Survey, p. 61
serious or habitual delinquents, p. 62
causal factor, p. 69
at-risk youth, p. 69
conceptual model, p. 69
biology and genetics, p. 69
personality, p. 69

family, p. 69
social environment, p. 69
ecological environment, p. 69
educational environment, p. 69
IQ, p. 70
broken home, p. 72
peers, p. 74
social class, p. 74
lifestyle, p. 77
cumulative effect, p. 80
outcomes and opportunities, p. 81

REVIEW QUESTIONS

1. What are the three main methods of collecting juvenile crime information used in the United States?

2. What is the UCR? What are index crimes?

3. What is the NCVS? Who is surveyed in the NCVS?

4. What are the three research projects that comprise the Causes and Correlates of Crime research?

5. List three strengths and three weaknesses of using official statistics to measure juvenile crime.

6. List three strengths and three weaknesses of using victimization surveys to measure juvenile crime.

7. List three strengths and three weaknesses of using self-report surveys to measure juvenile crime.

8. What role do biology and genetics play in juvenile delinquency?

9. What role does the family play in juvenile delinquency?

10. What role does personality play in juvenile delinquency?

11. What role does the social environment play in juvenile delinquency?

12. What role does the ecological environment play in juvenile delinquency?

13. What role does education play in juvenile delinquency?

14. What role do behavior and lifestyle play in juvenile delinquency?

15. How does lifestyle affect opportunities and outcomes for juveniles?

HANDS-ON ACTIVITIES

1. **Analyze Data** Go to an academic library and research the main sources of data on crime or access the website of the Office of Juvenile Justice and Delinquency Prevention at **www.ojjdp.ncjrs.org/ojstatbb/index.html** for a view of juvenile crime. You will find a variety of statistics, charts, and graphs on juvenile offending, juvenile victimization, and the juvenile justice system. Examine the data and determine the most interesting trends in juvenile justice.

2. **Visit a local probation officer** Go to your local juvenile probation authority and visit with a juvenile probation officer about the manner in which statistics are kept on juvenile crime. How is the officer bound by confidentiality standards? Ask about some problems experienced in the past in using juvenile records.

INTERNET ACTIVITIES

1. Bureau of Justice Statistics maintains a website with a variety of data on juvenile justice and juvenile crime. Go to **www.albany.edu/sourcebook/** and locate an interesting article on juvenile crime statistics. What trends does the article reveal?

2. Another good source for information about juvenile justice is the Sourcebook of Criminal Justice Statistics

Online, which can be found at **www.albany.edu/sourcebook/**. Visit the website and locate tables that present information based on the three main ways of measuring juvenile crime. What differences in information do you see among the tables that might be explained by the method through which the data was collected?

CRITICAL THINKING EXERCISES

1. **Analyze Data and Formulate Rationales about Crime**
   Examine the data presented in Figure 3.2 on page 57. What trends in juvenile offending do you see as most pronounced? What is causing the current decrease in violent juvenile offenses? Why are the figures for property offenses relatively stable? Do you think the trend in violent offenses will change in the next few years? Why or why not?

2. **Develop Data-Gathering Techniques** You have been asked by a local school to analyze how much crime exists in the school. What method(s) of measuring crime would you use to determine the level of crime in the school? What characteristics of the method(s) you choose make it/them better than the others? If you believe that the method(s) you have used show the most accurate level of crime in the school, what are your reasons for holding this position?

ANSWERS TO SELF-CHECKS

3.1 Self-Check

What factors help explain the elusive nature of juvenile delinquency in the United States?
Several factors affect the realities and perceptions surrounding delinquency. One is that the various methods of data collection for juvenile statistics are different and sometimes contradictory. For instance, self-report surveys show that social class does not affect delinquency, but official statistics show that it does. This, in turn, creates problems for those who wish to define the causes of juvenile delinquency before they attempt to fight it.

3.2 Self-Check

1. Explain the concept of victimless crime.
Victimless crimes are crimes that are said to not have a victim because the victim is a willing participant, such as in the crimes of prostitution or drug use.

2. Why do you think the report percentage for crimes involving juveniles is low compared with that of crimes involving adults?
Factors may include juveniles' perceived sense of helplessness, fear of being in trouble with school or family, and a belief that they should handle it themselves. Further, many times bullies in schools engage in tactics that make it less likely that a kid will report a crime. Finally, there is additional social stigma involved in a school setting that would lead a kid not to report a crime for fear of being labeled a snitch or a tattle tale.

3.3 Self-Check

What is the difference between a causal factor and a risk factor?
A **causal factor** is one that causes a juvenile to be delinquent. A **risk factor** is a variable that, by its presence or absence, is correlated with a youth's becoming delinquent. Even the presence of several risk factors, however, does not guarantee that delinquent behavior will emerge.

PART 2

THEORIES OF JUVENILE DELINQUENCY

CHOICE, DETERRENCE, BIOLOGICAL, AND PSYCHOLOGICAL THEORIES

CHAPTER FOUR

Chapter Outline

Theories of Juvenile Delinquency

Classical and Positive Schools of Thought

Classical School

Positive School

Choice Theory

Routine Activities

Deterrence Theory

Biological Theories

Morphological Approach

Genetics and Inherited Factors

Biochemical and Neurological Approach

Psychological Theories

Psychoanalytic Approach

Moral Development and Delinquency

Personality Disorders

Learning Theories

Chapter Objectives

After completing this chapter, you should be able to:

1. Contrast the classical and positive schools of criminological thought.

2. Understand choice theory.

3. Understand deterrence theory.

4. Explain Lombroso's atavism theory and Sheldon's somatotype theory.

5. Summarize twin and adoption studies.

6. Describe biochemical and neurological factors that impact delinquency.

7. Identify the major arguments presented by psychoanalytic theory.

8. Describe the relationship between moral development and delinquency.

9. Describe the impact of personality disorders on delinquency.

10. Summarize the three major learning theories.

Theories of Juvenile Delinquency

This chapter and Chapter 5 focus on the causes of juvenile delinquency. Since the development of the juvenile justice system, people have formulated theories in attempts to explain why juveniles commit delinquent acts. There are several theories that explain juvenile delinquency. A **theory** is a principle or an idea that attempts to define and explain a phenomenon, in this case, juvenile delinquency. Theories are also used to design programs and policies in efforts to decrease delinquency. Chapter 5 covers sociological and criminological explanations of juvenile delinquency.

This chapter focuses on choice, deterrence, biological, and psychological theories of delinquency. According to these theories, the reason juveniles commit delinquent acts is that they choose to do so or because of some biological factor or psychological malady. This chapter presents the classical and positive schools of thought and describes the major biological factors that lead to delinquency, including genetic, biochemical, and neurological factors. Finally, we discuss the major psychological theories about why juveniles break the law.

4.1 SELF-CHECK

Why do juvenile delinquents commit delinquent acts according to the choice, deterrence, biological, and psychological theories?

Classical and Positive Schools of Thought

Two major schools of criminological thought, the classical and the positive schools, are based on assumptions about individuals and their actions. For example, if someone states that juveniles choose to commit delinquent acts, that statement agrees with assumptions made by the classical school. On the other hand, if someone states that juveniles commit delinquent acts because they are poor and lack education, this statement agrees with assumptions made by the positive school. The differences in the assumptions of the classical and positive schools of thought have ramifications for the way juvenile delinquents are perceived and handled in the justice system.

CLASSICAL SCHOOL

The classical school of thought controlled judicial policy for juveniles in the United States until the late 1800s. According to the classical school, behavior is rational and a product of **free will;** juveniles choose to commit delinquent acts. They make rational decisions to commit crime because of the perceived pleasure derived from such acts. Cesare Beccaria (1738–1794), an Italian nobleman, is the best-known proponent of the classical school. Beccaria believed that people are naturally **hedonistic,**[1] which means that they attempt to maximize pleasure and minimize pain by performing acts that are pleasurable and avoiding acts that are painful. Therefore, as long as juveniles are deriving pleasure from committing delinquent acts, they will continue their delinquent behavior. Thus, delinquent behavior will cease only when the pain exceeds the pleasure. This is sometimes referred to as the *pleasure-pain principle*—or hedonistic calculus.

The classical school of thought focuses on the offense committed rather than on the offender. The offender's background, mental capacities, and extenuating circumstances are not important. The challenge for the law and society is to make the punishment fit the crime. The harm done by the offense must be proportional to the punishment; the more serious the offense, the more serious the punishment. If the punishment exceeds the pleasure derived from the crime, the person will be deterred. However, in order for the punishment to serve as a deterrent, it must be swift, certain, and severe.

theory A formalized idea or set of principles that attempts to define and explain a phenomenon.

free will The ability to make a choice among various alternatives.

hedonistic Attempting to maximize pleasure and minimize pain.

The punishment for a crime should be *just* severe enough to deter people from committing the act.[2] For example, in the 1700s in England, more than 200 offenses were punishable by death. Beccaria did not advocate *more* punishment but favored punishment that fit the crime. He believed that if people knew the punishment they faced, they would exercise their free will in deciding whether to commit the crime. The role of society is to increase the risks and decrease the benefits of crime so that people will choose not to commit crime.

POSITIVE SCHOOL

The positive school of thought began to influence juvenile justice practices in the late 1800s. This school believes that behavior is beyond an individual's control. In other words, juveniles do not commit crimes because they exercise free will and choose to commit crimes but rather because of factors beyond their control. The influence of the positive school of thought increased for two reasons: First, the emergence of the scientific method as a means to study phenomena developed in the 1800s. Scientific techniques became available to conduct research to determine factors that led to the development of delinquency. Before the development of the scientific method, it was impossible to empirically determine which factors led to crime. Unlike the classical school that is based on the logic that people choose to commit crime, the positive school is based on science. Second, the perception was that punishment, as encouraged by the classical school, had failed to reduce crime. Therefore, the argument was made that if juveniles commit crime because of forces beyond their control, punishing them for that behavior will not reduce the propensity to commit the act again. What will prevent the individual from continuing to commit crime is to identify the factors that lead to crime and develop treatment strategies to eliminate these factors. Therefore, the focus of the positive school is on rehabilitation rather than on punishment.

At first, positive criminologists looked at biological factors as the cause of crime. Over time, they emphasized isolating psychological factors and social factors that led to crime—family and school environments, and peer relationships. Cesare Lombroso is usually credited with having founded the positive school of thought. Lombroso believed that some individuals were less evolved than others, and that because of biological factors, they were unable to keep themselves from committing crime. (A discussion of Lombroso's theory appears in greater detail later in this chapter.)

Figure 4.1 contrasts the classical and positive schools. The classical school contends that juveniles commit delinquent acts because they choose to do so (free will). The positive school asserts that factors beyond the individual's control determine (or cause) delinquent acts. The classical school assumes that people are hedonistic and want to maximize pleasure and minimize pain; the positive school assumes that there are multiple causes of delinquency beyond the desire to maximize pleasure and minimize pain. Classical criminologists focus on the offense and prescribe a punishment that fits the offense. The

FIGURE 4.1	Comparison of Key Concepts from the Classical and the Positive Schools of Thought	
CLASSICAL SCHOOL	**POSITIVE SCHOOL**	
Free will	Determinism	
Hedonistic human	Multiple causes	
Emphasis on offense	Emphasis on offender	
Punishment	Rehabilitation	

4.2 SELF-CHECK

1. Briefly describe the classical school. Who was its best known proponent?
2. What beliefs were held by the positive school?

positive school posits that people's behavior is determined by their social surroundings and other characteristics that can cause or influence their behavior. As such, positive criminologists focus on the offender and support rehabilitation to eliminate factors that lead to delinquency.

Do you think rehabilitation is more effective in juvenile settings? If so, are juveniles more amenable to treatment?

Choice Theory

The classical school of thought controlled judicial policy until the late 1800s and presented the first theories of why individuals commit crime. Basically, individuals commit crime because they make a rational choice to do so by weighing the risks and benefits. When the positive school became prevalent, the tenets of the classical school began to have less influence on judicial policy.

In the late 1970s, the major beliefs of the classical school reemerged and are now often referred to as rational choice or choice theory. Three reasons explain this renewed interest in the classical school of thought:

1. Criminologists began to question the belief on which the positive school was based: that crime-producing traits and factors could be isolated and treatment could be administered to eliminate or control the trait/factor. However, by the late 1970s, researchers had failed to identify and isolate these factors and traits after almost 100 years of effort. Theorists who were dissatisfied with the positive school began to offer alternative reasons why juveniles commit crime.
2. The reported crime rate in the 1960s and 1970s increased significantly. This was evidence to some that the beliefs and practices of the positive school were unable to control the crime rate. Some began to look for means other than treatment and rehabilitation to control the crime rate.
3. The practice of rehabilitation came under attack.[3] In 1974, Robert Martinson wrote an article reviewing 231 studies of prison programs aimed at rehabilitating inmates. Martinson concluded that "with few and isolated exceptions, the rehabilitative efforts that have been reported so far have had no appreciable effect on recidivism."[4] Critics of prison programs used this finding, which was picked up by the mass media, to argue against rehabilitation as a primary purpose for incarceration. The results of the article are commonly referred to as "nothing works."

Since it appeared that the efforts of the positive school had failed, many called for a change in judicial policy to emphasize the need for punishment—not rehabilitation—as the primary reason for incarceration.

Based on the preceding factors, judicial policy began to focus on the offense and not the offender. Rational choice theory supports the idea that since the offender has made a rational choice to commit the offense, the focus should be on the offense and not on the offender. Rational choice theorists believe that the way to control delinquency is to have offenders fear the punishment and be deterred from committing the act. Because people are hedonistic and seek pleasure and the avoidance of pain, the role of punishment is to make the risks of committing delinquent acts greater than any pleasure they experience in committing the delinquent acts. Those who support the use of punishment to control delinquency assume that juveniles are making a choice to commit delinquent acts and can be deterred if the risks outweigh the benefits. The policies that have gained widespread acceptance in juvenile court, such as mandatory waiver to adult court, are also based on rational choice theory.

ROUTINE ACTIVITIES

Routine activities theory is based on rational choice. Developed by Lawrence Cohen and Marcus Felson, the theory contends that the motivation to commit crime and the supply of offenders are constant.[5] Many say that changes in the crime rates are due to changes in the number of motivated offenders. However, Cohen and Felson argue that there is always a steady supply of offenders who are motivated to commit crime. Instead, changes in crime rates are due to changes in the availability of targets and to the absence of capable guardians.[6] Therefore, crime occurs when there is a convergence in time and space of the following three factors:

Juveniles are responsible for many auto thefts each year. *Why do you think this offense is occurring?*

- a motivated offender (for example, a drug-abusing juvenile who needs money for drugs)
- a suitable target (for example, a home with easily transportable and valuable property)
- the absence of a capable guardian (for example, homeowners and neighbors are not home)[7]

All three factors must be present in order for a crime to occur. For example, if you leave your car running unattended with the doors unlocked on a cold winter morning in your apartment parking lot, it does not mean that your car will be stolen. Probably only two of the three factors are present: your vehicle is a suitable target and there is an absence of a capable guardian. However, in order for your vehicle to be stolen there must be a motivated offender at that time and place. Since it is unlikely that such a person will be present, your car will not be stolen. However, when motivated offenders are present, they make rational choices by selecting suitable targets that lack capable guardianship. This also reduces their chances of apprehension.

Deterrence Theory

Deterrence theory follows directly from choice theory. According to the deterrence theory, juveniles commit crime because they make a choice to do so, and this choice is based on the perceived risks and benefits of committing the delinquent act. If the risks (apprehension and punishment) outweigh the benefits, the person

4.3 SELF-CHECK

1. What are the three reasons for the renewed interest in the classical school?

2. How do Lawrence Cohen and Marcus Felson explain the changes in crime rates?

will not commit the act. The juvenile will be deterred from committing the delinquent act because of the threat of punishment.

General deterrence discourages would-be delinquents from committing delinquent acts because of the threat of punishment. General deterrence occurs when would-be delinquents choose not to commit a certain act because they fear the sanction that may be imposed. Sometimes, judges make examples of one offender to keep others from committing the same act. For example, one 18th century judge reportedly told a defendant, "You are to be hanged not because you have stolen a sheep but in order that others may not steal sheep."[8]

Specific deterrence is designed to impose a sanction on adjudicated delinquents to prevent them from continuing to commit delinquent acts. In other words, the sanction is so distasteful to delinquents that they do not want to commit any more delinquent acts. For example, a teenage girl who is arrested for shoplifting and is given 50 hours of community service as a sanction will not like spending several weekends doing community service just because she stole something from the grocery store. This girl will not commit any further acts of delinquency because of the sanction imposed. She has been specifically deterred.

The deterrence theory involves at least four assumptions.

- The most important assumption is that individuals are rational actors.[9] In other words, juveniles weigh the potential risks and benefits of committing a delinquent act and then make a conscious decision whether to commit the offense.
- Juveniles must be aware of the penalty for particular crimes.[10]
- Juveniles must view the risks as unpleasant.[11] If a juvenile does not think apprehension and incarceration are unpleasant, then he or she will not be deterred.
- In order for deterrence to be effective, the sanction must be swift, certain, and severe.

The sanction must be imposed quickly to have the greatest deterrent effect and there must be a high probability that a sanction will be imposed. It is not the actual certainty, severity, and swiftness of the sanction that serves as a deterrent but rather the juvenile's perception that the sanction is severe and swift. If juveniles believe that the certainty of arrest is high for shoplifting, then they will be deterred from committing the offense even if, in reality, there is little chance of arrest. Similarly, if juveniles perceive juvenile detention as a terrible place where they do not want to go, they may be deterred from committing offenses. On the other hand, if juveniles do not believe that being placed in a detention center is anything to fear, then they are less likely to be deterred. Thus, if juveniles do not believe that the sanctions in juvenile court are severe, then they are unlikely to be deterred from committing delinquent acts.

Minimal evidence supports the argument that the threat of arrest and punishment deters juvenile delinquency.[12] In fact, evidence supports the contention that informal sanctions from parents and friends serve as more of a deterrent than legal sanctions.[13] Fearing disapproval from parents and peers for delinquent acts is more likely to keep juveniles from committing those acts than the fear of arrest and punishment.

Why doesn't the fear of sanctions deter juveniles from committing delinquent acts? First, as mentioned earlier, many juveniles are not rational actors. They do not calculate the risks and benefits before deciding their course of action. Instead, they frequently commit delinquent acts spontaneously. Many delinquent acts are not planned events. Further, many juveniles are under the influence of alcohol and/or drugs during the commission of the offense.[14] Second, juveniles may not perceive the risk of apprehension and punishment to be high. If juveniles do not believe they have a good chance of being caught,

Certainty versus Severity

On the certainty of punishment, Beccaria wrote: "The certainty of a punishment, even if it be moderate, will always make a stronger impression than the fear of another which is more terrible but combined with the hope of impunity; even the least evils, when they are certain, always terrify men's minds."

Source: Beccaria, Cesare. *On Crimes and Punishments*. New York: Macmillan 1963, p. 58.

general deterrence Seeks to discourage would-be delinquents from committing delinquent acts because of the threat of punishment.

specific deterrence A sanction imposed on adjudicated delinquents in order to prevent them from continuing to commit delinquent acts in the future.

the threat of a sanction will not deter. Their perceptions also have been validated through experience. If juveniles have committed delinquent acts in the past but have not been arrested or punished, there is little likelihood that they believe they will be caught next time. This perception is also supported by reality. Only approximately 20 percent of all index crimes reported to the police are cleared by arrest.

Biological Theories

Choice and deterrence theories are based on the classical school of criminological thought. The first theories developed from the positive school of criminology were biological theories. They support the argument that biological differences exist between delinquents and nondelinquents.

MORPHOLOGICAL APPROACH

The morphological approach is the oldest of biological theories of crime. In this approach, criminals are viewed as biologically inferior to noncriminals. Biological inferiority produces physical characteristics that make the appearance of criminals and noncriminals different. Therefore, according to the morphological approach, criminals are biologically different from noncriminals and the symptoms of this difference can be found in physical appearance.[15] Two theories related to the physical appearance of criminals are Lombroso's atavism theory and Sheldon's somatotype theory.

LOMBROSO'S ATAVISM THEORY Cesare Lombroso (1835–1909), the father of the positive school, was a doctor in the Italian army. Although he identified several factors that might influence crime, including population density, education, unemployment, and newspaper crime coverage, he is most readily recognized for his idea that some individuals are born criminal. The term **atavism** means reversion to a primitive type. His discovery came during an autopsy of a notorious criminal. In observing the skull, he noticed a depression where there should have been a protrusion. This led Lombroso to believe that the brains of criminals were biological throwbacks to primitive man, making criminals both more aggressive and savage.

> At the sight of that skull, I seemed to see all of a sudden, lighted up as a vast plain under a flaming sky, the problem of the nature of the criminal—an atavistic being who reproduces in his person the ferocious instincts of primitive humanity and the inferior animals. Thus were explained anatomically the enormous jaws, high cheekbones, prominent superciliary arches, solitary lines in the palms, extreme size of the orbits, handle-shaped or sessile ears found in criminals, savages and apes, insensibility to pain, extremely acute sight, tattooing, excessive idleness, love of orgies, and the irresistible craving for evil for its own sake, the desire not only to extinguish life in the victim, but to mutilate the corpse, tear its flesh and drink its blood.[16]

Juvenile taken into detention center. *How will this youth be deterred from committing similar offenses in the future? Do you think this experience will deter this youth?*

atavism Reversion to a primitive type.

Cesare Lombroso

Lombroso, a doctor in the Italian army, became interested in studying the criminal activity of soldiers from southern Italy, including Sicily, when he learned that Italian politicians were calling people from southern Italy inferior, lazy, and barbaric.

SOURCE: Bernard, Thomas J., Jeffrey B. Snipes, and Alexander L. Gerould. *Vold's Theoretical Criminology*, 6th ed. New York: Oxford University Press, 2009.

In all, he studied the cadavers of 66 male criminals and discovered several characteristics that were unique to these individuals. These characteristics, known as *atavistic anomalies*, included:

1. skulls that were noticeably larger or smaller than normal
2. large protruding jaws
3. canine teeth
4. high foreheads
5. flattened noses
6. deep, close-set eyes
7. especially large or small ears
8. very long arms or legs
9. asymmetrical face[17]

These characteristics were similar to those found in primitive humans. Therefore, Lombroso argued that some individuals were genetic "throwbacks" to a more primitive time and were less evolved than other people. He estimated that 40 percent of all criminals were atavistic (genetic throwbacks).

Lombroso's research has been discredited because he failed to compare criminals with noncriminals. By studying only criminals, he found characteristics that were common to criminals. However, if Lombroso had studied a group of noncriminals, he would have discovered that these characteristics are just as prevalent among noncriminals. Lombroso's greatest strength is that he provided the point of view that factors beyond the individual's control, not only rational choice and free will, may influence crime. Lombroso's work later gave way to psychological and social factors that influence crime. Still, his theories did originate the positive frame of reference.

The mesomorph is more likely to be delinquent. *What characteristics lead the mesomorph to be more criminogenic in comparison to the endomorph and the ectomorph?*

SHELDON'S SOMATOTYPE THEORY William Sheldon also attempted to link physical appearance to delinquency. Sheldon focused on somatotype (body type) as the link to delinquency.[18] Sheldon believed that there would be differences between the somatotypes of delinquents and nondelinquents. Sheldon identified three somatotypes and argued that an individual's temperament was tied to his or her somatotype.

The first somatotype was **endomorph**. Endomorphic body structures are soft, round, and fat. Endomorphs are comfort-seeking and have extroverted personalities. The second somatotype was **mesomorph**. Mesomorphic body structures are muscular, firm, and strong. Mesomorphs have assertive and aggressive personalities. The third somatotype was **ectomorph** and consisted of a thin and frail body structure. Ectomorphs have introverted personalities and a strong ability for self-control.[19] Figure 4.2 presents a more detailed description of the three somatotypes and the corresponding temperaments.

endomorph Body structure that is soft, round, and fat.

mesomorph Body structure that is muscular, firm, and strong.

ectomorph Body structure that is thin and frail.

Sheldon did not believe that anyone was a pure endomorph, mesomorph, or ectomorph. Instead, he developed a system whereby levels of individuals' endomorphy, mesomorphy, and ectomorphy could be measured. The scores ranged from the lowest value, 1, to the highest value, 7. Therefore, someone who was a 1-1-7 would be an extreme ectomorph while a person rated as 3-6-1 would exhibit an average amount of endomorphic characteristics, a great amount of mesomorphic characteristics, and few ectomorphic characteristics. Sheldon studied 200 youths who were in a home for delinquent boys in Boston between

FIGURE 4.2	Sheldon's Somatotypes

SOMATOTYPE 1

Endomorphic relatively great development of digestive viscera; tendency to put on fat; soft roundness through various regions of the body; short tapering limbs; small bones; soft, smooth, velvety skin

ACCOMPANYING TEMPERAMENT

Viscerotonic general relaxation of body; a comfortable person; loves soft luxury; a "softie" but still essentially an extrovert

SOMATOTYPE 2

Mesomorphic relative predominance of muscles, bone, and the motor organs of the body; large trunk; heavy chest; large wrists and hands; if "lean," a hard rectangularity of outline; if "not lean," they fill out heavily

ACCOMPANYING TEMPERAMENT

Somotonic active, dynamic person; walks, talks, gestures assertively; behaves aggressively

SOMATOTYPE 3

Ectomorphic relative predominance of skin and its appendages, which includes the nervous system; lean, fragile, delicate body; small, delicate bones; droopy shoulders; small face; sharp nose; fine hair; relatively little body mass and relatively great surface area

ACCOMPANYING TEMPERAMENT

Cerebrotonic an introvert; full of functional complaints, allergies, skin troubles, chronic fatigue, insomnia; sensitive to noise and distractions; shrinks from crowds

Source: Bernard, Thomas J., Jeffrey B. Snipes, and Alexander L. Gerould, *Vold's Theoretical Criminology*, 6th Ed. New York: Oxford University Press, 2009. By permission of Oxford University Press, Inc.

1939 and 1942. He compared the somatotype measurements of these youths with the somatotype measurements of 4,000 college students. He discovered that the delinquent youths had a tendency to be more mesomorphic than the college students.[20] Therefore, according to Sheldon, individuals with mesomorphic body structures are more likely to be delinquent, because body structure influences an individual's temperament, and mesomorphs are more aggressive and assertive than other body types.

GENETICS AND INHERITED FACTORS

A common observation is that delinquent activity by one family member is related to the delinquent activity of another family member. Criminal activity tends to run in families; when one family member is delinquent, it is highly likely that another family member also will be. What explains this phenomenon? Some argue that this relationship in families is a function of learning: juveniles who are raised in households where criminal activity takes place will also learn to commit crime. However, could crime be inherited from one's parents? Is there a genetic influence on delinquency?

TWIN STUDIES One way to examine the impact of genetics on delinquency is to analyze the behavior of **monozygotic** or **identical twins**. Monozygotic twins develop from one egg and one sperm. Therefore, monozygotic twins are genetically identical, and so it is reasonable to expect that their delinquent behavior would be similar. The behavior of identical twins is compared to **dizygotic** or **fraternal twins**. Dizygotic twins develop from two eggs and two sperm and are no more genetically alike than other siblings (that is, 50 percent genetic similarity). If heredity plays a role in delinquency, one would expect that identical twins have a higher concordance rate of delinquent behavior than that of fraternal twins. A **concordance rate** is the similarity of delinquent behavior. Therefore, if an identical twin is delinquent, there is a greater likelihood that the other twin will also be delinquent in comparison to fraternal twins.

monozygotic or **identical twins** Twins that develop from one egg and one sperm.

dizygotic or **fraternal twins** Twins that develop from two eggs and two sperm.

concordance rate The similarity of delinquent behavior.

Karl O. Christiansen conducted a study in Denmark on the criminal convictions of identical and fraternal twins.[21] He found that if one identical twin had a criminal conviction, then in 35 percent of the cases, the other identical twin also had a criminal conviction. Therefore, the concordance rate was 35 percent. On the other hand, the concordance rate for fraternal twins was 12 percent.[22] Therefore, when one fraternal twin had a criminal conviction, the other fraternal twin also had a conviction in only 12 percent of the cases. This study lends support to the idea that there is a biological/genetic influence on delinquency. In fact, the majority of twin studies demonstrates a greater similarity in delinquent behavior between identical twins compared to delinquent behavior between fraternal twins. However, it does not mean that genetic influences cause delinquency because there are no controls for contributing environmental factors such as similarities in child rearing practices. By comparison, more identical twins than fraternal twins believe that they are reared and treated alike.[23] Therefore, their similar delinquent behavior may be a function of socialization, not heredity.

ADOPTION STUDIES Another way researchers have analyzed the relationship between heredity and delinquency has been to conduct adoption studies. Adoption studies focus on individuals who were adopted soon after birth. Therefore, biological and environmental factors that influence delinquency can be separated. Adoption studies are better than twin studies to isolate biological influences on delinquency because the environmental influence of the biological parents is absent. The only influence biological parents have on their children is genetic. In twin studies, the twins are usually raised by their biological parents. Therefore, it is extremely difficult to determine if the delinquency was influenced more by biological than by environmental influences.

Adoption studies are conducted by comparing the delinquent behavior of adopted children with the criminal behavior of the biological and adoptive parents. Four possible combinations may exist:

1. The biological and adoptive parents do not have a criminal record.
2. The biological parents have a criminal record, but the adoptive parents do not, thus pointing to a biological influence on delinquency since the behavior of the juvenile is more like that of the biological than the adoptive parents.
3. The biological parents do not have a criminal record, but the adoptive parents do. If this were the case, this would point to an environmental influence on delinquency.
4. The biological and adoptive parents both have criminal records. In this case, both biological and environmental factors influence delinquency.

In which combination does an adopted child have the greatest chance of being a delinquent? To answer this question, Sarnoff Mednick and his colleagues conducted a study of adoptions in Denmark. When the biological and adoptive parents had no criminal record, 13.5 percent of the adopted children had a criminal record. When the biological parents had a criminal record, but the adoptive parents did not, about 20 percent of the adopted children had a criminal record. When the biological parents did not have a criminal record, but the adoptive parents did, about 15 percent of the adopted children had a criminal record. When both biological and adoptive parents had a criminal record, almost 25 percent of the adopted children had a criminal record.[24] What do these findings mean? The greatest impact on delinquency in Mednick's adoption studies was seen when both biological and adoptive parents had criminal records. Therefore, both biological and environmental factors influence delinquency. This study does not dispute the argument that there is a genetic influence on delinquency but does indicate that biological factors interact with environmental and social factors to bring about delinquent behavior.

BIOCHEMICAL AND NEUROLOGICAL APPROACH

Most biological theories today focus on **biosocial factors**, interactions between biological and social factors that lead to delinquency. Biological factors, in and of themselves, rarely lead to delinquency. In order to lead to delinquency, biological factors must interact with something in the environment (i.e., social factors). Individuals may possess biological factors that put them at higher risk for delinquency. However, they may never commit delinquent acts unless faced with social factors that pull the trigger, so to speak, on the biological factors. These social factors include lack of opportunity, failure in school, unemployment, and substance abuse, among other things. Biosocial factors include biochemical factors that can lead to delinquency when mixed with social factors.

BIOCHEMICAL FACTORS In recent years, a biochemical explanation of delinquency has found a wide audience. It suggests that chemical deficiencies or abnormalities in the body can affect a juvenile's behavior, especially acts of aggression. The body needs certain chemical and mineral levels for normal brain functioning and growth. A decrease or increase in these levels can hinder juveniles' abilities to control their behavior. Research has found several biochemical factors related to delinquency.

Dietary Influences Certain vitamins and minerals and other food items have been tied to delinquency: high sugar intake, high calcium intake, too much or too little vitamin B and vitamin C, and high intake of magnesium and zinc. Therefore, the diet of a juvenile may influence delinquent behavior. However, evidence of a relationship between diet and delinquency is not conclusive. Some studies have identified a link between diet and delinquency while others have not. For example, Susan Schoenthaler and Walter Doraz studied whether a change in sugar intake had an influence on the behavior of 276 juveniles incarcerated in an institution.[25] They found that reducing the sugar intake of these juveniles significantly reduced the number of disciplinary violations, including assaults, within the institution. In response, some institutions removed candy machines from the premises in an effort to limit sugar intake.

Fetal Alcohol Syndrome and Prenatal Drug Use There is concern regarding the influence of prenatal alcohol and drug use on children. Children who are born to drug-addicted mothers are frequently called "crack babies." Crack cocaine is not the only drug that infants may have been exposed to. They are also exposed to heroin, amphetamines, marijuana, alcohol, nicotine, and others.[26] Evidence shows that these children frequently suffer from neurological problems as they grow older. These problems, including impulsivity and short attention spans, are similar to those associated with Attention Deficit Hyperactivity Disorder (ADHD). However, little is known about the long-term effects on children of drug consumption by pregnant women.[27] It is expected that many of these children will perform poorly in school, which may lead to delinquency. A discussion about the link between school performance and delinquency was included in Chapter 3. An explanation of the relationship between ADHD and delinquency will follow in greater detail in a later section of this chapter. Chapter 14 also discusses the relationship between juvenile drug use and delinquency.

Albert R. Roberts and Judith A. Waters believe that **Fetal Alcohol Syndrome (FAS)** is a more prevalent threat to babies than the consequences of other drugs.[28] If a woman drinks heavily during pregnancy, she could cause FAS, a condition in which alcohol affects the developing fetus. According to D. Maplin, "to be diagnosed with Fetal Alcohol Syndrome, a

biosocial factors Interaction between biological and social factors that lead to delinquency.

Fetal Alcohol Syndrome (FAS) A condition caused by the effect that alcohol has on a developing fetus.

Fetal Alcohol Syndrome and prenatal drug use are related to delinquency. *What factors influence a female to consume alcohol or drugs during pregnancy? What impact does this consumption have on the child?*

person must exhibit characteristics in the following areas: (1) pre- and/or post-natal growth retardation, (2) evidence of central nervous system (brain) involvement, and (3) a constellation of physical features."[29] There is limited research on the relationship between FAS and delinquency. However, one study found that 60 percent of the males and 40 percent of the females with FAS reported trouble with the law.[30] These numbers are significantly higher than one would expect to find among a sample of youth. In fact, 45 percent of the youth between 12 and 20 with FAS had committed a violent crime.[31]

Hormones A person's body naturally produces **hormones** that control such bodily functions as central nervous system functioning and reproduction. Researchers have studied the relationship between testosterone and aggression. Criminal activity peaks during the teenage years when testosterone levels are at their highest. In a similar way, criminal activity begins to reduce for most individuals in their twenties, a fact that can be linked to decreases in testosterone as one ages. Some research has shown that offenders who commit violent crimes have higher testosterone levels than those who have committed nonviolent crimes. However, the research on the link between testosterone and aggression is not conclusive. Regardless, Depo-Provera(®), a drug that inhibits the production of testosterone, has been used in the treatment of sex offenders.

Researchers have also studied the relationship between female premenstrual cycles and aggression. Studies show that the premenstrual cycle is linked to irritability and aggression. Diana Fishbein found that a small percentage of women are influenced by hormonal changes, which can result in an increase in hostility.[32] This increase in hostility is linked to changes in female hormones and a rise in testosterone.[33] In fact, premenstrual syndrome (PMS) has been used as a mitigating factor at the sentencing phase of criminal trials. (A mitigating factor is a situation, fact, or condition that may reduce the sentence an individual receives.)

AUTONOMIC NERVOUS SYSTEM The **autonomic nervous system** controls the body's involuntary functions such as blood pressure and heart rate. The autonomic nervous system produces a "fight or flight" response. It prepares the body for "fight or flight" when a person is presented with an unpleasant stimulus or stressful situation by increasing the heart and respiratory rate and by stimulating the sweat glands.[34] When a person is presented with an unpleasant stimulus, such as the threat of punishment, the person's heart and breathing rates increase, and they begin to perspire.

Children are conditioned by their parents to anticipate punishment when they have done something wrong. The expectation of punishment causes anxiety in many children, so they avoid situations that cause anxiety.[35] If a juvenile is presented with a situation that causes anxiety, he or she may flee the situation to lessen the anxiety. Anxiety and fear reduction serve as a reinforcement for flight in the future. If fleeing the situation reduced anxiety, then the individual is likely to flee similar situations. Therefore, if a juvenile becomes anxious about the fear of punishment for committing a delinquent act, he or she is likely to withdraw from the situation and not commit the act. However, if the juvenile does not become anxious and fearful, then

hormones Substances produced by the body that control such bodily functions as central nervous system functioning and reproduction.

autonomic nervous system Controls the body's involuntary functions such as blood pressure and heart rate.

withdrawal from the situation is less likely and delinquent activity is more likely to occur. Fear and anxiety reduction is the most powerful, naturally occurring reinforcement of behavior.[36] Mednick and his colleagues describe the process as follows:

1. Child A contemplates aggressive action.
2. Because of previous punishment or the threat of punishment, the child suffers fear.
3. Because of fear, the child inhibits aggressive response.
4. Because the child no longer entertains the aggressive impulse, the fear will begin to dissipate, or be reduced. Fear reduction is the most powerful, naturally occurring reinforcement that psychologists have discovered. The reduction of fear (which immediately follows the inhibition of the aggression) can act as a reinforcement of this inhibition and will result in learning inhibition of aggression.[37]

Anxiety is related to the autonomic nervous system's "fight or flight" response. Whether or not children have been conditioned by their parents to anticipate punishment for wrongdoing may impact the functioning of the autonomic nervous system. If the autonomic nervous system is slow to produce a "fight or flight" response, then the individual will not anticipate punishment and will not be anxious about committing the prohibited act. The anxiety the individual feels when presented with these situations is usually called conscience or guilt.[38] Some believe that psychopaths do not develop adequate consciences because of the way their autonomic nervous systems function.[39] Some perceive psychopaths as being incapable of experiencing fear or anxiety or of having a high threshold for fear and anxiety.

LEARNING DISABILITIES School failure has been linked to dropout rates and delinquency. Some argue, however, that the underlying reason for many school failures is an undiagnosed learning disability.[40] Learning disabilities are biologically determined factors that impose difficulty on an individual's ability to learn. More than half of juvenile offenders who were tested for learning disabilities were diagnosed with a serious learning disability, despite the fact that only 10 percent of all youths have a learning disability.[41] Two theories explain the link between learning disabilities and delinquency: the school failure rationale and the susceptibility theory. According to the school failure rationale, a juvenile who is performing poorly in school may develop a negative self-image because of school failure. This may lead to delinquency, especially if the juvenile associates with school dropouts and desires to be successful at something (for example, drug dealing or auto theft).[42] On the other hand, the susceptibility theory postulates that juveniles with learning disabilities have traits that make them more likely to commit delinquent acts. The traits include impulsivity (lack of impulse control) and the inability to predict the consequences of one's actions.[43] Juveniles with learning disabilities more frequently act on impulse.

One learning disability that has been linked to delinquency is **Attention Deficit Hyperactivity Disorder (ADHD)**. The symptoms of ADHD are inattention, hyperactivity, and impulsivity. Although the actual cause is still unknown, some experts point to neurological damage to the frontal lobes of the brain, while others focus on the impact of prenatal stress as the cause of ADHD. The

Myth Fact

Myth: Biological factors do not impact delinquency.

Fact: Several biological theories, and the research conducted to form these theories, have shown a relationship between biological factors and delinquency.

Source: Bernard, Thomas J., Jeffrey B. Snipes, and Alexander L. Gerould. *Vold's Theoretical Criminology*, 6th ed. New York: Oxford University Press, 2009.

Attention Deficit Hyperactivity Disorder (ADHD) A learning disability characterized by inattention, hyperactivity, and impulsivity.

4.5 SELF-CHECK

1. What factors affect a juvenile's chances of becoming delinquent according to William Sheldon?
2. Define biosocial factors.

Sigmund Freud developed psychoanalytic theory. *According to Freud's thoughts, how does delinquency occur?*

id The part of one's personality that is comprised of unconscious biological and psychological desires and instincts.

ego The part of one's personality that represents the identity of the individual and actual behavior.

superego The part of one's personality that represents the conscience and moral character of the individual.

diagnostic criteria for ADHD are shown in the Focus on Policy. It is estimated that 3 to 5 percent of school-age children have ADHD.[44] Children who have ADHD are more likely to have contact with the juvenile justice system.

Psychological Theories

A second set of theories derived from the positive school of criminological thought are psychological theories. They support the contention that there are psychological differences between delinquents and nondelinquents.

PSYCHOANALYTIC APPROACH

Psychoanalytic theory was developed by Sigmund Freud. He believed that an individual's personality was formed early in childhood and that, as the child developed, a three-part personality structure formed, called in turn: id, ego, and superego. The **id** is a collection of unconscious biological and psychological desires and instincts including sex and aggression. The **ego** represents the identity and actual behavior of an individual, while the **superego** represents conscience and moral character. According to August Aichhorn, an uncontrolled id is the basis for delinquent behavior.[45] He argued that juvenile delinquents frequently have underdeveloped superegos that are unable to regulate the id adequately. The id, comprised of unconscious urges, desires, and instincts, is counteracted by the superego where conscious and moral character reside. The superego helps an individual decide what is acceptable or unacceptable behavior. Juveniles who do not have an appropriate superego will be more apt to commit delinquent acts because their behavior is less likely to be controlled by their conscience and moral values.

The ego is the resulting outgrowth of the struggle between the id and superego. The ego, which represents the actual behavior of an individual, is the attempt to satisfy the needs of the id while trying to fulfill the requirements of the superego. If the id is stronger than the superego, delinquency is more likely to occur than in cases where the superego is stronger than the id. The conflict between the id and superego is an unconscious activity. The goal of psychoanalysis is to bring the conflict to consciousness so that people can learn to deal with the conflict.

Erik Erickson, another theorist, argued that delinquency occurred because of an underdeveloped ego (not an underdeveloped superego).[46] He argued that young people need to develop an ego identity which is a clear sense of themselves and their beliefs. Individuals who do not develop an adequate ego identity are susceptible to the influence of delinquent peers.

FOCUS ON POLICY

DIAGNOSTIC CRITERIA FOR ATTENTION DEFICIT HYPERACTIVITY DISORDER

A. Either (1) or (2):

(1) six (or more) of the following symptoms of *inattention* have persisted for at least six months to a degree that is maladaptive and inconsistent with developmental level:

Inattention

   a. often fails to give close attention to details or makes careless mistakes in schoolwork, work, or other activities

   b. often has difficulty sustaining attention in tasks or play activities

   c. often does not seem to listen when spoken to directly

   d. often does not follow through on instructions and fails to finish schoolwork, chores, or duties in the workplace

   e. often has difficulty organizing tasks and activities

   f. often avoids, dislikes, or is reluctant to engage in tasks that require sustained mental effort (such as schoolwork or homework)

   g. often loses things necessary for tasks or activities (e.g., toys, school assignments, pencils, books, or tools)

   h. is often easily distracted by extraneous stimuli

   i. is often forgetful in daily activities

(2) six (or more) of the following symptoms of *hyperactivity-impulsivity* have persisted for at least six months to a degree that is maladaptive and inconsistent with developmental level:

Hyperactivity

   a. often fidgets with hands or feet or squirms in seat

   b. often leaves seat in classroom or in other situations in which remaining seated is expected

   c. often runs about or climbs excessively in situations in which it is inappropriate (in adolescents or adults, may be limited to subjective feelings of restlessness)

   d. often has difficulty playing or engaging in leisure activities quietly

   e. is often "on the go" or often acts as if "driven by a motor"

   f. often talks excessively

Impulsivity

   g. often blurts out answers before questions have been completed

   h. often has difficulty awaiting turn

   i. often interrupts or intrudes on others (e.g., butts into conversations or games)

B. Some hyperactive-impulsive or inattentive symptoms that caused impairment were present before age 12 years.

C. Some impairment from the symptoms is present in two or more settings (e.g., at school [or work] and at home).

D. There must be clear evidence of clinically significant impairment in social, academic, or occupational functioning.

Source: *Diagnostic and Statistical Manual of Mental Disorders,* 4th ed. Text Revision. Washington, DC: American Psychiatric Association, 2000, pp. 83–84. Criteria in DSM-5 have not been changed from DSM-IV. http://www.dsm5.org/Documents/ADHD%20Fact%20Sheet.pdf.

Reprinted with permission from the *Diagnostic and Statistical Manual of Mental Disorders,* 4th ed, Text Revision (Copyright 2000), American Psychiatric Association

---

The conflict between the id and superego does not always lead to delinquent behavior. Individuals may develop one or more of the following defense mechanisms to deal with the conflict.

1. **Repression** An automatic exclusion of threatening impulses, wishes, and feelings from consciousness
2. **Denial** A blocking out of part of *external* reality rather than *internal* reality which involves repression
3. **Displacement** The use of a substitute person or object to gratify an impulse

repression A defense mechanism in which threatening impulses, wishes, and feelings are automatically kept from consciousness.

denial A defense mechanism that refers to blocking out part of external rather than internal reality.

displacement A defense mechanism that uses a substitute person or object to gratify an impulse.

4. **Regression** The return to a pattern of reaction characteristic of a less mature mode of adjustment
5. **Reaction formation** The replacement of a forbidden impulse with its opposite. For example, sometimes crusaders against pornography, alcohol, and gambling are those who have once been most susceptible to these vices
6. **Rationalization** The justification of behavior with socially acceptable reasons[47]

MORAL DEVELOPMENT AND DELINQUENCY

The relationship between moral development and delinquency focuses on cognitive development. Cognitive development theory assumes that individuals develop in a sequential manner, that is, a person passes through one step in development, then another step, and so on. Lawrence Kohlberg argued that there are sequential stages in moral reasoning that individuals pass through as they develop. At each stage, they make decisions about right and wrong for different reasons. Delinquency, then, may be explained by the arrested development of moral reasoning at certain stages. Kohlberg stated that there are six stages of moral development:

Stage 1   Punishment and Obedience Orientation: "Right" is obedience to power and rules and the avoidance of punishment.

Stage 2   Hedonistic Orientation: "Right" corresponds to seeing one's own needs met, taking responsibility for oneself, and allowing others to do the same.

Stage 3   Interpersonal Concordance: "Right" is having good intentions and motives, and being concerned for others.

Stage 4   Law and Order Orientation: "Right" is doing one's duty to society and others, and maintaining the rules of society.

Stage 5   Social Contract, Legalistic Orientation: "Right" is defined as upholding the rules and values agreed upon by society (a social contract).

Stage 6   Orientation to Universal Ethical Principles: "Right" is an obligation assumed by the individual to principles, such as justice and equality, which apply to all individuals; the individual recognizes the moral rightness of behavior.[48]

The first two stages are usually completed by the time a person reaches age 7. Stages 3 and 4 are passed through and completed from pre-adolescence through adolescence, while the last two stages begin in early adulthood.

Where do delinquents stop in their moral development in comparison to nondelinquents? Research has found that delinquents frequently are found in Stage 1 or Stage 2 of moral development while nondelinquents frequently fall into Stage 3 or Stage 4.[49] In Stage 1, children comply with authority out of fear. Something is viewed as morally right if punishment is avoided. Juveniles who did not progress through this stage will think that their delinquent behavior is permissible as long as they are not punished for it. Obviously, this stage of moral development does not take into account the feelings of other people or an obligation to society. In Stage 2, children define what is right as that which satisfies their needs. That is why it is referred to as the "Hedonistic Orientation Stage." At this stage, children define something as right if they are not punished for it (Stage 1) and it satisfies their needs. Some argue that many delinquents have stopped their moral development at Stage 1 or Stage 2. In Stage 3, children begin to take into account the feelings of others. This insulates young persons from delinquency because they have become concerned about others, not just their own needs. Therefore, juveniles who proceed into Stage 3 and perhaps beyond are far less likely to commit delinquent acts.

regression A defense mechanism that involves going back to a reaction pattern characteristic of a less mature mode of adjustment.

reaction formation A defense mechanism which occurs when a forbidden impulse is replaced with its opposite.

rationalization A defense mechanism by which one justifies one's behavior with socially acceptable reasons.

PERSONALITY DISORDERS

According to psychologists, certain personality characteristics of an individual may influence delinquency. **Personality** refers to the emotional and behavioral attributes of an individual. Researchers have attempted to find support for the belief that individuals with certain personality types are much more likely to commit delinquent acts. These attempts have focused on identifying differences in the personalities of delinquents and nondelinquents. Sheldon and Eleanor Glueck identified these personality characteristics after they compared 500 delinquent and nondelinquent boys. The characteristics of delinquents included extroversion, impulsivity, lack of self-control, hostility, resentment, suspicion of others, destructiveness, less fear of failure, ambivalence toward authority, assertiveness, and feeling unappreciated.[50]

One personality test used in studying delinquency is the Minnesota Multiphasic Personality Inventory-2 (MMPI-2), which consists of 567 true-false items. Individuals who take the MMPI are assessed on ten scales designed to measure different aspects of the personality, including psychopathic deviation, social introversion, and schizophrenia. The MMPI has consistently differentiated delinquents from nondelinquents. Delinquents and nondelinquents are most different on the original Scale 4, which is called the "psychopathic deviate" scale. Therefore, delinquents are more "psychopathic" than nondelinquents. This finding should not be surprising when one analyzes the questions asked on Scale 4. Scale 4 includes 14 items that measure self-reported delinquency. For example, statements include, "I have never been in trouble with the law" and "Sometimes when I was young I stole things." One would expect that delinquents are more likely than nondelinquents to respond "false" to the first statement and "true" to the second statement.

ANTISOCIAL PERSONALITY DISORDER Frequently, the terms *psychopath* or *sociopath* are used to describe some delinquents. These terms technically refer to a condition known as antisocial personality disorder. According to the *Diagnostic and Statistical Manual of Mental Disorders* (DSM) of the American Psychiatric Association, "the essential feature of antisocial personality disorder is a pervasive pattern of disregard for, and violation of, the rights of others that begins in childhood or early adolescence and continues into adulthood."[51] Some of the characteristics of antisocial personality disorder are:

1. repeatedly performing acts that are grounds for arrest
2. deceitfulness
3. impulsivity
4. irritability and aggressiveness
5. reckless disregard for safety of self or others
6. consistent irresponsibility
7. lack of remorse[52]

Juveniles in institutions are frequently diagnosed with conduct disorder. *What do you think institutional staff can do to assist youths in overcoming this disorder?*

In order to be diagnosed with this disorder, an individual must be 18 years of age or older. Therefore, a juvenile cannot be diagnosed with antisocial personality

personality The emotional and behavioral attributes of an individual.

FOCUS ON POLICY

DIAGNOSTIC CRITERIA FOR CONDUCT DISORDER

A. A repetitive and persistent pattern of behavior in which the basic rights of others or major age-appropriate societal norms or rules are violated, as manifested by the presence of three (or more) of the following criteria in the past 12 months, with at least one criterion present in the past 6 months:

Aggression to people and animals

1. often bullies, threatens, or intimidates others
2. often initiates physical fights
3. has used a weapon that can cause serious physical harm to others (e.g., a bat, brick, broken bottle, knife, gun)
4. has been physically cruel to people
5. has been physically cruel to animals
6. has stolen while confronting a victim (e.g., mugging, purse snatching, extortion, armed robbery)
7. has forced someone into sexual activity

Destruction of property

8. has deliberately engaged in fire setting with the intention of causing serious damage
9. has deliberately destroyed others' property (other than by fire setting)

Deceitfulness or theft

10. has broken into someone else's house, building, or car
11. often lies to obtain goods or favors or to avoid obligations (i.e., "cons" others)
12. has stolen items of nontrivial value without confronting a victim (e.g., shoplifting, but without breaking and entering; forgery)

Serious violations of rules

13. often stays out at night despite parental prohibitions, beginning before age 13
14. has run away from home overnight at least twice while living in parental home (or once without returning for a lengthy period)
15. is often truant from school, beginning before age 13

B. The disturbance in behavior causes clinically significant impairment in social, academic, or occupational functioning.

Source: *Diagnostic and Statistical Manual of Mental Disorders,* 4th ed. Text Revision. Washington, DC: American Psychiatric Association, 2000. Criteria in DSM-5 have not changed from DSM-IV. http://www.dsm5.org/Documents/Conduct%20Disorder%20Fact%20Sheet%20Rev%209%206%2013.pdf

Reprinted with permission from the *Diagnostic and Statistical Manual of Mental Disorders,* 4th ed, Text Revision (Copyright 2000). American Psychiatric Association.

---

disorder. Instead, juveniles who exhibit characteristics similar to antisocial personality disorder are diagnosed with conduct disorder. **Conduct disorder** is basically the juvenile version of antisocial personality disorder. Individuals with conduct disorder may have little concern for the feelings and well-being of others and may lack remorse or feelings of guilt for their behavior.[53] Conduct disorder can be caused by several factors including parental rejection and neglect, inconsistent child-rearing practices with harsh discipline, physical or sexual abuse, and lack of supervision.[54] Focus on Policy illustrates the diagnostic criteria for conduct disorder.

conduct disorder A personality disorder that involves the commission of delinquent acts and little concern for the feelings and well-being of others.

learning Habits and knowledge that develop as a result of the experiences of an individual in entering and adjusting to the environment.

LEARNING THEORIES

Some believe that juveniles commit delinquent acts because they learn ideas and behaviors that support such actions. **Learning** is both a psychological and social process. Learning as used here "refers to habits and knowledge that develop as a result of the experiences of an individual in entering and adjusting to the environment."[55] Behaviorists, also referred to as learning theorists, feel that individuals learn by associating stimuli with certain responses; individuals learn by observing how others react to their behavior or to the behavior of someone else.

CLASSICAL CONDITIONING One way that individuals learn is through **classical conditioning**. This learning theory states that one learns by connecting a stimulus with a response and is most closely associated with psychologist Ivan Pavlov and his experiments with dogs. Pavlov would ring a bell before he gave a dog a piece of meat. Pavlov discovered that after he had repeated this process several times, the dogs would salivate at the sound of the bell even if they were not given a piece of meat. Behaviorists believe that individuals learn by associating stimuli with certain responses. The dog's salivation, for example, was a response to the stimulus of the bell. Individuals can learn a conditioned response to a particular stimulus.

Author G. Trasler argued that children experience anxiety when their parents negatively react to their behavior.[56] If children consistently receive punishment for wrongdoing, they may develop anxiety as a conditioned response to the stimulus. Those individuals who experience anxiety when presented with a particular stimulus will frequently withdraw from the situation in order to remove the anxiety. According to the theory, then, juveniles who have been conditioned to experience anxiety (conditioned response) when presented with an opportunity to do something wrong (stimulus) are not likely to take advantage of the opportunity presented. In this situation, the juvenile has learned *not* to commit delinquent acts. Trasler argued that inhibition of delinquency is a learned, conditioned response that is designed to reduce anxiety.[57] Individuals learn to avoid delinquent behavior because they have been conditioned to anticipate punishment for their wrongdoing. Even if punishment is absent, individuals will avoid wrongdoing because they experience anxiety.

MODELING Individuals also learn through modeling. **Modeling**, perhaps the most basic learning theory, states that people learn delinquent behavior by modeling or imitating the behavior of others, including parents, peers, and siblings. Albert Bandura and Richard W. Walters focus on the aspect of aggression in the relationship between modeling and delinquency. They argue that juveniles have a tendency to copy the aggressive behavior of those around them when the models are rewarded for their aggression and not punished.[58] These juveniles who are presented with models acting aggressively in certain situations may also act aggressively in similar situations. Children can learn behavior through the observation of others. If a child is raised in a household where there is violence, that child may learn that such behavior is acceptable and rewarding.

In fact, some experts contend that children can learn aggressive and violent behavior from television, movies, video games and the Internet. There is evidence showing a relationship between watching violence through these media and aggression. However, there is a debate over whether watching violence through these media has a short- or long-term impact on aggressive behavior. Does watching violence on television increase levels of aggression for the next few hours or days or does it have a long-term impact by conditioning individuals to believe that violence and aggression are acceptable? Evidence confirms that there is a

Myth **Fact**

Conduct disorder occurs frequently among adolescents.

The American Psychiatric Association estimates rates for conduct disorder range from 6 percent to 16 percent for males and 2 percent to 9 percent for females.

Source: American Psychiatric Association. *Diagnostic and Statistical Manual of Mental Disorders*, 4th ed. Washington, DC: American Psychiatric Association, 1994.

FYI

Ivan Pavlov, a psychologist as well as a physiologist, first studied to be a priest, until he discovered his keen interest for science. He went on to win the 1904 Nobel Prize for his study of the digestive glands.

classical conditioning A learning theory that states people learn by associating stimuli with certain responses.

modeling A learning theory that states people learn by imitating the behavior of others.

Many studies show a relationship between playing violent video games and behavior. *How can violence in video games cause delinquency?*

4.6 SELF-CHECK

1. Name the six stages of moral development. Beyond which level are people less likely to commit delinquent acts?
2. What do learning theorists believe?

short-term impact of television violence on aggression, but it is difficult to establish the long-term impact.[59] Obviously, violence on television and other media sources does not impact everyone equally. Millions of children watch violence on television and movies and play violent video games daily and yet they do not act aggressively or commit violent delinquent acts.

CAREERS IN JUVENILE JUSTICE

Juvenile Corrections Caseworker

Caseworkers work in institutional settings with juveniles. These settings can include halfway houses, treatment facilities, secure institutions, and even detention centers. Caseworkers are employed by private and public agencies at both the state and the local levels.

Caseworkers are the primary treatment staff for juveniles who have been committed to a juvenile institution. Their responsibilities include making sure that the juvenile is meeting the requirements of his or her treatment plan such as attending school and receiving group counseling. The caseworker meets with the juvenile on a regular basis to determine his or her progress during confinement and to explore any issues that may be confronting the juvenile. Caseworkers also provide group and individual counseling to youth.

Caseworkers usually follow one of two career paths. First, the individual is hired to become a caseworker and has no prior experience with the agency. Second, the individual works for the agency as a juvenile corrections officer or in some other capacity and applies for and receives a caseworker position. Most caseworkers have a bachelor's degree in criminal justice or other related discipline such as psychology. Some also hold master's degrees, but it is usually not a requirement for the position.

CRITICAL THINKING

What personality characteristics do you think a good caseworker would have? Would you like to become a caseworker? Explain.

Another way individuals learn is through **operant conditioning**, a theory based on the work of B. F. Skinner. Whereas classical conditioning deals with involuntary reactions (anxiety) to stimuli, Skinner focuses on voluntary reactions. According to the theory of operant conditioning, behavior—including delinquent activity—is controlled by the consequences of that behavior. Consequences that increase the behavior are called *reinforcers* and consequences that decrease the behavior are called *punishers*. Reinforcers, such as praise and money, are designed to increase the behavior because the individual has received a reward for his or her behavior. Punishers, such as parental disapproval, arrest, and punishment, are designed to decrease the behavior. If a juvenile commits a delinquent act and receives support and praise (reinforcers) from his or her peer group, then it is *likely* that the juvenile will continue the behavior. However, if the same juvenile is arrested and placed in juvenile detention (punishers are present), then it is *unlikely* that he or she will continue.

operant conditioning A learning theory that states people learn based on the consequences of their behavior.

SUMMARY BY CHAPTER OBJECTIVES

1. Contrast the classical and positive schools of criminological thought

The key concepts of the classical school of thought are free will, hedonistic human, emphasis on offense, and punishment. On the other hand, the key concepts of the positive school are determinism, multiple causes, emphasis on offender, and rehabilitation.

2. Understand choice theory

Choice theory contends that juveniles commit delinquent acts because they make a rational choice to do so. Routine activities theory posits that three factors must converge in time and space in order for delinquency to occur: namely, a motivated offender, a suitable target, and the absence of a capable guardian.

3. Understand deterrence theory

The assumptions of deterrence theory include (a) individuals are rational actors, (b) individuals must be aware of the penalty for particular crimes, (c) individuals must view the risks as unpleasant, and (d) the sanction must be swift, certain, and severe. According to deterrence theory, if sanctions were swift, certain, and severe, there would be less crime.

4. Explain Lombroso's atavism theory and Sheldon's somatotype theory

Lombroso thought that individuals were born criminal. He believed that criminals exhibited atavistic anomalies, such as large protruding jaws, high foreheads, and very long arms that differentiated them from noncriminals. Sheldon thought that criminals had different body types than noncriminals. He thought that criminals were most likely to have a mesomorphic body type which was muscular, firm, and strong.

5. Summarize twin and adoption studies

The majority of twin studies demonstrate a greater similarity in delinquent behavior between identical twins than between fraternal twins. Mednick found in adoption studies that when biological parents had a criminal record but the adoptive parents did not, about 20 percent of the adopted children had a criminal record. When both biological and adoptive parents had a criminal record, almost 25 percent of the adopted children had a criminal record. The results mean that there is a biological influence on crime, but it is not the only influence.

6. Describe biochemical and neurological factors that impact delinquency

Certain vitamins, minerals, and food have been tied to delinquency, including high sugar intake, high calcium, too much or too little vitamin B and vitamin C, and high intake of magnesium and zinc. Prenatal drug and alcohol use can lead to higher rates of delinquency. One study found that 45 percent of the youth between 12 and 20 years of age with Fetal Alcohol Syndrome had committed a violent crime. The hormone testosterone has been linked to delinquency because of its influence on aggression. A slow autonomic nervous system and learning disabilities have an impact on delinquency as well.

7. Identify the major arguments presented by psychoanalytic theory

Some theorists believe that an uncontrolled id is the basis for delinquent behavior. They contend that juvenile delinquents frequently have underdeveloped superegos that are unable to adequately regulate the id. Juveniles who do not have an appropriate superego will be more apt to commit delinquent acts because their behavior is less likely to be controlled by their conscience and moral values. Other theorists argue that delinquency occurs because of an underdeveloped ego. Those who do not develop an adequate ego identity are more susceptible to the influence of delinquent peers.

8. Describe the relationship between moral development and delinquency

Delinquency can be explained by arrested development of moral reasoning at certain stages. Kohlberg stated that there are six stages of moral development. Most delinquents frequently fall into Stage 1 or Stage 2 of moral development.

9. Describe the impact of personality disorders on delinquency

Conduct disorder, in particular, is related to delinquency. Conduct disorder is basically the juvenile version of antisocial personality disorder. Individuals with conduct disorder may have little concern for the feelings and well-being of others and may lack remorse or feelings of guilt for their behavior.

10. Summarize the three major learning theories

The classical conditioning learning theory states that individuals can learn a conditioned response to a particular stimulus. The modeling learning theory states that people learn delinquent behavior by "modeling" or imitating the behavior of others. The operant conditioning learning theory states that behavior is controlled by the consequences of that behavior.

KEY TERMS

theory, p. 90
free will, p. 90
hedonistic, p. 90
general deterrence, p. 94
specific deterrence, p. 94
atavism, p. 95
endomorph, p. 96
mesomorph, p. 96
ectomorph, p. 96
monozygotic or identical
  twins, p. 97

dizygotic or fraternal
  twins, p. 97
concordance rate,
  p. 97
biosocial factors, p. 99
Fetal Alcohol Syndrome
  (FAS), p. 99
hormones, p. 100
autonomic nervous
  system, p. 100

Attention Deficit
  Hyperactivity Disorder
  (ADHD), p. 101
id, p. 102
ego, p. 102
superego, p. 102
repression, p. 103
denial, p. 103
displacement, p. 103
regression, p. 104

reaction formation, p. 104
rationalization, p. 104
personality, p. 105
conduct disorder, p. 106
learning, p. 106
classical conditioning,
  p. 107
modeling, p. 107
operant conditioning,
  p. 109

REVIEW QUESTIONS

1. What are the major differences between the classical and positive schools of criminological thought?

2. According to choice theory, why do juveniles commit delinquent acts?

3. According to routine activities theory, what three factors must converge in time and space in order for delinquency to occur?

4. What are the major assumptions of deterrence theory?

5. What were Sheldon's three somatotypes, and which one is most likely to lead to delinquency?

6. What were the findings of twin and adoption studies? What do the results mean?

7. What effects do dietary influences, prenatal drug use, and hormones have on delinquency?

8. How does the autonomic nervous system influence delinquency?

9. What is the relationship between learning disabilities and delinquency? What are the characteristics of someone with Attention Deficit Hyperactivity Disorder?

10. How do the id, ego, and superego affect delinquency?

11. According to Kohlberg, in what stages of moral development are delinquents most likely to be found?

12. What are the characteristics of someone with conduct disorder?

13. What are three major learning theories, and how does each argue that learning occurs?

HANDS-ON ACTIVITIES

1. **Interview and Analyze** Ask fellow students, family members, and friends why they think juveniles commit delinquent acts. Write down their responses. Note if anyone mentioned biological and psychological factors. Match the responses with the biological and psychological theories in this chapter. Identify which theory received the most responses.

2. **Research Opinions** Ask a group of juvenile justice practitioners such as police officers and probation officers if they believe that biological factors such as testosterone, diet, genetics, and learning disabilities lead to delinquency. Document which of these biological factors received the most support from the juvenile justice practitioners.

INTERNET ACTIVITIES

1. Research the work and theories of psychologist Carol Gilligan. She provides criticism of Kohlberg's work on moral development. She argues that the moral development of males and females differs. Write a one-page synopsis of her thoughts on moral development.

2. Go to **mentalhealthamerica.Net/conditions/conduct-disorder/** According to the website, what does the research say about conduct disorder?

CRITICAL THINKING EXERCISES

1. Assessment Unit You work in the assessment unit of a juvenile institution for violent juvenile offenders. A juvenile is brought to the assessment unit who has been adjudicated delinquent for robbery and sexual assault. It is your job to find out what caused this individual to commit these acts and then develop a treatment plan for the juvenile. You evaluate the individual and find the following:

a. The juvenile is a well-muscled youth who has an aggressive personality.

b. The juvenile reports that his diet has been primarily comprised of "junk food," especially foods that are high in sugar content.

c. The juvenile reports that his mother is currently in prison for dealing drugs. Upon further questioning, you discover that the mother has been abusing drugs for the past 20 years.

d. The juvenile does not appear to feel anxiety when faced with negative stimuli.

e. During the assessment, the juvenile is inattentive and has had a prior history of hyperactivity and impulsivity.

What factors can explain the juvenile's delinquent acts? What treatment would you prescribe for this juvenile in order to overcome his biological problems?

Which of the biological factors cannot be treated inside the institution?

2. Psychological Treatment You are employed at a facility that provides psychological treatment to juvenile delinquents. A juvenile is in your office who has committed several burglaries and auto thefts. Upon assessing the juvenile, you discover the following:

a. The juvenile does not feel remorse for his actions and argues that he committed the acts because it satisfied his need for money to repair his car so he could find a job. In addition, he states that committing delinquent acts really is not wrong unless the criminal is caught.

b. The juvenile also says that within the past six months he has been involved in several fights with strangers and acquaintances, and has set two cats on fire by pouring gasoline on them.

c. The juvenile has not been attending school on a regular basis since he was 12 years old.

d. The juvenile says that his friends also commit delinquent acts and they approve of his actions.

What psychological factors can explain the juvenile's delinquent acts? What treatment would you prescribe for this juvenile?

ANSWERS TO SELF-CHECKS

4.1 Self-Check

Why do juvenile delinquents commit delinquent acts according to the choice, deterrence, biological, and psychological theories?
According to the choice theory, juveniles choose to commit delinquent acts. According to deterrence theory, juveniles commit delinquent acts when they choose to do so and when the benefits outweigh the risks. Biological theories look at body types, genes, and prenatal conditions for answers about the causes of delinquency. Finally, psychological theories look at the juvenile's ability to develop morals and self-control; another psychological model is learning theory, which states that juveniles learn through reinforcement or through modeling themselves after other delinquents.

4.2 Self-Check

1. Briefly describe the classical school. Who was its best-known proponent?

The classical school stated that behavior is the rational product of free will. Therefore, juveniles who commit delinquent acts make the rational decision to do so, because of the pleasure they hope to gain from such acts. Its best-known proponent is Cesare Beccaria.

2. What beliefs were held by the positive school?

The positive school states that behavior is beyond an individual's control. At first, positivists looked at biological factors for the causes of crime and delinquency; over time, though, they turned to social and psychological factors.

4.3 Self-Check

1. What are the three reasons for the renewed interest in the classical school?

- Criminologists began to question the premises on which the positive school was founded, because after 100 years of effort the positivists were unable to isolate and treat that cause of crime.
- Crime rates soared in the 1960s and 1970s, which proved to some that the positive approach was not controlling crime.
- Rehabilitation came under attack because many believed that it had little or no effect on recidivism.

2. How do Lawrence Cohen and Marcus Felson explain the changes in crime rates?

Cohen and Felson would explain changes in crime rates by changes in the amounts of suitable targets and capable guardians.

4.4 Self-Check

1. Name the four assumptions underlying the deterrence theory.

The four assumptions are that:

- Juveniles are rational actors.
- Juveniles are aware of the penalty for their particular offenses.
- The risks involved in committing offenses are unpleasant.
- In order for deterrence to be effective, sanctions must be swift, certain, and severe—at least in the eyes of juveniles, who will be deterred by this knowledge.

2. How effective is the deterrence theory?

In general, there is little evidence to support the belief that arrest and incarceration deter crime.

4.5 Self-Check

1. What factors affect a juvenile's chance of becoming delinquent according to William Sheldon?

Sheldon believed that mesomorphic body types are more likely to lead to delinquency than are endomorphic or ectomorphic body types. (For a full explanation of Sheldon's somatotypes, refer to Figure 4.2 on page 97.)

2. Define biosocial factors.

Biosocial factors are interactions between biological and social factors that lead to delinquency. These factors include biochemical factors, such as dietary influences, Fetal Alcohol Syndrome and prenatal drug use, and hormones; the underdevelopment of the autonomic nervous system; and learning disabilities.

4.6 Self-Check

1. Name the six stages of moral development. Beyond which level are people less likely to commit delinquent acts?

The six stages are:

- Punishment and Obedience Orientation
- Hedonistic Orientation
- Interpersonal Concordance
- Law and Order Orientation
- Social Contract, Legalistic Orientation
- Orientation to Universal Ethical Principles

Beyond stage 2, people are less likely to become delinquent.

2. What do learning theorists believe?

Learning theorists believe that juveniles commit delinquent acts because they learn ideas and behaviors that support such actions. This is either through **classical conditioning,** which states that one learns by connecting a stimulus with an expected response; through modeling, which states that people learn delinquent behavior by **modeling** or imitating the behavior of others; or through **operant conditioning,** which states that behavior is controlled by the consequences of that behavior.

Social Structure, Social Process, and Social Reaction Theories

Chapter Outline

Chapter Objectives

After completing this chapter, you should be able to:

1. Define and contrast the four types of social theories of delinquency.

2. Describe three social structure theories.

3. Summarize three learning theories.

4. Describe three social control theories.

5. Understand life course theories.

6. Explain labeling theory.

7. Explain conflict theory.

Social Theories of Delinquency

This chapter presents the four major social theories of delinquency and specific theories in each. These social theories focus on factors that influence delinquency, including association with delinquent peers, lack of opportunity, and family relationships. Four major types of social theories of delinquency are social structure theories, social process theories, life course theories, and social reaction theories.

- Social structure theories focus on the economic and social conditions in which lower-class youths live.
- Social process theories analyze the impact on delinquency of factors such as peer group relationships, family relationships, and failure in school.
  - Life course theories focus on the creation of criminal careers and the different influences on individuals as they age.
  - Social reaction theories examine the role that societal institutions, including the juvenile justice system, play in perpetuating delinquent behavior.

5.1 SELF-CHECK

List the four major types of social theories of delinquency.

Social Structure Theories

Social structure theories examine why lower-class youths are more likely to commit crime than middle- and upper-class youths. Middle- and upper-class youths do commit crime, but their crimes are usually less serious than those committed by lower-class youths. Basically, social structure theories focus on two major factors that influence delinquency: socioeconomic conditions and cultural values. These conditions and values, in turn, are based on social and economic inequality in the social structure. Three social structure theories include ecological theory, strain theory, and subculture theory.

ECOLOGICAL THEORY

Ecological theory seeks to explain delinquency based on *where* it occurs. The environment of an area has an impact on delinquency. The most prominent ecological theory is Clifford R. Shaw and Henry D. McKay's social disorganization theory.

SHAW AND McKAY'S SOCIAL DISORGANIZATION THEORY When Shaw and McKay developed their theory in the 1920s, it was one of the first attempts to focus on the social conditions that lead to delinquency. They sought to explain why juvenile crime rates were so high in areas of a city characterized by urban decay. Shaw and McKay argued that the ecological condition of the city influenced delinquency. They studied the juvenile court and police records of juvenile delinquents from Chicago to determine the areas of the city that had the highest delinquency rates. They then mapped the delinquency rates and found that delinquent patterns were distributed in five concentric circles moving from the central business district to the suburbs.[1] (See Figure 5.1.)

Zone 1—Factory zone: The central business district
Zone 2—Zone in transition: One of the oldest areas of the city and surrounding the central business district. It is frequently invaded by businesses as the central business district expands
Zone 3—Zone of working people's homes: Comprised of the homes and apartments of working people who have left the zone in transition

Zone 4—Residential zone: Comprised of more expensive homes and apartments

Zone 5—Commuters' zone: The suburbs[2]

After studying crime rates in the various zones, Shaw and McKay discovered stable and significant differences in crime rates in the different zones. These differences had existed for more than 65 years. The zone in transition consistently had the highest delinquency rate in comparison to the other zones.[3] This zone, frequently referred to as an **interstitial area,** is one in which factories and commercial establishments exist along with private residences.

CULTURAL HETEROGENEITY Why was there increased delinquency in the zone in transition? Shaw and McKay identified three characteristics of interstitial areas: cultural heterogeneity, mobility, and poverty.[4] Up through the 1920s, a large number of immigrants from many countries came to the United States and frequently lived in the zone in transition where housing was cheapest. Therefore, a variety of cultures coexisted in this area which did not necessarily exist in the other zones. This variety led to the lack of a common value system among the residents. For example, neighbors who may not understand each other's cultural differences would not interact. Thus, the informal social control mechanisms that existed in the other zones, such as having neighbors who watched each other's children and a general feeling of cohesiveness with neighbors, did not exist in the zone in transition. The limited group cohesion in these neighborhoods due to cultural heterogeneity made delinquency more likely because informal social control mechanisms were less powerful.

| FIGURE 5.1 | **Concentric Zones in the Greater Chicago Area** |

Lake Michigan

5 4 3 2 1   Chicago

Source: Clifford R. Shaw and Henry D. McKay, *Juvenile Delinquency and Urban Areas.* Copyright 1942 by the University of Chicago. Reprinted by permission of the University of Chicago Press.

This neighborhood is socially disorganized. *What neighborhood factors would influence the delinquent behavior of a youth who lives in this neighborhood?*

interstitial area Area of a city characterized by high delinquency rates in which factories and commercial establishments exist along with private residences.

FOCUS ON POLICY

LOOTING AFTER HURRICANE KATRINA

In the aftermath of Hurricane Katrina in New Orleans, widespread looting occurred in the city. For example, in the city's Carrollton section, looters stole a forklift and used it to push up the storm shutters and break the glass of a Rite-Aid pharmacy. People ran into the store carrying out necessities such as ice, water, and food. However, in some cases it was hard to tell whether the looting was used as a mechanism to obtain necessities or used by common criminals as a means to obtain merchandise. New Orleans' homeland security chief, Terry Ebbert, said looters were breaking into stores all over town and stealing guns. At the time, there were gangs of armed individuals moving around the city. On New Orleans' Canal Street, dozens of looters ripped open the steel gates on clothing and jewelry stores and grabbed merchandise. In Biloxi, Mississippi, people picked through casino slot machines for coins and ransacked other businesses. Because law enforcement and other governmental officials were concerned with search and rescue of survivors first, additional officers and resources had to be called in to respond to the looting.

How can social disorganization theory be used to explain the looting in New Orleans? What neighborhood factors can lead to this type of behavior?

Source: www.cbsnews.com/stories/2005/08/31/national/main809442.shtml

MOBILITY Another characteristic of interstitial areas is the mobility of its residents. Usually, individuals would obtain better jobs and move away from the zone of transition. Therefore, there was rapid turnover in the population of interstitial areas, which hindered the development of a common set of neighborhood **norms** (prescriptions for appropriate behavior) and values. Still true today, the mobility of residents influences the level of informal social control in the neighborhood. Informal social control—family, neighbors, friends, school, and church—are far more powerful mechanisms to regulate people's behavior (including delinquency) than are formal social control mechanisms such as police and the juvenile justice system. In interstitial areas, then, informal social control mechanisms are not well developed. Therefore, delinquency is more likely (See Focus on Policy).

POVERTY The third characteristic of interstitial areas is poverty. Those who live in poverty are more likely to commit delinquent acts. To review the relationship between poverty (i.e., social class) and delinquency, refer to Chapter 3.

Prior to the work of Shaw and McKay and others in the Chicago School, many of the theories focused on biological and psychological factors. (See Chapter 4.) Shaw and McKay provided evidence that social factors, not biological and psychological factors, impact delinquency. Recall that a characteristic of the zone in transition is high mobility. As individuals obtain jobs, they begin to move to other areas of the city. If biological or psychological factors cause the delinquency in the interstitial areas, it might be expected that the delinquency would continue in the other zones as individuals from the zone in transition move there. However, this is not the case. As individuals move to Zone 3 and to other zones, delinquency does not continue. Therefore, Shaw and McKay argued that factors in the environment of these interstitial areas of a city led to delinquency (See Focus on Programs: Chicago Area Project on page 119).

STRAIN THEORY

The second major type of social structure theory is strain theory. Strain theorists see delinquency as a result of a lack of opportunity, in particular of economic opportunity. American society instills in citizens a desire for financial success but does not provide all individuals equal opportunity to achieve that financial success. Those who do not have equal opportunity are "strained" and consequently more likely to be delinquent.

norms Prescriptions for appropriate behavior.

CHICAGO AREA PROJECT

In 1932, Clifford Shaw began the Chicago Area Project, based on his social disorganization theory. He thought that delinquency could be reduced by programs that can effect change in the conditions of life in interstitial areas. The project included the establishment of 22 neighborhood centers in six areas of Chicago. These centers had two primary functions. First, they were to coordinate such community resources as churches, schools, labor unions, industries, clubs, and other groups in addressing and resolving community problems. Second, they were to sponsor a variety of activity programs including recreation, summer camping and scouting activities, handicraft workshops, discussion groups, and community projects. The Chicago Area Project operated for 25 years until 1957.

CRITICAL THINKING

Explain how Shaw and McKay's theories relate to the goals of the Chicago Area Project. Do you think the program would also be considered valuable by the proponents of biological and psychological theories? Why or why not?

Source: Bernard, Thomas J., Jeffrey B. Snipes, and Alexander L. Gerould. *Vold's Theoretical Criminology*, 6th ed. New York: Oxford University Press, 2009.

MERTON'S STRAIN THEORY Every society provides a cultural goal and the means to obtain it. According to Robert Merton, the cultural goal of American society is economic success.[5] Merton argues that the primary goal of U.S. citizens is material wealth and that this goal is made widespread through the media, cultural messages, and other mechanisms. In our society, institutionalized means of reaching the primary goal are education, occupation, and deferral of gratification. However, not everyone has equal access to the institutionalized means to obtain financial success. Poorer members of society have less access to education and good jobs than do members of the middle and upper classes. Strain theory is sometimes referred to as "blocked opportunity" theory. People are blocked in their ability to access education and good jobs; therefore, they experience a discrepancy between the desire to obtain economic success and the ability to do so. These individuals suffer from strain (See Focus on Programs: Job Corps on page 121).

If people are strained, how do they adapt to the strain? Merton developed five modes of adaptation.[6] The modes of adaptation vary depending on an individual's acceptance or rejection of the cultural goal of economic success and the institutionalized means to obtain the goal. Adaptations also vary on the propensity for delinquency (see Figure 5.2).

The first and most common mode of adaptation is **conformity**. A *conformist* both accepts the cultural goal of economic success and accepts the

FIGURE 5.2	Merton's Modes of Adaptation	
MODE OF ADAPTATION	CULTURAL GOAL	INSTITUTIONALIZED MEANS
Conformity	+	+
Ritualism	–	+
Innovation	+	–
Retreatism	–	–
Rebellion	+/–	+/–

+ means acceptance
– means rejection
+/– means rejection and substitution

Source: Reprinted with the permission of The Free Press, a Division of Simon & Schuster Adult Publishing Group, from *Social Theory and Social Structure* by Robert K. Merton. Copyright © 1957 by The Free Press. Copyright © renewed 1985 by Robert K. Merton. All rights reserved.

conformity A mode of adaptation that involves acceptance of the cultural goal of economic success and acceptance of the institutionalized means to obtain it.

institutionalized means to obtain success. A conformist is highly unlikely to commit delinquent acts and will continue to pursue the goal of economic success through the institutionalized means.

The second mode of adaptation is **ritualism.** A *ritualist* rejects the cultural goal of economic success but accepts the institutionalized means to obtain the cultural goal. Ritualists respond to strain by lowering their aspirations for financial success, but they still accept the means to obtain it, such as employment and education. It is unlikely that ritualists, who are heavily represented in the lower middle class, will commit delinquent acts.

The third mode of adaptation is **innovation.** An *innovator* accepts the goal of economic success but rejects the institutionalized means to obtain it. In this adaptation, the individual invents new means to obtain economic success other than education and employment. The innovator may commit offenses such as drug dealing, robbery, burglary, auto theft, fraud, bribery, and prostitution in an effort to obtain financial success. Innovators want to be financially successful and will commit delinquent acts that move them forward to this goal. Innovation is the mode of adaptation that is most likely to lead to delinquency.

The fourth mode of adaptation is **retreatism.** A *retreatist* rejects both the cultural goal of economic success and any institutionalized means to obtain it. Retreatists do not aspire to financial success nor are they concerned with education and employment. They frequently escape into drug addiction and may commit crimes to support their drug use. The retreatist's strain is reduced by abandoning both the goal and the means to obtain it.

The fifth mode of adaptation is **rebellion.** A *rebel* rejects the cultural goal and the means to attain it but substitutes new goals and new means to obtain them. This adaptation is likely to lead to delinquency and can be represented by some gangs, militias, cults, and countercultures. Delinquency is likely to occur among rebels, but it will not be as prevalent as delinquency among innovators.

AGNEW'S GENERAL STRAIN THEORY In 1992, Robert Agnew created General Strain Theory, which is sometimes referred to as GST. Agnew sought to explain why individuals who feel stress and strain are likely to respond to this stress by committing crimes. It is argued that Agnew's theory may be a better explanation of delinquency than Merton's strain theory because the cultural goal of economic success may not be as applicable to juveniles as adults. In addition, Agnew's theory does not focus exclusively on delinquency committed by members of the lower class but can be used as an explanation of delinquency among all social classes.

Agnew argues that crime is a response to negative affective states which are adverse emotions such as anger, frustration, disappointment, depression, and fear generated by negative social relations.[7] He maintains that these negative affective states occur not only as the result of failing to obtain economic goals (as offered by Merton), but also due to failure to achieve noneconomic goals, the removal of positive stimuli (e.g., divorce or ending a relationship with a boyfriend or girlfriend), and the introduction of negative stimuli (e.g., not getting along with your parents, getting bullied).[8]

Anger, along with other negative affective states, can increase the likelihood that delinquency will occur. Of the negative affective states, anger is the most important and is likely to occur when juveniles blame others for their misfortune. Anger increases a juvenile's perception of being wronged by someone else. In addition, anger also increases the desire for revenge and limits self-control. Chronic strain can lead to delinquency, especially when the strain causes an aggressive, hostile, and suspicious attitude on the part of the youth.[9] However, not all youths who face strain are going to commit delinquent acts. Some juveniles are able to cope with the anger and frustration caused by strain. Those unable to cope with strain and who thus commit delinquent acts are likely to

ritualism A mode of adaptation that involves rejection of the cultural goal of economic success and acceptance of the institutionalized means to obtain it.

innovation A mode of adaptation that involves acceptance of the cultural goal of economic success and rejection of the institutionalized means to obtain it.

retreatism A mode of adaptation that involves rejection of the cultural goal of economic success and rejection of the institutionalized means to obtain it.

rebellion A mode of adaptation that involves rejection and substitution of the cultural goal of economic success and rejection and substitution of the institutionalized means to obtain it.

FOCUS ON PROGRAMS

JOB CORPS

The Job Corps serves as an alternative learning program for disadvantaged young people who have difficulty in traditional school systems, who are high school dropouts, or who are facing challenges developing life goals. Almost 120 Job Corps campuses exist nationwide. It is the nation's largest and most comprehensive residential education and job training program for at-risk youth, ages 16 through 24. Since 1964, the program has provided more than 1.7 million disadvantaged young people with academic, vocational, and social skills training. Job Corps offers high school equivalency programs and training in various occupations, as well as advanced training in some areas. More than 80 percent of those who enroll in the Job Corps become employed, obtain further training, join the military, or enroll in college.

Eligibility requirements for Job Corps training include:

- Be at least 16 and not yet 25 years of age at the time of enrollment
- Be economically disadvantaged
- Be free of behavior problems that would prohibit self or others from benefiting from the program; must be free of face-to-face court or institutional supervision or court-imposed fines while in the Job Corps
- Be drug-free
- Live in an environment that is not conducive to getting a job or an education
- Must be a high school dropout or in need of further vocational training, education, or support services.

CRITICAL THINKING

Why do you think such a program would be helpful to potential juvenile delinquents?

Source: www.jobcorps.gov

---

be overly sensitive, have an explosive temperament, have a low tolerance for adversity, and have poor problem-solving skills.

SUBCULTURE THEORY

A **subculture** is a set of values, norms, and beliefs that differs from those within the dominant culture. According to subculture theory, delinquent youth hold values, norms, and beliefs in opposition to those held in the dominant culture. Therefore, youths who behave in a manner that is consistent with the values, norms, and beliefs of their subculture will often be in conflict with the law.

Three subculture theories are: Cohen's delinquency and frustration theory, Cloward and Ohlin's differential opportunity theory, and Miller's lower-class focal concern theory.

COHEN'S DELINQUENCY AND FRUSTRATION THEORY Albert K. Cohen believed that individuals from the lower class had different values, norms, and beliefs than those held by the middle class.[10] Despite this, Cohen argued that the goal of lower-class youths is middle-class membership. However, lower-class youths face developmental handicaps that place them at a disadvantage in obtaining their goal of middle-class membership. According to Cohen, these developmental handicaps include the lack of educational preparation and inability to delay gratification.[11] Because members of the lower class have norms and values that differ from those of the middle class, lower-class families cannot teach their children the proper socialization techniques necessary for middle-class membership.

How do young people of the lower class achieve middle-class membership? The primary means of becoming a member of the middle class is education. These youths, who have been socialized to be part of the lower class, frequently have difficulty in school because teachers and administrators are members of

JUVENILE JUSTICE ONLINE

Go to **www.acf.hhs.gov/programs/ohs** (Office of Head Start of the U.S. Department of Health and Human Services). Evaluate the statistics you find. Write a two-paragraph summary of what you learn. What trends did you observe? What theories presented in the chapter support the Head Start program?

subculture A set of values, norms, and beliefs that differ from those of the dominant culture.

Elementary school classroom. *Do you think each child has the same chance of succeeding at school? According to Cohen, what obstacles do lower-class youths face in school? What factors can influence school success?*

the middle class and hold the values, norms, and beliefs of the middle class. The standards and values used in school to evaluate youths, which Cohen calls **middle-class measuring rods,**[12] include ambition, responsibility, deferred gratification, courtesy, ability to control aggression, constructive use of time, and respect for property.[13] Essentially, lower-class youths are being evaluated by measures grounded in middle-class values and norms to which they are not accustomed. These middle-class measuring rods make it difficult for lower-class children to succeed in school.

If lower-class students fail at school, they will not be able to attain their goal of middle-class status. Inability to fulfill this goal is known as **status frustration.** Frequently, students who are not performing well in school seek others like themselves with whom to associate. In other words, these young people may associate with others like themselves who are failing in school and are facing status frustration. These young people form delinquent subcultures and gangs. In gangs, youths develop new norms, values, and beliefs; they also establish new means to obtain status. Cohen argued that these youths invert norms, values, and beliefs of the middle class.[14] These young people then perform actions opposite those consistent with middle-class values. Therefore, they value exactly what is despised by the middle class. Cohen describes this as nonutilitarian, malicious, and negativistic.[15] The delinquent behavior of these youths does not serve a purpose. They commit unprovoked assaults and steal items they do not need or want. Since gang members will not be able to reach their goal of middle-class status, they develop new means to obtain status, which include using violence and committing delinquent acts. Cohen argued that this delinquent behavior is actually a protest against the norms, values, and beliefs of the middle-class culture.[16]

CLOWARD AND OHLIN'S DIFFERENTIAL OPPORTUNITY THEORY Richard Cloward and Lloyd Ohlin focused on serious delinquency committed by urban, male gang members.[17] They asserted that two goals pursued by lower-class

middle-class measuring rods The standards and values used to evaluate youths in school.

status frustration Occurs due to a person's inability to obtain the goal of middle-class status.

youth were economic success and/or middle-class membership.[18] Youths who had little ability to achieve these goals through legitimate means would form delinquent subcultures/gangs in an effort to obtain the goals.

According to Cloward and Ohlin, the works of Merton and Cohen were too simplistic. Merton's strain theory and Cohen's delinquency and frustration theory made it seem that if juveniles could not achieve their goals, then they would commit crime. However, Cloward and Ohlin believed that illegal opportunities, like conventional opportunities, are stratified unequally.[19] This means that there is an **illegitimate opportunity structure** just as there is a legitimate opportunity structure for success. The legitimate opportunity structure involves education, hard work, and a good occupation, and not everyone has access to this opportunity structure to obtain economic success. Cloward and Ohlin argued that not everyone has access to the illegitimate opportunity structure, either. The illegitimate opportunity structure includes criminal enterprises in neighborhoods where there are criminal mentors to assist youths in becoming successful criminals. Because having a mentor and other types of opportunities do not exist in every neighborhood, not everyone has access to the means to be a criminal.

Think of it this way: Could you be a "successful" criminal? If you stole a car, would you then have the contacts necessary to dispose of the vehicle by taking it to a chop shop or some other location? Likewise, you may be able to break into someone's house, but can you fence the items you stole from the house? Do you have the connections to be a drug dealer? Obviously, you would not only have to know where to buy quantities of drugs, but you would also have to associate with individuals who are willing to buy drugs. Most of your answers to these questions will be "No." That is the exact point Cloward and Ohlin make. Achieving success by new means is more than a matter of choosing to commit crime. Although there are illegitimate opportunity structures in many neighborhoods, not everyone has equal access to these structures.

illegitimate opportunity structure
Neighborhood structures such as established criminal enterprises and criminal mentors that lead youths to become criminals.

CAREERS IN JUVENILE JUSTICE

School Counselor

There are approximately 90,000 school counselors employed in public elementary, middle/junior high, and senior high settings in the United States. School counselors work with all students, including those who are considered at-risk and those with special needs. Therefore, they deal with students who are delinquents as well.

School counselors are specialists in human behavior and relationships who provide assistance to students. They provide counseling and advice to youths on academic issues, vocational training opportunities, and college pursuits. Counseling and advice is also provided for social issues such as family problems and problems with alcohol and drugs.

School counselors are student advocates who work cooperatively with other individuals and organizations to promote the development of children, youth, and families in their communities. School counselors consult and collaborate with teachers, administrators, and families to assist students in becoming successful academically, vocationally, and personally.

School counselors frequently receive extensive training and education. Most school counselors have a degree in education, counseling, psychology, or a related discipline. Many school settings require that counselors have graduate degrees and teaching experience. The graduate degrees are frequently in counselor education or psychology. In addition, counselors receive specialized training through seminars and courses available to counselors.

Critical Thinking

What characteristics/skills must a counselor possess in order to be successful?

Inner-city youth gang. *What behaviors would these youths participate in if they were members of a criminal, conflict, or retreatist gang?*

Myth | Fact

Policies and programs are not influenced by theory.

On many occasions, policies and programs are influenced by theories. For example, the Chicago Area Project was developed on the basis of Shaw and McKay's social disorganization theory. Cloward and Ohlin's differential opportunity theory became the basis for Lyndon Johnson's War on Poverty.

Source: Bernard, Thomas J., Jeffrey B. Snipes, and Alexander L. Gerould, *Vold's Theoretical Criminology*, 6th ed. New York: Oxford University Press, 2009.

criminal gangs Gangs in organized communities in which younger offenders can gain the necessary knowledge and skills to be successful criminals from older offenders.

conflict gangs Gangs that develop in highly disorganized areas in which there are not adult criminal role models.

retreatist gangs Gangs that retreat into drug and alcohol use.

When delinquent subcultures/gangs are established with a different set of values, norms, and beliefs, the type of delinquent gang that develops will depend on the neighborhood in which the youths live and whether they have access to illegitimate opportunity structures. According to Cloward and Ohlin, three distinct types of gangs might form in neighborhoods: criminal gangs, conflict gangs, and retreatist gangs.[20] **Criminal gangs** exist in organized communities in which younger offenders can gain the necessary knowledge and skills to be successful criminals from older offenders. Criminal gangs are likely to commit crimes such as drug dealing, commercial theft, burglary, and other crimes with an economic motive. They have access to illegitimate opportunity structures to obtain their goals. On the other hand, **conflict gangs** do not have access to these illegitimate opportunity structures to obtain their goals. The neighborhoods in which conflict gangs develop are highly disorganized; there are no adult criminal role models to tutor these youths. Since there are no older offenders to teach the appropriate skills and knowledge, most of the crime is individualistic and unorganized. Frequently, youths in these neighborhoods may commit acts of violence out of anger and frustration. **Retreatist gangs** may exist in neighborhoods that either do or do not have illegitimate opportunity structures, or they may not have access to those structures. Retreatist gangs are comprised of members who are either unable or unwilling to be successful criminals. However, they may commit petty crimes, such as selling small amounts of drugs to support their drug and alcohol use.

MILLER'S LOWER-LASS FOCAL CONCERNS THEORY Walter B. Miller was an anthropologist who studied the lower-class areas of Boston in 1955 and formulated his lower-class focal concerns theory based on his field observations. Miller's basic tenet was that society is composed of various social groups, each with its distinctive subculture. For example, he recognized that delinquency may occur because youths are following certain norms and values of the lower class, which puts them in violation of the law. He also examined factors that contribute to gang formation and delinquency. Miller identified six focal concerns that describe six values of a lower-class subculture.[21] These focal concerns differentiate the lower class from the middle and upper classes.

1. **Trouble**—value by which people are evaluated on the basis of their involvement in trouble-making activity
2. **Toughness**—value of physical strength, fighting ability, and masculinity
3. **Smartness**—value of the ability to be streetwise and to con people
4. **Excitement**—value of thrill-seeking through gambling, fighting, and getting intoxicated
5. **Fate**—value or belief that most things that happen to people are beyond their control
6. **Autonomy**[22]—value of personal freedom resulting in an active disdain of authority.

To review, three social structure theories support the argument that socioeconomic conditions and cultural values in the lower class lead to delinquency. Thus, delinquency occurs for one of the following reasons:

- the environment in which one lives (social disorganization theory)
- the inability to obtain goals due to lack of equal access to legitimate means to obtain the goal (strain theory)
- the adherence to lower-class values (subculture theory).

5.2 SELF-CHECK

1. What factors lead to delinquency according to Shaw and McKay?
2. Briefly describe the three subculture theories.
3. Review Miller's focal concerns theory. What flaw can you find in this view of society?

Social Process Theories

Social process theories focus on the relationship between socialization and delinquency. In particular, social process theories analyze the relationship to delinquency of certain factors such as peer group relationships, family relationships, and failure in school. Individuals who associate with delinquent peers are themselves at significant risk of committing acts of delinquency. Individuals who have been raised in a dysfunctional family or without proper nurturing are at greater risk of delinquency. Finally, individuals who drop out of school are also at risk for delinquency. Chapter 3 includes a discussion of these factors, but the *theories* that relate to these factors are presented here. Two primary branches of social process theory, learning theory and social control theory, focus on the relationship between socialization and delinquency.

LEARNING THEORY

According to learning theory, juveniles commit delinquent acts because they learn the attitudes, skills, and rationalizations necessary to commit these acts. This learning may take place in interaction with parents and peers. Delinquents differ from nondelinquents in the extent of their exposure to definitions and situations that portray delinquent acts as appropriate. Three learning theories are: Sutherland's differential association theory, Akers's differential reinforcement theory, and Sykes and Matza's techniques of neutralization/drift theory.

SUTHERLAND'S DIFFERENTIAL ASSOCIATION THEORY At the time of Edwin H. Sutherland's work, social structure theories—social disorganization and strain—were prevalent. However, Sutherland asserted that delinquent behavior is a function of learning and not a function of either the ability to obtain economic success or of living in a socially disorganized area of a city. He made nine formal propositions that demonstrate that social interaction and learning lead to delinquency.[23]

1. *Criminal behavior is learned.* Sutherland argued that delinquency is not a function of a biological or psychological malady nor one of the social structure but is rather a function of learning.

2. *Criminal behavior is learned in interaction with other persons in a process of communication.* This communication is verbal and involves interaction with others.

3. *The principal part of the learning of criminal behavior occurs with intimate personal groups.* Learning involves interaction with significant others such as parents, siblings, and peers. Therefore, families and peers have the greatest influence on learning delinquent behavior and attitudes. Sutherland did not see a significant role for movies and the media as a way to learn delinquent behavior; however, he did formulate his theory prior to the development of television and other technology, such as video games or the Internet.

4. *When criminal behavior is learned, the learning includes techniques of committing the crime, specific directions of motives, drives, rationalizations, and attitudes.* In the process of learning delinquent behavior, a juvenile will learn how to commit the offense. For example, in learning how to steal a car or how to break into a house, a juvenile also learns appropriate attitudes and rationalizations necessary to justify the delinquent behavior.

5. *The specific direction of motives and drives is learned from definitions of the legal codes as favorable or unfavorable.* Sutherland argued that an individual may be surrounded by persons who define the legal codes as rules to be observed. In this case, delinquency is unlikely because the juvenile believes the law is something to be followed. However, some individuals associate with people who define the legal code in ways that are favorable to the violation of the law. Obviously, delinquency is much more likely in the second instance.

6. *A person becomes delinquent because of an excess of definitions favorable to violation of the law over definitions unfavorable to violation of the law.* According to Sutherland's principle of **differential association,** people learn definitions favorable and unfavorable to the violation of the law. A favorable definition occurs when a youth is exposed to ideas or behaviors (e.g., friends who deal drugs) that are deviant. When, through association with others, a juvenile has obtained more definitions that are favorable to the violation of the law than are unfavorable, then delinquency is likely to occur. In other words, the juvenile has learned to commit certain acts of delinquency. This principle explains why delinquents may think that some delinquent acts are appropriate while others are not. For example, a juvenile may think that committing burglary is appropriate but committing robbery is wrong. How can this be justified? According to Sutherland, the juvenile has received enough definitions in interaction with others to believe that committing burglary is appropriate. On the other hand, the same juvenile has not received enough definitions to believe that robbery is appropriate. Think of definitions favorable to violation of the law on one side of a scale while definitions unfavorable to violation of the law are weighing on the other side. If a juvenile receives more definitions favorable to the violation of the law, the balance will be tipped in favor

differential association The theory that delinquency results from social interaction and learning.

of committing the delinquent act. The balance may vary from offense to offense and from action to action. For example, a juvenile may believe that using marijuana is acceptable while using cocaine is not. The juvenile has received many more definitions that favor marijuana use than favor cocaine use.

7. *Differential associations may vary in frequency, duration, priority, and intensity.* Associations with delinquent and/or nondelinquent behavior vary depending on the quality and number of social interactions. The *frequency* and *duration* of the interactions will determine how much attention juveniles will pay to definitions. They will pay more attention to definitions obtained from those who are frequent contacts or from those with whom they have been in contact for a long period of time. Therefore, families and peers have more impact on the learning of delinquency than others who have less contact with the juvenile. *Priority* involves the importance of delinquent or nondelinquent behavior to the juvenile. Sutherland assumed that when lawful behavior developed in early childhood it was likely to persist throughout life. When delinquent behavior developed in early childhood, it was also likely to persist. Sutherland also argued that adolescents frequently place a higher priority on the interactions with their peers than with their parents. While parents may provide definitions that are unfavorable to violation of the law, juveniles may view their interactions with peers as more important. Thus, the influence of parents' definitions will be minimized. *Intensity* involves the prestige of the source of a delinquent or nondelinquent pattern and the emotional reactions related to the associations.

8. *The process of learning criminal behavior by association with criminal and anticriminal patterns involves all of the mechanisms that are involved in any other learning.* Learning delinquent behavior is not different than learning any other behavior. Sutherland did not, however, apply one of

Associating with delinquent peers is related to delinquency. *According to Sutherland, if one of these youths is delinquent, how may he influence the behavior of his peers? How likely is it that the other youths will also commit delinquent acts?*

the learning theories discussed in Chapter 4. Instead, he simply made the basic statement that delinquency is a learned behavior like other learned behaviors.

9. *While criminal behavior is an expression of general needs and values, it is not explained by those general needs and values, since noncriminal behavior is an expression of the same needs and values.* Sutherland argued that thieves steal in order to obtain money, but workers work to obtain money as well. One cannot say that a juvenile commits a delinquent act to get money because that is the same reason why another juvenile works at a local restaurant. In other words, the need for money explains unlawful behavior as well as it explains lawful behavior.

To summarize Sutherland's differential association theory, delinquency is a learned behavior.

Myth / Fact

Myth: The theories developed between the 1920s and the 1950s such as the theories by Shaw and McKay, Merton, and Sutherland have no relevance to delinquency today.

Fact: These theories are common and valid explanations of delinquency today.

Source: Bernard, Thomas J., Jeffrey B. Snipes, and Alexander L. Gerould, *Vold's Theoretical Criminology*, 6th ed. New York: Oxford University Press, 2009.

AKERS'S DIFFERENTIAL REINFORCEMENT THEORY

Sutherland did not apply a specific learning theory to his theory of differential association. Instead, he just stated that delinquent behavior is learned in the same way as any other behavior. He did not explain *how* other behavior or delinquent behavior is learned. (Chapter 4 includes a discussion of three learning theories: classical conditioning, modeling, and operant conditioning.) Ronald Akers's differential reinforcement theory integrated differential association and the learning theory of operant conditioning.[24] **Operant conditioning** holds that behavior is controlled by the consequences of that behavior. Everyone receives positive and negative reinforcements for behavior. According to differential reinforcement theory, a **positive reinforcement** is a reward and is designed to increase the behavior being rewarded. For example, if a girl is given money for cleaning up her room, then the positive reinforcement of the reward is likely to lead her to continue cleaning up her room. On the other hand, a **negative reinforcement** is a punishment designed to decrease the behavior. For example, if a teenage girl is caught skipping school and her parents punish her, it is unlikely that she will skip school in the future. Therefore, behavior is controlled by the rewards and punishments people receive for their behavior.[25]

If a positive reinforcement is given after a person commits a delinquent act, the person has received a reward for that behavior. It is to be expected that the person will continue the behavior. For example, if a young male breaks into a house and steals jewelry and a laptop, he has received a positive reinforcement for that behavior. If the juvenile then tells his friends, and they express support and award prestige for the delinquent actions, then he is likely to continue. Learning theorists argue that rewards are more powerful than punishments in shaping behavior. However, in some cases, a juvenile may be expecting to receive a reward (positive reinforcement) for behavior, but the reward is withheld. If this occurs, the person has received an indirect punishment for the behavior, and the behavior is less likely to continue. For example, if a young male commits a robbery but fails to obtain any money or valuables, he has received an indirect punishment, and he is less likely to continue the delinquent behavior.

A juvenile may also receive negative reinforcement for a behavior. If this occurs, the juvenile has received a direct punishment and is less likely to continue the behavior. For example, if a juvenile steals a car, is arrested by the police, and is put on probation, the juvenile has received a direct punishment

operant conditioning Learning theory that argues that behavior is controlled by the consequences of that behavior.

positive reinforcement Rewarded behavior.

negative reinforcement Punished behavior.

and is less likely to continue his or her delinquent behavior than if the juvenile had not been arrested and sanctioned. Recall, however, that learning theory argues that rewards are more powerful in shaping behavior than punishments. If a juvenile receives rewards from his or her peer group for committing delinquent acts, that delinquency may continue—even with punishment by the juvenile justice system. A juvenile may also anticipate that a punishment (negative reinforcement) is going to occur after delinquent behavior. If no punishment follows, the juvenile has received an indirect reward for the behavior and is likely to increase the behavior. The juvenile justice system does not do a good job of arresting and sanctioning people who have committed delinquent acts. The clearance rate for index crimes is about 20 percent. This means that a person is arrested for only one of every five offenses reported to the police. This statistic indicates that many juveniles receive an indirect reward for committing delinquent acts because they are never arrested. Therefore, delinquent behavior is reinforced by association with delinquent peers, a lack of punishment from parents, and the ineffectiveness of the juvenile justice system.

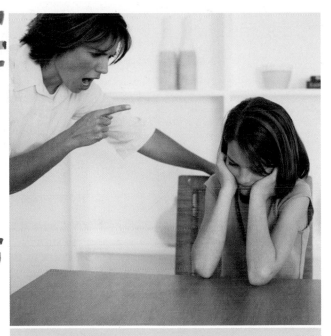

Scolding children for their behavior can serve as a negative reinforcement. *According to Akers, is this youth likely to continue the behavior for which she received the scolding?*

SYKES AND MATZA'S TECHNIQUES OF NEUTRALIZATION/DRIFT THEORY

Gresham M. Sykes and David Matza also took the position that the process of becoming delinquent is a learning experience. They argued that most delinquents hold conventional values, norms, and beliefs and must learn to neutralize the values before committing delinquent acts. Most delinquents are not committed to a delinquent lifestyle and only commit delinquent acts on rare occasions. These same delinquents hold values and beliefs that delinquent behavior is wrong. How can they commit delinquent acts but still hold conventional values? Juvenile delinquents use techniques of neutralization that shield them from any sense of guilt and allow them to drift into delinquency and then back into conventional behavior. Thus, this theory is sometimes referred to as *drift theory*.[26] Sykes and Matza stated that juveniles learn the techniques of neutralization before they commit delinquent acts. The five techniques of neutralization are as follows[27]:

1. **Denial of responsibility** This technique of neutralization occurs when juveniles state that their behavior was an accident or resulted from forces beyond their control—unloving parents, bad companions, or living in a criminogenic neighborhood—they deny responsibility. In effect, these juveniles saying, "I did not mean to do it" reflects denial of responsibility.

2. **Denial of injury** This technique of neutralization occurs when juveniles deny the wrongfulness of their action or express their beliefs that the offense does not really cause any harm. A statement such as, "I did not really hurt anybody because insurance will pay for it" reflects denial of injury.

3. **Denial of victim** This technique of neutralization occurs when juveniles believe that the victim deserved the injury or the victim caused the offense to occur. In other words, they deny that there is a victim. Saying, "They had it coming to them" reflects denial of victim.

4. **Condemnation of the condemners** This technique of neutralization occurs when juveniles shift the blame to others by focusing attention on the motive and behavior of those who disapprove of their actions. In this

instance, they are condemning the condemners. Using this neutralization technique, juveniles challenge those who condemn their actions. These juveniles argue that the police are corrupt and parents take out their frustrations on their children. A statement such as, "Why is everybody picking on me?" reflects a condemnation of the condemner.

5. **Appeal to higher loyalties** This technique of neutralization occurs when juveniles allow their peer group to take precedence over the rules of society. A statement such as, "I did not do it for myself but for my friends" reflects appeal to higher loyalties.

SOCIAL CONTROL THEORY

The theories discussed in Chapter 4 and in this chapter have sought to answer the question "Why do juveniles commit delinquent acts?" Social control theory is different in that it seeks to answer the question "Why *don't* juveniles commit delinquent acts?" Social control theory assumes that people will violate the law. So why don't they? The answer to this question, according to social control theorists, lies in the strength of an individual's ties to the foundations of society (family, friends, and school). Those who have close ties with their families and nondelinquent friends as well as those who possess high self-esteem are unlikely to commit delinquent acts. These individuals are bonded to the larger society. Individuals who are not bonded to the larger social order are free from constraints to violate the law.

RECKLESS'S CONTAINMENT THEORY Walter Reckless believed that both internal and external forces operate when juveniles make decisions to avoid or commit delinquent acts. Some internal forces inhibit people from committing delinquent acts while others encourage delinquent behavior. The same is true for external forces; some inhibit while others encourage delinquent acts. Reckless identified four motivating and restraining forces for delinquency.[28]

1. **Inner pressures and pulls** lead juveniles toward committing delinquent acts. Inner forces include an individual's desires, needs, and wants such as money. These also include feelings of restlessness, hostility, and the need for immediate gratification.

2. **Inner containments** inhibit delinquent behavior. Inner containments are internal personal controls that lead someone to *not* commit delinquent acts. These include self-esteem, strong sense of responsibility, internalized moral codes, tolerance of frustration, and positive goal orientations. Some argue that inner containments are the most powerful inhibitors to delinquency. If individuals are internally restrained from committing delinquent acts because of their belief systems, they are highly unlikely to commit delinquent acts.

3. **Outer pressures and pulls** lead to delinquent behavior. External pressures in the environment that may lead to delinquency include the influence of one's peer group, unemployment, and living conditions. Associating with delinquent peers, not having a job, and living in substandard conditions are external pressures on juveniles to commit delinquent acts. External forces also include the rewards for committing delinquent acts such as status and financial gain.

4. **Outer containments** inhibit delinquent behavior. These include forces that provide discipline and supervision including parents, police, schools, and the juvenile justice system.

FIGURE 5.3	Motivating and Restraining Forces for Delinquency according to Reckless	
FORCE	LEADS TO DELINQUENCY	EXAMPLES
Inner pressures and pulls	Yes	Desires, needs, wants, feelings of restlessness, hostility, and the need for immediate gratification
Inner containments	No	Self-esteem, strong sense of responsibility, internalized moral codes, tolerance of frustration, and positive goal orientations
Outer pressures and pulls	Yes	Pressures—influence of one's peer group, unemployment, and living conditions Pulls—Status and financial gain
Outer containments	No	Parental supervision and discipline, police, schools, and the juvenile justice system

Inner containments are more effective at inhibiting delinquent activity than are outer containments. Outer containments are not always present prior to the commission of delinquent acts, while inner containments such as internalized moral codes are. An individual's self-image and self-esteem are also major predictors of which of these forces will dominate behavior. Therefore, if individuals have a strong positive self-image, inner containments will dominate their behavior. However, if a strong, positive self-image does not exist, it is more likely that pressures and pulls will dominate behavior. In other words, a strong self-image insulates juveniles from delinquency. (See Figure 5.3.)

HIRSCHI'S SOCIAL CONTROL/SOCIAL BONDING THEORY According to Travis Hirschi, people usually do not commit delinquent acts because they fear that this behavior will damage their relationships with their parents, friends, families, teachers, and employers; thus, individuals do not commit delinquent acts because they are bonded to the larger society. When these social bonds are broken or diminished, delinquency is likely. Hirschi stated that there were four elements of the social bond[29] including attachment, commitment, involvement, and belief.

- **Attachment** describes the emotional and psychological ties a person has with others. It includes sensitivity to and interest in others as well as a sense of belonging. Hirschi believed that attachment to parents is more important than attachment to peers and school. Attachment is the most important element of the social bond.
- **Commitment** involves the time, energy, and effort expended in conventional action. For example, someone who has worked hard to get a good education is not likely to jeopardize those efforts by committing crime. This is also true for those who have good jobs. In both cases, the individuals are committed to conventional lines of action and are not likely to jeopardize their positions to commit crime. Therefore, the more conventional assets people have—such as an education, job, and home—the less likely they are to commit crime.
- **Involvement** means significant time and attention spent in conventional activities, which leaves little time for illegal behavior. The adage "Idle hands are the devil's workshop" applies here. People who are busy working, going to school, and raising children are far less likely to commit crime. They do not have the spare time to indulge temptations to commit crimes.
- **Belief** describes the acceptance of moral legitimacy of law and authority, with an understanding that the law should be obeyed.

Youths hanging out on street corners frequently get into trouble. *According to Hirschi, what elements of the social bond are these youths lacking?*

Hirschi argued that certain people do not commit crime precisely because they are bonded to society. However, those with a weakened bond because of lack of attachment, commitment, involvement, and belief are likely to commit delinquent acts. When individuals do possess these elements of the social bond, they are insulated from delinquency.

GOTTFREDSON AND HIRSCHI'S SELF-CONTROL THEORY Michael Gottfredson and Travis Hirschi argued in a later control theory that the tendency to commit crime can be found in the level of self-control. **Self-control** is the ability to control one's own behavior. Gottfredson and Hirschi proposed that those who commit delinquent acts have low self-control; they tend to be impulsive, insensitive, and need immediate gratification.

What causes people to have limited self-control? Gottfredson and Hirschi stated that lack of self-control is caused by inadequate child rearing practices. Self-control, according to Gottfredson and Hirschi, is instilled in children by the age of eight and is relatively constant thereafter. They suggested that parents must monitor their child's behavior, recognize inappropriate behavior when it occurs, and punish the inappropriate behavior.[30] If this consistently occurs, the child will develop a high level of self-control. Over time, the child will internalize the parents' controls. If the parents are unwilling or unable to instill self-control, it is likely they will raise children who lack self-control.

Gottfredson and Hirschi also integrated elements of rational choice theory into the development of their theory. Individuals with little self-control must be presented with the opportunities to commit delinquent acts for delinquency to occur. If an individual has low self-control, but there is no criminal opportunity, then delinquency will not take place. On the other hand, if criminal opportunity presents itself to a juvenile with low self-control, delinquency is likely to occur.

All Individuals Are Capable of Crime

In *Causes of Delinquency*, Hirschi argued that it is not necessary to explain the motivation for delinquency because "we are all animals, and thus all naturally capable of committing criminal acts."

SOURCE: Hirschi, Travis. *Causes of Delinquency*, Berkeley, CA: University of California Press, 1969.

5.3 SELF-CHECK

Compare the two branches of social process theory—learning theory and social control theory.

self-control The ability to control one's own behavior.

Life Course Theories

A growing trend in theoretical development is to focus on the onset and termination of delinquency at different stages over the course of one's life: childhood, adolescence, young adulthood, etc. Life course theories, as they are commonly referred to, draw on the many biological, psychological, and social theories presented in the last two chapters to address the following questions:

- Why do juveniles begin committing acts of delinquency?
- Why do some stop while others continue?
- Why do some increase the severity of their delinquency while others decrease the severity and commit less serious crime as they age into adulthood?
- When juveniles stop committing delinquent acts, what, if anything, causes them to begin again?
- Why do some juveniles specialize in a certain type of crime (e.g., auto theft), while other juveniles are more generalists and engage in a wide variety of different types of delinquent acts?

Life course theories emphasize the importance that childhood problems have on delinquency, but the theories also emphasize that many youths exposed to childhood problems do not end up delinquent because various events during the life course (e.g., positive school experiences and peer relationships) may intervene. For example, even though youths who are raised in abusive households are more likely to be delinquent, many youths raised in such environments do not commit delinquent acts.

Many of the theories that have already been presented lack a developmental perspective. In other words, the theories fail to account for developmental changes that occur during the life course and thus fail to distinguish between different phases of criminal careers. Therefore, life course theories focus on the development of criminal careers and how various criminogenic influences impact individuals during the course of their lives. Life course theories frequently build upon social learning and social control theories.

THORNBERRY'S INTERACTIONAL THEORY

Terence Thornberry developed what is called an interactional theory of crime. The interactional theory combines aspects of social control and social learning theories. However, Thornberry also recognizes the influence of social class and other structural variables, including social disorganization, on delinquency. According to interactional theory, the fundamental cause of delinquency is weakened social bonds to society.[31] Individuals who are attached to their parents and strive to succeed through conventional lines of action (e.g., education) rarely become chronic delinquents. However, more than weakened social bonds are required for delinquency to develop. According to Thornberry, an environment in which delinquency can be learned and rewarded must also be present for delinquency to occur.[32] Frequently, this conducive environment is provided by delinquent peers and through gang participation.

The process of associating with delinquent peers and committing delinquent acts can become a causal loop in which those who commit delinquent acts are more likely to continue to associate with individuals like themselves.[33] This can lead to a significant increase in criminal behavior. If the delinquent behavior continues to be rewarded, delinquents will seek out more and more delinquent groups with which to associate. Therefore, delinquency from the interactional perspective changes and is modified over the life course. The relationship between weakened social bonds and delinquent peer association is bidirectional. For example, frequent involvement with delinquent peers and delinquency weakens social bonds. The weakened social bonds then make it difficult to reestablish relationships with nondelinquent peers. However, if delinquents are able to reestablish such relationships then their social bonds will improve as well.

SAMPSON AND LAUB'S AGE-GRADED THEORY

In their book *Crime in the Making,* Robert Sampson and John Laub identify the turning points in a criminal career.[34] Sampson and Laub argue that delinquent behavior can be impacted by events that occur later in life, even after a significant delinquent career has been established. In other words, the theory can address the following question, "What leads a juvenile who has established a delinquent career to desist from delinquent activity in early adulthood?" Critical to their approach is the idea of turning points in a criminal career. Two important turning points are marriage and employment.[35] For example, delinquents can stop delinquent activity and live conventional lives if they can obtain good jobs and develop successful careers. Similarly, when juvenile delinquents achieve adulthood, they are able to desist from criminal activity if they become attached to a spouse who supports them despite their troubled pasts. Likewise, spending time with one's spouse and family reduces exposure to delinquent peers, which also reduces the opportunity to engage in delinquent activities. Furthermore, individuals who are unable to sustain a marriage are less likely to desist from crime. Other important turning points can occur in association with leaving home, having children, and graduating from school. According to age-graded theory, even chronic delinquents can turn away from delinquency if they experience the right turning points, and even individuals without a delinquent past can begin a criminal career in response to certain events that undermine their social bonds.[36]

5.4 SELF-CHECK

What questions do life course theories seek to answer?

Social Reaction Theories

Social reaction theories examine the role that societal institutions, including the juvenile justice system, play in perpetuating delinquent behavior. These theories argue that the reaction of society to delinquent behavior may lead to continuation of the behavior. Two major types of social reaction theory are labeling theory and conflict theory.

LABELING THEORY

Labeling theory, which became popular in the 1960s, emphasizes explanations of why certain laws are passed and enforced and why police and juvenile court personnel process some offenders but not others. Labeling theorists argued that the law represents the values and interests of individuals and organizations that are able to organize resources to influence legislation.

Not everyone who commits a delinquent act is processed through the juvenile justice system and labeled a "delinquent." Labeling theory looks at the unanticipated and negative consequences of law and law enforcement, especially the label that is attached to certain offenders. It is not concerned with what causes the initial delinquent act—lack of opportunity, low self-control, or biological abnormality—but is concerned with what leads to continued delinquency. Howard S. Becker states that:

> Social groups create deviance by making rules whose infractions constitute deviance, and by applying those rules to particular people and labeling them as outsiders.

labeling theory A criminological theory that contends that juveniles who are labeled delinquent or criminal will eventually commit secondary delinquent acts to live up to the label.

From this point of view, deviance is not a quality of the act a person commits, but rather a consequence of the application of rules and sanctions to an "offender." The deviant is one to whom the label has successfully been applied; deviant behavior is behavior that people so label.[37]

LEMERT'S LABELING THEORY Edwin M. Lemert proposed that the reaction to delinquency is what causes it in the future.[38] Most juveniles commit acts of delinquency and are never brought into the juvenile justice system for processing. Lemert called these delinquent acts **primary deviance.** Individuals who commit acts of primary deviance are not considered delinquents by their parents, family, friends, or by the juvenile justice system because their behavior has gone undetected. Lemert felt that detection and processing in the juvenile justice system has a direct impact on a person's self-image.[39] Most people who have committed acts of only primary deviance do not see themselves as delinquents. However, those whose illegal actions are detected and who are processed in the system are more likely to see themselves as delinquent.

Lemert believed that processing a juvenile in the juvenile justice system can change juveniles' self-concepts from one where they see themselves as nondelinquent to one where they see themselves as delinquent. Once the system reacts in this way to the actions of the juvenile, people start to treat the individual differently. Now that the person has been labeled a "delinquent" by the system, system personnel (such as the police, along with teachers, peers, and others) treat the individual according to the new label. Once this occurs, individuals will internalize the label and will also see themselves as delinquents. After this, secondary deviance will occur. **Secondary deviance** involves continued delinquent behavior because individuals are now acting according to the change in their self-images.

System processing brings about continued delinquency. Official processing in the juvenile justice system leads to the application of labels to certain offenders. Others react to these labels in a way that forces individuals to continue to commit delinquent acts. Basically, the process involves a self-fulfilling prophecy: Individuals become the person others consider them to be. Harold Garfinkel referred to the process of labeling as a **status degradation ceremony.**[40] This involves lowering a person's status from nondelinquent to delinquent.

Labeling theory has had a significant impact on the juvenile justice system. Tenets of labeling theory support **diversion,** which is the practice of removing juveniles from the juvenile justice process and providing them with treatment services outside of the juvenile justice system. This keeps individuals from being labeled as "delinquent." (Chapter 6 offers a more detailed discussion of diversion.) Confidentiality standards for juvenile justice records and proceedings are also based on labeling theory. (See Chapter 8 for a discussion of confidentiality standards.) Records of juveniles in juvenile court are held to stricter confidentiality standards than adult court records because of the interest in minimizing the impact of the labeling process. A third practice that is based on labeling ideas is **deinstitutionalization,** which is the removal of juveniles from institutions and the placement of them in community-based corrections. Obviously, labeling theory has had a great influence on practices of the juvenile justice system.

CONFLICT THEORY

Conflict theorists state that delinquent behavior is due to conflict in society that arises from an unfair distribution of wealth and power. Conflict theorists are concerned with the role government plays in creating an environment that is conducive to crime. They are also concerned with the role that power has in

primary deviance Initial acts of delinquency that go undetected by parents, family, friends, and the juvenile justice system.

secondary deviance Continued delinquent behavior because the individual is now acting according to the delinquent label.

status degradation ceremony Term coined by Garfinkel to describe the labeling process.

diversion Practice of removing juveniles from the juvenile justice process and providing them with treatment services outside of the juvenile justice system.

deinstitutionalization The removal of juveniles from institutions because of the labeling effects and their placement in community-based corrections.

Labeling Theory

Labeling theory has had a significant impact on the practices of juvenile justice including confidentiality provisions and diversion.

SOURCE: Bernard, Thomas J., Jeffrey B. Snipes, and Alexander L. Gerould, *Vold's Theoretical Criminology*, 6th ed. New York: Oxford University Press, 2009.

JUVENILE JUSTICE
ONLINE

Go to **www.anu.edu.au/polsci/marx/ marx.html** to find links to sites giving information on contemporary Marxist theory. Evaluate the ideas presented. How have these ideas played a role in the development of the theories presented in this chapter?

5.5 SELF-CHECK

1. Describe how labeling theory has had a significant impact on the juvenile justice system.

2. Name two major conflict theorists and briefly explain their theories.

3. Explain the roles society plays in increasing the risk of delinquency for certain groups according to conflict theorists and labeling theory.

controlling and shaping the law. Finally, conflict theorists deal with bias within the juvenile justice system.

HAGAN'S POWER-CONTROL THEORY John Hagan proposed that delinquency must be explained in terms of power relationships.[41] Specifically, he discussed how power in the workforce and in the family interact to influence delinquency. Delinquency rates are a function of class position (power) and family functions (control). The power-control theory states that the family model reproduces its power relations in the workforce. Theorists use this phenomenon to explain why females have had lower delinquency rates than males. In the past, many households were paternalistic; the mother stayed at home taking care of the children while the father worked outside of the home. Thus, boys were more likely to be delinquent than girls because the boys were taught to be risk-takers and were given more freedom while the girls were more strictly controlled by the mother. With the shift to egalitarian families in which mothers and fathers work outside the home, according to Hagan, the delinquency rates between males and females will be similar.[42] The girls in egalitarian families will be taught to be risk-takers since the mother is now also part of the workforce. Therefore, female delinquency is expected to increase in egalitarian families and families headed by females.

COLVIN AND PAULY—INTEGRATED STRUCTURAL MARXIST THEORY Mark Colvin and John Pauly argued that delinquency occurs because of inadequate socialization within the family.[43] However, they stated that socialization within the family is controlled by participation in the workforce. If parents do not have much power or responsibility at work, then they are likely to try to control and dominate at home. If parents work in a coercive environment, they are likely to reproduce the same environment at home. Negative experiences in the workplace can lead to inconsistent and overly punitive discipline at home. In these situations, because parents have little power at work, they seek power within their families. The results (for example, inconsistent and overly punitive discipline) may lead to alienation of youths in the family. Youths alienated from their parents are likely to associate with other alienated youths. This may lead to subculture formation and delinquency. The factor that began the process of delinquency was a lack of power in the workplace.

1. Define and contrast the four types of social theories of delinquency

Four major social theories of delinquency are social structure theories, social process theories, life course theories, and social reaction theories. Social structure theories account for delinquency by focusing on the economic and social conditions in which lower-class youth live. In particular, these theories focus on two prominent factors that influence delinquency: socioeconomic conditions and cultural values. Social process theories focus on the relationship between socialization and delinquency. These theories analyze the impact on delinquency of factors such as peer group relationships, family relationships, and failure in school. Life course theories focus on the creation of criminal careers and the differential influences on individuals as they age. Social reaction theories look at the role that societal institutions, including the juvenile justice system, play in perpetuating delinquent behavior. These theories hold that the reaction of society to delinquent behavior may lead to continuation of that behavior.

2. Describe three social structure theories

Three major types of social structure theory include ecological theory, strain theory, and subculture theory. Ecological theory seeks to explain delinquency based on where it occurs. The environment of an area can impact delinquency. The most prominent ecological theory is Shaw and McKay's social disorganization theory.

The second major type of social structure theory is strain theory. Strain theorists see delinquency as a result of a lack of opportunity, particularly economic opportunity. American society instills in citizens a desire for financial success but does not provide all individuals equal opportunity to achieve financial success. Those who do not have an equal opportunity are strained and are thus more likely to be delinquent. Strained individuals are more prevalent in the lower class. The most prominent strain theory is the one presented by Robert Merton.

The third major type of social structure theory is subculture theory. A subculture is a set of values, norms, and beliefs that differ from the dominant culture. The main tenet of subculture theory is that delinquent youths hold values, norms, and beliefs in opposition to those held in the dominant culture. These youths behave in a manner consistent with the values, norms, and beliefs of this subculture. However, because their subculture is in opposition to the dominant culture, the youths will often be in conflict with the law. Three main subculture theories include Cohen's delinquency and frustration theory, Cloward

and Ohlin's differential opportunity theory, and Miller's lower-class focal concern theory.

3. Summarize three learning theories

Differential association theory presented by Sutherland, differential reinforcement theory presented by Akers, and techniques of neutralization/drift theory by Sykes and Matza are the three main social learning theories. These theories argue that juveniles commit delinquent acts because they learn the attitudes, skills, and rationalizations necessary to commit these acts.

4. Describe three social control theories

Social control theories argue that whether or not someone commits a delinquent act depends on the strength of the individual's ties to conventional individuals and society. The main social control theories include Reckless's containment theory, Hirschi's social control/social bonding theory, and Gottfredson and Hirschi's self-control theory.

5. Understand life course theories

Life course theories draw on the many biological, psychological, and social theories presented in the last two chapters to address the development of criminal careers and how various criminogenic influences impact individuals during the course of their lives. The two life course theories discussed in this chapter were Thornberry's interactional theory and Sampson and Laub's age-graded theory. From the interactional perspective, delinquency changes and is modified over the life course due to changes in control and learning factors. According to age-graded theory, even chronic delinquents can turn away from delinquency if they experience the right turning points, and even individuals without a delinquent past can begin a criminal career in response to certain events that undermine their social bonds.

6. Explain labeling theory

Labeling theory places an emphasis on explaining why certain laws are passed and enforced and why police and juvenile court personnel process some offenders but not others. Labeling theorists argue that the law represents the values and interests of individuals and organizations that are able to organize resources to influence legislation.

Not everyone who commits a delinquent act is processed through the juvenile justice system and labeled a delinquent. Labeling theory looks at the unanticipated and negative consequences of law and law enforcement, especially the label that is attached to certain offenders. Therefore, it is not a theory concerned with what causes the initial delinquent act—such as lack of opportunity, low self-control, or biological abnormality—but rather with what leads to continued delinquency. Becker, Lemert, and Garfinkel are labeling theorists.

7. Explain conflict theory

Conflict theorists argue that delinquent behavior is due to conflict in society, based on an unfair distribution of wealth and power. Conflict theorists are concerned with the role that the government plays in creating an environment conducive to crime. They are also concerned with the role that power has in controlling and shaping the law. Finally, bias within the juvenile justice system is also a concern of conflict theorists.

KEY TERMS

interstitial area, p. 117
norms, p. 118
conformity, p. 119
ritualism, p. 120
innovation, p. 120
retreatism, p. 120
rebellion, p. 120
subculture, p. 121

middle-class measuring
   rods, p. 122
status frustration, p. 122
illegitimate opportunity
   structure, p. 123
criminal gangs, p. 124
conflict gangs, p. 124
retreatist gangs, p. 124

differential association,
   p. 126
operant conditioning, p. 128
positive reinforcement,
   p. 128
negative reinforcement,
   p. 128
self-control, p. 132

labeling theory, p. 134
primary deviance, p. 135
secondary deviance, p. 135
status degradation
   ceremony, p. 135
diversion, p. 135
deinstitutionalization,
   p. 135

REVIEW QUESTIONS

1. How do social structure, social process, and social reaction theories differ?

2. What are the three characteristics of interstitial areas and how do these factors influence delinquency?

3. What are the five modes of adaptation? Which is most likely to lead to delinquency?

4. According to Cohen, why do juveniles commit delinquent acts?

5. How did Cloward and Ohlin's theory of differential opportunity differ from the theories presented by Merton and Cohen?

6. What are the six focal concerns presented by Miller?

7. What are the nine propositions presented by Sutherland?

8. How do positive and negative reinforcements lead to delinquency?

9. What are the five techniques of neutralization?

10. What are the four elements of the social bond?

11. How does self-control influence delinquency?

12. What is the difference between primary and secondary deviance?

13. According to conflict theory, why does delinquency occur?

HANDS-ON ACTIVITIES

1. **Investigate Causes of Delinquency** Ask fellow students, family members, and friends why they think juveniles commit delinquent acts. Write down their responses. Match the responses with the sociological theories in this chapter. Identify which theory received the most responses.

2. **Use Theory to Explain Delinquency** Identify a case in the news involving a juvenile accused of a violent offense. On the basis of information provided, identify the sociological theory which best explains why the juvenile committed the delinquent act.

1. Go to **www.acolumbinesite.com/event/index.html** and read the information on the Columbine High School shootings. After reading the information presented, identify several sociological theories that might explain the actions of the two offenders.

2. Go to **www.courts.ca.gov/rules.htm** (California law on confidentiality of juvenile records is located in Title Five Rule 5,552). Write a brief summary of the law highlighting the restrictions put on juvenile records.

1. **Apply Your Knowledge of Social Theories** Jacob came from a lower-class family and had a normal childhood until he entered school. At school, his academic achievement was low, and he did not pay much attention in class. He wanted to be friends with the middle-class kids in school and wanted the material possessions they had. Because he did not have the material possessions of other kids in school, he began to steal from local department stores. He was caught by store security attempting to steal a leather jacket. The police came and arrested Jacob and placed him in juvenile detention. He was adjudicated delinquent in juvenile court for theft. His peers and teachers heard about Jacob's arrest and adjudication and started to treat him as a thief. Nobody would leave their possessions unattended with Jacob, and he became a social outcast in school. He began to associate with other outcasts, and they developed their own code of conduct and their own means to obtain status. Jacob continued to commit other acts of delinquency through his youth.

What social theories can be used to explain Jacob's behavior? Of the theories used to explain his behavior, which one best explains his behavior?

2. **Extended Practice with Social Theories** Elizabeth grew up in a tough, lower-class neighborhood that was characterized by several cultures and high mobility. She never felt close to her parents, and she did not perform well in school. She valued such things as her fighting ability and ability to con people. When she was 10 years old, she began to associate with delinquent peers who taught her how to steal cars and burglarize houses. She received rewards from her peers for her behavior and did not feel guilty for her delinquent acts. Instead, she would say that the people she stole from were wealthy enough to afford to replace the items, and most had insurance anyway.

What social theories can be used to explain Elizabeth's behavior? Of the theories used to explain her behavior, which one best explains her behavior?

5.1 Self-Check

List the four major types of social theories of delinquency.

The four major types are:

1. Social structure theories, which focus on economic and social conditions.
2. Social process theories, which focus on how peer group relationships, family relationships, and failure in school can affect delinquency.
3. Life course theories, which focus on the creation of criminal careers and the different influences on individuals as they age.
4. Social reaction theories, which examine the roles that social institutions play in perpetuating delinquency

5.2 Self-Check

1. What factors lead to delinquency according to Shaw and McKay?

The three factors described by Shaw and McKay are:

a. Cultural heterogeneity, where residents of a community lack similar characteristics and shared values;
b. Mobility, where residents do not stay in one home for long and thus cannot build community ties; and
c. Poverty.

2. Briefly describe the three subculture theories.

According to subculture theory, delinquents hold values, norms, and beliefs in opposition to those held in the dominant culture—but which are in agreement with those of the subculture to which the delinquents belong. The three subculture theories are:

a. Cohen's delinquency and frustration theory, which states that although lower-class youths have different values, norms, and beliefs than do middle-class youths, their goal is middle-class membership.

b. Cloward and Ohlin's theory of differential opportunity. Cloward and Ohlin believed that juveniles did not commit crime merely because they could not achieve their goals. Rather, they believed that illegal opportunities, just like legal ones, are stratified unequally.

c. Miller's lower-class focal concerns theory, which states that delinquency occurs when youth follow certain lower-class norms that violate the law.

3. Review Miller's focal concerns theory. What flaw can you find in this view of society?

Miller's focal concerns theory creates a stereotype of the lower class that may or may not be accurate. Miller may be accurate with regard to the lower class of Boston in the 1950s; however, he does not compare his observations against those of other cities or other times.

5.3 Self-Check

Compare the two branches of social process theory—learning theory and social control theory.

Learning theory states that juveniles commit delinquent acts because they learn the attitudes, skills, and rationalizations necessary to commit these acts. Social control theory assumes that people will violate the law but withhold themselves from doing so because of the effect of social controls—such as the disapproval of their families, friends, and school.

5.4 Self-Check

What questions do life course theories seek to answer?

- Why do juveniles begin committing acts of delinquency?
- Why do some stop while others continue?

- Why do some increase the severity of their delinquency while others decrease the severity and commit less serious crime as they age into adulthood?
- When juveniles stop committing delinquent acts, what, if anything, causes them to begin again?
- Why do some juveniles specialize in a certain type of crime (e.g., auto theft), while other juveniles are more generalists and engage in a wide variety of different types of delinquent acts?

5.5 Self-Check

1. Describe how labeling theory has had a significant impact on the juvenile justice system.

Labeling theory has had a significant impact on the practices of juvenile justice including confidentiality provisions, diversion, and deinstitutionalization.

2. Name two major conflict theorists and briefly explain their theories.

John Hagan believed that delinquency must be explained in terms of power relationships, such as how power in the workforce and family interact to create delinquency. Mark Colvin and John Pauly worked together to argue that delinquency resulted from inadequate socialization within the family, which is in turn affected by the parents' ability to feel self-control and power in the workforce.

3. Explain the roles society plays in increasing the risk of delinquency for certain groups according to conflict theorists and labeling theory.

According to conflict theorists, society contributes to delinquency because of its uneven distribution of wealth and power. Labeling theory contends that delinquency is encouraged because society views some first-time offenders in a negative light, thereby making youths fulfill the role of delinquents.

DELINQUENCY PREVENTION AND INTERVENTION

Chapter Outline

Chapter Objectives

After completing this chapter, you should be able to:

1. Describe the different types of delinquency prevention programs.

2. Explain the concept of diversion.

3. Describe the different areas of delinquency prevention programs.

4. Give examples of programs that fall under delinquency prevention programs.

5. Describe the types of programs that generally do not work in delinquency prevention.

6. Describe the types of programs that do tend to work in delinquency prevention.

Delinquency Prevention Programs

Delinquency prevention is the subject of strong opinions and political arguments. The idea is simple enough: the best way to deal with juvenile delinquency is to prevent it from occurring in the first place. The philosophy behind many delinquency prevention programs is very appealing: teach juveniles the skills they need, educate juveniles so they will not recidivate, and provide programs to occupy their time so they will not commit crimes. The programs that are started in the name of delinquency prevention all have some variation of these phrases in their mission statements and goals. The goals of these programs are very commendable. The people responsible for conceptualizing and running these programs typically have the best interest of the child at heart. Unfortunately, the history of delinquency prevention has sometimes been a search for the **panacea** that will prevent juveniles from becoming delinquent. There is a variety of solid programs that are effective at preventing delinquency, however the costs associated with these interventions can sometimes be high. There have been many attempts at identifying inexpensive juvenile prevention programs that appeal to politicians and the general public, but too often these programs are fads, coming and going as the latest craze in juvenile justice. Meanwhile, effective delinquency prevention programs typically go unheralded and unnoticed. Many of the programs in this chapter are rooted in the theories discussed in Chapters 4 and 5.

There are several different types of general delinquency prevention programs. Many programs fall under the heading of diversion, the idea that first-time juvenile offenders deserve a second chance. Many others attempt to identify juveniles who are most at risk of becoming delinquent and try to intervene before it is too late. Still others focus on those juveniles who have already committed a variety of delinquent acts and attempt to change their behavior. The variety and sheer number of programs that could be classified as delinquency prevention programs are staggering. The programs are at every level of government, and there are also a substantial number of private programs involved in prevention. Focus on Programs on page 148 profiles the governmental agency responsible for coordinating and researching delinquency prevention efforts in the United States, the Office of Juvenile Justice and Delinquency Prevention (OJJDP). OJJDP is responsible for wide-ranging tasks that are all related to bettering the juvenile justice system. Reviewing all of the different types of strategies and programs that could be called delinquency prevention is impossible; however, there are some common approaches to delinquency prevention. This chapter gives an overview of delinquency prevention efforts and the effectiveness of these efforts. As you will see, some programs are quite effective and have proven track records. Unfortunately, others are not as successful, yet we continue to fund them because they are politically popular. Nonetheless, efforts to prevent delinquency are worthy of discussion and review.

As discussed in Chapter 3, numerous risk factors are related to whether or not a juvenile becomes delinquent. The programs discussed in this chapter are based on several of the theories discussed in Chapters 4 and 5 as well as the risk factor research.

As shown in Figure 6.1, a developmental pattern of behaviors and characteristics leads to increasing levels of delinquency. The figure also shows that opportunities exist to break this pattern and intervene in the life of the child before that child becomes seriously delinquent or develops into an adult criminal. These developmental pathways to delinquency are the basis for several of the programs discussed in this chapter. This chapter is presented conceptually in terms of the age of the child who is the focus of the program. For example, very young at-risk children are targeted in programs such as Head Start, while early at-risk elementary school children are targeted by programs that focus

delinquency prevention A broad term used to identify a variety of programs designed to prevent juveniles from becoming delinquent.

panacea A quick fix, a cure-all. In juvenile delinquency prevention, panaceas are often very short-term, not individualized, and offer nothing in the way of follow-up or aftercare services.

| FIGURE 6.1 | Approximate Developmental Ordering of Risk Factors Associated with Disruptive and Delinquent Behavior |

RISK FACTORS EMERGING DURING PREGNANCY AND FROM INFANCY ONWARD

Child	Pregnancy and delivery complications
	Neurological insult
	Exposure to neurotoxins after birth
	Difficult temperament
	Hyperactivity/impulsivity/attention problems
	Low intelligence
	Male gender
Family	Maternal smoking/alcohol consumption/drug use during pregnancy
	Teenage mother
	High turnover of caretakers
	Poorly educated parent
	Maternal depression
	Parental substance abuse/antisocial or criminal behavior
	Poor parent-child communication
	Poverty/low socioeconomic status
	Serious marital discord
	Large family size

RISK FACTORS EMERGING FROM THE TODDLER YEARS ONWARD

Child	Aggressive/disruptive behavior
	Persistent lying
	Risk-taking and sensation-seeking
	Lack of guilt, lack of empathy
	Harsh and/or erratic discipline practices
	Maltreatment or neglect
Community	Television violence

RISK FACTORS EMERGING FROM MIDCHILDHOOD ONWARD

Child	Stealing and general delinquency
	Early onset of other disruptive behaviors
	Early onset of substance use and sexual activity
	Depressed mood
	Withdrawn behavior
	Positive attitude toward problem behavior
	Victimization and exposure to violence
Family	Poor parental supervision
School	Poor academic achievement
	Repeating grade(s)
	Truancy
	Negative attitude toward school
	Poorly organized and functioning schools
Peer	Peer rejection
	Association with deviant peers/siblings
Community	Residence in a disadvantaged neighborhood
	Residence in a disorganized neighborhood
	Availability of weapons

RISK FACTORS EMERGING FROM MIDADOLESCENCE ONWARD

Child	Weapon carrying
	Drug dealing
	Unemployment
School	School dropout
Peer	Gang membership

DIVERSION PROGRAMS

Diversion programs take many forms and can be either general, in the sense that most offenders can be eligible, or specific, meaning that only certain types of offenders are diverted to them. However, serious or violent juveniles are not eligible for diversion, even to general programs. Indeed, diversion is designed for first-time offenders as a means for a second chance and as a gateway to needed services. Many jurisdictions have strict rules regarding who is eligible for diversion either in juvenile court policy or in state statute. For example, in some diversion programs the criteria for eligibility are specifically spelled out so there can be no confusion regarding who can be placed on diversion. The age criteria are generally restricted to young offenders under 14 years of age. Exceptions can be made for older juveniles who commit a minor offense and who have no previous record. Most diverted juveniles are first-time offenders. Depending on the jurisdiction, some juveniles who have had informal contact with the police previously or who have committed only a minor status offense might also be considered for diversion. Finally, certain offenses are generally excluded from diversion programs, including:

- violent offenses
- sexual offenses
- weapons offenses
- drug offenses
- serious property offenses

While on diversion, a juvenile will typically have to participate actively in a treatment program of some type. Failure to adhere to diversion guidelines or the commission of a new crime usually results in automatic termination from diversion.

There are several problematic issues related to juvenile diversionary programs. The first involves the concept of **net widening**. Net widening means using diversion and prevention programs as a means to bring more juveniles under court control instead of as an alternative to formal processing. Some studies have found that diversion is frequently used in cases that might otherwise have been dismissed from formal processing. A true diversion program takes youths who would ordinarily be processed within the juvenile justice system and places them, instead, in an alternative program.[13] When diversion is used to handle cases that would otherwise not have to be processed, there can be no benefits for the juvenile or the overcrowded juvenile system diversion was designed to help.

A second issue involves the constitutionality of diversion in terms of both due process and equal protection issues. It can be argued that diversion is simply a disposition without the benefit of an adjudication. The juvenile is simply agreeing to probation without ever being given the chance of a hearing. In fact, some research has shown a disproportionate impact of diversion on minorities. In other words, white juveniles are offered diversion, and minority juveniles are formally processed. This issue relates to how decisions are made regarding who will benefit from diversion. Some research has found that diversion decisions are made haphazardly with no formal criteria to determine who will be diverted.[14]

DIVERSION EFFECTIVENESS

Most juveniles who come into contact with the system never come back into contact with the system again. One diversion program in Washington State implemented a fast-track system that diverts first- and second-time offenders charged with misdemeanors or gross misdemeanors to a Community Accountability Board (CAB). To be eligible for the program, offenders must be between

net widening Use of diversion and prevention programs as a means to bring more juveniles under court control instead of as an alternative to formal processing.

the ages of 8 and 17 and must admit to the charges. The CAB meets with the youth and his or her parent(s) or guardian(s) to discuss the diversion process, the reasons the offender committed the offense, and the impact of the offense. The CAB then formulates a diversion agreement that may include community service, restitution to the victim, or counseling. A juvenile diversion case manager monitors the juvenile's completion of the agreement. An evaluation of the program by the Washington State Institute for Public Policy examined the re-offending rates before and after diversion. They specifically compared the rate at which youths re-offended six months before the program with the rate at which they re-offended six months after the program. They found that 24.7 percent of the "before" group re-offended with either a felony or a misdemeanor while 19.1 percent re-offended "after" participating in the diversion program. In addition, the program saves about $2,775 of future justice system costs per participant, and it costs taxpayers only about $140 per youth.[15]

Like many issues in juvenile justice, the research on the effectiveness of diversion is mixed. A large body of research has found that diversion is successful in reducing the system's overload and in deterring future recidivism. The most successful diversion programs are those that provide intensive and comprehensive services. One diversion program was extended to include juveniles accused of serious crimes, and subsequent evaluation found that diversion can be safely extended to these offenders. Even though most of the juveniles who were on diversion admitted to subsequent crimes, the program resulted in lower recidivism rates than those reported for normal court-processed cases.[16] Nonetheless, other research has shown that diversion programs are not successful. In some instances, diversion programs were found to have detrimental properties.[17] Much of this research found net-widening effects and little, if any, formal intervention.

Myth / Fact

Myth: Most juvenile delinquents are chronic offenders who have multiple contacts with the juvenile justice and criminal justice systems.

Fact: A study of the court history of juvenile offenders in Arizona and Utah found that 71 percent of females and 54 percent of males who had contact with the juvenile court had only one referral.

Source: Kurlychek, Megan, Patricia Torbet, and Melanie Bozynski, "Focus on Accountability: Best Practices for Juvenile Court and Probation." *JAIBG Bulletin* August 1999. Washington, DC: Office of Juvenile Justice and Delinquency Prevention, 1999.

6.4 SELF-CHECK

What problems exist with diversion programs?

School-Based Programs

Many delinquency prevention programs target children at a very early age; as such, many of these programs are school-based. Juveniles spend a great deal of time in school, so it is logical for schools to offer a variety of programs designed to prevent delinquency. An analysis of potential school-based programs concluded:

1. A school district serving an area with a high rate of delinquency should offer a program of preschool education aimed at three- and four-year-old children.
2. The preschool program need not be a government venture. Public funds should pay for those programs that are intended to reach low-income, high-risk families, but these funds can be distributed in whole or in part by a voucher system, allowing parents to spend their voucher on whatever program appeals to them.
3. The school system should designate a counselor whose special responsibility would be to collate information from preschool teachers, guidance counselors, social service agencies, and law enforcement agencies in order to identify children with serious behavior problems.

4. Families of children with serious behavior problems should be contacted to explore the possibility and desirability of enrolling one or both parents in a program designed to improve the management of difficult young children.

5. Parents in such programs should be brought into contact with families who have had similar experiences and benefited from the treatment program.

6. Public and private agencies should experiment with a home visitor program. Regular visits to the homes of multi-problem families provide continuous contact between clients and agencies, supply clients with valuable health and nutritional advice, and build positive relationships between people in need of someone who will listen and people who are willing to be involved.

7. A significant part of a city program would be managed on an experimental basis with independent evaluation.[18]

Such a program would be targeted at children in preschool, prior to the development of serious problem behaviors. In addition, the program would seek to incorporate the parents, the school, and the criminal justice system into the treatment goals.[19] Research shows that programs incorporating all of the youth's primary caregivers are more successful in the long run.

6.5 SELF-CHECK

What component of a school-based program has been shown to yield the most successful results?

Community-Based Programs

In an effort to develop a more holistic approach to delinquency prevention, many jurisdictions attempt to move beyond the criminal or juvenile justice system alone and involve more community groups and organizations. The idea is that we all have a stake in preventing delinquency and ultimately caring for our communities. Focus on Programs describes the Communities That Care (CTC) program in Pennsylvania. The program is designed to bring together key community leaders to work on mechanisms for delinquency prevention. As such, it combines several key ingredients thought to be related to successful delinquency prevention programs including a holistic effort, involvement of multiple actors, and long-term planning for prevention.

Many community programs focus on education and awareness of topics that are problematic in the community. The Hands Without Guns program is a public health and education campaign that gets youths involved in violence prevention in their communities. A series of sessions teaches youths about the problems of violence and guns, and trains them to initiate a violence prevention program in their neighborhoods. Research showed that youths who could identify with a program were ten times less likely to carry a gun.[20]

Many other community-based programs attempt to bring about greater involvement and accountability of youth in their communities. Giving youths a stake in their communities is thought to develop new friends and interests, give a heightened sense of responsibility to peers and the community, improve leadership skills, increase self-esteem, and provide a sense of accomplishment.[21] One example of this type of program is Youth Advisory Councils (YACs), which are comprised of juveniles who regularly advise policymakers on youth issues. YACs offer youths civic roles, a voice in the legislative process, and opportunities to learn about the legislative process firsthand. Another example of a community-based program is the Youth Town Hall Meetings (YTHMs) which are one- to two-hour discussions between panels of youths and adults and diverse audiences about "hot" topics such as gun violence, curfews, and substance abuse. YTHMs provide youth and adults ways to communicate, work,

FOCUS ON PROGRAMS

PENNSYLVANIA'S COMMUNITIES THAT CARE

Communities That Care (CTC) is a community empowerment strategy that emphasizes assessment and planning as the basis for program development and implementation. CTC is a violence and delinquency prevention program that provides communities with a process to mobilize the community, identify risk and protective factors, and develop a comprehensive prevention plan. This model is based on the premise that to prevent a problem from happening, risk factors must be identified and strategies must be formulated and implemented to enhance protective factors.

The involvement of key community leaders (mayor, judge, superintendent of schools, chief of police, religious leaders, business leaders, etc.) in this process is essential, since they have the status, resources, and authority to implement comprehensive prevention efforts. The community is required to establish a Policy Prevention Board to oversee the local assessment, planning, and program implementation process. The Board ultimately develops a long-term (three years) comprehensive delinquency prevention plan based on an assessment of delinquency risk factors existing within the local community.

CTC is no longer limited to county units of government but is available to municipalities, townships, and school districts in partnership with local units of government that wish to undertake this risk-focused prevention strategy. CTC provides communities with a conceptual framework for reducing risk factors and enhancing protective factors utilizing a social development model. This approach requires the participation of the entire community in developing and implementing a comprehensive strategy for reducing juvenile crime and violence.

CRITICAL THINKING

What do you think makes CTC unique?

Source: www.pccd.state.pa.us/

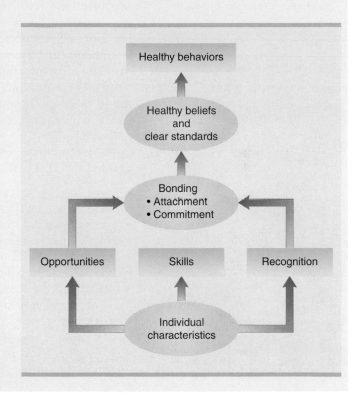

and act together on issues they care about or that have affected them.[22] Both of these initiatives attempt to prevent delinquency by giving youths a voice and a stake in their communities.

School-based and community programs are rooted in lessons from social disorganization and strain theories. The idea is that increasing the effectiveness of school and community institutions has benefits not only for the youth, but for the school and community as a whole. Strong social institutions are crucial for a strong, crime-free community. Further, a strong education can have secondary benefits by providing additional educational benefits and opportunities for youths.

MENTORING

Mentoring programs began in the late 1800s when several adults began serving as role models for children of the poor.[23] In 1904, a new organization was founded that used big brothers as role models and mentors to guide children in need. Big Brothers/Big Sisters (BBBSA) of America was created and continues to operate today as the largest mentoring organization of its kind.[24] Mentoring programs combine many of the positive aspects of delinquency prevention and have been a prime outlet for volunteers who wish to donate their time.

Mentoring programs focus on a wide variety of activities as well as prevention and treatment, and are typically based in churches, colleges, communities, courts, and schools. There is no overall measure of the numbers of volunteer mentors in the United States, but the numbers of organizations providing such services is staggering. Mentoring programs provide youths with positive role models and peers that give youths positive interactions.

BBBSA is a federation of about 350 agencies that serve children and adolescents. Its mission is to make a difference in the lives of young people through a professionally supported one-on-one relationship with a caring adult. BBBSA seeks to assist children in need in reaching their highest potential by providing committed volunteers, national leadership, and standards of excellence. The organization's goals include increasing the number of children served; improving the effectiveness, efficiency, and impact of services to children; and achieving a greater racial and ethnic diversity among volunteers and staff. BBBSA volunteers come from all walks of life and occupations, but they share the goal of being a caring adult who can make a difference in the life of a child. The volunteer mentor and the juvenile make a substantial time commitment, meeting for about four hours, two to four times a month, for at least one year. The national average cost of making and supporting a match relationship is $1,000 per year.[25]

Research compared children participating in BBBSA with those who have not and found that BBBSA children:

- were 46 percent less likely to initiate drug use during the study period.
- were 27 percent less likely to initiate alcohol use.
- were 52 percent less likely to skip school.
- were 37 percent less likely to skip class.
- were more confident in schoolwork performance.
- were almost one-third less likely to hit someone.
- were better in academic behavior, attitudes, and performance.
- were more likely to have higher quality relationships with their parents or guardians.
- were able to get along better with their families.
- were more likely to have higher quality relationships with their peers at the end of the study period.[26]

JOB SERVICES

There are a multitude of vocational and job-related services that are available to youths in the community. Some of these programs are designed specifically with delinquency prevention in mind while others simply focus on preparing youth for the job market without specific attention to delinquency prevention. One of the most prominent federal programs is the Job Corps. The Job Corps is a national residential education and training program for severely disadvantaged youths ages 16 to 24. The program prepares youths for stable, productive employment and entrance into vocational and technical schools, junior colleges, military service, or other institutions for further education and training. The Job Corps targets the most disadvantaged youths, who face multiple barriers to employment. The program provides a comprehensive mix of services in an integrated and coordinated manner. Students spend about half of their time in basic education and about half in vocational skills training. Those who remain enrolled in the Job Corps for longer periods of time are more likely to earn a high school equivalency diploma, finish skills training, and find employment at higher wages than early dropouts. During program year 2011, over 80 percent of all Job Corps students were placed in jobs, enrolled in educational programs, or joined the military. Additionally, more than 30,000 students obtained a high school diploma or GED certificate, while 62 percent of students completed career technical training.

According to Job Corps figures, 72 percent of all enrollees are minorities, 63 percent are high school dropouts, and 51 percent are from families on public assistance.

Another notable group of programs are the youth apprenticeship programs that place young people in work and learning settings with training by skilled workers. These programs benefit youths in two distinct ways: (1) by occupying their time and letting them earn money, and (2) by teaching them a marketable trade or skill that will benefit them for life. A federal program that ran from 1994 to 2002 incorporated the principles of vocational training and apprenticeships in order to reduce the number of youth who drop out of school or graduate from high school without career direction, marketable skills, and knowledge about workplace expectations. The federal School-to-Work (STW) Opportunities Act included three core elements:

1. School-based learning that includes blended academic and vocational training based on high academic expectations and industry-defined occupational skill standards
2. Work-based learning that involves youth in workplace settings for career exploration, work experience, structured training, and mentoring
3. Connected activities that identify work-based learning opportunities, match students with employers, train mentors, and build other bridges between school and work[27]

STW included academic and work preparation programs, including vocational education, work-study, Tech Prep, youth apprenticeship, internship programs, Junior Achievement, and other programs designed to serve both students who are college bound and those who are not.[28] These programs addressed the teaching of blocked opportunity and strain theory by providing legitimate opportunities and resources to youth who are traditionally denied these benefits.

RECREATIONAL AND TIME-OCCUPYING PROGRAMS

Although juveniles are enrolled in school for as much as eight hours a day, the majority of a juvenile's time is unstructured and unsupervised. Estimates vary, but for some juveniles, as much as 50 percent of time falls into these categories and is essentially unproductive. The time directly after school is particularly unstructured and unsupervised. Research has found that after school is also prime time for juveniles' committing delinquent acts. With these facts in mind, a variety of after-school and evening recreational programs have been developed to better structure and occupy a juvenile's free time. A popular recreation initiative is midnight basketball, so named because the early leagues played well past midnight in some communities. The idea is simple: provide youths with both a place to go and an activity to occupy their time during the most crime-prone hours. Many leagues begin in the early evening and last until late into the morning. Although evaluations of the program have not been conclusive, many of the youths who participate in midnight basketball would be out on the streets late at night with nowhere else to go.

Other programs in this area work not only to focus unstructured time for juveniles, but also to provide a service back to the community. For example, the Boys and Girls Clubs of America (BGCA) formed an initiative in Washington, DC, to provide inner-city children with a valuable set of opportunities, including a chance to contribute something to their community, develop a work ethic, and learn about nature and the environment. The initiative targeted juveniles aged 8 to 14 who come from low-income families, often residing in public housing. The

FOCUS ON PROGRAMS

Boys and Girls Clubs of America

Officially founded in 1906, Boys and Girls Clubs of America (BGCA) have club facilities and programs in each of the 50 states, Puerto Rico, and the U.S. Virgin Islands. Primarily located in communities and areas where children are the most disadvantaged, BGCA have provided at-risk girls and boys with an opportunity to lead productive, meaningful lives.

In 1987, recognizing that young people in public housing are at high risk for alcohol and other drug use, health problems, pregnancy, crime, violence, delinquency, and failure in school, BGCA launched a major initiative to establish new clubs in public housing communities nationwide. A subsequent three-year independent study conducted by Columbia University confirmed that BGCA in public housing had a significant impact on juvenile crime (reduced 13 percent), drug activity (reduced 22 percent), and the presence of crack cocaine (reduced 25 percent). The study also found that the clubs improved the overall quality of life for the children and families who reside in public housing.

BGCA help their members build self-esteem, acquire positive values, and pursue productive futures. The clubs achieve these goals by providing a safe haven away from the negative influences of the street. Juveniles receive guidance, discipline, and values modeling from caring adult leaders who focus on constructive youth development activities and programs in supervised supportive environments. Programs often include supplementary education, health and fitness, drug abuse prevention, teen pregnancy education and prevention, career exploration, arts and crafts, leadership development, community service, and environmental awareness.

Boys and girls "join" their local BGCA by completing a simple membership application and paying an annual membership fee that ranges from $1 to $5. In addition to extensive on-site consultations and regional training events, BGCA develops, prepares, and distributes detailed program models and guides to local clubs.

CRITICAL THINKING

What do you think is the single most important factor in BGCA's success?

Source: Bureau of Justice Assistance. *Boys & Girls Clubs of America*. Bureau of Justice Assistance Fact Sheet. Washington, DC: National Institute of Justice, 1995.

Programs such as midnight basketball are thought to reduce the chances of juveniles' becoming delinquent and to provide them with a positive outlet for their time. *How effective do you think this program is at reducing delinquency in a community?*

program works in conjunction with the National Park Services. Juveniles attend educational workshops, assist with trail cleanup and park maintenance, and also participate in recreational activities in the park.[29] BGCA is one of the oldest recreational programs for youth in the United States servicing at-risk youths.

6.6 SELF-CHECK

1. When did mentoring programs begin?
2. Describe one of the job services programs.

Teen Courts

Teen courts (also referred to as youth, peer, and student courts) have become extremely popular; growing from a handful of programs in the 1960s. According to the National Association of Youth Courts, the number of teen courts now operating in the United States is currently 1,050.[30] The number of programs grew from an estimated 50 courts in 1991 to between 400 and 500 courts in 1998.[31] Most teen courts service relatively small caseloads, and about half handle less than 100 cases per year.[32] Teen courts usually handle first-time offenders charged with minor offenses. Most of the juveniles processed by teen courts involve juveniles under the age of 16 who do not have a prior arrest record.[33]

A national survey of teen court programs found at least four potential benefits of the programs:

- **Accountability** Teen courts may help to ensure that young offenders are held accountable for their illegal behavior, even when their offenses are relatively minor and would not likely result in sanctions from the traditional juvenile justice system.
- **Timeliness** An effective teen court can move young offenders from arrest to sanctions within a matter of days rather than the months that may pass with traditional juvenile courts.
- **Cost savings** Teen courts usually depend heavily on youths and adult volunteers. If managed properly, they may handle a substantial number of offenders at relatively little cost to the community. The average annual cost for operating a teen court is $32,822.
- **Community cohesion** A well-structured and expansive teen court program may affect the entire community by increasing public appreciation of the legal system, enhancing community/court relationships, encouraging greater respect for the law among youth, and promoting volunteerism among both adults and youths.[34]

Most teen courts are operated by probation departments (42 percent); however, a variety of other agencies including schools (36 percent), and community-based nonprofit organizations (22 percent) operate teen courts.[35] As shown in Figure 6.6, teen courts handled a variety of offenses in their communities.

TEEN COURT MODELS AND PROCESS

Juveniles are referred to teen courts in various models from just about every component in the juvenile justice system. Figure 6.7 depicts a model of how cases get to teen court and the flow of the process of referral. Most juveniles referred to teen court are offered the program as a voluntary alternative in lieu of formal processing. While the process in teen court mirrors that of a formal juvenile justice adjudication, all parts in teen court are typically staffed by other juveniles. In fact, teens who go through the process are often required to serve as jurors on a subsequent proceeding. The specific processes vary; however, many courts allow a panel of juveniles to determine factual guilt and other juveniles to serve as attorneys and judges in the proceeding. Typically, the only adults involved in the process are those that administer the program; however, in some courts adults serve as attorneys and judges as well.

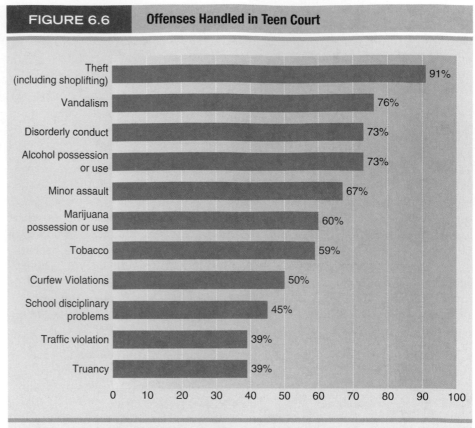

FIGURE 6.6 — **Offenses Handled in Teen Court**

Source: http://www.youthcourt.net/?page_id=24

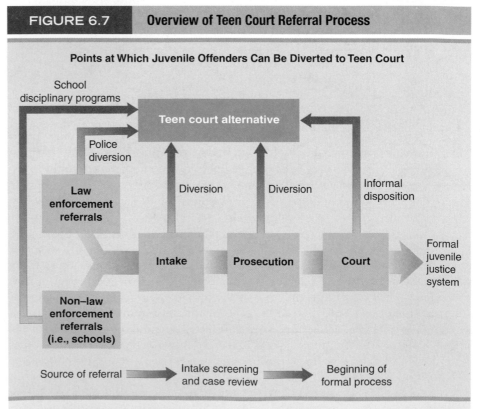

FIGURE 6.7 — **Overview of Teen Court Referral Process**

Points at Which Juvenile Offenders Can Be Diverted to Teen Court

Source: Butts, Jeffrey A. and Janeen Buck, "Teen Courts: A Focus on Research." *Juvenile Justice Bulletin*, October 2000. Washington, DC: Office of Juvenile Justice and Delinquency Prevention and the Urban Institute.

FIGURE 6.8	Characteristics of American Teen Courts			
	COURTROOM MODEL			
CHARACTERISTIC	ADULT JUDGE	YOUTH JUDGE	PEER JURY	YOUTH TRIBUNAL
Judge	Adult	Youth	Adult (limited role)	Youth (often 3)
Youth attorneys	Yes	Yes	No	Yes
Role of the youth jury, if any	Recommends disposition	Recommends disposition	Questions defendant recommends disposition	No jury
Percentage of teen courts using this model for at least some cases	53%	18%	31%	10%

Source: http://www.youthcourt.net/?page_id=24

Teen courts generally follow one of four models: the adult judge model, the youth judge model, the youth tribunal model, and the peer jury model.[36] As the name implies, the adult judge model has an adult serving as a judge on legal terminology and courtroom procedure. Under this model, youths serve in all of the other roles within the court. The youth judge model has a juvenile taking the role of the judge in the proceedings. In the youth tribunal model, there is no jury in the case; rather, the proceedings are argued before a three-judge youth panel. Finally, in the peer jury model, adults are typically used to argue the cases to a jury of youths who decide guilt and disposition. Most teen courts do not determine guilt or innocence during their proceedings; rather, they serve as diversion alternatives and youths must admit to the charges against them before the teen court proceedings.[37] Figure 6.8 summarizes the various models of teen courts and shows several interesting findings of a national survey of teen court programs.

Youths processed through teen courts can expect to be sanctioned in several different ways. The most common disposition reported is community service of some type. In addition, youths are often sentenced to write apology letters to victims, write academic essays, serve on future teen court juries, participate in drug and alcohol programs, and pay restitution. Essays are a very common sanction in teen courts and are used to reinforce both the experience and the sanction.[38] In fact, many conclude that the dispositions handed out in most teen courts are far more severe than the youth would have gotten if they were referred to juvenile court. In addition, the net-widening argument has merit in teen courts as it is likely that many of the cases that get to teen court would not have been processed formally anyway.

A number of states have passed legislation that endorses the implementation and operation of teen courts—important because specific juvenile diversion programs are not often supported by statute. Much of this legislation was passed after 1995. State laws usually define the critical characteristics of teen courts and describe their program mission. They also address program eligibility, confidentiality, sentencing alternatives, the respective roles of adults and teens in court hearings, and other aspects of teen court programs.

The objective, scope, and content of teen court legislation vary by state. Statutes may be used to provide start-up funds for local jurisdictions and to specify general eligibility guidelines for teen court programs. Some states specify which entities may establish teen courts. The authority to begin a program may be limited to courts, probation departments, and prosecutor's offices.

TEEN COURT EFFECTIVENESS

As with many other diversion and delinquency prevention programs, the research on the effectiveness of teen courts has resulted in mixed findings. A review of the research conducted on teen courts over the past 20 years found that many of the studies were rudimentary and offered little insight into true effectiveness. One report cites three studies that were relatively sound; however, the findings from the three studies were mixed with one reporting lower recidivism rates and two finding no differences between teen court participants and a similar group of juvenile offenders who went through the formal system.[39] Beyond recidivism, proponents of teen courts argue that youths and victims are more satisfied with the teen court experience and that youths learn a greater respect for the legal system in the process. Research conducted on teen court participants supports these claims as well.[40]

Programs Focusing on Status Offenses

Cities around the country more actively enforce existing status offense laws, particularly curfew and truancy, than they have in the past. In several cities, curfew laws have been passed that specifically target juveniles. As the programs that focus on these crimes have increased, so have the research and evaluation of these programs. The idea is based on the research finding that many juvenile delinquents and serious adult criminals were unsupervised, particularly after school and at night, and that many were undereducated and frequently truant. The philosophy of these programs is to aggressively target juveniles who violate curfew, who are truant, or who are otherwise at risk for becoming a delinquent. The programmatic interventions frequently target habitual truants, curfew violators, or runaways. The law enforcement efforts are typically crackdowns on these types of offenses. Several strategies are emerging, yet for the most part these interventions are not being extensively evaluated. The **deinstitutionalization** of status offenders under the JJDP Act prevents agencies from incarcerating juveniles for prolonged periods for status offenses. Yet, the children who are the chronic truants, curfew violators, and runaways are typically the most at risk and the most in need of intervention.

Law enforcement efforts in this area typically focus on aggressively enforcing the status offenses. Many in juvenile justice are frustrated by the lack of programs available for such offenders, yet more and more of these offenses are being taken seriously and are being heralded as a good delinquency prevention mechanism. In Phoenix, Arizona, an innovative curfew-enforcement program was set up which allows officers to enforce the curfew by giving them a place to take the juvenile and a mechanism to shorten the amount of time spent on enforcing the curfew. Curfew violators are detained and taken to one of several curfew centers in the city. The violator is then processed by officers who staff the facility full-time, allowing patrol officers to get back on the streets. Upon arrival, the juvenile's parents are called and required to come and pick up their sons and daughters. Many parents are surprised to learn their child was even out of the house; many more are angry that their child wasn't where they were supposed to be. Although no formal evaluation of the program is known, the Phoenix Police Department reported drops in juvenile crime, but more important are the drops in juvenile victimization. An evaluation of an aggressive police program designed to reduce gang violence found that aggressive enforcement of curfew and truancy was more effective in reducing gang crime than were saturation patrols or gang sweeps.

Many scholars question the constitutionality of these tactics and the effectiveness of them as well. However, the evidence at this point is mixed. Although

deinstitutionalization The removal of certain classes of juvenile offenders from incarceration. The deinstitutionalization of status offenders was brought about under the JJDP Act of 1974.

FOCUS ON PROGRAMS

ABOLISH CHRONIC TRUANCY (ACT)

This program deals primarily with pre–high school children and seeks to cover not only seriously truant children but those who are just starting to develop truant behavior. The program focuses on improving school attendance through parental and child accountability by addressing attendance problems before the child's behavior is ingrained and while the parent still exercises control over the child. The hope is that this will prevent delinquency and other problems later in life. The program operates in the following manner:

1. School provides list of students with attendance problems.
2. Letter is sent to parents advising them of their responsibilities under California law.
3. Parents and child are invited to a meeting with a deputy district attorney.
4. Community-based organizations and school personnel are present at the meeting to offer parenting classes, counseling, and other needed services.

Parents are advised that continued attendance problems could result in court action against the parent and/or the child.

Those parents and children who do not attend this meeting will receive a second letter informing the parent that the district attorney's office will monitor the child's attendance. The parent is advised that he/she is liable for prosecution for the child's truancy under the Education Code and the Penal Code with a penalty of up to one year in the county jail and/or a $2,500 fine. The child could also be subject to prosecution for truancy.

Those parents whose children continue to have attendance problems will be invited to a School Attendance Review Team (SART) meeting. The team will include a deputy district attorney, school representatives, probation officer, and members of community-based organizations. At this meeting, the student's attendance is reviewed, a plan is developed for the future, the student is referred to other agencies if appropriate, and a contract is signed outlining the agencies', parents', and children's responsibilities.

School attendance of the subject individuals will continue to be monitored by school officials. Students who continue to have attendance problems will be referred to the School Attendance Review Board (SARB). This group is similar to the SART, but with a broader membership. Subsequent failure to attend school will result in district attorney mediation hearings being conducted. If all of the above steps fail, a case will be filed against the parent and/or the child. From beginning to end the process takes about 8 to 12 months.

The ACT program started in 1991 in one school in South Central Los Angeles. In 1993, the program became fully implemented with the assignment of three attorneys to the program on a full-time basis. There are currently 29 school districts involved with the ACT program in Los Angeles County.

CRITICAL THINKING

Do you think this program approach is too severe? Why or why not?

Sources: http://da.co.la.ca.us/cr/act.htm

the delinquency prevention potential of these programs is probably minimal, the aggressive enforcement of these status offenses has great potential for reducing juvenile victimization. Recent research found that juveniles are most likely to become victims in the hours after school and at night.

6.8 SELF-CHECK

What is the philosophy underlying programs that focus on status offenses?

What Doesn't Work

Unfortunately, the search for a cure for delinquency or a program that can prevent all delinquency has sometimes resulted in quick-fix solutions. These solutions are often termed panaceas, a quick fix for a complicated problem. In juvenile delinquency prevention, these types of programs are often very short term, are not individualized, and offer nothing in the way of follow-up or aftercare services. Claims of startling successes are often put forth by supporters of these programs. The fact that the solution and treatment is quick and typically shocking can place national attention on the program and lead many to conclude that the program works. This conclusion is typically followed by adoption of the program or something similar in jurisdictions around the country. These early claims of success and subsequent national attention are frequently crushed when evaluation research reveals that the program is no more successful than traditional interventions.

The search for a panacea is part of human nature. We would all like to see a program that could cure crime and delinquency. Politicians and criminal justice system personnel tend to want to do something, and the quick fix is typically easily adoptable and garners great attention. Boot camps (see Chapter 12) are an example of a correctional sanction that spread quickly across the country. While the idea of a boot camp sounds appealing, the fact remains that research shows most boot camp programs were no more successful than traditional correctional sanctions. As a result, many boot camps altered their formats and have backed off the militarism in favor of educational and vocational programming. In delinquency prevention and intervention, the classic example of a panacea solution is Scared Straight.

More and more, jurisdictions are aggressively enforcing status offenses such as truancy in an effort to prevent more serious forms of delinquency. *Do you think this tactic is effective at reducing or preventing delinquency? What kinds of crimes would enforcing truancy and curfew laws prevent?*

SCARED STRAIGHT

Scared Straight was a program popularized by a television program that aired in 1979. The program took youths who had already committed delinquent acts and youths who were at risk of delinquency inside the prison system to be confronted by inmates from the correctional facility. The inmates then yelled and threatened the juveniles with violence and homosexual rape. All of this was in an effort to scare the juvenile into not committing any more delinquent acts. The film showed the juveniles entering the prison acting very cocky and showing off to others in the group. When leaving the prison, many of the juveniles were shown to be scared, crying, and lacking whatever attitude they had brought to the prison. The final scenes of the show claimed a high rate of success in deterring future delinquency among the juveniles who had participated in the program. Following the airing of the program, politicians and criminal justice officials around the country raced to start their own version of Scared Straight. Whatever semblance of treatment was included in the program was lost as inmates became more and more aggressive and less supportive of the juveniles who went into the correctional facilities.

The Scared Straight program was hailed as the best way to cure delinquency, and since it was extremely cheap to operate, many jurisdictions adopted their own. The juveniles were typically at the prison for only a few hours, and little if any follow-up was done with the juveniles who went through the programs. Claims of success came abruptly to a halt when research showed that the program's claims of success were grossly exaggerated and in fact less successful than other interventions.[41] Indeed, perhaps the only positive thing about the program was the cathartic effect it had on the inmates who participated in yelling at and threatening the juveniles. Scared Straight is a classic example of a panacea cure, a quick-fix solution to a complex problem. The idea that two hours of yelling and threats from inmates would fix years of poor socialization and psychological problems is misguided. In addition, the fact that little follow-up or aftercare was provided demonstrates a lack of commitment to serious intervention and delinquency prevention. Any deterrent effect from the program was quickly lost as the youths returned to the situation that created their problems in the first place. Scared Straight is an excellent example of the problem with many delinquency prevention "cures." Instead of long-term solutions to complex problems, there is a tendency to look for the quick fix where none exists.

6.9 SELF-CHECK

Describe the Scared Straight program.

What Does Work?

The notion that nothing works in juvenile justice is one of the leading reasons why some have called for abolition of the system entirely. However, compared to other aspects of criminal justice, the juvenile justice system is extraordinarily successful. Juvenile court judges, social workers, police officers, and other juvenile justice personnel all agree that most juveniles who come into contact with the system do not recidivate. Unfortunately, the majority of these juveniles go untracked and unmeasured by national statistics. Most juveniles who commit delinquent acts are handled informally by schools, social service programs, and the police. Many of the programs that exist to divert juveniles from the system have not been systematically analyzed or evaluated. In recent years, however, a growing body of evidence demonstrates that many programs are helping youths—including those who are at risk or disadvantaged—develop into responsible, self-sufficient citizens.[42] In addition, many of these "unknown" programs are being evaluated by federal, state, and local officials; and the results of this research are only now coming to light.

The results of recent program evaluations show that the programs that are working share common characteristics. Through an analysis of over 150 program evaluations, the American Youth Policy Forum identified the following ten program principles leading to positive outcomes for young people:

- Quality of implementation
- Caring, knowledgeable adults
- High standards and expectations
- Parent/guardian participation
- Community involvement
- Holistic approaches
- Youth as resources
- Community service and service-learning
- Work-based learning
- Long-term services, support, and follow-up[43]

Research has shown that some delinquency prevention programs are effective, indeed those that are share common qualities. An analysis of several evaluation studies of delinquency prevention programs found that the successful programs use a comprehensive, multifaceted approach rather than a single type of intervention. All of the most successful programs had an aftercare component built in, and they served relatively small numbers of juveniles.[44] Although the different areas of delinquency prevention have all been evaluated to some extent, there is no clear evidence of success on a wide scale. Part of the difficulty in evaluating the success of these programs lies in the diverse nature of the programs as well as the varying communities they are intended to serve. Nonetheless, growing evidence reveals that there are some common characteristics of successful delinquency prevention programs.

COST EFFECTIVENESS OF PREVENTION

One question about delinquency prevention that always concerns policymakers and practitioners is the cost of such programs relative to their benefits. A popular method of examining the effectiveness of delinquency prevention is to compare the costs of the program per child relative to what it would cost the system to handle the juvenile in the future. Many evaluations of delinquency-prevention programs have found that well-designed programs lead to:

- Increased emotional or cognitive development for the child, typically in the short run, or improved parent-child relationships.
- Improved educational processes and outcomes for the child.
- Enhanced economic self-sufficiency, initially for the parent and later for the child, through increased participation in the labor force, decreased participation in welfare, and higher incomes.
- Decreased criminal activity.
- Improved health-related indicators such as child abuse, maternal reproductive health, and substance abuse.[45]

These outcomes are obviously encouraging, but at what cost? A review of several prominent delinquency prevention programs concluded that, at least for some disadvantaged children and their families, cost savings could be achieved through early intervention.[46] The research concludes that carefully targeted early childhood interventions can yield measurable benefits and that some of those benefits endure for some time after the program has ended. The report estimated savings to the government ranging from $13,000 to $18,000 per family participating in the programs reviewed. The authors concluded that some targeted early intervention programs have substantial favorable effects for participants, and when targeted to families who will benefit most, these programs have generated savings to the government that exceed program costs.[47] The Rand Corporation estimated the cost-to-benefit ratio of several programs: the Perry Preschool in Ypsilanti, MI, the Prenatal/Early Infancy Project in Elmira, NY, and the Chicago Parent Centers. The study found a 4.1 to 1, a 5.1 to 1, and a 3.7 to 1 cost-to-benefit ratio, respectively, for each of these programs.

Another research study examined several diversion programs in California and compared them with the cost of the three-strikes program. Three-strikes reportedly resulted in a 21 percent reduction in crime, saving $5.5 billion a year. The study found that several prevention programs including high school graduation incentive programs, parent-training interventions, and delinquent-supervision programs resulted in cost savings as good as or better than the cost of the three-strikes program.[48] The authors concluded that investments in some interventions for high-risk youths may be several times more cost-effective in reducing serious crime than long mandatory sentences for repeat offenders. These programs could reduce the financial burden of prisons and divert youths from a life of crime. Carefully designed delinquency prevention programs targeting the appropriate juveniles and their families can both reduce delinquency and provide cost savings to the government.

6.10 SELF-CHECK

What common characteristics do successful prevention programs share?

1. Describe the different types of delinquency prevention programs

There are several different general types of delinquency prevention programs. Many programs fall under the heading of diversion, the idea that first-time juvenile offenders deserve a second chance. Many others attempt to identify those juveniles who are most at risk for becoming delinquent and try to intervene before it is too late. Still, others focus on those juveniles who have already committed a variety of delinquent acts and attempt to change their behavior.

2. Explain the concept of diversion

Diversion is a general term for a wide range of programs that keep juveniles who commit crimes out of the formal juvenile justice system. Diversionary programs are akin to probation; however, in exchange for not being formally adjudicated, juveniles will typically agree to participate in treatment programs tailored for their needs. Diversion programs are in place to correct or prevent future and more serious problems from occurring and to prevent further involvement with the juvenile and criminal justice systems.

3. Describe the different areas of delinquency prevention programs

Delinquency prevention and intervention programs can be grouped into several different categories. First, a growing number of programs are focusing on early pre-delinquent intervention and prevention where attempts are made to target pregnant mothers and children in the very early stages of life. Second, a large number of programs fall under the general heading of diversion where first-time offenders are diverted away from formal processing and into a number of service programs. The remaining areas of delinquency prevention and intervention take in all juveniles who are at risk of becoming delinquent, have shown early problem behaviors and other warning signs, or are very early in their delinquent careers. These areas include school-based programs, community-based programs, job services, recreational and time-occupying programs, and programs that focus on status offenders.

4. Give examples of programs that fall under delinquency prevention programs

There are several areas of delinquency prevention that were discussed in this chapter, and examples of each type of program were offered. Examples of early pre-delinquent programs included the Perry Preschool Program and Project Head Start. Risk-focused prevention programs included the SHIELD program and the Children At Risk Program. Family treatment and intervention programs included Healthy Families and Project FAST. Several community-based programs seek to rally community members in the delinquency prevention effort and include Youth Advisory Councils, Youth Town Hall Meetings and Hands Without Guns. Other community-based programs include mentoring programs such as Big Brothers and Big Sisters, and job services and vocational programs such as Job Corps and School to Work programs, and recreational programs such as the Boys and Girls Clubs of America and midnight basketball programs. Teen courts are diverse but are becoming increasingly common across the United States. Finally, some programs focus on status offenders such as the Abolish Chronic Truancy program.

5. Describe the types of programs that generally do not work in delinquency prevention

Silver bullet panacea-type programs that offer a quick-fix solution to delinquency. These programs tend to take off quickly because of their initial appeal and the desire to do something about delinquency. However, research eventually shows no differences in outcomes between these programs and traditional ones; in fact, traditional programs tend to outperform these types of initiatives.

6. Describe the types of programs that do tend to work in delinquency prevention

Successful programs use a comprehensive, multifaceted approach rather than a single type of intervention. In addition, all of the most successful programs have an aftercare component built in, and they serve relatively small numbers of juveniles. Through an analysis of over 150 program evaluations, the American Youth Policy Forum identified the following ten program principles leading to positive outcomes for young people:

- Quality of implementation
- Caring, knowledgeable adults
- High standards and expectations
- Parent/guardian participation
- Community involvement
- Holistic approaches
- Youth as resources
- Community service and service-learning
- Work-based learning
- Long-term services, support, and follow-up

KEY TERMS

delinquency prevention,
   p. 144
panacea, p. 144

early pre-delinquent
   intervention and
   prevention, p. 147

Blueprints Model
   Programs, p. 148
holistic approach, p. 151

net widening, p. 154
deinstitutionalization,
   p. 164

REVIEW QUESTIONS

1. What is the main function of the Office of Juvenile Justice and Delinquency Prevention?

2. What are the two primary interventions under the broad heading of delinquency prevention?

3. What are the primary areas of delinquency prevention currently in use in the United States?

4. What are the Blueprints Model Programs?

5. What is the Perry Preschool Program?

6. What is Project Head Start?

7. What is the purpose of the Prenatal and Infancy Home Visitation program?

8. What types of youths are targeted by the SHIELD program?

9. What four areas does the FAST program focus on to promote protective factors for juveniles at risk of becoming delinquent?

10. What is the theoretical foundation of diversion programs?

11. What types of offenses are generally excluded from diversion programs?

12. What are two problematic issues in diversion programs?

13. What is the goal behind Youth Advisory Councils and Youth Town Hall Meetings?

14. Give two examples of mentoring programs in the United States.

15. What are the two distinct ways that apprenticeship programs benefit youth?

16. What percentage of a juvenile's time is unstructured and unoccupied?

17. What is the goal of midnight basketball programs?

18. What are four potential benefits of teen courts?

19. What are the four primary teen court models?

20. What is the most common disposition given in teen courts?

21. Which delinquency prevention program is a classic example of a panacea?

22. What can be said about the cost effectiveness of delinquency prevention programs?

HANDS-ON ACTIVITIES

1. **Volunteer in an Intervention Program** Most communities around the country have a variety of programs designed to intervene in the lives of at-risk children. Find the programs in your community that seek to help these at-risk children and volunteer some of your time. Most likely, the program administrators will be overjoyed to see you, and the donation of your time can go a long way in preventing future problems with children in your community. You should share your experiences in volunteering with the rest of the class.

2. Visit a local organization devoted to juveniles such as the Boys and Girls Club, Volunteers in Action, the YMCA or YWCA, or Big Brothers/Big Sisters and volunteer some time to the organization. You can donate a small amount of your time on a weekly basis. How did your time change your perception of the juveniles that these programs serve?

1. Go to the Blueprints for the Prevention of Violence home page at **www.blueprintsprograms.com** and examine the model programs that it references. What common characteristics are there among these programs? Why are these programs so successful when many others have failed?

2. The Office of Juvenile Justice and Delinquency Prevention maintains an extensive library of materials relating to diversion and delinquency prevention at its website, **www.ojjdp.gov/publications/index.html.** Examine some of its online publications about the effectiveness of, and overall strategy for, delinquency prevention. What areas of research do you think are most promising?

1. **Find Help for a Juvenile in Trouble** Craig is a 12-year-old juvenile who has been caught shoplifting at a local convenience store. Craig comes from a broken home and currently lives with his paternal grandmother. Craig's father is in prison and his mother cannot be located. There is a history of substance abuse in the family and criminal behavior on the part of both parents and other siblings.

   Recently, Craig's school performance has been dropping, and he has become a disciplinary problem. Although his grandmother cares for him, she is physically unable to keep up with him these days. Assume you are a social worker who has just received this case. Considering the variety of potential programs Craig could be referred to, which program(s) would you use? Develop a statement as to why you chose the option(s) you did and a justification as to why this is the best course of action.

2. **Determine the Appropriate Type of Delinquency Prevention Program** Skip is a 15-year-old juvenile who was arrested as a minor in possession of alcohol. Skip is currently enrolled in school, getting below-average grades, and has had disciplinary problems in the past. Skip lives with both his parents in a middle-class community and there is no history of substance abuse or criminal history in his family.

   Assume you are a probation officer who has just received this case. Considering the variety of potential programs Skip could be referred to, which program(s) would you use? Develop a statement as to why you chose the option(s) you did and a justification as to why this is the best course of action.

6.1 Self-Check

What is meant by delinquency prevention?
Delinquency prevention is a broad term that covers the many programs and strategies that are used to prevent juveniles from becoming delinquent. Delinquency prevention seeks to intervene in at-risk groups on the basis of prior knowledge of the characteristics of juvenile offenders and work to prevent the juvenile from engaging in delinquency.

6.2 Self-Check

Explain why a growing number of programs are focusing on intervention and prevention.

Many believe that at-risk juveniles and other juveniles who are most in need of intervention are identifiable, such as by determining whether or not the juveniles possess risk factors. This early identification is believed to be helpful in early treatment and prevention.

6.3 Self-Check

1. What programs focus on risk factors?
Some programs that focus on risk factors are prenatal and infancy home visitation by nurses, SHIELD, CAR, and Healthy Families.

2. What is meant by the holistic approach?
The holistic approach is a comprehensive approach that targets multiple aspects of a problem

simultaneously, by using multiple agencies and groups instead of a single intervention method.

6.4 Self-Check

What problems exist with diversion programs?
There are some problems with diversion. An example is the problem with net widening, which is the use of diversion to bring more juveniles (whose cases would otherwise have been dismissed) under formal control. Another example is the constitutionality of using diversion while not maintaining due process and equal protection issues.

6.5 Self-Check

What component of a school-based program has been shown to yield the most successful results?
Programs incorporating all of a youth's primary caregivers are the most successful in the long run.

6.6 Self-Check

1. When did mentoring programs begin?
Mentoring programs began in the late 1800s, when several adults began serving as role models for poor children. This led to the founding of Big Brothers/Big Sisters in 1904.

2. Describe one of the job services programs.
Job services programs include any of the following:
- Job Corps, which is a national residential education and training program that provides several services in an integrated and coordinated manner.
- Youth apprenticeship programs, which place juveniles in work and educational settings with training by skilled workers.
- The School-to-Work Opportunities Act, which offers school-based learning, work-based learning, and connected activities. STW includes school and work preparation programs such as vocational education, work-study, Tech Prep, youth apprenticeships, internship programs, and Junior Achievement.

6.7 Self-Check

1. How are teens referred to teen court?
They are referred from nearly every component of the system. (Refer to Figure 6.8 on page 163 for examples of the many ways in which teens may be referred.)

2. Do adults play a role in teen court?
Adults play several different roles, some of them depending on the model of teen court being used. In some teen courts, the judge is an adult; in others, adults typically argue the cases to a jury of youths. In addition, all referrals to teen court come from adults, and all teen courts operate under the supervision of the adult-run juvenile court in that jurisdiction.

6.8 Self-Check

What is the philosophy underlying programs that focus on status offenses?
Their philosophy is that aggressively targeting juveniles who violate curfew, are truant, or who are otherwise at risk will significantly prevent juvenile crime. Programs such as the textbook example from Phoenix, Arizona, appear to be successful.

6.9 Self-Check

Describe the Scared Straight program.
This program, a classic example of a panacea that provides a quick fix for a complicated problem, was popularized by a television program that aired in 1979. Basically, it took delinquent and at-risk juveniles inside the prison system to be confronted by adult inmates who yelled at them and threatened them with violence and rape. This was done in an attempt to "scare" juveniles into stopping their delinquent behavior, thus making them go "straight."

The television program claimed high rates of success, and on the basis of these claims, policymakers rushed to develop their own version of Scared Straight; some of the main appeal was that it was cheap and seemed like an easy solution. Over time, though, the program's actual success rates revealed that Scared Straight was considerably less successful than other interventions.

6.10 Self-Check

What common characteristics do successful prevention programs share?
Successful programs share the following ten principles:
- Quality of implementation
- Caring, knowledgeable adults
- High standards and expectations
- Parent/guardian participation
- Community involvement
- Holistic approaches
- Youth as resources
- Community service and service-learning
- Work-based learning
- Long-term services, support, and follow-up

In addition, they also share a comprehensive, multifaceted approach rather than a single type of intervention, a built-in aftercare component, and a relatively small number of juveniles under their care.

PART

3

POLICING JUVENILES, THE LAW, AND THE COURTS

CHAPTER SEVEN

POLICE AND JUVENILES

Chapter Outline

The Central Role of Police Agencies in the Juvenile Justice System

Role of the Police in Dealing with Juvenile Offenders

Early Policing in Juvenile Justice and Police Matrons

The Changing Role of the Police

Definitions of Police Roles and Responsibilities

Community and Problem-Oriented Policing

Processing of Juvenile Delinquents by Police

Policing Status Offenders and Abused or Neglected Children

Police Discretion in Dealing with Juvenile Offenders

Police Attitudes toward Juveniles

Juveniles' Attitudes toward Police

Police-Based Programs for Juveniles

D.A.R.E. and Other School-Based Programs

New Directions in Working with Juveniles in Policing

Chapter Objectives

After completing this chapter, you should be able to:

1. Explain the role of police through the history of juvenile justice.

2. Describe the various police styles.

3. Explain how the police process juvenile cases.

4. Describe the role of police in handling status offenders and abused or neglected children.

5. Explain the discretionary options a police officer can exercise in juvenile cases.

6. List factors that influence police decisions in juvenile cases.

7. Compare police attitudes about juveniles with juveniles' attitudes about police.

8. Identify some intervention programs operated by police agencies.

9. Explain how community-oriented policing affects juvenile cases.

The Central Role of Police Agencies in the Juvenile Justice System

The role of police in the juvenile justice system is relatively complex and multi-fold. This role can be divided into four main categories: arresting delinquents, processing juvenile delinquents and status offenders, preventing juvenile delinquency, and protecting juveniles from victimization. The most familiar roles involve the arrest and processing of juvenile delinquents. The police are also responsible for attempting to prevent both juvenile delinquency and juvenile victimization. In fulfilling this role, police agencies around the country operate a variety of programmatic interventions. It is important to remember that just like other aspects of the juvenile justice system, the programs and specific police responsibilities vary greatly by jurisdiction. One common characteristic of all police agencies is that they are the gatekeepers of the juvenile justice system. Police officers are often the first point of contact between the system and a juvenile delinquent, juvenile status offender, or juvenile in need of protection. In this chapter, you will see that a variety of factors influence how police handle juvenile matters.

In 2010, police agencies in the United States made an estimated 1.6 million arrests of juveniles.[1] Those juveniles accounted for 14 percent of all violent crime arrests and 22 percent of all property crime arrests. This is, no doubt, still a larger number than we should be comfortable with, but it should be noted that the overall number of arrests among juveniles in 2010 was a full 43 percent less than those measured in 1996[2] (see Figure 7.1). As a group, in 2010, juveniles were involved in:

- 9 percent of murder arrests
- 11 percent of aggravated assault arrests
- 23 percent of burglary arrests
- 24 percent of robbery arrests
- 20 percent of weapons arrests
- 14 percent of forcible rape arrests

While juveniles do account for a substantial portion of arrests for serious **index felonies,** the numbers are even higher for misdemeanors and status offenses. However, as any juvenile justice scholar will note, juveniles in many jurisdictions are not technically "arrested"; instead, they are taken into custody. This is further evidence, to some, that the punitive movement has had multiple impacts on the system.

Police agencies in the United States are being called upon to deal with a growing number of social issues. Crimes committed by juveniles and other juvenile issues are rooted in social problems being relegated to the police.

Police agencies deal with juvenile issues in a variety of ways, ranging from the aggressive enforcement of curfew and truancy laws to the sponsorship of midnight basketball games for gang-involved youths. Because of their central role in the juvenile justice process, the police are at the forefront of initiatives designed to prevent delinquency and reduce juvenile crime.

The ways in which the police deal with juvenile delinquents have changed since the beginning of the juvenile justice system. Police agencies have been called upon to be more innovative in their approaches to dealing with juvenile crime.

Female Delinquents' Arrest Rates

Between 2000 and 2009, arrests for aggravated assaults decreased more (from 26 percent) for males than for females (only 20 percent). Arrests for simple assaults for females actually rose by 4 percent, while their male counterparts actually experienced a decrease in arrests for the same offense. In 2009, females accounted for 30 percent of juvenile arrests for the same offense. In 2009, females accounted for 30 percent of juvenile arrests for an estimated total of 578,500 girls under the age of 18.

SOURCE: Puzzanchera, Charles and B. Adams. "Juvenile Arrests 2009." *Juvenile Justice Bulletin,* December 2011. Washington, DC: Office of Juvenile Justice and Delinquency Prevention. Online, available at: http://www.ojjdp.gov/pubs/236477.pdf. Retrieved May 5, 2013.

7.1 SELF-CHECK

Why are police considered the gatekeepers of the juvenile justice system?

---

index felonies The eight felonies that comprise the FBI's Uniform Crime Report: murder, rape, robbery, aggravated assault, burglary, larceny/theft, auto theft, and arson.

FIGURE 7.1	Update: Juvenile Arrests in 2009

MOST SERIOUS OFFENSE	2009 ESTIMATED NUMBER OF JUVENILE ARRESTS	PERCENT OF TOTAL JUVENILE ARRESTS			PERCENT CHANGE		
		FEMALE	YOUNGER THAN 15	WHITE	2000– 2009	2005– 2009	2008– 2009
Total	1,906,600	30%	27%	66%	−17%	−11%	−9%
Violent Crime Index	85,590	18	26	47	−13	−10	−10
Murder and and nonnegligent manslaughter	1,170	7	9	40	0	−7	−7
Forcible rape	3,100	2	32	65	−30	−22	−6
Robbery	31,700	10	18	31	15	9	−10
Aggravated assault	49,900	25	30	56	−24	−19	−11
Property Crime Index	417,700	38	28	64	−19	0	−4
Burglary	74,800	11	27	61	−21	−4	−10
Larceny-theft	317,700	45	28	65	−12	8	−1
Motor vehicle theft	19,900	17	20	54	−61	−47	20
Arson	5,300	13	59	77	−37	−33	−17
Nonindex							
Other assaults	219,700	34	37	59	−6	−12	−5
Forgery and counterfeiting	2,100	30	13	67	−66	−49	−17
Fraud	6,200	35	17	62	−62	−21	−15
Embezzlement	600	42	7	64	−68	−47	−52
Stolen property (buying, receiving, possessing)	18,700	19	22	55	−28	−16	−10
Vandalism	90,500	14	39	79	−20	−13	−15
Weapons (carrying, possessing, etc.)	33,900	10	31	61	−7	−25	−15
Prostitution and commercialized vice	1,400	78	12	40	−4	−16	−8
Sex offense (except forcible rape and prostitution)	13,400	11	48	71	−23	−21	−7
Drug abuse violations	170,300	16	16	72	−14	−12	−5
Gambling	1,800	3	11	7	67	−13	9
Offenses against the family and children	4,500	36	28	74	−49	−21	−22
Driving under the influence	13,500	25	2	92	−37	−25	−15
Liquor law	110,300	39	9	89	−15	−11	−15
Drunkenness	13,800	25	12	88	−37	−13	−11
Disorderly conduct	170,100	33	36	57	6	−17	−10
Vagrancy	2,700	28	24	72	−24	−29	−32
All other offenses (except traffic)	323,300	26	23	69	−17	−12	−10
Suspicion (not included in totals)	200	22	27	42	−82	−61	−20
Curfew and loitering	112,600	31	25	61	−27	−20	−15
Runaways	93,400	55	31	65	−34	−14	14

- In 2009, there were an estimated 317,700 juvenile arrests for larceny-theft. Between 2000 and 2009, the number of such arrests fell by 12%.
- All four offenses that make up the Violent Crime Index decreased in the last year: murder (down 7%), rape (6%), robbery (10%), and aggravated assault (11%).
- In 2009, females accounted for 18% of juvenile Violent Crime Index arrests, 38% of juvenile Property Crime Index arrests, and 45% of juvenile larceny-theft arrests.
- Youth younger than age 15 accounted for more than one-fourth of all juvenile arrests for Violent Crime Index offenses and Property Crime Index offenses in 2009 (26% and 28%, respectively).

Source: Puzzanchera, Charles and B. Adams. "Juvenile Arrests 2009." *Juvenile Justice Bulletin*, December 2011. Washington, DC: Office of Juvenile Justice and Delinquency Prevention. Online, available at: http://ojjdp.gov/pubs/236477.pdf. Retrieved May 5, 2013

Many people think juveniles commit a large number of violent crimes; in fact, juveniles commit many more property crimes and status offenses than violent crimes. Nonetheless, the focus of police attention in juvenile matters in recent years has been toward juveniles who commit violent offenses. *What reasons can you think of for why so much attention has been paid to juveniles who commit violent crimes in recent years?*

Role of the Police in Dealing with Juvenile Offenders

Before the inception of the juvenile justice system, police treated juveniles as they would adult criminals. As discussed later in this chapter, many police departments today have separate divisions to handle juveniles, with certain officers designated to deal specifically with juvenile offenders.

EARLY POLICING IN JUVENILE JUSTICE AND POLICE MATRONS

Before the establishment of the first juvenile courts in the United States and during the early history of juvenile justice, juveniles were subject to the same laws, punishments, and treatment by police as adults. The child savers advocated a separate system of justice for juveniles. By 1925, such a system had been established in every state. An outgrowth of this new institution was the new role police would play. When the juvenile court was created to separate juveniles from the criminal justice system, police agencies began to play a dual role: dealing with adult crime and dealing with juvenile delinquency. Police agencies often responded to this new demand by creating a separate juvenile division within their agency.

During the early years of the juvenile justice system in the United States, the need for the police to deal with juveniles led to the hiring of females into policing.[3] The first women in policing were often assigned to the juvenile division. This assignment was based on the stereotypical assumption that women, because of their traditional maternal role, would be better able to deal with juveniles than male police officers. Women hired into police work were called police matrons and were given different duties than their male counterparts. Police matrons assumed clerical duties, minor ordinance enforcement (such as writing parking tickets), and dealing with juveniles. The feeling was that police matrons acted as benefactors to juveniles, whether they were criminals, runaways, or in need of supervision. This assumption also reflected the early-20th-century philosophy of being protective toward juveniles. Thus, for a long time, women officers dealt with many aspects of the juvenile justice system, especially the younger offender and the status offenders. However, as the juvenile justice system matured and became more formalized in the American justice system, the role of police changed dramatically.

THE CHANGING ROLE OF THE POLICE

Police history is generally divided into three periods: the *traditional* or *political period*, the *professional period*, and the *community-oriented* period. During the **traditional period** of law enforcement, police officers treated juveniles no differently than other offenders. As a result, juveniles were jailed with adults, interrogated like adults, and also experienced the same commonplace civil rights abuse. At that time, police in the United States were, for the most part, tools of the political apparatus. Before the reforms of the professional period, police agencies did not pay much attention to juvenile problems. Juveniles who were not serious criminals were handed off to police matrons or other social institutions.

The **professional period** of law enforcement began in the early part of the 20th century just after the creation of the juvenile justice system. The era ushered in efforts to remove politics from policing. Professional period reforms resulted in many changes in law enforcement. Yet, while the juvenile justice system was taking shape in the United States and these reforms were being instituted, the police treatment of juveniles remained largely unchanged. Juvenile offenders were still treated like any other criminal, but now they were at least removed from adults when incarcerated and adjudicated. Not until the reforms

Crimes against Juveniles

National Crime Victimization Survey data indicates that only 28 percent of violent crimes against juveniles become known to police. Juveniles are even less likely to report property crimes; only 10 percent of thefts against juveniles become known to police. Interestingly, juveniles report both violent and nonviolent victimization to other authorities outside law enforcement, such as school officials. An additional 16 percent of violent crimes against juveniles and an additional 29 percent of thefts are reported to some authority other than the police.

SOURCE: Finkelhor, David and Richard Ormrod. "Reporting Crimes against Juveniles." *Juvenile Justice Bulletin* November 1999. Washington, DC: Office of Juvenile Justice and Delinquency Prevention, 1999.

The role of women in policing was limited in the early part of the 20th century. Many police matrons worked with juveniles in some capacity. *How has the role of women changed over the past century?*

traditional or political period The era in law enforcement marked by political corruption and political control of policing.

professional period The era in law enforcement when the goal was to increase the professionalization of policing, thus removing it from political pressures.

of the 1960s and 1970s did substantial changes in the criminal and juvenile systems of justice surface and signal a truly new era for criminal justice.

One important push for change was the Juvenile Justice and Delinquency Prevention Act of 1974 (JJDP Act), which initiated widespread changes in juvenile justice. The act gave legislative weight to the requirement that juvenile offenders be separated from adult offenders. In addition, labeling theory (discussed in detail in Chapter 5) resulted in a shift in the treatment of juveniles who had been charged with a crime. The idea that labeling juveniles as criminals had a negative impact on them and drove them to behave criminally was implicit in labeling theory. Therefore, this theory caused a push to remove all stigmatization and potential for self-fulfilling prophecy from the processing of youths in the juvenile justice system. Consequently, fingerprinting, photographing, and record keeping (the law and case precedents for these areas are discussed in detail in Chapter 8) were substantially restricted. Even today, the treatment of juveniles who come into contact with the police remains fundamentally different from the treatment of adult offenders.

During the 1970s and 1980s, police theorists began to question the operational tactics and overall philosophy of policing in the United States. The assumption that the police were out of touch with the community led to the third period in law enforcement, the community-oriented period. During this period, the role that police played in juvenile justice expanded greatly. The philosophy of policing moved away from the concept of police as crime fighters and instead embraced the idea that the police are one of many organizations delivering quality of life services to the community. The new operational tactics used in juvenile matters would now embrace a prevention and intervention philosophy.

DEFINITIONS OF POLICE ROLES AND RESPONSIBILITIES

James Q. Wilson, in his book *Varieties of Police Behavior,* defined three fundamental functions in which police officers engage: law enforcement, order maintenance, and community service.[4] Although he wrote this book 30 years ago, Wilson's definitions are still being applied and researched.

In addition to defining the three primary functions, Wilson identified three styles of law enforcement agencies—legalistic, watchman, and service. While all police agencies engage in all three of the functions, there is typically more emphasis on one function. Figure 7.2 outlines these three functions and the various styles police agencies manifest.

Departmental style typically determines juvenile dispositions and the attitudes of officers toward juvenile issues. It also determines, in large part, the number and types of programs the law enforcement agency supports. For example, a watchman-style or a service-style department is much more likely to support educational and recreational programmatic interventions for juveniles than is a legalistic-style department. Clearly, the role of police officers is much larger in juvenile matters in both watchman-style and service-style departments.

There are substantial differences among the three styles of policing. It should be understood that very few, if any, police departments could be characterized as embracing only one of the styles listed in the figure. For example, while the style of a department may be decidedly legalistic, that does not mean that the department will not operate a Drug Abuse Resistance Education (D.A.R.E.) or Gang Resistance Education and Training

Myth / Fact

Myth: The police role in juvenile justice matters is exclusively related to arrests.

Fact: In fact, police have a wide range of discretion in dealing with juveniles. They can choose to formally process and refer a juvenile to court, or they can take informal measures to deal with some types of offenders. Police can also be actively involved in delinquency prevention activities and intervention programs.

FIGURE 7.2	Police Style and Juvenile Matters		
STYLE	**LEGALISTIC**	**WATCHMAN**	**SERVICE**
Mission	Law enforcement	Order maintenance	Community service
Techniques	Use of criminal law; black and white world (either there was a violation or there was not)	Use of criminal law, threats, temporary custody, and problem solving to keep the peace. Handle problem temporally and move on	Use of traditional police mechanisms is discouraged in favor of looking outside the criminal justice system for responses that will not only solve the community's problems but also improve the quality of life for the residents
Goals	Crime prevention and arrests	Keeping the peace and public order	Improving the quality of life
Role of Criminal Law	Central and rigid	One tool, a threat used to keep peace	One of the many tools, the last resort
Role of the Officer	1. Recognize violations 2. Follow due process 3. Follow orders and SOP 4. Administer law	1. Know how peace is defined in the beat 2. Know how the beat expects peace to be supported 3. Exercise judgment to "keep the beat quiet"	1. Measure and assess what the community wants (may or may not involve crime) 2. Co-actively work with community to identify needs and strategies 3. Perform service to meet needs and increase quality of life
Officer's Function	Militaristic	Problem solver	Social worker
Discretion	Low	Medium	High
Attitude toward Juveniles	Age is not a factor in disposition other than what is required under law. Determining factor in dispositions is which law was violated	Juveniles are perhaps the greatest threat to keeping the peace. Juveniles are treated in a paternalistic manner. Order breakers are typically ordered to leave the area, go home, or keep quiet. Determining factor in dispositions is typically attitude of the juvenile	Juveniles become problems when they are unsupervised and have unoccupied time. Juveniles need a role model, structure, and guidance
Programs for Juveniles	Not a police problem. It is up to the courts, probation, and corrections to service juveniles	Programs that keep youth off the streets and keep them busy are preferable. Curfew centers and truancy programs are frequently used	Programmatic interventions need to go beyond simply occupying a juvenile's time. Programs are used for corrections as well as delinquency prevention. D.A.R.E., G.R.E.A.T., and other educational programs are frequently used
Role of the officer in Juvenile Matters	Same as adult—enforce the criminal law and process the offender	To serve as a monitor for the community. Prevent juveniles from becoming problems by watching them and maintaining order	To serve as a parent to juveniles in need within the community

(G.R.E.A.T.) program. Departmental style simply characterizes the operational philosophy and common tactics used in the agency. Officers in a legalistic-style department would tend to approach juvenile matters "by the book." If a violation of the law is not present, the officer would likely not take any action. A legalistic police department would have little if any prevention or intervention programs and would instead seek to find violations of the criminal law. In contrast, officers in a watchman-style department would tend to take a more active role in juvenile matters to the extent that juveniles were creating problems in the community. These officers would use the criminal law as a last resort and instead try to disperse disruptive juveniles. Finally, service-style officers would essentially adopt the role of surrogate parent seeking to intervene in the lives of juveniles in a prevention capacity. These officers approach juvenile matters with a focus on prevention and intervention.

Police involvement with juveniles is common in areas such as public disturbances, family violence, home burglaries, vandalism, complaints from the elderly, traffic enforcement, and offenses against children. According to the Office of

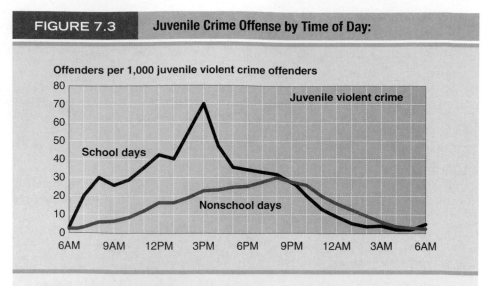

FIGURE 7.3   Juvenile Crime Offense by Time of Day:

Offenders per 1,000 juvenile violent crime offenders

Note: Violent crimes include murder, violent sexual assault, robbery, aggravated assault, and simple assault. Data are from law enforcement agencies in 35 states and the District of Columbia.

- Juvenile violence peaks in the afterschool hours on school days and in the evenings on nonschool days.
- On nonschool days, the incidence of juvenile violence increases through the afternoon and early evening hours, peaking between 7 P.M. and 9 P.M.
- The number of school days in a year is essentially equal to the number of nonschool days in a year. Despite this split, most (63%) violent crimes committed by juveniles occur on school days. Nearly one-fifth (19%) of juvenile violent crimes occur in the 4 hours between 3 P.M. and 7 P.M. on school days. A smaller proportion of juvenile violent crimes (15%) occurs during the standard juvenile curfew hours of 10 P.M. to 6 A.M. (inclusive of both school and non-school days).

Source: *OJJDP Statistical Briefing Book*. Online. Available: http://www.ojjdp.gov/ojstatbb/offenders/qa03301.asp?qaDate=2008. Retrieved on May 17, 2013.

Juvenile Arrests

The racial composition of the entire American juvenile population ages 10 through 17 in 2009 was 77 percent white, 16 percent black, 5 percent Asian/ Pacific Islander, and 1 percent American Indian (Hispanic juveniles are generally included under the "white" category). In juvenile arrests, black youth are significantly statistically overrepresented, accounting for 51 percent of all arrests despite making up less than one-fifth of the total population.

SOURCE: Puzzanchera, Charles and B. Adams. "Juvenile Arrests 2009." *Juvenile Justice Bulletin,* December 2011. Washington, http://www.ojjdp.gov/pubs/236477.pdf. Retrieved May 5, 2013.

Juvenile Justice and Delinquency Prevention, these areas account for at least 50 percent of the total requirement for police service. This figure grows significantly when informal contacts and general order maintenance duties are added. It has been estimated that 70 to 90 percent of police/juvenile encounters involve maintaining order or providing service.[5] The National Advisory Committee on Criminal Justice Standards and Goals[6] states that police agencies are responsible for the following:

- Exerting every possible effort toward discovery of potential delinquents and conditions conducive to delinquent behavior.
- Working closely with other agencies to remove or control environmental conditions conducive to creating juvenile problems.
- Advising and assisting all agencies and organizations concerned with juvenile problems when the police agency is not directly involved in the activity.
- Using preventive patrol techniques in areas where there is potential for juvenile problems.
- Conducting thorough investigations into delinquency problems that lead to the commission of juvenile offenses. This includes apprehension and prosecution of adults who contribute to, or are involved in, delinquency problems.
- Detecting and apprehending juvenile offenders as prescribed by existing juvenile law and procedures. There should be guidelines for the release of juveniles into parental or guardian custody, or for their detention.
- Follow-up as needed in the referral of the offender, obtaining the necessary legal process and obtaining the disposition of each action involving the juvenile offender.
- Retaining prescribed juvenile records as indicated by the courts and required by law.

FIGURE 7.4	Violent Crime Offenses by Time of Day: Adults versus Juveniles

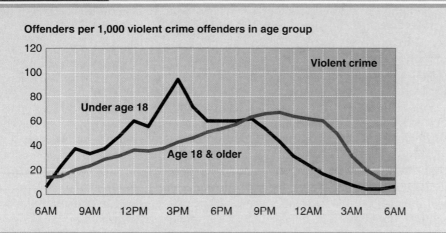

Note: Violent crimes include murder, violent sexual assault, robbery, aggravated assault, and simple assault. Data collected from law enforcement agencies in 35 states and the District of Columbia.

- In general, the number of violent crimes committed by adults increases hourly from 6 a.m. through the afternoon and evening hours, peaks at 10 P.M., and then drops to a low point at 6 a.m. In contrast, violent crimes by juveniles peak in the afternoon between 3 p.m. and 4 p.m., the hour at the end of the school day.
- Nearly one-third (29%) of all violent crime committed by juvenile offenders occurs between 3 P.M. and 7 P.M. In comparison, 26% of all violent committed by adult offenders occurs between 8 P.M. and 12 P.M.

Source: *OJJDP Statistical Briefing Book*. Online. Available: http://www.ojjdp.gov/ojstatbb/offenders/qa03301.asp?qaDate=2008. Retrieved on May 17, 2013.

The standards advocated by the National Advisory Committee on Juvenile Justice and Criminal Justice Standards and Goals are adopted by many police agencies in their policies. Because the standards are often recommendations rather than requirements, there is substantial variation in the role the police play in juvenile matters from department to department.

Many of the unilateral crime commissions of the 1960s and 1970s concluded that the police needed to become closer to the communities they served. Urban unrest and other problems of this era were often sparked by police/citizen confrontations. As a result of the shifts in thinking about the role the police should play, a new philosophy emerged—**community-oriented policing (COP)**. COP is a proactive policing philosophy which advocates that police and citizens should become co-active partners in policing their community. Proactive and innovative programs for juveniles sponsored by police agencies were a natural outgrowth of this movement.

COMMUNITY AND PROBLEM-ORIENTED POLICING

Beginning in the mid-1970s, following a series of research studies that questioned fundamental police practices, the COP movement began to take shape. Influenced by many authors and police officials, COP held the promise of creating a co-active bond between police and the communities they serve. Juvenile matters became much more prominent for police administrators as it was assumed that a fundamental goal of COP was to influence the next generation of citizens. Further, COP advocates held the belief that greater attention to juvenile and family matters would result in crime reductions and would focus police resources on the root causes of crime and disorder, rather than the effects.

community-oriented policing (COP) A philosophical movement in policing designed to make the community a co-active partner with law enforcement.

Another philosophy and policing strategy emanating from this period was the idea of **problem-oriented policing (POP)** conceptualized by Herman Goldstein. POP is a policing philosophy that attempts to take the focus of the police away from responding to calls and crime problems in a reactive fashion. Instead, POP holds that by "solving" underlying problems, the police can instead prevent or eliminate repetitive calls generated by underlying problems. Officers are instructed to *scan* for potential problems, *analyze* the contributing factors and causes, craft a tailored *response* that may or may not include traditional law enforcement practices, and then *assess* the results of their intervention—a process knows as the SARA model.

Applications of this process to juvenile problems become readily apparent. For example, it is commonly known that a significant proportion of crimes involving juveniles occur in the homes immediately after school. As such, a program or policy should be adopted that takes this into consideration. Rather than simply "rounding up" all of the kids after school, POP would attempt to look for underlying causes and reasons concerning why the spike in crime and victimization was occurring. An example cause is the fact that many kids are out of school before their guardians get home from work. These kids are essentially unsupervised for several hours. POP would say the best way to prevent these kids from misbehaving or from becoming victims would be to provide them with activities to occupy their time during these crime-prone hours. Examples would include police athletic leagues, after-school programs, and in some cases, some types of police explorer programs. All of these programs are outside of traditional police thinking and responses.

While COP and POP were certainly popular philosophies, in recent years the effectiveness and time implementation of the philosophies have come into question. Credible evaluations of the effectiveness of COP and POP are lacking, and recent scholarship has seriously questioned how much law enforcement has truly implemented these philosophies. Nonetheless, both philosophies brought out the need for police to be more involved with juveniles in their daily activities. Oftentimes, this interaction is not what some would consider "real" police work. Indeed, some even question the utility of having officers "taking kids to the zoo."

PROCESSING OF JUVENILE DELINQUENTS BY POLICE

Although the role of the police in juvenile matters varies across jurisdictions, procedures followed by police when a juvenile is accused of committing a crime are fairly consistent. Some processing based on state statute or local ordinances may vary, but the handling of juveniles and the procedures followed are relatively consistent. The investigatory process the police follow is essentially unchanged until a juvenile becomes the suspect in a crime. In other words, the police investigate all crimes in a similar manner; however, once it is clear that a juvenile is the suspect, there are some procedures and safeguards that the police follow. For example, confidentiality laws still exist in many states, and the police must take extra precaution with juvenile records. In addition, schools are typically involved, and there may be confidentiality provisions attached to school records as well (confidentiality and other restrictions are discussed fully in Chapter 8). Often state laws, municipal ordinances, and police agency policies guide and restrict police officials in handling juvenile offenders. An example of the restrictions placed on police can be seen in Figure 7.5.

Police departments often feel hampered by many of the restrictions placed on their ability to investigate juvenile offenders. **Confidentiality laws** typically prohibit police from photographing juveniles, fingerprinting them, or maintaining juvenile records. Where these routine police investigative practices are not prohibited, they are severely limited. In addition, police in many jurisdictions cannot question or interrogate juveniles in custody without their parents, a lawyer, or a guardian present.

problem-oriented policing (POP) A philosophical movement in policing that attempts to take the focus of the police away from responding to calls and crime problems in a reactive fashion.

confidentiality laws Statutes that protect the identity and records of juvenile offenders in an attempt to avoid the stigmatization that comes with adjudication.

FIGURE 7.5	Georgia State Statute Authorizing Police Custody of Juveniles

(a) A child may be taken into custody:

(1) Pursuant to an order of the court under this article, including an order to an employee of the Department of Juvenile Justice designated in accordance with paragraph (2) of subsection (i) of Code Section 49-4A-8 or to an employee of the Department of Corrections, to apprehend a child who has escaped from an institution or facility operated either by the Department of Juvenile Justice or the Department of Corrections or a child who has been placed under supervision and who has broken the conditions thereof;

(2) Pursuant to the laws of arrest;

(3) By a law enforcement officer or duly authorized officer of the court if there are reasonable grounds to believe that the child has committed a delinquent act or if there are reasonable grounds to believe that he or she is an unruly child;

(4) By a law enforcement officer or duly authorized officer of the court if there are reasonable grounds to believe that the child is suffering from illness or injury or is in immediate danger from his or her surroundings and that his or her removal is necessary;

(5) By a law enforcement officer or duly authorized officer of the court If there are reasonable grounds to believe that the child has run away from his or her parents, guardian, or other custodian;

(6) By a law enforcement officer or duly authorized officer of the court if a parent or guardian of a child has contacted a law enforcement agency and reported that the child is absent from parental custody without consent and a facility created pursuant to paragraph (2) of subsection (e) of Code Section 15-11-19 is available; or

(7) By a law enforcement officer or duly authorized officer of the court if a child is violating a curfew and a facility created pursuant to paragraph (2) of subsection (e) of Code Section 15-11-19 is available.

(b) The taking of a child into custody is not an arrest, except for the purpose of determining its validity under the Constitution of this state or of the United States.

(c) When a child who is taken into custody pursuant to this article has committed an act which would constitute a felony under the laws of this state if committed by an adult, the juvenile court, within 48 hours after it learns of the taking into custody, shall notify the district attorney or duly authorized assistant district attorney of the judicial circuit in which the juvenile proceedings are to be instituted.

Source: Georgia Code Annotated 15-11-17

Federal and state laws frequently limit the time and manner in which police may detain a juvenile. The JJDP Act mandates that juveniles detained by police cannot be mixed with adults at the police facility, jail, or temporary detention facility. Juveniles must be **sight and sound separated** from adults while in custody. Although the laws vary greatly from state to state, many common police practices are still restricted when it comes to juvenile offenders. For example, legislatures placed numerous restrictions on the police regarding the investigation, arrest, interrogation, booking, and detention of juveniles (see Figure 7.5). Several states have *per se* **attorney laws** that require that a juvenile be represented by a lawyer in all critical phases of the process.

There are numerous circumstances that police officers encounter in dealing with juveniles that could lead to the juvenile's being taken into **custody**. When the offense is serious, custody is essentially the same as arrest. However, nonserious juvenile offenders can also be taken into custody by police for a range of offenses much broader than those allowable for adults. In addition to state, county, and municipal criminal codes, a juvenile can be taken into custody for status offenses including **curfew, truancy**, and being a runaway. These statutes are rather broad; however, their intent is not to punish juveniles but to protect them. These statutes define a class of juveniles who are literally in need of supervision for some reason. The police are also frequently called to take into custody juveniles who are uncontrollable or unruly. In many jurisdictions, parents or schools can call police to remove an uncontrollable child for placement. The reasons and justifications for detaining and taking juveniles into custody are wide-ranging.

Model policies dealing with juvenile offenders serve as guides to police departments.[7] A common model policy states that juveniles should not be handcuffed to a stationary object for more than four hours and they should never be left unattended while handcuffed. Another model policy states that the police are to make every effort to notify the parents of any juvenile taken into custody. The formal processing of juveniles by police is controlled by several sources including federal mandates, state law, municipal law, and departmental policy.

sight and sound separated The concept that juveniles should not be able to see or hear adult offenders when taken into police custody.

***per se* attorney laws** Laws that require a juvenile to have an attorney present during critical police proceedings. *Per se* means that a juvenile cannot waive this right.

custody Essentially the same as arrest for adults.

curfew A municipal ordinance that restricts the hours a juvenile can be out in public.

truancy A status offense making It illegal for youths not to attend school.

model policies Written policies composed by national organizations in an effort to standardize operating procedures at the local level.

In addition to more traditional law enforcement responsibilities, police officers are called upon to deal with a variety of other juvenile issues. *How is the police role in dealing with juveniles different from that of dealing with adults?*

Once police have taken a juvenile into custody, there must usually be a detention hearing within 48 hours (this can vary depending on state or local requirements). If the police have detained a youth, he or she is typically taken to a detention facility to await processing by the courts. However, if a juvenile is taken into custody for investigative purposes, many other procedures and restrictions become important. For example, many states have statutory restrictions regarding the interrogation of juveniles. In some states, officers must take juveniles before a magistrate to be advised of their rights. Other states require the presence of a lawyer, parents, or other neutral party. Many states allow juveniles to waive their rights in a manner similar to adults. As discussed in Chapter 8, fingerprinting, photographing, and the records of a juvenile are all restricted by state law. Juvenile records must typically be kept separate from adult records and the confidentiality of juvenile records is often safeguarded.

POLICING STATUS OFFENDERS AND ABUSED OR NEGLECTED CHILDREN

Police officials are often called upon to deal with status offenders and children in need of protection. The enforcement of status offenses by police officers requires a proactive response. Status offenders typically don't turn themselves in to police, nor is there a victim to report the offender. The responsibility for a status offense enforcement lies solely with the police officer. Although enforcing status offenses might seem like just another way the police can arrest juveniles, it is more akin to protective custody. In other words, police officers typically enforce curfew, truancy, and runaway offenses to protect, not prosecute them. Status offenses give police a mechanism to control wayward juveniles who are not committing delinquent acts. Requiring a juvenile to be at home by a certain hour, to attend school, and to maintain a residence is more akin to parenting duties than traditional law enforcement duties. Nonetheless, enforcing status offenses and getting juveniles off the streets is a worthy pursuit.

In addition to dealing with juvenile criminals and status offenders, police officers are typically the first contact in many child abuse and neglect cases. Police officers have to be aware of the variety of social services that they can refer these cases to. *Do you think it should be the role of police to act as more of a social worker in these cases? Why or why not?*

In addition to delinquency cases, there are cases where the safety of a juvenile is in question. In these cases, police officers have to make a decision whether to take a juvenile into **protective custody**. Police are at the forefront of efforts to protect children from abuse, neglect, and other victimizations. The decision to remove a child from the home is a serious one, and some families have been ruined by false accusations of abuse. Unfortunately, many more children are the victims of abuse and neglect by their parents or other significant adults in their lives. There are numerous situations involving children where a police officer has to intervene in the family and take the child out of the home. Factors that influence an officer's decision whether or not to intervene include the following:

- Physical evidence of abuse such as bruises, burns, or other injuries
- An obvious lack of adult supervision or protection
- Any evidence of sexual abuse
- Any evidence of neglect, including the failure to provide for a child's basic needs

Police officers must be able to maintain a professional attitude in these matters in order to file charges and investigate the case thoroughly. Often these investigations involve multiple agencies such as child welfare or social service agencies that the police must work with in processing the case.

Police Discretion in Dealing with Juvenile Offenders

The police have a great deal of **discretion** in determining how to handle calls for service. They exercise even greater discretion in dealing with juvenile offenders. In any situation, the course of action the police choose to take is based on

protective custody Taking a minor into police custody to protect him or her from possible harm.

discretion The decision-making power police officers have in determining how to handle calls for service. The police have increased discretion in determining juvenile matters.

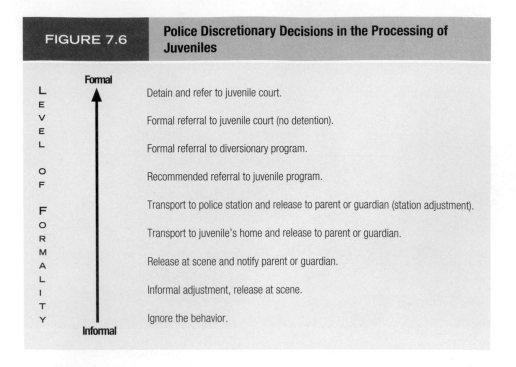

FIGURE 7.6 | **Police Discretionary Decisions in the Processing of Juveniles**

LEVEL OF FORMALITY

Formal

Detain and refer to juvenile court.

Formal referral to juvenile court (no detention).

Formal referral to diversionary program.

Recommended referral to juvenile program.

Transport to police station and release to parent or guardian (station adjustment).

Transport to juvenile's home and release to parent or guardian.

Release at scene and notify parent or guardian.

Informal adjustment, release at scene.

Ignore the behavior.

Informal

state law, departmental policies and practices, and the thoughts and practices of individual officers. The options shown in Figure 7.6 range from more typical, at the most informal level, to atypical at the most formal level. The number of juveniles *formally* charged and referred to juvenile court is very small when compared to the total number of police/juvenile encounters. Even when relatively serious crimes occur, a station adjustment is generally the preferred option—especially when the juvenile is young. Many times the decision to take informal action is based on the attitude of the juvenile or the fact that the officer views juvenile matters as a hassle.

Some police departments attempt to control police officer discretion by implementing structured policies that officers must follow. However, there is a trade-off involved in implementing written policies in police agencies between too detailed policy and too little policy.

GUIDANCE VERSUS PRESCRIPTION As with many other types of situations, the more successful policies regarding juveniles are those that provide guidance for action without rigidly ascribing each specific step for the officer to follow. Reasons for this approach include:

1. It is impossible to predict every situation that officers might find themselves in when dealing with juveniles.
2. Even if the majority of situations could be written into policy, such a compilation would be enormous and difficult to understand. Indeed, in police departments where the **standard operating procedure (SOP) manual** is long and complex, officers frequently don't know about the policy or are confused as to its meaning and directions.
3. Many SOPs are created in response to a mistake made by an officer in a prior case. As such, many SOP manuals are very negative sounding and typically create a difficult atmosphere in the department.

The level of discretion officers may exercise is also related to the departmental style. For example, the more legalistic a department is, the less discretion officers typically exercise. Officers in legalistic departments tend to view the

SOP manual Standard operating procedure manual. The compilation of policies and procedures for each law enforcement agency.

FOCUS ON POLICY

POLICE DISCRETION

The words *discretion* and *policies* may not seem fully compatible, but officers must rely on certain guidelines—whether formal or informal—when making decisions about how to handle juvenile cases. Officers should obviously employ department guidelines in their decisions, which generally include some or all of the following considerations:

- Public safety
- The nature of the alleged offense and the role that the juvenile played in that offense
- The age of the involved juvenile
- Any past history of police involvement or arrest
- Whether the juvenile has a gang affiliation
- The juvenile's relationship with family, school, and community
- The attitude of both the alleged offender and his/her parents toward the offense and toward any referral for treatment or rehabilitation
- Availability of community-based programming for the youth
- The likelihood that any alternative referrals will prevent further delinquent behavior
- The impact that police discretion will have on the victim

- Any recommendations from other professionals or agencies in contact with the alleged offender

Officers should never use any of the following factors to influence their decision about whether to proceed formally or informally with a juvenile offender:

- Race or ethnicity of the youth and his/her family
- Sex, sexual preference, or gender identity of the youth and his/her family
- Economic status of youth and his/her family

In any case, no matter what its ultimate disposition, officers should fully document any incident involving a juvenile. A full incident report, including the actions of both the juvenile and the officer, should be filed; all demographic information related to the juvenile should be included.

CRITICAL THINKING

What are some of the implications of using discretion in dealing with juveniles for the offender, the officer, and the victim of the crime?

Source: Connecticut Juvenile Justice Advisory Committee, "Children, Youth and the Police: Recommended Policies and Procedures, 2011." State of Connecticut Office of Policy and Management. Online. Available at http://www.ct.gov/opm/cwp/view.asp?q=383636. Retrieved May 7, 2013.

world, intentionally or not, in terms of those who violate the law and those who do not. Officers in departments with more peacekeeping or service styles are more likely to take a broader view of their roles. This is especially true in departments embracing an SOP philosophy.

Although discretion, departmental style, and policy are important, police officers also consider other factors while making decisions about how to handle juveniles. Focus on Policies: Police Discretion explores some common variables that come into play when the police deal with delinquent juveniles, and variables that should not be considered at all. There is also another important variable that has been researched in the past: the youth's appearance and demeanor.[8] Youths who are neatly dressed have a lesser chance of being stopped, questioned, or arrested by police. How a youth talks to the police and the mannerisms and attitudes he or she demonstrates to the police are also determining factors in how the youth will be treated.

Despite policies, statutes, and other checks, abuse of discretion can occur. On occasion, youths are detained without sufficient reason by police. The characteristics of the youths who are most likely to be targeted for increased police attention include minorities, suspicious behavior, living or loitering in high-crime areas, dressing sloppily or in a gang fashion, and any indication of disrespect for the officer.

Thus, while there are many factors that play a large role in how officers handle juveniles—law, policy, departmental style, dress, and behavior of the youth—the attitudes or perceptions of officers toward juveniles play a part in police discretion.

An inherent tension often exists between police agencies and other agencies that deal with juveniles. If a police agency adopts a more legalistic attitude toward juvenile matters, officers may find themselves disagreeing with the juvenile court or the juvenile department in the area. Juvenile departments are typically county-based and deal with several law enforcement agencies. A legalistic department tends to look at behavior by juveniles as either being a law violation or not, while most juvenile departments tend to view things in terms of what is best for the child. Juvenile departments must deal with a wide range of issues relevant to delinquency including placement, bed space, funds, and parents. A police officer may very well arrest a juvenile for a serious crime only to see that juvenile back in the community within hours. On occasion, the **intake officer** at a detention facility may refuse to admit a juvenile. This could be due to a lack of bed space or some other factor. Nevertheless, it is frustrating to police officers to keep detaining the same juveniles and see them being released. As a result, a natural tension between the police and other juvenile justice agencies is bound to exist. Police agencies with an open, service-oriented style are more likely to agree with the idea that all the agencies should be working toward what is best for the child and the community as a whole.

intake officer The person at a detention facility responsible for processing a juvenile into the facility. They often have the authority to refuse to take a juvenile into custody.

CAREERS IN JUVENILE JUSTICE

Juvenile and School Resource Officers

Many police departments have separate juvenile divisions or specific officers assigned to deal with juvenile offenders. Many departments also have school resource officers whose job is to deal with schools in the department's jurisdiction. In addition, in several states, school districts operate separate police departments that deal exclusively with the schools and crimes committed on school property. In Texas, for example, the largest school districts (Houston, Dallas) have separate police departments that deal with security and crime on school campuses. They are stand-alone police departments complete with a chief, rank structure, sworn police officers, and investigative capabilities. They file cases with the district attorney just like municipal police departments and have exclusive jurisdiction over crimes committed on school campuses.

A career as a juvenile officer or school resource officer begins with being hired into a police agency. This hiring process varies depending on the department and is guided by civil service requirements. Officers transfer into the juvenile division or are designated as the juvenile officer in much the same way as they are assigned to the property crimes division or are promoted to detective. A juvenile officer is a specialist who understands the different laws and procedures governing juveniles. In addition, the scope of an officer's responsibilities increase dramatically once he or she becomes a juvenile or school resource officer. Unlike a typical police officer, the juvenile or school resource officer deals with a large number of people who are involved in the lives of the juveniles they serve. The officer must deal with parents, teachers, counselors, and others who are responsible for the care and education of the juvenile. With the advent of community-oriented policing, the officer's responsibilities have grown even further. The role of the juvenile or school resource officer focuses more on prevention and education than it did in the past. These officers make multiple community contacts and conduct training and presentations all over their community. In short, the juvenile officer is expected to coordinate the various criminal and juvenile justice agencies that deal with children in their community in addition to their order maintenance and law enforcement responsibilities.

Critical Thinking

What do you think of the Texas model of specialized policing devoted to school districts?

POLICE ATTITUDES TOWARD JUVENILES

Some police officers view juvenile matters with disdain. For some officers, dealing with juveniles might seem pointless because their local juvenile justice system does little or nothing with most juvenile offenders, especially minor and status offenders.[9] Research indicates that many police officers now spend less time with juveniles and delinquency prevention to focus more time on serious crimes or answering calls for service. To some police officers, dealing with juveniles is a hassle because of a great deal of paperwork, increased time in processing, detention center problems, and various other procedures unique to juvenile cases. They view juvenile problems such as runaway, truancy, and curfew as low-priority crimes.[10] However, if these minor problems are ignored, they tend to lead to bigger problems with the juvenile and the community. The potential for the eventual occurrence of big problems is even greater when low-priority crimes are gang-related.

Officers in police departments where juvenile units exist tend to take a "that's their problem" approach, referring to the juvenile unit's responsibilities. In cases that involve juveniles, some police officers either ignore or abandon the problem, using the justification that such matters are handled by the juvenile division.

Sometimes, a police officer takes a juvenile into custody and transports him or her to a detention facility only to have the intake officer at the detention facility refuse to admit the juvenile. Intake officers have broad discretion to admit or refuse juveniles into their facilities. This level of discretion varies across the nation based on local practices and state law, and it may indeed be against the law for a detention facility to accept a juvenile in some locations. The decision to hold a juvenile is often based on the seriousness of the crime; however, available bed space is also a common factor. Some police officers have complained about situations where they have taken a juvenile into custody for a serious property crime such as auto theft only to have the detention facility intake officer tell them to take the juvenile home. This attitude is not universal in policing, however, and a substantial portion of officers are very committed to juveniles and related matters.

Many officers view juvenile issues as fundamental to crime prevention. Seeking to intervene before a problem is created, these officers often participate in youth programs offered by the police such as police athletic leagues (PAL), D.A.R.E., G.R.E.A.T., and various other programs involving youths. They often volunteer their free time and spend a great deal of energy on activities for juveniles and juvenile issues, sometimes with little support from their departments or colleagues. All police officers, whatever their attitude about other juvenile issues in general, view juvenile victimization as a problem, especially in cases of child abuse and child sexual abuse. Police officers, like most people, are very intolerant of people who victimize children.

Myth	Fact
The police are required to make an arrest when a juvenile commits a crime or other delinquent act.	Many times, juveniles are not referred to juvenile court. Police officers typically do a station adjustment, which involves lecturing the juvenile at the station. Records are not kept in station adjustments, so it is difficult to measure their exact frequency.

Once a juvenile is processed at a police station, the juvenile is taken to a detention facility where they will be held until a detention hearing in juvenile court. Detention facilities are for juveniles awaiting adjudication. *What factors should go into the decision to keep a juvenile in detention until adjudication?*

In sum, police officers tend to have a kind of love/hate relationship with juveniles. When juveniles are victimized, police officers take the situation *very* seriously. However, when juveniles are the offenders or creating problems in the community, officers tend to be divided in their views about the best way to handle the situation.

JUVENILES' ATTITUDES TOWARD POLICE

This love/hate relationship is also a good way to describe how juveniles view the police. When juveniles are the victims, especially young children, the police are often their saviors and the only role model the juveniles have. When juveniles are the offenders or creating problems, they tend to view police as harassing them or creating problems in their lives.

Several factors influence a juvenile's perception of the police including race, income, and where they live. Juveniles who live in urban areas tend to have a more negative view of the police than those in suburban or rural areas. Police departments in recent years have initiated a variety of programs to change their image in the eyes of the public, and reach out to juveniles.

7.3 SELF-CHECK

1. What are the responsibilities of juvenile departments?
2. What role do intake officers play when a juvenile is taken into custody?

Police-Based Programs for Juveniles

Two of the most prominent police-based programs targeting juveniles are the **D.A.R.E. program** and the **G.R.E.A.T. program**. Both of these programs bring officers together with juveniles in school settings. (The evaluation of G.R.E.A.T. is covered in Chapter 13 on gangs.) Taken together, these programs account for a large amount of resources expended by both the federal government and local law enforcement agencies. They have recently come under increased scrutiny with evaluation research showing the limited effect of these programs, especially for the D.A.R.E. program. Despite the negative results of this particular research, many police agencies sponsor a wide variety of community programs designed to address juvenile problems.

D.A.R.E. AND OTHER SCHOOL-BASED PROGRAMS

Proponents argue that D.A.R.E. not only warns young people about the use of illicit drugs, it also improves youths' self-esteem and decision-making skills. D.A.R.E. also has the added benefit of allowing police officers to interact with students in a positive environment. Mutual trust, increased communication, and support for healthy families and positive peer groups have been noted as the benefits associated with D.A.R.E. In some communities and for many departments, the program is touted as an example of effective community policing efforts, a police strategy designed to bring traditionally isolated segments of the community (e.g., homeless people, minorities, youth) and police closer together. Recently, this strategy has also come under controversy as calls for measurable effectiveness are raised and federal monies disappear.[11]

The first significant studies showing problems with D.A.R.E. began to appear in 1994 when the Bureau of Justice Assistance commissioned an evaluation of the program. Upon completion of the project, the Justice Department refused to publish the report, which found that D.A.R.E. was less effective in every

D.A.R.E. A controversial school-based program designed to encourage youths to avoid drugs.

G.R.E.A.T. A police program in which officers go to schools to educate youths on the dangers of gangs.

FOCUS ON PROGRAMS

DRUG ABUSE RESISTANCE EDUCATION (D.A.R.E.)

Description: Officer-led, in-classroom antidrug program for school children around the world.

Founded: September 1983

Headquarters: Los Angeles, California

Development: D.A.R.E. originated as a cooperative effort of the Los Angeles Police Department (LAPD) and the Los Angeles Unified School District (LAUSD).

Mission: D.A.R.E.'s primary mission is to provide children with the information and skills they need to live drug-and-violence-free lives. Additionally, it establishes positive relationships between students and law enforcement, teachers, parents, and other community leaders.

Curriculum: D.A.R.E.'s innovative and highly effective curriculum was developed by LAUSD health education specialists. Police officers receive 80 hours of special training to be equipped with all the tools they need to teach a course in drug resistance and violence avoidance techniques.

D.A.R.E. Lessons Focus: providing accurate information about alcohol and drugs, teaching students decision-making skills and showing them how to resist peer pressure by giving them ideas for alternatives to drug use.

Grade Levels Reached: Originally designed for elementary school students, D.A.R.E. has been expanded to reach students in kindergarten through 12th grade.

D.A.R.E. + PLUS: After school, on-campus program that offers middle and high school students safe, enjoyable, educational alternatives to the local streets.

Participating States and Countries: All 50 states, U.S. Department of Defense Schools worldwide, and 44 countries around the world.

Trained Officers: About 40,000

More information about D.A.R.E., including course curriculum, can be found at the D.A.R.E. website www.dare.com.

CRITICAL THINKING

Do you think there might be some downfalls to the D.A.R.E. program? Explain.

---

category at discouraging drug abuse than other more "interactive" teaching methodologies.[12] Other studies were less compelling concerning the effectiveness of D.A.R.E. Then, in 1998, authors D. P. Rosenbaum and G. Ganson concluded a six-year, multi-level analysis of the attitudes, beliefs, social skills, and drug use behaviors of students in urban, suburban, and rural schools to measure the long-term effects of the Drug Abuse Resistance Education program. They concluded that D.A.R.E. had no long-term effects on a wide range of drug use measures. Refer to Focus on Programs.

American society believes that drug education is the best way to reduce the use of illegal drugs by youth. The public continues to believe that antidrug education in schools is more effective than increased funding for police to interdict and prosecute drug users and dealers. There is promise for drug education as an effective prevention technique; however, to be effective, future drug education programs must conform to proven teaching and pedagogical methodologies as well as be research-based. This means that future drug education programs must be continuous throughout all age and school levels, consistent in message and content, honest in presentation material, interactive with students, continually evaluated for improvement, and, most important, developed on strong research findings relating to the drug subculture. In short, the role of the police in this process is still being debated and refined.

Some police programs focus on order maintenance, such as *midnight basketball*, while others are more service-oriented. A service-oriented program that attempts to occupy a juvenile's time is a **police athletic league (PAL)**. PAL programs offer recreation and sports activities to at-risk youths. Officers serve as

police athletic leagues (PAL) A police program focusing on recreation and sports designed to reduce delinquency and increase youth's commitments to legitimate activities.

SUMMARY BY CHAPTER OBJECTIVES

1. Explain the role of police through the history of juvenile justice

Prior to the existence of the juvenile justice system, juveniles were treated like any other criminals by police officers. Following the founding of the juvenile justice system in the early 1900s, police matrons generally assumed responsibility for handling juvenile matters. Many police departments established separate divisions to handle juveniles and designated certain officers to deal with juvenile offenders. Today the role of the police in the juvenile justice system is that of "gatekeeper"; the police are usually the initial point of contact between the system and the juvenile.

2. Describe the various police styles

The three styles of law enforcement presented by James Q. Wilson distinguish among the different methods police use to deal with juvenile crime and juvenile criminals. A more legalistic department sees juvenile offenders as not being very different from their adult offenders. Officers in a legalistic department would generally not want to intervene with juveniles unless they violated a law of some type. Once a law is broken, juveniles are treated like any other criminal except that they are taken to a detention facility instead of a jail. In a watchman-style department, juveniles are viewed as being just another threat to public order. Juveniles are treated in a more parent-child manner and are typically handled informally by police officers. Juvenile order-breakers may be told to leave the area, go home, or to keep quiet. The criminal law is invoked only when a juvenile crosses the line and becomes unruly toward an officer or violates a serious law. Finally, in a service-oriented police department, the juveniles are a problem only when they are unoccupied or unsupervised. Therefore, it is more important that the police use the criminal law only as a last resort. Police are preventing juvenile crime by providing youth with role models and activities to keep them out of trouble.

3. Explain how the police process juvenile cases

Juveniles, once detained by police, are subject to different laws and procedures than adults are. Depending on state law, the juvenile's parents or attorney might have to be present prior to any police questioning. State law also restricts the ability of the police to fingerprint or photograph juveniles in some cases. In addition, federal law requires that juveniles be "sight and sound separated" from adult offenders while in police custody. Juveniles are taken to different facilities for processing and are subject to different detention procedures. The steps in the processing of juveniles are similar to those for adults; however, there are typically many more safeguards and requirements present for juveniles.

4. Describe the role of police in handling status offenders and abused or neglected children

The police, in addition to their criminal law responsibilities, are also charged with the authority to remove from the home or restrict the freedom of children who are status offenders or who need protection. Juvenile status offenders include runaways, curfew violators, and truants. The police take these children into custody for their own protection rather than for the protection of society. In addition, officers are directed by law to protect children from abuse and neglect at the hands of their parents or anyone else. In these cases, the police act as a parent to the juveniles rather than police officers.

5. Explain the discretionary options a police officer can exercise in juvenile cases

Discretion plays a large part in the way police officers do their jobs, and the level of discretion by police in juvenile matters is even greater. Police officers are more likely to use discretion in handling juveniles than any other person they come into contact with. The range of discretionary options a police officer can use when dealing with a juvenile is typically not exercised with other offenders. Such options include releasing the juvenile to his or her parents or guardian, taking the juvenile into protective custody for both delinquent and nondelinquent behavior, and a variety of field and station adjustments.

6. List factors that influence police decisions in juvenile cases

Many factors determine how a juvenile will be processed by the police, including the demeanor, age, and maturity of the juvenile, his or her home situation, the type of crime committed, and the policing style of the department (see Figure 7.2). The police officer weighs these factors when making decisions about how to handle a juvenile offender.

7. Compare police attitudes about juveniles with juveniles' attitudes about police

The attitude that police and juveniles have toward each other is best characterized as a love/hate relationship. Police officers typically cite juvenile issues as their main "headaches." Juveniles sometime complain that officers harass them in public. However, these feelings are often tempered by the parental quality of most police officer interactions with juveniles.

8. Identify some intervention programs operated by police agencies

Police agencies operate a wide variety of programs for juveniles in their communities. These programs are aimed at delinquency prevention, education, or occupying a juvenile's free time. Some of the more prominent programs include D.A.R.E., G.R.E.A.T., police athletic leagues, and police explorer posts.

9. Explain how community-oriented policing affects juvenile cases

Community-oriented policing (COP) broadens the police mission concerning juveniles. The goal of COP is to form a co-active bond between the police and the community. To strengthen this bond, many police departments are increasing the programs that they offer for juveniles. In addition, they are looking for more creative ways to deal with juvenile issues in their communities beyond traditional criminal law interventions.

KEY TERMS

index felonies, p. 176
traditional or political period, p. 179
professional period, p. 179
community-oriented policing (COP), p. 183
problem-oriented policing (POP), p. 184

confidentiality laws, p. 184
sight and sound separated, p. 185
per se attorney laws, p. 185
custody, p. 185
curfew, p. 185
truancy, p. 185

model policies, p. 185
protective custody, p. 187
discretion, p. 187
standard operating procedure (SOP) manual, p. 188
intake officer, p. 190
D.A.R.E. program, p. 192

G.R.E.A.T. program, p. 192
police athletic leagues (PAL), p. 193
police explorer posts, p. 194
police cadet programs, p. 194

REVIEW QUESTIONS

1. How has the police role in dealing with juveniles changed over the history of the juvenile justice system?

2. Why were women police officers viewed as better able to deal with juvenile offenders?

3. What are the three periods of law enforcement, and how did these periods affect the police administration of juvenile matters?

4. What are the three styles of policing? How does each style view the role of the police in juvenile matters?

5. What do each of the three styles of policing hold about how juveniles should be treated?

6. What role do the police play in the juvenile justice system?

7. How is the process of handling juvenile offenders different from the process used with adults?

8. What are the discretionary options a police officer has in dealing with a juvenile?

9. What factors are involved in a police officer's decision on how to deal with a juvenile offender?

10. What are the various reasons for which a police officer may take a juvenile into custody?

11. What are the attitudes of police officers toward juveniles? What are the attitudes of juveniles toward police?

12. What are some of the police-based programs available for juveniles?

13. How has community-oriented policing affected the relationship between police and juveniles?

HANDS-ON ACTIVITIES

1. Visit your local high school or middle school and meet with the school resource officer assigned to the school. What tasks does this person perform and how are they different from those of regular police officers?

2. Learning from police officers. Contact the juvenile or school resource officer at a local police department. If possible, ride along with the officer during a shift. If it is not possible to ride along, interview the officer and inquire about his or her job. What differences do you see between the tasks a juvenile officer performs and those performed by a typical police officer?

INTERNET ACTIVITIES

1. Visit the Dallas, Texas, PAL website at http://dallaspal.com/dallaspal/youthprog.htm and read about the different programs that are offered for youth. How are each of these aimed at reducing juvenile delinquency?

2. Visit the national D.A.R.E. website at http://www.dare.com. Do you think the D.A.R.E. program is an effective use of resources for police departments? Why or why not? Where does the D.A.R.E. program fit in with the theoretical framework developed by James Q. Wilson?

CRITICAL THINKING EXERCISES

1. **Decide How to Process a Case** You are a police officer responding to a disturbance call. Upon arriving at the scene, you discover that two adolescents are restraining a younger child. The two adolescents inform you that the younger child was caught stealing a toy from a neighbor's backyard, and they held him till you arrived. The child is 8 years old and has not had any prior contact with the juvenile justice system or your police agency. The neighbor from whom the child took the toy is not at home. The two adolescents state that they want you to arrest the boy because he is a problem in their neighborhood. The boy is crying and pleading with you not to arrest him and that he will never do it again. The boy lives about two blocks away from where the incident occurred and states that his parents are home.

   a. What would you do in this case?

   b. Which of the discretionary options discussed in this chapter would you likely follow?

   c. What factors would you base your decision on?

   d. Is it possible to satisfy everyone involved in this case?

2. **Take Action within Your Police Department** You have just taken over as commander of the juvenile unit of your police department. The chief tells you that the department needs to improve its image in the eyes of the public concerning juvenile matters. In the past, the department has been accused of harassing juveniles in the community and being too aggressive with juveniles. The officers in your department generally take a legalistic- or watchman-style approach to dealing with juveniles. The chief would like you to develop a plan to improve the image of the department as well as expand the services the department currently provides for juveniles.

   a. What steps would you take in this case? What types of programs or policies would you adopt?

   b. What philosophy or style would you urge the department to adopt to achieve the chief's wishes?

3. **Find Alternatives to Juvenile Detention** You have just arrested a 12-year-old youth for auto theft. After processing the juvenile at the police station, you transport the juvenile to the county detention facility. The intake officer at the detention facility informs you that they are currently full to capacity and are admitting only violent offenders. Upon hearing the conversation with the detention officer, the youth looks at you and smirks, indicating his pleasure at not being locked up that evening.

   a. What would you do in this case?

   b. How would you try to get the message through to the juvenile that the charges he is facing are serious?

   c. What alternative steps or placements might you try at this point to handle the juvenile?

7.1 Self-Check

Why are police considered the gatekeepers of the juvenile justice system?

Because they are given the ability to use discretion; that is, to make decisions about whether to take a juvenile into custody and, if necessary, process him or her further into the system. There are many options available to police, and they essentially determine whether or not a juvenile enters the system.

7.2 Self-Check

How do police typically respond to status offenders?

This depends on whether the policing style in use is legalistic, watchman, or service-oriented. Legalistic police may crack down on status offenders, especially repeat status offenders, by taking them into custody and possibly even referring them to juvenile court. The typical watchman response is to stop the status offense, warn the juvenile, and send him or her home, without taking further action. The service-oriented police officer will probably try initiating a conversation with the juvenile to explain why the offense is wrong, in a way that will appeal to the juvenile's best interests (e.g., "Smoking will stunt your growth and give you cancer," "Missing school will make it harder for you to reach your goals in life"). The service-oriented officer may be more likely than the watchman-style one to take juveniles into custody, but would probably refer them into a diversionary program that could help them give up delinquent behavior.

7.3 Self-Check

1. What are the responsibilities of juvenile units in police departments?

They employ officers who, in effect, become juvenile justice specialists; this equips them to deal more effectively not only with juvenile offenders, but also with the special procedures, court system, and placement options that are unique to the juvenile justice system. They also understand the unique demands and procedures of the juvenile justice system.

2. What role do intake officers play when a juvenile is taken into custody?

Intake officers are the people at detention facilities who decide whether to admit the juvenile into the facility; they are responsible for processing the juvenile into the facility. They can refuse to take the juvenile into custody, which sometimes places them in conflict with police officers who would like a particular juvenile to be detained.

7.4 Self-Check

Describe the PAL program.

Police athletic leagues (PAL) have been in use since the 1930s. In this program, police provide positive influences for children by playing sports with them and forming bonds of friendship and trust.

7.5 Self-Check

What are the peak hours for juvenile crime?

Recent research has indicated that the peak hours that juveniles commit crime are between 2 P.M. and 8 P.M. About 20 percent of violent juvenile crime occurs in just the four-hour period between 3 P.M. and 7 P.M. on school days. The biggest spike is between 2 P.M. and 3 P.M. and then the numbers decline steadily until the next day. In other words, the peak level is around the time that school is finished, and continues through the dinner hour. This is why many people feel that after-school programs would be the best remedy for juvenile delinquency.

JUVENILE LAW AND PROCEDURE

Chapter Outline

Chapter Objectives

After completing this chapter, you should be able to:

1. List the changes in rights and procedures since the due process revolution.

2. Describe four landmark Supreme Court cases on juvenile justice.

3. Explain what totality of circumstances means.

4. List situations where a juvenile is entitled to an attorney.

5. Describe the different ways police are allowed to handle juveniles.

6. Define confidentiality and anonymity.

7. Explain current legal issues in juvenile justice.

8. Compare rights and procedures in an adult criminal trial with rights and procedures in juvenile proceedings.

The Development of Juvenile Law and Procedures

The juvenile justice system is much more decentralized than the adult criminal justice system. Unlike most of the criminal justice system, the juvenile justice system is not constitutionally guaranteed. There is absolutely no mention of a separate system of justice for juveniles in the U.S. Constitution. States are free to create, abolish, or alter the juvenile justice system at their will. As a result, much of the juvenile law in the United States varies from state to state, county to county, and even city to city. Several chapters in this book discuss or review juvenile law and procedure. However, there are some universal laws and procedures that guide the operation of the juvenile justice system that are presented here. This chapter consolidates law and procedure in juvenile justice in order to present these topics together to aid in a conceptual understanding of the legal operation of the system.

Compared to the criminal justice system, the juvenile justice system has received little specific attention from the U.S. Supreme Court—relatively few juvenile court cases have been heard before the Court. The Supreme Court essentially adopted a **hands-off approach** to juvenile justice for most of the system's existence, except during the **due process revolution** of the 1960s. At that time, the U.S. Supreme Court created additional protections for individuals, which greatly affected the operations of the juvenile justice system. Before these Court rulings, juveniles who came under the jurisdiction of the juvenile court were denied most of the basic rights and due process available in the criminal courts because it was presumed that the fundamental purpose of the juvenile court was to be different from that of the criminal court.

Prior to the 1960s, juvenile justice operated under the **medical model**, and the goal of a juvenile proceeding was to "cure" a wayward juvenile. Thus, there was a more **civil nature of juvenile proceedings**, and as a result, the court was less formalized procedurally than the adult criminal court. This relaxed procedural atmosphere was thought to be a necessity to allow the court flexibility to deal with individual juveniles and tailor a treatment program to fit each juvenile's needs. This flexibility was questioned by many juvenile justice experts as it became clear that abuses were occurring with regularity in the juvenile system.

Several landmark U.S. Supreme Court juvenile justice cases fundamentally transformed the traditional juvenile justice system and instituted a variety of **procedural** and **substantive rights** into juvenile justice. Today, these landmark cases still serve as the foundation of juvenile justice procedure and law. Even so, much of the existing juvenile law differs from the criminal law in a variety of ways. As you will see, the juvenile justice system differs from the criminal justice system in terminology, purpose, law, and procedure.

There are relatively few "always" or "never" statements that can be made about juvenile law and procedure. There are some minimum standards and procedural rights that are available to juveniles as the result of U.S. Supreme Court cases and federal law. However, states are free to add to or alter these rights and procedures as long as they conform to the federal case law. In recent years, the fundamental purpose of the juvenile justice system has been altered in several states.[1] The move to a more punitive and accountability-based juvenile justice system has facilitated the rewriting of juvenile law in several states. It is not practical to review all relevant state law pertaining to juveniles in this chapter; the focus will be on the landmark cases in juvenile justice where the U.S. Supreme Court mandated that certain minimal procedural rights be afforded to juveniles. In addition, several other issues in juvenile law are reviewed, and examples of state statutes are given where applicable.

hands-off approach The idea that day-to-day operations of the juvenile justice system should be left up to the professionals working in the system without court review or intervention.

due process revolution Period of time during the 1960s and early 1970s when the U.S. Supreme Court made several rulings that created or applied additional due process protections to juvenile justice.

medical model The basic philosophy behind the creation of the juvenile court. The court was more of a hospital where juveniles went to be cured of their illness.

civil nature of juvenile proceedings The juvenile court was operated and proceeded similarly to a civil court rather than a criminal court.

procedural rights Rights that govern the process by which a hearing or court action will proceed.

substantive rights Rights that protect an individual against arbitrary and unreasonable action.

8.1 SELF-CHECK

What roles have the courts played in the administration of juvenile justice in the United States?

Early Juvenile Law

The freedom of the juvenile court to intervene in the lives of children and family was rooted in two doctrines: *parens patriae* and *in loco parentis*. As described in Chapter 2, *parens patriae* translates as "parent of the country" and *in loco parentis* translates to "in place of the parents." These principles led to the belief that when children came into contact with the juvenile justice system, they were not being charged with a crime. The juvenile justice system served as a parent and intervened for the best interest of the child. Because intervention was assumed to be benign, nonadversarial, and a good thing for the child, no formalized due process was instituted or required in juvenile proceedings. Courts recognized *parens patriae* as a legitimate governmental philosophy and state interest.[2] Children were not viewed as persons in their own right by the legal system; instead, they were considered similar to property. Court intervention in the lives of children was viewed as child saving and not child sanctioning. As noted in several court opinions and writings of early American jurisprudence, a child did not have the right to liberty, but to custody.

After World War II, some legal philosophers and juvenile justice specialists began to question the supposed benevolence of the juvenile court. The challenge arose because a majority of the juvenile offenders were not being saved but, instead, continued their antisocial behavior despite guidance from fatherly judges. Although the juvenile courts proclaimed salvation, scrutiny of actual performance showed that, in practice, the courts were punishing juvenile offenders rather than treating them. Juveniles were subject to long terms of confinement without any due process or formalized rights. Prior to landmark decisions by the U.S. Supreme Court in juvenile justice, juveniles were

- arrested without warrant or cause
- interrogated by police at length without parental notification or legal counsel
- not advised of any rights
- incarcerated for lengthy periods at the whim of a juvenile court judge

In the 65 years following the creation of the first juvenile court in 1899, the U.S. Supreme Court did not hear a single case regarding the juvenile justice system. Then within a span of seven years during the due process revolution, the U.S. Supreme Court established new parameters and procedures that still govern juvenile justice today.

Myth / Fact

Myth: Juveniles are entitled to the same full due process rights as adults when facing criminal charges.

Fact: The U.S. Supreme Court has repeatedly stopped short of granting juveniles all of the rights adult criminal defendants have. Instead, the Court has come down with a series of decisions that define which rights juveniles who face criminal charges do have and which they do not have.

8.2 SELF-CHECK

How were juveniles treated by the legal system prior to the due process revolution?

Landmark U.S. Supreme Court Cases in Juvenile Justice

During the 1960s, the U.S. Supreme Court subjected the American juvenile justice system to substantial scrutiny. Four landmark U.S. Supreme Court decisions mandated fundamental due process in juvenile justice. Some states already had such measures in their systems; however, these four cases made due process mandatory across the country. Each case outlined what form the process would take as well as what rights juveniles accused of a crime would be afforded. Each case clarified the process and rights of juveniles; the procedure of the juvenile justice system was fundamentally altered nationwide.

KENT v. UNITED STATES[3]

The case of **Kent v. United States** was the first landmark U.S. Supreme Court case regarding juvenile justice. A 14-year-old when he first came into contact with the juvenile court of the District of Columbia in 1959, Morris A. Kent, Jr. was charged with several burglaries and robberies and as a result was placed on probation. At age 16 and still on probation for his earlier offenses, Kent was again arrested and charged with burglary, robbery, and rape. This time, the juvenile court decided that Kent should be waived to adult court for criminal proceedings (see Chapter 10 for a complete explanation of waiver to adult court). In reaching the decision to waive Kent, the juvenile court did not hold a hearing; did not confer or consult with Kent, his parents, or his lawyer; did not publish any findings or statements of fact; and did not give a reason for the waiver. The juvenile court simply entered an order waiving Kent to adult court. Kent was convicted in criminal court on six counts and was sentenced to serve 5 to 15 years on each count for which he was found guilty, for a total of 30 to 90 years in prison.

In the *Kent* v. *United States* case, the U.S. Supreme Court considered whether a juvenile was entitled to due process in the juvenile system. The Court examined the waiver provisions of the District of Columbia Juvenile Court Act in reaching its decision. The Act explicitly stated the circumstances in which juveniles could be waived to adult court and required that a full investigation be conducted prior to waiver. However, the Act did not state any elements that must be considered in making the decision to waive.[4]

The U.S. Supreme Court decided that the District of Columbia Juvenile Court Act entitled Kent to certain fundamental due process rights. The Court stated that juveniles could not simply be waived to adult court because a juvenile court wants to or as a matter of routine. The court ruling required a judgment in each case based on an inquiry not only into the facts of the alleged offense, but also into whether the *parens patriae* plan of procedure was desirable and proper in each particular case. The Court stated:

> It is inconceivable that a court of justice dealing with adults. . . would proceed in this manner. It would be extraordinary if society's special concern for children. . . permitted this procedure. . . The Juvenile Court is theoretically engaged in determining the needs of the child and of society rather than adjudicating criminal conduct. The objectives are to provide measures of guidance and rehabilitation for the child and protection for society, not to fix criminal responsibility, guilt and punishment. The State is *parens patriae* rather than prosecuting attorney and judge, but the admonition to function in a parental relationship is not an invitation to procedural arbitrariness.[5]

The Court concluded that juvenile justice was seeking to serve a noble purpose, but it noted that many juvenile courts lacked the personnel, facilities, and techniques to perform adequately in a *parens patriae* capacity. In a famous quote, the Court held:

> there is evidence, in fact, that there may be grounds for concern that the child receives the worst of both worlds: that he gets neither the protections accorded to adults nor the solicitous care and regenerative treatment postulated for children.[6]

Kent v. *United States* First U.S. Supreme Court case in which it was ruled that juveniles facing waiver to adult court are entitled to some basic due process rights.

The U.S. Supreme Court's ruling stopped short of requiring due process in all juvenile proceedings. The rights given in *Kent* were applicable only in waiver proceedings; as a result, the *Kent* decision was limited in scope. Nonetheless, the case marked the first time the Court was willing to extend due process rights to juvenile proceedings. Many of the statements made in the decision foreshadowed a much more important case where juveniles were given many of the due process rights that were already required in adult criminal proceedings.

IN RE GAULT[7]

One year after the Kent decision, the case of Gerald Francis Gault would forever alter the nature of the juvenile justice system and create a storm of controversy in the United States. The facts of this 1967 Supreme Court case would no doubt today receive a great deal of media attention because the treatment of Gault in the juvenile system was nothing short of ridiculous. The Focus on Policy box details exactly what happened to Gault in an Arizona juvenile court. The Gault case would firmly establish the concept that *parens patriae* was not an excuse to abuse or neglect the rights of juveniles.

The question for the Supreme Court in the *Gault* case was, "Does a juvenile have due process rights during the adjudication stage of a delinquency proceeding?" The Supreme Court did affirm and extend procedural rights to juveniles in delinquency proceedings. It did not, however, specifically grant juveniles all of the procedural rights given defendants in criminal proceedings. The rights it did grant are:

- Right to reasonable notice of the charges
- Right to counsel as well as appointed counsel if indigent
- Right to confront and cross-examine witnesses
- Right against self-incrimination, including the right to remain silent

The U.S. Supreme Court concluded in **In re Gault** that the original purposes of the juvenile court—that a fatherly judge would look into each situation thoroughly and prescribe a treatment plan to save a juvenile from a life of crime—were not being served. Research showed that juveniles were not being rehabilitated by the juvenile system. As a result, the U.S. Supreme Court decided that the essentials of due process were needed not only to protect juveniles, but to aid in their treatment. While acknowledging that due process requirements would introduce more order, formality, and in some cases aspects of the adversarial system, the Court ruled that the juvenile court could still retain the "kindly juvenile court judge." The justices refused to extend these rights to all stages of juvenile proceedings and also did not extend all of the rights given to adults in criminal cases to juveniles.

One reason the U.S. Supreme Court decided to grant juveniles some due process was that many juvenile court proceedings ended the same as criminal proceedings—that is, incarceration of the offender. The Court stated:

> It is of no constitutional consequence—and of limited practical meaning—that the institution to which he [the child] is committed is called an Industrial School. The fact of the matter is that, however euphemistic the title, a "receiving home" or an "industrial school" for juveniles is an institution of confinement in which the child is incarcerated for a greater or lesser time. His world becomes "a building with whitewashed walls, regimented routine and institutional hours . . . ." Instead of mother, father, sisters, brothers, friends, and classmates, his world is peopled by guards, custodians, state employees, and "delinquents" confined with him for anything from waywardness to rape and homicide.[8]

In essence, the Court reasoned that whatever the terminology and/or stated purpose, when the end result was loss of liberty, due process protections must be followed.[9]

If Gault had been three years older and subject to criminal court jurisdiction, the Court noted that the maximum punishment would have been a fine of $5 to $50, or imprisonment in jail for not more than two months. Under the juvenile

In re Gault U.S. Supreme Court case in which it was ruled that a juvenile in a delinquency proceeding is entitled to the essentials of due process, including right to notice of the charges, right to counsel, right to confront and cross-examine witnesses, and the right to remain silent.

FOCUS ON POLICY

IN RE GAULT

Gerald Francis Gault and a friend were taken into custody by the Sheriff of Gila County, Arizona, on Monday, June 8, 1964. At the time of his arrest, Gault was on probation from being in the company of another boy who had stolen a wallet from a woman's purse. Gault was detained on the basis of a neighbor's verbal complaint about an obscene phone call made to her. No attempt was made to notify Gault's parents of his arrest, and he was taken to the Children's Detention Home. Gault's mother learned of his arrest from the mother of the other boy. She went to the detention facility where she learned that Gault was arrested for making an obscene telephone call and that a hearing would be held in juvenile court at 3 P.M. the following day.

A petition was filed with the juvenile court on the hearing day; however, it was not served on the Gaults. The petition made no reference to any facts of the case or the basis for the judicial action which it initiated. It stated only that "said minor is under the age of eighteen years, and is in need of the protection of this Honorable Court; [and that] said minor is a delinquent minor." On June 9, 1964, Gault, his mother, his older brother, and Probation Officers Flagg and Henderson appeared before the juvenile court judge in his chambers. Gault's father was not there; he was at work out of the city. Mrs. Cook, the complainant, was not there. No one was sworn at this hearing. No transcript or recording was made. No memorandum or record of the substance of the proceedings was prepared. The information concerning the hearing was based entirely on the testimony of the juvenile court judge, Mrs. Gault, and Officer Flagg. During the June 9 hearing, Gault was questioned by the judge about the telephone call. There was conflict as to what he said. His mother recalled that Gault said he only dialed Mrs. Cook's number and handed the telephone to his friend. Officer Flagg recalled that Gault had admitted making the obscene remarks. Judge McGhee testified that Gault had admitted to making one of the obscene statements. At the conclusion of the hearing, the judge said he would "think about it." Gault was taken back to the detention home. On June 11 or 12, after having been detained since June 8, Gault was released and driven home. There is no explanation in the record as to why he was kept in the detention home or why he was released. At 5 P.M. on the day of Gault's release, Mrs. Gault received a note signed by Officer Flagg. Its entire text was as follows:

"Mrs. Gault:

Judge McGhee has set Monday June 15, 1964 at 11:00 A.M. as the date and time for further hearings on Gault's delinquency.

/s/Flagg"

At the appointed time on Monday, June 15, Gault, his father and mother, Gault's friend and his father, and Officers Flagg and Henderson were present before Judge McGhee. No record or transcripts were kept of this hearing either. Mr. and Mrs. Gault later stated that Gault again testified that he had only dialed the number and that the other boy had made the remarks. Officer Flagg agreed that at this hearing Gault did not admit making the obscene remarks. Officer Flagg also testified that Gault had not, when questioned at the detention home, admitted having made any of the obscene statements, but that each boy had sought to put the blame on the other. However, Judge McGhee recalled that "there was some admission again of some of the lewd statements. He didn't admit any of the more serious lewd statements." Judge McGhee also testified that Gault had not denied "certain statements" made to him at the hearing by Officer Henderson. Again, the complainant, Mrs. Cook, was not present. Mrs. Gault asked that Mrs. Cook be present "so she could see

court's jurisdiction, Gault was sentenced to a possible six-year commitment without any due process, without a witness testifying against him, and without the assistance of counsel.

In re Gault is the most important case decided by the U.S. Supreme Court in the area of juvenile justice. This case moved juvenile delinquency adjudications from an informal, almost secret proceeding into a more formalized, consistent process. The case now serves as a foundation for all other significant cases related to the juvenile justice system and juvenile rights. In addition, *Gault* signaled the end of the traditional model of juvenile justice and the beginning of the due process model of juvenile justice.

which boy that done the talking, the dirty talking over the phone." The juvenile judge said "she didn't have to be present at that hearing." The judge did not speak to Mrs. Cook or communicate with her at any time. Probation Officer Flagg had talked to her once over the telephone on June 9.

At this June 15 hearing a "referral report" made by the probation officers was filed with the court, although not disclosed to Gault or his parents. This listed the charge as "lewd phone calls." At the conclusion of the hearing, the judge committed Gault as a juvenile delinquent to the State Industrial School "for the period of his minority [that is, until 21], unless sooner discharged by due process of law." The judge then entered an order that concluded "after a full hearing and due deliberation the Court finds that said minor is a delinquent child, and that said minor is of the age of 15 years."

No appeal was permitted by Arizona law in juvenile cases. On August 3, 1964, a petition for a writ of *habeas corpus* was filed with the Arizona Supreme Court and referred to the Superior Court for hearing. At the *habeas corpus* hearing on August 17, Judge McGhee was vigorously cross-examined concerning the basis for his actions. He testified that he had taken into account the fact that Gault was on probation. Some of the questioning at the appeal centered on the statute under which Gault was convicted.

In substance, Judge McGhee concluded that Gault came within an Arizona statute which specifies that a delinquent child includes one "who has violated a law of the state or an ordinance or regulation of a political subdivision thereof." The law which Gault was found to have violated stated that a person who "in the presence or hearing of any woman or child . . . uses vulgar, abusive or obscene language, is guilty of a misdemeanor . . . ." The penalty specified in the criminal code, which would apply to an adult, is $5 to $50, or imprisonment for not more than two months. The judge also testified that he acted under

Arizona law that stated the definition of a delinquent child as one who is "habitually involved in immoral matters." The section of the Arizona Juvenile Code, which defines a delinquent child, reads:

"Delinquent child includes:

(a) A child who has violated a law of the state or an ordinance or regulation of a political subdivision thereof.

(b) A child who, by reason of being incorrigible, wayward or habitually disobedient, is uncontrolled by his parent, guardian or custodian.

(c) A child who is habitually truant from school or home.

(d) A child who habitually so deports himself as to injure or endanger the morals or health of himself or others."

Asked about the basis for his conclusion that Gault was "habitually involved in immoral matters," the judge testified, somewhat vaguely, that two years earlier, on July 2, 1962, a referral was made concerning Gault, "where the boy had stolen a baseball glove from another boy and lied to the Police Department about it." The judge said there was no hearing, and no accusation relating to this incident, because of lack of material foundation. Yet it seems to have remained in the judge's mind as a relevant factor. The judge also testified that Gault had admitted making other nuisance telephone calls in the past, which, as the judge recalled the boy's testimony, were "silly calls, or funny calls, or something like that."

And what did Gault and his friends actually say in the phone call to Mrs. Cook? "Are your cherries ripe today" and "Do you have big bombers?"

CRITICAL THINKING

Explain how this case shows violations of the rights to notice of charges, to counsel, to confront and cross-examine witnesses, and to remain silent.

IN RE WINSHIP[10]

The *Gault* case instituted four fundamental due process rights to juveniles. However, juvenile proceedings were still assumed by many to be more civil than criminal, more informal than formal. In addition, many of the rights outlined in the U.S. Constitution and applied by the courts to criminal cases had not been specifically applied to juvenile cases. In the years following *Gault*, the U.S. Supreme Court would selectively incorporate portions of the Constitution into juvenile proceedings. One such area is in the standard of proof necessary for conviction. **Proof beyond a reasonable doubt** is the standard in

proof beyond a reasonable doubt The facts and evidence are entirely convincing and satisfy that the person committed the act beyond any reasonable doubt, sometimes equated with 95 percent certainty.

criminal courts for conviction; however, in civil court the standard of proof is a **preponderance of the evidence**. The question, now that juvenile proceedings had to follow some due process, was what level of proof is necessary to adjudicate a child delinquent.

The case of **In re Winship** (1970) presented this exact issue to the U.S. Supreme Court. Winship, age 12, faced a delinquency proceeding in a New York Family Court because he stole money from a woman's purse in a locker. The juvenile court judge found that Winship had engaged in delinquent conduct and committed him to a training school for an initial period of 18 months subject to extensions under New York law. In the case, the juvenile court judge noted that guilt might not have been proven beyond a reasonable doubt in criminal court, but the standard for the juvenile court under New York law was simply a preponderance of the evidence. In the juvenile court judge's view, the case met the lower standard of proof.

With *In re Winship*, the U.S. Supreme Court ruled that when a juvenile is faced with a proceeding where incarceration might result, the standard of proof beyond a reasonable doubt applies. In making this decision, the Court noted that the stakes are substantially higher when a juvenile is charged with an act that would

preponderance of the evidence Evidence which is of greater weight or more convincing than evidence that is offered in opposition to it. Sometimes referred to as more than 50 percent, more than half of the level of certainty.

In re Winship U.S. Supreme Court case that decided the standard of proof in juvenile delinquency proceedings is proof beyond a reasonable doubt.

CAREERS IN JUVENILE JUSTICE

Juvenile Court Attorney

Subsequent to the ruling in the Gault decision, attorneys began to play a much more prominent role in the juvenile justice system. In contrast to the adult criminal justice system, attorneys in the juvenile court adopt a bifurcated role, balancing legal representation and child counseling. Juvenile court attorneys are frequently involved in determining what is best for the child as well as protecting society (the district attorney) and protecting the child's rights (the juvenile defense attorney). Many juvenile attorneys specialize in family law, which in many states governs juvenile justice.

Attorneys in the juvenile court are responsible for the law; however, in practice and in actual court proceedings, the atmosphere is much less formal. The juvenile district attorney is primarily responsible for preparing the case against the juvenile. However, the district attorney works closely with probation to both assess the juvenile and determine what the appropriate disposition is. The juvenile's defense attorney is frequently a party to determining what is best for the child in these proceedings as well. The defense attorney's primary responsibility is protecting the child's rights and informing the child and his or her guardians of the process and proceedings. The juvenile courtroom workgroup (judge, district attorney, defense attorney, and probation officer) work as a team to adjudicate and determine the best disposition. This approach is much more team oriented and cohesive than their counterparts in the adult criminal justice system.

To work as a juvenile attorney you must have an undergraduate college degree, a law degree, and some jurisdictions require a specialty in juvenile or family law. The training for a juvenile attorney is much greater than that of a typical criminal attorney in that not only does the attorney have to know the criminal law, he or she must also know the special laws and procedures that govern juvenile proceedings. In very large jurisdictions, the district attorney's office often has a special section of attorneys that work specifically in juvenile court. The same is true for the public defender's office. In other jurisdictions, there may be one or two attorneys that handle all of the juvenile cases in the juvenile court or an assistant district attorney that has juvenile responsibilities in addition to all of his or her other cases. Juveniles can be represented by the public defender's office or a private attorney of their choice. Although this is a growing area of specialty for attorneys, district attorneys and public defenders will frequently rotate through juvenile court as well as other areas of specialty.

The American Bar Association is home to two organizations that support juvenile court attorneys. Information about juvenile district attorneys and juvenile defense attorneys can be found on the ABA website http://www.americanbar.org/aba.html

Critical Thinking

What do you think is the most difficult task for a juvenile court attorney? Why?

constitute a crime if committed by an adult. In addition, the court concluded that setting the minimum level of proof higher than preponderance of the evidence would not impose any burden on the juvenile court or change the nature of the proceeding, the informality of the proceeding, or the speed of the proceeding. As in the cases cited, the Court did *not* extend this level of proof to all juvenile proceedings, but only to delinquency proceedings where incarceration might be the result. *Winship* was one of the first cases in which the U.S. Supreme Court began to selectively incorporate portions of adult criminal rights into juvenile proceedings. The view among practitioners and juvenile court judges was that it would be only a matter of time before all criminal trial rights would be given to juveniles.

McKEIVER v. PENNSYLVANIA[11]

In 1971, one year after the decision in *Winship*, the U.S. Supreme Court had the opportunity to apply another constitutional right to juvenile proceedings in the case **McKeiver v. Pennsylvania**. In 1968, Joseph McKeiver, age 16, was charged with robbery, larceny, and receiving stolen goods in Philadelphia and adjudicated in juvenile court. Represented by counsel at his delinquency proceeding, McKeiver requested trial by jury. His request for a jury trial was denied, and the judge adjudicated McKeiver a delinquent and placed him on probation. He appealed and his case eventually reached the U.S. Supreme Court. In a stunning reversal to the trend of applying due process protections to juveniles, the U.S. Supreme Court refused to apply the right to a jury trial to juvenile proceedings.

In *McKeiver*, the U.S. Supreme Court outlined four reasons for denying juveniles the right to jury trial:

1. The Court stated that its decisions on juvenile justice thus far had already formalized and protected juveniles enough so that jury trials were unnecessary.
2. The Court noted that jury trials would put an effective end to what has been the idealistic prospect of an informal, protective proceeding. The Court did not want to abandon all of the rehabilitative goals of the juvenile justice system. In its decision, the Court noted that a jury trial brings with it the traditional delay, formality, and clamor of the adversary system.
3. The Court stated that jury trials would not greatly strengthen the fact-finding function of the juvenile court and that nothing prevents juvenile court judges from using juries when they think it necessary.
4. The Court stated that to grant jury trials would end the distinction between the criminal and juvenile systems.[12]

The decision in *McKeiver* clearly showed that the Court was unwilling to create a "junior criminal court" where there would be no distinction in process other than the age of the defendant. Further, they were not ready to eliminate the juvenile justice system entirely. As a result, the rights granted to juveniles would proceed haphazardly on a case-by-case basis with many states adopting rights and procedures that differ from other states.

IMPACT OF THE LANDMARK CASES

The only other U.S. Supreme Court case that applied a fundamental right to juvenile proceedings was the 1975 **Breed v. Jones**[13] case where juveniles were given the right against double jeopardy. In *Breed*, a juvenile, Gary Breed, age 17, was found to be delinquent in a juvenile proceeding and then transferred to criminal court for a criminal proceeding. The U.S. Supreme Court ruled that double jeopardy applied and prevented a juvenile from being tried twice for the same crime. Future U.S. Supreme Court decisions would generally be concerned with issues presented by the rights given by these landmark cases or special circumstances unique to juveniles.

McKeiver v. *Pennsylvania* U.S. Supreme Court case in which it was ruled that juveniles are not entitled to trial by jury in delinquency proceedings.

Breed v. *Jones* Case in which the U.S. Supreme Court ruled that juveniles are protected against double jeopardy by the U.S. Constitution.

In the criminal justice system, the names Miranda, Mapp, and Gideon are remembered because their cases fundamentally altered the way the criminal justice system operated. In the juvenile justice system, the names Gault, Kent, and Winship have a similar impact. Until these decisions, the juvenile justice system was not required to follow any formalized procedure or due process. Juveniles were subjected to long terms of incarceration for minor offenses without any due process protections. At the time, many in the juvenile justice system opposed the U.S. Supreme Court decisions and regarded the changes as effectively abolishing the juvenile justice system. Without doubt, the juvenile justice system was forever changed as a result of these landmark cases.

8.3 SELF-CHECK

1. What specific rights were granted by the Supreme Court to juveniles in the cases of *Kent*, *Gault*, and *Winship*?

2. What right did the U.S. Supreme Court refuse to grant to juveniles in the *McKeiver* decision?

3. Why were the Supreme Court decisions discussed in this section originally opposed by many in the juvenile justice system?

Issues in Juvenile Law

Although the U.S. Supreme Court set parameters for the basic procedure of juvenile justice, many questions and unresolved issues still persist in juvenile law and juvenile rights. These questions have taken on greater importance in recent years as the juvenile justice system has become more punitive. In the past 20 years, many states revised their laws governing juveniles and juvenile justice. The changes reflect new attitudes toward juvenile crime and juveniles who commit violent crimes in particular. Many, if not all, of the changes reflect a desire to "get tough" on juvenile crime or hold juveniles more accountable for their actions. As a result, many scholars and juvenile justice philosophers have begun to question whether juveniles should receive greater rights than adults in proceedings which, in many states, can result in long terms of incarceration.

The full rights given to adults are still not given to juveniles. States generally have greater authority to restrict the rights of children than they do the rights of adults. The decision as to which rights are applicable and which are not is now generally a case-by-case determination, and there are wide discrepancies among the states in the juvenile rights that are granted or restricted.[14] Many states have fundamentally different purposes and philosophies behind their juvenile codes. Figure 8.1 describes differences in purpose between the juvenile justice systems in New Jersey and Texas. The two states have clear differences in their thinking about what to do with juveniles who commit crimes. Many times, these differences manifest themselves in other areas of the law and rights given to juveniles.

The differences in rights given to adults and those given to children are justified primarily because the courts have ruled that states have a more compelling interest in restricting juveniles than they do in restricting adults. Special concerns about children provide the rationale behind many of the restrictions.[15] These restrictions are justifiable in many cases since there is little doubt that children are different from adults. Because their capacities of reason and emotion are not yet fully formed, children are more likely, in certain situations, to make decisions or to take actions that may cause serious damage to the children themselves or others, or may even alter the course of their entire lives.[16]

The U.S. Supreme Court suggested that restrictions of juvenile rights need only serve a "significant state interest . . . not present in the case of an adult."[17] The U.S. Supreme Court has refused to apply a consistent standard that governs all juvenile rights or the restriction of those rights. This unwillingness probably results from the tension caused by the recognition that, while children are persons for constitutional purposes, they are simultaneously the subject of special state concern.[18] As a result, juvenile rights and procedure can be altered by an individual state if that state can show a legitimate interest in regulating these rights. One issue in particular is the varying standards that exist regarding how a juvenile can waive his or her rights.

FIGURE 8.1	Differing Views in Juvenile Justice

The stated goals and philosophy of juvenile justice can vary greatly from state to state. The following two statutes from New Jersey and Texas illustrate the different philosophies operating in juvenile justice today.

NEW JERSEY CODE OF JUVENILE JUSTICE

2A:4A-21. Purposes

2. Purposes. This act shall be construed so as to effectuate the following purposes:

   a. To preserve the unity of the family whenever possible and to provide for the care, protection, and wholesome mental and physical development of juveniles coming within the provisions of this act;

   b. Consistent with the protection of the public interest, to remove from children committing delinquent acts certain statutory consequences of criminal behavior, and to substitute therefore an adequate program of supervision, care and rehabilitation, and a range of sanctions designed to promote accountability and protect the public;

   c. To separate juveniles from the family environment only when necessary for their health, safety or welfare or in the interests of public safety;

   d. To secure for each child coming under the jurisdiction of the court such care, guidance and control, preferably in his own home, as will conduce to the child's welfare and the best interests of the State; and when such child is removed from his own family, to secure for him custody, care and discipline as nearly as possible equivalent to that which should have been given by his parents;

   e. To insure that children under the jurisdiction of the court are wards of the State, subject to the discipline and entitled to the protection of the State, which may intervene to safeguard them from neglect or injury and to enforce the legal obligations due to them and from them.

   f. Consistent with the protection of the public Interest, to insure that any services and sanctions for juveniles provide balanced attention to the protection of the community, the imposition of accountability for offenses committed, fostering interaction and dialogue between the offender, victim, and community, and the development of competencies to enable children to become responsible and productive members of the community.

   g. to insure protection and a safe environment for those sexually exploited juveniles who are charged with prostitution or who are alleged to be victims of human trafficking; and to provide these juveniles with appropriate shelter, care, counseling and crisis intervention services from the time they are taken into custody and for the duration of any legal proceedings.

TEXAS FAMILY CODE TITLE 3. JUVENILE JUSTICE CODE CHAPTER 51. GENERAL PROVISIONS

Sec. 51.01. Purpose and Interpretation.

This title shall be construed to effectuate the following public purposes:

   (1) to provide for the protection of the public and public safety;

   (2) consistent with the protection of the public and public safety:

   (A) to promote the concept of punishment for criminal acts;

   (B) to remove, where appropriate, the taint of criminality from children committing certain unlawful acts; and

   (C) to provide treatment, training, and rehabilitation that emphasizes the accountability and responsibility of both the parent and the child for the child's conduct;

   (3) to provide for the care, the protection, and the wholesome moral, mental, and physical development of children coming within its provisions;

   (4) to protect the welfare of the community and to control the commission of unlawful acts by children;

   (5) to achieve the foregoing purposes in a family environment whenever possible, separating the child from the child's parents only when necessary for the child's welfare or in the interest of public safety and when a child is removed from the child's family, to give the child the care that should be provided by parents; and

   (6) to provide a simple judicial procedure through which the provisions of this title are executed and enforced and in which the parties are assured a fair hearing and their constitutional and other legal rights recognized and enforced.

JUVENILE WAIVER OF RIGHTS

The circumstances under which a juvenile is permitted to waive his or her constitutional rights depends on the state in which the case takes place. The U.S. Supreme Court has decided on a particular case that outlines a test to determine whether or not a juvenile's waiver of rights was knowing and voluntary (the adult standard). However, the Court has not ruled on a ***per se test*** or circumstance under which juveniles can or cannot waive their rights.

FARE V. MICHAEL C.[19] Michael C., a juvenile with a long history of police and court contact, was implicated in a murder in California. Police in Van Nuys, California, who were investigating the murder, arrested him and took him to the police department for questioning. At the time of his arrest, Michael C. was 16 years old and on probation from the juvenile court. On probation for over four years, he had been committed previously to a secure juvenile facility and had a long history of violent and property crime arrests.

Police recorded their questioning of Michael C. The officers were the only persons in the room with Michael C. during the interrogation. Michael C. was fully advised of his right to remain silent and his right to have an attorney present. The following is a court transcript of the conversation that occurred:

Q: Do you understand all of these rights as I have explained them to you?
A: Yeah.
Q: Okay, do you wish to give up your right to remain silent and talk to us about this murder?
A: What murder? I don't know about no murder.
Q: I'll explain to you which one it is if you want to talk to us about it.
A: Yeah, I might talk to you.
Q: Do you want to give up your right to have an attorney present here while we talk about it?
A: Can I have my probation officer here?
Q: Well I can't get a hold of your probation officer right now. You have the right to an attorney.
A: How do I know you guys won't pull no police officer in and tell me he's an attorney?
Q: Huh?
A: How do I know you guys won't pull no police officer in and tell me he's an attorney?
Q: Your probation officer is Mr. Christiansen.
A: Yeah.
Q: Well I'm not going to call Mr. Christiansen tonight. There's a good chance we can talk to him later, but I'm not going to call him right now. If you want to talk to us without an attorney present, you can. If you don't want to, you don't have to. But if you want to say something, you can, and if you don't want to say something you don't have to. That's your right. You understand that right?
A: Yeah.
Q: Okay, will you talk to us without an attorney present?
A: Yeah, I want to talk to you.

Michael C. subsequently made statements and drew sketches that incriminated him in the murder. Largely on the basis of his incriminating statements, his probation was revoked, and he was remanded to the juvenile court for adjudication. Michael C. challenged the validity of his confession, alleging that the statements had been obtained in violation of his rights because his request to see his probation officer amounted to a request to remain silent, just as if he had requested the assistance of an attorney. Michael C.'s probation officer

per se test Something is required in all circumstances regardless of the facts of a case.

Fare v. *Michael C.* Case that established ground rules for determining whether a juvenile has knowingly and voluntarily waived his or her rights.

Judges and attorneys play a pivotal role in the juvenile justice process today. *Do attorneys in the juvenile court detract from the goals of juvenile justice? Why or why not?*

eventually testified that he had indeed instructed Michael C. to inform him if he ever had "a police contact." The juvenile court denied the motion to suppress, the appeals court reversed and suppressed the confession, and the case eventually made its way to the U.S. Supreme Court.

In *Fare* v. *Michael C.*, the U.S. Supreme Court had to decide under what circumstances a juvenile, without consulting a parent, attorney, or other interested adult, can make an intelligent, understanding, and voluntary waiver of his or her rights. The Court applied the **totality of circumstances** approach as the standard applicable to juveniles. The majority held that the determination of the validity of a waiver of rights should not be based on any one characteristic or procedure, but should be based on all of the relevant circumstances of the case. Thus, the determination of whether statements obtained during police interrogation are admissible against a juvenile is based on the totality of the circumstances surrounding the waiver. The Court noted:

> The totality approach permits—indeed, it mandates—inquiry into all the circumstances surrounding the interrogation. This includes evaluation of the juvenile's age, experience, education, background, and intelligence, and into whether he has the capacity to understand the warnings given him, the nature of his Fifth Amendment rights, and the consequences of waiving those rights.[20]

The U.S. Supreme Court then applied this test and determined that Michael C.'s request to see his probation officer was not the same as asking for an attorney. In addition, the Court specifically refused to apply the exclusionary rule or a *per se* attorney appointment rule to juvenile proceedings.[21] The Court concluded that Michael C. had waived his rights under the totality of circumstances and noted that he had repeated contacts with the juvenile system and that his statements clearly indicated he understood his rights.

States are free, however, to impose more stringent requirements on the waiver of juvenile rights than are required by the courts. For example, many

totality of circumstances The test used to determine if a juvenile's waiver of rights was knowing and voluntary.

states require that police make an immediate and reasonable attempt to notify the parents of a juvenile taken into custody within a specified time. Several states require that a parent, an attorney, or other guardian be present during all police interrogations of the juvenile. The courts have had numerous cases in which to apply the totality of circumstances test to decide the validity of a juvenile's waiver of rights; some cases are upheld and some are thrown out.[22]

A number of factors surround the issues of juveniles' waiver of their rights. Research has shown that only a small percentage of juveniles are capable of understanding their rights, let alone being able to knowingly and intelligently waive them.[23] Also, simplifying the explanation of the rights has not had a greater effect on juveniles' understanding.[24] Several other studies debate the mental processes of juveniles, as well as their capacity to understand and competently waive their legal rights.[25] The police attempt to interrogate almost 75 percent of the juveniles referred to courts on felony charges, yet only 10 percent of these juveniles choose not to waive their rights.[26] Thomas Grisso researched the capacity of juveniles to waive their rights,[27] and some of his findings have been incorporated in subsequent judicial decisions.[28] Grisso found that:

1. Juveniles demonstrated less comprehension than adults of the actual **Miranda rights**. Fifty-five percent of the juveniles had an inadequate understanding of the Miranda warnings compared to 23 percent of adults.
2. Juveniles demonstrated less understanding of the words used in Miranda warnings. Sixty-three percent of the juveniles misunderstood at least one crucial word compared to 37 percent of adults.
3. Juveniles, more than adults, misunderstood the right to counsel. Forty-five percent of the juveniles misunderstood the right to counsel compared to 15 percent of the adults.
4. Although most juveniles understood the meaning of the right to remain silent, many did not grasp the comprehensiveness of the right, believing that they could later be punished for exercising the right and be made to tell their criminal activity. Sixty-two percent of the juveniles believed they could be penalized by the judge for silence.

Some research has found that only 9 to 11 percent of the juveniles interrogated refused to waive their rights to avoid potential self-incrimination, as contrasted with a study of adult interrogation in which 40 percent refused to waive their rights.[29] Several studies have found that pre-adolescents are significantly less capable of foreseeing the full consequences of their decisions.

Related to the issue of waiving rights is a juvenile's right to counsel. Effective counsel for juveniles who are charged with a crime becomes more important with likely serious consequences of a delinquency adjudication.

JUVENILE RIGHT TO COUNSEL

A juvenile's right to an attorney in all delinquency proceedings has gathered considerable attention and support.[30] Some believe that the introduction of increased due process protections and lawyers into the juvenile court will take away the informal nature of the court and the court's ability to rehabilitate and treat juveniles and may result in more punitive sanctions.[31] The U.S. Supreme Court in *In re Gault* stated that a juvenile is entitled to an attorney, and if the child could not afford one, one would be appointed.[32]

In several cases following *Gault*, the U.S. Supreme Court further defined the role of an attorney in juvenile justice.[33] The U.S. Supreme Court decided that juveniles are entitled to an attorney only after adversarial proceedings have commenced against them.[34] In many states, less than half of the juveniles accused of delinquency receive the assistance of counsel.[35] This lack of counsel has been attributed to the following factors:

Miranda rights The right to remain silent, the right to an attorney, and the right to indigent appointment of an attorney.

- parents' reluctance to retain an attorney
- inadequate public defender legal services in nonurban areas
- judicial ambivalence toward advocacy in treatment-oriented juvenile courts

The latter factor often results in pressure on juveniles and parents to waive counsel.[36]

One research study examined the right to counsel as applied in all 50 states.[37] Figure 8.2 reports the status of all the states concerning juvenile right to counsel and waiver of rights by juveniles. The first column indicates whether or not the state has a statute specifying the juvenile right to counsel. The second column reveals whether or not the judge in a specific state in a juvenile case has the option of appointing counsel where "it is in the interests of justice." The third column lists states which have adopted a *per se* rule or other strict requirements for waiver of rights. Finally, the fourth column indicates whether or not a state juvenile justice system is statutorily bound to provide counsel at "all critical stages" of proceedings or when there is a threat of loss of liberty or confinement. According to Figure 8.2, all states but New Hampshire, Delaware, Hawaii, Michigan, Mississippi, and Missouri have specific statutory language dictating the provision of legal counsel to youths in all delinquency proceedings. However, only seven states require mandatory appointment of counsel to juveniles in delinquency proceedings.

Many juveniles and their parents waive their right to an attorney. *Do you think this is a problem specific to the juvenile justice system? Explain.*

The majority of states (27) are less protective of a juvenile's right to counsel in that they make appointment of counsel discretionary or do not provide strict waiver requirements. Thus, while the right to counsel exists, provision of an attorney to juveniles is conditional in many states.

The Institute for Judicial Administration/American Bar Association (ABA) Joint Commission on Juvenile Justice Standards developed standards that require children to be represented by counsel in all proceedings arising from a delinquency action, beginning at the earliest stage of the decision process.[38] Research conducted by the ABA discovered a number of problems in children's representation. In particular, the problems facing public defenders in juvenile court included:

1. Annual caseloads of more than 500 cases, with up to 300 of these being juvenile cases
2. Lack of resources for independent evaluations, expert witnesses, and investigatory support
3. Lack of computers, telephones, files, and adequate office space
4. Juvenile public defenders' inexperience, lack of training, low morale, and salaries lower than those of their counterparts who defend adults or serve as prosecutors
5. The inability to keep up with rapidly changing juvenile codes

Heavy caseloads appear to be the most significant barrier to effective representation. Attorneys are often unable to keep their clients appropriately informed or to adequately develop detention and dispositional alternatives.[39]

In conclusion, one of the most important areas of juvenile rights involves a child's legal representation and the circumstances under which juveniles waive their rights. These issues will probably receive additional attention by the courts as the juvenile justice system becomes more punitive.

FIGURE 8.2	State Statutory Provisions of Juvenile Right to Counsel			
STATE	SPECIFIC JUVENILE RIGHT TO COUNSEL STATUTE	DISCRETIONARY APPOINTMENT OF COUNSEL BY COURT	STRICT WAIVER OF RIGHTS REQUIREMENTS	MANDATORY APPOINTMENT OF COUNSEL
Alabama	X	X		
Alaska	X			
Arizona	X	X		
Arkansas	X	X	X	
California	X	X		X
Colorado	X	X	X	
Connecticut	X	X	X	
Delaware				
Florida	X			
Georgia	X	X		
Hawaii				
Idaho	X	X		
Illinois	X	X		X
Indiana	X		X	
Iowa	X		X	
Kansas	X			
Kentucky	X			X
Louisiana	X		X	
Maine	X			
Maryland	X	X	X	
Massachusetts	X	X	X	X*
Michigan				
Minnesota	X			
Mississippi				
Missourl				
Montana	X	X	X	
Nebraska	X			
Nevada	X			
New Hampshire				
New Jersey	X		X	
New Mexico	X	X	X	X
New York	X			
North Carolina	X		X	X
North Dakota	X			
Ohio	X	X	X	
Oklahoma	X	X	X	
Oregon	X	X		
Pennsylvania	X	X		
Rhode Island	X			
South Carolina	X			
South Dakota	X	X		
Tennessee	X	X		
Texas	X	X	X	X
Utah	X	X		
Vermont	X	X		
Virginia	X	X	X	
Washington	X			
West Virginia	X			
Wisconsin	X	X		
Wyoming	X			

*The Massachusetts waiver requirements are defined by case law.

Source: Caeti, Tory J., Craig Hemmens, and Velmer Burton. "Juvenile Right to Counsel: A National Comparison of State Legal Codes." *American Journal of Criminal Law, 23:3,* Spring 1996.

SEARCH AND SEIZURE

Although law enforcement searches of juveniles have not been directly addressed by the U.S. Supreme Court, juveniles have fewer rights than adults concerning searches and seizures. All appellate courts that have specifically considered Fourth Amendment cases have ruled that the Fourth Amendment does apply to juveniles. The exclusionary rule has not yet been directly applied to juvenile proceedings by the U.S. Supreme Court. The U.S. Supreme Court has not decided cases regarding a juvenile's rights in many common police practices (temporary detainment, temporary protective custody, or arrest). Many states and courts require that the police have probable cause prior to taking a juvenile into custody. However, there are circumstances where police can detain a juvenile but not an adult. For example, juveniles can be taken into custody for a variety of status offenses, which include curfew violations, truancy, and running away. In many states, the police often need only a reasonable suspicion to detain a juvenile rather than the probable cause required to arrest an adult.

The Uniform Juvenile Court Act (UJCA) states that

> a child may be taken into custody pursuant to an order of the court under that act or pursuant to the laws of arrest; or, by a law enforcement officer if there are reasonable grounds to believe that the child is suffering from illness or injury, or is in immediate danger from his surroundings, and that his removal is necessary; or, by a law enforcement officer if there are reasonable grounds to believe that the child has run away from his parents or guardian.

In short, a juvenile can be taken into custody without a warrant if the law enforcement officer reasonably believes the juvenile to be delinquent, dependent, abused, neglected, or a status offender.

The U.S. Supreme Court did address a search and seizure issue, but not related to police proceedings. In *New Jersey v. T.L.O.*,[40] school officials searched a student's belongings and found drugs and evidence that implicated her in drug dealing. A school official searched her purse without probable cause and in response to the student's denial of an allegation that she was smoking in the bathroom. Upon inspection, the school official found cigarettes, and a more thorough search revealed the other evidence. The girl was eventually charged in juvenile court for dealing marijuana. The juvenile court moved to have the evidence suppressed alleging that the search was illegal.

In *New Jersey* v. *T.L.O.*, the U.S. Supreme Court ruled that school officials do not have to have a warrant, nor do they have to have probable cause to justify a search. The Court reasoned that the privacy interests of a student are outweighed by a higher level of need for school officials to maintain security and a healthy school environment. School officials need only "reasonable grounds" to suspect a search will produce evidence that the student is violating a school rule. While the rule enables school officials, it does not apply to police officers who are still bound by probable cause requirements. What happens if the officer is employed by the school? In several school districts across the country, schools employ both private security and school district police to maintain security in their schools. The Court made no specific reference to what rule would apply in these cases.

A 1995 case[41] allows more leeway to school officials in investigating perceived threats to student and staff safety. Locker searches, the use of drug-sniffing dogs, and strip searches of students raise more complex problems if drugs or weapons are found in such a search. Many school systems are now using metal detectors, and courts generally uphold their use for safety purposes rather than on the grounds that they are present for crime-detection purposes.[42]

New Jersey v. T.L.O. The court decision that school officials only need reasonable grounds, not probable cause, to search a student when they suspect that the search will turn up illegal evidence.

In 2009, the U.S. Supreme Court placed restrictions on strip searches in public schools. The Court ruled that the facts in the case did not indicate the danger presented to students by the object of the search; in this case, drugs. Also, the Court ruled that the school officials did not have sufficient suspicion that the drugs were being concealed in the student's undergarments. Therefore, the Court determined that the strip search was too intrusive under the circumstances.[43]

INTERROGATIONS AND CONFESSIONS

The U.S. Supreme Court has ruled that confessions that were coerced by police are not admissible in adult proceedings against a juvenile.[44] In the case considered, police questioned a juvenile for a lengthy period and held him **incommunicado** for over three days during which his lawyer was not allowed to see him. In a similar case, the Court ruled that isolating a juvenile for long periods of time may result in involuntary confessions.[45] The U.S. Supreme Court has also established age as a factor in determining whether or not a confession was voluntary. The *Fare* v. *Michael C.* case established some boundaries for police interrogations and station confessions. However, unless specified by state statute, there is no higher standard the police must adhere to when questioning juveniles.

incommunicado Holding a person charged with a crime without allowing him or her to communicate with anyone.

As described in the discussion on waiver of rights, several states do require that a juvenile's parents be present, that a lawyer is present, or that the juvenile receive counsel and guidance concerning his or her rights prior to police questioning.

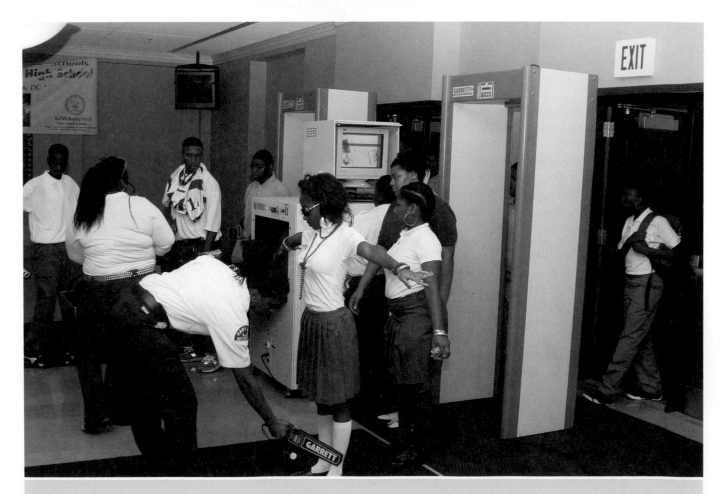

The rights of people in their homes are different from a juvenile's rights at school. *Should police and school officials be allowed to search students and their lockers whenever they want to? Why or why not?*

In Texas, for example, a juvenile must be taken before a magistrate and the magistrate must judge that the juvenile has been informed of and understands his or her rights prior to police interrogation. Most courts and law enforcement recognize the age of the juvenile as a factor in determining the level, length, and parameters of questioning by police. The U.S. Supreme Court mandated in *Fare v. Michael C.* that several factors be taken into account under the totality of circumstances framework to determine whether a confession was knowingly and voluntarily given. These might include, but are not limited to:

- The juvenile's age
- Education
- Knowledge of the substance of the charge
- Knowledge and understanding of his or her rights
- Whether the juvenile is allowed contact with parents, guardian, attorney, or other interested adult
- The methods used in interrogation
- The length of interrogation

JUVENILE PROCEEDINGS

When the juvenile justice system was founded, one of the early concerns was the "taint of criminality" that a child could receive if not protected. As a result, state legislation established laws to protect the anonymity of the child and the confidentiality of the proceeding. Many older court cases involving juveniles do not include their full name or use a fictitious name in the case title (for example, *In re Gault* or *Fare v. Michael C.*). Juveniles were assumed to have a right to confidentiality and anonymity; in fact, many states had laws guaranteeing this. Juvenile records were sealed or destroyed, fingerprinting and photographing juveniles was not allowed, and court proceedings were closed to the public.

The shift in juvenile justice to a more punitive, more accountability-based system has resulted in the eroding or elimination of many of the early systems' confidentiality provisions. Many state statutes now explicitly authorize fingerprinting and photographing as well as centralized record keeping. In addition to the use of juvenile records for additional and future court proceedings, the right of a juvenile to remain anonymous and to have the proceedings kept confidential is becoming outdated in many states.

FINGERPRINTING AND PHOTOGRAPHING JUVENILES The police practice of fingerprinting and photographing juveniles works most directly against the issues of confidentiality and anonymity. Traditionally, law enforcement officers were either prevented from fingerprinting and photographing juveniles or, at least, these records had to be kept confidential. Fingerprinting juveniles who are taken into custody has become more common in recent years. Currently, all states authorize police to fingerprint detained juveniles under certain circumstances. The taking of fingerprints is limited in some states on the basis of the type of crime or age limitations. Some states have a minimum age (most commonly 14 years), and others limit fingerprinting of juveniles to those taken into custody for acts that would be felonies if committed by an adult. Florida's statute on fingerprinting and photographing, detailed in Figure 8.3, provides an example of some of the restrictions states provide for juveniles.

Many state legislatures recently changed laws in this area by lowering the age threshold or adding to the list of offenses for which fingerprints can be taken. Several states now require photographs be taken with fingerprints at the

---

Myth / Fact

Myth

When police interrogate juveniles, their parents and/or a lawyer must be present.

Fact

States vary with respect to the conditions under which a juvenile can be interrogated by police. Juveniles in some states can waive their rights without a parent, lawyer, or anyone else being present. In fact, some states do not set an age limit on who can and cannot waive their rights.

JUVENILE JUSTICE ONLINE

Go to **www.law.cornell.edu/states/listing** or **www.njdc.info/state_data.php.** Find examples of state laws on juvenile rights to counsel, juvenile waiver of rights, confidentiality of juvenile proceedings, fingerprinting and photographing juveniles. Are there any unique laws pertaining to juveniles in your state?

| FIGURE 8.3 | **Fingerprinting and Photographing Juveniles** |

FLORIDA STATUTE 985.11 FINGERPRINTING AND PHOTOGRAPHING

(1) (a) A child who is charged with or found to have committed an offense that would be a felony if committed by an adult shall be fingerprinted and the fingerprints must be submitted to the Department of Law Enforcement.

(b) A child who is charged with or found to have committed one of the following offenses shall be fingerprinted and the fingerprints shall be submitted to the Department of Law Enforcement.

1. Assault
2. Battery
3. Carrying a concealed weapon
4. Unlawful use of destructive devices or bombs
5. Negligent treatment of children
6. Assault on a law enforcement officer, a firefighter, or specified officers
7. Open carrying of a weapon
8. Exposure of sexual organs
9. Unlawful possession of a firearm
10. Petty theft
11. Cruelty to animals
12. Arson, resulting in bodily harm to a firefighter
13. Unlawful possession or discharge of a weapon or firearm at a school-sponsored event or on school property.

A law enforcement agency may fingerprint and photograph a child taken into custody upon probable cause that such child has committed any other violation of law, as the agency deems appropriate. Such fingerprint records and photographs shall be retained by the law enforcement agency in a separate file, and these records and all copies thereof must be marked "Juvenile Confidential."

These records shall not be available for public disclosure and inspection, but shall be available to other law enforcement agencies, criminal justice agencies, state attorneys, the courts, the child, the parents or legal custodians of the child, their attorneys, and any other person authorized by the court to have access to such records. In addition, such records may be submitted to the Department of Law Enforcement for inclusion in the state criminal history records and used by criminal justice agencies for criminal justice purposes. These records may, in the discretion of the court, be open to inspection by anyone upon a showing of cause. The fingerprint and photograph records shall be produced in the court whenever directed by the court. Any photograph taken pursuant to this section may be shown by a law enforcement officer to any victim or witness of a crime for the purpose of identifying the person who committed such crime.

(c) The court shall be responsible for the fingerprinting of any child at the disposition hearing if the child has been adjudicated or had adjudication withheld for any felony in the case currently before the court.

(2) If the child is not referred to the court, or if the child is found not to have committed a violation of law, the court may, after notice to the law enforcement agency involved, order the originals and copies of the fingerprints and photographs destroyed. Unless otherwise ordered by the court, if the child is found to have committed an offense which would be a felony if it had been committed by an adult, then the law enforcement agency having custody of the fingerprint and photograph records shall retain the originals and immediately thereafter forward adequate duplicate copies to the court along with the written offense report relating to the matter for which the child was taken into custody. Except as otherwise provided by this subsection, the clerk of the court, after the disposition hearing on the case, shall forward duplicate copies of the fingerprints and photographs, together with the child's name, address, date of birth, age, and sex, to:

(a) The sheriff of the county in which the child was taken into custody, in order to maintain a central child identification file in that county.

(b) The law enforcement agency of each municipality having a population in excess of 50,000 persons and located in the county of arrest, if so requested specifically or by a general request by that agency.

(3) This section does not prohibit the fingerprinting or photographing of child traffic violators. All records of such traffic violations shall be kept in the full name of the violator and shall be open to inspection and publication in the same manner as adult traffic violations. This section does not apply to the photographing of children by the Department of Juvenile Justice or the Department of Children and Family Services.

time of the juvenile's arrest.[46] In short, many states have repealed laws that prevented the fingerprinting and photographing of juveniles in response to increasing demands for more accountability in juvenile justice.

Federal law requires that when a juvenile is found guilty of an act that would be a violent felony if committed by an adult, the juvenile must be photographed and fingerprinted. The federal court must send fingerprints, photographs, and the record to the FBI if the juvenile has twice been adjudicated for a felony, or if the juvenile is 13 years or older and has been convicted of a felony crime of violence with a firearm.[47]

CONFIDENTIALITY AND ANONYMITY OF JUVENILE PROCEEDINGS The U.S. Supreme Court has had to decide if juveniles are entitled to privacy and confidentiality as a result of coming into contact with the juvenile justice system. The Court has ruled that despite state confidentiality laws, the probation status of a juvenile witness could be brought out during cross-examination at trial.[48] The Court has also ruled that a state law that made it illegal to publish the name of a juvenile charged with a crime is unconstitutional.[49]

A case involving three juveniles charged with a federal hate crime tested the ability of a juvenile court to deny access to the media.[50] The federal government charged three youths with civil rights violations after they allegedly conspired to infringe upon the civil rights of Jews and African Americans. The three, initially prosecuted in 1994 under a federal hate crime statute, purportedly had been members of a white supremacy skinhead group.[51] *The Boston Globe* filed suit over this case in order to gain access to the court materials and proceedings. Although the court gave the newspaper a few documents, it denied the media access to the proceedings stating that the Federal Juvenile Delinquency Code[52] required the closure of a federal juvenile delinquency proceeding if a juvenile is amenable to rehabilitation and has no prior criminal or juvenile delinquency record. The U.S. Court of Appeals for the First Circuit decided that the newspaper could be refused access because the federal law was sufficient to allow the judge discretion in this area. The U.S. Supreme Court refused to hear the case, allowing judges to retain the ability to determine if and when protecting the privacy of a minor during delinquency proceedings will serve the broader interest of furthering the juvenile's rehabilitation.[53]

Even though early juvenile justice legislation did not include specific provisions for protecting the confidentiality of juvenile court proceedings or records, confidentiality was practiced by most early juvenile courts where it was thought to provide the juvenile with a measure of protection against being labeled a criminal and the inhibiting effects on a youth's rehabilitation.[54] However, in the interest of accountability of juveniles, an increasing number of state legislatures have passed laws that erode confidentiality provisions and practices. An increasing number of states are allowing public access to and victim participation in juvenile proceedings, broadening access to juvenile records, and altering expungement laws for juvenile records. As the punitive model of juvenile justice became prominent, community protection and the public's right to know have begun to displace confidentiality and privacy issues as an underpinning in the juvenile court system.[55]

Although most agencies that collect records on juvenile offenders are restricted in the collection and dissemination of juvenile record information, many states are changing their laws.[56] In spite of various existing confidentiality statutes and practices, courts have held that there is no constitutional confidentiality right for an alleged or adjudicated delinquent. In cases processed over the past 25 years, the courts have disregarded the confidentiality provision when it impedes the constitutional rights of another.[57] More and more states are also allowing the public access to juvenile proceedings. Most states require or permit the court to open juvenile proceedings if the case involves a serious

FIGURE 8.4 | **Confidentiality of Juvenile Delinquency Hearings**

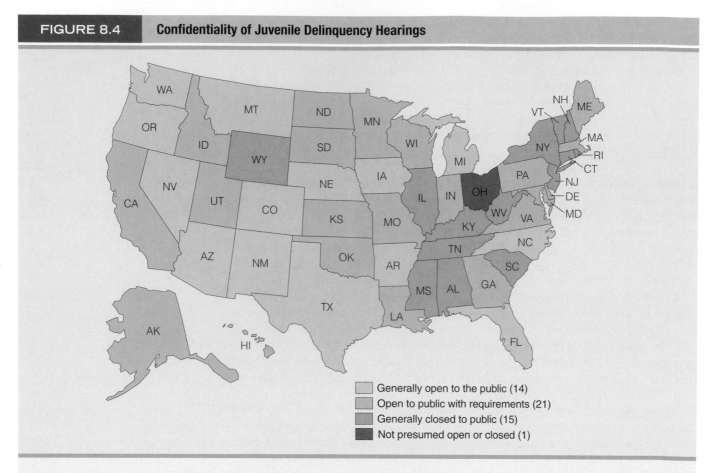

Generally open to the public (14)
Open to public with requirements (21)
Generally closed to public (15)
Not presumed open or closed (1)

Source. Szymanski, L. "Confidentiality of Juvenile Delinquency Hearings (2008 Update)." *NCJJ Snapshot*, 13(5). Pittsburgh, PA: National Center for Juvenile Justice, 2008.

offense or if the youth is a habitual offender (see Figure 8.4).[58] Georgia enacted a provision of this sort in 1995 when the State legislature voted to open juvenile courtrooms to the public for the first time. The law allows the general public admission to adjudicatory hearings for youth accused of committing acts that would be felonies if committed by adults or youth who have previously been adjudicated delinquent.[59] The provision also requires written notice to school officials of such adjudicatory proceedings.[60]

Despite these changes in several states, many states still protect the confidentiality of the proceedings in one form or another. Figure 8.5 depicts the status of confidentiality in the United States concerning the public release of juvenile names. The U.S. Supreme Court has affirmed the right of courts, in general, and juvenile courts, in particular, to close proceedings to the press and public. However, the Court has also ruled that news organizations can publish or broadcast juvenile names and other information once they obtain this information.[61] Now almost all states allow public release of a juvenile offender's name and photographs, in some circumstances. This is up from 30 states in 1995. Those circumstances customarily involve violent or serious crimes or repeat offenders.[62] The confidentiality of juvenile proceedings will likely continue to be eroded over the next few years. An example of how different today's system is from the traditional system can be seen in a syndicated television program called "Juvies." The program, which originally aired in 2007, showed actual juveniles being processed in Indiana's Lake County Juvenile Center. The juvenile's name, crimes, prior adjudications, and the entire court process were shown in each episode.

| FIGURE 8.5 | **Public Release of Juvenile Names** |

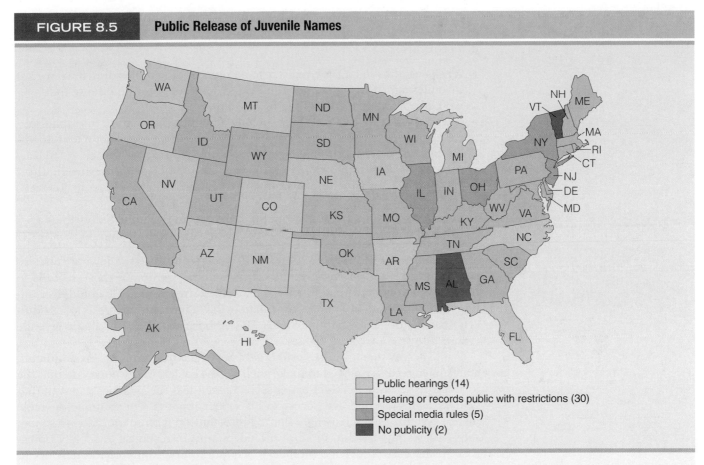

Public hearings (14)
Hearing or records public with restrictions (30)
Special media rules (5)
No publicity (2)

Source: "Releasing Names of Juvenile Offenders to the Media/Public (2004 Update)." *NCJJ Snapshot*, 9(4). Pittsburgh, PA: National Center for Juvenile Justice, 2004 update.

JUVENILE RECORDS

Laws relating to juvenile records, record keeping, access, and sharing of juvenile record information are driven by trends in juvenile justice practices. Neil Miller, an expert in juvenile records, noted that there are three trends involving juvenile justice records that are particularly striking:

1. More juveniles are subject to transfer to adult court
2. Juvenile justice record information is increasingly available outside the juvenile system
3. Integration of juvenile and adult records is increasing

The relaxation of confidentiality and the drive for increased accountability and punishment of juvenile offenders have prompted several states to alter their laws regarding juvenile records. The policy initiatives in this area focus on five issues: centralized record keeping and storage; who has access to juvenile records; information sharing; use of juvenile records in subsequent proceedings or sentencing; and sealing and expungement.[63]

At one time, juvenile records were haphazardly collected or not collected at all. Even today, the record of a juvenile disposition is frequently located only in the county where the offense occurred. However, the formalized collection and the storing of juvenile records are changing. For example, in 1988 only 13 out of 50 state central repositories maintained juvenile record information.[64] By 1996, 44 states specifically authorized the keeping of juvenile records in central record repositories.[65] Miller reported that, in 1995 alone, four states reportedly took legislative action that addressed the centralization of juvenile justice records:[66]

- Alaska established a DNA registry to contain DNA samples drawn from juveniles age 16 or older and adjudicated delinquent for an offense that would be a felony if committed by an adult.[67]
- Iowa's legislature took action to include juvenile adjudication information for aggravated misdemeanors or felonies in the adult rap sheet maintained by the state central criminal history repository.[68]
- Minnesota's legislature called for the preparation of a report regarding the creation of a separate information and tracking system for juvenile justice information.[69]
- Texas amended its law to require the Department of Public Safety to establish and maintain a statewide juvenile justice information system.[70]

In 1992, the FBI reversed its previous policy and began allowing states to submit records on serious juvenile offenses and to maintain those records in the FBI's national criminal history system. In addition, the FBI would disseminate juvenile criminal history information the same as it currently does adult criminal history information. States may choose whether to submit juvenile record information to the FBI.

While access to a juvenile's criminal history has, traditionally, been difficult, states have recently moved to make such access easier. Many conclude that the juvenile justice system might better serve a juvenile if the agencies and staff that deal with the juvenile had access to his or her records. For example, juvenile justice systems are increasingly sharing information with schools due to school safety issues, the need to monitor offenders, and in response to society's pressure to increase a juvenile offender's accountability. Many of the barriers to sharing such information have been eroded in recent years.[71] Figure 8.6 illustrates which states require juveniles to register as sex offenders, thus allowing this information to be shared with the community.

One of the fears of the early founders and practitioners of the juvenile justice system was that records of juvenile proceedings would someday be used against the juvenile as an adult. Today, that is exactly what is happening. Many states have sentencing laws that dictate adjudication record use in adult court.[72] In fact, California and Louisiana, for example, include the juvenile record as a potential strike in their **three-strikes laws**.[73] Adult courts frequently use juvenile records in sentencing determinations. Most states have statutes that prescribe the inclusion of a juvenile record in a pre-sentence report or authorize the adult court to consider a defendant's juvenile record in sentencing.[74] Also, most of the states authorize prosecutors to use juvenile records in charging determinations.[75]

Even though a number of states have moved to include juvenile records in future prosecutions or sentencing decisions, all but Rhode Island, as of 2009, have provisions for **expunging or sealing** juvenile records. Some states seal and/or destroy all records, except those where a serious or violent crime was committed. The policy of sealing or expunging records remains in many states as a sort of reward for juvenile offenders. Juvenile court personnel will typically expunge or seal the records of a juvenile who has successfully completed probation. Because the records are destroyed in expungement, court orders are almost always required. In addition, access to sealed records is strictly regulated. In many jurisdictions, consent of the court is required to open sealed records. Many states allow the record to be opened if the juvenile is convicted of another crime or adjudicated delinquent. The courts have made it clear that there is not a constitutional right to seal or expunge juvenile records and that a court may unseal records.[76]

three-strikes laws Mandate that three felony convictions result in life imprisonment.

expunging or sealing Allows for the erasure or destruction of juvenile records once a juvenile reaches the age of majority.

| FIGURE 8.6 | Judicial Discretion over Registering Juveniles as Sex Offenders |

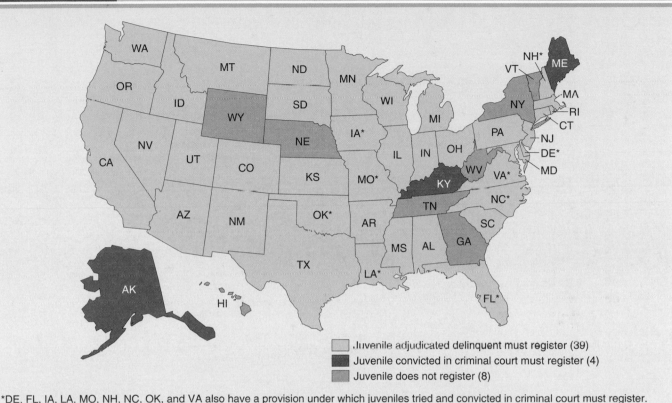

Juvenile adjudicated delinquent must register (39)
Juvenile convicted in criminal court must register (4)
Juvenile does not register (8)

*DE, FL, IA, LA, MO, NH, NC, OK, and VA also have a provision under which juveniles tried and convicted in criminal court must register.

Source: Szymanski, Linda "Megan's Law: Juvenile Sex Offender Registration (2009 Update)." NCJJ Snapshot, 14(7). Pittsburgh, PA: National Center for Juvenile Justice.

BAIL

Bail is a qualified right granted by the Eighth Amendment to the U.S. Constitution. However, adults can be held without bail, and juveniles have not expressly been given the right to bail by the U.S. Supreme Court. Juveniles may often be held in preventive detention or protective custody. More typically, juveniles are released to their parents or another guardian who is responsible for caring of the juvenile and making sure he or she complies with the orders of the court. Several states authorize bail for juveniles in their statutes; however, several others specifically forbid the use of bail for juveniles.

DETENTION

The U.S. Supreme Court has ruled on one case involving the detention of juveniles. In **Schall v. Martin**[77] the Court had to decide whether or not the **preventive detention** of juveniles is constitutional. Martin was arrested for robbery, assault, and possession of a weapon. The juvenile court judge ruled that Martin presented a threat to the community and, under a New York statute, ruled that he be held in preventive detention prior to the trial. Martin was held for a total of 15 days prior to being dispositioned. The Court ruled that the preventive detention of juveniles is constitutional and concluded that such a detention protects both society and the juvenile. Thus, the Court found that "the practice serves a legitimate regulatory purpose compatible with the 'fundamental fairness' demanded by the

Schall v. Martin Court case that decided juveniles can be held in preventive detention prior to adjudication.

preventive detention The holding of a juvenile without bond or bail prior to his or her adjudication hearing.

FIGURE 8.7	Juvenile Delinquents' Right to a Jury Trial

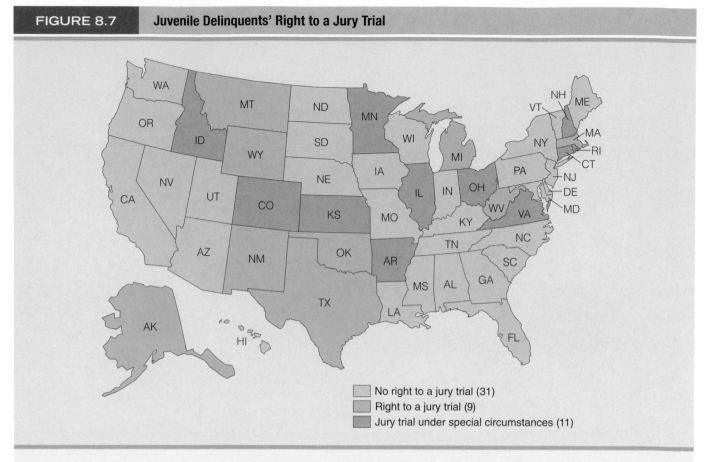

☐ No right to a jury trial (31)
◩ Right to a jury trial (9)
◼ Jury trial under special circumstances (11)

Source: Szymanski, L. "Juvenile Delinquents' Right to a Jury Trial." *NCJJ Snapshot,* 13(2). Pittsburgh, PA: National Center for Juvenile Justice, 2008.

Due Process Clause in juvenile proceedings." The Court also noted that every state allows pretrial detention of juveniles accused of crime, and that some states have expressly upheld their statutes permitting preventive detention. In *Schall* v. *Martin,* the Court for the first time permitted the states to restrain liberty for a reason other than to ensure the accused's presence at trial.[78] The basis for this confinement is a judge's independent determination that a juvenile is likely to engage in criminal behavior prior to trial. Although predictions of future dangerous conduct have been allowed in other cases, these predictions have never before been implemented in a situation before the adjudication of guilt.[79]

JUVENILE RIGHT TO JURY TRIAL

The U.S. Supreme Court decision in *McKeiver* v. *Pennsylvania* clearly denied juveniles the right to a jury trial in delinquency proceedings. However, as the Court noted, states are free to enact statutes that extend this right if they so desire. Some states do not grant juveniles a right to a jury trial and some grant them this right in limited circumstances. Figure 8.7 lists the states that provide this right and those that do not. A Colorado statute, for example, provides a juvenile the right to a jury trial in some circumstances; a juvenile is assumed to have waived his or her right to trial unless he or she made a specific request otherwise (see Figure 8.8).

FIGURE 8.8	**Juvenile Right to a Jury Trial**

COLORADO 19-2-107

(1) In any action of delinquency in which a juvenile is alleged to be an aggravated juvenile offender, or is alleged to have committed an act that would constitute a crime of violence if committed by an adult, the juvenile or the district attorney may demand a trial by a jury of not more than six persons or the court, on its own motion, may order such a jury to try any case brought under this title, except as provided in subsection (2) of this section.

(2) The juvenile is not entitled to a trial by jury when the petition alleges a delinquent act which is a misdemeanor, a petty offense, a violation of a municipal or county ordinance, or a violation of a court order.

(3) Unless a jury is demanded pursuant to subsection (1) of this section, it shall be deemed waived.

(4) Notwithstanding any other provisions of this article, in any action in delinquency in which a juvenile requests a jury pursuant to this section, the juvenile shall be deemed to have waived the 60-day requirement for holding the adjudicatory trial.

Several arguments have been presented defending why a juvenile should or should not have the right to a jury trial. Some reasons why states do not give juveniles the right to a jury trial are:

1. The juvenile courts are unique.
2. Juvenile court proceedings would become adversarial.
3. Juvenile courts are separate and unequal.
4. Jury trials would introduce substantial delay into juvenile proceedings.[80]

States that do give juveniles the right to a jury trial offer these reasons:

1. The proceedings sound criminal.
2. The proceedings look criminal.
3. The proceedings are more criminal than civil.
4. Jury trials are a due process right.
5. There is little delay in juvenile court.[81]

JUVENILE CORRECTIONAL LAW

A large body of federal case law and U.S. Supreme Court rulings relate to adult probationers, prisoners, parolees, and the conditions of confinement. However, there are no U.S. Supreme Court and relatively few federal cases dealing specifically with juveniles or juvenile facilities. Again, it is assumed by many that the adult standards apply to juveniles. However, the Court has demonstrated that such conclusions are premature pending rulings. One method that is increasingly being used as an attempt to ensure the civil rights of incarcerated juveniles is civil action by the Department of Justice against a juvenile facility under the Civil Rights of Institutionalized Persons Act (CRIPA). CRIPA allows the United States Attorney General to file a federal complaint against a juvenile facility when there are systemic violations of the rights of youth. Since Congress enacted CRIPA, there have been investigations into over 100 juvenile correctional institutions. Some of the investigations were closed before any litigation ensued because the Justice Department concluded that a pattern or practice of unlawful conditions did not exist or because the facility closed its doors.[82]

Incarcerated juveniles rarely file court cases concerning their conditions of confinement or their legal rights. Some research has indicated that a lack of appeals from the juvenile court is due to the lack of formalized procedures. In addition, juveniles are probably less likely than the adult prisoners to have access to legal resources. Indeed, several states do not allow appeals from juvenile courts; however, most states do not restrict or even address this right. A federal case concluded that incarcerated juveniles have a right to access to the courts, including access to a lawyer, and access to legal assistance.[83]

Juvenile Court Trial Delay

Nearly half of the formal cases in large jurisdictions take more than 90 days to reach disposition—the maximum time suggested by professional standards.

SOURCE: Knoll, Crystal and Melissa Sickmund. 2012, October. *Delinquency Cases in Juvenile Court, 2009.* Washington DC: Office of Juvenile Justice and Delinquency Prevention.

RIGHT TO TREATMENT

Does a juvenile have a right to rehabilitational treatment? While the right to rehabilitational treatment is grounded in the historical development of the juvenile court, it developed only recently into a legal right for challenging the conditions in juvenile facilities.[84] Following *Gault*, several cases centered on complaints about conditions of confinement in juvenile facilities. These attempted to enforce the juvenile court's promise to provide rehabilitative care by asserting a "right to treatment."[85] The courts have found that juveniles do have a right to treatment under the Constitution and some state statutes. However, the form of treatment and how treatment should be prescribed is generally still left up to correctional authorities.[86]

JUVENILE RIGHTS AT SCHOOL

Students facing disciplinary action have due process protections similar to those that juveniles receive in juvenile court. The U.S. Supreme Court ruled in 1975 that students who face temporary suspension from school have liberty interests that require due process protection.[87] The Court concluded that students facing suspension must receive notice of the charges, an explanation of the evidence if the student contests the charges, and an opportunity to be heard on the charges. This process must occur prior to the suspension if possible. Since the Court applied due process protections in school disciplinary matters, more serious processes in school would also require some type of due process.

At present, many fundamental rights are not granted to students, including the unlimited right to free expression. The U.S. Supreme Court has ruled that free speech rights of students in public schools are not necessarily as extensive as the rights of adults in other settings. A school newspaper is not automatically a forum for public expression—especially if the paper is published as part of the educational curriculum. If a school authority believes a student's expression will substantially interfere with the rights of other students or the work of the school, the expression can be limited.

Some states allow school officials to use corporal punishment on students. *Do you agree with this practice? Why or why not?*

FIGURE 8.9	Corporal Punishment in Schools: State-by-State Analysis

CORPORAL PUNISHMENT LEGAL		CORPORAL PUNISHMENT ILLEGAL	
Alabama	Mississippi	Alaska	Nebraska
Arizona	Missouri	California	Nevada
Arkansas	North Carolina	Connecticut	New Hampshire
Colorado	Oklahoma	Delaware	New Jersey
Florida	South Carolina	Hawaii	New Mexico
Georgia	Tennessee	Illinois	New York
Idaho	Texas	Iowa	North Dakota
Indiana	Wyoming	Maine	Ohio
Kansas		Maryland	Oregon
Kentucky		Massachusetts	Pennsylvania
Louisiana		Michigan	Rhode Island
		Minnesota	South Dakota
		Montana	Utah
			Vermont
			Virginia
			Washington
			West Virginia
			Wisconsin

Source. The Center for Effective Discipline. Columbus, OH. www.stophitting.com

Another area of debate is the use of corporal punishment in schools. May a teacher or other school official inflict corporal punishment on a child who misbehaves in school? Several states and school systems have rules and legislation that specifically allow corporal punishment in schools and delineate when and how it should be applied. Figure 8.9 lists the states that allow and forbid the use of corporal punishment. The U.S. Supreme Court decided a case on corporal punishment and upheld its use in school as a legitimate disciplinary device. The Focus on Policy box on page 233 describes the U.S. Supreme Court case about the use of corporal punishment in the school.

Although corporal punishment of students is allowable and may even be somewhat severe where it is authorized, school officials are usually very wary about the use and/or abuse of corporal punishment in their schools. There is, after all, potential legal liability if a teacher does use corporal punishment on a student. In light of the U.S. Supreme Court ruling in this matter, it is interesting that the Court banned the use of corporal punishment on prisoners some time ago. Figure 8.10 shows the Georgia statute outlining the parameters of corporal punishment.

Recently, other issues involving school safety and school-related violence have come to the forefront of public scrutiny. Efforts to make schools safer have become common; however, many legal scholars worry that students' rights will be compromised in the process.[88] Many states now require that juvenile courts report the adjudication of certain offenses to the local school system. Recent legislative trends have even led to statutes that require that schools be notified of juvenile arrests or petitions when the offense involves drugs or weapons.[89] Some statutes limit the dissemination of this information to the superintendent or principal of the school, but other states have no such protections. In addition, many juveniles are suspended from school or placed in alternative programs prior to any final adjudication of the charge in court.

Many schools have adopted "zero tolerance" policies regarding drugs, weapons, or violence.[90] These zero tolerance policies raise several issues regarding student rights, including searches, seizures, and statements or confessions. Courts have held that school authorities may question a student without giving a Miranda warning, although much of that case law is predicated on the recognition that

FIGURE 8.10	Corporal Punishment in Georgia's Schools

GEORGIA 20-2-731

An area, county, or independent board of education may, upon the adoption of written policies, authorize any principal or teacher employed by the board to administer, in the exercise of his sound discretion, corporal punishment on any pupil or pupils placed under his supervision in order to maintain proper control and discipline. Any such authorization shall be subject to the following requirements:

(1) The corporal punishment shall not be excessive or unduly severe;

(2) Corporal punishment shall never be used as a first line of punishment for misbehavior unless the pupil was informed beforehand that specific misbehavior could occasion its use; provided, however, that corporal punishment may be employed as a first line of punishment for those acts of misconduct which are so antisocial or disruptive in nature as to shock the conscience;

(3) Corporal punishment must be administered in the presence of a principal or assistant principal, or the designee of the principal or assistant principal, employed by the board of education authorizing such punishment, and the other principal or assistant principal, or the designee of the principal or assistant principal, must be informed beforehand and in the presence of the pupil of the reason for the punishment;

(4) The principal or teacher who administered corporal punishment must provide the child's parent, upon request, a written explanation of the reasons for the punishment and the name of the principal or assistant principal, or designee of the principal or assistant principal, who was present; provided, however, that such an explanation shall not be used as evidence in any subsequent civil action brought as a result of the corporal punishment; and

(5) Corporal punishment shall not be administered to a child whose parents or legal guardian has upon the day of enrollment of the pupil filed with the principal of the school a statement from a medical doctor licensed in Georgia stating that it is detrimental to the child's mental or emotional stability.

GEORGIA 20-2-732

No principal or teacher who shall administer corporal punishment to a pupil or pupils under his care and supervision in conformity with the policies and regulations of the area, county, or independent board of education employing him and in accordance also with this subpart shall be held accountable or liable in any criminal or civil action based upon the administering of corporal punishment where the corporal punishment is administered in good faith and is not excessive or unduly severe.

school personnel are not law enforcement personnel or even agents of the police. Arguments that the principal or assistant principal fully intended to turn a youth over to the police have usually been unsuccessful, unless it can be shown that the actions are solely for the purpose of criminal or juvenile prosecution.[91]

VICTIMS' RIGHTS IN JUVENILE JUSTICE

Victims' rights have received increased attention in the criminal justice system, and numerous innovative programs designed to involve and empower victims have resulted. The mission and laws governing juvenile justice have traditionally served to block those outside the juvenile justice system from any of the stages of adjudication or disposition. Indeed, according to the traditional paradigm of juvenile justice, neither the guilt of the offender nor the rights of the victim were of much interest to the court.[92] However, the relaxation of confidentiality restrictions and the change in the philosophy of the juvenile court have opened avenues for victims to become more involved. Including victims in juvenile justice proceedings has had consequences, not the least of which is the requirement that practitioners incorporate the needs, rights, and wants of yet another actor onto an already crowded stage.[93] Inclusion of the victim in juvenile justice proceedings also has implications for the disposition of cases. Restitution, community service, and victim/offender mediation, for example, become integral components of the juvenile court's dispositional philosophy and hence the dispositions ordered by the court.

States typically have victim bill of rights amendments in their constitutions;[94] some specifically include victims of juvenile crime. Alabama and Arizona legislatures established a victim bill of rights in 1995 to apply expressly to victims of

FOCUS ON POLICY

THE U.S. SUPREME COURT: CORPORAL PUNISHMENT

According to students, assistant principal Lemmie Deliford displayed brass knuckles as he patrolled the corridors. Solomon Barnes, another assistant to the principal, was said to sport both brass knuckles and a large wooden paddle at the school. One day, because 14-year-old James Ingraham was slow to leave the auditorium stage, he was held face down on a table by Deliford and Barnes while the principal, Willie J. Wright, hit him on the buttocks at least 20 times with the paddle. Later that day Ingraham's mother took him to a hospital where painful bruises on his backside were diagnosed as a hematoma. A doctor prescribed ice packs, pain pills, sleeping pills, and a laxative and advised Ingraham to rest at home for at least a week. More than a week after the beating, another doctor examined him and found that the hematoma was still "swollen, tender, and purplish in color" and was discharging fluid. This doctor prescribed rest at home for an additional 72 hours. Ingraham could not sit comfortably for about three weeks.[i]

Ingraham was not the only student to feel the sting of the paddle. Roosevelt Adams was paddled, on about ten different occasions, during the year. Once, in a school bathroom, he was whacked by Barnes on the leg, arm, back, and neck. Another time, for an infraction, which Adams claims he did not commit, Wright hit him on the wrist. A doctor prescribed pain pills and an ice pack for the resulting swelling. Adams could not use the arm for about a week. Daniel Lee, who claimed to be an innocent bystander to a paddling incident, was asked by Barnes to bend down and "get a little piece of the board." Barnes rapped Lee on the hand four or five times; the hand was fractured, enlarged, and disfigured. For the grievous infraction of standing up in the study hall to wipe some foreign matter off the seat of his chair, Rodney Williams was beaten on the head and back with a paddle and whipped with a belt. Williams was out of school for about a week to undergo surgery to remove a lump on the side of his head caused by the beating. Other beatings by Deliford and Wright caused Williams to cough blood and receive treatment at a hospital.

Ingraham and Adams filed suit in U.S. District Court on January 7, 1971. They sought compensatory and punitive damages under 42 U.S.C. 1981–1988 for personal injuries caused by the unconstitutional infliction of corporal punishment. They also included a class-action claim seeking declarative and injunctive relief against the use of corporal punishment on Dade County public school children.

The U.S. Supreme Court granted certiorari on the questions of cruel and unusual punishment and procedural due process while denying review of the question of whether corporal punishment was so arbitrary, capricious, and unrelated to any legitimate educational objective that it violated the concept of substantive due processes.[ii] The Court first examined the common law tradition permitting the reasonable use of corporal punishment by public school teachers. The Court noted that of the 23 states which have enacted legislation on corporal punishment, only two (Massachusetts and New Jersey) have banned it (at the time of the decision), while the remainder have retained the common law standard or modified it only slightly. The Court stated, "The schoolchild has little need for the protection of the Eighth Amendment."[iii]

Turning to procedural due process, the Court found that insofar as corporal punishment involves restraint and physical punishment, it implicates a liberty interest entitled to due process protection. These procedures should "minimize the risk of wrongful punishment and provide for the resolution of disputed questions of justification."[iv] These standards are fully met, in Powell's view, by existing procedures in state law. The Court stated that the imposition of procedural safeguards on the administration of corporal punishment could have deleterious effects on discipline in the schools. If a teacher's recommendation to paddle a student was rejected at a hearing, it could negatively affect a teacher's ability to maintain discipline. Individual teachers and entire school systems might abandon corporal punishment in favor of disciplinary measures, which they believe are less effective. This might exacerbate the already serious disciplinary problem in the nation's schools. Therefore, while procedural safeguards might "marginally" reduce the risk of unwarranted corporal punishment, the Court concluded that the costs are far too great to justify such "a significant intrusion into an area of primary educational responsibility."[v]

CRITICAL THINKING

Are you in favor of corporal punishment? Explain your position.

NOTES:

i. Testimony regarding the level of corporal punishment. Drew Junior High School in 1970–71 is summarized p. 498 F.2d 248, 253259 (5th Cir. 1974).

ii. 97 S. Ct. 1401 (1977).

iii. *Ibid* p. 1415.

(Continued)

iv. *Ibid* p. 1416 n.46. Elsewhere in the opinion, the Court conceded that teachers "often" failed to follow school board procedural requirements. *Ibid* p. 1405.

v. *Ibid* p. 1418. The Court made clear, however, that this case does not decide "whether, or under what circumstances corporal punishment of a public school child may give rise to an independent federal cause of action to vindicate substantive rights under the Due Process Clause." *Ibid* p. 1416–17, n.47.

Source: Excerpted from Thomas J. Flygare. "*Ingraham v. Wright:* The Return of Old Jack Seaver." *Inequality in Education,* Center for Law and Education, Number 23, Cambridge, Massachusetts, September 1978

juvenile crime, and Idaho and Utah amended their bills to include juveniles.[95] Even though states have victim rights laws, many of the provisions do not apply to juvenile proceedings.[96] Some of the juvenile victims-of-crime legislation includes provisions for:

- Notifying the victim upon release of the offender from custody
- Increasing opportunities for victims to be heard in juvenile court hearings
- Expanding victim services to victims of juvenile crime
- Establishing authority for victims to submit a victim's impact statement
- Requiring victims to be notified of significant hearings (e.g., bail, disposition)
- Providing for release of the name and address of the offender and the offender's parents to the victim upon request
- Enhancing sentences if the victim is elderly or handicapped[97]

Victims' issues appeal to politicians and voters alike. It is likely that more legislation of this type will be passed in the future.

However, in cases where juveniles are assessed restitution, the amounts are frequently very large and the juvenile frequently owes an insurance company and not the direct victim who had already been compensated for his or her loss by insurance. Juveniles with multiple property crime records typically owe tens of thousands of dollars in restitution, and it is unlikely that they could ever afford to pay it.[98]

CURFEW LAWS

Curfew laws apply only to juveniles. As previously discussed, breaking a curfew is an example of a status offense. Not only must juveniles attend school and not run away from home, they can also be restricted in both the areas they frequent and the times of day they are allowed in public. In essence, their rights under the First, Fourth, Fifth, Ninth, and Fourteenth Amendments to the Constitution are limited by curfew, truancy, and other status offenses. As a result, many of the laws regarding status offenses have been challenged in federal courts under these Amendments.[99]

One study revealed an upsurge in the passing and use of curfews in the largest cities in the United States.[100] Curfews provide an easy mechanism for law enforcement to get youth off the streets. However, courts have ruled that some curfews violate the aforementioned amendments and others do not.

To be constitutional, a curfew law must adhere to two tests: (a) the law must demonstrate that there is a compelling state interest, and (b) the law must be narrowly tailored to serve the compelling state interest. A curfew law in Dallas, Texas, was ruled constitutional and served as a guide for other jurisdictions.[101] The Dallas City Council adopted its curfew ordinance in 1991 after hearings included testimony on increased incidences of late-night juvenile violence. Challenged by the ACLU, Dallas's curfew ordinance was upheld in 1993 by the U.S. Court of Appeals for the Fifth Circuit,[102] and in May 1994, the U.S. Supreme Court refused to hear an appeal of the case. The refusal to hear the case allowed

Juvenile Arrests for Curfew and Loitering

Juvenile arrests for curfew and loitering violations exceeded 110,000 in 2009, representing a 27 percent decrease from 2000-2009. In 2009, 25 percent of curfew arrest involved juveniles under age 15 and 31 percent involved females.

Source: Puzzanchera, Charles, Benjamin Adams, and Sarah Hockenberry. 2012, May. *Juvenile Court Statistics 2009.* Pittsburgh, PA: National Center for Juvenile Justice.

the Fifth Circuit's decision to stand. The decision ruled that the Dallas curfew passed the test because the city demonstrated a compelling state interest in reducing juvenile crime and victimization and because the ordinance was narrowly tailored to juveniles while respecting the rights of the affected minors.[103]

The Dallas curfew applied to youth under age 17 and was in effect from 11 P.M. through 6 A.M. Sunday through Thursday and from midnight to 6 A.M. Friday and Saturday. The statute exempted juveniles who were:

- Accompanied by an adult
- Engaged in activities related to interstate commerce or protected by the First Amendment
- Traveling to or from work
- Responding to an emergency
- Married
- Attending a supervised school, religious, or recreational activity

The Fifth Circuit found that the exemptions that permitted juveniles to exercise their fundamental rights and remain in public demonstrated that the ordinance was narrowly tailored to meet the city's legitimate objectives.

8.4 SELF-CHECK

1. Do public school students have the same rights at school as when they are at home?
2. List three trends involving juvenile records.
3. Explain the nature of curfew laws and ordinances and which situations they typically encompass.

FIGURE 8.11	Comparison of Criminal and Juvenile Court Rights Based on U.S. Supreme Court Rulings		
RIGHT	ADULT CRIMINAL COURTS	JUVENILE COURTS	CASE
Right to due process	Yes	Yes—limited	Kent v. United States, In re Gault, In re Winship
Right to counsel	Yes	Yes	In re Gault
Right to indigent appointment of counsel	Yes	Yes	In re Gault
Right to notice of charges	Yes	Yes	In re Gault
Right to confront and cross-examine witnesses	Yes	Yes	In re Gault
Right against self-incrimination	Yes	Yes	In re Gault
Right to remain silent	Yes	Yes	In re Gault
Reasonable doubt standard of proof	Yes	Yes	In re Winship
Right against double jeopardy	Yes	Yes	Breed v. Jones
Right to jury trial	Yes	No	McKeiver v. Pennsylvania
Preventive detention	Yes	Yes	Schall v. Martin
Waiver of rights	Yes	Yes	Fare v. Michael C.
Right to a transcript of court proceedings	Yes	Undecided	
Right to bail	Qualified right	Undecided	
Probable cause for police searches	Yes	Undecided	
Arrest based on probable cause	Yes	Undecided	
Right to a speedy trial	Yes	Undecided	
Right to court access (habeus corpus)	Yes	Undecided	
Right to probation or parole revocation due process	Yes	Undecided	
Right to treatment	Yes	Undecided	
Right to appeal	Yes	Undecided	
Public trials	Yes	Undecided	
Right to grand jury indictment	Yes	Undecided	
Evidence illegally obtained excluded at trial	Yes	Undecided	

Juveniles do not have the same rights to liberty and freedom of movement as adults. *Do you think curtailing juveniles' rights reduces juvenile crime?*

8.5 SELF-CHECK

1. List some of the rights granted to juveniles by the U.S. Supreme Court.

2. Review each of these rights and explain what difference they make in the juvenile justice process.

3. Are juvenile justice laws uniform across the country?

Adult Criminal Trials versus Juvenile Adjudicatory Proceedings

There is no central authority or body of laws that govern all juvenile justice systems or juvenile law in general. In contrast, the U.S. Constitution does provide a central authority for the adult criminal system. Attempts have been made to provide uniformity to juvenile law. The Uniform Juvenile Court Act of 1968 (UJCA) was one such effort. The UJCA outlined several fundamental rights that adults have in criminal cases and applied them to juvenile proceedings. Some of these rights include legal representation, rules of evidence, right against self-incrimination, right to confront witnesses, and several others. However, this does not mean that all juvenile courts are uniform in practice or procedure. Several issues have been ruled on by the U.S. Supreme Court; however, many others vary from jurisdiction to jurisdiction. As a result, juvenile law and procedure vary greatly when compared to adult proceedings from state to state and county to county. Nonetheless, a body of federal case law does establish certain basic juvenile rights. Figure 8.11 depicts some of the rights that the U.S. Supreme Court has granted juveniles and the associated cases compared with adult criminal proceedings.

As the juvenile justice system changes at the state level, issues regarding the rights of juveniles will undoubtedly come to the forefront of juvenile justice. As the system becomes more punitive, many scholars are arguing that the full realm of due process and rights of the accused in criminal matters be applied to juvenile proceedings.[104] Some have argued that the current state of affairs in juvenile justice warrants the abolition of the system.[105] Juvenile law will predictably continue to be an area of controversy and change.

SUMMARY BY CHAPTER OBJECTIVES

1. List the changes in rights and procedures since the due process revolution

Prior to the due process revolution of the 1960s, juveniles essentially only had the right to intervention by the state. Juvenile justice officials had virtually unbridled discretion in their handling of juvenile cases. In addition, many times juveniles were subjected to more severe punishments than adults who were charged with similar crimes. Today, a juvenile who is facing adjudication as a delinquent for a crime where incarceration is a possibility has many of the same rights adults do in criminal proceedings.

2. Describe four landmark Supreme Court cases on juvenile justice

Four landmark U.S. Supreme Court cases govern juvenile proceedings today. In *Kent* v. *United States*, the Court decided that juveniles facing waiver to adult court are entitled to some basic due process rights. This was the first U.S. Supreme Court case that applied rudimentary due process rights to juvenile adjudicatory proceedings. In *In re Gault*, the Court held that a juvenile in a delinquency proceeding is entitled to the essentials of due process, including the right to notice of the charges, the right to counsel, the right to confront and cross-examine witnesses, and the right against self-incrimination, including the right to remain silent. The Court held in *In re Winship* that the standard of proof in juvenile delinquency proceedings is proof beyond a reasonable doubt. Finally, in *McKeiver* v. *Pennsylvania* the U.S. Supreme Court stopped short of requiring all adult criminal rights to juveniles by deciding that juveniles are not entitled to trial by jury in delinquency proceedings.

3. Explain what totality of circumstances means

Whenever a juvenile waives any of his or her constitutional rights, the court must decide whether or not the waiver was knowing and voluntary. In the case of *Fare* v. *Michael C.*, the U.S. Supreme Court decided that the test to determine whether or not a juvenile has knowingly and voluntarily waived his or her rights is the totality of circumstances. The totality of circumstances includes an evaluation of the juvenile's age, experience, education, background, and intelligence when determining whether or not a waiver was knowing and voluntary.

4. List situations where a juvenile is entitled to an attorney

A juvenile is entitled to be represented by an attorney at all critical stages of the proceedings against him or her. Representation by counsel is especially important whenever a juvenile is facing incarceration as the result of a delinquency proceeding. In general, the critical stages include police investigatory proceedings (interrogations and line-ups), most court proceedings (adjudication stage), and sentencing. Nonetheless, a juvenile can waive his or her right to counsel at any or all of these stages. The circumstances of the waiver vary from state to state.

5. Describe the different ways police are allowed to handle juveniles

In general, the police are more restricted in the way in which they process and deal with juvenile offenders. Many of these additional restrictions are specified in state statutes. For example, in some states the police cannot interrogate a juvenile without an attorney or the juvenile's parents being present. Additional restrictions on where the police can conduct investigations include the fact that juvenile offenders must be sight and sound separated from adult offenders. Finally, many standard record-keeping procedures are limited by state law as well.

6. Define confidentiality and anonymity

In some instances, state and federal law prevent law enforcement agencies from maintaining a centralized record system for juveniles, fingerprinting or photographing juveniles, and maintaining records of juvenile offenses into adulthood. The confidentiality and anonymity statute that was a hallmark of the juvenile justice system has been relaxed in recent years due to policy changes designed to get tough on juvenile offenders. Many more states are now allowing records to be kept and used against a juvenile after he or she reaches the age of adulthood. In addition, states have begun to house juvenile records in a central location.

7. Explain current legal issues in juvenile justice

Recent juvenile justice legislation at the state level reflects a desire to get tougher on juvenile offenders and maintain greater accountability over juveniles who are adjudicated delinquent. Laws, such as curfew laws, are being passed to restrict juveniles from being out in the community. In addition, the victims' rights movement has led to states adopting a victims' bill of rights for victims of juvenile offenders. These victims' rights frequently include more accountability-based mechanisms for juveniles. Juvenile rights at school are more limited than they are at home or out in public. While juveniles do have a right to some due process in school, these rights are very limited. Juveniles are entitled to rehabilitative treatment within the juvenile justice system; however, the form this treatment is supposed to take is unclear.

8. **Compare rights and procedures in an adult criminal trial with rights and procedures in juvenile proceedings**

Figure 8.11 on page 235 depicts the differences between juvenile and adult court proceedings in the United States. Juveniles are entitled to many of the same due process rights as their adult counterparts in criminal courts. The notable exception is the right to a jury trial, which was specifically denied by the U.S. Supreme Court in *McKeiver* v. *Pennsylvania*. Although many of the rights are similar, the atmosphere of the juvenile court remains fundamentally more relaxed and informal than an adult criminal proceeding.

KEY TERMS

hands-off approach, p. 204
due process revolution, p. 204
medical model, p. 204
civil nature of juvenile proceedings, p. 204
procedural rights, p. 204
substantive rights, p. 204

Kent v. *United States*, p. 206
In re Gault, p. 207
proof beyond a reasonable doubt, p. 209
preponderance of the evidence, p. 210
In re Winship, p. 210

McKeiver v. *Pennsylvania*, p. 211
Breed v. *Jones*, p. 211
per se test, p. 214
Fare v. *Michael C.*, p. 214
totality of circumstances, p. 215
Miranda rights, p. 216

New Jersey v. *T.L.O.*, p. 219
incommunicado, p. 220
three-strikes laws, p. 226
expunging or sealing, p. 226
Schall v. *Martin*, p. 227
preventive detention, p. 227

REVIEW QUESTIONS

1. How were juveniles traditionally treated by the law before the creation of the juvenile justice system in the United States?

2. What two legal doctrines allowing the state to intervene in the lives of children govern the operation of the juvenile justice system?

3. What legal issue was resolved in the case of *Kent* v. *United States*?

4. What changes to the juvenile justice system were initiated by the case of *In re Gault*?

5. What legal standard of proof is required in juvenile cases according to *In re Winship*?

6. According to *McKeiver* v. *Pennsylvania,* are juveniles entitled to a trial by jury?

7. Can juveniles waive their constitutional rights in the same way that adults do? What additional protections or safeguards are present in some state statutory laws regarding how a juvenile waives his or her rights?

8. Why are juvenile records sometimes sealed or expunged?

9. Can juveniles be fingerprinted and photographed when they are taken into custody?

10. Do juveniles have a right to treatment once they are incarcerated?

11. Under what circumstances is a CRIPA suit filed by the Department of Justice?

12. Can juveniles receive corporal punishment at schools? What legal issues are involved in the use of corporal punishment at school?

13. What rights do the victims of juvenile offenders have?

14. What are juvenile curfews? Are these curfews legal?

15. What rights granted to adults in criminal proceedings are not granted to juveniles in delinquency proceedings?

HANDS-ON ACTIVITIES

1. **Ask an Attorney** Speak with an attorney specializing in juvenile law. Ask what changes in juvenile law and procedure the attorney has witnessed in the recent past. Ask him or her if these changes are good or bad. From what you have learned from this chapter and from your interview with an attorney, state whether or not you agree with the attorney's reasons.

2. Contact your local juvenile court and determine how attorneys are assigned in juvenile cases. If there is a public defender–style system, inquire about volunteer opportunities with the office. If there is an appointment system, inquire about the offices that are usually selected for juvenile cases and contact those firms and inquire about volunteering. In your work there, you will find a host of problems and issues relating to legal representation in the juvenile system; which of these are most problematic?

INTERNET ACTIVITIES

1. Go to **http://apps.americanbar.org/dch/committee. cfm?com=CR200000**, the website for the American Bar Association's Juvenile Justice Committee. Review some of the material in this section. What are some of the new issues concerning juvenile justice that are being discussed at the state and federal level?

2. Visit the National Juvenile Defender Center at **www.njdc.info/.** What are the most prominent priorities of this group? What does this group advocate in terms of changes to the juvenile justice legal system? What are the most pressing problems in the juvenile justice system according to this group?

CRITICAL THINKING EXERCISES

1. **Explain the Differences between Juveniles and Adults in the Justice System** The police take Amy, a 16-year-old juvenile, into custody for auto theft. Describe the differences in law and procedure between juveniles and adults at each of the following stages: detention, adjudication, corrections, and record keeping that would apply to this scenario.

2. **Decide Whether to Admit a Confession** The police take Bob, a juvenile age 15, into custody for a sex offense. Police picked him up at his house when his parents were not home and transported him to the police station. Upon arrival, the police question Bob about his role in the crime. Bob never asks to see his parents or an attorney and the interrogation continues for two hours. Bob eventually confesses to the crime and signs a sworn confession admitting his responsibility. Bob is currently enrolled in high school, has average intelligence, and lives in a middle-class neighborhood.

   You are a state supreme court justice in your state of residence. Using the criteria established in *Fare v. Michael C.* make a determination as to whether this confession is admissible. What criteria did you use to make your final judgment?

3. **Describe Booking Procedures** You are a police officer processing a juvenile offender accused of committing a burglary. Describe the restrictions on the booking procedures of which you may have to be aware while processing this juvenile.

4. **Determine the Right to Jury Trial** Doug is a 16-year-old juvenile accused of committing a murder during the course of a convenience store robbery. Doug is not going to be waived to adult court. Under state law, Doug is eligible for a 40-year determinate sentence from the juvenile court. With reference to the issues discussed in the McKeiver v. Pennsylvania case, should Doug have the right to a jury trial? Has anything changed since the U.S. Supreme Court decision which you think should guarantee juveniles the right to a trial by jury?

ANSWERS TO SELF-CHECKS

8.1 Self-Check

What role have the courts played in the administration of juvenile justice in the United States?

Before the 1960s, juvenile courts followed the "medical model" and saw delinquents as needing treatment rather than punishment; however, since this treatment was also punitive, juveniles were deprived of due process rights. The U.S. Supreme Court maintained a hands-off approach toward juvenile matters until the granting of due process rights and substantive rights.

8.2 Self-Check

How were juveniles treated by the legal system prior to the due process revolution?

A child did not have the right to liberty, but to custody. Adults viewed children not as people, but essentially as the property of the people who were in charge of them. Court intervention in the lives of children was considered "child saving," not punishment.

8.3 Self-Check

1. What specific rights were granted by the Supreme Court to juveniles in the cases of *Kent*, *Gault*, and *Winship*?

Kent v. *United States:* Juveniles facing the possibility of waiver to adult court are entitled to some basic due process rights.

In re Gault: Juveniles in delinquency proceedings are entitled to essential due process rights, including the right to notice of the charges, right to counsel, right to confront and cross-examine witnesses, and the right against self-incrimination (including the right to remain silent).

In re Winship: The standard of proof in juvenile delinquency proceedings is "beyond a reasonable doubt," as it is with criminal proceedings.

2. What right did the U.S. Supreme Court refuse to grant to juveniles in the *McKeiver* decision?

The U.S. Supreme Court refused to guarantee the right to a jury trial for juveniles. This does not mean that juveniles cannot have a jury trial, but that the courts are not required to guarantee one.

3. Why were the Supreme Court decisions discussed in this section originally opposed by many in the juvenile justice system?

Many people in the juvenile justice system opposed the major Supreme Court decisions involving juveniles because they felt the changes would abolish the juvenile justice system. As juveniles were given many of the same rights as adults, these people thought that the differences between the juvenile and criminal justice systems were becoming more and more blurred. With these distinctions disappearing, the juvenile justice system would move from its paternalistic role to a more punitive one.

8.4 Self-Check

1. Do public school students have the same rights at school as when they are at home?

No, many fundamental rights are not granted to students, including freedom of expression and the Miranda warning.

2. List the three trends involving juvenile records.

These trends are:

- More juveniles are subject to transfer to adult court.
- Juvenile justice record information is increasingly available outside the juvenile system.
- Integration of juvenile and adult records is increasing.

3. Explain the nature of curfew laws and ordinances and which situations they typically encompass.

Curfew laws must meet two requirements to be constitutional: (a) there must be a compelling state interest, and (b) the curfew must be designed to serve that state interest. Many cities that have curfews follow the Dallas, Texas, model. This model was designed to help reduce juvenile crime and victimization. It applies to youth under age 17, but it allows for exceptions such as being accompanied by an adult, traveling to and from work, or responding to an emergency.

8.5 Self-Check

1. List some of the rights granted to juveniles by the U.S. Supreme Court.

Answers can include the rights to any of the following, which can be found in Figure 8.11 on page 235.

- Due process (limited)
- Counsel
- Indigent appointment of counsel
- Notice of charges
- Confront and cross-examine witnesses
- Protection from self-incrimination
- Remain silent
- Standard of proof that is "beyond a reasonable doubt"
- Protection from double jeopardy

2. Review each of these rights and explain what difference they make in the juvenile justice process.

- Due process: The right to due process in cases that involve waiver to adult court provides youths with the same rights that adults would have when being tried under similar circumstances.
- Counsel: Attorneys help keep juveniles aware of their rights. However, some believe that the right to counsel has turned the juvenile justice system more adversarial than it used to be.
- Indigent appointment of counsel: As with adult offenders, this right ensures that the poor have the right to the same privileges that the wealthy do.
- Notice of charges: The right to notice of charges prevents juveniles from being punished without knowing why. Previously, juveniles could be sentenced without having committed a crime, perhaps in order to remove them from bad environments.
- Confront and cross-examine witnesses: This right allows juveniles to defend themselves by confronting those who claim they have committed a crime. This is important because, as evidenced in In re Gault, cross-examining witnesses could help prove a juvenile's innocence.
- Protection from self-incrimination: Juveniles do not have to take the stand against themselves.
- Remain silent: As with the right to protection from self-incrimination, juveniles do not have to contribute to the case against them.
- Standard of proof that is "beyond a reasonable doubt": Juveniles are held to the same standard of proof as adults, making their prosecution more rigorous and less subject to mistakes. The standard of proof had previously been a preponderance of evidence, the same standard used in civil cases.
- Protection from double jeopardy: This right protects juveniles from being tried twice for the same charge. It also protects them from being tried in both the juvenile justice system and the criminal justice system for the same charge.

3. Are juvenile justice laws uniform across the country?

No, juvenile justice laws vary from state to state and from city to city. There are some rules, however, that are uniform throughout the country, particularly those that are based on Supreme Court decisions.

THE JUVENILE COURT

Chapter Outline

Chapter Objectives

After completing this chapter, you should be able to:

1. Describe the jurisdiction of the juvenile court.

2. Describe juvenile court key personnel and their primary responsibilities.

3. List the major steps in the juvenile court process.

4. Explain what occurs during the decision to detain and the decision to petition a case.

5. Describe decisions made by the prosecutor.

6. Explain what happens during adjudication.

7. Describe a predisposition report.

8. Analyze what occurs at a disposition hearing.

The First Juvenile Justice Courts

Before the establishment of the first juvenile court, there was only one system of justice in the United States, and all offenders were processed by the same system regardless of age. This meant that juveniles were treated the same as adults and in many instances received the same punishment as adults. Although some were kept separated from adults prior to the establishment of the first juvenile court, many juveniles were housed in prisons with adults and sometimes subjected to the death penalty. (Under common law, a juvenile age seven or older could receive the same punishment as an adult.) In the 1800s, changes in the social and economic structure included urbanization, industrialization, and immigration which led to various juvenile reform efforts. Concerned about the number of youths who appeared to be unsupervised and out of control, juvenile justice reformers led efforts to create the first juvenile court in 1899. This juvenile court was established in Cook County, Illinois, by the passage of the Juvenile Court Act.

Juveniles are taken into custody for offenses that are crimes if committed by adults. *What is going to happen to this youth after being taken into custody? What impact will this have on the youth?*

Juvenile courts were instituted rapidly throughout the country. By 1910, 22 states had established juvenile courts, and by 1925, only two states lacked juvenile courts. Finally, in 1945, the last two states without juvenile courts—Maine and Wyoming—created juvenile court systems.

The juvenile court was founded on the concept of *parens patriae* (see full definition in Chapter 1), roughly translated as the "state as parent." The state, through the juvenile court judge, acts in the role of parent for a juvenile when parents are deemed incapable or unwilling to control their children. Therefore, the juvenile court was designed to do what was in the best interest of the juvenile, just as a parent would. As discussed in Chapter 2, the juvenile court has undergone significant changes since its development in 1899. This chapter analyzes the juvenile court process. Each major step in the process will be discussed including intake, prosecutor decision making, adjudication, and disposition. Personnel who work in the juvenile court will also be studied, including the juvenile court judge, juvenile court referee, prosecuting attorney, defense attorney, and probation officer.

9.1 SELF-CHECK

How were juveniles treated prior to the establishment of juvenile courts?

The Juvenile Court Today

What is the **jurisdiction** of the juvenile court? Generally, the juvenile court has jurisdiction over all acts of delinquency. Delinquency is any behavior that is prohibited by the juvenile law of the state. Therefore, each legislature defines what delinquency is in that particular state. In most states, however, delinquency consists of two general categories. First, delinquency is any act committed by a juvenile that would be a crime if committed by an adult. Therefore, acts such as theft, burglary, assault, and robbery are acts of delinquency.

jurisdiction The court authority granted by law to hear a case.

The second category consists of acts known as status offenses. A status offense is an act committed by a juvenile that would not be considered a crime if committed by an adult. These acts are forbidden because of the status (based on age) of the individual as a juvenile. Status offenses include such acts as running away from home, skipping school (truancy), violating curfew, not obeying one's parents (incorrigibility or ungovernability), illegal purchase of alcohol, smoking tobacco, and underage drinking.

CATEGORIES OF DELINQUENCY

About one half of the states include status offenses as delinquency. The other states have established categories that distinguish juvenile delinquents from status offenders. These states classify status offenders as CINS, CHINS, PINS, JINS or MINS. These acronyms stand for children in need of supervision (CINS, CHINS), persons in need of supervision (PINS), juveniles in need of supervision (JINS), and minors in need of supervision (MINS), respectively. Separating juvenile delinquents from status offenders removes the stigma of being classified as a juvenile delinquent and demonstrates that these juveniles have special problems and needs that are not criminal in nature.

The juvenile court not only has jurisdiction over delinquent acts and status offenses but also has jurisdiction over child abuse and neglect matters, adoption, termination of parental rights, child custody matters, and child support.

In some jurisdictions, juvenile courts may be structured to be completely separate courts that hear only cases involving juveniles. This is likely to occur in areas with large populations. On the other hand, some juvenile courts may be a component of a larger court that has jurisdiction over adult cases and other matters as well.

Juvenile courts in the United States processed nearly 1.5 million delinquency cases, excluding status offenses, in 2009. The number of delinquency cases processed by juvenile courts increased 30 percent between 1985 and 2009.[1] Between the peak year 1997 and 2009, the delinquency caseload declined 20 percent.[2] More specifically, the number of juvenile court cases involving violent offenses (criminal homicide, forcible rape, robbery, aggravated assault, simple assault, other violent sex offenses, and other person offenses) declined 18 percent between 2000 and 2009, while property crime index offenses (burglary, larceny-theft, motor vehicle theft, arson, vandalism, trespassing, stolen property offenses, and other property offenses) processed in juvenile court declined 19 percent during the same time period.[3] In 2009, the most serious charge brought was a property offense (such as burglary, larceny, motor vehicle theft, or vandalism) in 38 percent of the cases, a person offense (such as simple or aggravated assault, robbery, sex offenses, or homicide) in 24 percent, a public order offense (such as disorderly conduct or weapons offenses) in 27 percent, and a drug offense (including trafficking or possession of controlled substances or paraphernalia) in 11 percent.[4]

DELINQUENCY CASE OUTCOMES

When a delinquency case is referred to juvenile court, an intake officer, prosecutor, or judge determines whether to handle the case formally or informally. Formal handling involves the filing of a petition to request that the court hold an adjudicatory or waiver hearing. More than half (55 percent) of the delinquency cases processed in 2009 were handled formally.[5] The remaining 45 percent of the cases were dismissed (19 percent) or were handled informally (27 percent), which generally means that the juvenile was placed on informal adjustment or **diversion**. Of the cases that were petitioned, or handled formally, 59 percent were adjudicated delinquent, that is, found to have committed the act, and less than 1 percent were waived to adult court.[6] Of the delinquency cases adjudicated

---

Drug Offenses

In juvenile court, the number of cases involving drug offenses were relatively flat from 1985 through 1993 (increasing 17 percent), rose sharply (up 110 percent) from 1993 through 1997, and then slightly decreased through 2009 (down 12 percent from 1997).

SOURCE: Knoll, Crystal and Melissa Sickmund. 2012, October. *Delinquency Cases in Juvenile Court, 2009.* Washington DC: Office of Juvenile Justice and Delinquency Prevention.

---

diversion A procedure by which the juvenile is removed from the juvenile justice process and provided with treatment services.

COMMUNITY SERVICE PROGRAM'S JUVENILE DIVERSION PROGRAM

Community Services Program, Inc. is a non-profit agency which was established in 1972 as a field study project for students at the University of California Irvine. Since that time, CSP has grown dramatically in size and scope and has designed and implemented some of the most respected intervention programs in Southern California. One such program is CSP's Juvenile Diversion Program. It is designed to provide diversion services to youths ages 10–17 and their families. The goals of the program are to provide early intervention for delinquent juveniles who come into contact with police, probation, and school personnel.

The following services are provided in CSP's Diversion Program:

- *Individual and Family Counseling*
  Professional counselors work with youths and their families on a short-term basis to help them improve communication and develop coping and decision-making skills. The goals are to increase positive family interactions and to promote responsible law-abiding behavior by youth.

- *Drug/Alcohol Education Groups*
  Small groups of youths meet for three 2-hour sessions led by counselors. The youths become aware of their behavior patterns and understand the consequences of drug and alcohol use. These groups also help young people learn effective problem-solving and decision-making skills.

- *Anger Management Groups*
  The anger management group addresses the needs of juveniles who are identified by schools or the juvenile justice system for an inability to express their anger appropriately. A psychoeducational approach is utilized to develop new skills and recognize the ineffectiveness of the old behavior. The group involves three sessions.

- *Truancy Reduction Intervention Program*
  TRIP is designed to assist students in understanding the short- and long-term consequences of truancy, to assist them in learning to make sound decisions, and assist them in goal setting for the future. Additionally, TRIP provides students with pre-employment skills such as determining their transferable skills, completing job applications, and interview techniques. The program involves two 2-hour classes.

Source: www.cspinc.org

in juvenile court in 2009, 27 percent resulted in residential placement, and 60 percent were placed on probation.[7] In 13 percent of adjudicated delinquency cases, the court ordered some other sanction, such as requiring a juvenile to pay restitution or a fine, to participate in some form of community service, or to enter a treatment or counseling program.

Juvenile Court Personnel

The juvenile court is composed of several individuals who make decisions on what to do with cases involving delinquents and status offenders. This section will examine the key personnel in the juvenile court as well as their primary responsibilities.

JUVENILE COURT JUDGE

A **juvenile court judge** has the primary responsibility for the operation of the juvenile court and is an important decision maker in the juvenile court. Although a court administrator may relieve the judge of some duties, the juvenile court judge is usually responsible for hiring and firing staff, establishing court policies, and budgeting. However, the most important duties of a juvenile court judge involve the disposition of cases involving delinquents. The judge possesses tremendous power over the delinquent and has the ability to remove

juvenile court judge Position or office primarily responsible for the operation of the juvenile court including deciding guilt or innocence and disposition of cases.

The juvenile court judge hears cases against juveniles. *What decisions does the juvenile court judge make? What factors do you think impact the judge's decisions?*

the delinquent from his or her family and place the juvenile in a secure or nonsecure facility outside the home. The judge can also impose requirements on the delinquent and even the parents. For example, the judge can require a juvenile to attend counseling sessions, school, or any other program the judge deems necessary. The judge can also require parents to assist in the treatment of their child by ensuring that the juvenile abides by the judge's orders. Failure

JUVENILE JUSTICE ONLINE

Go to **www.ncjfcj.org**, the National Council of Juvenile and Family Court Judges Web page. Click on "About Us" and "Membership." Read the information provided. Who are members of NCJFCJ? What services does the organization provide to its members?

CAREERS IN JUVENILE JUSTICE

Juvenile Court Judge

A juvenile court judge is primarily responsible for the operation of the juvenile court. The most important duties of a juvenile court judge involve the disposition of cases involving delinquents. A juvenile court judge determines whether the juvenile committed the offense and then decides the appropriate disposition of the case. If a juvenile is adjudicated for a delinquent act, the judge determines the sanction. Juvenile court judges also hear cases involving abuse, neglect, adoption, and custody of children.

Judges who exclusively hear juvenile cases are present only in large jurisdictions where there is enough juvenile crime to justify the use of one or more full-time judges. In smaller jurisdictions with less juvenile crime, the juvenile court judge is also responsible for hearing other cases not involving juveniles. These cases could include adult criminal cases as well as civil cases.

Juvenile court judges possess law degrees. Some juvenile court judges are elected while others are appointed. The career paths of juvenile court judges are varied. Many have been prosecutors or practicing attorneys before becoming juvenile court judges. Others are judges in other capacities such as adult court who transfer into the position of juvenile court judge.

Critical Thinking

What do you think the differences are between a juvenile court and an adult court judge?

to do so can lead to sanctions for both the juvenile and parents, including incarceration.

A juvenile court judge provides the leadership to determine how the juvenile court in that jurisdiction will be managed. For example, the judge can dictate which types of cases have priority in juvenile court. If a judge decides that runaways, truants, and curfew violators should not be handled by the juvenile court, then these types of offenders will be diverted from the juvenile court. In some jurisdictions, status offenders are handled in municipal or other courts of limited jurisdiction. As another example, a judge may also provide informal leadership on what types of outcomes are expected in certain cases. The judge may believe that many offenders need to be detained prior to adjudication in order to protect the community and that incarceration in an institution should be a readily used sanction after adjudication. If a judge believes this is what should be done with juvenile offenders, then the court staff is likely to respond in a manner consistent with the judge's perspective. Similarly, if a judge feels that juveniles should be waived to adult court only under extreme circumstances, then very few juveniles will be waived to adult court in that jurisdiction.

How are juvenile court judges selected to serve? Depending on the state, juvenile court judges are selected by one of the following ways:

1. Elected—This is how judges are selected in most states
2. Appointed by the governor
3. Appointed by the legislature
4. Appointed via the Missouri plan (The Missouri plan combines number one and two above. In other words, the governor usually appoints an individual to serve as a juvenile court judge. After the first term is completed, usually four to six years, the judge must run for reelection in an uncontested election. If a judge is not reelected because of poor performance on the bench or some other reason, then the governor appoints another person to serve as judge and the process starts all over.)

JUVENILE COURT REFEREE

Judges must tend to a large volume of cases on a daily basis. In order to assist with the workload, **referees** are frequently appointed by the juvenile court judge to assist with the duties of the court. Referees, sometimes called **commissioners** or **masters**, are usually, although not always, attorneys that have been appointed by the juvenile court judge.

The duties of a referee vary from jurisdiction to jurisdiction, but the primary responsibility of a referee is to hear cases and tend to preadjudication hearings. The referee usually hears the less serious cases so that the juvenile court judge can focus on the more serious felony offenses. Therefore, a juvenile who has been referred to juvenile court for a theft may have the case heard by a referee rather than a juvenile court judge. The referee also presides over preadjudication hearings such as detention hearings and arraignments. For example, referees who preside over detention hearings will determine whether a juvenile should remain in detention or be released into the community.

PROSECUTING ATTORNEY

The prosecutor represents the interest of the state in bringing the case against a juvenile. In large jurisdictions with a large volume of juvenile cases, a prosecutor may handle only juvenile cases. In smaller jurisdictions with fewer cases, a

referees, commissioners, masters Individuals who hear cases in juvenile court and tend to preadjudication hearings.

prosecutor may be responsible for both juvenile and adult cases. The prosecutor has several key responsibilities in the juvenile court:

- The prosecutor frequently makes the decision of whether a case should be dismissed, adjudicated, or diverted. The prosecutor makes this decision based on several factors: the seriousness of the offense, prior record of the juvenile, sufficiency of evidence, and other relevant issues.
- If the prosecutor decides that the juvenile should be adjudicated for the offense, the prosecutor decides what charges to bring against the juvenile. The juvenile may be accused, for example, of auto theft, burglary, and vandalism. The prosecutor will decide whether to charge the juvenile with each offense or reduce the charges.
- The prosecutor is also responsible for the disposition of the case; in many instances, through the use of *plea bargaining*. When a case is plea-bargained, the prosecutor negotiates an appropriate disposition of the case with the juvenile's attorney.
- The prosecutor is usually responsible for initiating the proceedings that lead to waiving a juvenile to adult court for prosecution. The prosecutor decides whether to petition the juvenile court to waive the case to the adult system.

DEFENSE ATTORNEY

The primary responsibilities of the defense attorney are to present the best case possible to the judge or jury (if applicable) during the adjudication hearing regardless of the offense committed, to negotiate settlement of the case through plea bargaining if applicable, and to ensure that the rights of the juvenile are not violated during the juvenile justice process. Juveniles may retain their own attorney to represent them or may have one appointed for them by the court. Chapter 8 discusses the *In re Gault*[8] case, which gave juveniles the right to representation by counsel. Despite the ruling in *In re Gault*,

Defense attorneys protect the rights of their clients. *What role does the defense attorney play in the juvenile justice process? When do they usually become involved in a case?*

less than 50 percent of juveniles accused of delinquency receive assistance of counsel.

PROBATION OFFICER

Probation officers are critical players in the juvenile court process. Their responsibilities will be briefly mentioned here; they are covered in much greater detail in Chapter 11. Probation officers perform three basic functions for the juvenile court:

- Probation officers perform intake screenings that determine if the case is initially handled formally or informally by the juvenile justice system.
- They complete predisposition reports that assist juvenile court judges in determining the most appropriate disposition of the case after adjudication.
- They monitor juveniles on probation to make sure that they are abiding by their conditions of probation and accessing the services required by the court.

9.3 SELF-CHECK

What persons work in juvenile court and what are their responsibilities?

Intake

How does a juvenile enter the juvenile justice system? The juvenile enters the system by being referred to juvenile court. There are two main sources of referrals to juvenile court: (1) law enforcement (police) agencies and (2) others such as parents, victims, schools, and probation officers. The vast majority of cases alleging that a juvenile has committed a delinquent act are referred to the juvenile court by a law enforcement agency.

After a case has been referred to juvenile court, it is sent to intake. Intake is usually the responsibility of the juvenile probation department or the prosecutor's office. At this point in the process, two important decisions are made: (1) the decision to detain the juvenile and (2) the decision to petition the case.

DECISION TO DETAIN

When a police officer has taken a juvenile into custody, the officer may take the juvenile to the detention center. A **detention center** is a facility designed for short-term, secure confinement of a juvenile prior to court disposition or execution of a court order. Not all juveniles taken into custody are sent to the detention center. Instead, the arresting officer files the case with juvenile intake for processing. If the juvenile is taken to a detention center, the juvenile goes through a screening process to determine whether the juvenile should be released back into the community or detained in the detention center. The individual conducting the detention center screening is usually a probation officer or detention center staff member. Screening officers may speak with the juvenile's parents and the officer who took the juvenile into custody in making their decision. In addition, the screening officer will determine if the juvenile has a pending offense against him or her in juvenile court and if the juvenile is currently on probation. The screening officer will look at the criteria established by state law and departmental regulations in making the decision. The criteria may specify who can be detained, who must be detained, and who cannot be detained. For example, departmental regulations may require that all juveniles accused of a violent felony offense be detained while forbidding the detention of certain offenders such as those committing minor delinquent acts.

Most juveniles are not held in a detention center prior to adjudication, but a juvenile is likely to be detained if: (1) the juvenile is determined to be

detention center A facility designed for short-term, secure confinement of the juvenile prior to court disposition or execution of a court order.

Intake is a significant step in the juvenile justice process. *What decisions are made during the intake process? How are these decisions made?*

a threat to the community; (2) the juvenile will be in danger if returned to the community; or (3) the juvenile is a flight risk and may not appear at the adjudication hearing.[9] A juvenile may also be detained if a parent who can provide suitable supervision for the juvenile cannot be located. Therefore, juveniles are held in secure detention facilities before adjudication and disposition in some cases. This serves to protect the community and the juvenile, ensure the juvenile's appearance at scheduled hearings, and allow for evaluation if needed.[10]

In 2009, 318,000 juveniles who were accused of a delinquent offense were detained (21 percent of total delinquency cases). Over 31 percent of the juveniles detained prior to adjudication were accused of a violent offense while 30 percent were accused of a property offense. The remaining juveniles who were detained were accused of public order offenses (30 percent) and drug offenses (9 percent). What is the probability of a juvenile's being detained prior to adjudication? Only 27 percent of juveniles accused of a violent offense were detained prior to adjudication while 17 percent accused of property offenses were detained.[11]

If the juvenile is detained, every state requires that a **detention hearing** be held within 24 to 72 hours of detention.[12] At the detention hearing, the judge decides whether the current detention is justified and whether continued detention is warranted. It is estimated that approximately 50 percent of all detained juveniles are released after a detention hearing.[13] In other words, the juvenile court judge decides that continued detention is not warranted in about half of the cases. In the remaining cases, the juvenile may continue to be detained until

Myth / Fact

Myth

Most youths who are taken into custody are placed in a detention center prior to adjudication.

Fact

Only 27 percent of juveniles accused of a violent offense are detained prior to adjudication while 17 percent accused of property offenses are detained.

Source: Puzzanchera, Charles, Benjamin Adams, and Sarah Hockenberry. 2012, May. *Juvenile Court Statistics 2009.* Pittsburgh, PA: National Center for Juvenile Justice.

detention hearing A hearing held in juvenile court during which the judge decides whether the current detention of the juvenile is justified and whether continued detention is warranted.

the adjudication hearing. The practice of detaining juveniles until adjudication is known as preventive detention. The practice of preventive detention (upheld as constitutional by the U.S. Supreme Court in *Schall* v. *Martin*.[14]) is discussed in Chapter 8.

QUALIFIED RIGHT TO POST BAIL

Traditionally, juveniles have not been afforded the qualified right to post bail although the use of bail is a growing trend. Bail is not designed to be a punishment, but is expected to ensure the individual's appearance at subsequent stages of the court process including adjudication. Most juveniles are released to the custody of their parent or guardian and are not required to post bail. Some states do *not* have bail for juveniles. This practice is based on the concept of *parens patriae* discussed earlier in this chapter. A judge acts as a parent and if the judge believes the juvenile should be detained, then the juvenile is detained. On the other hand, if the judge believes the juvenile should be released, then the juvenile is released. However, with the "get tough on juvenile crime" attitude that has dominated juvenile justice in recent years, many argue that the concept of *parens patriae* has eroded. With this view has come the increased use of bail for juveniles. Some states grant juveniles the qualified right to bail. As mentioned in Chapter 8, juveniles have not expressly been given the qualified right to post bail by the U.S. Supreme Court.

DECISION TO PETITION THE CASE

The second major decision made at intake is whether to petition the case. A **petition** is a document that states the allegations against the juvenile and requests the juvenile court to adjudicate the individual. This decision is usually made by a probation officer, although the prosecuting attorney has played an increasing role in jurisdictions in recent years. Once intake receives a referral from a police officer or from another referral source, the intake process commences. The decision usually involves choosing among three alternatives:

1. Dismiss the case against the juvenile and release the individual to his or her parent or guardian
2. Handle the matter informally by placing the juvenile on informal probation
3. Petition the case by referring the case further into the juvenile justice system for formal intervention by the court[15] See Figure 9.1.

In making the decision on what to do with the case, an intake officer may take into account several factors, including seriousness of the offense, prior record of the accused, age of the accused, demeanor of the juvenile, and harm inflicted on the victim. The intake officer also takes into account state law and departmental regulations in making the decision. Many states and departmental regulations require that petitions be filed for certain offenses. For example, a juvenile court may require that all cases involving violent offenses or where a gun was involved be petitioned. If state law or departmental regulation does not restrict their decision, then the intake officer has a great deal of discretion in deciding what to do with the case. The intake officer may also speak with the juvenile's parents and school, as well as the arresting officer, prior to making the decision.

CASE DISMISSALS Cases that are dismissed at intake usually involve minor offenses or first-time offenders, or lack substantial evidence to support the allegations against the juvenile. If the case is dismissed, the intake officer will explain to the juvenile that future violations of the law will lead to formal

---

Cases Involving Males and Females

The number of delinquency cases involving female juveniles increased 86 percent between 1985 and 2009, while cases involving males increased 17 percent.

SOURCE: Puzzanchera, Charles, Benjamin Adams, and Sarah Hockenberry. 2012, May. *Juvenile Court Statistics 2009*. Pittsburgh, PA: National Center for Juvenile Justice.

---

petition A document that states the allegations against a juvenile and requests the juvenile court to adjudicate the juvenile.

Juveniles in Adult Jails

The Juvenile Justice and Delinquency Prevention Act of 1974 limits the placement of juveniles in adult institutions. The act states that, ". . . juveniles alleged to be or found to be delinquent shall not be detained or confined in any institution in which they have contact with adult persons incarcerated because they have been convicted of a crime or are awaiting trial on criminal charges or with the part-time or full-time security staff or direct-care staff of a jail or lockup for adults."

Subsequent rulings have interpreted the act to permit juveniles to be held in secure adult facilities if the juvenile is being tried as an adult for a felony or has been convicted of a felony. In institutions other than adult jails or lockups, confinement is permitted, if the juvenile and adult inmates cannot see each other and no conversation between them is possible. This latter requirement is commonly referred to as "sight and sound separation." There is a six-hour grace period that allows the temporary holding of delinquents in adult jails or lockups until other arrangements can be made, provided there is sight and sound separation.

In rural areas, delinquents may also be held in adult jails or lockups for no more than 24 hours under the following conditions:

- The juvenile is awaiting an initial court appearance
- There is no alternative placement available
- There is sight and sound separation

In rural and less populous communities, juvenile detention centers are rare. Therefore, juveniles are sometimes placed in adult jails prior to adjudication. It is unknown whether "sight and sound separation" between juveniles and adults is maintained or whether the two groups are mixed. Despite efforts to remove juveniles from adult jails, several thousand juveniles are confined in adult jails annually.

CRITICAL THINKING

Do you think juvenile offenders should be held in adult facilities at all (even with the provisions of the JJDP Act)?

Source: Sickmund, Melissa. *Juveniles in Corrections.* Washington, DC: Office of Juvenile Justice and Delinquency Prevention, 2004.

handling within the court system. Depending on the seriousness of the subsequent offense and the amount of time since the previous offense, this warning may or may not be enforced. Approximately 19 percent of all cases referred to juvenile court are dismissed.[16]

9.4 SELF-CHECK

What decisions are made during intake?

| FIGURE 9.1 | Intake Decisions, 1999 |

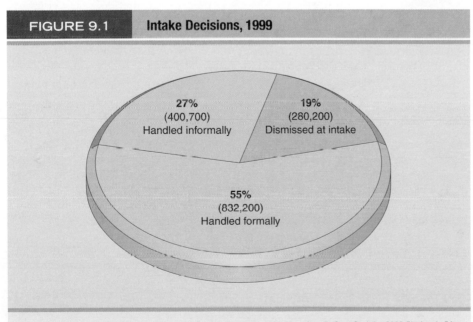

27%
(400,700)
Handled informally

19%
(280,200)
Dismissed at intake

55%
(832,200)
Handled formally

Source: Puzzanchera, Charles, Benjamin Adams, and Sarah Hockenberry. 2012, May. *Juvenile Court Statistics 2009.* Pittsburgh, PA: National Center for Juvenile Justice.

CASES HANDLED INFORMALLY About 25 percent of all cases referred to juvenile court are handled informally at intake.[17] In many instances, a juvenile will agree to complete certain requirements in exchange for having the case handled informally and not processed further in the system. The juvenile is typically required to pay **victim restitution**, perform **community service**, attend school, or meet some other related requirement. In recent years, victim restitution and community service have become popular ways of handling cases informally in many jurisdictions. In addition, the juvenile may be referred to agencies within the community that can assist the juvenile. For example, a juvenile may be referred to a drug counseling program or a mental health agency. If the juvenile completes the requirements, then nothing further occurs with the case (i.e., the case is dismissed). This process is sometimes called **informal probation, informal adjustment, and deferred prosecution**.[18] However, if the juvenile does not complete the requirements, then the case can be sent to juvenile court for further processing within the juvenile justice system. For example, suppose a 15-year-old girl is referred to juvenile court for vandalizing her neighbor's vehicle by breaking two windows. An intake officer reviews the police report and decides to place the girl on informal probation. The juvenile is required to pay the victim $400 for the replacement of the windows and attend counseling sessions on appropriate ways to deal with aggression. The girl has 60 days to complete these requirements. If both requirements are satisfactorily met by the end of the 60 days, then the case against the juvenile is dismissed. However, if the requirements are not met, then a petition will be filed in juvenile court alleging the juvenile has committed vandalism. If the intake officer decides to file a petition, the case is forwarded to the prosecutor for action. Prosecutor decision making is discussed in the next section.

Prosecutor Decision Making

Once the intake decision to further process the juvenile in the system has been made, the prosecutor receives the case. Frequently, the decision by the intake

victim restitution A sanction by which an offender pays the victim for the harm done due to the offense.

community service A sanction imposed requiring the individual to perform a predetermined number of hours of volunteer work in the community.

informal probation, informal adjustment, deferred prosecution A procedure by which the juvenile agrees to meet certain requirements in exchange for having the case dismissed.

Most juveniles are not placed in a detention center after they are taken into custody. *What factors increase the likelihood that a juvenile will be placed in a detention center prior to adjudication?*

officer to file a petition must be approved by the prosecutor. The prosecutor determines if there is enough evidence to substantiate the complaint against the juvenile and that the offense occurred in the court's jurisdiction. As mentioned in the previous section, the prosecutor plays a larger role today in the intake decision in many jurisdictions than in the past. In some jurisdictions, prosecuting attorneys handle the intake function instead of probation officers. In deciding what to do with the case, a prosecutor decides between many of the same options as the intake officer. The choices are:

1. Dismiss the case
2. Handle the matter informally by placing the juvenile on informal probation (if the prosecutor makes this decision, the juvenile is usually sent back to the intake unit for processing)
3. Petition the case by requesting adjudication of the juvenile
4. Waive the juvenile to adult court for prosecution

The first three alternatives are the same for the prosecutor and for the intake officer. The unique alternative for the prosecutor is the decision to waive a juvenile to adult court, which involves the juvenile court relinquishing its jurisdiction over the offender and allowing the juvenile to be sent to adult court for prosecution. Waiver to adult court is a serious decision, but as the trend toward tougher sanctions for juvenile delinquents continues, this option also receives more attention. Once waived to adult court, the juvenile is treated as an adult and, if convicted, may be eligible for the same punishment as adults, including life imprisonment. (See Chapter 10 for a detailed discussion of waiver to adult court.)

9.5 SELF-CHECK

1. What choices does a prosecutor have in deciding what to do with a case?

Adjudication

At this stage in the juvenile court process, there is an arraignment and adjudication hearing.

ARRAIGNMENT

If a petition is filed by the prosecutor against a juvenile alleging delinquent conduct, then the next step in the process is an **arraignment**. At the arraignment hearing, the juvenile is made aware of the following rights:

1. Right to counsel and right to court-appointed counsel if indigent
2. Right to an adjudication hearing
3. Right to confront and cross-examine witnesses
4. Right to have witnesses testify on behalf of the juvenile[19]

In addition to being made aware of their rights, juveniles are notified of the charges against them and are asked to enter a plea in the case. Many delinquents plead guilty during the arraignment and receive a sanction for their delinquent act. It is estimated that only 5 percent of all juvenile delinquency cases petitioned to the juvenile court actually involve an adjudication hearing. In other words, about 95 percent of the cases do not go to an adjudication hearing. Sometimes the cases are disposed of through plea bargaining. **Plea bargaining** is the process by which a juvenile pleads guilty in exchange for concessions made by the prosecutor. For example, a juvenile may be charged with five counts of burglary. The prosecutor may agree to dismiss four of those counts in exchange for a guilty plea on one count of burglary. It is unknown how many guilty pleas in juvenile court are the result of plea bargaining and how many are the result of an open admission of guilt.

arraignment A hearing held in juvenile court prior to the adjudication hearing in which the juvenile is made aware of his or her rights and is asked to enter a plea to the charges.

plea bargaining The process by which a juvenile pleads guilty in exchange for concessions made by the prosecutor.

Until recently, plea bargaining was not needed in juvenile court because the doctrine of *parens patriae* dictated that the juvenile court act in the role of the parent and decide what was in the best interest of the juvenile. As the juvenile court process began to resemble criminal court processes, plea bargains became more and more common.

Defense attorneys who represent juveniles usually ask for these concessions in a plea bargain discussion:

1. A reduction of charges either by reducing the number of charges or charging the juvenile with a less serious offense than originally intended
2. An agreement on the disposition to be imposed on the juvenile (i.e., what sentence the juvenile should receive)
3. An agreement not to waive the case to adult court in exchange for a guilty plea

ADJUDICATION HEARING

If a juvenile does not admit to the offense at the arraignment, then an **adjudication hearing** is scheduled. Adjudication hearings are held in juvenile court to determine if the juvenile committed the offense. The adjudication hearing is much like a trial in the adult court except trials by jury are far less frequent in the juvenile justice system. A juvenile court judge or referee hears evidence and testimony from the prosecutor and defense attorney and determines whether sufficient evidence exists that proves beyond a reasonable doubt the juvenile committed the offense.

A prosecutor presents the state's case against the juvenile first. The prosecutor calls witnesses, including the arresting officer, to provide oral testimony regarding the juvenile's guilt. In addition, the prosecutor presents other evidence that has a bearing on the case. The defense attorney has an opportunity to cross-examine the prosecution witnesses. Once the state has brought forth evidence and testimonies in the case, the defense attorney presents its case. The defense attorney calls witnesses and gives evidence that is favorable to the

adjudication hearing A hearing to determine whether there is evidence beyond a reasonable doubt to support the allegations against a juvenile.

Jury trials do not frequently occur in juvenile court. *What distinguishes an adjudication hearing from a trial?*

defense's case. In addition, the juvenile may take the stand and testify on his or her own behalf. The prosecutor also has an opportunity to cross-examine the witnesses presented for the defense. After this has been completed, both the prosecutor and defense attorney present a summary of the case to the judge or referee. After the summary statements have been made and the judge or referee has had time to deliberate on the case, he or she renders a decision on whether the juvenile committed the offense. The determination of guilt is usually done by the judge or referee, but in some states, juries are used in juvenile court.

As discussed in detail in Chapter 8, juveniles have several rights during the adjudication hearing. The U.S. Supreme Court in *In re Gault*[20] granted juveniles the right to counsel, as well as court-appointed counsel if indigent, the right to confront and cross-examine witnesses, and the right against self-incrimination. Therefore, juveniles should be represented by counsel during the adjudication hearing. However, research has found that less than half of the juveniles accused of delinquency receive assistance of counsel.[21] In addition, a juvenile does not have to testify against himself or herself because of the protection against self-incrimination. Furthermore, the case against a juvenile must be proven beyond a reasonable doubt pursuant to the U.S. Supreme Court decision in *In re Winship*.[22] Unlike adult court, juveniles do not have a constitutional right to a trial by jury. The U.S. Supreme Court decided this issue in *McKeiver* v. *Pennsylvania*.[23] However, some states have enacted legislation that grants juveniles a right to a jury trial under certain circumstances.

9.6 SELF-CHECK

1. What happens during an arraignment?
2. What occurs during an adjudication hearing?

Disposition

At this stage in the juvenile court process, a predisposition report is completed and a disposition hearing is held.

PREDISPOSITION REPORT

After the juvenile has been adjudicated delinquent, the juvenile court judge may order a **predisposition report** in order to assist the judge in making an appropriate disposition in the case. These reports are typically completed by probation officers. A predisposition report contains background information on the juvenile, a description of the circumstances surrounding the juvenile's delinquent acts, as well as a disposition recommendation from the probation officer. Predisposition reports serve three main functions:

1. Provide a comprehensive picture of the juvenile and his or her delinquency history, including any aggravating or mitigating circumstances.
2. Assist the judge in determining which disposition will most appropriately meet the needs of the juvenile.
3. Include the juvenile's treatment history which may indicate which dispositions may be effective and which have not been effective in the past.[24]

During the completion of the predisposition report, a probation officer is likely to interview the juvenile as well as his parents or guardians, contact the juvenile's school and place of employment, and speak with other agencies that have worked with the juvenile including child protective services among others. All information that is relevant to the disposition of the case and the juvenile is compiled in the predisposition report. This includes information about the juvenile's physical and emotional health, family and home environment, friends and associates, school history, employment experience, prior contact with the juvenile justice system, prior dispositions, and use of alcohol and drugs.[25] At

predisposition report Report that contains background information on the juvenile, a description of the circumstances surrounding the juvenile's delinquent acts, as well as a disposition recommendation from the probation officer.

Myth

The most typical disposition of a delinquency case is residential placement.

Fact

Of all the delinquency cases adjudicated in juvenile court in 2009, 27 percent resulted in residential placement and 60 percent were placed on probation.

Source: Puzzanchera, Charles, Benjamin Adams, and Sarah Hockenberry. 2012, May. *Juvenile Court Statistics 2009*. Pittsburgh, PA: National Center for Juvenile Justice.

the end of the predisposition report, the probation officer typically makes a recommendation regarding the appropriate disposition of the case. Although the judge is not required to follow the recommendation of the probation officer, the judge frequently agrees with the disposition recommendation.

DISPOSITION HEARING

Most juvenile courts today are bifurcated. A **bifurcated** court exists when the adjudication and **disposition hearing** are held separately. They are held separately because the disposition hearing typically has relaxed rules of evidence, such as allowing hearsay and other testimony and evidence that would not be allowed at an adjudication hearing. At the beginning of the disposition hearing, the probation officer frequently provides a summary of the information contained in the predisposition report. Many states grant juveniles the right to counsel and the right to confront and cross-examine witnesses at the disposition hearing. The defense attorney is also afforded the opportunity to challenge information contained in the predisposition report.

At the completion of the disposition hearing, the judge decides on the appropriate disposition of the case. The judge has wide discretion in making the disposition decision. Dispositions can include the following basic options:

- *Suspend judgment in the case.* In this instance, the judge does not prescribe a disposition in the case. Instead, the judge postpones the disposition decision if the juvenile agrees to abide by certain conditions. If the juvenile abides by the conditions, then the judge will not impose a more serious disposition. This practice is similar to informal probation which was discussed in this chapter. For example, the judge may be willing to impose a term of six months' probation on the juvenile for shoplifting but is willing to give the juvenile another chance. Instead of sentencing the juvenile to probation, the judge orders the juvenile to attend a shoplifting intervention program and pay restitution to the victim. If the juvenile abides by these conditions within a certain amount of time, then the judge does not sentence the juvenile to a term of probation. If the juvenile does not abide by these conditions, then the juvenile is sentenced to probation.

- *Probation.* This is the most common disposition in juvenile court. Probation allows a juvenile to remain in the community as long as the individual abides by certain conditions of probation. Many times, probation orders require a juvenile to attend counseling programs (e.g., drug counseling), perform community service, and pay victim restitution, along with other conditions. The probation term is usually for a specified period of time (one year, for example). If the juvenile successfully abides by the conditions of probation for the specified period of time, then the case is completed and no further action in the case is warranted. However, if the juvenile does not abide by the conditions of probation, the probationary sentence can be revoked, and the juvenile may be sentenced to residential placement.

- *Residential placement.* A residential placement can include being sent to an institution, camp, ranch, or group home. The placement may be for a

9.7 SELF-CHECK

1. What are the purposes of a predisposition report?
2. What types of decisions are made at the completion of a disposition hearing?

bifurcated Type of juvenile court where the adjudication and disposition hearings are held separately.

disposition hearing A hearing held after a juvenile has been adjudicated to determine what sanction should be imposed on the juvenile.

specified period of time, or it may be indeterminate. The facility may be a ranch-type environment or a prison-like environment and may be publicly or privately operated.

The disposition made by the judge typically involves probation or residential placement. These dispositional alternatives as well as others are detailed in Chapters 11 and 12.

The Future of the Juvenile Court

The juvenile court has changed significantly since its inception over a century ago. The concept of *parens patriae* was, until recently, the very solid foundation of the juvenile court process. However, this basic principle has weakened in recent years—in its place has emerged a juvenile court that is more similar to an adult court than the juvenile courts of the early 1900s. The current trends lead away from *parens patriae* and toward the formalization of the juvenile court. The juvenile court will probably continue to resemble adult courts more and more, which has some asking the question "Are juvenile courts needed any more?" This question will remain the focus of debate in the coming years.

9.8 SELF-CHECK

What founding concept of the juvenile court has eroded in recent years?

SUMMARY BY CHAPTER OBJECTIVES

1. Describe the jurisdiction of the juvenile court

The juvenile court has jurisdiction over all acts of juvenile delinquency. Delinquency typically involves status offenses and acts that would be a crime if committed by an adult.

2. Describe juvenile court key personnel and their primary responsibilities

The key personnel in the juvenile court are the juvenile court judge, juvenile court referee, prosecuting attorney, defense attorney, and probation officer.

A judge is primarily responsible for the operation of the juvenile court. The most important duties of a juvenile court judge involve the disposition of cases involving delinquents. A juvenile court judge determines whether a juvenile committed the offense and then decides the appropriate disposition of the case. If a juvenile is adjudicated for a delinquent act, the judge determines the sanction.

The primary responsibilities of a referee are: (1) to hear less serious cases so that the juvenile court judge can focus on more serious felony offenses; and (2) to preside over preadjudication hearings, such as detention hearings and arraignments.

The primary responsibilities of a prosecuting attorney are: (1) to make the decision of whether a case should be dismissed, adjudicated, or diverted; (2) to decide what charges to bring against the juvenile; (3) to dispose of the case, in many instances, through the use of plea bargaining; and (4) to initiate the proceedings that lead to waiving a juvenile to adult court for prosecution.

The primary responsibilities of the defense attorney are: (1) to present the best case possible to the judge or jury during the adjudication hearing; (2) to negotiate settlement of the case through plea bargaining if applicable; and (3) to ensure that the rights of the juvenile are not violated during the juvenile justice process.

The main responsibilities of a probation officer are: (1) to perform intake screenings; (2) to complete predisposition reports; and (3) to monitor juveniles on probation.

3. List the major steps in the juvenile court process

The major steps in the juvenile court process are intake, prosecutor decision making, adjudication, and disposition.

4. Explain what occurs during the decision to detain and the decision to petition a case

A probation officer or detention center staff member usually makes the initial decision to detain a juvenile.

In making this decision, the individual may speak with the juvenile's parents and the officer who took the juvenile into custody. A screening officer will determine if the juvenile has a pending offense against him or her in juvenile court and if the juvenile is currently on probation. In addition, the screening officer will look at the criteria established by state law and departmental regulations in making the decision.

The decision to petition the case is usually made by a probation officer although the prosecuting attorney may also play an active role in this decision. In making the decision, the probation officer or prosecutor may take into account several factors, including seriousness of the offense, prior record of the accused, age of the accused, demeanor of the juvenile, and harm inflicted on the victim, to name a few.

5. Describe decisions made by the prosecutor

The prosecutor decides whether or not to: (1) dismiss the case; (2) handle the matter informally by placing the juvenile on informal probation; (3) petition the case by requesting adjudication of the juvenile; or (4) initiate the proceedings to waive the juvenile to adult court for prosecution.

6. Explain what happens during adjudication

During adjudication, two stages occur in juvenile court: arraignment and adjudication hearing. At an arraignment, a juvenile is made aware of certain rights and asked to enter a plea in the case. At an adjudication hearing, it is determined whether or not the juvenile committed the offense.

7. Describe a predisposition report

A predisposition report assists the judge in making an appropriate disposition in the case. A report typically contains background information on the juvenile, a description of the circumstances surrounding the juvenile's delinquent acts, as well as a disposition recommendation from the probation officer who completes the report. It also includes information about the juvenile's physical and emotional health, family and home environment, friends and associates, school history, employment experience, prior contact with the juvenile justice system, prior dispositions, and use of alcohol and drugs.

8. Analyze what occurs at a disposition hearing

At the beginning of a disposition hearing, the probation officer frequently provides a summary of the information contained in the predisposition report. Many states grant juveniles the right to counsel and the right to confront and cross-examine witnesses at the disposition hearing. At the completion of the

disposition hearing, a judge decides on the appropriate disposition of the case. Dispositions typically include suspend judgment in the case, probation, or residential placement.

KEY TERMS

jurisdiction, p. 244
diversion, p. 245
juvenile court judge,
  p. 246
referees, commissioners,
  masters, p. 248
detention center, p. 250

detention hearing, p. 251
petition, p. 252
victim restitution, p. 254
community service,
  p. 254
informal probation,
  informal adjustment,

deferred prosecution,
  p. 254
arraignment, p. 255
plea bargaining,
  p. 255
adjudication hearing,
  p. 256

predisposition report,
  p. 257
bifurcated, p. 258
disposition hearing,
  p. 258

REVIEW QUESTIONS

1. What is the jurisdiction of a juvenile court?

2. Who are the key personnel in the juvenile court?

3. What are the main responsibilities of a juvenile court judge?

4. What are the main responsibilities of a juvenile court referee?

5. What are the main responsibilities of a prosecuting attorney?

6. What are the main responsibilities of a defense attorney?

7. What are the main responsibilities of a probation officer?

8. What are the two major decisions that are made at intake? Who makes these decisions?

9. What occurs during an arraignment and adjudication hearing?

10. What is a predisposition report and what information does it contain?

11. What are the three main disposition options available to the juvenile court judge?

12. What is the trend or direction in juvenile justice?

HANDS-ON ACTIVITIES

1. **Experience an Adjudication Hearing** Go to a juvenile court and observe an adjudication hearing. Document what juvenile court personnel are present at the hearing. What roles and responsibilities are each fulfilling? How does the adjudication hearing differ from your perception of an adjudication hearing prior to attending?

2. **Find Out More about the Role of the Intake Officer** Interview an intake officer at a local detention center. Ask the intake officer what his or her responsibilities are and what factors are taken into account in making the decision to detain and the decision to petition. How is the information provided by the intake officer similar and different from the information in the book?

INTERNET ACTIVITIES

1. Go to **www.nationalcasa.org/,** the website for the National Court Appointed Special Advocates Association. Provide a two-paragraph summary of the website including the history of Court Appointed Special Advocates (CASA) and the role of CASA.

2. Go to **www.journalofjuvjustice.org/JOJJ0101/JOJJ0101.pdf** and review the article entitled "Impact of Juvenile Drug Courts on Drug Use and Criminal Behavior." What are juvenile drug courts? What are the goals of juvenile drug courts? What are the key elements of a juvenile drug court program? What are the major findings of this study?

CRITICAL THINKING EXERCISES

1. **Assume the Role of an Intake Officer** You are a juvenile probation officer who is assigned to the intake unit. On Friday afternoon, a 15-year-old juvenile is brought to the intake unit by a police officer for stealing clothing worth $250 from a local department store. The officer states that the juvenile has been cooperative since the arrest, and the officer has never arrested this juvenile before. You check the county records to obtain the delinquency history of this juvenile. You discover that two years ago the juvenile was taken into custody for running away from home and was released to the custody of his parents. After looking at the juvenile's prior history, you contact the juvenile's parents. The parents do not seem concerned that their son has been taken into custody and make the remark that they expected this to occur sooner or later. The parents also tell you that the juvenile has begun to skip school but has not been arrested for this behavior.

   What do you do with the case? Do you petition the case to juvenile court, handle the matter informally by placing the juvenile on informal probation, or dismiss the case altogether? What factors led you to make your decision?

2. **Assume the Role of a Juvenile Court Judge** You are a juvenile court judge who has just adjudicated a 14-year-old juvenile for committing a burglary. He broke into a convenience store when it was closed and stole two cases of beer and five cartons of cigarettes. You have ordered that a predisposition report be

   completed. Once completed, the report contains the following information:

   a. The juvenile has one prior adjudication for auto theft. For this offense, the juvenile was placed on probation for one year and successfully completed the probationary term;

   b. The juvenile lives with both parents. The juvenile's father is currently employed as a bookkeeper while the mother is currently unemployed;

   c. The juvenile reports to have used alcohol and marijuana in the past. The juvenile has admitted to consuming about five alcoholic drinks a week and has used marijuana about once a week for the past year;

   d. The juvenile has failed one school grade and currently averages a "C" on his report card. The juvenile rarely misses school;

   e. Most of the juvenile's friends have been involved in delinquent activity in the past. In fact, his best friend has two prior adjudications for auto theft.

   How do you dispose of the case? Do you sentence the juvenile to probation, to an institution, or something else? What factors impacted your decision?

3. **Review the Qualified Right to Post Bail** Review the concept of parens patriae and explain why some states deny juvenile offenders the qualified right to post bail. Give your own opinion about the qualified right to post bail.

ANSWERS TO SELF-CHECKS

9.1 Self-Check

How were juveniles treated prior to the establishment of juvenile courts?

All offenders, whether juvenile or adult, were handled through the same court system. In many instances, juveniles received the same punishments as adult offenders.

9.2 Self-Check

What acts are handled by the juvenile court?

These acts can be broken into two categories: acts of delinquency, which are acts committed by a juvenile that would be considered a crime if committed by an adult, and status offenses, which are acts committed by a juvenile that would not be considered a crime if committed by an adult (e.g., truancy and running away).

9.3 Self-Check

What persons work in juvenile court and what are their responsibilities?

The key personnel are the juvenile court judge, juvenile court referee, prosecuting attorney, defense attorney, and probation officer. The juvenile court judge has the primary responsibility for the operation of the juvenile court. The juvenile court referee assists a juvenile court judge in handling the court caseload. The prosecuting attorney's main responsibility is to try juveniles for the offenses with which they are charged; other responsibilities include negotiating plea bargains and initiating waivers to adult court. The defense attorney presents the best possible case on the defendant's behalf during adjudication, negotiates plea bargains, and works to ensure that the juvenile is allowed due process throughout the process. Finally, the probation officer performs intake screenings, completes predisposition reports, and monitors juveniles on probation.

9.4 Self-Check

What decisions are made during intake?

The two major decisions made at intake are (1) the decision to detain the juvenile, and (2) the decision to petition the case.

9.5 Self-Check

1. What choices does a prosecutor have in deciding what to do with a case?

The prosecutor's choices are to: (1) dismiss the case, (2) handle the case informally by ordering informal probation, (3) petition the case by requesting adjudication of the juvenile, and (4) waive the juvenile to adult court for prosecution.

9.6 Self-Check

1. What happens during an arraignment?

At an arraignment, a juvenile is made aware of his or her basic rights and asked to enter a guilty or not-guilty plea in the case.

2. What occurs during an adjudication hearing?

In an adjudication hearing, it is determined whether the juvenile committed the offense for which he or she has been charged.

9.7 Self-Check

1. What are the purposes of a predisposition report?

A predisposition report provides a comprehensive picture of the juvenile and his or her delinquency history, assists the judge in determining which disposition will most appropriately meet the needs of the juvenile, and includes the treatment history of the juvenile, which may indicate which dispositions may be effective and which may not have been effective in the past.

2. What types of decisions are made at the completion of a disposition hearing?

The judge decides on the appropriate disposition of the case, which may include suspended judgment in the case, probation, or residential placement.

9.8 Self-Check

What founding concept of the juvenile court has eroded in recent years?

The concept of *parens patriae* has eroded, with the concept of a more formalized (and thus adult-like) system rising in its place. With this erosion has come the decrease in the rehabilitative aspects of juvenile justice; these have been replaced by an increase in punishment and deterrence.

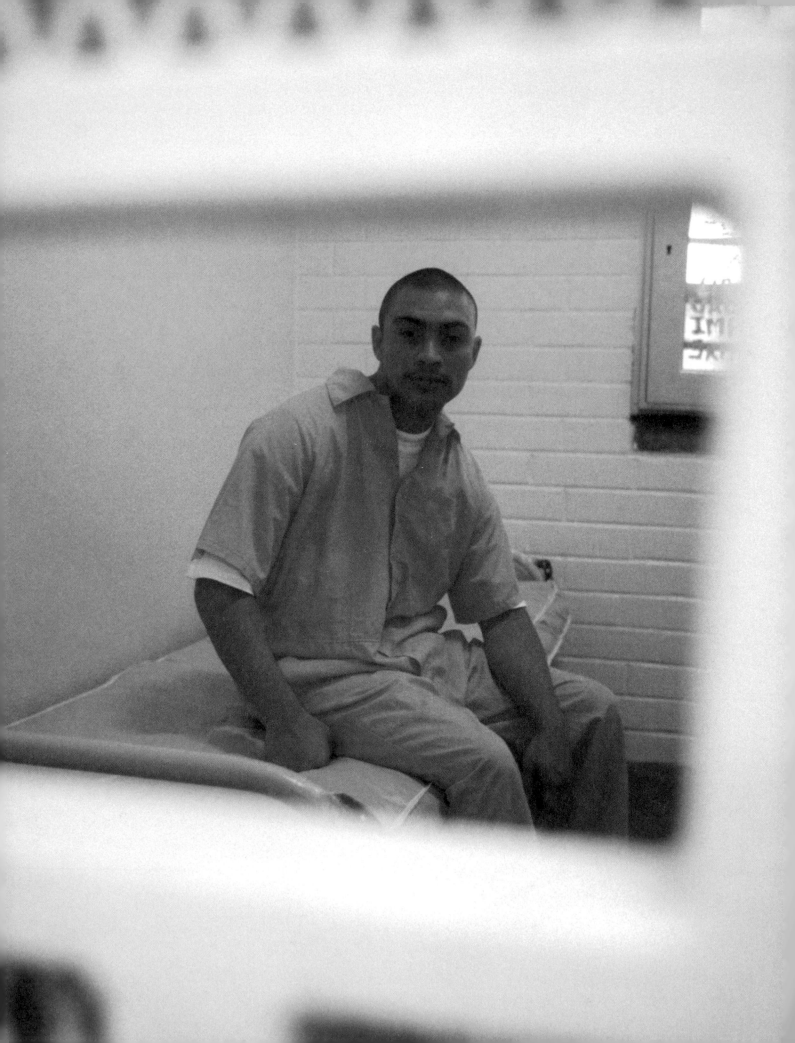

JUVENILES IN THE CRIMINAL JUSTICE SYSTEM

Chapter Outline

Chapter Objectives

After completing this chapter, you should be able to:

1. Explain waiver to adult court.

2. Name the main purposes for waiving a juvenile to adult court and explain the process.

3. Compare and contrast the three main types of waiver to adult court.

4. List the deciding factors in waiving a juvenile to adult court.

5. Evaluate the effectiveness of the waiver to adult court.

6. Describe and contrast the five types of blended sentencing.

7. Analyze major U.S. Supreme Court cases that address the constitutionality of the death penalty for juvenile offenders.

Changing Beliefs about the Purpose of Juvenile Justice

In the late 1800s, interested individuals and experts began to advocate the establishment of a separate juvenile justice system. They believed that juveniles lacked the maturity and level of culpability (intent to commit a crime) that were required to impose traditional criminal sanctions such as incarceration in prison. Consequently, they reasoned that juvenile offenders should not only be treated as less blameworthy, but also as more amenable to treatment and rehabilitation than hardened adult criminals.[1] The belief that the juvenile justice system's primary purpose was to treat the delinquent child remained a cornerstone of the U.S. juvenile justice system for decades.

The credibility of the juvenile justice system deteriorated in the 1970s and 1980s. The juvenile crime rate increased, and the types of crimes juveniles committed were thought to be more serious. As crime rates escalated, many lost faith in the ability of the juvenile justice system to rehabilitate offenders. Some began to blame the juvenile justice system's emphasis on rehabilitation and treatment for the failure to halt the growth of crime.

Because the juvenile justice system has been under attack for being too lenient, there has been a trend in juvenile justice to "get tough" on serious and violent juvenile offenders. Many states now model their juvenile justice system after the more punitive criminal justice system. The adult system holds offenders more accountable for their actions.

This chapter examines three mechanisms designed to deal with juvenile offenders in the criminal justice system. First, we discuss the process of waiver to adult court. Waiver to adult court is the process through which a juvenile court relinquishes jurisdiction over a juvenile offender, and the case is processed in adult court. A juvenile who has been waived to adult court is treated like an adult and in many cases subject to the same punishments as adults. Second, we examine blended sentences. Blended sentencing refers to the imposition of juvenile and/or adult correctional sanctions for serious and violent juvenile offenders who have been processed in the juvenile or adult court. The differences between waiver to adult court and blended sentencing will be discussed. Third, we discuss the imposition of the death penalty on juvenile offenders along with the major United States Supreme Court cases which address this issue.

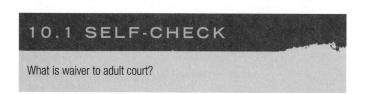

10.1 SELF-CHECK

What is waiver to adult court?

Waiver to Adult Court

Waiver to adult court (also called *certification, transfer, remand,* and *binding over*) is the means by which a juvenile is processed in the criminal justice system instead of in the juvenile justice system. With the "get tough" attitude toward juvenile crime that is prevalent in many states, the options available for waiver to adult court for serious and violent juvenile offenders, including legislative and prosecutorial waiver, have grown. In 2009, juvenile court judges waived jurisdiction over an estimated 7,600 delinquency cases, sending them to criminal court. This represents less than 1 percent of all delinquency cases handled. The number of cases judicially waived was relatively flat from 1985 to 1988, rose sharply from 1988 to 1994 (105 percent), and then fell to the level of the mid-1980s and remained there through 2009.[2] One probable reason for the decline in the number of judicial waivers immediately after 1994 was the large increase in the number of states that passed legislation excluding certain

waiver to adult court The process through which a juvenile court relinquishes jurisdiction over a juvenile offender and the case is processed in adult court.

FIGURE 10.1	Minimum Age a Juvenile May Be Waived to Adult Court by State

No Minimum Age Specified (21 states): Alaska, Arizona, Delaware, Florida, Georgia, Hawaii, Idaho, Indiana, Maine, Maryland, Nebraska, Nevada, Oklahoma, Oregon, Pennsylvania, Rhode Island, South Carolina, South Dakota, Tennessee, Washington, West Virginia

Age 10 (3 states): Kansas, Vermont, Wisconsin

Age 12 (3 states): Colorado, Missouri, Montana

Age 13 (6 states): Illinois, Mississippi, New Hampshire, New York, North Carolina, Wyoming

Age 14 (16 states): Alabama, Arkansas, California, Connecticut, Iowa, Kentucky, Louisiana, Massachusetts, Michigan, Minnesota, New Jersey, North Dakota, Ohio, Texas, Utah, Virginia

Age 15 (1 state): New Mexico

Source: *OJJDP Statistical Briefing Book.* Online. Available: http://www.ojjdp.gov/ojstatbb/structure_process/qa04105. asp?qaDate=2011. Retrieved on December 17, 2012.

serious offenses from juvenile court jurisdiction and legislation permitting the prosecutor to file certain cases directly in criminal court.[3]

Of the 7,600 cases judicially waived in 2009, 46 percent involved a violent offense, 31 percent involved a property offense, 13 percent involved a drug law violation, and 10 percent involved a public order offense as the most serious charge.[4]

The use of waiver to adult court is a relatively rare event. Less than 1 percent of all cases formally processed in juvenile court are waived to adult court for prosecution.[5] Therefore, less than 10 out of every 1,000 cases processed in juvenile court are waived to adult court. Once waived to adult court, juveniles are usually subject to the same penalties as adults. This includes life sentences and, in some states, life without parole possibilities for homicide. As discussed later in this chapter, juveniles are no longer eligible for the death penalty.

During the 1920s, only 10 states allowed juveniles to be waived to adult court for prosecution; but today all states allow certain juvenile offenders to be waived to adult court. The three types of waiver discussed in this chapter differ primarily by who makes the decision to try a juvenile in adult court. A juvenile judge decides to waive a juvenile to adult court under judicial waiver provisions, a prosecutor decides under prosecutorial waiver, and a legislature decides under legislative waiver.

The offender's age and the offense committed have usually been the criteria to determine who is eligible to be waived to adult court. These restrictions depend on state law. Some states allow only older juvenile offenders (14-, 15-, 16-, and 17-year-olds) to be waived to adult court, while some allow any juvenile regardless of age to be waived (See Focus on Practice). Figure 10.1 illustrates the minimum age a juvenile may be waived to adult court by state. Some states allow only offenders who have committed violent offenses to be waived to adult court, while other states allow juveniles who have committed property and drug offenses to be eligible for such waiver.

PURPOSE OF WAIVER TO ADULT COURT

Juveniles are waived to adult court for prosecution for three basic reasons:[6]

- To remove juvenile offenders charged with heinous, violent offenses that frequently generate media and community pressure
- To remove chronic offenders who have exhausted the resources and the patience of the juvenile justice system
- To impose longer potential sentences than are available within the juvenile justice system

Some juveniles accused of murder are waived to adult court. *What factors, besides the offense committed, should a judge consider in deciding to waive a juvenile to adult court?*

Sometimes a juvenile offender commits an act that is particularly violent and shocking. Consider the case of a male juvenile who stabs a victim 67 times during a robbery. An event such as this will generate substantial media attention, and there will be a great deal of community pressure on the prosecutor and other juvenile justice system personnel to waive the offender to adult court. In such cases, the community and public are not generally concerned with rehabilitating the juvenile, but rather with giving the juvenile the deserved punishment. Because of the violent nature of the offense and the pressure to punish the juvenile, a case like this will often be waived to adult court.

The first reason to waive a juvenile to adult court applies to serious and violent offenders. The second reason applies primarily to chronic property offenders. Once a juvenile has been exposed to the available resources in the juvenile justice system but continues to commit crime, there is not much choice but to waive the juvenile to adult court. For example, a young female juvenile begins her career of crime stealing cars at the age of 10. At age 12, she is arrested for the third time for stealing cars and is placed on probation. She continues to commit crime, including burglary. By the time she is 13 years old, she has become a runaway and has been arrested on two additional occasions for burglary and auto theft. She is then placed in a boot camp for three months. After her release, she continues to commit crime. At age 14, she is once again arrested for burglary and this time is placed on electronic monitoring. She continues to break into houses and to steal cars. She is arrested six months later for several burglaries and auto thefts and is sentenced to a juvenile institution. She spends nine months in the institution and is released at age 15½. She continues to commit crime and once again goes back to juvenile court on more burglary charges. At this point the prosecutor and the judge may decide to waive her to adult court because she has exhausted the resources of the juvenile justice system and continues to commit crime. This young girl has been placed on probation,

FOCUS ON PRACTICE

JONESBORO, ARKANSAS, SCHOOL SHOOTERS RELEASED

On March 24, 1998, Mitchell Johnson, age 13, and Andrew Golden, age 11, pulled a fire alarm at Westside Middle School in Jonesboro, Arkansas, and waited for students to exit the building. The two youths opened fire on the crowd of students and teachers with a Ruger .44-caliber rifle and a 30.06-caliber hunting rifle. Four students and one teacher were killed, and ten others were wounded during the shooting rampage. The juveniles were charged with five counts of murder and ten counts each of first-degree battery.

Mitchell Johnson and Andrew Golden could not be waived to adult court for prosecution because Arkansas law allowed only juveniles 14 years of age or older to be waived to adult court at the time the offense was committed.

Since Mitchell Johnson and Andrew Golden were younger than 14 at the time of the offense, they had to be processed in juvenile court. They were not eligible to receive a long prison sentence in adult court. Instead, they were adjudicated delinquent in juvenile court and sentenced to the state Division of Youth Services, scheduled to be released before their 21st birthdays. In August 2005, Mitchell Johnson turned 21 and was released from custody after serving seven years for the murders. Andrew Golden was released when he turned 21 in May 2007 after serving nine years for the murders.

After Andrew Golden was released in 2007 he changed his name and enrolled at a community college. However, he made news in December 2008 when police revealed that he had applied for a state concealed weapons permit and was turned down. Since his release in 2005, Mitchell Johnson was sentenced to a four-year prison sentence for a federal conviction for gun and drug possession stemming from an arrest in 2007. Most recently, he was sentenced to a total of 18 years in state prison for theft by receiving and financial identity fraud for the use of a debit card he stole.

CRITICAL THINKING

Should state laws on minimum ages for waiver to adult court be amended? Explain.

Sources: Breed, Allen G. "The Boys: From Church and Computer Games to Jailhouse: Who Are the Suspects?" The Associated Press, March 26, 1998; "Arkansas School Shooter Gets 6 years for Theft." *USA Today.* January 23, 2009. Online Available http://www.usatoday.com/News/Nation/2009-01-23-shooting-theft_N.htm

sentenced to a boot camp, placed on electronic monitoring, and sentenced to a juvenile institution, but none of these has reduced her criminal behavior. It may now be time to send her to adult court for prosecution because everything that can be done in the juvenile justice system has been done but has failed.

Some people argue that the primary reason for waiver to adult court is to impose more severe sanctions than are allowed in juvenile court.[7] More specifically, the primary justification for waiver is to impose terms of incarceration that are in excess of the maximum terms available within the juvenile court.[8] The juvenile justice system cannot incarcerate a juvenile forever. Each state sets what is known as a **jurisdictional age limit** which specifies the age when a juvenile court no longer has jurisdiction over a juvenile offender. In other words, a juvenile must be released from a juvenile institution when he or she reaches a certain age. Depending on the state, the jurisdictional age limit is usually between ages 19 and 21. Figure 10.2 illustrates the age at which the juvenile justice system in each state must relinquish jurisdiction over juvenile offenders.

Therefore, a juvenile processed in juvenile court in Iowa must be released from a juvenile institution by age 19, regardless of the offense committed. Many argue that certain juvenile offenders, especially violent offenders, need

Myth | Fact

Myth	Fact
Youths under age 16 are likely to be waived to adult court.	Youths age 16 or older accounted for 88 percent of all waived cases in 2010. Therefore, it is relatively rare for a youth under age 16 to be waived to adult court. Source: C. Puzzanchera and W. Kang. 2013. "Easy Access to Juvenile Court Statistics: 1985-2010," Online. Available: www.ojjdp.gov/ojstatbb/ezajcs/

jurisdictional age limit The age limit when a juvenile court no longer has jurisdiction over a juvenile offender, usually between ages 19 and 21.

FIGURE 10.2	Age at Which Juvenile Court Must Relinquish Jurisdiction over Juvenile Offenders
AGE	STATES
19 (7 states)	Alaska, Iowa, Kentucky, Nebraska, Oklahoma, Rhode Island, Texas
20 (1 state)	Mississippi
21 (31 states)	Alabama, Arizona, Arkansas, Connecticut, Delaware, District of Columbia, Georgia, Idaho, Illinois, Indiana, Louisiana, Maine, Maryland, Massachusetts, Michigan, Minnesota, Missouri, Nevada, New Hampshire, New Mexico, New York, North Carolina, North Dakota, Ohio, Pennsylvania, South Carolina, South Dakota, Utah, Virginia, Washington, West Virginia, Wyoming
22 (2 states)	Florida, Vermont
23 (1 state)	Kansas
25 (4 states)	California, Montana, Oregon, Wisconsin
Until the full term of the disposition order (4 states)	Colorado, Hawaii, New Jersey, Tennessee

Note: Extended ages of jurisdiction may be restricted to certain offenses or juveniles (such as violent offenses, habitual offenders, and juveniles under correctional commitment).

Source: *OJJDP Statistical Briefing Book*. Online. Available: http://www.ojjdp.gov/ojstatbb/structure_process/qa04106.asp?qaDate=2011. Released on December 17, 2012.

to be incarcerated for a longer period of time than is allowed in the juvenile justice system.

For example, a 15-year-old in Kentucky who commits two murders during a drive-by shooting must be released from a juvenile institution by age 19. Therefore, the maximum term of incarceration available if the juvenile is kept in juvenile court is four years. Many would argue this is not a long enough sentence for such a crime. However, if the juvenile is waived to adult court, he could potentially spend the remainder of his life in prison. In summary, there is a limit to how long a juvenile may remain incarcerated in a juvenile institution, but a juvenile waived to adult court may spend the rest of his or her life in prison. It is in cases where a long term of incarceration is warranted that waiver to adult court becomes an acceptable option.

The United States Supreme Court has decided cases that have dictated the standards for giving a life without the possibility of parole sentence to a juvenile. In 2009, the Court ruled that a juvenile offender cannot be sentenced to life in prison without parole for a non-homicidal crime (*Graham* v. *Florida*, 560 U.S. 48 (2010) because such a sentence violates the Eighth Amendment's cruel and unusual punishment clause. In 2012, the Court ruled that the Eighth Amendment forbids a sentencing scheme that mandates life in prison without the possibility of parole for juvenile homicide offenders. (*Miller* v. *Alabama*, 132 S.Ct. 2455 (2012). Based on the decisions, the only juvenile offenders who can be sentenced to life without the possibility of parole are homicide offenders, but the sentence cannot be mandatory. Instead, the sentence must be based on the discretion of the judge or jury.

TYPES OF WAIVER TO ADULT COURT

Three main types of waiver to adult court are judicial waiver, legislative waiver, and prosecutorial waiver.

JUDICIAL WAIVER The most common method of waiver to adult court and the one with the longest history is **judicial waiver.** Originally, this was the only means of waiving a juvenile to adult court. Judicial waiver involves the use of discretionary authority by a juvenile court judge to waive jurisdiction and to send the case to adult court. A juvenile court judge decides to waive the

judicial waiver A type of waiver to adult court in which a juvenile court judge makes the decision to waive a juvenile to adult court.

case to adult court for prosecution. If the case is transferred to adult court, the offender is treated as an adult and in many cases is subject to the same punishments as adults.

Three types of judicial waiver are discretionary, mandatory, and presumptive. The most frequently used is **discretionary judicial waiver.** Usually a prosecutor files a petition with a juvenile court requesting that the juvenile court waive its original jurisdiction over the juvenile offender and send the juvenile to adult court. In some states, a judge may decide to waive a case to adult court without the prosecutor previously filing a petition. In either case, a judge makes the final decision to waive the juvenile to adult court. Forty-four states and the District of Columbia have discretionary judicial waiver. The only states that do not have this type of waiver are Connecticut, Massachusetts, Montana, Nebraska, New Mexico, and New York.[9]

The discretionary judicial waiver laws in each state usually vary based on two factors:

1. The offenses they allow to be waived to adult court
2. The minimum age at which a juvenile can be waived to adult court

For example, Alabama allows any juvenile over age 14 to be waived to adult court for any criminal offense. A juvenile under age 14 in Alabama cannot be tried in adult court regardless of the offense. On the other hand, Kansas allows any juvenile, age 10 or older, to be waived to adult court for any offense. Many states, however, restrict the offenses for which juveniles can be waived to adult court, frequently restricting to violent offenses only. For example, Louisiana allows any juvenile age 14 or older to be waived to adult court if the offense is a violent crime such as murder, aggravated kidnapping, aggravated rape, or aggravated battery.

Before a judge makes the decision to waive a juvenile to adult court under discretionary judicial waiver, a **waiver hearing** will be held in juvenile court. At the waiver hearing, the prosecutor and defense attorney present evidence on whether or not the juvenile should be waived to adult court. After the evidence is presented, the judge decides whether the case should be waived to adult court or remain in juvenile court.

discretionary judicial waiver A type of judicial waiver that involves the prosecutor filing a petition with a juvenile court requesting that the juvenile court waive a juvenile to adult court.

waiver hearing A hearing held in juvenile court in which a prosecutor and defense attorney may present evidence on whether or not the juvenile should be waived to adult court.

CAREERS IN JUVENILE JUSTICE

Prosecutor

The prosecutor represents the interests of the state in bringing a case against a juvenile. The prosecutor makes the decision of whether a case should be dismissed, adjudicated, or diverted. In addition, the prosecutor decides what the juvenile should be charged with and also is responsible for the disposition of the case. Prosecutors are usually responsible for initiating the proceedings that lead to waiving a juvenile to adult court for prosecution.

In large jurisdictions with a heavy volume of juvenile cases, the prosecutor may handle only juvenile cases. In fact, there may be a juvenile division with several prosecutors within the prosecutor's office who work only on juvenile cases. In smaller jurisdictions with fewer juvenile cases, the prosecutor may be responsible for both juvenile and adult cases.

Prosecutors are employees of the government—either local, state, or federal—and receive wages and benefits according to a government scale. To become a prosecutor, an individual must first receive a bachelor's degree and then a law degree from a qualified law school. Finally, prosecutors must pass the bar exam in the state where they wish to work.

Critical Thinking

If you were a prosecutor, would you want to work only on juvenile cases? Why or why not?

Juvenile Sentencing

Criminal courts sometimes sentence juveniles waived to adult court for murder to longer prison terms than adults convicted of murder. On average, the maximum prison sentence imposed on transferred juveniles convicted of murder was 23 years 11 months. This was 2 years and 5 months longer than the average maximum prison sentence for adults.

SOURCE: Snyder, Howard N. and Melissa Sickmund. *Juvenile Offenders and Victims: 1999 National Report.* Washington, DC: Office of Juvenile Justice and Delinquency Prevention, 1999.

How does a judge decide whether to waive a juvenile to adult court? Most states require that judges look at certain criteria based on the United States Supreme Court decision in *Kent* v. *United States* (383 U.S. 541 [1966]). This case was discussed in Chapter 8 but applies specifically to waiver to adult court. At age 16, Morris Kent was accused of committing several burglaries, robbery, and sexual assault. Since Kent was already on probation, the juvenile court judge presiding over the case waived Kent to adult court without a hearing and without a thorough investigation of the allegations that warranted waiver. Kent's sentence was 30 to 90 years in prison. The United States Supreme Court overturned the conviction of Kent and ruled that a juvenile has the following rights if waived to adult court:

1. Right to a hearing where evidence can be presented as to why the juvenile should *not* be waived to adult court.
2. Right to counsel at waiver hearings.
3. Right to access any reports and records used by the court in deciding waiver.
4. Right to a statement issued by the judge justifying waiver to adult court.

In addition, the United States Supreme Court outlined eight factors that a juvenile court judge should take into consideration in deciding whether or not to waive a juvenile to adult court for prosecution. These factors, sometimes referred to as the ***Kent* criteria,** are[10]:

1. *The seriousness of the alleged offense to the community and whether the protection of the community requires waiver.* A juvenile court judge determines how serious the offense was and whether the community can be adequately protected if the juvenile is processed in juvenile court. Remember that the criminal justice system can impose longer terms of incarceration than the juvenile justice system. Therefore, if a long term of incarceration is needed in order to protect the public, then waiver to adult court may be warranted.
2. *Whether the alleged offense was committed in an aggressive, violent, premeditated, or willful manner.* A juvenile court judge takes into consideration whether the offense was particularly violent or heinous. Previously, it was mentioned that the juvenile justice system was established on the belief that a juvenile offender cannot develop the same level of intent that an adult offender can; therefore, juvenile offenders should be handled differently. However, this factor looks at the level of intent by focusing on whether the offense was committed in a premeditated or willful manner.
3. *Whether the alleged offense was against persons or against property, greater weight being given to offenses against persons, especially if personal injury resulted.* A juvenile court judge should be more willing to waive violent offenders to adult court than those who have committed property crimes or crimes involving drugs. This criterion specifically addresses violent offenders when a judge is deciding who should be waived to adult court and who should not.
4. *The prosecutive merit of the complaint.* A juvenile court judge determines whether a grand jury indictment can be obtained in the case and whether there is enough evidence to obtain a conviction in adult court. If the judge believes that a conviction can be obtained in adult court, waiver to adult court may be warranted.
5. *Whether the juvenile's associates in the offense were adults.* A juvenile court judge determines if the accomplices in the case were adults. If a juvenile commits an offense with an adult, the judge may decide to waive the juvenile to adult court to maintain consistency in how the offenders are handled by the justice system.
6. *The sophistication and maturity of the juvenile.* A juvenile court judge looks at the home life of the juvenile as well as his or her environmental

***Kent* criteria** The factors established by the United States Supreme Court in *Kent* v. *United States* that a juvenile court judge should take into consideration when deciding whether or not to waive a juvenile to adult court.

situation and emotional attitude. For example, if a juvenile exhibits an adult lifestyle, such as living away from home, then waiver to adult court may be warranted. This factor also addresses the issue of intent by asking the judge to analyze the sophistication and maturity level of the juvenile although, when the juvenile justice system was established, it was assumed that juveniles were not as mature as adults. This factor takes into consideration that some juveniles are as mature as adults and should be treated as such.

7. *The record and previous history of the juvenile.* A juvenile court judge considers the previous criminal history of the juvenile, including previous contacts with law enforcement, the juvenile court, and prior periods of probation or commitments to juvenile institutions. The more extensive the juvenile's prior offense history, the more likely the juvenile will be waived to adult court.

8. *The prospects for adequate protection of the public and the likelihood of reasonable rehabilitation of the juvenile by the use of procedures, services, and facilities currently available to the juvenile court.* A juvenile court judge determines if the public can be adequately protected from the offender if the offender remains in juvenile court. In addition, the judge determines whether or not the person can be rehabilitated in the juvenile justice system. If the juvenile court judge determines that the juvenile cannot be rehabilitated, then the judge may waive him or her to adult court for prosecution.

A juvenile court judge does not always take into account all eight factors when deciding whether or not to waive a juvenile to adult court. The factors that play the greatest role in deciding whether or not to waive a juvenile to adult court are (a) the seriousness of the offense; (b) the juvenile's previous record; and (c) whether the juvenile can be rehabilitated.[11] In other words, if a juvenile has committed a serious offense, has an extensive prior record of contact with the juvenile justice system, and cannot be rehabilitated, then it is likely that the juvenile will be waived to adult court.

A second type of judicial waiver is **mandatory judicial waiver.** As mentioned, under discretionary judicial waiver, a juvenile court judge looks at the *Kent* criteria to determine whether or not a juvenile should be waived to adult court. Under mandatory judicial waiver, a juvenile court judge, at the waiver hearing, looks for only probable cause that a juvenile offender committed a serious offense. Probable cause is the level of proof required to justify an arrest. It means that the police have enough evidence to believe that the individual arrested committed the offense. If a judge finds that probable cause exists, then the judge *must* waive the juvenile to adult court. Mandatory judicial waiver is different from discretionary judicial waiver because under mandatory judicial waiver a judge looks only at probable cause, not at the *Kent* criteria, in making the waiver decision.

As of 2012, 15 states allowed mandatory judicial waiver (see Figure 10.3). Once again, the waiver provisions are bounded by age and offense restrictions and vary from state to state. For example, North Carolina has a mandatory waiver statute that applies to any juvenile who is accused of committing a capital crime (that is, a crime in which an adult could potentially receive the death penalty) and the individual is at least 13 years old. However, the law in Rhode Island requires the juvenile to be at least 17 years old and be accused of murder, first degree sexual assault, or assault with intent to commit murder. As Figure 10.3 shows, many states have more than one way in which they can waive a juvenile to adult court.

Presumptive waiver is a third type of judicial waiver. Typically, a prosecutor who is seeking the waiver of a juvenile to adult court must prove to the judge

mandatory judicial waiver A type of judicial waiver in which a juvenile court judge must waive a juvenile to adult court if the juvenile court judge finds probable cause that the juvenile committed the offense.

presumptive waiver A type of judicial waiver in which the defense bears the burden of proof and must justify to the judge why the juvenile should not be waived.

FIGURE 10.3	Summary of Current Juvenile Waiver Provisions

STATE	JUDICIAL WAIVER			LEGISLATIVE WAIVER		
	DISCRETIONARY	PRESUMPTIVE	MANDATORY	PROSECUTORIAL WAIVER	STATUTORY EXCLUSION	ONCE AN ADULT ALWAYS AN ADULT
TOTAL STATES:	45	15	15	15	29	34
Alabama	*				*	*
Alaska	*	*			*	
Arizona	*			*	*	*
Arkansas	*			*		
California	*	*		*	*	*
Colorado	*	*		*		
Connecticut			*			
Delaware	*		*		*	*
District of Columbia	*	*		*		*
Florida	*			*	*	*
Georgia	*		*	*	*	
Hawaii	*					*
Idaho	*				*	*
Illinois	*	*	*		*	*
Indiana	*		*		*	*
Iowa	*				*	*
Kansas	*	*				*
Kentucky	*		*			
Louisiana	*		*	*	*	
Maine	*	*				*
Maryland	*				*	*
Massachusetts						
Michigan	*			*		*
Minnesota	*	*			*	*
Mississippi	*				*	*
Missouri	*					*
Montana				*	*	
Nebraska				*		
Nevada	*	*			*	*
New Hampshire	*	*				*
New Jersey	*	*	*			
New Mexico					*	
New York					*	
North Carolina	*		*			*
North Dakota	*	*	*			*
Ohio	*		*			*
Oklahoma	*			*	*	*
Oregon	*				*	*
Pennsylvania	*	*			*	*
Rhode Island	*	*	*			*
South Carolina	*		*		*	
South Dakota	*				*	*
Tennessee	*					*
Texas	*					*
Utah	*	*			*	*
Vermont	*			*		
Virginia	*			*		*
Washington	*				*	*
West Virginia	*		*			
Wisconsin	*				*	*
Wyoming	*			*		

Legend: * indicates the provision(s) allowed by each state as of the end of the 2011 legislative sessions.

Source: *OJJDP Statistical Briefing Book.* Online. Available: http://www.ojjdp.gov/ojstatbb/structure_process/qa04115.asp?qaDate=2011.

that the juvenile should be waived. In other words, the prosecution typically bears the burden of proof in a discretionary waiver proceeding, but under presumptive waiver the burden shifts to the defense. As of 2012, 15 states have presumptive waiver laws which designate certain cases in which waiver to adult court is presumed to be appropriate. In such cases, if a juvenile meeting the criteria for the presumption fails to make an adequate showing against transfer, the juvenile court judge must waive the juvenile to adult court. Under presumptive waiver, the defense bears the burden of proof and must justify to the judge why the juvenile should not be waived. Statutory criteria triggering presumptive waiver fall into three categories: offense-based, age-based, and record-based.[12] In some states with presumptive waiver it is the offense that matters most. For example, Alaska and Maine allow juveniles of any age to be waived to adult court under presumptive waiver if the offense is among a list of violent offenses. In other states, older offenders are singled out for presumptive waiver even when less serious offenses have been committed. In a few states, the juvenile's prior delinquency history is emphasized.

LEGISLATIVE WAIVER Another mechanism for transferring juveniles to adult court is **legislative,** or statutory, **waiver.** This type of waiver brings certain juvenile offenders into the criminal justice system at the point of arrest and bypasses the juvenile court altogether.[13] A

Judges frequently decide whether juveniles should be waived to adult court for prosecution. *What factors, besides those identified in* Kent, *do you think a juvenile court judge should take into consideration when deciding to waive a juvenile to adult court?*

juvenile who has committed an offense covered by a legislative waiver statute is treated as an adult from the beginning of the judicial process. Legislative waiver is sometimes referred to as automatic waiver because juvenile court jurisdiction is removed automatically, without a motion by a prosecutor or a decision by a juvenile court judge. In this way, legislative waiver differs from mandatory judicial waiver, which is the result of a hearing held in a juvenile court about a case originating in juvenile court.

Legislative waiver has received much support in recent years and is preferable to judicial waiver because it is a rational, nondiscretionary, and easily administered method for deciding who is waived to adult court for prosecution.[14] Neither the juvenile court judge nor the prosecutor decides who should be waived to adult court under legislative waiver. Instead, the state legislature has passed a law that mandates certain juvenile offenders be waived to adult court.

One type of legislative waiver is referred to as **statutory exclusion.** It excludes certain offenses from the jurisdiction of a juvenile court, usually violent crimes such as murder and sexual assault.[15] A typical legislative waiver statute states that a juvenile who commits murder, aggravated robbery, or aggravated sexual assault is automatically waived to adult court for prosecution. Frequently, a juvenile has to be a certain age in order to fit the criteria for statutory exclusion. For example, any juvenile in New Mexico who is 15 years old and is accused of committing first degree murder is automatically treated as an adult.[16] Offenders charged with such offenses are excluded from the juvenile justice system because juvenile courts cannot impose sufficiently long sentences for such offenses.[17] Twenty-nine states have laws that exclude certain offenses from juvenile court jurisdiction (see Figure 10.3).

A second type of legislative waiver concerns juveniles who have been previously waived to adult court and continue to commit crime. The potential exists that a juvenile can be waived to adult court and once convicted may be placed

legislative waiver A type of waiver to adult court in which a juvenile is automatically sent to adult court because of the type of offense that was committed.

statutory exclusion A type of legislative waiver that excludes certain offenses, usually violent crimes, from the jurisdiction of the juvenile court.

Policing Juveniles, the Law, and the Courts

Prosecutors have the ability to waive youth to adult court in some states without approval from a juvenile court judge. *Do you think this can lead to abuses by the prosecutor? Why or why not?*

JUVENILE JUSTICE
ONLINE

Go to **www.ncjrs.gov/pdffiles/ 172835.pdf** and read the report on state legislative responses to violent juvenile crime. Write a two-paragraph summary of the responses to serious and violent juvenile crime in the 1990s.

"once an adult always an adult" law A type of legislative waiver that mandates that all offenses a juvenile commits after having been waived to adult court and convicted will also be handled in adult court.

prosecutorial waiver A type of waiver to adult court that occurs when there is concurrent jurisdiction between juvenile and adult courts and the prosecutor has the option of filing charges against the juvenile offender in either court.

on probation or receive a short term of incarceration. What happens to a juvenile if he or she continues to commit crime and is still young enough to be classified as a juvenile? Is the case handled in juvenile or adult court? Many states have remedied this situation by passing **"once an adult always an adult" laws.** According to these laws, if a juvenile has been waived to adult court previously and convicted, then all other offenses that the juvenile commits thereafter are processed in adult court, even if the person is still young enough to be classified as a juvenile under state law. Thirty-four states have these types of laws that prohibit juveniles who have previously been convicted in adult court from ever being processed in juvenile court again (see Figure 10.3).

PROSECUTORIAL WAIVER Prosecutorial waiver occurs when there is concurrent jurisdiction in the juvenile and adult courts and the prosecutor has the option of filing charges against the offender in either court. This type of waiver is sometimes referred to as *direct file.* This method of waiver is the most controversial because it gives a great deal of discretion to the prosecutor, whose primary duty is to secure convictions and who is traditionally more concerned with retribution than rehabilitation.[18] Fifteen states have prosecutorial waiver provisions (see Figure 10.3). For example, a law in Virginia allows a prosecutor to file a case in either juvenile or adult court if the person is at least 14 years old and has committed a designated violent offense. A law in Florida even allows juveniles who have committed certain misdemeanor offenses to be waived to adult court if they are at least 14 years old and have a serious enough prior record. Under prosecutorial waiver, a juvenile offender is not given a waiver hearing as occurs under judicial waiver. Instead, the decision of whether to waive a juvenile to adult court under prosecutorial waiver rests solely with the prosecutor.

TRENDS IN THE USE OF WAIVER TO ADULT COURT

The waiver to adult court is perceived as a way to get tough on juvenile offenders. Since the punitive model of juvenile justice emerged, many states have passed laws that make it easier to try juveniles as adults. This legislative action has resulted in three trends.

- Legislatures have passed laws that lowered the age at which a juvenile can be waived to adult court. For example, Texas lowered the minimum age at which a juvenile can be waived to adult court from age 15 to age 14.
- Legislatures have enacted laws that expand the number of offenses eligible for waiver to adult court. Some states that have targeted primarily violent offenders for waiver to adult court have now allowed more property offenders to be eligible for waiver.
- States have enacted or modified legislative or prosecutorial waiver statutes. Since legislative transfers automatically waive certain offenders to adult court, this mechanism fits well with the current "get tough" attitude toward juvenile offenders. In addition, because prosecutorial waiver bypasses the waiver hearing used in judicial waiver, it expedites the judicial process.

Therefore, the use of legislative and prosecutorial waivers as mechanisms to send juveniles to adult court has expanded and increased in recent years.

As mentioned previously, the increased use of legislative and prosecutorial waivers is seen as the primary reason for the decreased use of judicial waivers after 1994.

EFFECTIVENESS OF WAIVER TO ADULT COURT

Many argue that the primary reason for waiver to adult court is to impose more severe sanctions, in particular, longer sentences, than are allowed in juvenile court.[19] Many also believe that waiver to adult court should be reserved primarily for violent offenders rather than for property offenders.[20] Thus, the effectiveness of waiver is usually based on the answer to two questions:

1. Are most juveniles waived to adult court accused of violent offenses? If the answer is yes, waiver is seen as effective.
2. Do juveniles waived to adult court consistently receive more severe sanctions than are available in juvenile court? Once again, if the answer is yes, waiver is seen as effective.

Studies have not definitely determined whether waiver is effective in meeting these two objectives. Historically, the literature appears to be evenly balanced on the issue of whether or not violent or property offenders are waived to adult court more frequently. Some studies have found that violent offenders were waived more frequently, while others have found the opposite.[21] Overall, in 2009, 46 percent of the cases waived to adult court involved a violent offense, 31 percent involved a property offense, 13 percent involved a drug law violation, and 10 percent involved a public order offense as the most serious charge.[22]

Why are juvenile property offenders frequently waived to adult court? Some argue that waiver is frequently used to get rid of juveniles who have been through the juvenile justice system several times. Earlier in the chapter, we stated that juveniles are waived to adult court when they have exhausted the resources of the juvenile court (that is, been put on probation, subjected to an intermediate punishment, and sentenced to a juvenile institution) and continue to commit crime. Since property offenders generally commit more offenses than violent offenders, property offenders are more likely to have had more contacts with the juvenile system.

Once waived, do juveniles receive more severe sanctions in adult court? Most of the studies that have analyzed sanction severity as it applies to waiver to adult court have focused on one of two outcomes: sentence type and sentence length. Studies that analyze sentence type answer the questions: What types of sentences do juveniles receive once waived to adult court? Is a juvenile waived to adult court more likely to receive probation, an intermediate punishment such as a sentence to a boot camp, or a prison sentence? According to several studies, juveniles waived to adult court are more likely to be sentenced to prison than any other potential disposition such as probation.[23] Other studies have found that juveniles waived to adult court are less likely to receive a prison sentence than they are to receive a probationary sentence, an intermediate sanction, or even dismissal of their cases.[24]

Myth Once a juvenile is waived to adult court, it is rare for the case to be dismissed by the prosecutor.

Fact The prosecutor or the court dismisses charges in 25 percent of the cases waived to adult court.

Source: Snyder, Howard N. and Melissa Sickmund. *Juvenile Offenders and Victims: 1999 National Report.* Washington, DC: Office of Juvenile Justice and Delinquency Prevention, 1999.

Waived youths are presumably the most serious and violent offenders in the juvenile justice system. Still, there is no guarantee that they will receive a lengthy prison sentence if waived to adult court. One reason for this is that waived juveniles can be viewed as first-time offenders whose age tends to mitigate, rather than aggravate, sentencing decisions. Figure 10.4 shows what happens to juveniles waived to adult court. Barry C. Feld refers to this as the

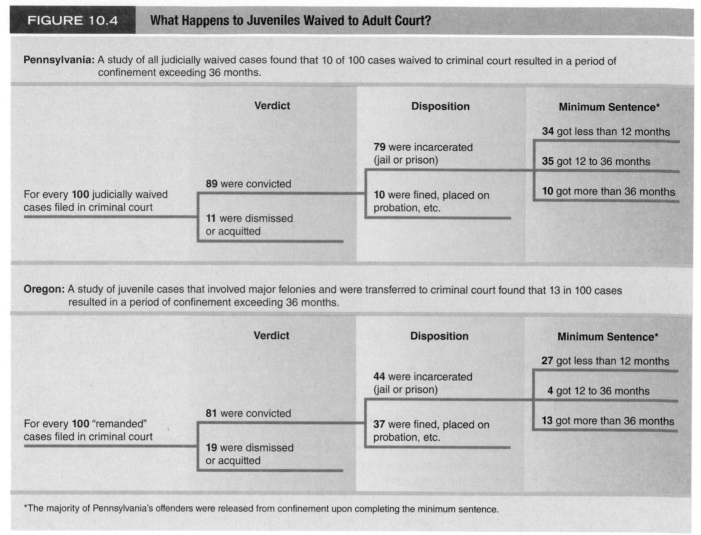

FIGURE 10.4   What Happens to Juveniles Waived to Adult Court?

Pennsylvania: A study of all judicially waived cases found that 10 of 100 cases waived to criminal court resulted in a period of confinement exceeding 36 months.

Verdict	Disposition	Minimum Sentence*
For every **100** judicially waived cases filed in criminal court — **89** were convicted	**79** were incarcerated (jail or prison)	**34** got less than 12 months **35** got 12 to 36 months **10** got more than 36 months
11 were dismissed or acquitted	**10** were fined, placed on probation, etc.	

Oregon: A study of juvenile cases that involved major felonies and were transferred to criminal court found that 13 in 100 cases resulted in a period of confinement exceeding 36 months.

Verdict	Disposition	Minimum Sentence*
For every **100** "remanded" cases filed in criminal court — **81** were convicted	**44** were incarcerated (jail or prison)	**27** got less than 12 months **4** got 12 to 36 months **13** got more than 36 months
19 were dismissed or acquitted	**37** were fined, placed on probation, etc.	

*The majority of Pennsylvania's offenders were released from confinement upon completing the minimum sentence.

Source: Snyder, Howard N. and Melissa Sickmund. *Juvenile Offenders and Victims: A National Report,* Washington, DC: Office of Juvenile Justice and Delinquency Prevention, 1995.

punishment gap.[25] Juveniles waived to adult court for the first time are usually given the leniency accorded to first-time adult offenders.

Recall that the juvenile justice system must release a juvenile from a juvenile institution by a particular age, usually between ages 19 and 21, depending on the state law. Most studies have found that juveniles waived to adult court and sentenced to prison usually receive longer sentences than are available in juvenile court.[26]

PUBLIC ATTITUDES TOWARD WAIVER TO ADULT COURT

A survey of citizens' attitudes toward waiver to adult court found that 86.5 percent of the respondents felt that a juvenile charged with a serious violent offense should be tried as an adult, while 69.1 percent of the respondents felt the same way for a juvenile charged with selling illegal drugs. In addition, 62.6 percent of the respondents felt that a juvenile charged with a serious property crime should be waived to adult court for prosecution.[27]

Figure 10.5 shows the results of a national survey conducted by The Gallup Organization, Inc. Respondents were asked, "In your view, how should juveniles between the ages of 14 and 17 who commit violent crimes be treated in the criminal justice system—should they be treated the same as adults, or

punishment gap The discovery that juveniles waived to adult court for the first time are usually given the leniency accorded to first-time adult offenders.

should they be given more lenient treatment in a juvenile court?" Regardless of how the data is broken down, the majority of respondents in each category, with the exception of respondents with college post-graduate education, were in favor of juveniles being treated the same as adults.[28] However, the public does not always approve of juveniles being sent to prison after having

10.2 SELF-CHECK

1. What is the purpose of waiving a juvenile to adult court?

2. Briefly describe the three types of waivers.

FIGURE 10.5	**Attitudes toward the Treatment of Juveniles Who Commit Violent Crimes**

Question: "In your view, how should juveniles between the ages of 14 and 17 who commit violent crimes be treated in the criminal justice system—should they be treated the same as adults, or should they be given more lenient treatment in a juvenile court?"

	SAME AS ADULTS	MORE LENIENT TREATMENT	DEPENDS[a]	DON'T KNOW/ REFUSED
National	59%	32%	8%	1%
Sex				
Male	64	29	5	1
Female	55	34	10	1
Race				
White	59	32	8	1
Nonwhite	58	32	8	1
Black	54	36	9	1
Age				
18 to 29 years	62	34	3	0
30 to 49 years	57	31	11	1
50 to 64 years	65	27	6	2
50 years and older	59	31	7	2
65 years and older	52	36	8	3
Education				
College post-graduate	42	49	9	(b)
College graduate	51	41	7	1
Some college	61	27	9	2
High school graduate or less	68	25	6	1
Income				
$75,000 and over	58	36	5	1
$50,000 to $74,999	54	35	9	1
$30,000 to $49,999	63	28	8	1
$20,000 to $29,999	59	31	8	1
Under $20,000	58	31	7	4
Community				
Urban area	62	29	8	1
Suburban area	57	34	7	1
Rural area	60	31	7	2
Region				
East	57	34	7	2
Midwest	51	37	10	1
South	66	25	7	1
West	59	34	6	1
Politics				
Republican	64	24	10	1
Democrat	55	35	9	1
Independent	59	35	5	1

[a]Response volunteered.
[b]Less than 0.5%.

Source: www.albany.edu/sourcebook. Table constructed by *Sourcebook* staff from data provided by Gallup, Inc. 2003. Reprinted by permission.

been convicted in adult court. Most state laws, however, do allow juveniles who are waived to adult court and convicted to be sent to prison.

Blended Sentencing

Traditionally, the juvenile justice system and criminal justice system have been separate, and there has not been any crossover between the two systems. If a person were processed in juvenile court, the maximum punishment available would be a term of confinement in a juvenile institution until the individual reaches the age of majority, usually age 19 to 21, depending on the state. At this point, the juvenile had to be released from the institution and was no longer under the jurisdiction of the juvenile court. The only way to impose a longer sentence on the individual was to waive the juvenile to adult court and sentence the juvenile to prison upon conviction. If convicted in adult court, the juvenile could receive life imprisonment. Processing in juvenile court or waiving them to adult court were the two options available for processing a juvenile offender.

Since the punitive model of juvenile justice began, a new form of disposition and sentencing, known as *blended sentencing*, has become popular. **Blended sentencing** refers to the imposition of juvenile and/or adult correctional sanctions for serious and violent juvenile offenders who have been processed either in the juvenile or adult court;[29] it blurs the traditional dividing line between the juvenile and criminal justice systems. Certain juveniles processed in juvenile court may receive adult sanctions, and, certain juveniles tried in adult court may receive juvenile sanctions. Blended sentences, where juveniles can receive a mix of both juvenile and adult sanctions, are unprecedented at any prior time in the history of the juvenile justice system.

TYPES OF BLENDED SENTENCING

In three of the five types of blended sentencing, a juvenile offender is processed in juvenile court but is eligible to receive an adult punishment (for example, incarceration in prison). In the other two types, a juvenile offender is processed in adult court but is eligible to receive a juvenile punishment (for example, incarceration in a juvenile institution). The various types of sentencing are based on (a) where the case is processed (juvenile or adult court), and (b) what sentencing options are available (see Figure 10.6). The following are the five types of blended sentencing:

1. **Juvenile-exclusive blend** The case against the juvenile offender is processed in juvenile court. If the individual is adjudicated, the juvenile is eligible to receive a sentence either in the juvenile correctional system or in the adult correctional system. This is known as an exclusive blend because a judge must decide between either a juvenile or an adult sanction. A judge decides if the juvenile should be placed in a juvenile institution or sent to an adult prison. A judge cannot impose both a juvenile sanction and an adult sanction under this type of sentencing.

2. **Juvenile-inclusive blend** The case against the juvenile offender is processed in juvenile court. The difference between this type of sentencing and the previous one is the type of sanction that is available after adjudication. A judge can simultaneously impose both a juvenile and adult correctional sanction. The adult correctional sanction is suspended, pending a revocation or further criminal activity, at which point the juvenile will be required to complete the adult sanction. For example, a juvenile is convicted of aggravated robbery and the judge sentences him to a term of incarceration in a juvenile institution and 10 years in adult prison. The juvenile offender will be sent to the juvenile institution and will be required to complete only the juvenile sanction if he behaves appropriately

blended sentencing Involves the imposition of juvenile and/or adult correctional sanctions for serious and violent juvenile offenders who have been processed in either the juvenile or adult court.

juvenile-exclusive blend A type of blended sentence in which the case is processed in juvenile court; and, once the case is adjudicated, a juvenile offender may receive a sentence in either the juvenile or adult correctional system.

juvenile-inclusive blend A type of blended sentence in which the case is processed in juvenile court; and, once the case is adjudicated, a juvenile offender may receive a sentence in both the juvenile and adult correctional systems.

| FIGURE 10.6 | Types of Blended Sentencing |

Juvenile Court — or — Juvenile / Adult	**Juvenile–Exclusive Blend:** The juvenile court has original jurisdiction and responsibility for adjudication of the case. The juvenile court has the authority to impose a sanction involving either the juvenile or adult correctional systems.	New Mexico
Juvenile Court — and — Juvenile / Adult	**Juvenile–Inclusive Blend:** The juvenile court has original jurisdiction and responsibility for adjudication of the case. The juvenile court has the authority to impose a sanction involving both the juvenile and adult correctional systems. In most instances, the adult sanction is suspended unless there is a violation, at which point it is invoked.	Alaska, Arkansas, Connecticut, Illinois, Kansas, Massachusetts, Michigan, Minnesota, Montana, Ohio
Criminal Court Juvenile ▲ Adult	**Juvenile–Contiguous Blend:** The juvenile court has original jurisdiction and responsibility for adjudication of the case. The juvenile court has the authority to impose a sanction that would be in force beyond the age of its extended jurisdiction. At that point, various procedures are invoked to determine if the remainder of that sanction should be imposed in the adult correctional system.	Colorado, Rhode Island, Texas
Criminal Court — or — Juvenile / Adult	**Criminal–Exclusive Blend:** The criminal court tries the case. The criminal court has the authority to impose a sanction involving either the juvenile or adult correctional systems.	California, Colorado, Illinois, Kentucky, Massachusetts, Nebraska, New Mexico, Oklahoma, West Virginia
Criminal Court — and — Juvenile / Adult	**Criminal–Inclusive Blend:** The criminal court tries the case. The criminal court has the authority to impose a sanction involving both the juvenile and adult correctional systems. In most instances, the adult sanction is suspended unless there is a violation, at which point it is invoked.	Arkansas, Florida, Idaho, Iowa, Michigan, Missouri, Virginia

Source: Graphic adapted from Torbet, Patricia, Richard Gable, Hunter Hurst IV, Imogene Montgomery, Linda Szymanski, and Douglas Thomas. *State Responses to Serious and Violent Juvenile Crime.* Washington, DC. Office of Juvenile Justice and Delinquency Prevention, 1996.

Updates in *OJJDP Statistical Briefing Book.* Online. Available: http:www.ojjdp.gov/ojstatbb/structure_process/qa04113.asp?qaDate–2011; OJJDP Statistical Briefing Book. Online. Available: http:www.ojjdp.gov/ojstatbb/structure_process/qa04115.asp?qaDate=2011.

there. If he or she does not behave appropriately in the juvenile institution, the judge can revoke that sentence and force him to serve the 10-year prison sentence in an adult correctional facility.

3. **Juvenile-contiguous blend** The case against the juvenile offender is processed in juvenile court. Once the juvenile is adjudicated, a judge can impose a sentence that can exceed the jurisdictional age limit of the juvenile corrections agency. Before the juvenile reaches the jurisdictional age limit, the sentence is continued in the adult correctional system. As previously discussed, each state has a jurisdictional age limit of its juvenile corrections agency, most frequently age 21. All juveniles incarcerated in a juvenile institution must be released by this age. The juvenile contiguous type of blended sentencing allows correctional sanctions to be continued from the juvenile to the adult system (See Focus on Policy).

4. **Criminal-exclusive blend** The last two types of blended sentencing are different from the previous three because the case against the juvenile

juvenile-contiguous blend A type of blended sentence in which the case is processed in juvenile court, and once the case is adjudicated, a judge can impose a sentence on the juvenile offender that can exceed the jurisdictional age limit of the juvenile corrections agency.

criminal-exclusive blend A type of blended sentence in which the case is processed in adult court, and, once convicted, the juvenile offender may receive a sentence in either the juvenile or adult correctional system.

FOCUS ON POLICY

TEXAS' JUVENILE CONTIGUOUS TYPE OF BLENDED SENTENCE

The juvenile contiguous blended sentence in Texas is known as the "determinate sentence law." The law allows any juvenile, age 10 to 16, who commits one of 23 offenses to receive up to a 40-year sentence. The potential sentence depends on the offense committed. Some offenses allow for a maximum of a 10-year sentence while some allow for up to a 40-year sentence (see Table 10.1). Offenses that are classified as capital and first-degree felonies by state law can receive up to a 40-year sentence. Offenses that are classified as second-degree felonies by state law can receive up to a 20-year sentence, while offenses classified as third-degree felonies can receive up to a 10-year sentence.

A juvenile offender in Texas is processed in juvenile court, and if found guilty, sentenced under the determinate sentence law. A juvenile who receives a determinate sentence is sent to a juvenile institution. Prior to the juvenile's 18th birthday, a release hearing is held before a juvenile court judge. At the release hearing, the judge hears testimony of whether or not the juvenile should be transferred to adult prison to serve the remainder of the sentence, be recommitted to the juvenile institution, scheduled to be released by age 19, or be immediately released from the juvenile institution. If the juvenile has been sufficiently rehabilitated, then the judge may decide to recommit the juvenile to a juvenile institution with a scheduled release by age 19. If the rehabilitation is not successful, then the judge decides to send the juvenile to adult prison for the remainder of the sentence. Once in adult prison, the juvenile is subject to the state parole laws and may be released before serving his or her entire sentence or may remain incarcerated for the rest of the sentence.

Conceivably a 10-year-old juvenile convicted of capital murder or another offense listed in Table 10.1 could receive a 40-year sentence. The juvenile would serve less than eight years in a juvenile institution because the juvenile must receive a release hearing prior to his 18th birthday. If the judge decides to send the juvenile to adult prison for the remainder of the sentence, the juvenile could serve an additional 32 years in prison, totaling 40 years of incarceration. Therefore, a 10-year-old who commits capital murder or another specified offense could be incarcerated until he or she is 50 years old.

CRITICAL THINKING

How would you propose to determine whether a delinquent has been sufficiently rehabilitated?

TABLE 10.1

OFFENSE	MAXIMUM SENTENCE AVAILABLE		
	40 YEARS	20 YEARS	10 YEARS
Aggravated assault	X		
Aggravated controlled substance felony	X		
Aggravated kidnapping	X		
Aggravated robbery	X		
Aggravated sexual assault	X		
Arson causing bodily injury or death	X		
Attempted aggravated kidnapping		X	
Attempted aggravated robbery		X	
Attempted aggravated sexual assault		X	
Attempted capital murder	X		
Attempted indecency with a child			X
Attempted murder		X	
Attempted sexual assault			X
Capital murder	X		
Criminal solicitation	X		
Criminal solicitation of a minor	X		
Deadly conduct with a firearm			X
Indecency with a child		X	
Injury to a child, elderly or disabled individual	X		
Intoxication manslaughter		X	
Manslaughter		X	
Murder	X		
Sexual assault		X	

offender is processed in the adult criminal court. Under the criminal-exclusive blend, a judge must decide whether to impose a juvenile or adult correctional sanction, but not both, after the juvenile is convicted in adult court. If a judge believes that a juvenile offender should be sent to adult prison, then the judge can sentence the individual to prison. However, if a judge believes that it is best to sentence the offender to a juvenile correctional sanction such as confinement in a juvenile institution, then the judge will impose this sanction despite the fact that the case was processed in adult court. This is similar to the juvenile-exclusive type of blended sentencing previously discussed except the case is processed in adult court.

5. **Criminal-inclusive blend** The case against a juvenile offender is processed in adult criminal court. After conviction, a judge will impose both a juvenile and an adult correctional sanction but suspend the adult sanction, pending a violation or revocation. Therefore, the juvenile will begin to serve his or her sentence in a juvenile institution. If a violation or revocation occurs, the judge may revoke the juvenile sanction and impose the adult sanction. This is similar to the juvenile-inclusive type of blended sentencing previously discussed except the case is processed in adult court.

Juveniles in Adult Prisons

Where is a juvenile incarcerated once he or she has been waived to adult court, convicted or subjected to a blended sentence, and has received an adult correctional sanction? Almost all states allow juveniles who have been sentenced as adults or subjected to a blended sentence to be sent to an adult prison facility. In some states, the juvenile offender is housed in the general adult population (known as **straight adult incarceration**). Other states house the juvenile offender in a separate facility for younger adult offenders, usually between ages 18 and 25 (known as **segregated incarceration**).

Some states place restrictions on incarcerating juveniles in adult prison. Six states (Arizona, Hawaii, Kentucky, Montana, Tennessee, and West Virginia) either prohibit juveniles from being incarcerated in prison or require a juvenile offender to be housed separately from all adults. Other states require a juvenile to be a certain age in order to be sent to prison. For example, laws in California and North Dakota require that juveniles be 16 years old before being housed in an adult prison. Juveniles in North Dakota and California can be waived to adult court if they are 14 years or older. However, if a 14- or 15-year-old in either state is convicted in adult court, the juvenile cannot be sent to prison until age 16. Until that time, the person remains in a juvenile institution.

Usually, juveniles incarcerated in adult prisons are subject to the same policies and procedures as other inmates regarding housing, health care services, education, vocation and work programs, and recreational activities.[40] They are treated the same as the rest of the inmates. Juveniles in adult prisons represent a small percentage of all inmates. Less than 1 percent of state prison inmates

In some states, juveniles convicted in adult court are sentenced to prison. *Do you think this is the appropriate place to put juveniles convicted in adult court? What other options may be feasible alternatives to incarceration?*

10.3 SELF-CHECK

Describe the different types of blended sentences.

criminal-inclusive blend A type of blended sentence in which the case is processed in adult court, and, once convicted, the juvenile offender may receive a sentence in both the juvenile and adult correctional systems.

straight adult incarceration The practice of housing juveniles convicted in adult court in the general adult prison population.

segregated incarceration The practice of housing juveniles convicted in adult court in a separate prison facility for younger offenders, usually between the ages of 18 and 25.

Describe the different types of living arrangements juveniles can encounter once they are sentenced to an adult prison.

are 17 years old or younger. Many people are concerned about the victimization of juveniles in adult prisons. Juveniles who are incarcerated in prison are more likely to be victimized by other inmates than juveniles who remain in a juvenile institution.[31] Despite this fact, the most common practice is to incarcerate juveniles in prison once they are convicted in adult court.

Death Penalty for Juvenile Offenders

On March 1, 2005, the United States Supreme Court ruled in *Roper* v. *Simmons* that the imposition of the death penalty on juvenile offenders is unconstitutional. The Court ruled that the Eighth and Fourteenth Amendments of the U.S. Constitution forbid imposition of the death penalty on offenders who are under the age of 18 when their crimes are committed.[32] This section will discuss the prevalence of use of the death penalty prior to *Roper* as well as the prior U.S. Supreme Court decisions on the juvenile death penalty. At the end of this section, a detailed discussion of the *Roper* case will be presented.

PREVALENCE AND USE PRIOR TO *ROPER*

Prior to the *Roper* decision, the death penalty was rarely imposed for offenses committed when the offender was a juvenile. There have been only 366 documented juvenile executions, accounting for only 2 percent of all documented executions in American history. However, the practice of executing juveniles has a long history. Under common law doctrine, which was the legal system the American colonists brought from England, a juvenile age 7 or older could receive the same punishment as adults, including death. The first documented case of a juvenile being executed for a crime in the American colonies occurred in 1642 when 16-year-old Thomas Graunger was executed in Plymouth Colony, Massachusetts, for bestiality.[33] Interestingly, juveniles as young as age 10 when they committed their offense have been executed in the United States.

From 1973 to 2003, only 226 individuals who were younger than age 18 when they committed the offense were sentenced to death. This is only 2 percent of the offenders who have received the death penalty since 1973. However, some of the offenders counted in the above figure were legally adults at the time the offense was committed because they were older than the maximum age of juvenile court jurisdiction in their state. Remember that in some states, 16- and 17-year-olds are considered adults because the maximum age of juvenile court jurisdiction is set below age 18. From 1973 to 2005, 22 offenders were executed for offenses they committed under age 18 (see Figure 10.7).[34] All but five of these offenders were legally adults when they committed their offenses. For example, in 1998, Virginia executed a juvenile who had been transferred to criminal court under judicial waiver provisions. Oklahoma has executed juveniles who were 16 and 17 at the time of their crimes. Oklahoma statutes exclude 16- and 17-year-old offenders charged with murder from juvenile court.[35] Thirteen of the 22 offenders were from Texas, and they were all 17 years old when they committed their crimes. In Texas, a 17-year-old is an adult.

UNITED STATES SUPREME COURT CASES PRIOR TO *ROPER*

In 1988, the U.S. Supreme Court ruled on the constitutionality of the death penalty for juveniles in a case brought by William Wayne Thompson, who was convicted and sentenced to death for murdering his former brother-in-law.[36]

FIGURE 10.7	Juveniles under 18 Executed from January 1, 1973, until *Roper* Decision				
NAME	EXECUTION DATE	STATE	RACE	AGE AT OFFENSE	AGE AT EXECUTION
Scott Allen Hain	4/3/2003	Oklahoma	White	17	32
Toronto Patterson	8/28/2002	Texas	African American	17	24
T.J. Jones	8/8/2002	Texas	African American	17	25
Napoleon Beazley	5/28/2002	Texas	African American	17	25
Gerald Lee Mitchell	10/22/2001	Texas	African American	17	33
Gary L. Graham	1/22/2000	Texas	African American	17	39
Glen C. McGinnis	1/25/2000	Texas	African American	17	27
Steve E. Roach	1/19/2000	Virginia	White	17	23
Christopher Thomas	1/10/2000	Virginia	White	17	26
Sean R. Sellers	2/4/1999	Oklahoma	White	16	29
Dwight A. Wright	10/14/1998	Virginia	African American	17	26
Robert A. Carter	5/18/1998	Texas	African American	17	34
Joseph John Cannon	4/22/1998	Texas	White	17	38
Chris Burger	12/7/1993	Georgia	White	17	33
Ruben Cantu	8/28/1993	Texas	Latino	17	26
Frederick Lashley	7/28/1993	Missouri	African American	17	29
Curtis Harris	7/1/1993	Texas	African American	17	31
Johnny Garrett	2/11/1992	Texas	White	17	28
Dalton Prejean	5/18/1990	Louisiana	African American	17	30
Jay Pinkerton	5/15/1986	Texas	White	17	24
J. Terry Roach	1/10/1986	South Carolina	White	17	25
Charles Rumbaugh	9/11/1985	Texas	White	17	28

Source: Adaptation and update of Victor Streib, *The Juvenile Death Penalty Today: Death Sentences and Executions for Juvenile Crimes.*

Thompson shot his former brother-in-law twice in the head, cut his throat, chest, and abdomen and threw his body in a nearby river. William Thompson was 15 years old at the time of the offense. The Court ruled that executing juveniles who were under age 16 at the time of the offense would violate the Eighth Amendment prohibition against cruel and unusual punishment. The U.S. Supreme Court stated that it was cruel and unusual punishment to execute anyone who was under 16 years old at the time of the offense. Therefore, prior to *Roper,* no juvenile in the United States could be executed for an offense that he or she committed when age 15 or younger.

Despite the decision of the U.S. Supreme Court in *Thompson* v. *Oklahoma,* the question remained unanswered as to whether juveniles who commit offenses at age 16 or 17 could be executed for their crimes. The question was answered the next year in 1989 in *Stanford* v. *Kentucky*[37] and its companion case *Wilkins* v. *Missouri.*[38] Kevin Stanford at age 17 repeatedly raped and sodomized a gas station attendant during a robbery. He then drove the victim to a secluded area and shot her in the face and the back of the head. Stanford was convicted of capital murder and was sentenced to death. In the other case, Heath Wilkins was convicted of first-degree murder and sentenced to death for the stabbing death of a convenience store owner. Wilkins was 16 at the time of the offense. The U.S. Supreme Court ruled that the execution of an offender who was 16 years of age or older at the time of the offense did not violate the Eighth Amendment prohibition against cruel and unusual punishment.

In making its decision in these cases, the U.S. Supreme Court looked at the current practice of the death penalty in the United States and stated that the imposition of the death penalty on 16- or 17-year-old offenders was not contrary to the "evolving standards of decency that mark the progress of a

Juvenile Death Sentences

Even prior to *Roper* most juvenile death sentences were reversed. From 1973 to the *Roper* decision, 51 percent of under-18 death sentences were reversed, 9 percent resulted in executions, and 39 percent were still in force at the time of the *Roper* decision.

Source: Sickmund, Melissa. *Juveniles in Corrections.* Washington, DC: Office of Juvenile Justice and Delinquency Prevention, 2004.

maturing society." In other words, there was not a clear national consensus that the imposition of the death penalty on 16- and 17-year-old offenders violated the contemporary standards of decency in the United States. Therefore, prior to *Roper* a juvenile who was at least age 16 at the time of the offense *could* receive the death penalty. Prior to *Roper*, the United States was one of only eight countries in the world that allowed the execution of juvenile offenders. The seven other countries were Iran, Pakistan, Saudi Arabia, Yemen, Nigeria, the Congo, and China. However, all of these countries have either abolished the death penalty for juveniles or have disavowed the practice.[39]

Christopher Simmons is serving a sentence of life without the possibility of parole. *Do you think he should be executed for the murder he committed when he was 17 years old?*

ROPER V. *SIMMONS* [40] (2005): THE DEATH PENALTY FOR JUVENILES IS RULED UNCONSTITUTIONAL

At the age of 17, when he was still a junior in high school, Christopher Simmons committed murder. About nine months later, he was tried and sentenced to death. There is little doubt that Simmons was the instigator of the crime. Before its commission, Simmons said he wanted to murder someone. In chilling, callous terms he talked about his plan, discussing it for the most part with two friends, Charles Benjamin and John Tessmer, then aged 15 and 16, respectively. Simmons proposed to his friends to commit a burglary and murder by breaking and entering, tying up a victim, and throwing the victim off a bridge. Simmons assured his friends they could "get away with it" because they were minors.

The three met at about 2 A.M. on the night of the murder, but Tessmer left before the other two set out. Simmons and Benjamin entered the home of the victim, Shirley Crook, after reaching through an open window and unlocking the back door. Simmons turned on a hallway light. Awakened, Mrs. Crook called out, "Who's there?" In response, Simmons entered Mrs. Crook's bedroom, where he recognized her from a previous car accident involving them both. Simmons later admitted this confirmed his resolve to murder her.

Using duct tape to cover her eyes and mouth and bind her hands, the two perpetrators put Mrs. Crook in her minivan and drove to a state park. They reinforced the bindings, covered her head with a towel, and walked her to a railroad trestle spanning the Meramec River. There they tied her hands and feet together with electrical wire, wrapped her whole face in duct tape, and threw her from the bridge, drowning her in the waters below.

Soon after the murder, Simmons was bragging about the killing, telling friends he had killed a woman "because the bitch seen my face." The next day, after receiving information of Simmons' involvement, police arrested him at his high school and took him to the police station in Fenton, Missouri. They read him his *Miranda* rights. Simmons waived his right to an attorney and agreed to answer questions. After less than two hours of interrogation, Simmons confessed to the murder and agreed to perform a videotaped reenactment at the crime scene.

The State charged Simmons with burglary, kidnapping, stealing, and murder in the first degree. As Simmons was 17 at the time of the crime, he was outside the criminal jurisdiction of Missouri's juvenile court system. He was tried as an adult. At trial, the State introduced Simmons' confession and the videotaped reenactment of the crime, along with testimony that Simmons discussed the crime in advance and bragged about it later. The defense called no witnesses in the guilt phase. The jury returned a verdict of murder; then the trial proceeded to the penalty phase.

The State sought the death penalty. As aggravating factors, the State submitted that the murder was committed for the purpose of receiving money; was committed for the purpose of avoiding, interfering with, or preventing lawful arrest of the defendant; and involved depravity of mind and was outrageously and wantonly vile, horrible, and inhuman. The State called Shirley Crook's husband, daughter, and two sisters, who presented moving evidence of the devastation her death had brought to their lives.

In mitigation, Simmons' attorneys first called an officer of the Missouri juvenile justice system, who testified that Simmons had no prior convictions and that no previous charges had been filed against him. Simmons' mother, father, two younger half-brothers, a neighbor, and a friend took the stand to tell the jurors of the close relationships they had formed with Simmons and to plead for mercy on his behalf. Simmons' mother, in particular, testified to the responsibility Simmons demonstrated in taking care of his two younger half-brothers and of his grandmother and to his capacity to show love for them.

During closing arguments, both the prosecutor and defense counsel addressed Simmons' age, which the trial judge had instructed the jurors they could consider as a mitigating factor. Defense counsel reminded the jurors that juveniles of Simmons' age cannot drink, serve on juries, or even see certain movies, because "the legislatures have wisely decided that individuals of a certain age aren't responsible enough." Defense counsel argued that Simmons' age should make "a huge difference to the jurors in deciding just exactly what sort of punishment to make." In rebuttal, the prosecutor gave the following response: "Age, he says. Think about age. Seventeen years old. Isn't that scary? Doesn't that scare you? Mitigating? Quite the contrary I submit. Quite the contrary." The jury recommended the death penalty after finding the State had proved each of the three aggravating factors submitted to it. Accepting the jury's recommendation, the trial judge imposed the death penalty.

After the proceedings in Simmons' case had run their course, the U.S. Supreme Court held in *Atkins* v. *Virginia* that the Eighth and Fourteenth Amendments prohibit the execution of a mentally retarded person. Simmons filed a petition for state postconviction relief, arguing that the reasoning of *Atkins* established that the Constitution prohibits the execution of a juvenile who was under 18 when the crime was committed. The Missouri Supreme Court agreed and set aside Simmons' death sentence and resentenced him to life without the possibility of parole.

FIGURE 10.8	Juveniles on Death Row at Time of *Roper* Decision
STATE	NUMBER ON DEATH ROW
Texas	28
Alabama	13
Mississippi	5
Arizona	4
Louisiana	4
North Carolina	4
Florida	3
South Carolina	3
Georgia	2
Pennsylvania	2
Vermont	1
Nevada	1

Source: Adapted from *USA Today*, March 2, 2005, p. 1.

10.5 SELF-CHECK

1. Prior to *Roper,* did juveniles receive the death penalty in the United States?

2. What did the U.S. Supreme Court rule in *Roper* v. *Simmons?*

The State of Missouri appealed and the U.S. Supreme Court agreed to hear the case. On March 1, 2005, the U.S. Supreme Court decided the *Roper* case and ruled that the Eighth and Fourteenth Amendments of the U.S. Constitution forbid the imposition of the death penalty on offenders who were under the age of 18 when their crimes were committed. The Court reasoned that the evolving standards of decency have now reached a point at which the execution of a juvenile is considered cruel and unusual punishment by U.S. society.

At the time of the *Roper* decision, there were 70 individuals on death row in the United States for offenses committed when they were less than 18 years of age (see Figure 10.8). The sentences of these individuals were commuted to life imprisonment. In states that have a sentence of life without the possibility of parole, these individuals will remain in prison for the remainder of their lives. However, in states that do not have such a sentence, these individuals will become eligible for parole at some time in the future.

1. Explain waiver to adult court

Waiver to adult court is the process by which a juvenile is processed in the criminal justice system instead of in the juvenile justice system.

2. Name the main purposes of waiving a juvenile to adult court and explain the process

The main purposes for waiving juveniles to adult court are:

a. To remove juvenile offenders charged with heinous, violent offenses that frequently generate media and community pressure

b. To remove chronic offenders who have exhausted the resources and the patience of the juvenile justice system

c. To impose longer potential sentences than are available within the juvenile justice system

The most prevalent form of waiver to adult court is discretionary judicial waiver. The prosecutor files a petition with the juvenile court requesting that the juvenile court waive its original jurisdiction over the juvenile offender and send the juvenile to adult court. In other forms of waiver, the prosecutor or the legislature makes the decision to waive a juvenile to adult court.

3. Compare and contrast the three main types of waiver to adult court

The three main types of waiver (judicial, legislative, and prosecutorial) are similar in that they all may lead to a juvenile being waived to adult court. The primary difference between the three types is who makes the decision to try a juvenile in adult court. It is the decision of the juvenile judge to waive a juvenile to adult court under judicial waiver provisions, the prosecutor under prosecutorial waiver, and the legislature under legislative waiver.

4. List the deciding factors in waiving a juvenile to adult court

The following factors are taken into consideration in deciding whether or not to waive a juvenile to adult court:

a. The seriousness of the alleged offense to the community and whether the protection of the community requires waiver

b. Whether the alleged offense was committed in an aggressive, violent, premeditated, or willful manner

c. Whether the alleged offense was against persons or against property, greater weight being given to offenses against persons—especially if personal injury resulted

d. The prosecutive merit of the complaint

e. Whether the juvenile's associates in the offense were adults

f. The sophistication and maturity of the juvenile

g. The record and previous history of the juvenile

h. The prospects for adequate protection of the public and the likelihood of reasonable rehabilitation of the juvenile by the use of procedures, services, and facilities currently available to the juvenile court

5. Evaluate the effectiveness of the waiver to adult court

Prior literature appears to be evenly balanced on the issue of whether violent or property offenders are waived to adult court more frequently. When analyzing sentence severity, several studies have found that juveniles waived to adult court are more likely to be sentenced to prison than any other potential disposition such as probation. On the other hand, some studies have found that juveniles waived to adult court are less likely to receive a prison sentence than they are to receive a probationary sentence, or intermediate sanction, or even to have their cases dismissed.

6. Describe and contrast the five types of blended sentencing

Blended sentencing refers to the imposition of juvenile and/or adult correctional sanctions for serious and violent juvenile offenders who have been processed in either the juvenile or the adult court.

The two factors that distinguish the five types of blended sentencing are (a) where the case is processed (juvenile or adult court) and (b) what sentencing options are available.

7. Analyze major U.S. Supreme Court cases that address the constitutionality of the death penalty for juvenile offenders

In *Thompson* v. *Oklahoma* (1988), the U.S. Supreme Court ruled it *unconstitutional* to execute a person who was 15 years old at the time of the offense. In *Wilkins* v. *Missouri* (1989) and *Stanford* v. *Kentucky* (1989), the U.S. Supreme Court ruled it *constitutional* to execute a person who was 16 or 17 years old, respectively, at the time of the offense. In 2005, the U.S. Supreme Court decided the *Roper* v. *Simmons* case and ruled that the Eighth and Fourteenth Amendments forbid imposition of the death penalty on offenders who were under the age of 18 when their crimes were committed.

KEY TERMS

waiver to adult court,
    p. 266
jurisdictional age limit,
    p. 269
judicial waiver, p. 270
discretionary judicial
    waiver, p. 271
waiver hearing, p. 271
Kent criteria, p. 272

mandatory judicial
    waiver, p. 273
presumptive waiver,
    p. 273
legislative waiver, p. 275
statutory exclusion, p. 275
"once an adult always an
    adult" laws, p. 276
prosecutorial waiver, p. 276

punishment gap, p. 278
blended sentencing,
    p. 280
juvenile-exclusive blend,
    p. 280
juvenile-inclusive blend,
    p. 280
juvenile-contiguous blend,
    p. 281

criminal-exclusive blend,
    p. 281
criminal-inclusive blend,
    p. 283
straight adult
    incarceration, p. 283
segregated incarceration,
    p. 283

REVIEW QUESTIONS

1. What is waiver to adult court? What terms are used interchangeably with this term?

2. Describe three main purposes for waiving juveniles to adult court for prosecution.

3. What are the three main types of waiver to adult court? What primary factor distinguishes the three types?

4. What are the three types of judicial waiver? Define each.

5. What rights were granted juveniles in *Kent* v. *United States?*

6. What factors were established in *Kent* v. *United States* that assist the juvenile court judge in deciding whether to waive a juvenile to adult court?

7. What are the two types of legislative waiver? Define each.

8. What is prosecutorial waiver? How does it differ from judicial and legislative waivers?

9. What are the current trends in the use of waiver to adult court?

10. Is waiver to adult court effective?

11. What is blended sentencing? What are the five types of blended sentencing? What two factors distinguish the five types of blended sentencing from each other?

12. What major United States Supreme Court cases decided the constitutionality of the death penalty for juvenile offenders?

HANDS-ON ACTIVITIES

1. **Analyze a Waiver to Adult Court** Identify an article in a newspaper involving a juvenile waived to adult court. On the basis of the information provided in the article, identify the factors that led to the juvenile being waived to adult court. Compare these factors with the factors identified by the U.S. Supreme Court in *Kent* v. *United States.*

2. **Witness a Waiver Hearing** Attend a waiver hearing at the local juvenile court. What occurs during the hearing? What arguments do the defense attorney and prosecuting attorney make? What statements does the judge make? What factors led to the juvenile being waived to adult court or retained in juvenile court?

INTERNET ACTIVITIES

1. Go to **www.deathpenaltyinfo.org/juveniles-and-death-penalty**. Review the table on the Reported Executions of Juvenile Offenders in Other Countries since 1990. Compare this table with Figure 10.7 in the chapter and write a one-page summary.

1. **Waive a Juvenile to Adult Court?** Joseph has been taken into custody for robbery of a convenience store. He was 14 years old at the time he allegedly committed the offense. During the robbery, Joseph displayed a handgun, but the store attendant was not physically injured. Joseph committed this offense with his 18-year-old brother.

   Joseph has been taken into custody on three prior occasions. Two involved auto theft and the other involved possession of marijuana. Joseph was on probation when he was taken into custody on the robbery charge. He has not been sent to a boot camp or other intermediate sanction program.

   Using the *Kent* criteria for guidance, would you waive Joseph to adult court for prosecution or retain the case in juvenile court? What factors led you to waive or retain the case? What sentence do you think Joseph should receive?

2. **Sentence a Juvenile** You are a juvenile court judge in a suburban county. A case involves a 16-year-old juvenile female accused of murder in the stabbing death of her mother during an argument over curfew time. The juvenile has had one prior contact with the juvenile justice system in which she was accused of assault and received one-year probation. She completed her probation term more than a year before her arrest for murder. On the basis of the evidence you hear during the adjudication hearing, you find the juvenile guilty of murder.

   On the basis of the offense committed, you are allowed by law to sentence the juvenile to either a juvenile institution or an adult prison. Would you sentence the juvenile to prison or an institution? What factors most strongly affected your decision? What impact do you think the institution or prison will have on the juvenile?

10.1 Self-Check

What is waiver to adult court?

Waiver to adult court is the process through which a juvenile court relinquishes jurisdiction over a juvenile offender, and the case is processed in adult court. A juvenile who has been waived to adult court is treated like an adult and, in many cases, subject to the same punishments as adults.

10.2 Self-Check

1. What is the purpose of waiving a juvenile to adult court?

The three main purposes are:

- To remove juvenile offenders charged with heinous, violent crimes, partly as a result of community and media pressure.
- To remove chronic offenders who have exhausted the resources of the juvenile justice system.
- To impose longer potential sentences than are available within the juvenile justice system.

2. Briefly describe the three types of waivers.

The three types of waivers are:

- Judicial waiver, which occurs when a judge waives jurisdiction and thereby sends the juvenile's case to adult court. There are three types of judicial waiver: discretionary judicial waiver, in which a juvenile

court judge holds a waiver hearing to decide whether to waive the case to adult court; mandatory judicial waiver, and presumptive waiver.
- Legislative waiver, a type of waiver created by a legislature, which orders an automatic waiver to adult court when certain offenses are committed.
- Prosecutorial waiver, which occurs when there is concurrent jurisdiction between the adult and juvenile courts and the prosecutor is given the choice of which court should handle the case.

10.3 Self-Check

Describe the different types of blended sentences.

There are five types of blended sentences.

- Juvenile-exclusive blend: The case against the juvenile offender is processed in juvenile court. If the individual is adjudicated, the juvenile is eligible to receive a sentence either in the juvenile correctional system or in the adult correctional system. This is known as an exclusive blend because a judge must decide between either a juvenile or an adult sanction. A judge decides if the juvenile should be placed in a juvenile institution or sent to an adult prison. A judge cannot impose both a juvenile sanction and an adult sanction under this type of sentencing.
- Juvenile-inclusive blend: The case against the juvenile offender is processed in juvenile court.

The difference between this type of sentencing and the previous one is the type of sanction that is available after adjudication. A judge can simultaneously impose both a juvenile and adult correctional sanction. The adult correctional sanction is suspended, pending a revocation or further criminal activity at which point the juvenile will be required to complete the adult sanction.

- Juvenile-contiguous blend: The case against the juvenile offender is processed in juvenile court. Once the juvenile is adjudicated, a judge can impose a sentence that can exceed the jurisdictional age limit of the juvenile corrections agency. Before the juvenile reaches the jurisdictional age limit, the sentence is continued in the adult correctional system. Each state has a jurisdictional age limit of its juvenile corrections agency, most frequently age 21. All juveniles incarcerated in a juvenile institution must be released by this age. The juvenile-contiguous type of blended sentencing allows correctional sanctions to be continued from the juvenile to the adult system.

- Criminal-exclusive blend: The case against the juvenile offender is processed in the adult criminal court. A judge must decide whether to impose a juvenile or adult correctional sanction, but not both, after the juvenile is convicted in adult court. If a judge believes that a juvenile offender should be sent to adult prison, then the judge can sentence the individual to prison. However, if a judge believes that it is best to sentence the offender to a juvenile correctional sanction such as confinement in a juvenile institution, then the judge will impose this sanction despite the fact that the case was processed in adult court. This is similar to the juvenile-exclusive type of blended sentencing previously discussed except the case is processed in adult court.

- Criminal-inclusive blend: The case against a juvenile offender is processed in adult criminal court. After conviction, a judge will impose both a juvenile and an adult correctional sanction but suspend the adult sanction, pending a violation or revocation. Therefore, the juvenile will begin to serve his or her sentence in a juvenile institution. If a violation or revocation occurs, the judge may revoke the juvenile sanction and impose the adult sanction. This is similar to the juvenile-inclusive type of blended sentencing previously discussed except the case is processed in adult court.

10.4 Self-Check

Describe the different types of living arrangements juveniles can encounter once they are sentenced to an adult prison.

They can either encounter straight adult incarceration, which places them among the general prison population, or segregated incarceration, which is the practice of housing juveniles, usually between the ages of 18 and 25, in a separate prison facility.

10.5 Self-Check

1. Prior to *Roper*, did juveniles receive the death penalty in the United States?

Yes, as long as they were aged 16 or older, juvenile murderers were eligible for the death penalty. Since 1973, 22 juveniles (all but one aged 17 at the time of the offense) were executed for their crimes.

2. What did the U.S. Supreme Court rule in *Roper* v. *Simmons*?

The court ruled that the Eighth and Fourteenth Amendments forbid imposition of the death penalty on offenders who were under the age of 18 when their crimes were committed.

COMMUNITY-BASED CORRECTIONS FOR JUVENILES

CHAPTER ELEVEN

Chapter Outline

Chapter Objectives

After completing this chapter, you should be able to:

1. Describe the differences between juvenile community corrections and institutional corrections.

2. Identify the different correctional sanctions available to the juvenile court.

3. Explain the juvenile probation process.

4. Identify typical juvenile probation conditions.

5. Describe the duties and responsibilities of probation officers.

6. Identify and explain the variations in juvenile probation.

7. Describe what intensive supervision probation (ISP) is and which juveniles are eligible for ISP.

8. Identify and explain alternative sanctions available to the juvenile court.

9. Describe what aftercare services are provided for juveniles released from secure incarceration.

Introduction and Overview of Juvenile Corrections

The three main governmental agencies that encompass the juvenile justice system are the police, juvenile courts, and the juvenile correctional system. Of these three, the juvenile correctional system in the United States is the most diverse and unique. A whole host of facilities, programs, and processes exist to deal with at-risk juveniles, delinquent juveniles, and juveniles who are under some type of court sanction. There are multitudes of public and private correctional agencies and social service agencies that deal exclusively with juveniles. In addition, from state to state and county to county, there is a wide variation in terms of the number and kinds of correctional services provided for juveniles. As such, a detailed description of all of the types of correctional services for juveniles is impossible. It is important to remember that it is possible for each and every county in the United States to have a separate juvenile correctional system (especially community corrections), and the diversity of these institutions is immense.

There are several different correctional sanctions that are available to the juvenile court. On average, approximately 27 percent of all juveniles adjudicated delinquent are placed in an out-of-home placement.[1] Research demonstrates:

- In dispositional hearings, juvenile court judges must determine the most appropriate sanction for delinquent youth. Disposition options include commitment to an institution or another residential facility; probation; or a variety of other dispositions, such as referral to an outside agency or treatment program, community service, fines, or restitution. Very often the court imposes some combination of these sanctions.
- The number of adjudicated delinquency cases resulting in residential placement increased 27 percent from 1985 to 2009. In 2009, adjudicated juveniles were ordered to residential placement in 133,800 delinquency cases—27 percent of all adjudicated delinquency cases.
- The number of adjudicated delinquency cases resulting in formal probation increased 51 percent from 1985 to 2009. In 2009, formal probation was the most restrictive disposition ordered in 60 percent of all adjudicated delinquency cases.

Clearly, the majority of juveniles who are adjudicated delinquent are sentenced to some type of community sanction (See Figure 11.1). This chapter examines the various forms of **community corrections** for juveniles. Juvenile detention, boot camps, youth ranches, and reform schools are discussed in Chapter 12. Community corrections simply means that the youth is released back to the community and is most typically allowed to remain at home.

In the United States, the juvenile correctional system is as decentralized as the rest of the juvenile justice system—if not more so. The primary difference is that many states have a central administrative body in charge of overseeing juvenile corrections. These bodies are typically called Department of Youth Services or Department of Juvenile Justice. In addition, the facilities for more serious youthful offenders are typically run by the state. However, there are also a multitude of facilities and services available for delinquent and at-risk youth that are too numerous to name. The primary difference between juvenile and adult corrections is that there are many more placements (and much greater diversity) available for juveniles than there are for adults. In addition, the fundamental goal of juvenile correctional facilities remains rehabilitation, whereas most adult facilities embrace a punitive and custodial orientation.[2] Placements do not always come directly from juvenile court. Many times youths

Myth / Fact

Myth: Most juveniles who are formally adjudicated by the juvenile court are placed out of their homes.

Fact: Only 133,800 (27 percent) of the juveniles formally adjudicated in the American juvenile justice court system in 2009 were placed in a secure facility.

Source: Puzzanchera, Charles, Benjamin Adams, and Sarah Hockenberry. 2012. *Juvenile Court Statistics 2009*. Pittsburgh, PA: National Center for Juvenile Justice.

JUVENILE JUSTICE ONLINE

Find your state's department of juvenile justice or another state-level juvenile justice authority's Web page. Determine which kinds of correctional facilities and programs are governed by the state-level body. Which of the programs listed in Figure 11.2 are not listed on the Web page? What goals and objectives are listed or discussed on the Web page for the juvenile correctional system in the state?

community corrections Correctional programs and facilities located in the community where the delinquent youth lives.

FIGURE 11.1	Case Processing Overview, 2009

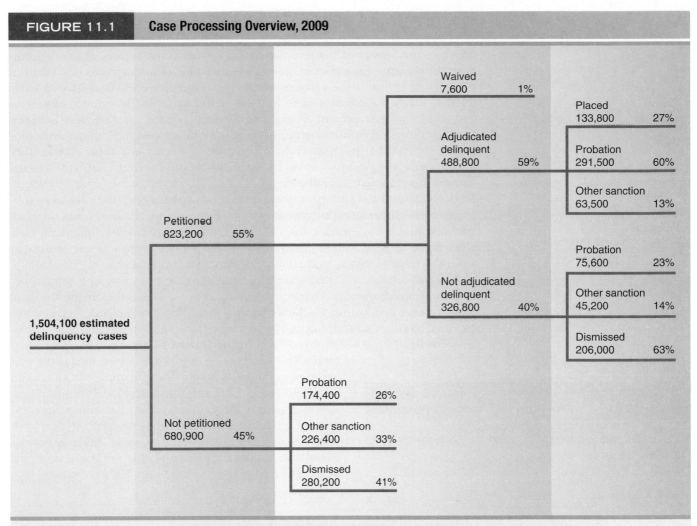

Source: Puzzanchera,Charles, Benjamin Adams, and Sarah Hockenberry. *Juvenile Court Statistics 2009*. Pittsburgh, PA: National Center for Juvenile Justice, 2012.

are referred or placed by their parents, police, community groups, teen courts, diversionary systems, schools, district attorneys, and many other formal and informal agencies of juvenile justice. Because of this, it is impossible to fully categorize or characterize the entire variety of juvenile corrections. Nonetheless, there are several levels of placements that serve juveniles and are fairly common across the United States. Figure 11.2 lists the various types of possible placements and sanctions for juveniles adjudicated delinquent.

11.1 SELF-CHECK

1. What is the most common correctional sanction imposed on juvenile offenders?

2. What are the different correctional alternatives available in the juvenile justice system?

FIGURE 11.2	Juvenile Correctional Alternatives

- Juvenile detention (juveniles awaiting trial or placement)
- Counseling and specialized treatment programs
- Alternative sanctions: restitution and community service
- Vocational and apprenticeship programs
- Short-term shelter and placement facilities
- Foster care
- Juvenile probation
- Shock probation
- Intensive supervision probation

- Home confinement and house arrest
- Day treatment and monitoring facilities
- Wilderness camps, adventure camps, outward bound
- Boot camps
- Youth ranches, camps, and farms
- Group homes, community facilities, halfway houses
- Reform, training, and secure schools
- Juvenile parole and aftercare

History of Juvenile Corrections

Much of the history of the juvenile justice system is the history of the development of separate correctional facilities for juvenile delinquents as described in Chapter 2. Up until the reforms of the Victorian Era (middle 1800s to early 1900s), juvenile offenders were housed in the same facilities and subject to the same harsh treatment as their adult counterparts. The earliest facilities for the correction or housing of juveniles were developed in England and colonial America. Charles Dickens described part of this system in his classic story *Oliver Twist;* the picture painted by Dickens was not far from reality. Wayward juveniles (orphaned, abandoned, and those considered incorrigible) were collectively housed at a variety of workhouses and orphanages. Juveniles were subjected to harsh treatment in these early facilities where the focus was on work and learning a trade rather than general education and development. In fact, the advent of the juvenile justice system was a direct result of the treatment juveniles were receiving in these facilities and adult prisons.

The juvenile correctional system in the United States grew in a bifurcated, or two-pronged, manner. Originally developed as an alternative to adult prison, state reform and training schools formed one prong of juvenile corrections. Some of the original training and industrial schools that opened during the Progressive Era (late 1800s–early 1900s) in the United States are still operational today. The other prong of juvenile corrections is the vast array of community-based and private institutions and programs run by philanthropists and local communities. Any mid-sized or large American city has numerous community programs and institutions designed to deal with wayward children. Indeed, the range of available correctional alternatives serves as one of the primary strengths of the juvenile justice system in the United States.

11.2 SELF-CHECK

What does the statement "the juvenile correctional system developed in a bifurcated manner" mean?

Juvenile Community Corrections

Community corrections is a broad term used to capture a variety of correctional alternatives with one common characteristic: they are less restrictive than institutional corrections and are literally operated in the community. There is no centralized community correctional system. Instead, there is a haphazard collection of both public and private placements and referral alternatives for youths who are adjudicated delinquent or who are at risk of becoming delinquent. Once a youth is adjudicated delinquent, the youth is placed on a dispositional plan by the juvenile court. The disposition plan outlines educational, training, counseling, and other goals for youth while they are on probation. It is usually up to the probation department to coordinate the treatment and correctional goals outlined in the dispositional plan and ensure that the youth is complying with the plan. This may involve placement in a group home, field supervision, referral to treatment programs, job training, and a host of other options. In some circumstances, a youth may reside at home and be required to attend school, work, and receive programmatic treatment supervised by a probation officer. In other circumstances, a youth might be taken out of his or her home and placed in foster care, a temporary shelter, or group home where treatment is more continual and supervision is increased. Community corrections programs place importance on youths remaining in their communities as well as developing consistent relationships with positive adult role models.[3] These programs provide treatment interventions that reflect the expectations of the community and society and attempt to prevent the youth from becoming further involved with the court system.

The majority of juveniles under sanction in the United States are under some form of community corrections. Depending on the state, typically well under 5 percent of the juveniles who are arrested end up in a maximum security facility. There are a variety of factors that can potentially influence whether a juvenile is committed to an out-of-home placement or sentenced to some form of community corrections. Although the final determination is up to the juvenile court judge, several guidelines and research studies have suggested a finite list of variables which influence disposition:

- The circumstances of the offense committed:
  - Violent or not
  - Number and type of victims
  - Weapon used
- Prior history with the juvenile justice system:
  - Prior arrests
  - Prior adjudications
  - Previous probation sentences
  - Prior secure commitments
- Characteristics of the juvenile:
  - Education, IQ, social skills
  - Attitude during proceedings
  - Admission of guilt
  - Substance abuse
- The juvenile's family situation
- The juvenile's social situation
- Availability of community resources and alternative placements
- Availability and workload of staff and correctional personnel

Many probation departments and juvenile courts use **classification instruments** to determine the most appropriate placement for an adjudicated juvenile. Figure 11.3 is a model scale developed by the National Council on Crime and Delinquency (NCCD). Individual jurisdictions can adopt any classification scale they wish, and the juvenile court judge is typically not under any obligation to follow the scale in all cases. Nonetheless, the scale is an attempt to provide more consistency to the placement process. As shown in Figure 11.3, the scale takes into account the severity of the present offense, and prior criminal history, as well as prior placements and adjudications. Note that certain offenses listed in the scale merit automatic secure placement.

The availability of a multitude of correctional alternatives for juveniles helps individualize juvenile corrections to a large extent. Rather than sending all juveniles to the central correctional authority, juvenile court judges have several non-secure and alternative placements for juveniles. The juvenile court seeks to match the needs of the juvenile with the type of placement and takes a prominent role in determining what is in the best interest of the child.

Juvenile community corrections encompasses a variety of treatment alternatives. *What criteria do you think a juvenile judge should follow when determining if a juvenile should be allowed to remain in the community?*

11.3 SELF-CHECK

1. Explain what is meant by juvenile community corrections.
2. List some of the factors that are used to determine whether a juvenile is sentenced to a secure facility or sentenced to some form of community corrections.
3. What are classification instruments and what role do they play in selecting correctional alternatives for juveniles?

classification instruments Instruments that are used to determine which placements are most appropriate for an adjudicated juvenile.

FIGURE 11.3	NCCD Juvenile Classification Scale

	SCORE
1. Severity of Current Offense	
Murder, rape, kidnapping	10
Other offense involving use of a weapon or use of force	5
2. Most Serious Prior Adjudication	
Any offense involving use of a weapon or use of force	5
No prior offense or property offense only	0
3. Number of Prior Out-of-Home Placements	
Three or more	5
Two or less	0
	Total Items 1–3 _____

Total Items 1–3. If score is 10 or higher, secure placement is recommended.
If less than 10, score the remaining items.

	SCORE
4. Prior Placement in a Juvenile Correctional Institution	
Yes	2
No	0
5. Age at First Delinquent Adjudication	
14 or under	2
15 or over	0
6. History of Mental Health Outpatient or Drug/Alcohol Care	
Yes	1
No	0
7. Prior Runaways	
Three or more	1
Two or fewer	0
	Total Items 1–7 _____

Recommendations

10 or above: Secure placement   5–9: Short-term secure care   0–4: Community placement

Source: Krisberg, Barry, Deborah Neuenfeldt, Richard Wiebush, Orlando Rodriguez. *Juvenile Intensive Supervision: Planning Guide*. Washington, DC: National Council on Crime and Delinquency and Office of Juvenile Justice and Delinquency Prevention, 1994.

Juvenile Probation

The juvenile court is the centerpiece of the juvenile justice system, and the **juvenile probation department** is the operational arm of that centerpiece. Most juveniles who are formally processed by the juvenile justice system end up on some type of probation. **Probation** is a sanction where the court releases a youth to a parent or other guardian to live in the community under certain rules and conditions. These rules and conditions attempt to balance the need to protect society with what is in the best interest of the child.

A juvenile probation officer's job is to assure that the juvenile delinquent under his or her supervision is following the disposition plan of the juvenile court. This supervision often leads to the juvenile probation officer becoming a kind of surrogate mother or father to juveniles who are formally sanctioned by the juvenile court. The juvenile probation department is typically responsible for maintaining juvenile records, monitoring juveniles throughout the system, and coordinating the treatment and supervision of juvenile offenders. Probation is the preferred alternative for the vast majority of offenses for a variety of reasons, the least of which is cost. It costs fundamentally more to incarcerate or place a juvenile in a facility than it does to monitor him or her on probation.

The development of juvenile probation in the United States was equally important as the development of a separate juvenile court system. Probation

juvenile probation department The agency in charge of monitoring all youths on probation within a jurisdiction.

probation A sanction where the court releases a youth to a parent or other guardian to live in the community with certain rules and conditions.

in America began with the work of **John Augustus** in Boston, Massachusetts, in the mid-1800s. Augustus vouched for offenders in court and posted their bail. Augustus monitored and supervised their behavior while on bail release. Over time, he personally supervised thousands of offenders and developed many of the common practices and programs of modern probation. Although he began with adults, Augustus extended his work to juvenile offenders. He personally monitored several youths aged 7 to 15 in 1847. He reported to the court monthly and after a period of time, all of the boys were released from supervision. In 1869, Massachusetts formalized this process when the Board of State Charities commissioned agents to act for the board in juvenile criminal matters. Agents were responsible for investigating juvenile cases in the court system, attending trials, and placing certain juveniles in placements and foster homes. In 1878, Massachusetts established a state law that authorized full time, paid probation officers.[4] When the separate system of juvenile courts was established in the United States in the early 20th century, probation systems were already in place. The role of probation in the juvenile justice system would be prominent and would evolve to be the centerpiece of the modern juvenile justice system in America.

The juvenile probation systems that operate in the United States are clearly the central and coordinating agencies in charge of monitoring all aspects of juveniles who are adjudicated delinquent. Since statistics have been kept (1929), probation has been the overwhelming dispositional choice of juvenile courts.[5] Hence, the system has also been dubbed a "catch basin," meaning that most juveniles who are processed end up on probation. There are several reasons for this:

- Probation is limitless: unlike training schools or private providers, probation departments cannot limit or control their intake.
- It is inexpensive and cost efficient, relative to other sanctions.
- It is reasonably satisfactory: most juvenile offenders never recidivate.[6]

Because of its popularity and broad function, juvenile probation affects decision making and service delivery at every stage of juvenile justice processing and holds the potential to ensure that accountability is stressed at all points from initial entry through final discharge.[7]

JUVENILE PROBATION PROCESS

Because of the widespread use of juvenile probation, there are several different types of probation systems. Sometimes, probation is used in lieu of adjudication in a sanction known generally as **deferred adjudication** or informal probation. In deferred adjudication, a youth agrees to follow certain probation conditions without going to court. There is generally no direct supervision by the probation department and the probation is terminated within a short period of time as long as the juvenile does not commit any new offenses. The advantage of this for the juvenile is that there is no formal adjudication and hence no record of a proceeding. The placement of the youth on deferred adjudication probation can be made by the police, intake, prosecutor, or juvenile court.

A variety of information about a juvenile is collected at intake to determine the correctional needs of the juvenile.

John Augustus The initiator of probation. He was a cobbler in Boston, Massachusetts, who posted bail for a few men charged with drunkenness. Later, he would vouch for both adult and juvenile offenders promising the court to personally monitor their behavior and treatment in the community.

deferred adjudication Situation in which a youth agrees to follow certain probation conditions without going to court. There is generally no direct supervision by the probation department and the probation is terminated within a short period of time, as long as the juvenile does not commit any new offenses.

Probation is also used for many, if not all, first-time, low-risk offenders. Most juveniles who are formally referred to the juvenile court for the first time are typically facing status offense charges or property offense charges. These youths will undoubtedly be sentenced to short-term probation with minimal supervision. If the youth gets into more trouble, the conditions of probation and the supervision level are usually increased. The level of supervision, the types of programs the youth will be required to attend, and the length of probation are direct functions of the offense the juvenile committed. The offense is the ultimate determinant of whether the youth will be granted probation and remain in the community or be sentenced to secure incarceration. However, in some instances, even serious or habitual offenders will receive probation because of overcrowding or other mitigating circumstances involved in the case.

The process of involvement by the probation department begins with intake screening to determine how the case should be processed and whether detention should be maintained. The probation department also prepares predisposition reports on most cases and provides some supervision of youths awaiting adjudication.[8] During the adjudication phase, the probation department is frequently asked to testify or be present at hearings. Once a juvenile is adjudicated delinquent, the probation department's role in the life of the juvenile increases substantially. The probation department often conducts review hearings to monitor the progress of youth on probation and may terminate the probation if all the conditions are met.[9] Even after the probation is terminated, some probation departments maintain responsibility for aftercare service for the juvenile.

Executive agencies administer juvenile probation services in 14 states. Executive agencies that administer probation services are mainly at the state level and include correctional agencies, child protection agencies, and social or human services agencies. Less often, adult corrections agencies are responsible for administering probation. In a few states, local government agencies, such as county commissioners, administer probation. In 22 states, judicial agencies administer probation services. The judicial agencies can be at the state level, such as the administrative office of the courts, or local juvenile courts. Finally, in 14 states, a combination of executive and judicial agencies administer probation. There are several ways that this can be arranged. In some states, like Georgia and Louisiana, urban areas have locally court-administered probation departments, while the state administers probation in other areas. In other states, like Nevada, district courts administer probation services except in the most populous county, where probation is administered by the county executive agency. There are some states where the state-level judicial and executive agencies share administration responsibilities, and other states, such as Ohio, where probation services can be contracted out.[10]

PROBATION CASELOAD

Juvenile probation caseloads vary substantially by region as well as by the demographics of who is on probation. In the late 1980s and early 1990s, probation caseloads increased dramatically around the country in response to the significant rise in juvenile crime during that period. There was not an actual increase in the use of probation by the juvenile court system, but there was simply a substantial increase in the number of cases going to juvenile court. In 1999, almost 400,000 adjudicated delinquents were placed on probation in the United States, reflecting an 80 percent increase from 1990 through 1999.[11] Over the same time period, informal probation caseloads rose only 12 percent, which is indicative of the trend toward more formal processing of delinquency cases. A national survey of juvenile probation officers revealed that they

---

Probation Demographic Profile

In 2010, 68 percent of cases placed on probation involved white juveniles, 29 percent involved African-American juveniles, and 3 percent involved juveniles of other races. Most cases (73 percent) placed on probation in 2010 involved males.

Source: Puzzanchera, C., and W. Kang. 2013. "Easy Access to Juvenile Court Statistics: 1985–2010." Online. Available: http://www.ojjdp.gov/ojjstatbb/ezajcs/

thought their optimal caseload was 30 juveniles, while their actual caseload was 41 juveniles. A number of variables can affect the caseload of probation departments and individual officers.

Obviously, the number of referrals from the juvenile court is the prime determinant of the size of the caseloads. Other factors can include resources, turnover, and management within the probation department itself. Some probation departments, especially those in rural areas, may handle both juvenile and adult clients. The age at which a juvenile becomes an adult can affect caseload as well. For example, in a state where the age of adulthood is 18, the caseload on a juvenile probation department will be less than where the age of adulthood is 21. As one researcher notes, several other variables that impact department or caseload size include the range of functions performed by juvenile probation, the range of juvenile behaviors prohibited by law, and the number of crimes excluded from juvenile court jurisdiction.[12] Finally, other system factors such as the extent to which laws are enforced in an area, the clearance rate of juvenile crimes, and the use of diversion or informal handling can all affect caseload.[13]

PROBATION CONDITIONS

Juveniles sentenced to probation can expect to be under the supervision of a probation officer and a host of conditions. Probation conditions can vary substantially from jurisdiction to jurisdiction; however, there are some standard conditions to which most juveniles are required to adhere. Common juvenile probation conditions include:

- Attend school regularly
- Attend work regularly
- Do not use alcohol or drugs
- Submit to random drug screenings
- Check in with probation officer regularly

Overcrowding in juvenile facilities leads to a number of juveniles being placed on probation who would otherwise be incarcerated. *What other problems in institutional corrections do you think affect probation caseloads?*

FOCUS ON POLICY

WOOD COUNTY, OHIO JUVENILE PROBATION AGREEMENT

Name: _____ DOB: _____ Case No.: _____

Address: _____

_____ Phone: _____

Offense: _____

You have been placed on probation on this date _____ by the Honorable _____ Judge of the Wood County Juvenile Court. It is the Order of this Court that you shall abide by the following general and specific conditions of probation:

General Conditions

1. You will obey all laws (federal, state, and local) and will report immediately to your probation officer if arrested or questioned by a law enforcement officer.
2. You will attend school daily, be on time, and obey all school regulations. You will exert your best efforts in completing your school assignments.
3. You will report for probation appointments as directed and be prompt to all such appointments. If, for any excusable reason, you are unable to report for an appointment, it is your responsibility to call your probation officer.
4. The use, possession, or sale of alcohol or drugs of abuse is strictly forbidden unless prescribed by a licensed physician.
5. You shall not own or possess any deadly weapon or dangerous weapon, as defined by the Ohio Revised Code, except with the specific knowledge and permission of your probation officer.
6. You will not leave or remain away from your home without the permission of your parents. Your parents must have knowledge of your whereabouts at all times.
7. You will obey your parent(s), guardian(s), school teachers, school authorities, law enforcement officers, and probation officer and will treat, answer, and address them with respect at all times.
8. You will be in your home by the time designated by your parents or guardians. The maximum curfew hours are _____ p.m. until 6:00 a.m., Sunday through Thursday, and _____ p.m. until 6:00 a.m. Friday and Saturday. Exceptions to these hours are when you are with your parent or guardian, or with the special permission of your probation officer.
9. You shall submit your person and/or property to search or seizure by a probation officer, without probable cause, with or without a warrant, at any time.
10. You will not leave the State of Ohio without the permission of your probation officer.

- Attend special counseling or treatment
- Do not associate with known criminals
- Do not commit any crimes
- Maintain established curfew
- Do not possess a weapon of any type
- Pay restitution
- Perform community service
- Obey parents or other guardian

probation agreement Explains the probation process and outlines the general conditions of probation and any special conditions imposed.

Judges are free to add special conditions at their discretion. Probation is not a right but a privilege. As such, the conditions can be creative rather than oppressive in some situations. Once a juvenile is placed on probation, the juvenile is then obligated to sign a **probation agreement** with the juvenile court. The probation agreement outlines the general conditions of probation, any special

11. Any involvement with gang activity is strictly forbidden. This includes all forms of gang paraphernalia; the wearing of colors or hats associated with gangs; writing or displaying graffiti; using gang signs; and associating with gang members.
12. You will abide by the advice of your probation officer and any other special conditions established by the court and/or your probation officer.
13. Any order of the court requiring a fine, court costs and/or restitution must be complied with strictly.

Special Conditions

Fine and costs: _____ To be paid by: _____

Restitution: _____ To be paid by: _____

Community Service Work: _____ Hours scheduled for _____

Detention Time Ordered: _____ Days ordered to serve _____ Days suspended _____

_____ Counseling as ordered by the court _____

_____ Counseling as deemed appropriate by the probation officer.

_____ Theft Offender Program on _____

_____ Parenting Classes beginning _____

_____ Drug/Alcohol evaluation and complete recommended treatment.

_____ House Arrest until _____

_____ Dr.'s excuse required for any school absence.

_____ Driver's License/Right to apply suspended for _____

_____ No association with: _____

Other: _____

_____

   The length of time that you remain on probation will depend on your attitude, behavior and successful completion of all court orders (minimum six months). If you violate your probation rules or any state or federal laws, you subject yourself to further court action and possible institutionalization. This is an opportunity for you to prove to yourself, and to the court, that you can conduct yourself in a law-abiding manner and remain in your own home.

   The above conditions have been explained to me by a probation officer. I understand them and agree to follow them. I will contact my probation officer if any questions arise. I also understand that the court may revoke my probation, modify the conditions of my probation, and extend the length of my probation. I also understand that my probation officer may arrest me without a warrant.

Probation Officer _____ Date _____ Probationer _____ Date _____

   I/We understand that as the parent(s)/guardian(s) involved in this matter, I/we must notify the Probation Department concerning any probation violations that arise or subject myself/ourselves to another court appearance. Further, I understand that I am responsible for the payment of counseling services, including assessments, as ordered by the court.

Parent/Guardian _____ Date _____ Parent/Guardian _____ Date _____

conditions imposed, and explanations regarding the probation process. (See Focus on Policy.)

   Many times, the parents or guardians of the juvenile will also sign the probation agreement. The probation agreement serves as a contract between the juvenile and the juvenile court that clearly documents what is expected and what is prohibited. Any juvenile who fails to adhere to the contract violates his or her probation and is then subject to increased or additional conditions, or **probation revocation** resulting in incarceration.

ISSUES IN JUVENILE PROBATION

Several problematic issues in juvenile probation affect the delivery of service and the effectiveness of the sanction. First, because juvenile probation is the "catch basin" of the juvenile justice system, probation departments cannot

probation revocation The termination of an unsuccessful probation. The youth is typically sent to a secure placement as a result.

control or limit their caseloads.[14] Issues of supervision, burgeoning caseloads, and more violent juveniles are prominent. Second, issues of safety on the job have led many jurisdictions to begin arming probation officers and requiring them to become certified law enforcement officers. Research has revealed that approximately one-third of juvenile probation officers were assaulted at some point in their careers.[15] In the course of supervising their caseload, probation officers make home visits and might have to travel to dangerous areas where their clients may reside. Finally, perhaps the biggest issue facing probation concerns the ultimate goals of juvenile probation itself. New state laws have increased the punitive ability of the juvenile court as well as the accountability of juveniles accused of committing crimes.

New laws regarding record keeping, fingerprinting, and photographing place new responsibilities on already overburdened probation departments. In addition, probation has to balance the treatment goals for the juvenile with the accountability measures now in place. Indeed, in the face of rising caseloads, fixed resources, public demand for more accountability, and serious safety concerns, the mission of probation will need to evolve even further to respond to both the needs of the juveniles and the needs of the community.[16]

WORKING IN JUVENILE PROBATION

Juvenile probation officers are dedicated individuals who work to ensure community safety and serve the best interests of their clients. As such, they must walk a tenuous line between what is best for the juvenile and what is best for community safety. In that pursuit, they perform a variety of duties and functions and are responsible for ensuring that the juvenile court's directives are followed. Although specific duties vary across the nation, probation officers are typically responsible for the following:

- Making intake decisions. Intake can include screening to determine if formal processing or detention is warranted.
- Preparing **pre-sentence investigations** for the juvenile court. Pre-sentence investigations, also known as predisposition reports, involve psychological assessments, risk score evaluations, educational assessment, social history reports, criminal history reports, and documentation of the facts surrounding the current offense and reasons why the youth is delinquent.
- Functioning as a liaison for the juvenile court. Probation officers work with the juvenile court judge in all aspects of the juvenile justice system and often coordinate information flow between all agencies of the juvenile justice system.
- Preparing **dispositional plans**. The probation officer takes the lead in determining what is best for the juvenile and works to advise the juvenile judge on dispositional issues.
- Supervising juveniles on probation. Probation officers monitor all aspects of the juvenile's disposition plan to assure compliance. They make regular reports to the juvenile court regarding a juvenile's progress on probation.
- Making decisions about the progress of juveniles on probation. Probation officers make recommendations to the juvenile court regarding successful termination of probation, revocation of probation, and modification of probation rules.
- Overseeing **aftercare** for juveniles released from secure placement. Some states have specific juvenile parole departments; however, in some jurisdictions this job falls to the juvenile probation officer.

11.4 SELF-CHECK

1. Describe the process of juvenile probation.
2. What are some common conditions of probation imposed by the juvenile court?
3. What are some of the issues facing probation today?
4. What are the typical duties of a juvenile probation officer?

---

pre-sentence investigations Reports prepared by the probation department overviewing a juvenile's case, social history, criminal history, and treatment needs.

dispositional plans Plans that are imposed on juveniles adjudicated delinquent that outline their entire course of treatment.

aftercare The monitoring and support of juveniles who have been released from custody or supervision by the juvenile court.

Clearly, juvenile probation officers are essential to the operation of the juvenile justice system. The Focus on Practice details the work involved in probation through the eyes of a Florida probation officer.

Variations in Juvenile Probation

Whenever a juvenile receives a disposition from the juvenile court, there is almost always a term of probation assigned to the youth. While the probation sentence is common, there are a number of other community correctional alternatives that a judge may choose to impose. In addition, there are a number of variants to standard juvenile probation that focus on increased supervision, increased security and control, and increased treatment and counseling. Each of the variations in juvenile probation has become fairly common in the United States over the past 25 years.

INTENSIVE SUPERVISION PROBATION (ISP)

One specialized type of juvenile probation increases the level and amount of supervision of juveniles in the community. **Intensive supervision probation (ISP)** programs are characterized by high levels of contact and intervention by the probation officer or caseworker, small caseloads, and strict conditions of compliance. Juvenile ISP is designed as an alternative to secure institutionalization. Some programs include treatment/services components, while others emphasize surveillance and controls. Although juvenile ISP can be defined in many ways (depending upon the goals of the individual jurisdiction), a common definition is a post-adjudication, nonresidential program for serious juvenile offenders used as an alternative to secure institutional placement.[17]

There are five common key elements to ISP programs that have been identified by the National Council on Crime and Delinquency (NCCD). First, ISP is based on a philosophy of risk control, which incorporates incapacitation and rehabilitative goals while stressing accountability and supervision. Second, proper identification of juveniles who need ISP or who will be eligible for ISP is essential. There is a danger of both over- and under-inclusion; therefore, decisions on who receives ISP should be based on research of the target population of juvenile offenders in a jurisdiction. The target population for ISP is postadjudication delinquents who would otherwise be in a secure juvenile correctional institution because of the seriousness of their offenses or their risk of continued delinquent activity. Third, ISP requires a comprehensive effort encompassing highly structured supervision and a broad array of treatment alternatives. ISP includes a phased system of controls, case planning, continuous case management, core service requirements, and a system of rewards and graduated sanctions. Fourth, it is assumed that ISP will be most effective when it has a broad base of ongoing community support and is used in conjunction with other community resources. The comprehensive program of supervision and services requires the coordinated efforts of multiple agencies as well. Finally, there must be a financial commitment to ISP in the jurisdiction. Because of the comprehensive nature of the ISP design, the cost of this program will be considerably more than traditional probation.[18]

ISP assumes that these relatively serious delinquents can be safely and effectively served in the community given the demands of the program. Two types of offenders are targeted for ISP: chronic offenders and those who have committed serious but nonviolent offenses. Chronic offenders are defined as juveniles who have committed multiple offenses, both status offenses and delinquent offenses. They have most probably been through and failed a variety of correctional programs prior to being eligible for ISP. These offenders are at risk for continued problems and committing future crimes. The other group is nonviolent offenders who have committed serious property crimes or drug offenses.

intensive supervision probation (ISP)
A form of probation characterized by increased supervision and treatment. The caseload of officers is typically reduced so they can spend greater amounts of time with smaller numbers of riskier juveniles.

FOCUS ON PRACTICE

A FLORIDA JUVENILE PROBATION OFFICER SPEAKS OUT

The job of the juvenile probation officer (once known as the case manager) is to capably steer and monitor a youth through the delinquency system. This process lasts from arrest, through assessment of the child and his family, recommendations to the state attorney and juvenile judge, and then shadowing that young person, whether he's home on community control or returning from a residential program, to make sure he doesn't stray. Or, if he does get into trouble, that there is immediate fallout.

In Baker County, Florida, Alisa Alred has performed this job for four years, and her case management unit is one of the top three in the state. "My kids know I'm serious. If I say, 'Do this, or I'm taking you back to court,' I do it. You set limits, and if they cross those limits, you set consequences. You have to let them know it's serious. Otherwise they think it's a joke," says Alred. "I tell my kids the first time they come through, they get basically one shot. I tell them everybody can get into trouble. You learn from it. But if you don't learn from it, something needs attention, and you go to court. I believe if you scare them the first time, hopefully they won't come back."

First-time offenders here may land in diversion programs like Teen Court. If they are allowed to stay at home, they may be subject to curfews. Alred checks their school attendance, and she rides with a police officer to see if they're home at night when they're supposed to be.

"I try to help them develop skills so they don't commit more crimes, or I send them to programs where they can learn it there. A lot of my kids are pretty good. They just need a little guidance. A lot of them don't come back. But the ones that come from a family where dad's in jail and the aunt's selling drugs, it's almost impossible to keep that child out of trouble. One of my frustrations is you have a child who's gone to a residential program and made such progress and completed his GED and learned some job skills and you've seen a change in attitude. And the only option when he gets out is to put him back in that same environment."

From parents who think discipline means just beating children, to parents who refuse to set limits and enforce them (or waited to do that until it was too late), Alred says she sees the end result of "a lack of parenting skills." She also sees a lot of delinquent youth who have been abused (physically or sexually) or who have mental problems or substance abuse problems. And parents who just want to shed all responsibility for their kids.

Among her caseload, "Girls can be the most difficult. Boys will be honest about not doing something. Girls are very manipulative. And they run more than boys." She counts stopping one girl from hitchhiking everywhere and seeing another girl put on a dress and stop painting her fingers black as some of her small successes. There is also the girl, once charged with assaulting her mother, who got a chance to live independently, finish school and earn $2,000 on a job. She's now heading to community college.

"I enjoy it. You have to go into this job knowing you're not going to save all of them. But I just hope something they've learned while they're with us helps them down the road. That the next time somebody wants to steal a car, they have the sense to say 'no.'"

CRITICAL THINKING

Do you think this probation officer is more akin to a parent or to a police officer? Explain.

Source: www.djj.state.fl.us/delinquency2.html

This group of offenders would typically be sent to secure placement on the first offense or soon thereafter because of the seriousness of the delinquent act. As noted by the NCCD, ensuring the appropriate selection of the target population for ISP is the single most important element in the prototype implementation.[19] Figure 11.4 depicts a selection matrix developed by NCCD for ISP programs. The model shows which offenders between the most serious offense level and the least serious should be selected for ISP.

Once a juvenile is selected for ISP placement, the National Council on Crime and Delinquency recommends that a phase system of five levels be followed. The initial phase has the greatest level of control, and subsequent phases lessen restrictiveness. The five phases and their anticipated duration are:

Phase 1 Residential or institutional placement—15 to 45 days.
Phase 2 Day treatment—4 to 6 months.

FIGURE 11.4	ISP Selection Matrix		
OFFENSE OR OFFENSE HISTORY	**RISK OF RECIDIVISION**		
	LOW	**MODERATE**	**HIGH**
Major Violent and Multiple Violent Offense[i]	Institutional Placement	Institutional Placement	Long-Term Institutional Placement
Violent Chronic Offense[ii]	ISP/Institutional Placement	ISP/Institutional Placement	Institutional Placement
Violent Chronic Offense (single violent episode)[iii]	ISP/Probation	ISP	ISP/Institutional Placement
Serious Chronic Offense[iv]	ISP	ISP	ISP
Nonserious Chronic Offense[v]	Probation	Probation	ISP
Nonserious Nonchronic Offense[vi]	Probation	Probation	Probation

Notes:
  i. Murder, rape, kidnapping, or history of violent offenses (e.g., two + aggravated assault).
 ii. Instant offense is violent (robbery, aggravated assault); no other violent, but five or more delinquent offenses.
iii. Instant offense is violent (robbery, aggravated assault); but less than five or more delinquent priors.
 iv. Instant offense is not violent (burglary); and has five or more priors.
  v. Instant offense is nonserious (theft); and has five or more priors.
 vi. Instant offense is nonserious (theft); and has less than five priors.

Source: Krisberg, Barry, Deborah Neuenfeldt, Richard Wiebush, Orlando Rodriguez. *Juvenile Intensive Supervision: Planning Guide*. Washington, DC: National Council on Crime and Delinquency and Office of Juvenile Justice and Delinquency Prevention, 1994.

Phase 3 Outreach and tracking (Reintegration)—3 to 4 months.
Phase 4 Regular supervision (Transition)—2 to 3 months.
Phase 5 Discharge and follow-up—1 to 2 months.[20]

Evaluations of the effectiveness of ISP are mixed. Some research has found lower rates of recidivism among juveniles who received ISP versus a comparison group that did not. Other research found no significant differences between juveniles who went through ISP versus those who did not.[21] Several research studies found problems with the implementation of the ISP criteria and programs. In one study, the number of contacts between the youths and their ISP officer were substantially less than what was mandated. Further, the goals and criteria in some programs that were evaluated were not clear, and there was high turnover in the staff. In other projects, the juveniles who participated in ISP were not subjected to the higher levels of increased treatment that were expected.[22] Therefore, the interpretation of the research on the effectiveness of ISP is unclear.

CAREERS IN JUVENILE JUSTICE

Juvenile Probation Officer

Eighty-five percent of the juvenile probation professionals in the United States are involved in the delivery of basic intake, investigation, and supervision services at the line officer level; the remaining 15 percent are involved in the administration of probation offices or the management of probation staff. Caseloads within departments range between 2 and more than 200 cases, with a typical (median) active caseload of 41. The optimal caseload suggested by respondents to a national survey was 30 cases.

Most entry-level probation department positions require a college degree. In addition, many agencies require some experience in a criminal or juvenile justice position. Usually this experience will be in juvenile detention or juvenile corrections.

Critical Thinking

What do you think is the main drawback of being a probation officer? Explain.

SHOCK PROBATION

Shock probation is a relatively unique correctional strategy that involves shocking juvenile delinquents with a brief commitment to an institutional facility and then releasing them on probation. In some instances, juveniles are not informed that they will be released from the institution after a short stay. This is to increase the shock value of both the incarceration and the release onto probation. In other instances, the juveniles are informed that they will be spending a certain amount of time in the institution in hopes they will become aware of what they are facing and then they will be released. The incarceration can be at a detention facility, group home, temporary placement, boot camp, or secure long-term institution. In some jurisdictions, this is a formal program option judges can use as a regular disposition. In others, it can be an informal arrangement between a judge or probation department and selected institutions.

Most often, the shock incarceration occurs at the beginning of a juvenile's disposition following adjudication. However, the technique is also used when juveniles are not following their dispositional plan or rules of probation. Typically, a probation revocation hearing is held where the judge, juvenile, probation department, and parents or guardians are present. The probation conditions are typically modified at these hearings or probation can be revoked altogether. In some instances, the judge will put the juvenile in detention for a weekend or send him or her to a secure placement for a brief period in order to convince the juvenile that if the rules are not followed, incarceration is next. The ultimate hope is that the brief experience in secure custody will have a shock effect on the juvenile such that they change their behavior and conform with the dispositional plan.

SCHOOL-BASED PROBATION

An interesting form of probation blends the supervisory capacity of juvenile probation and the school system. **School-based probation** is a model where the probation officer works and is housed within the walls of the school. Since

shock probation A relatively unique correctional strategy that involves shocking juveniles with a brief commitment to an institutional facility and then releasing them on probation.

school-based probation A model where the probation officer works and is housed within the walls of the school.

ISP officers spend a great deal of time monitoring a smaller caseload of juveniles in the community. *Which types of juveniles do you think should be on intensive supervision probation?*

most juveniles on probation are enrolled in school and must attend school as a probation condition, this model allows probation officers more frequent and immediate contact with their clients. In addition to increased supervision and contact time, school-based probation adopts a different case management style compared to regular probation. Because the program is housed within the school, the probation officer can adopt a dual role of both supervisor and educator. He or she is also in a very good position to monitor the juvenile's progress in school and other extracurricular activities.

School-based probation is administered in one of two ways. In some jurisdictions, the school-based probation officer is responsible for all aspects of a juvenile's case, including intake and court appearances. In others, the school-based probation officer is responsible only for supervision and related paperwork with other probation personnel handling the remaining administrative duties.[23] Research on the Pennsylvania system revealed that school-based probation officers had an average caseload of 27 juveniles and spent approximately 70 percent of their time on school property. The research also found that the school-based probationers were similar to regular juvenile probationers in terms of demographics. However, the school-based group had significantly more time in the community without additional charges being filed or additional placements being utilized. When they did get new charges, it was likely to be a status offense or probation violation rather than a new serious crime. Finally, the study found that school-based probation saved more than $6,600 per client more than other placements.[24]

HOUSE ARREST AND ELECTRONIC MONITORING

When a juvenile commits a serious offense or is thought to be a security or flight risk, a judge can order that a juvenile stay at home under **house arrest**. This order can be given while the juvenile is awaiting adjudication or as part of the juvenile's probation plan. The idea is simple: The juvenile is not permitted to leave the home for any reason other than school, work, court, or treatment programming. The juvenile is monitored by home visits by the probation officer and random phone calls from the probation department. The juvenile is placed on a schedule by the probation department and must be where he or she says he or she is supposed to be at any given time. In addition, a juvenile who is placed on house arrest must be monitored by a parent or guardian at all times. Parents and guardians will typically sign an agreement not only to supervise the juvenile but also to report any deviation from the treatment plan or unauthorized absence from the home. If they fail to report the juvenile missing or fail to supervise him or her, they can be subject to a contempt of court citation and incarcerated. House arrest is frequently for a given amount of time at the beginning of the juvenile's probation or in response to a juvenile's failing to follow the rules of probation.

When a juvenile is judged to be an increased security risk by a probation department or juvenile court judge, another option is for the juvenile to be placed on **electronic monitoring**. The process of electronic monitoring operates in juvenile justice in much the same way as in the adult criminal justice system. The juvenile is fitted with an electronic monitoring device, usually attached to his or her ankle. The device typically works in conjunction with a monitoring system that is located in the juvenile's home and connected to a phone line. Although the specific systems vary, the operating principle is basically the same—once a juvenile who is wearing an electronic

house arrest Confining juveniles to their homes when they are not at school or undergoing treatment.

electronic monitoring Restricting a juvenile through the use of an electronic tracking device.

There are many ways to increase the amount of supervision for juvenile delinquents. *Under what circumstances should high-risk juveniles be allowed to remain in the community?*

monitoring device gets outside the device's range, an alarm sounds and the probation department is called electronically. Recent technological advances in global positioning systems (GPS) have eliminated the home monitoring device, and the juveniles are monitored via satellite.

The rationale of this system is to assure the probation department that the juvenile is where he or she is supposed to be without 24-hour-a-day monitoring with a probation officer. The juvenile and his or her family are often given a choice between electronic monitoring or secure detention. The juvenile and/or his or her family are often required to pay for the costs of the system and the monitoring. Electronic monitoring is not a right; it is a privilege and an option in lieu of detention. As such, the juvenile court can recoup the costs for the program. In some jurisdictions, the juvenile does not have to pay for the costs, especially if they cannot afford it. The costs of electronic monitoring are substantially lower than the costs of incarceration.

Alternative Sanctions in Juvenile Community Corrections

As the term implies, **alternative sanctions** are those that provide a means to hold juveniles accountable outside traditional mechanisms such as probation or incarceration. Interestingly, most often these sanctions are not used as an alternative but in addition to probation and incarceration. As such, some critics point out that they are anything but alternative and are simply a means to place additional sanctions on juveniles. However, when used appropriately and judiciously, alternative sanctions have the promise of restoring the wrongs done by juveniles who commit delinquent acts. These sanctions are receiving additional attention under the Balanced and Restorative Justice (BARJ) philosophy (described in Chapter 15). BARJ focuses on three interrelated components: community safety, competency development, and accountability. The latter component implies accountability to the individual victims of crime, not society in general. As such, this model and other accountability-based laws focus on such sanctions as victim/offender mediation, restitution, and community service.

MEDIATION

The role of victims in the criminal justice process has increased substantially in recent years. The effect has been in both the criminal justice system and the juvenile justice system. **Victim impact statements** are now fairly commonplace in most juvenile justice proceedings and allow the victim a voice in a formerly closed proceeding. In addition to these types of statements being allowed in juvenile court, several **mediation** programs for juveniles have started around the country. These programs attempt to bring together juvenile delinquents and their victims to mediate the situation between the parties. In some instances, this is used as a diversionary tactic to keep a juvenile offender out of juvenile

alternative sanctions A range of correctional sanctions that are designed to take the place of traditional ones such as probation or incarceration.

victim impact statements Questionnaires distributed to victims of crime where they report their financial losses, mental and physical injuries, and impact of the crime on their lives.

mediation These programs attempt to bring together juvenile delinquents and their victims, hoping to mediate the situation between the parties.

court. Other times, this is done in addition to probation proceedings or as part of a juvenile's disposition plan.

In some jurisdictions, the mediation takes place under the guise of the juvenile court or through the juvenile probation department. In other jurisdictions, the mediation is done through a public or private mediator or mediation program that receives direct referrals from the juvenile court. Most often the cases referred involve property crimes, minor assaults, or other minor offenses. Both parties (juvenile and victim) must agree to participate in the mediation, and the mediation session is typically run by a professional mediator or court representative trained in victim-offender mediation. The mediation typically involves two phases or two separate meetings. In the first part, the victim expresses his or her feelings directly to the juvenile about the crime and the juvenile can attempt to explain his or her actions and motives for the offense. In the second part, the actual losses the victim incurred are discussed and documented and a plan is developed for compensation by the juvenile directly to the victim.[25] These programs are becoming very popular, and most juvenile courts in larger jurisdictions now either operate a mediation program or can refer cases out to mediation.

RESTITUTION

Another popular alternative sanction in juvenile justice is the use of **restitution**. Restitution is the payment of money or the rendering of restorative service or work to the individual victim of a crime, either a person or a business. The victim will report the total amount of loss to the court and the juvenile offender is then sentenced by the court to repay the victim for the losses. Most often the payment is in cash; however, it is also fairly common for the juvenile to work off restitution for the person or business directly. For example, in a vandalism case where a juvenile caused property damage the juvenile would be sentenced to repair the damage he or she caused under the supervision of the victim or the victim's representative. Juvenile court judges around the country can be very creative in their restitution orders. There are documented instances where juveniles have been sentenced to repaint houses, landscape properties, brand cattle, and even wash cars and dogs for their victims. Some judges find a dual purpose of restitution can be both a restoration for the victim and an embarrassment for the juvenile.

Several problems exist with juvenile restitution. For example, chronic juvenile offenders can accumulate quite a hefty sum of owed restitution. In many instances, the victims will receive restitution in an amount sufficient to cover their insurance deductible with the remainder of the restitution being owed to an insurance company. In one case, a juvenile supervised in a community correctional facility by one of the authors of this textbook had accumulated over $70,000 in restitution owed to victims—approximately $2,000 was owed to individual victims and the rest was to insurance companies. This particular juvenile had totaled three sport-utility vehicles that he had stolen and had been sentenced to full restitution for the vehicles. The juvenile worked a minimum-wage job while in custody and 50 percent of his money was automatically deducted for restitution. The message got through to the juvenile; however, it is unlikely that all of the restitution sentenced was ever paid off.

In many cases, juveniles cannot afford the restitution they are sentenced to pay. Several jurisdictions have started programs where juveniles can work in community improvement projects or for private companies for money to pay restitution. In addition, many states now operate victim compensation funds, which aid victims in recouping their losses. An example of a comprehensive juvenile restitution program in Ohio is detailed in the Focus on Programs. Restitution is a popular sanction and will undoubtedly continue to be part of

Property Offense Cases

Between 1985 and 2009, the number of cases adjudicated delinquent that resulted in an order of probation increased 51 percent, compared with a 27 percent increase in the number of cases that resulted in out-of-home placement.

SOURCE: Puzzanchera, Charles, Benjamin Adams, and Sarah Hockenberry. *Juvenile Court Statistics 2009*. Pittsburgh, PA: National Center for Juvenile Justice, 2012.

restitution The payment of money or the rendering of restorative service or work to the victim of a crime, whether a person or a business.

FOCUS ON PROGRAMS

ROSS COUNTY, OHIO, RESCUE RESTITUTION PROGRAM FOR JUVENILES

The RESCUE Program is one of two components of Ross County, Ohio, Juvenile Court's restitution program. The court may adjudicate a juvenile to make restitution for whatever material loss he or she may have caused. If the youth is unable to pay the restitution to the victim, the RESCUE Program has a system in place for the youth to earn the money through work to pay the court-ordered restitution. Generally, this adjudication is a term of probation, so RESCUE is operated by an officer from the Ross County Juvenile Court Probation Department. Through coordinated efforts within the county, nonprofit organizations will accept adjudicated youth to work at unskilled tasks at the equivalent of minimum wage to pay the restitution. These organizations include fire stations, cemeteries, apartment complexes, parks, and occasionally schools. The original objective of the RESCUE Program was to adjudicate juvenile offenders to pay restitution. That goal evolved into providing juvenile offenders the opportunity to work for money to pay restitution, rather than ask parents to pay the restitution or leave youths with no means of working to earn money to pay restitution. Not only do juvenile offenders learn work ethics, but worthwhile services are performed for community organizations. Work is limited to nonprofit organizations.

Property offenders make up the majority of the youth involved, but no youth is excluded if qualified for probation/diversion, and if the Court feels there can be a benefit from an adjudication to pay restitution. About 80 percent of youth ordered to pay restitution are in the RESCUE Program. As a condition of probation, juvenile offenders are given a deadline to complete the necessary number of work hours. The community organizations that provide work for juvenile offenders keep a time sheet they pass on to the RESCUE Program Officer, as well as make periodic verbal reports on the juvenile offenders' progress and compliance. Youth who fail to comply are given an official warning; then, if they still do not comply, they are brought back before the court for further adjudication. Generally, juvenile offenders serve 30-, 60-, or 90-day terms in the RESCUE Program, depending on the amount of restitution and the work scheduling.

CRITICAL THINKING

What do you think the possible drawbacks of a restitution program might be?

Source: www.co.ross.oh.us/

many dispositional plans for juvenile delinquents. A study evaluated a group of juveniles who had gone through a restitution program, both voluntarily and involuntarily. The offenders who agreed to restitution had a recidivism rate of 11 percent, compared with 18 percent for juveniles who received other dispositions. In formal probation cases, 32 percent of the probationers ordered to pay restitution recidivated, compared with 38 percent of those not paying restitution.[26]

COMMUNITY SERVICE

While restitution is used to compensate individual victims, **community service** sentences are used to compensate society. Community service means that as part of his or her disposition a youth is required to work a set number of hours doing community improvement work. This work can take many forms ranging from picking up trash along highways to working shifts as a volunteer in community programs. Governmental agencies can apply to the juvenile court for community service work. Juveniles under court sanction are then provided to the agency free of charge for the number of hours they are sentenced to by the court. In many jurisdictions, there are formal community service agencies that coordinate the work efforts for the juvenile court. In such cases, the juvenile will show up at the community service agency and then be assigned to a work detail. The work typically involves general city clean-up, cleaning public housing projects, cleaning parks, or new construction and city improvement work.

community service As part of their disposition, youths are required to work a set number of hours doing community improvement work.

Many juvenile judges use alternative sanctions in addition to probation sentences. *Which alternative sanction do you think is most effective at preventing future delinquency?*

In many cases, juvenile judges attempt to fit the community service work to the offense the juvenile committed. For example, juveniles who spray paint graffiti are typically sentenced to graffiti clean-up crews where they will spend long hours sandblasting graffiti from walls, scrubbing graffiti from road signs, and repainting houses and other structures. In certain cases of vandalism of city property or city buildings, juveniles are sometimes assigned to work crews repairing the damage or renovating existing city property. One juvenile judge stated that she attempts to assign community service that best represents restoring whatever a juvenile has destroyed in a manner consistent with the juvenile's attitude and offense. When a juvenile displays an attitude in her court, she has been known to assign them to police stables to clean up after the mounted patrol. When one juvenile graffiti artist stated that he didn't want to perform community service because he really didn't do that much harm, she sentenced him to 40 hours of scrubbing floors in city buildings.[27] The goal is to teach the juvenile a lesson and in the process gain some restoration for society in the form of public service.

11.6 SELF-CHECK

1. Describe the process of victim-offender mediation.
2. What role does restitution play in juvenile justice? What are some problems with restitution?
3. What is community service and how is it used in juvenile corrections?

Community Correctional Alternatives to Incarceration

In addition to probation and the wide variety of alternative sanctions, a multitude of programs for juveniles exist as alternatives to incarceration. Juveniles can be directly sentenced to these programs or referred as an alternative to juvenile court by another juvenile agency. Oftentimes, a sentence to a community correctional program or facility is part of the probation plan. There are many programs designed for delinquency prevention (discussed in Chapter 6) and intervention. One of the most well-known examples of a facility designed for wayward children is Boys Town, which was profiled in the classic movie starring Spencer Tracy and Mickey Rooney. Located in Nebraska, Boys Town accepts all kinds of wayward children, including direct sentences from juvenile courts around the country. Since the creation of Boys Town in the early part of the 20th century, a host of programs and facilities have been established and designed to be a last chance for delinquent children before they are sentenced to a secure institution.

COUNSELING AND SPECIALIZED TREATMENT PROGRAMS

A variety of programs are based locally and serve the juvenile courts in their jurisdictions as well as social service agencies, children's agencies, and the general public. Many of these programs are operated by private individuals and corporations. Some of the better-known examples advertise on television and actively seek out referrals for treatment. The common theme in these programs is a short-term, focused treatment that attempts to intervene with the juvenile before he or she becomes further involved in the system. In some instances, referral to these programs is an alternative to secure incarceration and if the juvenile fails the program, he or she will be sent to a secure placement. One such program that has received national attention is VisionQuest (see Focus on Programs). This program has a unique treatment philosophy that embraces Native American ideals and rituals. It is typical for programs of this type to have some sort of slant that distinguishes it from other similar programs.

Counseling and specialized treatment programs can be located in rural or urban areas. In rural locations, they tend to adopt a work ethic style. Youths learn to farm, raise livestock, face challenges, and work hard in the course of the program. In urban settings, the youths tend to work more outside the facility. What is common is that the duration of these types of programs typically ranges from one to three months. In some programs, the juvenile is broken down and then built back up. In others, the juvenile progresses through a series of levels or steps sometimes culminating in a level where the juvenile helps other juveniles just starting the program. Besides individual treatment goals, there is usually a common goal the whole group is striving for. The counseling and therapy can be very intense in some of the programs, and group sessions with other juveniles are common.

DAY TREATMENT PROGRAMS

Day treatment programs are a type of community correctional facility where the juveniles report during the day for school, vocational, and other treatment programs. The environment of such programs is highly structured and focused on keeping stricter supervision on a juvenile than just through probation alone. Youths in day treatment facilities can live at home, be in foster care, or even be housed in another group home. Day treatment is used as both a front- and back-end correctional sanction. In some cases, the youth has been released from a secure facility or other treatment facility and is being moved back into the community. In other cases, day treatment is used as a direct sentence by the juvenile court when additional structure and supervision are needed. If a youth is sentenced to day treatment, he or she is most likely supervised under an ISP program. Utah's day reporting center system is an example of a state-wide system. These facilities allow the state to maintain supervision of youths while they remain at home and attend school or work. To participate, a juvenile

day treatment programs A type of community correctional facility where juvenile offenders report during the day for school, vocational, and other treatment programs.

FOCUS ON PROGRAMS

VISIONQUEST

For over 40 years, VisionQuest has been providing innovative and effective intervention services to at-risk youth and families. VisionQuest's purpose is to provide nonlocked settings for jurisdictions looking for cost-effective, high-quality alternatives to incarceration and to provide prevention programs that work to keep youngsters out of the criminal justice system altogether. The name VisionQuest was borrowed from the Plains Indians and reflects the philosophy of the program. During a vision quest, Native American adolescents were sent into the wilderness to overcome challenges and discover a view of their futures. VisionQuest programs seek to give adjudicated youth this same opportunity to succeed in challenges, see a new future for themselves, and give them skills to accomplish their goals and reach their highest potential. Youth are referred to VisionQuest by county or state government staff in corrections, probation, mental health, and child welfare.

VisionQuest's treatment philosophy, Guided Centering, is aimed at helping troubled adolescents attain greater stability and balance in their perceptions, emotions, and behaviors. In the Guided Centering approach, adolescents are encouraged to explore fundamental problems in their lives related to abuse, abandonment, and boundary issues. They also learn the skills and attitudes necessary to achieve success academically, vocationally, and as a community member. As a result, youth learn to deal with challenging situations and feelings without responding automatically with violence, anger, and frustration. Program elements include:

- **New environments and experiences** to give youth an opportunity to break free from habitual expectations and behaviors.
- **Supportive staff** who encourage, nurture, and, when necessary, intervene to keep the environment safe, hold youth accountable to their commitments, and allow them to examine the motivations and beliefs underlying their actions.
- **Physical challenges** such as ropes courses, hiking, biking, and rock climbing.
- **Treatment** is provided as needed, based on individual assessment and planning.
- **Modalities** include individual and group counseling, therapy, and therapeutic experiences in working with animals.
- **Customs and ceremonies** borrowed from Native American culture are used to reinforce connections to community, acknowledge each youth's progress, and allow for healing and sharing of experiences.
- **Education** is provided through an on-site, fully accredited school and is designed to assist youth in mastering basic skills, and working towards graduation.
- **Community service** to teach the value of contributing, to learn skills, and to gain self-confidence.
- **Cultural competency** helping youth to understand their own culture and those of others through history and cultural diversity groups.
- **Family reunification** by involving the family and working to establish a successful interaction after the program.
- **Vocational assessment** and planning to ensure that youth are able to obtain employment, plan a career, and be successful in work.

CRITICAL THINKING

What do you think the possible pluses and minuses of this program might be?

Source: www.vq.com

---

delinquent must be ordered into the program by a juvenile court judge. The youth and parent or legal guardian must be willing to accept the strict rules of the program. The key benefit of the system is providing a stricter form of supervision with cost savings versus secure placement. In addition, youths have a greater opportunity for skill development in day/night reporting centers than if they were in a secure setting.[28]

The NCCD recommends day reporting centers as part of the ISP model program. The activities that are conducted during the day at these centers include educational programs. Educational programs typically focus on remedial education and vocational training. In addition, time is typically spent on activities such as community service, job skill preparation, group counseling, and life/survival skills counseling. Common strategies include efforts to link juveniles with appropriate role models and community organizations, intensive staff interactions with parents to shore up parenting authority and skills, and recreational programming.[29]

FOSTER CARE

Foster care is the term used to describe the care and custody of children by families willing to take them into their homes. Some foster families care for several children and some care for a few. Typical foster care is short term, and the children hope to return to their parents in many instances. In other circumstances, foster care is used for wards of the state raised until adulthood by the foster family. Foster care is also sometimes used for juvenile delinquents. In cases where the parents of a juvenile delinquent are either incarcerated or incapable of caring for the juvenile, the juvenile will be placed in foster care. Some foster families specialize in dealing with pre-delinquent and delinquent youths. The placement into foster care can occur while the child is awaiting adjudication from a juvenile court or while the child is on probation. Many juvenile delinquents come from broken homes, and oftentimes the juvenile's family situation is partly responsible for the juvenile's problems.

GROUP HOMES

Group homes could easily be classified as a community-based correction or an institutional one. However, since the majority of these facilities are nonsecure and operated in the community, it is perhaps more prudent to think of them as a community correctional option. Group homes, as the name implies, house groups of juveniles who have been adjudicated delinquent. Group homes also care for juveniles sentenced directly from the juvenile courts, transitioning juveniles coming out of secure placements prior to parole, and juveniles who have been referred for placement by other agencies of juvenile justice. Some group homes house only one of these groups, some house all three. For example, the North Carolina Department of Juvenile Justice and Delinquency Prevention contracts with private vendors to operate several homes designed to provide secure noninstitutional alternatives to training schools and secure detention. These eight-bed residential homes have residential counselors, a certified teacher, and a full-time family counselor. They provide up to 30 days of care for juveniles in need of secure detention prior to adjudication and up to 240 days of care as a treatment disposition. The facilities are designed to relieve the demands on the regional secure detention facilities; to reduce the time and expense of transporting juveniles to and from those facilities; and to lower the training school commitment rate in the target judicial districts by providing the courts with a realistic option involving families.[30] Some group homes house as few as three or four juveniles, some house as many as 50. Regardless of the size, the job of the group home is similar to that of a typical parental household.

Juveniles in a group home are expected to follow a structured lifestyle—school, work, and household chores. In addition, there is often counseling in the form of group therapy and individual therapy designed to rehabilitate the juvenile. The school may be on the premises or the juveniles in the home may attend the local school in the area. Work is typically done off-site, and the juvenile usually works all day and comes to the group home at night. The correctional treatment is similar to what might be expected in a more secure facility. The juveniles in the group can usually progress through some type of level system which eventually lets them have weekend passes out of the facility.

foster care The care and custody of children by families willing to take them into their homes.

group homes Homes for groups of juveniles who have been adjudicated delinquent similar to their institutional counterparts.

JOB TRAINING FOR JUVENILES —PROJECT CRAFT

A successful vocational training program for high-risk youths and juvenile offenders sponsored by the Home Builders Institute (HBI), the educational arm of the National Association of Home Builders (NAHB), is addressing youth crime and unemployment and helping reduce recidivism. Youths receive pre-apprenticeship training in residential construction trades, such as carpentry or building and apartment maintenance, job placement, and follow-up services. Key elements of the CRAFT model include: (1) partnership building and linkages; (2) comprehensive service delivery; (3) community training projects; (4) industry-driven responsive training; (5) motivation, esteem building, and leadership; (6) job placement, often with home builder association members; and (7) follow-up services. CRAFT operates as an alternative to incarceration, intervention, or aftercare programs.

Participants, age 17 or older, complete 21 weeks of training which include extensive hands-on, real work opportunities using community service projects. Through HBI's Pre-Apprenticeship Certificate Training (PACT), students learn the basics of carpentry, building, and apartment maintenance or any one of the trades. Throughout the training, the promotion of goal-oriented thinking helps the participants develop a sense of accomplishment. With certificate in hand and tools, graduates are placed in related employment and/or apprenticeships. An HBI project coordinator assists the graduate with community transition and other supportive services for six months.

The program works in partnership with juvenile corrections facilities, juvenile judges, juvenile justice system personnel, education agencies, community-based organizations, and other human service agencies. In some instances, juvenile judges and probation officers refer youth directly to Project CRAFT; in other cases, Project CRAFT staff provide vocational training while personnel from other partner agencies provide case management, substance abuse treatment, or other services that are part of care in a residential facility. Integration of these services and access to community aftercare services have been instrumental in ensuring that youth make a successful transition back into their communities. The program also has developed partnerships and relationships with community-based organizations, community development organizations, housing authorities, developers, housing agencies, Habitat for Humanity, local governments, historical societies, and other organizations.

An evaluation of the project showed:

- Project CRAFT has a high rate of job placement for its graduates. By the end of the national program, 94 of the 140 graduates in the three original demonstration sites had been placed in jobs in the home building industry.
- The cumulative recidivism rate for students participating in Project CRAFT at the three national demonstration sites was 26 percent, which is significantly lower than the national rate. The recidivism rate at the Nashville, TN, site was 15 percent the first year and 5.9 percent the second year.
- Project CRAFT also has been successful in providing long-term follow-up for juvenile offenders after release and community placement. This helps ensure the adjustment and stability of these offenders after they return to their communities.

CRITICAL THINKING

What type of juvenile offender would you send to this program, as opposed to asking for restitution?

Sources: Hamilton, Robin and Kay McKinney. "Job Training for Juveniles: Project CRAFT." *Juvenile Justice Update* August 1999 #116. Washington, DC: Office of Juvenile Justice and Delinquency Prevention, 1999. HBI's Web site at www.hbi.org

Although the juvenile is not committed to a secure institution, this sanction is much more restrictive than the other sanctions discussed in this chapter.

WILDERNESS AND ADVENTURE PROGRAMS

Wilderness and adventure programs became very popular for juveniles in the late 1970s and early 1980s.[31] These types of programs emphasize physical challenges, survival skills, and mental challenges through outdoor adventures and nature trips. One of the most popular of these programs that serves delinquents as well as nondelinquents is Outward Bound. A variety of these types of programs are still flourishing today and serve a variety of youth who are at risk for

wilderness and adventure programs Programs that emphasize physical challenges, survival skills, and mental challenges through outdoor adventures and nature trips.

There are a variety of vocational training programs for youths. *How important do you think learning a trade is in fighting juvenile delinquency?*

11.7 SELF-CHECK

1. What is meant by the term "alternatives to incarceration"?
2. Describe the various types of alternatives to incarceration.

delinquency or already are delinquent. Most programs are akin to summer camp for juvenile delinquents. In some programs, the juveniles are challenged to use the skills they learn in a final survival-type test. In others, the focus is on learning how to live in the wilderness while also developing life skills. Some programs are lengthy, while others may be for a weekend, or a week or two.

Wilderness programs are yet another correctional alternative that seeks to accomplish exactly what the other programs described thus far do—intervene in the lives of delinquent youth and prevent further delinquency. In some instances, the excursions are used for community service. Several programs have the youths clean up parks and resorts or help construct facilities, trails, and other useful projects within the wilderness. Some programs focus on teaching skills in ranching or farming. These programs are still very popular, but evaluations of their effect are rare. The studies that have been conducted have produced mixed results.[32]

VOCATIONAL AND APPRENTICESHIP PROGRAMS

A common practice in juvenile correctional programming is to refer juveniles to **job training programs and apprenticeship programs**. These programs are specifically designed to teach the juvenile a skill that is marketable in the real world. The assumption is that if a juvenile can learn a skill or apprentice a trade and subsequently get a good-paying, secure job, he or she is much less likely to engage in delinquent behavior. Many secure juvenile institutions operate a variety of vocational training programs; these programs are very similar to programs that exist in the community. Common trades and skills taught are various construction professions, automotive service repair, machinery operation and maintenance, and a growing number are teaching computer-related skills. Focus on Programs profiles a nationally known job training program called Project CRAFT (Community, Restitution, and Apprenticeship-Focused Training) that operates as an alternative to incarceration.

job training programs and apprenticeship programs Programs specifically designed to teach the juvenile a skill that is marketable in the real world.

determinate Term used when the juvenile delinquent is subject to aftercare supervision for a fixed period of time.

indeterminate Term used when a juvenile delinquent is placed on aftercare with either a maximum time allowed or based on treatment goals and objectives.

Aftercare for Juveniles, Juvenile Parole, and Parolee Services

There are several ways in which juvenile aftercare is managed, both indeterminately and determinately. Under a **determinate** structure, the juvenile is subject to aftercare supervision for a fixed period of time. The amount of time is determined by the state aftercare agency or by the amount of time remaining on the juvenile's sentence. Under an **indeterminate** structure, a juvenile is placed on aftercare with either a maximum time allowed or based on treatment goals and objectives. In other words, juveniles are under supervision until such time that they have completed a treatment plan in the eyes of the aftercare authority. There is substantial variation across the United States in aftercare laws, policies, procedures, and administration.[33]

Prior to a juvenile's being released from a secure program or other residential facility, an assessment is typically done to assess the juvenile on a variety of factors thought to be related to recidivism. Several jurisdictions have developed scales to evaluate educational achievement, job skills, emotional stability, maturity, independent living skills, social skills, and behavior.[34] The needs of a juvenile being released into the community in large part determine what type of supervision he or she will be subject to upon release. One of the principal concerns of professionals in the juvenile correctional field is the need for a solid system of aftercare. A perennial problem in juvenile corrections is that the juvenile can behave very well in the correctional facility and may have matured substantially prior to release. However, upon release, the juvenile is sent right back to the conditions that created the delinquency problem in the first place. Hence, there is a demonstrated need for an adequate system of follow-up and aftercare.

Some states have juvenile parole authorities that oversee the aftercare of juveniles released from secure custody. The Division of Juvenile Justice of the California Department of Corrections and Rehabilitation is responsible for parolee services for the state and offers a variety of programs to serve their clients. The juvenile parole system in California operates as a "step-down" process. As the parolee advances through his or her parole program, the need for supervision and services tends to lessen. Once on parole, the Division of Juvenile Justice assigns the juvenile to one of the four case management system components:

- **Electronically Enhanced Parole Release Program**—an institutional conditional release program designed to ease institution population while at the same time enhancing parole supervision. It reduces institutional length of stay by 60 days for selected wards who are released to a highly structured supervision program, augmented with electronic monitors, providing 24-hour surveillance.
- **Intensive Re-Entry Supervision with Related Services**—designed to increase public protection by early detection and prevention of parole violations and to provide maximum services during the most critical period of transition from institutional to community living.
- **Specialized Caseloads**—provides concentrated, intensive services for parolees with special needs, severe substance abusers, sex offenders, those with mental problems, those needing specialized placement, and/or parolees heavily involved in gang activity.
- **Case Management Caseloads**—Parolees are transferred to case management after intensive re-entry or upon transitioning from a specialized caseload to assist the parolee in maintaining acceptable levels of behavior and job and placement stability.[35]

In addition to these standard supervision practices, parolee services operates several specialized parole programs focusing on survival skills, vocational training and job placement, substance abuse counseling, and several other case-specific programs.[36]

In some states such as California, the system attempts to maintain a step-down process where juveniles released from secure custody are slowly reintegrated into the community through a series of placements with lessened security. Other states simply release juveniles to a halfway house for transition into the community for a short period of time. It is preferable to have at least some type of transition back into the community because of the need to **deinstitutionalize** the juvenile and to assess the juvenile's risk to the community in a less secure setting. However, in most states juveniles must be released when they reach a certain age, typically 19 or 21.

11.8 SELF-CHECK

1. What is the difference between determinate and indeterminate structures in aftercare?

2. What are some of the services and placements a juvenile can benefit from while on parole?

deinstitutionalize The process of teaching the juvenile how to remain in the community.

Qualities of Effective Juvenile Correctional Programs

The juvenile justice system has often been criticized for failing to fulfill its intended mission of rehabilitating juveniles. Making sweeping conclusions about effectiveness is difficult because of the decentralized nature of the juvenile correctional system. Nonetheless, there have been some good evaluations of programs, and the Office of Juvenile Justice and Delinquency Prevention published research outlining the characteristics of good juvenile correctional programs.[37]

The report noted that in order to implement effective intervention programs for delinquents it is first necessary to better understand the causes and risk factors associated with becoming a delinquent. However, it is also recognized that there is no single cause of delinquency or method currently in place that would cure all delinquency. Research has found that effective juvenile programs have several things in common.

1. They concentrate on changing behavior and improving social skills.
2. They focus on teaching problem-solving skills in their correctional programs.
3. The programs do not have one particular method of programming; the treatment plans are tailored to the individual.
4. The programs are highly structured and intensive.[38]

In addition, research shows that early detection and intervention works far better than post-serious delinquency correctional rehabilitation. The research reviewed several empirical studies and outlined the following conclusions about successful correctional intervention programs; the programs should:

- Concentrate on changing negative behaviors by requiring juveniles to recognize and understand thought processes that rationalize negative behaviors.
- Promote healthy bonds with, and respect for, law-abiding members within the juvenile's family, peer, school, and community network.
- Have a comprehensible and predictable path for client progression and movement. Each program level should be directed toward and directly related to the next step.
- Have consistent, clear, and graduated consequences for misbehavior and recognition for positive behavior.
- Recognize that a reasonable degree of attrition must be expected with a delinquent population.
- Provide an assortment of highly structured programming activities, including education and/or hands-on vocational training and skill development.
- Facilitate discussions that promote family problem solving.
- Integrate delinquent and at-risk youth into generally prosocial groups to prevent the development of delinquent peer groups (bringing together only at-risk or delinquent youth to engage in school or community activities is likely to be counterproductive).
- Involve the community to the greatest degree possible.[39]

It is important to remember that there is no one program or programs that have been completely successful in their mission. However, multiple evaluations have consistently shown that well-designed community-based programs for juveniles do not compromise public safety and that appropriate aftercare is effective at reducing recidivism.[40]

11.9 SELF-CHECK

1. What are the characteristics of successful juvenile correctional programs?

1. Describe the differences between juvenile community corrections and institutional corrections

Community corrections is a broad term used to capture a variety of correctional alternatives that all have one common characteristic: they are less restrictive than institutional corrections and are literally operated in the community. Community corrections programs place importance on youths' remaining in their communities as well as developing consistent relationships with positive adult role models. These programs provide treatment interventions that reflect the expectations of the community and society and attempt to prevent the youth from becoming further involved with the court system. Institutional corrections are secure facilities that do not allow the juvenile freedom of movement within the community. All aspects of the juvenile's life are controlled within the walls of the facility.

2. Identify the different correctional sanctions available to the juvenile court

The different correctional sanctions available to the juvenile court are: juvenile detention (juveniles awaiting trial or placement); counseling and specialized treatment programs; alternative sanctions: restitution and community service; vocational and apprenticeship programs; short-term shelter and placement facilities, foster care; juvenile probation; shock probation; intensive supervision probation; home confinement and house arrest; day treatment and monitoring facilities; wilderness camps, adventure camps, Outward Bound; boot camps; youth ranches and farms; group homes, community facilities, halfway houses; reform, training, and secure schools; and juvenile parole and aftercare.

3. Explain the juvenile probation process

The process of involvement by the probation department begins with screening where a determination is made about how the case should be processed and whether detention should be maintained. The probation department also prepares investigation reports on most cases and provides some supervision of youths awaiting adjudication. During the adjudication phase, the probation department is frequently asked to testify or be present at hearings. Once a juvenile is adjudicated delinquent, the probation department's role in the life of the juvenile increases substantially. The probation department is typically responsible for monitoring youths on probation, maintaining all juvenile records, and coordinating the disposition plan with the youth, his or her parents/guardian, and other agencies of juvenile justice. The probation department often conducts review hearings to monitor the progress of youths on probation and may terminate the probation successfully if all the conditions are met. Even after the probation is terminated, some probation departments maintain responsibility for aftercare service for the juvenile.

4. Identify typical juvenile probation conditions

The typical juvenile probation conditions include: attend school regularly; attend work regularly; do not use alcohol or drugs; submit to random drug screenings; check in with probation officer regularly; attend special counseling or treatment; do not associate with known criminals; do not commit any crimes; maintain established curfew; do not possess a weapon of any type; pay restitution; perform community service; and obey parents or other guardians.

5. Describe the duties and responsibilities of probation officers

The duties and responsibilities of probation officers include: making intake decisions; preparing presentence investigations for the juvenile court; being a liaison for the juvenile court; preparing dispositional plans; supervising juveniles on probation; making decisions about the progress of juveniles on probation; and planning aftercare for juveniles released from secure placement.

6. Identify and explain the variations in juvenile probation

Several variations exist in juvenile probation that alter the supervision level, treatment options, or location of probation programming. These variations address high-risk juveniles or juveniles in need of specialized treatment.

7. Describe what intensive supervision probation (ISP) is and which juveniles are eligible for ISP

ISP is a form of probation characterized by increased supervision and treatment. The target population for ISP is postadjudication delinquents who would otherwise be in a secure juvenile correctional institution because of the seriousness of their offenses or their risk of continued delinquent activity. Two types of offenders are targeted for ISP: chronic offenders and those who have committed serious but nonviolent offenses, and nonviolent offenders who have committed serious property crimes or drug offenses.

8. Identify and explain alternative sanctions available to the juvenile court

Alternative sanctions are those that provide a means to hold juveniles accountable outside traditional mechanisms such as probation or incarceration. Interestingly, most often these sanctions are not used as an alternative but in addition to probation and incarceration. Typical alternative sanctions include victim/offender mediation, restitution, and community service. Community correctional alternatives include counseling and specialized treatment programs, day treatment programs, foster care, group homes, wilderness and adventure programs, and vocational and apprenticeship programs.

9. Describe what aftercare services are provided for juveniles released from secure incarceration

Aftercare services can include parolee services for juveniles released from secure institutions and follow-up monitoring by juvenile probation departments. The goal is to maintain contact and supervision with juveniles to assure that they do not recidivate.

KEY TERMS

community corrections, p. 296

classification instruments, p. 299

juvenile probation department, p. 300

probation, p. 300

John Augustus, p. 301

deferred adjudication, p. 301

probation agreement, p. 304

probation revocation, p. 305

pre-sentence investigations, p. 306

dispositional plans, p. 306

aftercare, p. 306

intensive supervision probation (ISP), p. 307

shock probation, p. 310

school-based probation, p. 310

house arrest, p. 311

electronic monitoring, p. 311

alternative sanctions, p. 312

victim impact statements, p. 312

mediation, p. 312

restitution, p. 313

community service, p. 314

day treatment programs, p. 316

foster care, p. 318

group homes, p. 318

wilderness and adventure programs, p. 319

job training programs and apprenticeship programs, p. 320

determinate, p. 320

indeterminate, p. 320

deinstitutionalize, p. 321

REVIEW QUESTIONS

1. What sanction is the most common result of juvenile court adjudications?

2. What are the varying correctional sanctions available to juvenile court judges?

3. What is meant by the bifurcated manner in which the juvenile justice system developed?

4. What are the main factors that go into determining what type of sanction a juvenile will receive?

5. Who is the father of modern probation?

6. Why is probation referred to as the "catch basin" of juvenile justice?

7. What is deferred adjudication?

8. What are the factors that influence probation caseload?

9. What are the typical common probation conditions?

10. What is a probation agreement?

11. What is ISP?

12. What are the five common key elements to ISP programs?

13. What is shock probation?

14. What are the characteristics that distinguish school-based probation from regular probation?

15. What two systems are used to strictly monitor the whereabouts of particularly risky juveniles who are awaiting adjudication or are on probation?

16. What is the goal of victim/offender mediation?

17. What are the two parts of most victim/offender mediation programs?

18. What are the two types of victims most restitution is assigned to?

19. What criteria typically guide the nature of community service sanctions?

20. What areas do most specialized counseling programs focus on?

21. In what ways is day treatment a front-end and back-end correctional sanction?

22. What types of juveniles are placed in group homes?

23. What activities are emphasized in wilderness and adventure programs?

24. What is the difference between determinate and indeterminate aftercare models?

1. **Interview a Probation Officer** Contact a juvenile probation officer in your local jurisdiction and set up either a phone or an in–person interview. Ask the probation officer what the most important challenges are in the job. Also ask what is the most frustrating part of the job in supervising and treating juveniles.

2. **Visit a Juvenile Facility or Program** Arrange a visit and/or tour of a wilderness program, adventure program, Outward Bound, or other community youth facility in your area. On the basis of what you see, what differences do you perceive between these types of programs and facilities and more secure facilities for juveniles?

3. **Outline Program Features** On the basis of the characteristics of the most successful programs listed in this chapter, outline an ideal alternative to incarceration for lower-middle-class suburban youths found guilty of defacing property and possession of marijuana. Explain your choice of program features, length, etc.

1. Visit **www.ncjrs.gov/pdffiles1/ojjdp/208804.pdf** and read the article, which covers alternatives to incarceration. On the basis of what you read there and your own personal opinion, what are the main issues involved in utilizing alternatives to incarceration?

2. Visit the NCJRS page on alternatives to incarceration at **www.ncjrs.gov/App/Topics/Topic.** **aspx?topicid=131** and read some of the material on the different programs available to juveniles. How different are these options when compared with the available options for adult offenders? Are there more programs for juveniles than adults? Why do you think this is?

1. **Sentencing a Juvenile Car Thief** Dennis, a 15-year-old juvenile, has been adjudicated delinquent in a case where he stole a car. Dennis has had no prior adjudications in the juvenile court; however, he has been detained by police on two previous occasions for theft and disorderly conduct. In both of the previous detainments by police, Dennis was released to the custody of his parents with no formal charges filed. Dennis currently lives with both his parents at home, attends school fairly regularly, and has average grades. He does not currently have a job and expresses a wish to remain in school to finish his degree. On the basis of the factors discussed in this chapter, what sentence do you think Dennis deserves? What determining factors weighed most in your decision? If you decide to grant probation in this case, what conditions would you impose on Dennis? If you decide to commit Dennis to a placement, what factors weighed most heavily on your decision?

2. **Selecting an Alternative Program for Nonviolent Offenders** Given the range of alternatives discussed in this chapter, which of the community correctional programs do you think would be most appropriate for nonviolent offenders? Which components of these programs do you think would be most beneficial for nonviolent offenders? If the juvenile has a substance abuse problem, which program or programs would you think would be most effective in deterring the juvenile from committing future delinquent acts?

3. **Developing a Dispositional Plan** Assume that you are a judge in the juvenile court. Gina, a 14-year-old juvenile, is accused of aggravated robbery in your court. At the adjudication hearing, Gina admits her guilt in the offense in which she served as a lookout and getaway driver for her boyfriend and another accomplice. At the time of the robbery, Gina was under the influence of narcotics and alcohol. Gina was habitually truant from school, was living at home with her mother who is a single parent with two jobs, and was frequently out past curfew at home. Gina's mother testifies that she has trouble supervising Gina due to her two jobs and Gina's association with the wrong crowd. Gina tested relatively poorly on educational and social assessments conducted by the probation department. She has had no prior adjudications or detainments by police. She is currently pregnant by her boyfriend, who has been committed as a result of this offense. Develop a dispositional plan for Gina using the alternatives discussed in this chapter. What special treatment and conditions will you impose on Gina? Your decision can combine alternatives from this chapter and anything else you deem relevant.

INSTITUTIONAL CORRECTIONS FOR JUVENILES

Chapter Outline

Chapter Objectives

After completing this chapter, you should be able to:

1. List differences between detained juveniles and committed juveniles.

2. Profile the typical juvenile who is sent to an out-of-home placement facility.

3. Explain the differences between public and private facilities.

4. Describe the different types of secure institutional facilities.

5. Explain the nature of juvenile detention facilities and processing procedures.

6. Outline what is meant by a short-term secure facility.

7. Describe what boot camps are designed to do.

8. Explain what youth ranches and camps are.

9. Summarize the nature of state institutions and schools.

10. Outline the various types of programming that occur in juvenile institutions.

Juvenile Placement

If you'd taken a snapshot of juvenile corrections around 2005, you would have seen a much different picture than you do today: census numbers of juveniles in residential placements bordered on nearly 100,000 youth. Considering that secure placements for juveniles—which can include short-term facilities like detention centers or boot camps, or long-term facilities like state institutions or youth ranches—are the most severe and intrusive sanctions doled out in the juvenile justice system, this number was fairly mind-boggling. Juveniles end up in secure facilities through various circumstances, including detention prior to adjudication, **commitment** by a juvenile court, or placement by a **juvenile justice administrative body** or other social service agency. This still holds true, but in 2010, fewer than 71,000 juvenile offenders were in residential treatment facilities on any given day. See Figure 12.1.

We expect trends in residential placement to mirror the trends in juvenile arrests and juvenile court cases. We've already discussed in Chapter 3 how juvenile arrest rates have decreased on the order of about 20 percent since 2005—and how there was about an 11 percent decrease in delinquency cases handled by courts in the same span. But the drop in the number of juveniles in secure correctional institutions is much steeper during the same time frame.

It remains true that there are a greater proportion of youth incarcerated for less serious offenses—such as public order violations, technical violations (such as failing a probationary drug test or not paying fines assessed), drugs, and status offenses.[1] But even those numbers have dropped in the past decade: consider that the number of juveniles incarcerated for drug offenses dipped from 9,645 in 1999 to 4,986 in 2010.[2] This decrease fits easily into what we know about the current political and social climate as it relates to drug use, even among juveniles. In the 2012 elections, both Colorado and Washington State voted to legalize marijuana use. Beyond that, the Obama administration views

commitment An order by a juvenile court judge putting the juvenile in the custody of a state juvenile correctional authority or another specific juvenile correctional facility.

juvenile justice administrative body An organization responsible for the administration and management of juvenile justice placements within a state.

FIGURE 12.1	
COUNT	**2010**
Person Offenses: Criminal homicide	924
Person Offenses: Sexual assault	4,638
Person Offenses: Robbery	6,996
Person Offenses: Aggravated assault	6,097
Person Offenses: Simple assault	5,445
Person Offenses: Other person	1,910
Property Offenses: Burglary	7,247
Property Offenses: Theft	3,759
Property Offenses: Auto theft	2,469
Property Offenses: Arson	533
Property Offenses: Other property	3,029
Drug Offenses: Drug trafficking	1.034
Drug Offenses: Other drug	3,952
Public Order Offenses: Weapons	3,013
Public Order Offenses: Other public order	5,126
Technical violations	11,604
Status offenses	3,016
Total	70,792

Source: Sickmund, M., Sladky, T. J., Kang, W., and Puzzanchera, C. 2011. Easy Access to the Census of Juveniles in Residential Placement. Available: http://www.ojjdp.gov/ojstatbb/ezacjrp/

Secure juvenile facilities are the most severe sanction available in the juvenile correctional system. *What types of offenders do you think should be sent to secure facilities?*

drug abuse as a public health problem as opposed to a criminal justice issue—making a continuum of intervention at various stages in the justice process more likely than incarceration.

Furthermore, the decline in the number of juveniles committed to correctional institutions still speaks to the unwillingness of many to send young people into a system rife with sexual abuse, suicide risks, and high rates of recidivism. Combined with economic realities in state and local governments, there is a growing trend toward individualized services aimed at smaller groups of offenders, and a movement away from the large-scale incarceration of youth and "get tough" stances of a few decades ago.

12.1 SELF-CHECK

Explain the different ways a juvenile can be sent to an out-of-home placement.

The Population in Institutional Corrections

A commitment to an out-of-home placement is a serious sanction, and typically only a small portion of the juveniles arrested are eventually committed to a residential placement. For example, in 2009 there were 1.8 million juveniles taken into custody by police; 1.5 million cases processed by the juvenile courts; and yet, only about 71,000 offenders in a residential placement on any given day.[3] California, Texas, Pennsylvania, New York, and Ohio have the largest numbers of youth in custody, as has been the case for about two decades. These six states combined represent 44 percent of all juveniles in custody in the United States.[4] See Figure 12.2.

Most states have a central juvenile correctional authority that governs the administration and operations of juvenile correctional facilities in the state. If a judge decides to send a juvenile to a secure placement, the judge issues an

Florida Juvenile Commitments

In Florida, during the 2011–2012 fiscal year, juveniles committed to a residential treatment facility served at the following sanction levels:

- 9 percent are in low-risk residential settings, which include family group homes or short-term academy programs.

- About 67 percent are in moderate-risk residential programs, such as halfway houses, vocational programs, boot camps, and residential academies.

- 20 percent are in high-risk residential facilities, which provide 24-hour secure custody and care in intensive halfway houses, sex offender programs, and secure youth development centers.

- Only around 3 or 4 percent of offenders end up in maximum security settings, like long-term juvenile corrections facilities.

SOURCE: 2012 Florida Comprehensive Accountability Annual Legislative Reports. Online. Available at: www.djj.state.fl.us/docs/car-reports/(2012-car)-residential-(final-web)-(1-25-13).pdf?sfvrsn=0. Retrieved April 12, 2013.

JUVENILE JUSTICE ONLINE

Research your state's juvenile law regarding the incarceration of juveniles in institutions. You can find your state's code online at **www.law.cornell.edu/states/listing.html.** What does your state's law say about incarcerating juveniles in secure institutions? Does your state have sentencing recommendations? Does your state have aggravating and mitigating factors listed? If not, what should be the criteria for placing a juvenile in a secure institution?

| FIGURE 12.2 | Placement Status, 2011 |

PLACEMENT STATUS BY STATE, 2011

STATE OF OFFENSE	TOTAL	COMMITTED	DETAINED	DIVERSION
United States	**61,423**	**41,934**	**19,014**	**464**
Alabama	1,026	717	255	54
Alaska	222	123	99	0
Arizona	936	579	354	3
Arkansas	711	507	198	6
California	9,810	5,691	4,065	51
Colorado	1,254	879	375	0
Connecticut	252	144	105	0
Delaware	180	99	81	0
District of Columbia	258	123	135	0
Florida	3,744	2,883	753	108
Georgia	1,788	909	876	3
Hawaii	99	69	27	3
Idaho	399	267	132	3
Illinois	2,106	1,419	684	3
Indiana	1,878	1,365	513	3
Iowa	729	552	150	27
Kansas	813	501	309	0
Kentucky	747	501	240	6
Louisiana	957	606	345	6
Maine	165	138	24	3
Maryland	939	471	465	0
Massachusetts	543	363	180	0
Michigan	2,085	1,470	603	12
Minnesota	828	615	180	30
Mississippi	258	138	120	0
Missouri	1,122	867	252	3
Montana	168	114	48	3
Nebraska	669	486	183	0
Nevada	720	498	219	3
New Hampshire	90	87	3	0
New Jersey	1,005	615	390	0
New Mexico	522	360	162	0
New York	2,139	1,677	456	9
North Carolina	567	405	159	3
North Dakota	156	141	15	0
Ohio	2,490	1,554	930	6
Oklahoma	576	318	237	21
Oregon	1,098	936	156	0
Pennsylvania	3,075	2,505	567	3
Rhode Island	186	78	108	0
South Carolina	726	426	300	0
South Dakota	429	336	87	9
Tennessee	783	528	252	6
Texas	4,671	3,069	1,560	45
Utah	732	552	180	0
Vermont	36	24	12	0
Virginia	1,686	1,128	555	0
Washington	1,062	786	273	3
West Virginia	489	327	162	0
Wisconsin	915	657	258	3
Wyoming	249	228	18	3
Not Reported	2,325	2,097	210	18

Source: Sickmund, M., Sladky, T. J., Kang, W., and Puzzanchera, C. 2011. Easy Access to the Census of Juveniles in Residential Placement. Online. Available: http://www.ojjdp.gov/ojstatbb/ezacjrp/

order of commitment whereby the juvenile is removed from the custody of his or her parent or guardian and placed in the custody of the state juvenile correctional authority. It is then up to the correctional authority to determine placement, correctional treatment plan, time spent in the institution, and release from secure confinement. In some instances, the judge retains the authority to release the juvenile. Most state correctional authorities have a variety of placement options that address the offense committed, the risk associated with the juvenile, and the treatment needs of the juvenile.

The population of juveniles in secure placements is typically young males who have committed a serious offense or multiple offenses. There are varying levels of risk that are determined by the correctional authority prior to placing the juvenile in a facility. Most juveniles are sent to low- or medium-risk facilities. A high-risk facility handles only those juveniles who have repeatedly committed crimes, committed violent or sex crimes, or are guilty of a particularly heinous crime.

PUBLIC VERSUS PRIVATE FACILITIES

The juvenile correctional system in the United States uses a number of **private facilities** that contract with the state or local jurisdiction to house juvenile offenders. Interestingly, most juveniles in public facilities (97 percent) are held there by court order under a delinquency adjudication. However, private facilities hold about 88 percent of their population under delinquency offenses. A greater proportion of the population in private facilities are there for status offenses, or are detained for other reasons.[5] Juveniles in private facilities included youths referred for abuse, neglect, emotional disturbance, or mental retardation as well as youths who were voluntarily admitted (referred by parents or school officials or as part of a diversion program). In many instances, these juveniles are housed with delinquent populations in the same facilities. Figure 12.3 shows

private facilities Correctional institutions run by private corporations or private individuals.

FIGURE 12.3	Detailed Offense Profile in Public and Private Facilities for United States, 2010			
COUNT	STATE	LOCAL	PRIVATE	TOTAL
Person Offenses: Criminal homicide	458	401	65	924
Person Offenses: Sexual assault	2,262	788	1,588	4,638
Person Offenses: Robbery	3,436	2,336	1,224	6,996
Person Offenses: Aggravated assault	2,679	2,008	1,410	6,097
Person Offenses: Simple assault	1,655	1,612	2,178	5,445
Person Offenses: Other person	607	648	655	1,910
Property Offenses: Burglary	3,018	2,141	2,088	7,247
Property Offenses: Theft	1,402	1,172	1,185	3,759
Property Offenses: Auto theft	907	756	806	2,469
Property Offenses: Arson	231	135	167	533
Property Offenses: Other property	1,042	1,074	913	3,029
Drug Offenses: Drug trafficking	403	262	369	1,034
Drug Offenses: Other drug	1,103	1,109	1,740	3,952
Public Order Offenses: Weapons	983	1,185	845	3,013
Public Order Offenses: Other public order	1,812	1,633	1,681	5,126
Technical violations	2,467	6,474	2,663	11,604
Status offenses	416	497	2,103	3,016
Total	24,881	24,231	21,680	70,792

Suggested Citation: Sickmund, M., Sladky, T.J., Kang, W., and Puzzanchera, C. (2011). "Easy Access to the Census of Juveniles in Residential Placement." Available: http://www.ojjdp.gov/ojstatbb/ezacjrp/

FIGURE 12.4	Placement Facilities by State, 2008					
	JUVENILE FACILITIES			JUVENILE OFFENDERS		
STATE	TOTAL	PUBLIC	PRIVATE	TOTAL	PUBLIC	PRIVATE
U.S. total	2,458	1,150	1,300	81,015	56,157	24,757
Alabama	56	13	43	1,328	632	696
Alaska	18	8	10	249	178	71
Arizona	40	16	20	1,488	1,198	240
Arkansas	32	11	21	836	286	550
California	215	117	98	13,309	12,056	1,253
Colorado	56	13	43	1,688	853	835
Connecticut	12	3	9	303	180	123
Delaware	7	6	1	256	239	17
Dist. of Columbia	10	3	7	236	174	62
Florida	118	37	81	5,895	2,210	3,685
Georgia	40	26	14	2,692	2,168	524
Hawaii	8	3	5	130	118	12
Idaho	28	15	13	683	540	143
Illinois	42	28	14	2,440	2,141	299
Indiana	76	37	39	2,422	1,561	861
Iowa	66	15	51	1,060	297	763
Kansas	41	17	24	973	682	291
Kentucky	39	29	10	944	873	71
Louisiana	43	17	26	1,294	909	385
Maine	7	2	5	215	189	26
Maryland	35	14	21	787	615	172
Massachusetts	58	18	40	961	343	618
Michigan	82	37	45	2,659	1,252	1,407
Minnesota	76	21	55	1,332	697	635
Mississippi	16	14	2	413	351	62
Missouri	68	63	5	1,226	1,196	30
Montana	16	8	7	161	114	30

12.2 SELF-CHECK

1. Describe the characteristics of juveniles who are sent to secure correctional facilities.

2. Explain the nature of the differences between public and private juvenile correctional facilities.

3. Which organization oversees the placement of juvenile delinquents?

that most juveniles in out-of-home placements are housed in public facilities for serious offenses.

STATE VARIABLES The use of private facilities in juvenile corrections varies substantially from state to state, ranging from less than 10 percent of the juvenile correctional population to as many as 76 percent.[6] The individual state percentages can be seen in Figure 12.4. In addition, there is substantial variation across the United States in the custody rate, the rate of incarceration of delinquent and status offenders, and the use of private facilities. It is worth noting that several variables affect state custody rates: age differences in juvenile court jurisdiction, differences in the age at which a state can hold a juvenile in a correctional facility (some states are mandated to release juvenile delinquents at 18, others at 21), provisions for transfer to criminal court, demographic and offense profile differences, and available bed space. Therefore, state-level incarceration rates should be interpreted with caution.[7]

FIGURE 12.4	Placement Facilities by State, 2008 (continued)					
	JUVENILE FACILITIES			JUVENILE OFFENDERS		
STATE	TOTAL	PUBLIC	PRIVATE	TOTAL	PUBLIC	PRIVATE
Nebraska	16	4	12	773	438	335
Nevada	23	17	6	1,052	841	211
New Hampshire	8	2	6	157	86	71
New Jersey	49	39	10	1,564	1,428	136
New Mexico	19	15	4	409	397	12
New York	169	40	129	3,157	1,470	1,687
North Carolina	52	22	30	1,014	557	457
North Dakota	9	4	5	85	73	12
Ohio	87	66	21	3,871	3,521	350
Oklahoma	46	16	29	923	626	276
Oregon	47	25	22	1,437	1,106	331
Pennsylvania	152	34	118	5,034	1,263	3,771
Rhode Island	10	1	9	291	168	123
South Carolina	33	13	20	1,258	794	464
South Dakota	23	7	14	507	233	261
Tennessee	48	30	18	1,151	836	315
Texas	109	85	24	5,831	5,192	639
Utah	35	18	17	770	384	386
Vermont	4	1	3	48	24	24
Virginia	61	56	5	2,114	2,022	92
Washington	37	31	6	1,382	1,302	80
West Virginia	26	11	15	565	376	189
Wisconsin	69	20	49	1,395	884	511
Wyoming	21	2	19	247	84	163

Source: Hockenberry, Sarah, Melissa Sickmund, and Anthony Sladky. 2011, July. Juvenile Residential Facility Census, 2008: Selected Findings. *Juvenile Offenders and Victims:* National Report Series Bulletin. Office of Juvenile Justice and Delinquincy Prevention. Online. Available at: https://www.ncjrs.gov/pdffiles1/ojjdp/231683.pdf. Retrieved April 13, 2013.

Institutional Facilities for Juveniles

Institutional facilities for juveniles generally serve two classifications of youths: detained juveniles awaiting a detention or adjudication hearing and committed juveniles placed by a juvenile court or other juvenile justice administrative body. The youths referred by another juvenile justice administrative body are generally referred to as voluntary placements because either their parents turned them over to a social service agency or the social service agency placed them because they had committed delinquent acts but were not formally adjudicated. In 2010, of all juveniles in secure custody, 68 percent were committed, 30 percent were being detained, and the remaining 2 percent were diverted juveniles, including those voluntarily admitted to facilities in lieu of adjudication as part of a diversion agreement.[8] The nature of an institution is directly related to the role it plays in the juvenile justice process. Secure facilities include detention centers, orientation and diagnostic assessment centers, transfer facilities, boot camps, youth ranches and camps, institutions and state schools, and transitional facilities. The substantial variety in placement facilities reflects diversity in both function and correctional style of the local jurisdiction. Some states

institutional facilities Secure facilities including detention centers, orientation and diagnostic assessment centers, transfer facilities, boot camps, youth ranches and camps, institutions and state schools, and transitional facilities.

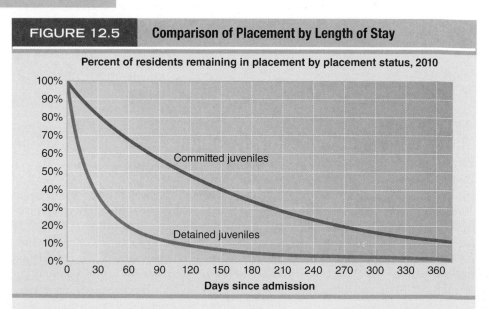

The makeup of the juvenile incarcerated population has changed in recent years. *Can you think of possible reasons why?*

have only large state-level training schools while others make use of a variety of secure placements. As shown in Figure 12.5, juveniles in the various types of secure facilities can expect to stay varying lengths of time prior to adjudication, transfer, or release.

Juveniles remain in detention until a judge at a detention hearing decides whether to release or keep them. Once adjudicated, the juvenile can be released based on acquittal, sentenced to a community sanction, or committed by the judge to the state-level department of corrections. In some instances, the judge may directly sentence a juvenile to a specific juvenile facility, but it is more common for the judge to transfer the juvenile to the custody of the state juvenile justice agency. Depending on statutory provisions, the state department of juvenile corrections may make placement and release decisions once a juvenile is committed. In other instances, the judge retains jurisdiction and may make determinations about placement and duration of confinement.[9] In the case of the former, once juveniles are released from the secure placement, they are typically placed on some type of juvenile parole or other aftercare. The costs of incarcerating juveniles can be exorbitant and cannot be dismissed as a factor in commitment and release decisions (see FYI box).

FIGURE 12.5   Comparison of Placement by Length of Stay

Percent of residents remaining in placement by placement status, 2010

Committed juveniles

Detained juveniles

Days since admission

- One-third (33 percent) of committed juveniles, but just 5 percent of detained juveniles, remained in placement six months after admission.
- Among detained offenders (those awaiting adjudication, disposition, or placement elsewhere), 73 percent had been in the facility for at least a week, 56 percent for at least 15 days, and 35 percent for at least 30 days. By 60 days, only 19 percent of these detained offenders remained in placement; and by 90 days, less than 13 percent remained.
- Among committed juveniles (those held as part of a court-ordered disposition), 80 percent had been in the facility at least 30 days, 68 percent for at least 60 days, and 58 percent at least 90 days. After a full year, 12 percent of committed offenders remained in placement.

Source: *OJJDP Statistical Briefing Book.* Online. Available: http://www.ojjdp.gov/ojstatbb/corrections/qa08401.asp?qaDate=2010. Retrieved April 18, 2013.

DETENTION

Juvenile detention facilities are short-term secure units that house juveniles awaiting court hearings or adjudications. They are similar to adult jails in operation; however, while adult jails also house criminals under sentence, juvenile detention centers are rarely used for this purpose. When a police officer detains a juvenile for an offense and decides to formally file charges, the juvenile is taken to a detention center. The juvenile may or may not be admitted into detention through a process called an intake, where detention staff or a probation officer processes the juvenile and makes a determination of whether or not to admit the juvenile into custody. Once a detention hearing is held (usually within 24 hours of arrest), a judge determines whether to continue the detention or release the juvenile. The original detention may continue beyond the adjudicatory and dispositional hearings while a juvenile is awaiting placement.[10]

The number of juveniles held in detention facilities increased 29 percent between 1985 and 2009. During the same period, the proportion of detained delinquency cases ranged somewhere between 18 and 23 percent.[11] Interestingly, the profile of the national detention population shifted during this period, with a greater proportion of juveniles charged with person offenses, a greater proportion of females, and a greater proportion of black youth in the detention population. Between 1985 and 2009, the percent increase in the number of cases involving detention was nearly nine times greater for black youth than white (72 percent versus 8 percent, respectively). The incidence among Asian youth increased a whopping 13 times more than the incidence among white youth. However, black youth were the most likely to be detained among all racial categories for each and every year in that span.

Despite a spike in property crime detentions in the early 1990s, the rates of detentions for those offenses have actually dropped 19 percent, but the number of person offense cases in which juveniles were detained increased 99 percent between 1985 and 2009. There was also a 117 percent increase in drug offense cases resulting in detention and a 108 percent increase in public order offense cases.[12] See Figure 12.6.

The Cost of Long-Term Incarceration

The California Department of Juvenile Justice (DJJ) determined in 2012 that it costs about $179,400 to incarcerate one juvenile for one year. This is a substantial increase from even five years earlier, due in part to new staffing and service mandates imposed due to lawsuits against the DJJ. The following is a breakdown of those costs:

- 26 percent for treatment programs
- 24 percent for health care
- 14 percent for education
- 11 percent for security (including transportation and detention costs)
- 8 percent for support (food, clothing, etc.)
- 17 percent for administration

SOURCE: http://www.lao.ca.gov/analysis/2012/crim_justice/juvenile-justice-021512.aspx

juvenile detention facilities Secure facilities that house juveniles on a short-term basis while they await court hearings or adjudications.

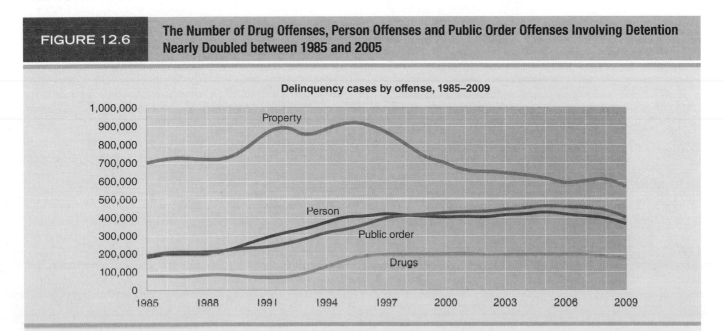

| FIGURE 12.6 | The Number of Drug Offenses, Person Offenses and Public Order Offenses Involving Detention Nearly Doubled between 1985 and 2005 |

Delinquency cases by offense, 1985–2009

Source: OJJDP Statistical Briefing Book. Online. Available: http://www.ojjdp.gov/ojctatbb/court/qa06205.asp?qaDate=2009. Retrieved April 23, 2013.

The detention facility is similar to other juvenile correctional facilities with a few exceptions. First, most of the juveniles who stay in detention stay for very short periods of time. Most are released following a detention hearing in juvenile court to the custody of their parents or guardians, to foster care, or to a non-secure short-term placement facility. Those who are held for adjudication do not typically stay much longer. During that time, a variety of assessments and tests are typically done by the probation department in the course of preparing a presentence investigation. The juveniles who are held for adjudication can and do receive treatment and other services, but not nearly as much as they would in a long-term secure facility. Detention facilities typically have minimal programming and instead focus on secure custody, assessment and evaluation, and assuring that the juveniles do not harm themselves or others. Working in a detention facility is somewhat similar to working in a secure juvenile correctional facility; however, the interaction with the juveniles is typically limited by the short duration of their stay.

SHORT-TERM SECURE FACILITIES

Many state juvenile justice correctional authorities operate several types of short-term secure facilities. One type is an **assessment facility**. Depending on the state and the number and variety of potential placements in a state, the assessment facility may be a stand-alone center that determines placements for all juveniles under secure commitment such as Virginia's Carroll R. Minor Reception and Diagnostic Center (see Focus on Programs). Central assessment units are responsible for orienting the juvenile to the correctional system in that particular state and to what the expectations are. In addition, these centers are responsible for conducting a thorough testing and diagnosis of each juvenile committed to the juvenile correctional authority. Once the orientation and diagnostic assessments are complete, a comprehensive profile of the juvenile is compiled and the juvenile is then transferred to the most appropriate unit in the system for his or her needs. In states where a centralized facility does not exist, the orientation and assessment is typically done at a regional office or within the correctional facility itself. Some states have only two or three long-term secure facilities for juveniles, so it does not make sense to have a separate unit for orientation and diagnostic assessments.

In addition to diagnostic and assessment centers, many states operate **transfer or transitional facilities** for juveniles. If juveniles are being transferred from a community placement to a secure unit or vice versa, it is often necessary to house them in a transfer unit until beds open up. Bed space in many states is at a premium, and it is therefore necessary to have a facility with space for juveniles awaiting placement or transfer. Juveniles in these facilities can expect to stay for a short time with very little in the way of programs, education, or other training.

A transitional facility is typically designed to house juveniles who are making the transition back to the community or into a specialized program of some type. Many experts believe that a transitional step between maximum security and community placement is advisable to equip juveniles with the skills they need to make it in the community. It is

Juvenile boot camps have come under increasing scrutiny in recent years. *Do you think boot camps should be used for juvenile offenders? Why or why not?*

also commonly assumed that a transitional facility lessens the shock of moving from a high-security placement to a low-security and low-supervision community facility. As such, transitional facilities typically operate programs designed to reintroduce the juvenile to the community and to lessened supervision. In addition to secure transitional facilities, many states operate community-based halfway houses that serve in a similar capacity (discussed in Chapter 11).

BOOT CAMPS The correctional sanction that has undoubtedly generated the greatest amount of controversy in recent years is **juvenile boot camps**. A boot camp is a secure correctional facility that emphasizes military-style discipline, physical training, and an extremely regimented schedule. The name boot camp is derived from the military, and the program follows a military regime and training style. The first correctional boot camps began in Georgia and Oklahoma in 1983, and by the end of the 1990s, there were about 75 boot camps operating nationally in over 30 states.[13] The concept started with adult prisoners but was soon implemented at the juvenile level. Boot camps became the rage across the nation and were soon present in state-level juvenile correctional systems, at the county level operated by either law enforcement or probation officials, and in private juvenile correctional corporations. The proliferation of boot camps was, however, unguided by comprehensive and methodologically rigorous evaluations.[14] Like other correctional panaceas, boot camps were extraordinarily popular during an era when the public and politicians saw them as a way of getting tough on juvenile crime. Furthermore, incidents like the 2006 death of a teen in a Florida boot camp have served to further slow the demand for these programs. Fourteen-year-old Martin Lee Anderson died after attending a juvenile boot camp in Bay County, Florida. Sheriff's office officials were seen on a widely distributed video tape beating and kicking the teen after

assessment facility Secure facilities responsible for orienting the juvenile to the expectations of the correctional system in that particular state. These centers are responsible for conducting testing and diagnosis of each juvenile committed to the juvenile correctional authority.

transfer or transitional facilities A temporary facility where juveniles are awaiting either transfer to another facility or release into the community.

juvenile boot camp A secure correctional facility that emphasizes military-style discipline, physical training, and an extremely regimented schedule.

CAREERS IN JUVENILE JUSTICE

Detention Care Workers Speak Out

Sgt. Margie McKinney, detention care supervisor and mother of two teenagers, works at Brevard Regional Juvenile Detention Center in Cocoa Beach, Florida, where she has been for eight years. The center was rated highly recently in its quality assurance review; its group sessions with youth have been ranked top in the state. Says McKinney, "I love this type of work. I have a strong will power to try to make a difference. . . .

"Our main goals are safety and security. We're like a holding facility for public safety and to make sure the kids are appearing in court. Because they're only with us for a short amount of time, while they're here we try to have an impact on their lives—letting them realize there's another way to insure they can do something positive with their lives. In group sessions, we discuss topics such as responsibility, recognizing where they went wrong, and what can be changed.

"Maybe it seems like they weren't listening. But down the road, we may run into one of them later and see them doing something positive, and he'll say, 'Ms. McKinney,

I remember what you said. I can be somebody and decide to be something positive.'"

Detention staff are responsible for monitoring and counseling juveniles within a short period of time. Their jobs frequently entail intake duties, supervision and security, counseling and intervention, education, and all other services necessary to house juveniles under their care. The requirements for working in detention vary across jurisdictions; however, many require a college education or experience working with juveniles. The detention facilities are open 24 hours a day, seven days a week, and staff can expect to work a variety of shifts and rotate days off. Many detention staff use their experience as a stepping stone into careers as juvenile probation officers.

Critical Thinking

What qualities do you think are essential for a good detention case worker?

Source: www.djj.state.fl.us/detention3.html

FOCUS ON PROGRAMS

VIRGINIA'S CARROLL R. MINOR RECEPTION AND DIAGNOSTIC CENTER

The Carroll R. Minor Reception and Diagnostic Center (RDC) serves as the central intake facility for all juveniles committed to the Virginia Department of Juvenile Justice (DJJ). The RDC receives and evaluates all youths who have been adjudicated as juveniles and committed to the DJJ by the courts throughout Virginia. The RDC also serves as the central file location for the master records for all juveniles committed to the DJJ. The facility has dedicated transportation staff responsible for the statewide transportation of committed juveniles from local detention facilities and jails to the facility, as well as the transportation of juveniles to the various juvenile correctional centers upon completion of the assessment process. Intakes are completed on a weekly basis.

The juveniles sent to the RDC include males and females of varying socioeconomic backgrounds who require different levels of supervision. The juveniles range in age from 10 through 20, and the average length of stay is approximately four weeks.

Once a juvenile arrives, a barrage of testing and evaluation begins that will last until the juvenile is ready for placement in a long-term facility. The standard assessment includes:

- Preliminary assessment and cottage assignment
- Medical evaluation
- Behavioral observations and management
- Educational/vocational evaluation
- Psychological and related evaluations
- Social/casework evaluation
- Drug abuse screening and evaluation

Once the various evaluations have been completed, a "staffing" is held to determine the appropriate placement for the juvenile. The counselor supervisor, the counselor, the psychologist, the educational evaluator, and the representative from the cottage life staff are voting members of the staffing who determine placement. The non-voting members that may be present at the staffing are the medical staff, court service unit staff, family members, and the juvenile.

Staffings are held weekly, and the function of the group is to review all evaluations from the various components, develop a needs assessment, and make a juvenile correctional center placement decision. In certain cases, this group determines special education eligibility. The juvenile is advised during the staffing process of the team's placement decision and the identified needs while in care. All juveniles have the opportunity to appeal their placement decision through a review board and the superintendent of the facility.

CRITICAL THINKING

Do you think the assessment process described above is effective? Explain your position.

Source: www.djj.state.va.us/resources/djj_publications/pdf/RDC.pdf

---

he collapsed during a mandatory one-mile run. The guards and a nurse involved in the case were found not guilty of aggravated manslaughter of a child in 2006, but all Florida boot camps were closed later in the year by order of the legislature. Nationally, the boot camp craze has fizzled out, fueled not only by fallout from incidents such as this one, but also by evaluations and studies that exposed other glaring problems in the system.

The boot camp correctional philosophy is essentially guided by the idea that a juvenile delinquent needs structure and discipline in his or her life. As in the military boot camps, the juvenile needs to be broken down and then built back up into a more productive citizen. The regimen varies, but the guiding principles are remarkably consistent and similar—strict discipline, structure, and tough love.

The Office of Juvenile Justice and Delinquency Prevention sponsored three demonstration boot camps for juvenile offenders in Cleveland, Ohio; Denver, Colorado; and Mobile, Alabama. The goal was to initiate and evaluate the concepts that led to the creation of the boot camp as a juvenile correctional alternative. The boot camps were designed as an intermediate sanction (an intervention less severe than long-term institutionalization but more severe than immediate supervised release) and targeted nonviolent offenders. The camps would operate a 90-day program that embraced military-like discipline

The make-up of the juvenile incarceration population has changed in recent years. Can you think of possible reasons why?

and structure in a comprehensive residential setting to be followed by supervised aftercare in the community for up to nine months.[15] In all three camps physical fitness, basic education, and life skills training were part of each day's regimen.[16]

The juveniles selected for the boot camps at the three sites varied somewhat in terms of their criminal history and socioeconomic status; however, most of the juveniles who went through the program were similar. Researchers compared the recidivism rates for juveniles who participated in the pilot programs with those of control groups. The research also compared the cost effectiveness of juvenile boot camps with other dispositional alternatives. Most juvenile boot camp participants completed the residential program and graduated to aftercare. Program completion rates were 96 percent in Cleveland, 87 percent in Mobile, and 76 percent in Denver. In Cleveland and Mobile, substantial improvements in academic skills were noted.[17] None of the three programs researched demonstrated a reduction in recidivism. In Denver and Mobile, no difference was found between the recidivism rates of juvenile boot camp participants and those of youth confined in state or county institutions, or released on probation. In Cleveland, boot camp graduates had higher recidivism rates than juveniles confined in traditional juvenile correctional facilities.[18]

Communities often implement juvenile boot camps, in part, to reduce costs. Research indicates that when boot camps are used as an alternative to traditional confinement, costs can be reduced considerably because of the significantly shorter residential stay. However, if boot camps are used as an alternative to probation, savings will not be realized. In response to many of the criticisms and issues raised in this and

Myth | Fact

Myth: Most juveniles in long-term secure correctional facilities have committed a violent offense.

Fact: Of the juveniles committed to correctional facilities in 2010, only about 38 percent had committed a violent crime. The remainder committed property offenses (25 percent), drug offenses (7 percent), public order offenses (11 percent), and technical violations (14 percent).

other research, many boot camps began to adopt a more holistic approach to correctional programming.

The evaluations of boot camps provide mixed findings of their utility as a correctional alternative. Additional criticism has been levied at the concept of boot camps themselves. One commentator concluded that the nature of boot camps does not fit well with the basic principles of adolescent development. Boot camps do not allow the juveniles to have a voice in their treatment and they tend to be very negative, especially at the outset.[19] In a broader sense, boot camps violate a primary principle of the juvenile justice system, which is individualized treatment.

Perhaps the most prominent criticism of the juvenile boot camp system is the idea of putting juveniles through a short program and then expecting the juveniles to turn their behavior around without anything in the way of follow-up or aftercare. Who said it was a good idea to instill military discipline in juvenile delinquents? Some might argue that the only effect the boot camp has on the juveniles is that they now commit crimes with military precision. Boot camps that have been founded more recently have taken a more holistic philosophy that includes a range of programming and aftercare services. In addition, the offenders who are selected for boot camp are screened more carefully than they were when the facilities first came into operation. Finally, future evaluations will determine if the boot camp is a viable alternative sanction that reduces recidivism and costs less than traditional secure facilities. Until that research is compiled, boot camps remain controversial.

YOUTH RANCHES AND CAMPS In the early history of the juvenile justice system (late 1800s–early 1900s), part of the Puritan philosophy operating at the time was the idea that youths in the inner cities of America were subjected to the evils of big-city living. As a result, delinquent youths were taken to remote facilities in the country to be rehabilitated through traditional country values and hard work. Many state training schools are to this day located in remote rural locations. A related type of correctional facilities is **youth ranches and camps**. The correctional programs in these facilities are akin to the wilderness and adventure programs discussed in Chapter 11; however, these facilities are secure, and the youths remain there until paroled. One such facility is the Idaho Youth Ranch, founded in 1952, which provides troubled children and their families a bridge to a valued, responsible, and productive future.

These facilities receive youths who are committed to state-level correctional authorities (however, in most cases they are a step below the most secure facilities in the state). Youth ranches and camps operate similarly to state institutions with one exception; the atmosphere is more like a year-round summer camp than a maximum-security facility. There are typically dorms or cottages, a school, vocational programs, and industry. The one component that sets them apart from other secure facilities is a program centering on some type of farming, ranching, or adventure. The idea is that youths need to be given the responsibilities that come with running a farm or ranch to teach them there is more to life than being delinquent. The process of rehabilitating youths at these facilities is keyed on their active participation in the work that goes on at the facility. If youths choose not to participate or disobey the rules of the camp, they are often dismissed from the program and sent to a more secure facility.

Juveniles sent to these facilities can expect to be subjected to a rigorous schedule of work and rehabilitational programming. Their day usually begins very early with tending to the livestock, crops, or whatever work program is part of the facility. During the day they will attend educational programs or other vocational programs depending on what their treatment needs are. The evenings are usually devoted to group counseling sessions and other types of psychological programming.

youth ranches and camps Facilities that operate similarly to state institutions with one exception: the atmosphere is more like a year-round summer camp than a maximum-security facility. There are typically dorms or cottages, a school, vocational programs, and industry. The one component that sets them apart from other secure facilities is a program centering on a type of farming, ranching, or adventure.

FOCUS ON PROGRAMS

CALIFORNIA WORKS TO DISMANTLE ITS STATE JUVENILE JUSTICE AGENCY

As with any large bureaucracy, the California Department of Juvenile Justice (formerly the California Youth Authority) has had its share of problems—and as the country's largest juvenile justice system, the system was strained to the point of breaking by the end of the 1990s. The department was flooded with lawsuits alleging grim living conditions, rampant abuse, and blatant security risks, and in 2006 it was ordered by the judicial system to institute sweeping reforms.

The DJJ did an about-face, shifting from a fully punitive organization to one that embraced rehabilitative measures such as intensive treatment programs and education services. Despite those improvements and subsequent small successes, Governor Jerry Brown made a stunning announcement in 2011: he would eliminate the Department of Juvenile Justice altogether.

Brown's reasoning for such dramatic action seems logical on many fronts: it eliminates a clunky bureaucracy; it embraces the move toward less punitive means of dealing with juvenile offenders; it allows communities to tailor programming to local needs and use innovative methods of rehabilitation; and it promises to decrease state budgetary constraints in a time of great economic uncertainty.

However, local communities—particularly rural ones—are not equipped to handle dangerous offenders for long-term incarcerations. Critics worry that such juveniles will be crammed into facilities meant only for short-term detention of nonviolent offenders, and that there is no structure in place to monitor for the abuses and neglect that once plagued the statewide agency. Furthermore, many believe that prosecutors may charge more juveniles as adults in order to ensure that they do end up in a more secure correctional environment.

The DJJ has had a declining population for nearly a decade, since lower-level offenders were not eligible for placement in the system starting in 2006. At the beginning of 2013, the DJJ housed only about 1,000 offenders, down from 9,700 in 1996. Current projections show that by mid-2015, the population of DJJ inmates will be zero; new admissions will not be received in 2013.

This realignment of juvenile justice to a county supervision model will be watched throughout the country and analyzed for its ability not only to save money but also to revolutionize and streamline the juvenile corrections process. [Insert right before "Clearly, more research. . . ."]

CRITICAL THINKING

Do you think California's plans will appeal to other states? What will this do to the juvenile corrections system as we know it?

Sources: Taylor, M. "The 2012–13 Budget: Completing Juvenile Justice Realignment." Legislative Analyst's Office, State of California. Online. Available: http://www.lao.ca.gov/analysis/2012/crim_justice/juvenile-justice-021512.pdf. March 22, 2013.

"In California, Justice for Juveniles." *Los Angeles Times*, March 27, 2012. Online. Available: http://articles.latimes.com/2012/mar/27/opinion/la-ed-juvenile-justice-california-20120327. Retrieved March 22, 2013.

STATE INSTITUTIONS AND SCHOOLS State institutions and schools are typically very self-contained and provide a variety of services for juveniles including rehabilitation, health, education, counseling, recreation, employment, and training. Historically, these facilities have been very large, housing up to 300 youths drawn from wide geographic regions of the state. Starting in the 1970s, some states opted to eliminate or reduce their dependence on large facilities. Instead, they developed smaller, community based facilities serving 10 to 50 youths. These smaller facilities typically allow youth to be placed closer to their homes and to the communities to which they will return upon release.[20] Surveys of prison wardens and juvenile facility directors have revealed that the degree of emphasis placed on rehabilitation counseling and programs is higher in juvenile corrections than it is in adult corrections. However, the degree of emphasis placed on maintaining institutional order and on inmate behavior is relatively the same. The only areas where prison wardens reported higher emphasis were related to punishment, preventing escapes, and preventing the flow of contraband into and within the facility.[21]

state institutions and schools Self-contained facilities that provide a variety of services for juveniles including rehabilitation, health, education, counseling, recreation, employment, and training.

The state institution takes on a much broader role in rehabilitating juveniles than do other juvenile correctional institutions. Most states currently embrace a broad organizational model in fulfilling their mission of juvenile corrections. There are a wide variety of programs and treatment services available to juveniles in most states, implementing a general mission and operational objectives throughout the state's facilities in programs. Many states operate separate institutions for female delinquents designed to address their needs. Although much of the programming is similar, facilities for female delinquents do have some treatments that differ from those used for male delinquents.

Programming in Institutional Corrections

All juvenile institutions follow some form of treatment or rehabilitation plan. The fundamental purpose of correctional treatment is to change the behavior of the youth so that they do not commit future delinquent acts. While the goal itself is simple, accomplishing the goal is anything but easy. The recidivism rates for juveniles who have been incarcerated rival those of adults; however, it is important to remember that incarceration in secure facilities is relatively rare and is reserved for the most serious repeat juvenile offenders. While it is true that recidivism is high for these juveniles, the overwhelming majority of juveniles who come into contact with the juvenile justice system do not return.

CORRECTIONAL TREATMENT

The various juvenile correctional institutions all have some type of treatment program or correctional mission that they use to treat the youths in their custody. The variety of correctional treatment approaches and philosophies are almost as numerous as the facilities themselves. Nonetheless, there are some standard treatment methods that have received attention in academic and practitioner circles. Sometimes the correctional approach of the facility changes when the administration changes; thus it is more a function of the person than it is the facility. In general, there are four primary goals in corrections: **rehabilitation**, **deterrence**, **incapacitation**, and **retribution**.

rehabilitation Methods of treatment and counseling used to reform juvenile offenders so that they will return to society in a constructive rather than a destructive way.

deterrence Arranging conditions in the law and corrections so that juveniles are aware of the risks and consequences involved in committing crimes. If the risks and consequences are greater than the rewards, juveniles will choose not to commit crime.

incapacitation Taking juveniles out of the community so that they are prevented from committing crimes. It means locking up juveniles so that they are incapacitated from causing any more harm.

retribution Punishing and paying juveniles back for the harm they caused society.

Rehabilitation means using methods of treatment and counseling in an effort to reform juvenile offenders so that they will return to society in a constructive rather than a destructive way. It has been the prime mission of juvenile corrections since its inception and remains so today in spite of the drive for increased punishment. Deterrence means that conditions in the law and corrections are such that juveniles are aware of the risks and consequences involved in committing crimes. If the risks and consequences are greater than the rewards, juveniles will choose not to commit crime. Incapacitation refers to taking juveniles out of the community so that they are prevented from being able to commit crimes. Literally, it means locking up juveniles so that they are incapacitated from causing any more harm. Finally, retribution refers to punishment and paying juveniles back for the harm they caused society. All four of these goals are operational in one way or another in the juvenile correctional system; however, some facilities may emphasize one over the others in their correctional programming. A national survey of juvenile facility directors revealed which correctional goals are emphasized the most in juvenile corrections and which activities were most important relating to those goals. Figure 12.7 shows the ranking of the correctional goals of the juvenile justice system compared with adult prisons. As you can see, juvenile correctional facilities emphasize

FIGURE 12.7	Differences in the Operational Goals and Philosophies of Juvenile and Adult Corrections		
		JUVENILE FACILITY DIRECTORS MEAN	PRISON WARDENS MEAN
Ranked Goal of the Correctional System			
Rehabilitation		1.45	2.51
Deterrence		2.13	2.50
Incapacitation		2.73	3.35
Retribution		3.66	1.66
Importance of Activity in Ideal Institution			
(assign 100 points total)			
Involving juveniles in rehabilitation programs		47	18
Maintaining security		23	29
Preventing escapes		13	16
Keeping inmates busy by having them work		15	27
To punish juveniles for the crimes they committed		6	12
Amenability to Treatment			
Percent of juveniles you believe will be rehabilitated (will not return to crime) because of their participation in institutional treatment programs		48.06	25.70

Source: Caeti, Tory J., Craig Hemmens, Francis T. Cullen, and Velmer S. Burton, Jr., "Management of Juvenile Correctional Facilities," *Prison Journal* 83 (2003): 383–405.

rehabilitation over all other goals while prisons emphasize retribution. In addition, juvenile facility directors believe that almost 50 percent of the youths they deal with will be rehabilitated while only 25 percent of prison wardens hold the same thoughts about their inmates.

The public, too, believes strongly in rehabilitation for juvenile offenders. A 2007 survey conducted by the Center for Children's Law and Policy showed that 89 percent of people in the United States agree with the following statement: "Almost all youth who commit crimes are capable of positive growth and have the potential to change for the better." Furthermore, less than 15 percent of those surveyed thought that simply incarcerating juveniles was a "very effective" way to rehabilitate youth. Respondents also believed that government funds should be shifted from incarceration to educational, rehabilitative, and vocational programs.[22]

CORRECTIONAL EDUCATION

One of the primary goals of juvenile institutional corrections is education. While the education level of the juveniles in secure facilities varies dramatically, most are well below where they should be in their educational achievement. In addition to overcoming past educational deficiencies, educators in correctional facilities must deal with youths who were not model students in academic study skills or classroom behavior. Educational programs in juvenile facilities often serve as the core program, consuming the largest portion of time. Educators in these facilities often feel isolated, alienated, and ill prepared to teach incarcerated juvenile offenders.[23] Research indicates that educators are indeed seldom prepared for the juvenile confinement setting, where students are rarely uniform in age, grade level, academic competency, or behavior. Youths in institutional settings manifest many problems beyond educational problems, and this often includes violent acting out. Teachers in these settings also are expected to work with other counselors and security staff to integrate aspects of treatment plans and institutional discipline into the classroom.[24]

FOCUS ON PRACTICE

ARTS PROGRAMS FOR JUVENILE OFFENDERS

Perhaps fine arts such as painting, dance, and drama seem out of place in a gritty juvenile facility, but in the late 1990s, the National Endowment for the Arts partnered with the Office of Juvenile Justice and Delinquency Prevention to both enhance existing arts programs and pioneer new ones in juvenile corrections settings, in hopes that such programming might decrease recidivism among the delinquent populations. What resulted was a set of best practices for similar programming that focused on cognitive, social, and civil development.

- **The Experimental Gallery Program:** This outreach program was enhanced with funding from the NEA and OJJDP and consisted of curriculum-based arts instruction with public presentation of work by inmates in gallery and community settings.
- **Fred C. Nelles Facility:** Another enhancement project, this one focusing on an exchange of ideas between incarcerated youth and established artists in Whittier, California. Features intensive, semester-long studies in dance, music, visual arts, and creative writing.
- **Bronx Writers Corps:** Creative writing program that also includes poetry slams, mentorships, and workshops for institutionalized youth.
- **Gainesville State School:** A pilot program in Texas offered arts instruction for visual arts, theater/creative writing, and music. Students were able to present their work, and those with promise were given referrals to community colleges or community-based arts programs upon discharge.
- **Monroe County Children's Center PAINTS Program:** Provided arts experiences to both short- and long-term clients, including skills-based instruction by community mentors specializing in ceramics/sculpture, woodworking, photography, and creative writing.
- **West Palm Beach Alternative Arts Center:** A prevention/intervention-based offering that uses arts as an incentive for avoiding delinquent behavior.

Each program blended community collaboration with careful planning, design, and evaluation. The Office of Juvenile Justice and Delinquency Prevention and the National Endowment for the Arts assert that such programming is "highly empowering and transforming for the participants. These programs support the premise that participation in arts programming reduces risk factors that cause youth to be more susceptible to problem behaviors and crime (e.g., social alienation, school failure, impulsivity) and enhances protective factors that reduce the impact of risk factors and enable youth to lead productive lives (e.g., by increasing communication skills, conflict management techniques, and positive peer associations)."

While such programs seem to be useful in a juvenile corrections setting, they face several obstacles. Funding is clearly an issue in an economic climate that can barely keep the doors open to many juvenile facilities. Furthermore, community connections necessary to bring artists into teaching roles may not be as ample in rural areas; or they may fall victim to high professional turnover in correctional settings.

CRITICAL THINKING

What benefits do you think artistic endeavors might have on juvenile offenders?

Source: Hillman, Grady. "Arts Programs for Juvenile Offenders in Detention and Corrections: A Guide to Promising Practices." Office of Juvenile Justice and Delinquency Prevention. Online. Available: http://ia600800.us.archive.org/32/items/artsprogramsforj00hill/artsprogramsforj00hill.pdf. Retrieved April 23, 2013.

Teachers in correctional institutions must incorporate innovative teaching methods to stimulate incarcerated youths to learn. The environment of the school and the attitude of the educators are directly related to the effectiveness of the school itself. Research on correctional education has revealed that education is regarded by facility administrators as the most important component of the rehabilitation process.[25] Recently, the Office of Juvenile Justice and Delinquency Prevention published a model that involves changes in educational philosophy, curriculum, and instructional techniques. The model recommends that correctional education adopt the following principles:

- The academic curriculum features comprehension and complex problem-solving tasks, allowing students to develop their cognitive skills.
- The curriculum integrates basic skills into more challenging tasks that allow students to apply these skills to real-life situations.

- The curriculum allows for a number of discrete skills to be combined and applied to perform more complex tasks.
- Knowledge sharing is emphasized through cooperative learning, peer tutoring, and team problem solving.
- Teachers model cognitive processes through a variety of instructional strategies, including externalizing thought processes, encouraging multiple approaches to problem solving, and focusing on dialog and reciprocal learning.
- A variety of assessment and evaluation measures are used. Progress is based on mutually defined student goals emphasizing competence.
- Instruction involves multiple strategies appropriate to each learner's interests and needs.
- Reading, writing, and oral expression are interrelated.[26]

One such model has been adopted by the Texas Juvenile Justice Department. Called CoNEXTions®, the system is an innovative, holistic program adopted in 2006 that represents a cross-disciplinary approach to treatment, with a focus on rehabilitation and education tailored to the individual needs of the juvenile offender. CoNEXTions® is integrated into almost every aspect of Texas Juvenile Justice Department programming, and it recognizes the link between educational achievement and success. The program emphasizes year-round coursework that leads to the receipt of a high school diploma or GED, while implementing a federally and state-mandated cognitive behavior program designed to increase positive education experiences among incarcerated youth.[27]

Every staff member in TYC has roles and responsibilities in the CoNEXTions® program, from administrators such as superintendants and principals to teachers and even caseworkers and corrections officers. Additionally, the TYC actively involves parents in the treatment program, keeping them apprised of progress and achievement in all levels of their rehabilitation. Including all educational components.

There are numerous vocational and job training programs in juvenile correctional institutions. *Why is this important in juvenile corrections?*

Juvenile correctional staff are required to perform a variety of functions in their jobs. *How much of an impact do you think staff can have in reforming juvenile delinquents?*

CORRECTIONAL INDUSTRY AND VOCATIONAL TRAINING

The majority of delinquents age 16 years and older do not return to school after release from a correctional setting. While correctional educators must find better ways to motivate students to return to school, they must also provide students with the knowledge, skills, and attitudes needed in entry-level jobs. Juveniles who will enter the workplace need training in working productively with others on teams, acquiring and using information, understanding and utilizing systems, and using technology.[28] To this end, many facilities develop relationships with business partners in a symbiotic fashion to train juveniles for work in the real world. Some facilities develop internships, apprenticeships, and mentorships with these business partners.

One example of this type of program is the California Division of Juvenile Justice Free Venture Program. The program lets a business set up and operate its industry within the confines of the correctional institution and hire the youthful offenders as its employees. The juveniles receive training for meaningful jobs, which aids in their rehabilitation. The program provides financial assistance to victims of crime, and funds generated also reduce incarceration costs. Under the program guidelines, inmates are paid comparable wage that is subject to deductions for:

- Federal, state, and local taxes
- Room and board
- Restitution fines or victims compensation
- Family support
- Mandatory inmate savings[29]

SPECIALIZED TREATMENT AND PROGRAMS

Specialized treatment includes programs designed specifically for the treatment of capital offenders, sex offenders, chemically dependent youths, youths with emotional disturbances, and mentally retarded youth. As many as 40 percent of youths in correctional facilities may have some form of learning disability. Special education typically focuses on:

1. Assessment of the deficits and learning needs
2. A curriculum that meets each student's needs.
3. Vocational training opportunities
4. Transitional services that link the correctional special education services to prior educational experiences and to educational and human services needed after release
5. A comprehensive range of educational and related services
6. Effective staff training[30]

Juvenile delinquents are often deficient in cognitive problem-solving skills, moral reasoning, communication skills, and social skills essential for successful functioning in daily life. Many programs offer specialized treatment focusing on problem-solving and social survival skills. These programs begin by assessing the juvenile's social skills and cognitive reasoning abilities. Some individualized treatment is offered and social skills education is integrated into life at the facility. The staff will consciously create opportunities for practicing and applying social skills in the community as well as giving the juveniles the opportunity to participate in school and facility governance. In addition, staff are trained in such techniques as modeling, small-group discussions, and cooperative learning.[31] The goals of these programs are to bring the juveniles to a level of social skills commensurate with their age as well as provide the juveniles with the cognitive skills they will need to make it on the outside.

PROGRAMS FOR SERIOUS AND REPEAT JUVENILE DELINQUENTS

Many states have facilities or programs that specifically target serious or repeat juvenile offenders. Serious juvenile offenders are usually categorized as juveniles who commit violent crimes or other crimes that result in a serious impact on society or a victim. For example, a juvenile murderer, a juvenile sex offender, or juvenile who commits a robbery with a deadly weapon would all be considered serious juvenile offenders. First-time offenders deemed serious by a juvenile court or state statute are likely to be sentenced to secure placement regardless of their social, educational, or psychological history. The Texas Juvenile Justice Department operates a program in the Giddings State School for juveniles convicted of murder or attempted murder. The program has been profiled in several national news programs and documentaries. Youths are required to reenact their crimes and play the role of both perpetrator and victim. Research shows that participation in this program reduces by 55 percent the likelihood of being reincarcerated for any offense, and by 43 percent the likelihood of being reincarcerated for a felony offense.[32]

Another program that has received national attention in the media is the Lighthouse Youth Center at Paint Creek in the Cincinnati, Ohio, area. The program is operated by a private, nonprofit corporation that accepts referrals from the Ohio Department of Youth Services of juveniles who have committed serious felonies. The program has been evaluated favorably, and the key features of the program include:

- The Problem Oriented Record System (PORS)—a systematic procedure for identifying each youth's most serious problems and specific activities for working on the problems.
- The peer (youth) booking system—negative behavior on the part of a youth is pointed out by a peer youth and the youth is warned to stop. If the behavior continues, the reporting youth is expected to report it to the discipline committee through the use of a "booking slip."
- Personality-based classification system—youths are categorized as either "expressive" or "instrumental" and assigned to a team leader of the same type.
- Pattern of program phases—a short orientation period is followed by promotion to successive phases which require accomplishment of specific behavioral goals and periods of sustained satisfactory performance.
- Team-based management system—initial inputs for the PORS are assembled and reviewed at a treatment team conference which occurs about six weeks after a youth has been placed in the program.
- Family program—families are informed of the treatment plan at the initial staffing and kept apprised of their children's progress throughout their stay. During the later phases, parents are encouraged to participate in special family group sessions on every other Sunday, in which parents sit in the regular treatment groups. These family groups focus on special family issues and utilize training material specifically developed for this purpose.
- Intensive aftercare supervision—when a peer leaves Paint Creek, he is virtually under house arrest on what is called "permission status," allowing him to leave his house only with the permission of his community caseworker and only for the purposes and periods specified. Over the next few weeks, this control is turned over to the parents and then gradually loosened under the close supervision of the caseworker who is also assisting the youth to obtain appropriate schooling or work.[33]

12.4 SELF-CHECK

Describe the various types of correctional programming available in juvenile facilities.

Staff at Paint Creek spend a good deal of time critiquing each other's performance and working out solutions to administrative problems as a group. A number of staff have been dismissed or encouraged to leave for not being able or willing to engage in this process with a sufficient degree of enthusiasm.

A review of several programs for serious youth concluded that they share some common characteristics.[34] First, the programs have well-defined treatment programs with a strong intuitive appeal. Second, the treatment plans have demonstrated positive effects on the youth. The recidivism rates in these programs are typically lower than simple incarceration in a secure facility. Finally, the report noted a strong following among judges and correctional administrators that work with the program. In addition, these programs are typically very intensive and service a small number of juveniles. Some programs take all juveniles who are deemed to be serious while others take only those who have committed certain offenses; sex offender programs are a prime example of a specialized program for certain offenders.

Institutional Life for Juveniles

Juveniles who are placed in an out-of-home placement respond differently to their new surroundings. Many times, the atmosphere in the facility is far better than their living environment prior to placement. In other instances, the last place the juvenile wants to be is in detention or a secure treatment facility. In contrast to adult prisons, juvenile facilities tend to have far fewer inmates (119 in juvenile facilities versus 862 in adult prisons[35]), and the transition into the facility can be eased by close interaction with a small number of fellow juveniles. Even in the larger institutions, the population is frequently divided into cottages or dormitories in such a way as to limit the interaction of the juvenile with other inmates in the facility. In the end, how a juvenile adjusts to the facility and the program is largely a function of their personality and prior history with the system.

FACILITY LIFE   The life on the inside for juvenile delinquents is fundamentally different from what they are used to in the community. Most prominent among the changes that juveniles have difficulty adjusting to is the structured life and programs in the facilities that dictate how juveniles will spend their time. Most juveniles who are committed are used to having more free time than structured programming. The juvenile's time is now occupied for them with regimented meals, standard wake-up and lights-out times, educational programming, individual and group counseling, vocational training, work responsibilities and chores, scheduled recreational activities, and a variety of other programming. It should not be surprising that a juvenile who has never had appropriate structure of any kind has difficulty in adjusting to such a regimented time schedule.

Another area of friction and problems concerns the emotional, social, and psychological problems the youths bring with them into the correctional facility. All of the youths that end up in a secure placement have problems in these areas; if they did not, they wouldn't have committed an offense serious enough to mandate incarceration in the first place. Many, if not all, of the juveniles have never had to take a serious inventory of themselves, let alone discuss their problems in a public forum. Odds are that the people juveniles should be talking to about their problems (their parents or other significant adults) were the source of their problems in the first place, or at least a contributing factor. Again, it is not hard to see how regular individual counseling sessions and group counseling sessions would be difficult for a juvenile upon arrival at the facility. These sessions are key to a juvenile's progress, and juveniles generally take varying amounts of time before they open up to staff or a group of their peers.

Finally, the other programming that occurs in juvenile correctional facilities revolves around educational, recreational, and vocational treatment. The juveniles in these facilities typically have learning dysfunctions, have never held a serious job of any kind, and do not know or understand how to participate appropriately in group recreational activity. Overcoming these dysfunctions takes time and positive reinforcements from staff and peers. All of these areas are the most difficult adjustments a juvenile faces in conforming to institutional life in the facility. Some juveniles conform rapidly and remain in full compliance with the program throughout their stay; however, the vast majority will experience successes and failures before they are in full compliance with the program. For those who never make it that far, their success is the learning of social survival skills they need to exist in the community. At the other end of the spectrum are the juveniles who earn diplomas and leave the institution to attend college. Somewhere in the middle are the majority of juveniles whom the institutions deal with.

The release of a juvenile from institutional life opens new problems and issues for the juvenile. The institutional programming typically leads to juveniles' manifesting "institutionalized" behavior upon release. In other words, they are so used to strict structure and programming that the transition to the community is difficult. Another related problem is that once juveniles complete their stay at an institution, they are typically returned right back into the situation that contributed to their problems in the first place. Behaving appropriately in a facility where staff are monitoring your every move is a great deal easier for some juveniles than it is to manage their behavior in the community. The freedom that they seek to regain in the correctional facility is often their worst enemy upon release. This revelation heightens the need for appropriate and effective aftercare in juvenile corrections.

Recent surveys of juvenile facility directors asked them to assess the juveniles in their institutions. Figure 12.8 depicts the results from these surveys and shows that the directors believe an almost equal number of juveniles will be rehabilitated as will be back in the criminal justice system. The juveniles labeled as troublemakers and those who are perceived to be in need of protection from other

12.5 SELF-CHECK

1. What problems do juveniles experience in adapting to institutional life?

2. What problems do juveniles experience when they are released from an institution?

FIGURE 12.8	Juvenile Facility Directors' Assessment of the Juveniles in Their Institution

ITEM	MEAN
What percentage of juveniles in your institution do you believe will be rehabilitated because of their participation in institutional treatment programs?	48.06
What percentage of juveniles in your institution do you believe will recidivate and be back in the criminal justice system?	41.69
What percentage of the juveniles in your institution might be called chronic "troublemakers"?	19.76
What percentage of the juveniles in your institution need to be protected from other juveniles in the institution?	18.44
What percentage of juveniles in your institution do you believe will be deterred or "scared straight" by their institutional experience?	13.37
What percentage of juveniles in your institution do you believe are dangerously violent and should not be released into society?	12.93

Source: Caeti, Tory J., Craig Hemmens, Francis T. Cullen, and Velmer S. Burton, Jr., "Management of Juvenile Correctional Facilities," Prison Journal 80 (2000): 383–405.

delinquents are equally divided as well. Finally, the directors do not believe that a large percentage of juveniles will be "scared straight" and deterred from future criminal activity. These findings confirm the fact that in the eyes of the correctional administrators about half of the juveniles they deal with will not return and only a small percentage are dangerously violent.

Suicide in Juvenile Corrections

One issue that is receiving increased attention in juvenile corrections research and policy circles is that of suicide during incarceration. From October 1, 2003, through September 30, 2004, there were 16 deaths attributed to suicide among juvenile facilities in the United States. This does represent an increase from 2000 and has spurred a variety of research on the topic. Although the number is low statistically, representing only a fraction of the overall juvenile offender population, the fact that these youths were in custody has a number of implications that affect public perception and overall evaluation of the way they are treated during incarceration.

During this study period, most juvenile suicides during incarceration happened after 75 days of incarceration, suggesting that those locked away for longer periods of time were more at risk than those detained for shorter stays.[36] According to a study that examined data from a four-year period from 1995 through 1999, the vast majority of suicide victims were male Caucasians,[37] though recent data shows an increase in the proportion of juvenile African-American males who committed suicide. The average age of the victims was 15.7, and the majority of the victims were confined for nonviolent offenses. Many of the victims had a prior history of violations. Furthermore, nearly three-quarters of the victims had a history of substance abuse and nearly 70 percent had a history of mental illness. Most had a history of suicidal behavior. Nearly all deaths were by hanging. The implications of these findings lead to a number of recommendations for suicide prevention in confinement including a written suicide prevention policy that implements training, identification and screening of at-risk individuals, as well as intervention plans. Training and education programs should be specifically tailored to juveniles, and should avoid using generalizations from adult populations. Environmental precautions should be taken, and supervisory practices should be informed by this risk.[38] Confinement practices need to weigh the risks of suicide against the punitive benefits of room or solitary confinement. Not only do suicides during incarceration increase liability for facilities and governmental agencies, they also rob juvenile offenders of the opportunity for rehabilitation, reintegration, and happiness.

Sexual Abuse in Juvenile Facilities

Sexual abuse in juvenile facilities is yet another issue of confinement that has reared its head in the recent past. It can certainly be argued that this issue has always been a factor in juvenile confinement, but a 2007 investigation by the *Dallas Morning News* exposed a horrific pattern of sexual abuse against juvenile inmates in Texas and systematic tolerance of those offenses by facilities, state agencies, and even federal oversight mechanisms. The DMN investigation revealed abuse of youth in a west Texas facility in Pyote. High-level facility staff were accused of engaging in repeated sexual activity with their charges, often under the threat of additional time.[39] The public furor was shared by the Texas legislature, which ordered a complete overhaul of the organization, resulting in a name change to the Texas Department of Juvenile Justice and extensive reforms, including extensive training, background checks for employees, and a meaningful grievance process for incarcerated youth.[40]

Texas is not the only state to experience this problem. A Department of Justice study released in 2010 found that about 12 percent of youth being held in state-run, local, or private facilities experienced some kind of sexual victimization. About 3 percent of the reports involved nonconsensual sex acts with another offender, and about 11 percent involved staff members. For those reporting incidents with staff, 4.3 percent involved force and 6.4 percent did not involve any force. Male juveniles were more likely to be involved in incidents with staff members. Female youth were more likely to report forced sexual contact with other youth[41]—a situation not only troubling from a victimization standpoint, but from a rehabilitation standpoint as well.

Working in Institutional Corrections

A variety of personnel work in secure juvenile justice facilities performing all of the tasks and roles necessary to not only raise but also rehabilitate the juvenile. The largest juvenile facilities are akin to self-sufficient small cities and require numerous staff to operate.

These correctional facilities have personnel working a variety of jobs including:

- Administration and management
- Psychological treatment and testing
- Educational teaching and assessment
- Correctional case management and counseling
- Security monitoring
- Recreational and physical education
- Medical treatment
- Food services
- Vocational training and industrial services
- Maintenance and operations

In larger facilities, there are separate groups of employees to handle each of these roles. In smaller facilities, the juvenile correctional staff may be responsible for several of the tasks. The best way to think about this is that the larger facilities tend to have specialists who focus on one or a few roles, and the smaller facilities have generalists who perform a variety of tasks.

The most problematic issues concerning working in juvenile corrections are appropriate training and retention of qualified personnel. The juvenile justice system is experiencing widespread changes at the philosophical level as it becomes more punitive. In addition, the nature and qualities of the youths who are being incarcerated are changing. Therefore, the training and expertise of the juvenile correctional staff need to change as well. Unfortunately, training is often a low priority due to uneven levels of pre-employment education, high staff turnover rates, increasingly complex needs of juvenile offenders, liability issues, and scarce agency funds.[42]

The adult prison system is fundamentally different from the juvenile correctional system in both the goals and operational strategies employed. In addition, the demographics of juvenile correctional personnel are somewhat different from their adult prison counterparts. Recent surveys of juvenile correctional facility directors and adult prison wardens point out several key differences. The data indicates that the directors and wardens are similar in terms of age and education. However, several notable demographic differences

12.6 SELF-CHECK

1. Explain the difference between task specialization and task generalization in juvenile correctional facilities.

2. Explain the differences between adult prison wardens and juvenile correctional facility directors.

include gender, race, and military experience. Although gender information was not collected in the prison warden survey, undoubtedly there are fewer female prison wardens. There are also more minorities in juvenile corrections, and far fewer of the directors have military experience.

The most striking differences are in the areas of correctional officer experience, experience working as treatment staff, and the number of inmates/juveniles they supervise at their facilities. These differences are reflected in the goals and operations of the facilities already discussed and show that working in juvenile corrections means more treatment and rehabilitation servicing fewer juveniles overall.

SUMMARY BY CHAPTER OBJECTIVES

1. **List the differences between detained juveniles and committed juveniles**

   A detained juvenile has not been adjudicated. The juvenile may be awaiting a detention hearing where it will be determined if the juvenile will remain in detention prior to adjudication or released. Alternatively, the juvenile is in detention awaiting adjudication or final disposition by the juvenile court. A committed juvenile has been adjudicated by the juvenile court and sentenced to a secure facility as a result. The juvenile is therefore committed to the custody of the state juvenile justice authority.

2. **Profile the typical juvenile who is sent to an out-of-home placement facility**

   The typical juvenile in secure custody has either committed a serious crime or has committed crimes in a chronic fashion.

3. **Explain the differences between public and private facilities**

   Public facilities are operated by the state, and private facilities are operated by private individuals or corporations. Most of the time, private facilities do not handle the most severe or violent offenders.

4. **Describe the different types of secure institutional facilities**

   Secure facilities include detention centers, orientation and diagnostic assessment centers, transfer facilities, boot camps, youth ranches and camps, institutions and state schools, and transitional facilities.

5. **Explain the nature of juvenile detention facilities and processing procedures**

   Juvenile detention facilities are short-term secure units that house juveniles awaiting court hearings or adjudications. They are most similar to adult jails in operation; however, while adult jails also house criminals under sentence, juvenile detention centers are rarely used for this purpose. When a police officer detains a juvenile for an offense and decides to formally file charges, the juvenile is taken to a detention center. The juvenile may or may not be admitted into detention through a process called an intake, where detention staff or a probation officer processes the juvenile and makes a determination of whether to admit the juvenile into custody. Once a detention hearing is held (usually within 24 hours of arrest), a judge determines whether to continue the detention or release the juvenile. The original detention may continue beyond the adjudicatory and dispositional hearings while a juvenile is awaiting placement.

6. **Outline what is meant by a short-term secure facility**

   A short-term secure facility typically is used for two purposes, assessment and transition. Assessment involves diagnosing the juveniles under their care and determining the best placement for the juvenile within the system. Transition can include a transfer to another facility or pending release into the community.

7. **Describe what boot camps are designed to do**

   The boot camp correctional philosophy is essentially guided by the idea that juvenile delinquents need structure and discipline in their lives. Therefore, as in the military boot camps, the juvenile needs to be broken down and then built back up into a more productive citizen. The regimen at the juvenile correctional boot camps varies; however, the guiding principles are remarkably consistent and similar—strict discipline, structure, and tough love.

8. **Explain what youth ranches and camps are**

   Youth ranches and camps operate similarly to state institutions with one exception; the atmosphere is more like a year-round summer camp than it is a maximum-security facility. There are typically dorms or cottages, a school, vocational programs, and industry. The one component that sets them apart from other secure facilities is a program centering on some type of farming, ranching, or adventure. The idea is that youths need to be put in charge of responsibilities that come with running a farm or ranch to teach them there is more to life than being delinquent. The process of rehabilitating youths at these facilities is keyed on their active participation in the work that goes on at the facility.

9. **Summarize the nature of state institutions and schools**

   State institutions and schools are typically very self-contained and provide a variety of services for juveniles including rehabilitation, health, education, counseling, recreation, employment, and training. Historically, these facilities have been very large, housing up to 300 youth drawn from wide geographic regions of the state.

10. **Describe the various types of programming that occur in juvenile institutions**

    Programming in juvenile institutions includes correctional treatment, correctional education, correctional industry and vocational training, and various specialized treatment and programs.

KEY TERMS

commitment, p. 332

juvenile justice administrative body, p. 332

private facilities, p. 335

institutional facilities, p. 337

juvenile detention facilities, p. 339

assessment facility, p. 340

transfer or transitional facilities, p. 340

juvenile boot camps, p. 341

youth ranches and camps, p. 344

state institutions and schools, p. 345

rehabilitation, p. 346

deterrence, p. 346

incapacitation, p. 346

retribution, p. 346

REVIEW QUESTIONS

1. What are the various ways a juvenile can end up in a secure facility?

2. What are central juvenile correctional authorities? What is their purpose?

3. What are the differences between youths in public and private facilities?

4. What two classifications of youth do institutional facilities generally service?

5. Describe the nature and operation of juvenile detention facilities. What is the process of intake in detention facilities?

6. What are the roles and responsibilities of central assessment units?

7. What is the role of a transitional facility? Why is it important to operate transitional facilities?

8. What has the research found regarding the rate of recidivism in juvenile boot camps?

9. What are the differences between juvenile facility directors and prison wardens regarding the role of rehabilitation in corrections?

10. What are the four primary goals of corrections?

11. What are the common characteristics of the programs for serious or habitual offender juveniles?

12. What are some of the tasks or jobs that are routinely performed inside a secure juvenile state institution?

13. What is the difference between a role specialist and a role generalist?

HANDS-ON ACTIVITIES

1. **Visit a Secure Placement Facility** Schedule a class tour at a local secure placement facility for juveniles (state institution, youth ranch or camp, boot camp, or detention facility). What about the conditions in the facility is most surprising to you? What about the facility did you expect to see?

2. **Research a Boot Camp or Youth Ranch** Select a boot camp or youth ranch and prepare a research report. What is the mission of the camp or ranch? Include a description of the activities the youths engage in on a daily basis. Does the camp or ranch include family members? Are career skills encouraged? How successful is the program? Report your findings to the class.

INTERNET ACTIVITIES

1. Visit your state's central juvenile justice authority's website (or another state's if your state doesn't have a website) and find the following information: the number of state-run secure juvenile institutions, the number of juveniles that those facilities house, and the operating mission of juvenile corrections in these facilities. If your state's website doesn't have this information, several other states do. Are you surprised by the number of facilities or the number of juveniles under secure commitment? Is the operating philosophy of the juvenile correctional authority comparable to what you think it should be? Why or why not?

2. Visit OJJDP's site on Model Programs at **www2 .dsgonline.com.mpg** and find an example of a model correctional program in your state. What characteristics

of the program appear to fit into the criteria discussed in this chapter? How does the program compare to the other criteria and programs listed on the website?

CRITICAL THINKING EXERCISES

1. **Create a Mission Statement** Write a mission statement for a long-term, secure, state-operated juvenile correctional institution. Your mission statement should reflect the correctional goals you think will be most effective in preventing recidivism among the juveniles you serve. Be sure to list several goals and related objectives in your statement.

2. **Outline Criteria to Determine Juvenile Placement** Develop a list of criteria you would use to make a determination of whether a juvenile should be sent to a secure placement facility. Your criteria should examine the following variables: the offense

committed, the impact of the offense on the victim, the juvenile's criminal history, the juvenile's socio-demographic profile, the juvenile's psychological profile, and any other characteristics you deem relevant.

3. **Think about how Scandals in Juvenile Justice Programs (such as the TYC Sex Abuse Scandal) Have Resulted in Policy Changes** What steps do you think are most critical to eliminating the abuses of juvenile inmates? Do you think that the steps taken in Texas go far enough?

ANSWERS TO SELF-CHECKS

12.1 Self-Check

Explain the different ways a juvenile can be sent to an out-of-home placement.

There are several ways, including:
- Detention prior to adjudication.
- Commitment by a juvenile court to a secure placement.
- Placement in a secure facility by a juvenile justice administrative body or other social service agency. Secure placements can include short-term facilities such as detention centers or boot camps, and long-term facilities such as youth ranches or state institutions.

12.2 Self-Check

1. Describe the characteristics of juveniles who are sent to secure correctional facilities.

Recent trends have revealed that the number of cases that resulted in out-of-home placement rose from 104,800 to 163,200, an increase of 56 percent, in the period between 1988 and 1997. During the same period, the number of violent offenses resulting in placement grew 103 percent, placements for drug offense cases and public order offense cases each grew 77 percent, and placement for property offense cases grew 27 percent. However, the overall proportion of cases that were placed out-of-home declined from 31 percent to 28 percent.

2. Explain the nature of the differences between public and private juvenile correctional facilities.

Most juveniles in public facilities (96 percent) are held there by court order under a delinquency adjudication. They are much more likely to have committed violent offenses, property offenses, and technical violations of probation agreements. Most juveniles in private facilities, which are facilities that are run by private corporations or private individuals, are either status offenders (14 percent) or nonoffenders (41 percent). In addition, many more status offenders are housed in private facilities as opposed to public ones (5,094 versus 1,782, respectively).

3. Which organization oversees the placement of juvenile delinquents?

In most states, the placement of juvenile delinquents is handled by a central juvenile correctional authority which also governs the administration and operation of juvenile correctional facilities in the state.

12.3 Self-Check

1. Describe the various types of secure correctional facilities to which a juvenile can be sent.

Juvenile detention facilities are short-term secure units that house juveniles awaiting court hearings or adjudications. There are other types of short-term secure facilities: the assessment facility is responsible for orienting the juvenile to the correctional system, and transfer or transitional facilities are for juveniles who are being transferred from a community placement to a secure unit or vice versa. A juvenile boot camp is a secure correctional facility that emphasizes military-style discipline, physical training, and an extremely regimented schedule. Youth ranches and camps are similar to the wilderness and adventure programs discussed in Chapter 11; the differences are that they are secure, and the youths remain there until paroled. State institutions and schools are typically large, very self-contained facilities that accommodate up to 300 youths.

2. Explain the different nature of each type of correctional facility.

- Juvenile detention facilities are most similar to adult jails in operation, but unlike adult jails, juvenile detention centers rarely also house delinquents under sentence.
- Assessment facilities are responsible for orienting the juvenile to the correctional system in that particular state and what the expectations are, and for conducting testing and diagnosis.
- Transfer or transitional facilities are used when bed space is limited in other facilities to which juveniles await placement or transfer. Juveniles in these facilities will find very few programs, education, or other training.
- The guiding principles of juvenile boot camps, which are modeled after military boot camps, are strict discipline and structure combined with tough love.
- Youth ranches and camps operate similarly to state institutions, except that the atmosphere is more like a year-round summer camp than it is a maximum-security facility.
- State institutions and schools provide a variety of services for juveniles including rehabilitation, health, education, counseling, recreation, and employment and training.

12.4 Self-Check

Describe the various types of correctional programming available in juvenile facilities.
These types are:
- Correctional education: Educational programs in juvenile facilities often serve as the core program, consuming the largest portion of time.
- Correctional industry and vocational training: Many facilities develop internships, apprenticeships, and mentorships with these business partners.
- Specialized treatment and programs: Specialized treatment includes programs designed specifically for the treatment of capital offenders, sex offenders, chemically dependent youth, youth with emotional disturbances, and mentally retarded youth.
- Programs for serious and repeat juvenile offenders: These small, intensive programs are welldefined, with a strong intuitive appeal; have demonstrated

positive effects on the youth; and have a strong following among judges and correctional administrators who work with the programs.

12.5 Self-Check

1. What problems do juveniles experience in adapting to institutional life?
Most prominent among juveniles' difficulties in adjusting are:
- The structured life and programs in the facilities that dictate how juveniles will spend their time, since most juveniles who are committed are used to having more free time than structured programming.
- The emotional, social, and psychological problems that juveniles bring with them into the facility. All youths in secure placement have these problems, and few, if any, have ever examined themselves.
- Educational, recreational, and vocational treatment. Juveniles in secure placement typically have learning dysfunctions, have never held a serious job of any kind, and do not know or understand how to participate appropriately in group recreational activity. Although some juveniles conform rapidly and remain in full compliance with the program throughout their stay, the vast majority will experience successes and failures before they become in full compliance with the program.

2. What problems do juveniles experience when they are released from an institution?
Often, juveniles show "institutionalized" behavior upon release: They are so used to strict structure and programming that the transition to the community is difficult. Also, juveniles are typically returned to the environment that contributed to their problems in the first place. In short, the freedom that juveniles long for is often their worst enemy upon release.

12.6 Self-Check

1. Explain the difference between task specialization and task generalization in juvenile correctional facilities.
Larger facilities tend to have role specialists, who focus on one or two specialized roles. Smaller facilities tend to have role generalists, who perform a variety of tasks.

2. Explain the differences between adult prison wardens and juvenile correctional facility directors.
Juvenile facility directors placed a greater emphasis on rehabilitation counseling and programs. Both placed an equal degree of emphasis on maintaining institutional order and on inmate behavior. Prison wardens reported a higher emphasis on punishment, preventing escapes, and preventing the flow of contraband into and within the facility.

GANGS AND DELINQUENCY

Chapter Outline

Chapter Objectives

After completing this chapter, you should be able to:

1. Explain the difficulties in accurately defining a gang, gang member, and gang-related crime.

2. Describe the extent of the gang problem.

3. Differentiate between types of gangs.

4. Identify the major characteristics of gangs.

5. Explain why youths join gangs.

6. Describe the major responses to gangs.

7. Summarize efforts to control gang activity.

Gangs in Society

Gang violence and the media frenzy that envelops such acts has led to widespread attention being paid to street gangs and policies to deal with them since the middle 1980s. While gangs have existed throughout history, the theoretical and political attention paid to them has increased and decreased over time. While there was a great deal of attention paid to gangs in the 1950s and early 1960s, little attention was paid to this social problem in the late 1960s and 1970s. Concern about gangs returned to the forefront of juvenile justice and American policy in the 1980s and continues today. This heightened concern grew for several reasons:

1. the emergence of youth gangs in small and rural communities;
2. the increased diversity of gang composition;
3. the increased use of highly dangerous weapons and the higher level of violence; and
4. the controversy surrounding the role of gangs in drug trafficking.[1]

The word *gang* has been the most commonly used term to label certain groups considered to be major social problems. The gang-related issues facing American society today are not all that new; in fact, many of the theoretical and political debates surrounding gangs are simply variations on a theme argued for some time now.[2]

The question of what to do about gangs has equally puzzled law enforcement and policymakers. The simple fact that gangs have existed for so long tells us that there is no simple solution. As law enforcement adopts new strategies to deal with gangs, the gangs respond by becoming more sophisticated in the manner in which they conduct their business. Gangs have changed throughout history and generally reflect the social and economic conditions of society.

Gangs are defined in many different ways. Many states define gangs by law. *Do the youths appear to fit the definition of a gang? What external characteristics do these youth display that makes them appear to be a gang?*

Periods of gang expansion seem to correlate with other transitional periods in U.S. history. For example, gang activity increased during the Industrial Revolution, Prohibition, wartime, and, more recently, during the transition from an industrial to an information society. The reasons underlying these booms are debatable. Since the middle 1980s, gangs have become more violent, more prevalent, and less susceptible to traditional law enforcement intervention.

This chapter will examine several issues related to gangs. We will discuss what is a gang, who is a gang member, and what is gang-related crime. Next, we will look at the extent of the gang problem in the United States and the types of gangs. Several key characteristics of gangs will be highlighted, including age, race and ethnicity, gender, gang migration, communication, and delinquent activity. Finally, approaches to control gang activity will be discussed, especially efforts by law enforcement officers, prosecutors, and legislators.

Defining Gangs

When the term *gang* or *gang member* is used, an image is projected in people's minds. The actual definitions of these terms are as varied as people's mental images. However, the definitions of these terms are vitally important. As we will discuss later in this chapter, gang members may receive more severe penalties for their offenses than nongang members. Therefore, it is crucial to be able to accurately define these terms. In fact, some state legislatures have made it illegal simply to be a gang member.

> ### 13.1 SELF-CHECK
>
> What circumstances caused members of the juvenile justice system to renew their concern about gangs?

> ## JUVENILE JUSTICE ONLINE
>
> Go to www.nationalgangcenter.gov/ Legislation, and under the subheading Gang-Related Legislation, click on Gang, Gang Crime, and Gang Member Definitions. What similarities and differences do you observe in how gangs, gang members, and gang-related crime are defined in different states?

It is difficult to accurately define the term *gang member*. What characteristics of the person lead you to believe he is a gang member? Are some of those characteristics also exhibited by nongang members?

FIGURE 13.1	State Statutory Definitions of the Term "Gang"

Arizona §13–105(7)

"Criminal street gang" means an ongoing formal or informal association of persons whose members or associates individually or collectively engage in the commission, attempted commission, facilitation or solicitation of any felony act and who have at least one individual who is a criminal street gang member.

CALIFORNIA §186.22(F)

"Criminal street gang" means any ongoing organization, association, or group of three or more persons, whether formal or informal, having as one of its primary activities the commission of one or more of the criminal acts enumerated in paragraphs (1) to (25), inclusive, or (31) to (33), inclusive, of subdivision (e), having a common name or common identifying sign or symbol, and whose members individually or collectively engage in or have engaged in a pattern of criminal gang activity.

CONNECTICUT 29–7N

"Gang" means a group of juveniles or youth who, acting in concert with each other, or with adults, engage in illegal activities.

NEVADA 193.168 (8)

"Criminal gang" means any combination of persons, organized formally or informally, so constructed that the organization will continue its operation even if individual members enter or leave the organization, which

(a) has a common name or identifying symbol
(b) has particular conduct, status and customs indicative of it
(c) has as one of its common activities engaging in criminal activity punishable as a felony, other than the conduct which constitutes the primary offense

WHAT IS A GANG?

While it is clear that gangs exist in today's society, there is very little consensus about how a **gang** should be defined. *Webster's Collegiate Dictionary* defines a gang as "a group of persons working to unlawful or antisocial ends, especially a band of antisocial adolescents," but there is not one single definition of a gang that everyone uses. Definitions vary in terms of their scope, range, and complexity—and whether or not delinquent behavior is a defining characteristic or a manifestation of the group. Here are two distinctive definitions of a gang:

1. Michael W. Klein, in his text *Street Gangs and Street Workers*, defined a gang as any denotable adolescent group of youngsters who (a) are generally perceived as a distinct aggregation by others in their neighborhood, (b) recognize themselves as a denotable group, and (c) have been involved in a sufficient number of delinquent incidents to call forth a consistent negative response from neighborhood residents and/or enforcement agencies.[3]
2. Walter B. Miller, in his article "Gangs, Groups, and Serious Youth Crime," defined a gang as a self-formed association of peers, bound together by mutual interests, with identifiable leadership, well-defined lines of authority, and other organizational features, who act in concert to achieve a specific purpose or purposes which generally include illegal activity and control over a particular territory, facility, or type of enterprise.[4]

These two definitions vary considerably. Klein's definition focuses more on the external factors in defining a gang such as community recognition and law enforcement response. On the other hand, Miller's definition focuses almost exclusively on the internal dynamics of a gang, including leadership and lines of authority. Klein's definition is much broader than the definition provided by Miller; Klein's would allow more youth groups to be classified as gangs.

Many states have defined gangs by law. This is necessary in those states that impose more severe punishments on gang members than on nongang members or that make gang membership illegal. Figure 13.1 depicts a few examples of how states have defined gangs. Once again, the definitions are quite variable. For example, Connecticut defines a gang as basically any group of juveniles who commit delinquent acts. Since much juvenile delinquency is committed in groups, a large number of groups could be classified as gangs using this definition. Other definitions are more restrictive, requiring that the delinquent activity must be a felony.

What is clear from the above definitions is that everyone has not and probably will not agree on a single definition. This is particularly true for issues such

gang Any denotable group of adolescents working to unlawful or antisocial ends.

| FIGURE 13.2 | Statutory Definitions of Gang Members |

ARIZONA (ARIZ. REV. STAT. ANN. § 13–105 (9))

"Criminal street gang member" means an individual to whom two of the following seven criteria that indicate criminal street gang membership apply:

    (a)　Self-proclamation.

    (b)　Witness testimony or official statement.

    (c)　Written or electronic correspondence.

    (d)　Paraphernalia or photographs.

    (e)　Tattoos.

    (f)　Clothing or colors.

    (g)　Any other indicia of street gang membership.

FLORIDA (FLA. STAT. ANN. § 874.03 (3))

"Criminal gang member" is a person who meets two or more of the following criteria:

    (a)　Admits to criminal gang membership.

    (b)　Is identified as a criminal gang member by a parent or guardian.

    (c)　Is identified as a criminal gang member by a documented reliable informant.

    (d)　Adopts the style of dress of a criminal gang.

    (e)　Adopts the use of a handsign identified as used by a criminal gang.

    (f)　Has a tattoo identified as used by a criminal gang.

    (g)　Associates with one or more known criminal gang members.

    (h)　Is identified as a criminal gang member by an informant of previously untested reliability and such identification is corroborated by independent information.

    (i)　Is identified as a criminal gang member by physical evidence.

    (j)　Has been observed in the company of known criminal gang members four or more times.

    (k)　Has authored any communication indicating responsibility for the commission of any crime by the criminal gang.

as how many members does it take to form a gang, what level of organization is necessary to be called a gang, and what level of delinquency, if any, is necessary to be defined as a gang.

How a gang is defined has implications for theory and policy. Popular definitions of gangs might lead to allocating resources in delinquency prevention and correctional treatment erroneously.[5] In other words, how a gang is defined has implications for how jurisdictions, such as state and local governments, react to and deal with gangs. Further, jurisdictions have to be careful in the formulation and application of gang laws because of the long history of over-inclusiveness in American justice. For example, the history of the juvenile court shows that well-intentioned statutes can have the effect of leaving too much discretion in the hands of justice officials. For juvenile justice, this meant that a juvenile charged with an offense was subjected to incarceration while an adult charged with the same offense might only face a fine and minimal jail time. Too many juveniles who were not seriously delinquent were caught in the wide discretionary net the state legislatures left open. Similarly, if a gang statute is overly broad, prosecutors who are trying to be "tough" on delinquency could target and prosecute individuals who don't really belong to a gang or members who associate with others in a gang-like group which is not really a gang, either. We have many negative examples of what widening the net does to the justice system. It is possible that the reactions of authorities to youths whom they perceive, whether justifiedly or not, as gang members can intensify the delinquency of the youths.[6]

WHO IS A GANG MEMBER?

At what point does an individual become a **gang member?** Research on gangs has concluded that *very few* youths are actually hard-core gang members.[7] It is difficult to distinguish gang members from nongang members because the criteria used to distinguish the two groups are not very clear-cut. Definitions of gang members used in Arizona and Florida in Figure 13.2 show that individuals can be identified as gang members if the individuals state they are a gang member (self-proclamation) and they are wearing particular clothing or colors. These criteria are not very helpful because nongang members frequently emulate the clothing style of gang members and may claim membership even if not a gang member. In fact, many states include gang membership criteria such as "self-admission" and identification from "other gang members" as a determining factor of who is and who is not in a gang. Indeed, many individuals believe most gang members are peripheral, transitory, or **wannabes.**

gang member An individual who actively participates in the activities of a gang.

wannabe A young individual who wants to be a gang member and emulates the behavior of gang members.

Several states have defined criteria for determining who is a gang member. These criteria are often used to impose additional penalties on those who fit the criteria or to sanction them for mere participation in a gang. Being a gang member can carry with it severe penalties. For example, a gang member in California can receive up to a three-year sentence in prison for participating in a gang.[8]

WHY DO YOUTHS JOIN GANGS?

We will examine three prominent reasons why youths join gangs.

1. Gangs provide youths with an opportunity to associate with their peers and to obtain a sense of belongingness. Many gang members have reported that they joined gangs to be affiliated with their friends because a number of their friends were already gang members.[9] Adolescence is a time when youths place a higher priority on their relationships with their peers than with their parents. People with friends who are gang members will be pulled into joining a gang. In addition, many youths may not feel a sense of attachment and belongingness with their families. Joining a gang may give some youths a sense of belongingness unavailable in their families, plus the gang may provide an opportunity to gain respect and status from their peers.

2. Youths join gangs because of the prospect of obtaining money through the commission of delinquent acts such as burglary and distributing drugs.[10] Many gangs exist in low-income areas where the prospect of adequate legitimate employment is limited. Therefore, joining a gang becomes an attractive option to make money. Furthermore, committing delinquent acts can produce quick profits, which is consistent with many adolescents' desire for immediate self-gratification.

3. Youths join gangs because they are seeking protection from other youths in the community.[11] The adage that "there is strength in numbers" applies here. Many potential gang members live in neighborhoods that are riddled with rival gangs and violence. In these areas, it is assumed that most youths are affiliated with gangs even if they are not. This puts pressure on youths to join gangs for protection. On the basis of where a youth lives, a rival gang may assume that the youth is a gang member. In fact, many youths have reported joining a gang because they got tired of being accused of being a gang member by other gangs.[12] Author James D. Vigil quoted a 14-year-old gang member as stating, "It was either get your ass kicked every day or join a gang and get your ass kicked occasionally by rival gangs."[13]

WHAT IS GANG-RELATED CRIME?

No matter how gangs and gang members are defined, there is concern about what is meant by **gang-related crime**. Authors Cheryl L. Maxson and Malcolm W. Klein researched the inherent difficulties in defining gang-related crime by examining differences in gang-related homicides between two jurisdictions.[14] The Los Angeles Police Department and Chicago Police Department use different definitions of what gang-related crime is as well as what is gang-related homicide. Los Angeles classifies a homicide as gang-related *if a gang member is a victim or an offender.* Chicago classifies only those homicides *with a gang-related motive* as *a gang-related homicide.* Therefore, the Chicago Police Department uses a *narrower* definition of gang-related homicide than the Los Angeles Police Department. This research determined that about half of the gang-related homicides in Los Angeles would not be similarly classified as gang-related in Chicago.[15] These differences in how terms are defined are important

Gang-related Homicides

In a typical year in the so-called "gang capitals" of Chicago and Los Angeles, around half of all homicides are gang-related; these two cities alone accounted for approximately one in five gang homicides recorded in the National Youth Gang Survey from 2010 to 2011.

Source: National Gang Center. *National Youth Gang Survey Analysis.* http://www.nationalgangcenter.gov/Survey-Analysis. Retrieved July 23, 2013.

gang-related crime Acts of delinquency in which the offender or the victim is a gang member.

because the amount of gang-related crime in a jurisdiction affects public perception of crime generally and the gang problem specifically in the community.

These differences reveal related issues. For instance, if an individual is a gang member, are all of the offenses he or she commits gang-related? Should only collective delinquent events be considered gang-related? In other words, should offenses that are committed only in groups be characterized as gang-related? Further, if an individual uses his or her gang reputation to commit individual offenses, should these acts be considered gang-related?

Some states have, by passing laws or statutes, enacted definitions of what constitutes gang-related crime. For example, in Illinois, *street gang-related* or *gang-related* means:

> any criminal activity, enterprise, pursuit, or undertaking directed by, ordered by, authorized by, consented to, agreed to, requested by, acquiesced in, or ratified by any gang leader, officer, or governing or policy-making person or authority, or by any agent, representative, or deputy of any officer, person, or authority: (1) with the intent to increase the gang's size, membership, prestige, dominance, or control in any geographical area; or (2) with the intent to provide the gang with any advantage in, or any control or dominance over any criminal market sector, including but not limited to, the manufacture, delivery, or sale of controlled substances or cannabis; arson or arson-for-hire; traffic in stolen property or stolen credit cards; traffic in prostitution, obscenity, or pornography; or that involves robbery, burglary, or theft; or (3) with the intent to exact revenge or retribution for the gang or any member of the gang; or (4) with the intent to obstruct justice, or intimidate or eliminate any witness against the gang or any member of the gang; or (5) with the intent to otherwise directly or indirectly cause any benefit, aggrandizement, gain, profit or other advantage whatsoever to or for the gang, its reputation, influence, or membership.[16]

As we have seen, there is no single definition of a gang, gang member, or gang-related crime. Although many state legislatures have defined these terms by law, the majority of jurisdictions develop their own definitions of these terms. Therefore, the term *gang* may be defined differently by the Minneapolis Police Department versus the Detroit Police Department. Although a mental image develops when these terms are mentioned in conversation, there is no agreed-upon definition for any of these terms.

The Extent of the Gang Problem

It is difficult to accurately estimate the number of gangs and gang members in the United States because of the different ways gangs are defined. What one jurisdiction defines as a gang and gang member may not be similarly labeled in another jurisdiction. Given these differences, the National Youth Gang Center's 2011 Survey surveyed more than 2,500 local police and sheriff's departments across the nation to obtain information about the presence of youth gangs and related delinquent activity.[17] About 85 percent of the agencies responded to the

Myth / Fact

Myth: All gangs frequently commit violent crimes.

Fact: Only 28 percent of gangs have a high degree of involvement in aggravated assault, only 13 percent in robbery.

Source: Office of Juvenile Justice and Delinquency Prevention. *1997 National Youth Gang Survey.* Washington, DC: Office of Juvenile Justice and Delinquency Prevention, 1999.

13.2 SELF-CHECK

1. Explain why defining gangs is so important.
2. Name three reasons why young people join gangs.

Myth / Fact

Myth: Gangs exist only in large cities.

Fact: More than 31% of cities with less than 50,000 population report that active youth gangs exist in their communities.

Source: National Gang Center. *National Youth Gang Survey Analysis.* http://www.nationalgangcenter .gov/Survey-Analysis. Retrieved July 23, 2013.

survey. The respondents estimated a total of 29,400 gangs and 756,000 gang members active in their jurisdictions (see Figure 13.3).[18]

Although these totals on the number of gangs and gang members in the nation are large, the actual numbers are likely to be higher. Not all law enforcement agencies were surveyed, and some of those surveyed did not participate. Therefore, we can reasonably assume that the youth gang problem is undoubtedly larger than the survey indicates.

Respondents to the National Youth Gang Survey estimated that 42 percent of their youth gangs were involved in the street sale of drugs and 33 percent were involved in drug distribution for the specific purpose of generating profits for the gang.[19] Respondents also said that gang members were responsible for:

- 33 percent of crack cocaine sales;
- 32 percent of marijuana sales;
- 16 percent of powder cocaine sales;
- 12 percent of methamphetamine sales; and
- 9 percent of heroin sales.[20]

13.3 SELF-CHECK

How many youth gangs and youth gang members are there in the United States?

Of the responding agencies reporting gang problems, 54 percent characterized their gang problem as staying about the same in 2011 while 31 percent indicated that their local gang problems were getting worse, leaving only 15 percent who felt the gang problem was improving.[21] The study concluded that no state is gang-free; few large cities are gang-free; and youth gangs are emerging in new localities.[22]

| FIGURE 13.3 | Gang Members Per Capita by State |

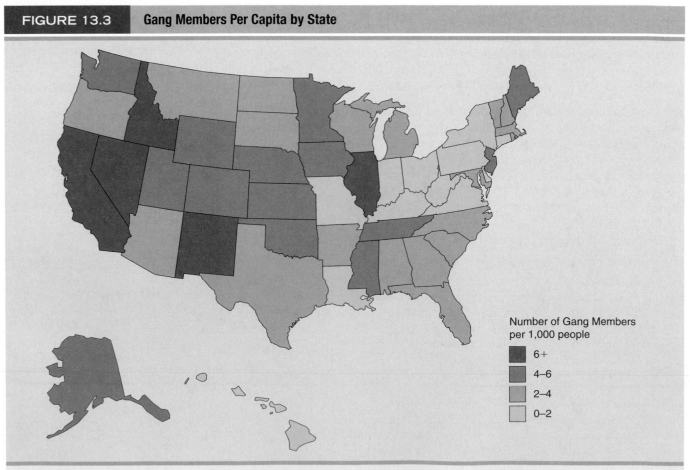

Number of Gang Members per 1,000 people

- 6+
- 4–6
- 2–4
- 0–2

Source: *National Gang Threat Assessment 2011*. National Gang Intelligence Center. Washington DC. www.fbi.gov/stats-services/publications/2011-national-gang-threat-assessment

Types of Gangs

There are many different types of gangs. Gangs are typically divided into categories based on their activity. C. Ronald Huff identified three major types of gangs in "Youth Gangs and Public Policy," his study of gangs in Cleveland and Columbus, Ohio.

- **Hedonistic gangs** are primarily involved in using drugs and getting high with little involvement in delinquency.[23] These types of gangs almost never commit acts of violence. Therefore, most of their activity involves partying and committing minor violations of the law.
- **Instrumental gangs** are primarily involved in committing property offenses such as burglary, auto theft, and theft. In addition, members in these types of gangs are actively involved in using drugs but seldom sell drugs.[24] Members in these types of gangs commit more serious offenses than members of hedonistic gangs, but members of both types rarely commit acts of violence.
- **Predatory gangs** are the most serious type of gang and are actively involved in serious offenses including violent crimes such as robbery. Members of these types of gangs are actively involved in using drugs such as crack cocaine, and many engage in selling drugs as well.[25] These are the most serious types of gangs.

While predatory gangs are the most stereotypical gang as portrayed in the media, they are the *least* prevalent. In other words, while many perceive that most gangs can be classified as predatory gangs, in comparison to the other types of gangs, predatory gangs are relatively *few* in number. However, gangs such as the Crips, Bloods, and Vice Lords certainly fit into this predatory category. These types of gangs are involved in polycrime, or multiple crime, and polydrug activity. They are actively involved in committing several different types of crime and using and distributing several different drugs.

OTHER CATEGORIES OF GANGS

Another typology was developed by Cheryl Maxson and Malcolm Klein. They categorized gangs based on their size, age range, duration of existence, territory, and delinquent acts.

1. The **traditional gang** is very large with perhaps as many as several hundred members. These gangs have been in existence for over 20 years and have members that range in age from 10 to over 30. These gangs are primarily territorial and have a well-defined turf.[26] This type of gang is typical of Hispanic gangs in large metropolitan areas such as Los Angeles.
2. The **neotraditional gang** is similar to the traditional gang but is smaller and newer than the traditional gang.[27] If the neotraditional gang stays in existence long enough, it may evolve into a traditional gang.
3. The **compressed gang** is usually a relatively new gang with less than 50 members around the same age. These gangs do not have a defined territory.[28] Compressed gangs are believed to be the most prevalent gangs in the United States. These gangs are not traditionally involved in serious acts of delinquency but participate in a gang for its social relationships.
4. The **collective gang** does not have many of the characteristics of the prior three types of gangs.[29] These gangs usually have a short history and may take on some of the characteristics of the other gangs.
5. The **specialty gang** is usually actively involved in serious delinquent activity including drug trafficking. The first four types of gangs have been more social than delinquent; however, specialty gangs are just the opposite. These gangs typically have a narrow age range of members and are usually smaller in size than traditional gangs. These gangs also have a

hedonistic gang A type of gang identified by Huff that is primarily involved in using drugs and getting high with little involvement in crime.

instrumental gang A type of gang identified by Huff that is primarily involved in committing property crime and is actively involved in using drugs.

predatory gang A type of gang identified by Huff that is actively involved in committing serious crimes including violent crime and selling drugs.

traditional gang A type of gang identified by Maxson and Klein that has as many as several hundred members and has been in existence for over 20 years. The gang has a well-defined territory and has members that range in age from 10 to over 30.

neotraditional gang A type of gang identified by Maxson and Klein that is smaller and newer than the traditional gang (see traditional gang).

compressed gang A type of gang identified by Maxson and Klein that is a relatively new gang with less than 50 members around the same age. The gang does not have a defined territory.

collective gang A type of gang identified by Maxson and Klein that has a short history, limited size, and little defined territory.

specialty gang A type of gang identified by Maxson and Klein that has a well-defined territory, has a narrow age range of members, and is small in size. The gang is actively involved in serious criminal activity including drug trafficking

defined territory that may be used for drug trafficking or other delinquent activities.[30]

The *least prevalent* types of gangs are the last two: collective and specialty gangs. As previously stated, the stereotypical gang is one that is actively involved in drug distribution and violence, but these types of gangs are actually relatively *few* in number in comparison to other types of gangs.

Characteristics of Gangs

Six major characteristics of gangs will be discussed: age, race and ethnicity, gender, gang migration, communication, and delinquent activity.

AGE

Gang members have typically been seen as being juveniles. Youths become interested in gang activity during their preteen years. Research has shown that juveniles first learn about gangs at about 9 years of age, get involved in violence about 10 or 11 years of age, and join a gang soon thereafter, usually by the age of 12.[31] Therefore, gang participation usually begins in adolescence. But what happens to juvenile gang members once they become adults?

Traditionally, once the juvenile gang member reached adulthood, he or she would stop participating in a gang and take on adult responsibilities such as employment and family. However, evidence has emerged that more and more gang members are continuing their participation in gangs into adulthood. What was once considered a juvenile phenomenon has become an adult problem as well. In fact, several police departments now report that the majority of the gang members in their jurisdiction are adults over the age of 18. Respondents to the National Youth Gang Survey reported less than 35 percent of the gang members in their jurisdictions were juveniles while over 65 percent were adults.[32]

Two primary reasons are cited for the change in age of gang members. First, the dramatic changes in the economic structure of the United States have had a significant impact. In particular, the decline in manufacturing jobs in the United States has been cited as the primary reason for the increasing age of gang members.[33] Manufacturing jobs typically require few skills but pay relatively well. These types of jobs were common in the 1950s, 1960s, and 1970s, but began to dramatically decline in many cities by the end of the century. There has been a dramatic increase in service jobs in the United States. The service jobs most gang members are able to obtain usually require few skills, but the pay is not high enough to attract juvenile gang members away from the gang.

Second, the increased emphasis on drug dealing has led to a stable supply of money into gangs. Gangs are more profit oriented today than in the past. The stable supply of money and the lack of employment alternatives outside of the gang have led to few options for gang members who want to leave the gang once they become adults. Instead, many gang members are continuing their participation into their twenties, thirties, and even forties.

RACE AND ETHNICITY

No racial or ethnic group is excluded from gang participation; gang members include Caucasian, African-American, Hispanic, and Asian members. According to the National Youth Gang Survey, it is estimated that 35 percent of gang members are African-American, 46 percent are Hispanic, 7 percent are Asian, and 12 percent are white.[34] Typically, gangs are racially or ethnically homogenous. In other words, most Hispanic gangs have only Hispanic members while most

No racial or ethnic group is excluded from gang participation. *What types of criminal activities do you think Asian gang members are likely to participate in?*

Asian gangs have only Asian members. However, the homogeneity of gangs varies from community to community. In cities such as Los Angeles and Chicago, gangs are usually racially and ethnically segregated, while gangs in Miami have a tendency to be racially mixed.[35] Despite these differences, most gangs are racially or ethnically homogeneous and most gang offenses are intraethnic. The conflict between gangs usually involves gangs of the same racial or ethnic background.

Female gang participation occurs more frequently than previously believed. *What association and relationship do female gangs have with male gangs?*

GENDER—FEMALES AND GANGS

Until recently, most research on gangs focused on male participation. The traditional role of females in gangs was to form an auxiliary unit to the male gang. Usually, the auxiliary female gang would take on a feminized version of the male gang name. For example, the **female auxiliary gang** for the Vice Lords is known as the Vice Queens. Traditionally, the role of females in gangs has been limited to acting as lookouts for male gang members who were committing delinquent acts, carrying guns and drugs, and being the girlfriends of the male gang members.

Over time, research has been conducted on female participation in gangs, which modified the traditional perspective of females in gangs. It was once thought that female participation in gangs was rare. It is estimated that about 7 percent of all gang members in this country are females.[36] However, data from the Rochester Youth Development Study has shown that females are even more likely to participate in gangs than males. Of the respondents, 22 percent of the females reported gang participation while 18 percent of the males reported the same.[37] Furthermore, it is argued that female gang members have become much more involved in drug use and delinquent activity. Writers Beth Bjerregaard and Carolyn Smith found that female gang members are just as likely to have previously participated in drug use and delinquent activity, but male gang members usually commit these acts more frequently.[38] Finally, there has been a trend in recent years toward the formation of autonomous female gangs without ties to a male gang. Although auxiliary gangs are still the most prevalent form of female gangs, it has been found that these gangs are much more independent from the male gangs than previously thought. They frequently have their own leadership, meetings, and rules, and make their own decisions on membership.

GANG MIGRATION

In the past 25 years, many communities have experienced gang problems for the first time. Most of the gangs in these communities are "homegrown." In other words, the gang is established in the community without any support or interference from gangs in other jurisdictions. However, some argue that the majority of the gang proliferation in the past several years is due to **gang migration**. There are two basic perspectives on gang migration:

1. One perspective is that established gangs from major cities such as Los Angeles and Chicago have migrated to other areas of the country in order to set up local chapters for drug distribution. This argument hypothesizes that gangs such as the Bloods and Crips from Los Angeles are highly organized gangs with the capability to develop a nationwide drug distribution network. Because of the need to expand drug distribution territory, these gangs move to other cities to establish chapters. The gang recruits local youths to deal drugs for the gang in exchange for membership. However, most of the empirical evidence of this type of gang migration is anecdotal and based on the fact that gangs in communities throughout the country are using the same names and colors as gangs from Los Angeles and Chicago.
2. Another perspective is that most migration of gangs is accidental rather than purposeful. It usually occurs under two circumstances. First, a gang member's family relocates to another city. The gang member then develops a chapter of his previous gang in the new city. The gang member may or may not maintain contact with his fellow gang members from where he moved. Therefore, the existence of gangs such as the Bloods, Crips, and Vice Lords in cities that have not previously experienced a gang problem is often due to the fact that a gang member from Los Angeles, Chicago, or some other major city has moved to the community. Second, a group of youths from a city with minimal to no prior exposure to gangs decides to

female auxiliary gang A female gang that is affiliated with a male gang and generally takes on a feminized version of the male gang's name.

gang migration The movement of gangs from large metropolitan areas such as Los Angeles and Chicago to other areas of the country.

establish a gang and borrow the name, colors, and other identifying symbols from the Crips, Bloods, Vice Lords, etc. This occurs in rural areas and communities with little prior gang activity. This is sometimes known as the "Copy Cat" phenomenon.[39] These individuals are considered renegades because they are independent gang members with no recognized connection to the same gang in other areas.[40]

In the 2010 National Youth Gang Survey, respondents rated a number of factors pertaining to their influence on gang member migration in their jurisdictions. Almost 47 percent of the respondents stated that gang member migration was due to social reasons.[41] Social reasons included concerns and efforts to improve quality of life, including moves with family for employment and/or educational opportunities. The remaining factors influencing migration included drug market opportunities (14 percent), to avoid law enforcement crackdowns (13 percent), other illegal ventures (10 percent), and to get away from gang life (6 percent).[42]

Based on the data from the survey, the following conclusions were drawn:

"These findings, coupled with the substantially lower prevalence rate of gang activity in smaller areas, strongly suggest that on the whole, gang member migration is far more the exception than the rule outside urban areas, and if present, gang member migrants are usually but a small part of the total gang population, have likely moved to the area for legitimate reasons, and have no prominent impact on local gang offenses."[43]

COMMUNICATION

Gangs want recognition from rival gangs as well as from the larger community. In order to gain recognition in the community, gangs must be able to effectively communicate. Gangs primarily communicate through **graffiti**, tattoos, hand signs, and clothing. Graffiti can be found in every large city in the United States and many smaller communities. Gangs use graffiti to identify their existence, to mark their territory, to challenge rival gangs, and to remember deceased

graffiti Public markings used by gang members to identify their existence.

Graffiti is one of the primary ways gangs communicate. *Why do gangs like using this method of communication?*

gang members. Graffiti is primarily used by gang members to communicate to rival gang members. It is used to let others know that a particular territory is under the control of a particular gang. Graffiti usually contains the gang's name or **logo**.[44] A logo is a descriptive emblem used to identify the gang and may include a group of Roman numerals, the gang's initials, or a picture or symbol such as a pitchfork, crown, or Playboy bunny.[45] In addition to the gang's name or logo, graffiti will usually include the nickname, or moniker, of the gang member who wrote the graffiti. Graffiti is used to mark the gang's territory and to notify rival gangs of territorial boundaries. Territorial areas that are disputed will frequently have "cross-outs" where one gang's graffiti will be crossed out by a rival gang and that gang's name or symbol will take its place.

Many, although not all, gang members will openly display signs of their membership in a gang. This is usually done through tattooing, flashing hand signs, and/or adopting a particular style of dress. Traditional Hispanic gangs use tattoos extensively. The tattoos frequently include the gang member's name or moniker and the name of their gang.[46] The tattoos are usually placed on the arms, hands, or shoulders. Another method of gang communication is the flashing of **hand signs**. The hand signs are designed to identify the user with a particular gang.[47] The flashing of hand signs between rival gangs can escalate into violence. In fact, inter-gang violence is frequently preceded by the flashing of hand signs.

Gang members also identify their gang affiliation by adopting a particular style of dress including wearing particular **colors**. Colors are designed to demonstrate the youth's affiliation with a particular gang. For example, Blood gang members typically wear an article of clothing that is red. It can be a hat or shirt or even a smaller piece of clothing such as a bandana or a shoelace. Many nongang members adopt a similar style of dress as gang members, which makes it difficult to differentiate between gang and nongang members on the basis of dress alone.

DELINQUENT ACTIVITY

There is little doubt that gang members commit more delinquent acts than nongang members. Bjerregaard and Smith found that gang members are more likely than nongang members to have committed delinquent acts and to have used alcohol and marijuana.[48] For example, they found that over 73 percent of gang youths studied had committed a serious delinquent act such as burglary and auto theft, while less than 9 percent of the nongang youths had previously committed such an act.

It is difficult to specify the delinquent activity committed by gang members because it varies by the type of gang. As previously mentioned, the majority of gangs do not actively participate in drug trafficking and violence, although these are the stereotypical offenses associated with all gangs. In fact, some gangs specialize in a particular type of offense such as extortion while other gangs can be classified as generalists, committing several different types of offenses such as theft, burglary, and vandalism. Some gangs are actively involved in distributing drugs while others are not. Some gang members do commit drive-by shootings, but in reality these offenses are rare among gang members in comparison to other offenses they commit.

It should be noted that most gang members do not spend the majority of their time committing delinquent acts. The gang members studied by Hagedorn spent the majority of their time "partying and hanging out."[49] When gang members do commit delinquent acts, it is typically a property offense such as theft or a less serious violent offense such as assault. The issue is not whether gang members commit delinquent acts, it is how much delinquency they commit. The involvement of gangs in drug use is also highly variable. Jeffrey Fagan

13.5 SELF-CHECK

What factors account for gang migration?

logo A descriptive emblem used to identify a gang and may include a group of Roman numerals, the gang's initials, or a picture or a symbol such as a pitchfork, crown, or Playboy bunny.

hand sign A method of communication used by gang members which identifies the user with a particular gang.

colors Clothing used by gang members to demonstrate their affiliation with a particular gang.

surveyed gang members in Los Angeles, San Diego, and Chicago and found that about 28 percent are rarely involved in drug use, while 42 percent were actively involved in drug use and sales.[50]

Responses to Gangs

What are communities doing to respond to the gang problem? The OJJDP comprehensive gang model includes five strategies used by various communities to address gang problems:

1. **Community organization** involves efforts to mobilize the community to deal with gangs. Strategies that involve community organization are usually broad-based strategies that include networking between many agencies and organizations. Community organization involves efforts at enhancing, modifying, or changing interorganizational relationships to deal with a gang problem.
2. **Opportunities provision** involves efforts to deal with gangs through employment, job training, and education. Strategies include job training, job placement, and tutoring.
3. **Organizational change and development** involve making adaptations that facilitate the application of other strategies. Organizational adaptations typically involve specialization that enables an organization to deal with the gang problem. For example, many large police departments have developed a special gang unit to deal with gangs.
4. **Social intervention** includes counseling and other direct attempts to change the values of youth in order to make gang involvement less likely. Social intervention includes several outreach efforts such as provision of role models, intergang mediation, and drug treatment. In addition, many of the programs attempt to build the self-esteem of the gang member. This strategy is frequently used when drug use is a problem for the gang member.
5. **Suppression** involves the use of the juvenile and criminal justice system to reduce gang behavior through the use of formal social control including arrest and incarceration. Under this approach, gang members are arrested, prosecuted, and incarcerated for short or long periods of time.[51]

All gangs actively deal drugs.

Less than 30 percent of gangs in the United States are estimated to have a high level of involvement in the street sale of drugs.

Source: www.fbi.gov/stats-services/publications/2011-national-gang-threat-assessment

13.6 SELF-CHECK

1. List the five strategies used by communities to respond to the gang problem.
2. What is the most frequently used strategy? The least frequently used?

According to the National Youth Gang Survey, over 44 percent of the respondents stated that suppression was the primary strategy used in their community to deal with gangs. The second most used strategy was social intervention (31 percent), followed by organizational change and development (11 percent), community organization (9 percent), and opportunities provision (5 percent).[52] It is clear that traditional juvenile and criminal justice responses such as arrest, prosecution, and incarceration are the typical ways in which most communities deal with gangs. It is interesting to note, however, that the survey respondents thought that suppression tactics, although the most used, were least effective. In fact, the survey respondents thought that opportunities provision, the least used strategy, was probably the most effective means to deal with gangs.[53]

Since suppression strategies are the primary strategy used in most communities, we will focus almost exclusively on the suppression efforts used by law enforcement agencies, prosecutors, and legislatures in the next section.

community organization A response to gangs which involves efforts to mobilize the community in an effort to deal with gangs.

opportunities provision A response to gangs that involves efforts to deal with gangs through employment, job training, and education.

organizational change and development A response to gangs that involves organizational adaptations that facilitate the application of gang control strategies.

social intervention A response to gangs that involves counseling and other direct attempts to change the values of youth in order to make gang involvement less likely.

suppression A response to gangs that involves the use of the criminal justice system to reduce gang behavior through the use of formal social control including arrest and incarceration.

Controlling Gang Activity

Efforts to control gang activity stem from three major parts of the juvenile justice system: law enforcement, prosecution, and legislature.

LAW ENFORCEMENT EFFORTS

Suppression by law enforcement includes such activities as gang "sweeps," surveillance, aggressive patrol, intelligence gathering, and follow-up investigations. Gang suppression tactics used by law enforcement vary from jurisdiction to jurisdiction. Some law enforcement agencies have adopted a philosophy of total suppression, in which any gang member or wannabe has been targeted. Others have adopted a philosophy of target suppression, in which the police target only hard-core gang members.[54] Still others have focused on information sharing and intelligence gathering to identify, arrest, and successfully prosecute gang members.[55] One study found that aggressive enforcement of truancy and curfew violations by police led to significant reductions in gang violence.[56]

In addition to their focus on suppressing gang crime, the police are actively involved in attempts to prevent individuals from participating in gangs. One such program is **Gang Resistance Education and Training** (G.R.E.A.T.). G.R.E.A.T. is a school-based program in which police officers teach a structured curriculum to students. G.R.E.A.T. is designed to help students set goals for themselves, resist pressures, learn how to resolve conflicts without violence, and understand how gangs and youth violence impact the quality of their lives (See Focus on Programs).

Gang Resistance Education and Training
A school-based gang prevention program that is designed to help students set goals for themselves, resist pressures, learn how to resolve conflicts without violence, and understand how gangs and youth violence impact the quality of their lives.

CAREERS IN JUVENILE JUSTICE

Gang Intelligence Officer

Gang intelligence officers work for police departments and are the gang specialists in the department. Gang intelligence officers document gang members and their affiliations and gather intelligence on and investigate gang-related criminal activity. They also perform these functions:

- Make gang information available to other officers in the agency;
- Assist in identifying suspects involved in gang activity and crimes and arrest those suspects;
- Provide training to officers and other agencies on the subject of gangs;
- Concentrate and monitor areas where there have been reports of gang activity; and
- Testify in court as gang experts.

Gang intelligence officers usually exist only in medium-size and large jurisdictions. Some police departments may have several gang intelligence officers who are banded together and classified as a gang unit. Medium-size departments may have only a few gang intelligence officers or just one. Smaller departments will not have a full-time gang intelligence officer. The functions usually performed by a gang intelligence officer are then the responsibility of the detective(s) in the department and the patrol officers.

To be qualified as a gang intelligence officer an individual must usually first work in the patrol division of a police department as a patrol officer and after a certain number of years of service in this position can seek the position of a gang intelligence officer.

Critical Thinking

How would you go about becoming an intelligence officer in your community?

Police use different suppression tactics to control gangs. *What reasons might this officer have for frisking the gang member?*

PROSECUTION EFFORTS

The primary mission of prosecutors as it applies to gangs is successful prosecution, conviction, and incarceration of gang offenders. Prosecutors have found numerous problems in prosecuting gangs, including difficulty obtaining cooperation of victims and witnesses, intimidation by gang members of victims and witnesses, and issues with victim and witness credibility.[57] Prosecutors have some unique tools at their disposal in dealing with gangs, including the Racketeer Influenced Corrupt Organization (RICO) Act, Street Terrorism Enforcement and Prevention (STEP) Acts, and Nuisance Abatement laws.

RICO The **Racketeer Influenced Corrupt Organization Act** (RICO) was enacted in 1970 with the specific intent of dismantling organized crime (e.g., Sicilian Mafia, Columbian Drug Cartels). RICO allows for the prosecution and conviction of participants in an ongoing organized criminal enterprise even if the participants have not been physically involved in the commission of criminal acts. While all states can assist the federal government in RICO prosecutions, several states have enacted their own RICO-style legislation to make this option more readily available to them. Although RICO has been a controversial piece of legislation in application, it has been essentially successful in dismantling large criminal organizations.[58]

Prosecutors using RICO note the similarities between the Mafia and some of today's urban street gangs. The question remains: Are most street gangs really organized criminal enterprises? Some gangs possess many of the same characteristics defined in RICO that are necessary for legal action. RICO requires that an organization:

- Operates with a criminal purpose over an extended period of time;
- Has an established managerial order;

Racketeer Influenced Corrupt Organization Act A federal statute which is used to prosecute gang members who participate in an organized criminal enterprise.

FOCUS ON PROGRAMS

GANG RESISTANCE EDUCATION AND TRAINING (G.R.E.A.T.)

In 1991, police officers from the Phoenix, Mesa, Glendale, and Tempe Police Departments and special agents of the Bureau of Alcohol Tobacco and Firearms developed Gang Resistance Education and Training (G.R.E.A.T.) to reduce adolescent involvement in gangs. G.R.E.A.T. is now a national, school-based gang prevention program in which uniformed law enforcement officers teach a 13-week curriculum to middle school students. To date, thousands of law enforcement officers from hundreds of agencies throughout the United States, Canada, Guam, and Puerto Rico and military personnel from overseas bases in Japan and Germany have been trained to present the core curriculum in middle school classrooms. The estimated cumulative number of students who have received the G.R.E.A.T. program is more than four million.

Philosophy of G.R.E.A.T.

The G.R.E.A.T. program is designed to help children set goals for themselves, resist pressures, learn how to resolve conflicts without violence, and understand how gangs and youth violence impact the quality of their lives. G.R.E.A.T. students discover for themselves the ramifications of gang and youth violence through structured exercises and interactive approaches to learning. It is believed that through the combined efforts of law enforcement, the schools, and the community, a difference can be made in the lives of children across America by providing them with the necessary skills and information to say "NO" to gangs and acts of random violence.

G.R.E.A.T. Program Composition and Curriculum

G.R.E.A.T. helps children learn to resolve conflicts without resorting to violence and to resist the pressure to join gangs. This program is implemented in areas where gangs are emerging or already exist. Through classroom instruction and other related activities, seventh graders are taught to respect themselves, set goals, and make sound choices. The children also can learn how cultural differences affect their community.

Taught by trained, uniformed police officers and federal agents, the G.R.E.A.T. curriculum is designed for the junior/middle school level. The program is generally taught one period per week for 13 consecutive weeks. An optional six-week curriculum for fifth/sixth graders and third/fourth graders also is available. A summer follow-up program reinforces the classroom lessons in a less structured one-on-one setting. The summer component also gives children an opportunity to become involved in community services.

Effectiveness of G.R.E.A.T.

A five-year longitudinal evaluation of G.R.E.A.T. found that the program had positive impacts on the attitudes of students and their delinquency risk factors. For example, students experienced lower levels of victimization, more negative views about gangs, more favorable attitudes about police, reduction in risk-seeking behaviors, and increased association with peers involved in pro-social activities. However, the study found no impact on their involvement in gangs or actual delinquent behaviors.

For more information, visit the G.R.E.A.T. website at www.great-online.org.

CRITICAL THINKING

At what age level do you think the G.R.E.A.T. program could be most effective? Why?

- Restricts membership in the gang through some means;
- Relies on criminal activity to generate the income that finances the organization;
- Achieves its goals often through violence; and
- Has a power/profit motive.[59]

The vast majority of gangs are not actively involved in drug distribution and the commission of violent crimes and do not meet the other criteria required for RICO prosecution. Therefore, most gangs cannot be classified as organized criminal enterprises. However, the fact that several gangs have been successfully targeted for prosecution under RICO shows that some gangs *are* organized criminal enterprises. All of the previous RICO cases were brought against gangs

FOCUS ON POLICY

UNITED STATES SUPREME COURT REJECTS CHICAGO'S ANTI-GANG LOITERING ORDINANCE

In 1992, Chicago enacted the Gang Congregation Ordinance that gave police the power to break up groups if an officer "observes a person whom he reasonably believes to be a criminal street gang member." Anyone who refused to leave the premises after the officer's request could be arrested. The law was designed to keep gang members from loitering on the streets. In three years, Chicago police issued more than 89,000 dispersal orders and arrested more than 42,000 resisters. The city suspended enforcement of the ordinance in 1995 amid legal challenges by the Illinois American Civil Liberties Union.

On June 10, 1999, the United States Supreme Court struck down the ordinance, stating that the ordinance was too vague and gave police too much discretion.

CRITICAL THINKING

Should the police be able to break up groups of gang members loitering on the street even if other law violations are not apparent? Or does this ordinance give the police too much power and infringe too much on an individual's rights?

who were strongly controlled by influential leaders, controlled an area or areas of a large metropolitan city, and were actively involved in violent activity and distributing large quantities of drugs.

Author L. S. Bonney notes that many somewhat fraternal gangs were transformed into violent criminal enterprises in the late 1980s and early 1990s because of crack cocaine sales.[60] The level of narcotics involvement is directly related to the size and complexity of the gang. The drug trade becomes the main source of income for sophisticated urban street gangs. Comparisons to the Mafia and bootlegging of liquor during Prohibition are obvious. Sophisticated urban street gangs have accrued much of the same economic and political power traditionally associated with the Mafia. For example, gangs like the Westies in Manhattan and the El Rukns in Chicago have been successfully prosecuted using RICO. The courts in both these cases upheld the notion that these gangs were ongoing criminal enterprises under the RICO definition.[61] Critics maintain that today's urban street gang is often younger and more impressionable than typical Mafia members. Conversely, the conclusion that these gangs are nothing more than a modern version of the Mafia is also defensible.[62]

STEP ACTS Street Terrorism Enforcement and Prevention (STEP) Acts are based on the RICO model. These acts use a series of predicate offenses as the basis for sentence enhancements and provide for civil forfeiture of a street gang's assets and the proceeds of its criminal activities.[63] These acts are valuable because they turn **specific intent** crimes like attempted murder or aggravated assault into **general intent** crimes. Specific intent occurs when the circumstances of the offense demonstrate that the offender must have consciously desired the result. This is the highest level of intent and is typically required for the most serious offenses. On the other hand, general intent is a lower level of intent and involves an act in which a prohibited result follows (e.g., death) in the absence of a desire for the particular result.

California's STEP Act was the first and served as a prototype for other states that have enacted these statutes. The California STEP Act links three definitions: "pattern of criminal gang activity," "criminal street gang," and "participation in a criminal street gang." A *pattern of criminal gang activity* in California means commission of one or more predicate offenses on two or more separate occasions. These offenses include assault with a deadly weapon, robbery, and sale of drugs, to name a few. A *criminal street gang* is an ongoing group that has as one of its primary activities the commission of one or more of these predicate crimes, plus a common name or common identifying sign or symbol whose

Street Terrorism Enforcement and Prevention (STEP) Acts A type of statute which uses a series of predicate crimes as the basis for sentence enhancements and provides for civil forfeiture of a gang's assets and the proceeds of its criminal activities.

specific intent A level of intent that occurs when the circumstances of the offense demonstrate that the offender must have consciously desired the result.

general intent A level of intent that involves an act in which a prohibited result follows (e.g., death) in the absence of a desire for the particular result.

FOCUS ON PRACTICE

RIVERSIDE COUNTY, CALIFORNIA, USES STEP ACT

Riverside County, California, "steps" both street gangs and gang members by bringing them within the parameters of the STEP Act. The street gang unit of the City of Riverside police department compiles three related notebooks on a targeted gang. The first notebook contains copies of all incident, arrest, investigative, supplemental, and field interrogation reports pertaining to the gang. The second notebook contains the personal records of gang members and affiliates, including pictures, prints, rap sheets, and copies of any reports in which their names appear. The third consists of pictures of gang members, individually and together, showing their colors, tattoos, signs, and other indicia of street gang affiliation. The notebook also includes pictures of gang graffiti, with places and dates carefully recorded.

Riverside police officers also serve certain gang members with written notices, developed by the prosecutor, which state that a specific gang is considered a criminal street gang under the STEP Act and that participation in the gang can subject an individual to a sentence of 1 to 3 years. The carefully preserved record of notification destroys any claim that a defendant did not know of the street gang's criminal activity, knowledge being one of the bases for STEP Act prosecution. In addition, prosecutors have reported that the notice itself has an inhibiting effect on many gang members.

CRITICAL THINKING

Why would STEP play a role in defining gangs?

Source: Johnson, Claire, Barbara Webster, and Edward Connors. *Prosecuting Gangs: A National Assessment* (Washington, DC: U.S. Department of Justice, 1995).

members individually or collectively engage in a pattern of criminal gang activity. *Participation in a criminal street gang* is a separate offense, carefully defined to guard against unconstitutional infringement of the rights of free association and free speech.[64] Therefore, if a criminal street gang is involved in a pattern of criminal gang activity, then the participants in the gang can be held liable for the offenses even if the participants did not physically commit the offense (See Focus on Practice).

NUISANCE ABATEMENT

Nuisance abatement statutes targeting gangs exist in several states including California, Florida, Louisiana, Missouri, and Texas, to name a few. Prosecutors in California deal with gangs in an innovative way, through civil process. They have entire gangs declared a public nuisance (see Figure 13.4). Prosecutors are increasingly pressing judges to use their blanket abatement power to grant injunctions against street gangs.

In the nuisance abatement process, the judge issues a court order against the members of the gang. The gang members are instructed to stop their delinquent activity along with other behaviors. If the gang members do not voluntarily stop their behavior, then the gang is classified as a nuisance. Each gang member is then given a court order which places restrictions on behavior including lawful behaviors such as wearing certain clothing, associating with certain people, and possessing cellular phones. If a gang member does not abide by the court order, then the gang member can be arrested for violation of a court order and incarcerated. A gang member who is subject to a nuisance abatement order can be arrested and incarcerated for carrying a cell phone if it is prohibited by the court order.

Judges have responded to nuisance abatement requests with orders that restrain gang members from fighting, possessing weapons, spraying graffiti, trespassing, and possessing gang-associated paraphernalia such as a cell phone.[65] Some orders have commanded individuals not to associate with one another or congregate publicly. "Through the magic of a judicial order, even purely social

nuisance abatement A method to deal with gangs that defines their behavior as a public nuisance and forbids certain legal and illegal behaviors.

FIGURE 13.4   Nuisance Abatement in Oxnard, CA

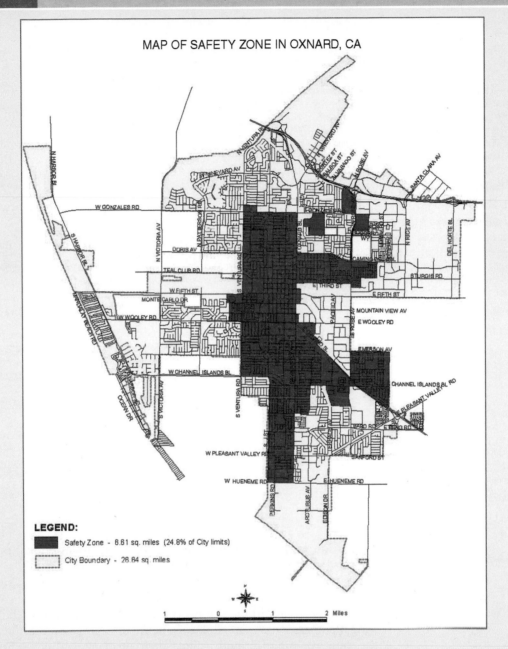

MAP OF SAFETY ZONE IN OXNARD, CA

LEGEND:
- Safety Zone - 6.61 sq. miles (24.8% of City limits)
- City Boundary - 26.64 sq. miles

WHAT IS A GANG INJUNCTION?

A gang injunction is a civil lawsuit against a street gang and its members based on the legal theory of "public nuisance." The allegation is that the conduct and activities of the street gang within a defined area constitute a public nuisance. It interferes with the community's comfortable enjoyment of life and their property.

HAS THIS BEEN DONE BEFORE?

Gang injunctions have been used for the past 10 years. There are currently about 40 injunctions in California. Their legality has been upheld in the California Supreme Court.

WHAT IS THE OBJECTIVE OF A GANG INJUNCTION?

To improve the quality of life for the people who live and work in the Safety Zone, suppress gang activity and help reduce gang crime, provide outreach

programs a better opportunity to work, reduce the ability for borderline gang associates to join the gang and give gang members and associates an excuse to leave the gang. It also allows the Police Department to use fewer resources to suppress the gang and devote more resources to other issues.

WHAT IS COLONIA CHIQUES?

Colonia Chiques is a predominantly Latino turf-oriented street gang. It is the largest street gang in Ventura County and claims as its "turf" neighborhoods in Oxnard including Colonia. The primary activities of the gang are to engage in violent and serious felonies among rival gangs and innocent members of the community.

The gang has about 1,000 members, uses Dallas Cowboys attire to "represent itself," and is associated with organized crime. The vast majority (90 percent) of the members of this gang are adults. This street gang has been involved (as suspects or victims) in 39 homicides since 1992. They are responsible for more than 2,000 crimes in recent years including hundreds of robberies and other serious crimes in the city.

WHO DOES THE INJUNCTION APPLY TO?

The gang injunction only applies to members of the Colonia Chiques gang who engage in acts prohibited by the lawsuit. These prohibitions would have to occur in the "safety zone" and in the area open to the public. Community members and citizens are not under any authority of the injunction. Essentially, 99.5 percent of Oxnard's population would not be subject in any way to the prohibitions of this injunction. This injunction is enforceable ONLY AGAINST COLONIA CHIQUES GANG MEMBERS who have been SERVED, and who are in the SAFETY ZONE, are IN PUBLIC, and in violation of one or more of the NEW RULES FOR LIVING as outlined in the injunction. If any of these five requirements are not present then the police department cannot take any action against the Person.

WHERE IS THE SAFETY ZONE?

The "geographical area" is a selected area based on the recent nuisance and criminal activity by the Colonia Chiques gang. It is bordered on the north side of Gonzales Road, on the west side of Ventura Road, on the south side of Hueneme Road and on the east side by Saviers Road. It also includes the neighborhoods of Cal-Gisler, Lemonwood, Colonia, Rose Park, as well as Pacifica High School, Shopping at the Rose, and St. John's Hospital.

HOW BIG IS THE SAFETY ZONE?

The safety zone is 6.6 square miles or about 24 percent of the City of Oxnard.

WHAT DOES THE INJUNCTION PROHIBIT?

- Do not intimidate witnesses.
- Do not associate with other Colonia Chiques gang members (some exceptions).
- Do not possess guns or dangerous weapons.
- Do not engage in fighting.
- Do not use gang gestures.
- Do not wear gang clothing.
- Stay away from drugs without a prescription.
- Do not engage in activities associated with drug sales.
- Stay away from alcohol.

- Do not graffiti or possess graffiti tools.
- Do not trespass on property without written consent of owner.
- Be out of public in the safety zone between 10:00 P.M. and sunrise (some exceptions).
- Do not act as a lookout.
- Obey all laws.

WHO CAN ENFORCE THE INJUNCTION?

Oxnard Police Officers who see gang members in violation of the injunction within the safety zone can make an arrest.

WHAT IS THE PENALTY?

Gang members who violate the injunction can be arrested for violation of a court order, a misdemeanor, and be sentenced up to six months in jail. This is a violation of Penal Code § 166(a)(4) (contempt of court).

HOW DOES A GANG MEMBER GET OUT FROM UNDER THE INJUNCTION'S AUTHORITY?

A gang member who is under the authority of the injunction may free themselves from the restrictions by disassociating himself from the Colonia Chiques gang. This usually involves not associating with other gang members, not wearing the clothing of the gang, nor representing the gang in any fashion.

WHAT ARE SOME THINGS THE INJUNCTION CANNOT DO?

The injunction is a prohibitory injunction and thus does not seek any monetary damages. It is not enforced outside of the Safety Zone, and is not effective inside their homes. The injunction is not a stay-away order or a banishment, nor is it a Municipal Code ordinance. It is enforceable only against the Colonia gang members who have been served. It does not prohibit the wearing of any particular attire for the 99.5 percent of the population not under the authority of the injunction.

HOW LONG WILL THE INJUNCTION BE IN PLACE?

Forever.

Source: Oxnard (CA) Police Department website, www.oxnardpd.org/misc/GangInjunction.htm.

association becomes a punishable offense, subjecting violators to months of incarceration and significant fines."[66]

For example, in a civil suit, *People* v. *Playboy Gangster Crips*,[67] the court issued a 23-point injunction against some 200 members of the gang. Among the orders were prohibitions against: wearing gang colors; associating with other gang members; possessing firearms, paint, or markers; remaining in public longer than five minutes; and leaving their residences after nightfall.[68] Under a similar order in another jurisdiction, a reputed gang member was convicted of violating an abatement order because he possessed a pager and a glass bottle, trespassed, and obstructed traffic. The man was sentenced to 90 days in jail and given three years' probation.[69]

Nuisance statutes are a powerful tool for local law enforcement. Because a nuisance abatement is a *civil* action, the burden of proof is lower than the reasonable doubt standard required in criminal cases. Thus, it is easier to establish the legal existence of a criminal street gang and a pattern of illegal activity. Abatement allows the permanent closure of buildings used by criminal street gang members to commit offenses such as selling drugs in crack houses. Personal property used to commit offenses may also be seized as a nuisance. This includes, but is not limited to, firearms and automobiles. As previously noted, gang members themselves can be held in contempt of court for violating the court order and jailed.

SOCIAL AND CONSTITUTIONAL QUESTIONS These anti-gang injunctions raise difficult social and constitutional questions. Civil court orders designed to eradicate gangs can prohibit otherwise legal conduct. Additionally, using civil remedies may deprive an individual or group of constitutional procedural protections that are given in criminal proceedings.[70] Subsequent legal challenges based on the freedom of association, freedom of speech, and the right to privacy were all found to be unsubstantiated by appellate courts.[71]

LEGISLATIVE EFFORTS

Policy directed toward juvenile gangs has taken a new direction in recent years. In the past, gang behavior was dealt with through law enforcement techniques and through prosecution under existing penal laws. More recently, legislatures around the country have begun to enact "gang-specific" legislation. These new laws are targeted specifically at street gangs and go so far as to make it illegal simply to be a member in a gang. Although RICO, STEP Acts, and nuisance abatement are all laws, the legislatures in several states have adopted additional strategies to deal with gangs. There are some unique efforts by legislatures to enact laws to control gang activity.

ENHANCED PENALTIES FOR GANG-RELATED CRIME One of the most popular legislative responses to gang activity has been to impose increased penalties for gang-related offenses. States vary in the amount of additional punishment given for gang-related crimes. Generally, states that enhance penalties increase their penalty range "one class," which means that the crime is punished as if it were the next highest degree (e.g., a second-degree felony is punished as a first-degree felony, etc.). Some states grant judges the option of adding additional years onto a gang member's sentence. Perhaps the most punitive statute is Nevada's; there a person convicted of a gang-related offense can have a sentence doubled, and the additional "gang-related" sentence must run consecutively with the sentence for the original offense.

The use of nuisance abatement to suppress gang activity has grown in popularity. *What is the purpose of nuisance abatement orders? Do you think they are effective?*

GANG MEMBERSHIP AND PARTICIPATION DEFINED AS ILLEGAL Some states have made gang membership or participation illegal. For example, Indiana law states "a person who knowingly or intentionally actively participates in a criminal gang commits criminal gang activity, a Class D felony.[72] California and Missouri both provide for imprisonment terms ranging from one to three years for gang participation.[73]

In order to punish an individual for active participation in a gang, it is crucial to first accurately define what a gang is, as previously discussed. The gang definitions vary from state to state, but all are similar in that the requirements for calling a group a "gang" are typically vague and overbroad.

Author R. H. Destro contends that the variations in definitions show the extent and nature of the gang problem in different states.[74] For example, the California, Louisiana, and Missouri definitions all contain a list of specific felonies which are considered gang-related. Arizona, in contrast, limits the extent of the definition to drug-related activities. Indiana and Iowa take a broader approach in that they include all felonies and several misdemeanors. These variations show that while states agree that there is a gang problem, they do *not* agree on what motivates gang membership, what constitutes a gang, and ways to address the problem. These variations become crucial when an individual receives a criminal penalty based on one definition in one jurisdiction that would not be a criminal penalty in a court located in a different jurisdiction.

DRIVE-BY SHOOTINGS DEFINED AS A SEPARATE OFFENSE The "drive-by" is perhaps the most infamous of gang offenses and receives the greatest media attention. Some states have chosen to enact legislation that specifically criminalizes drive-by shootings. While firing a weapon from a moving vehicle is a crime in any state, some statutes specifically target gang drive-bys. Statutes have been specifically developed to respond to drive-by shootings because of the potential leniency given offenders if an individual was not injured during a drive-by shooting. The only law which is violated by shooting a weapon from a moving vehicle is unlawful discharge of a weapon (usually a misdemeanor violation). If property is damaged, then the person could be charged with vandalism. Without someone being injured, the shooter does not face severe punishment. However, states that have created a specific drive-by shooting statute usually place severe sanctions on the offense. The laws allow states to hold juvenile gang members more accountable. For example, Colorado defines a drive-by as a first- or second-degree assault, and the vehicle that is used in the drive-by can be declared a nuisance subject to forfeiture.[75]

13.7 SELF-CHECK

1. Briefly describe G.R.E.A.T.'s philosophy and curriculum.

2. What strategies have been used by prosecutors and legislatures to respond to gangs?

The Future of Gangs

Is the gang problem going to get better or worse in the coming years? It is impossible to know for sure, but some indicators demonstrate that the gang problem in the United States is likely to get worse before it gets better. Despite significant efforts by juvenile justice system agencies to control gang activity, there is limited evidence that these strategies are effective in reducing the gang problem. It was noted previously that the primary strategy used in the United States to deal with gangs is suppression. However, it was also noted that many argue that suppression is the least effective mechanism to deal with gangs.[76]

According to the National Youth Gangs Survey, about 31 percent of the respondents characterized their gang problem as getting increasingly worse. By comparison, 54 percent of the agencies characterized their gang problem as staying about the same, while the remaining 15 percent felt their gang problem was improving. Overall, these findings underscore what is commonly referred to as gang cycles, or consistently changing patterns of gang activity and violence, that occur at the local level.[77] Although there is no definitive answer on whether the gang problem will get better or worse in the coming years, one thing is certain: jurisdictions will continue to experiment with programs and strategies to try to better manage gangs in their communities.

13.8 SELF-CHECK

Is the gang problem getting better or worse?

SUMMARY BY CHAPTER OBJECTIVES

1. Explain the difficulties in accurately defining a gang, gang member, and gang-related crime

There is very little consensus on how to define a gang, gang member, and gang-related crime. Therefore, numerous definitions exist in practice.

2. Describe the extent of the gang problem

According to the National Youth Gang Survey, there are over 29,400 gangs and 756,000 gang members.

3. Differentiate between types of gangs

Huff identified three major types of gangs. Hedonistic gangs are primarily involved in using drugs and getting high with little involvement in delinquency. These types of gangs almost never commit acts of violence. Therefore, most of their activity involves partying and committing minor violations of the law. Instrumental gangs are primarily involved in committing property offenses such as burglary, auto theft, and theft. In addition, members in these types of gangs are actively involved in using drugs but seldom sell drugs. Members in these types of gangs commit more serious offenses than members of hedonistic gangs, but members of both types of gangs rarely commit acts of violence. Predatory gangs are the most serious type of gang and are actively involved in serious offenses including violent crimes such as robbery. Members of these types of gangs are actively involved in using drugs such as crack cocaine, and many engage in selling drugs as well.

4. Identify the major characteristics of gangs

The major characteristics of gangs include age, race/ethnicity, gender, gang migration, communication, and delinquent activity. Although gang members have typically been perceived as being juveniles, the majority of gang members in some jurisdictions are adults. The majority of gang members are either African-American or Hispanic, but all racial and ethnic groups participate in gangs, including whites, Asian, and American Indian. The majority of gang members are male, but it is estimated that 7 percent of all gang members are female. Most of the evidence shows that gang migration is a rare occurrence. Gang members communicate through graffiti, colors, logos, and hand signs. Gang members commit more delinquent acts than nongang members, but the majority of gangs do not actively participate in drug trafficking and violence.

5. Explain why youths join gangs?

Youths join gangs for several reasons. First, gangs provide youth with an opportunity to associate with their peers and to obtain a sense of belongingness. Many gang members have reported that they joined gangs to be affiliated with their friends because a number of their friends were already gang members. Second, youths join gangs because of the prospect of obtaining money through the commission of delinquent acts such as burglary and distributing drugs. Many gangs exist in low-income areas where the prospect of adequate legitimate employment is limited. Therefore, joining a gang becomes an attractive option to make money. Third, youths join gangs because they are seeking protection from other youth in the community. The adage that "there is strength in numbers" applies here. Many potential gang members live in neighborhoods that are riddled with rival gangs and violence. In these areas, it is assumed that most youths are affiliated with gangs, even if they are not. This puts pressure on youths to join gangs for protection in the school or neighborhood.

6. Describe the major responses to gangs

The major responses to gangs include community organization, opportunities provision, organizational change and development, social intervention, and suppression.

7. Summarize efforts to control gang activity

Law enforcement, prosecution, and legislatures have all made efforts to control gang activity. The primary strategy used by law enforcement to deal with gangs can be best characterized as suppression and includes such activities as gang "sweeps," surveillance, aggressive patrol, intelligence gathering, and follow-up investigations. Prosecution efforts have included the use of the Racketeer Influenced Corrupt Organization (RICO) Act, Street Terrorism Enforcement and Prevention (STEP) Acts, and nuisance abatement. Legislatures have passed new laws targeting gangs including the provision for enhanced penalties for gang-related crime, defining gang membership and participation as illegal, and defining drive-by shootings as a separate offense.

KEY TERMS

gang, p. 366
gang member, p. 367
wannabe, p. 367
gang-related crime, p. 368
hedonistic gang, p. 371
instrumental gang, p. 371
predatory gang, p. 371
traditional gang, p. 371
neotraditional gang,
 p. 371
compressed gang, p. 371

collective gang, p. 371
specialty gang, p. 371
female auxiliary gang,
 p. 374
gang migration, p. 374
graffiti, p. 375
logo, p. 376
hand sign, p. 376
colors, p. 376
community
 organization, p. 377

opportunities provision,
 p. 377
organizational change
 and development,
 p. 377
social intervention, p. 377
suppression, p. 377
Gang Resistance
 Education and
 Training (G.R.E.A.T.),
 p. 378

Racketeer Influenced
 Corrupt Organization
 (RICO) Act, p. 379
Street Terrorism
 Enforcement and
 Prevention (STEP)
 Acts, p. 381
specific intent, p. 381
general intent, p. 395
nuisance abatement,
 p. 382

REVIEW QUESTIONS

1. Discuss the problems associated with defining the terms: gang, gang member, and gang-related crime.

2. What is the extent of the gang problem? How many gangs and gang members are there in the United States?

3. What are the major types of gangs? What characteristics distinguish each type of gang from one another?

4. What are the major characteristics of gangs including age, race and ethnicity, gender, gang migration, communication, and delinquent activity?

5. What are the three main reasons why youths join gangs?

6. What are the major responses to gangs?

7. Of the major responses to gangs, which is most used and which is seen as most effective?

8. What efforts have law enforcement officials, prosecutors, and legislators made to control gang activity?

9. How does the process of nuisance abatement work?

10. Why have legislatures defined drive-by shootings as a separate offense?

HANDS-ON ACTIVITIES

1. **Compare Statistics** Contact your local police department. Ask them how many gangs and gang members are documented in your community and how they define these terms. Compare these numbers and definitions with those in the chapter.

2. **Investigate Gang Migration** Contact criminal justice personnel in your community including prosecutors, judges, police officers, and probation officers, among others, and ask them about the existence of gang migration in your community. Document the evidence they provide for the existence or nonexistence of gang migration in your community.

INTERNET ACTIVITIES

1. Go to **www.fbi.gov/stats-services/publications/2011-national-gang-threat-assessment.** Review the *National Gang Threat Assessment 2009*. What does the document say about gangs in the region of the country in which you live?

2. Go to **www.nationalgangcenter.gov/Legislation/,** the website for the National Youth Gang Center. Go to **Gang-Related Legislation by State** and then click on the state in which you reside. Review the gang-related legislation in your state.

CRITICAL THINKING EXERCISES

1. **Community Action** You are an active citizen who is beginning to notice signs of gang activity in your community. You have begun to notice graffiti on telephone poles, trash dumpsters, and the sides of buildings. Most of the graffiti uses the terms "Crips" and "Bloods" which you relate to the gangs from Los Angeles. In addition, you have begun to notice that kids are hanging out on corners and in front of convenience stores. You speak with a few teachers who indicate that they are observing gang activity in the school as well.

   The city council has called a town meeting to identify measures to deal with gangs. You attend the meeting and are asked to speak for your neighborhood on what should be done with the gangs in the community.

   a. What recommendations would you make to the city council? What is the potential impact of these recommendations on your community?

   b. Do you think that law enforcement should be the primary response to the problem? Why or why not?

   c. What role can the schools play in dealing with gangs?

2. **Police Response to Gangs** You are a police officer in a city of 50,000 people who has recently been assigned to be the "gang officer" for the department. The chief of police tells you that currently there are 500 documented gang members in the city. Within the next year, she would like to see that number reduced to 250.

   You have been a police officer in this city for five years. Four years ago, two rival gangs were involved in a shooting in the parking lot of a local grocery store. Since then, the community has been concerned. The number of documented gang members indicates the gang problem is getting worse. However, the shooting in the parking lot of the local grocery store is the only shooting that has involved gang members in the past four years.

   a. What would you do to reduce the number of gang members in the community?

   b. Would your strategies be best identified as suppression or social intervention?

   c. What other agencies might help reduce the number of gang members in the community?

ANSWERS TO SELF-CHECKS

13.1 Self-Check

What circumstances caused members of the juvenile justice system to renew their concern about gangs?
The four reasons are:
- The emergence of youth gangs in small and rural communities
- The increased diversity of gang composition
- The increased use of highly dangerous weapons and the higher level of violence
- The controversy surrounding the role of gangs in drug trafficking

13.2 Self-Check

1. Explain why defining gangs is so important.
Defining gangs is important because simply being a gang member is illegal in some states. In addition, many other states offer sentence enhancements for gang-related crimes. Therefore, defining a gang and a gang member is crucial to prevent unfair sentencing.

2. Name three reasons why young people join gangs.
Three main reasons are:
- Gangs provide youths with an opportunity to associate with their peers and to obtain a sense of belongingness.
- Youths join gangs because of the prospect of obtaining money through the commission of delinquent acts.
- Youths join gangs because they are seeking protection from other youths in the community.

13.3 Self-Check

How many youth gangs and youth gang members are there in the United States?
According to the National Youth Gang Survey, there are 29,400 gangs and 756,000 gang members in the United States.

13.4 Self-Check

1. List the different types of gangs according to C. Ronald Huff.
Huff separates gangs into three categories: hedonistic gangs, which primarily get high and commit few

delinquent acts; instrumental gangs, which commit property offenses and will use, but rarely sell, drugs; and predatory gangs, which are actively involved in violent crimes such as robbery, and often use and sell drugs.

2. Which types of gangs are the least prevalent according to the classifications established by Maxson and Klein?

The least prevalent gangs are collective and specialty gangs.

13.5 Self-Check

What factors account for gang migration?

One perspective holds that gang members actively try to expand their territory by branching out to new cities and recruiting members there. This theory, however, is not supported by research. More likely is that gang members' families move and the gang members take their gang affiliation with them, starting new gangs in their new locale either with or without the help or approval of their old gang.

13.6 Self-Check

1. List the five strategies used by communities to respond to the gang problem.

The five most common strategies are:

- Community organization
- Opportunities provision
- Organizational change and development
- Social intervention
- Suppression (i.e., arrest and incarceration)

2. What is the most frequently used strategy? The least frequently used?

Suppression is the most frequently used, and opportunities provision is used least frequently.

13.7 Self-Check

1. Briefly describe G.R.E.A.T.'s philosophy and curriculum.

G.R.E.A.T.'s philosophy is that students can be taught gang prevention in the schools. It states that law enforcement can play an active role in teaching children to say "NO" to gangs. The curriculum teaches students how to resolve conflicts without violence and resist peer pressure to join a gang. It can be adjusted depending on the age of the students being taught, whether they are at the elementary, or middle-school level. For instance, middle-school students receive a 13-week curriculum.

2. What strategies have been used by prosecutors and legislatures to respond to gangs?

Responses include:

- RICO, STEP Acts, and nuisance abatement laws, which are three popular prosecutorial options; and
- Sentence enhancements for gang-related crimes, defining gang membership and participation as illegal, and defining drive-bys as a separate offense, which are three well-known legislative efforts.

13.8 Self-Check

Is the gang problem getting better or worse?

This question is difficult to answer because some evidence shows that the problem is getting worse, but most jurisdictions cycle between increases and decreases in gang activity.

SPECIAL POPULATIONS

Chapter Outline

Chapter Objectives

After completing this chapter, you should be able to:

1. Explain the difference between a rampage killing and a typical homicide.

2. Define paraphilia.

3. Define what drugs are and assess their impact on American youth.

4. Explain the concept of a chronic juvenile offender.

5. Describe the demographic profile of the juvenile hacker.

6. List the categories of hate groups and explain their attractiveness for juveniles.

7. Learn what the most common kind of child abuse is.

8. Describe the worlds of child prostitution and child exploitation.

Juveniles and Violence

Juveniles represent a unique and separate population within the criminal justice system. Thus far, we have discussed the various theoretical assumptions underlying juvenile delinquency and juvenile law, correctional treatment and diversion, and many of the unique aspects of the juvenile justice system. We also studied juveniles involved in gangs. In this chapter, we not only focus on juveniles as a separate offender category but also explore the ugly and disturbing world of juvenile victimization and exploitation.

While juvenile gang-related activity, especially that involving violent crime, remains high in many areas across the country, the overall homicide rate continued on a downward trend through 2011.[1] Violent crime overall was down in 2011 by 15.4 percent from the 2007 level and 15.5 percent from the 2002 level. Violent crime in cities with populations over 1 million people—typically seen as havens for serious criminal activity—actually dropped 4 percent from the previous year. This bucks conventional wisdom, which suggests that the number of at-risk youth is rising due to various socioeconomic factors and budget cuts in law enforcement make police agencies less effective in combatting juvenile crime.

During the late 1990s and early 2000s, criminologists suggested that a great surge in violent crime would plague large cities in America, primarily due to a new predatory generation of thrill-seeking adolescents, referred to as Generation X.[2] Gen X-ers, born between 1966 and the early 1980s, were supposed to be the next wave of violent criminals to overwhelm the juvenile justice system. So much for criminal soothsaying! Crime rates have actually decreased despite those seemingly logical inferences based on sweeping characterizations of a generation that was exposed to more graphic violence and sexualized images, as well as more family decay and abuse than any generation before it. Generation X grew up on daily doses of heavy metal music, rap and video games . . . and survived quite well.

Much the same was predicted of Generation Y and the Millenial Generation. Again, politicians, criminologists and sociologists have predicted doom and gloom for these generations of kids. Those born after the mid-1980s are in the historic position of being the first generation fully immersed in the digital world, as described by psychologist Don Tapscott in *Growing Up Digital*.[3] Indeed, this is a unique generation that has information at their fingertips at all times—who can use their phones to watch live television broadcasts or capture videos and send them to hundreds of recipients with the touch of a button. This is a generation who has seen unspeakable acts of violence played out as part of 9/11, wars in the Middle East, shooting rampages, and home-grown terror attacks.

These young people are a generation less likely to die in an auto accident or by disease, but more than twice as likely to die by suicide or homicide than their parents were at the same age.[4] Are they the generation that will force momentous change in the juvenile and criminal justice systems of America? Or conversely, is this group simply a new generation with its own unique problems and peculiarities, no better or worse than those generations preceding it? They are a large generation (some 50 million Americans) that has already marked the beginning of a new millennium—some for their outstanding achievements in information sciences and environmental responsibility, others for their high-profile involvement in school shootings, hate crimes, and drug trafficking.

SCHOOL VIOLENCE

As with other acts of random violence (serial killings, terrorism), the tragedies stemming from school shootings seem to have no logical explanation.

Since the late 1980s, every state in the nation has been touched by an incident involving a school shooting or an episode of school violence where students have lost their lives. Incidents have captured the nation's attention to the point where the incident is known simply by uttering the name of the town or school where it occurred. These include Jonesboro, Arkansas (March 24, 1998), Littleton, Colorado (April 20, 1999), Red Lake, Minnesota (March 21, 2005), Virginia Tech (April 16, 2007), and Sandy Hook (December 14, 2012).[5] In each case, large numbers of innocent children and teachers were killed as a result of irrational violence carried out by a fellow student or gunman.

SHOOTINGS AT COLUMBINE HIGH SCHOOL: Though the 2012 shooting at Newtown, Connecticut (which killed 20 small children and 6 adults) has probably eclipsed this event as the single most horrific school shooting in American history, Columbine will always be the singular event that forever changed the way American parents viewed the safety of their children in schools. Unlike Newtown, the two shooters were students—insidious insiders who attacked their classmates with homemade bombs and automatic weapons. The attack left 15 students (including the attackers) and two teachers dead and another 25 wounded. The shooters were part of a handful of students called the "trench coat mafia," but they were generally described as outsiders. Many assumed that the pair were bullied and were somehow exacting revenge on their tormentors, but in recent years, portraits of the two boys have emerged that make it clear that one was clinically mentally ill and the other was—from all indications—a psychopath.[6]

Myth	Fact
Juveniles involved in recent incidents of school violence were addicted to violent video games, movies, and rock music.	While the rampage killings at schools have caused many people to point to violent aspects of American culture, there is very little empirical evidence that video games, movies, or television shows that depict graphic violence encourage such attacks.

School shootings, like this one at Sandy Hook Elementary School just before Christmas 2012, shocked the nation. Twenty children and six adult staff members were killed in this tragic event. *What do you think are the causes of such random violence in the United States?*

FOCUS ON PRACTICE

BULLYING: THE *OTHER* SCHOOL VIOLENCE

Jennifer Elaine Davis-Lamm

When someone mentions school violence, most of us think immediately about the mass shootings at Columbine, Jonesboro, and Newtown. These events were horrifying, undoubtedly, and have left scars on the American psyche that will be visible in one way or the other for many, many years. But there is another type of violence in schools that breeds much fear—so much so that the victims of it live with constant dread and anxiety, and have been known to commit suicide to escape it. That violence manifests in school bullying, once thought to be no more than a rite of passage for schoolchildren. Now we know that the consequences of bullying are anything but harmless, resulting in decreased academic achievement, long-term psychological issues (anxiety, depression), and in rare cases, violent outbursts against antagonists. Suicide is also associated with bullying victimization, though those who do commit suicide usually present with more than one risk factor, including depression, past trauma, or identifying as gay or lesbian.

Bullying is characterized by constant harassment, but it can take many forms, including verbal taunts, physical assaults, threats, social isolation, and even cyber bullying. In cyber bullying, the bully takes to Facebook, Instagram, Twitter, or other social networks to post malicious statements about his or her victims. The large audiences that can be reached through these means make such attacks particularly devastating to those being bullied.

The problem of bullying is widespread in our schools. About 28 percent of 12- to 18-year-old American school students reported being bullied in 2008, the last year for which data is available. As a result, many schools have adopted "get tough" approaches to bullying that not only seek to intervene in bullying, but also attempt to prevent a climate where such behavior thrives. Such approaches include adopting a plan to respond to bullying that goes beyond obvious physical assaults, such as rumor-spreading or social ostracism; educating parents on how to identify and deal with both children who are victims and children who are perpetrators of bullying; guidelines for teachers and other staff on consistent responses to bullying; collaborations with mental health and law enforcement professionals to address the problem; encouraging students to report all incidents of bullying; and offering counseling programs for those victimized by bullies.

Bullying is not an easy topic for parents, administrators, and students to approach. It involves a lot of shame on the part of the victim, and denial on the part of school personnel and parents. Bullying prevention must be proactive, interactive, and collaborative in order to prevent a type of victimization that scars so many American juveniles.

CRITICAL THINKING

What role does bullying play in the overall culture of violence in American schools?

Sources: "Effects of Bullying." Stopbullying.gov. Online. Available at: http://www.stopbullying.gov/at-risk/effects/. Retrieved May 3, 2013.

Simpson Rana. "Bullying in Schools". *Problem-Specific Guides Series, Number 12*. Community Oriented Policing Services. May 2012. U.S. Department of Justice. Online. Available at: http://www.cops.usdoj.gov/Publications/e07063414-guide.pdf. Retrieved May 3, 2013.

"Student Reports of Bullying and Cyber-Bullying: Results from the 2009 School Crime Supplement to the National Crime Victimization Survey." August 2011. U.S. Department of Education. Online. Available at: http://nces.ed.gov/pubsearch. Retrieved May 3, 2013.

TRENDS IN SCHOOL VIOLENCE High-profile events like Columbine, the massacre at Virginia Tech in 2007, and Sandy Hook may make it appear that school campuses in our country are not safe places for our children. Research actually shows that children are safer on campuses than they are anywhere else—the chances of becoming a victim in a school-associated violent death is less than one in a million—much less than dying in an auto accident or at the hands of an abusive parent.[7] Less than 2 percent of all youth homicides happen at school.[8]

School violence in the United States reached a peak in 1993 and has been falling steadily since that time. And, though frightening, high-profile school violence—such as mass shootings described above—is anything but typical. Such random acts of violence account for an extremely small percentage

FOCUS ON POLICY

ZERO TOLERANCE

The term zero tolerance was coined in the 1980s for strict drug control policies adopted as part of the federal war on drugs. Beginning in 1989, school districts in California, New York, and Kentucky were the first to attach the term "zero tolerance" to policies mandating expulsion for drugs, fighting, and gang-related activity, according to the Center for Evaluation and Education Policy. It became national policy in 1994, after President Bill Clinton signed the Gun-Free Schools Act of 1994, which was passed in response to several school shootings across the country. The federal law required states to expel for at least one calendar year any student who brought firearms to school grounds.

State lawmakers and school boards have since expanded the punishment for weapons to include automatic expulsion or suspension for drugs and alcohol, fighting, swearing, disrupting class, disobedience, truancy, and more than a dozen other forms of misbehavior. But have zero-tolerance policies had an effect on school crime rates?

Probably not—and in fact, the policies may be counterproductive. Research has shown that the policies were applied inconsistently across the board and disproportionately to minorities, and that children who were disciplined under these models were more likely to re-offend. Furthermore, the suspensions involved may have a negative impact on future attendance—and be a precursor to a student dropping out of school altogether.

Evidence that zero-tolerance policies really work is scant, according to many experts, and a new push to move away from such models is underway. Crisis prevention scholars recommend now that schools adopt a "threat assessment approach" that gives schools the flexibility to identify students who might pose a risk to other students and intervene appropriately. Schools that have so far adopted such a practice have seen marked decreases in suspensions and bullying incidents.

CRITICAL THINKING

Why do you think zero-tolerance policies don't work?

Source: Peterson, Kavan. 2005, March 15. "Schools Re-Think Post-Columbine Discipline." Online.

Neuman, Scott. "Violence in Schools: How Big a Problem Is It?" National Public Radio. Originally broadcast March 16, 2012. Online.

Moll, Jeanette and Henry Joel Simmons. 2012, August. "Expelling Zero Tolerance: Reforming Texas School Discipline for Good". *Texas Public Policy Foundation Policy Perspective.* Online. Available at: http://www.texaspolicy.com/sites/default/files/documents/2012-08-PP18-ExpellingZeroTolerance-CEJ-JeanetteMoll.pdf

of homicides in this country. The number of those killed in mass shootings like Columbine between 1983 and 2012 is 550, which is by no means trivial. But consider that in 2011 alone, a total of 8,583 people in this country were killed by firearms—and it becomes clear that these mass shooting events are quite rare.[9]

Furthermore, these **rampage killings** are rarely impulsive acts. Instead, they are premeditated and highly staged or planned. Many of the suspects had openly expressed violence and, in a majority of cases, had actually threatened violence before the event. There is often a precipitating factor, or "a spark that sets off the tinder." In juvenile cases, this is often a seemingly unimportant event at school or the break-up of a girlfriend/boyfriend relationship. In many cases, the suspects killed themselves after committing their crime. The demographic profile of rampage killers is also significantly different from that of typical murderers (refer to Figure 14.1). However, the most important finding relating to rampage homicides is the link to mental health problems. In over half the cases reported from 1990 to 2007, the suspects had a history, or showed signs, of significant mental health disturbance. While rampage killings have caused many people to point to violent aspects of American culture, such

14.1 SELF-CHECK

1. Describe zero tolerance programs.
2. What are the differences between rampage killings and typical murders? Give some examples of rampage killings involving juveniles.

rampage killings Multiple-victim killings that are random in nature, characterized by violent and quick outbursts on the part of one or more suspects for seemingly no reason or motive.

| FIGURE 14.1 | How Rampage Killers Differ from Typical Murderers |

They are older . . .

Under 30 years old	43%
	60%
30 to 50	46%
	32%
Over 50	11%
	7%

. . . better educated . . .

No high school	8%
	57%
High school	33%
	26%
Some college	24%
	13%
Degree	35%
	1%

They don't get away . . .

| Apprehended by police | 100% |
| | 76% |

Percent (0 10 20 30 40 50 60 70 80 90 100)

. . . more likely to be white . . .

White (non-Hispanic)	71%
	36%
Black (non-Hispanic)	19%
	50%
Hispanic	2%
	11%
Other*	8%
	2%

*includes Asian, Indian, and unknown

. . . and out of work.

Unemployed	57%
	26%
Working	43%
	74%

. . . and many kill themselves

| Committed suicide | 33% |
| | 3% |

Percent (0 10 20 30 40 50 60 70 80 90 100)

■ Rampage killers   ■ Typical murderers

Sources: For rampage killers: *The New York Times* Database. For others: (Age, race, apprehension status) FBI Supplemental Homicide Reports, 1996; (Education, employment, military background) Survey of Inmates of State Correctional Facilities, 1991; (Time of day) Criminal Victimization in the United States, 1992, Bureau of Justice Statistics (for aggravated assault crimes); (Suicide) Estimates based on Marzuk, P. M. et al. "The Epidemiology of Murder-Suicide." *Journal of the American Medical Association*, June 1, 1992.

The New York Times Graphics. From Ford Fessenden, "They Threaten, Seethe and Unhinge, Then Kill in Quantity," *New York Times*, April 9, 2000, p. A28.

as video games, movies, television, and the Internet, the real problems may rest in society's failure to address serious mental health issues, particularly among juveniles.

Mentally Ill Juvenile Offenders

There is still much to be known about the prevalence of mental illness in juvenile offenders and the connection between mental illness and delinquency. Mentally ill juveniles are involved in the juvenile justice system, and research suggests that mental illnesses and disorders may be greater among delinquent youths than nondelinquent youths.[10] It is estimated that 20 percent of all youths in the juvenile justice system have serious mental disorders. A much higher percentage have less serious, but still significant, mental health problems.

Juvenile offenders who have a mental illness are often referred to as emotionally disturbed. These juveniles are not prone to commit any particular type of crime over another. Some delinquents have serious psychiatric disorders, are psychotic, or are diagnosed with schizophrenia. Others have less serious problems, such as poor self-esteem, depression, anxiety, simple phobias, and

FOCUS ON PROGRAMS

TREATMENT FOR MENTALLY ILL JUVENILE OFFENDERS

Compared to programs designed to meet the needs of other types of offenders, little is being done with regard to treatment and programs for delinquents with mental illnesses. Historically, the juvenile justice system has been ambivalent about how to respond to juvenile offenders with mental illnesses or disorders. This is not surprising given the multiple and complex needs of this particular group of offenders.

Juvenile offenders with mental illnesses may be formally processed by the juvenile justice system or diverted to mental health agencies for screening, assessment, and treatment. Some programs that deal with mental illness are offered for youths after they have become juvenile offenders. One of the more progressive programs in the country is offered by the Texas Juvenile Justice Department. TJJD has implemented an innovative *resocialization* program for emotionally disturbed and other types of juvenile offenders coming out of juvenile correctional institutions.

The program includes education, work, discipline, and cognitive–behavioral treatment. Early findings indicate that the program may reduce recidivism among the emotionally disturbed juvenile offenders.

Other programs are geared to the prevention of delinquency and may not necessarily be directed to youths who are diagnosed with a mental illness. These programs simply offer services to assist youths in developing skills to avoid hostile or aggressive behaviors as well as coping skills to be better prepared in dealing emotionally with difficult situations.

For juvenile justice agencies to respond effectively to mental illness among delinquent youths, much more research is needed on the association between mental illness and delinquency and the types of treatment and services most relevant for this population.

CRITICAL THINKING

Do you think the Texas program mentioned is preventative or correctional?

Source: Briscoe, Judy. "Breaking the Cycle of Violence: A Rational Approach to At-Risk Youth." *Federal Probation*, 61, March 1997, pp. 3–13.

Attention-Deficit/Hyperactivity Disorder (ADHD). Many juveniles who are incarcerated have been diagnosed with post-traumatic stress disorder. Significantly disturbing events (for example, witnessing domestic violence, incest, death of a parent) in the lives of children may also lead to other types of emotional and behavioral problems, later manifesting in psychiatric disorders.[11] The most prevalent disorders appear to be conduct disorders, antisocial personality disorders, and substance abuse disorders. Oftentimes, mentally ill juvenile offenders suffer from more than one diagnosable disease or disorder. Recent estimates suggest that nearly two-thirds of inmates in juvenile facilities have at least one type of mental illness. Such offenders overwhelm the juvenile justice system, which is a frequent resort for kids unable to find community treatment options to help them. Poor economic conditions that have resulted in deep cuts to social service agencies across the country mean that juvenile facilities can expect to see even more admissions of mentally ill kids dependent on powerful psychotrophic drugs and without access to meaningful therapeutic intervention.[12]

14.2 SELF-CHECK

What types of family events may lead to emotional and behavioral problems among juveniles?

Juvenile Drug Offenders

The use and abuse of drugs in society is not a new phenomenon. Indeed, the extent of drug use among humans can be traced to almost all civilizations during every period of time. It is not surprising that most individuals first come into contact with drugs during the high-risk and high-experimentation years associated with adolescence. **A drug** can be defined as a chemical that interacts

drug A chemical that alters normal body and mind functioning.

with the body and alters basic body functioning, usually through the central nervous cord and system. The drugs most commonly associated with abuse-are classified as opiates, stimulants, depressants, hallucinogens, and marijuana. However, there are thousands of substances that are capable of altering human perception and behavior.

The linkage of drug abuse with crime (or delinquency) is also not a new phenomenon. Researchers first explored the connection in the early urbanization periods of the 20th century, but the relationship was not fully analyzed until the crime wave of the 1960s. Called upon to explain and curb it, policymakers sought empirical evidence that drug addicts were responsible for the sudden upsurge of robberies, murders, property and street crime, and race riots indicative of the decade.[13] Many young Americans from every background and ethnicity experimented with drug use, including marijuana, lysergic acid diethylamide (LSD), barbiturates, cocaine, and heroin. At that time, most of the available research focused on heroin addiction and adult crime. However, subsequent work has explored the nexus between a variety of drug use, patterns of trafficking, and delinquency.[14]

Today, the abuse of drugs and alcohol among adolescents is considered one of the most serious public health problems facing America, and juveniles do seem to be taking drugs at a younger age than ever before. Rates of drug use remain high, and are increasing in some cases, particularly among high-risk youths. The spread of HIV/AIDS related to drug use and high-risk sexual behavior continues to be of concern, as does rates of overdose of both drugs and alcohol. While the overall stance on drug use in this country may have soften somewhat since the War on Drugs' heyday, the devastating impact of drugs on adolescent lives is still a critical issue.

DRUG USE AMONG ADOLESCENTS

In 2011, about 22.5 million Americans ages 12 and up were current illicit drug users; this number represents close to 9 percent of the total U.S. population ages 12 and older. This rate is similar to what it had been in 2010 and 2009, but it is actually a higher rate than what was seen in the years between 2003 and 2008.

Estimates count 18.1 million marijuana users currently in the United States. Marijuana is the drug most commonly used by illicit drug users; nearly 80 percent of them report using it.[15] This number also represents an increase from previous years. And heroin use has nearly doubled: in 2011, 620,000 users were reported, up from 373,000 just five years previously. However, cocaine use in the same period has fallen slightly, as has use of prescription pain relievers such as Oxycontin, Vicodin, Percoset, and others for nonmedical reasons.[16] The use of more traditionally abused drugs such as crack and cocaine, methamphetamines (including the "designer drug" MDMA—"ecstasy"), hallucinogens (including LSD ["acid"] and PCP ["angel dust"]), and a broad category of "club drugs" (including the date rape drugs rohypnol ["roofies"] and GHB ["soap"]) remains high but relatively constant.

The increase in marijuana use reflects changing attitudes about the drug. Perceived by many to be safe, the drug was legalized in 2012 elections in Washington State and Colorado. Surveys among youth show that they do not consider the drug to be dangerous. However, **synthetic marijuana** is a new concern. This drug, known as K2 or spice, is an herbal mixture laced with synthetically made cannabinoids—which act similarly in the brain to the active ingredient in marijuana, THC. Until recently, these mixtures could be purchased legally and were seen as a safer alternative to marijuana. However, it was linked to 11,406 drug-related emergency department visits in 2010 alone, and has been linked to a handful of fatalities. In 2011, 11.4 percent of

---

Binge Drinking in Adolescents

- Binge drinking is defined as consuming five or more drinks in a row.
- Binge drinking, often beginning around age 13, tends to increase during adolescence and peaks in young adulthood (ages 18–22).
- Binge drinkers are eight times more likely to miss class, fall behind in schoolwork, get hurt or injured, and damage property than nonbinge drinkers.
- Binge drinking during high school is strongly predictive of binge drinking in college.
- Binge drinking in college may be associated with mental health disorders such as compulsiveness, depression or anxiety, or early deviant behavior.

SOURCE: "Binge Drinking in Adolescents and College Students," www.health.org/govpubs/rpo995, November 1, 2005.

synthetic marijuana (K2 or "spice") An herbal mixture laced with synthetically made cannabinoids similar to the active ingredient in marijuana, THC.

12th graders reported using it in the past year. In 2012, 4.4 percent of eighth graders, 8.8 percent of 10th graders, and 11.3 percent of 12th graders reported past-year use.[17]

Alcohol continues to be a widely abused drug among juveniles. In 2011, about 9.7 million persons aged 12 to 20 reported drinking alcohol in the past month. Approximately 6.1 million (15.8 percent) were binge drinkers, and 1.7 million (4.4 percent) classified themselves as heavy drinkers.[18] One-third of traffic fatalities involving teenagers were attributed to alcohol use.[19]

DRUGS, DELINQUENCY, AND JUVENILE VIOLENCE

The relationship between drug use and delinquency, particularly as it relates to violent criminal activity, has been the subject of much study and debate. In 1985, author Paul Goldstein developed a theoretical framework in which to study the drugs/violence nexus.[20] One linkage is identified as psycho-pharmacological, which purports that drugs alter behavior by reducing inhibitions and instilling aggressive/violent tendencies. By contrast, economically compulsive violence occurs when individuals commit violent crime in their effort to secure money to purchase drugs for self use (for example, robbery). Systemic violence occurs during turf battles and struggles for control in the drug dealing and street trafficking subculture.[21] (See Figure 14.2 for data on drug-related homicides.) These categories provide a sound basis on which to study drug use and violence. However, a more recent review of the literature reveals the following four major changes that now characterize the drug subculture.

Drug use appears to be increasing among adolescents. *Do you think drinking and smoking lead to heavier drug use?*

First, in adolescence and adulthood, general forms of drug use and delinquency are not causally related. That is, drug use does not cause crime. However, recent studies on heroin addiction taken in Baltimore, New York, and Miami clearly established a strong relationship between drug use and crime.[22] According to these leading studies, even though heroin and other drug use did not necessarily initiate crime on the part of addicts, it did tend to intensify and perpetuate criminal activity among users. Author James Inciardi points out that "drug use freezes its devotees into patterns of criminality that are more acute, dynamic, unremitting, and enduring than those of other offenders."[23] Drug use, specifically among adolescents, seems to be much more spurious in nature, since crime, delinquency, and drug abuse are all forms of deviant behavior in which juveniles engage. These findings have far-reaching policy ramifications since the current American drug-control policy is based on demand reduction (that is, lessen the use or demand by the user). In turn, demand reduction reduces the amount of drug-related crime. If delinquency and drug use are only inconsistently correlated, then it makes sense to focus our efforts not on the enforcement of drug laws, but rather the intervention and treatment of adolescent drug users.

Second, there has been a historically erroneous misconception of the relationship between drugs and violence. In many instances, there has been a tendency to portray the individual drug user as a crazed maniac incapable of controlling his or her own behavior. Such depictions have been historical in nature, and were promoted more to fulfill religious and establishment goals rather than to

FIGURE 14.2	Drug-Related Homicides	
YEAR	NUMBER OF HOMICIDES	PERCENT DRUG RELATED
1987	17,963	4.9%
1988	17,971	5.6
1989	18,954	7.4
1990	20,273	6.7
1991	21,676	6.2
1992	22,716	5.7
1993	23,180	5.5
1994	22,084	5.6
1995	20,232	5.1
1996	16,967	5.0
1997	15,837	5.1
1998	14,276	4.8
1999	13,011	4.5
2000	13,230	4.5
2001	14,061	4.1
2002	14,263	4.7
2003	14,465	4.7
2004	14,210	3.9
2005	14,965	4.0
2006	14,990	5.3
2007	14,916	5.3
2008	14,224	5.0
2009	13,752	5.2
2010	13,164	5.2
2011	12,664	5.1
2012	12,449*	4.9*

*Data for 2012 is an estimate (see Federal Bureau of Investigation, *Preliminary UCR Crime Report: Crime in the United States-2012* published January 14, 2013).

Source: U.S. Department of Justice, Bureau of Justice Statistics, Drug Use and Crime and Federal Bureau of Investigation, *UCR Crime Reports, 2007, 2009, 2010,* and *2011.*

Heroin use is increasing among juveniles. Despite its fashionable, hip reputation, heroin consumption is a leading cause of death in the juvenile population. *Why do you think there is such a resurgence of heroin as a drug of choice among youths?*

FOCUS ON PRACTICE

SYNTHETIC DRUGS: A NEW THREAT FOR TEENS

Every few years, a new drug comes to the forefront of national consciousness due to a spike in popularity and the subsequent deaths or injuries of youth as a result of that drug. In the past, we've seen deadly substances like"cheese" and "chiva" in the spotlight; more recently, synthetic reproductions of drugs like marijuana and cocaine have taken their place. What's especially dangerous about these synthetics is that they were, until recently, legally sold in head shops and some gas stations—which gave the impression to many that they were safe.

However, these drugs are anything but safe. K2 (or spice) and bath salts are synthetically derived chemical compounds that stayed under the radar as legal substances for many years. Bath salts, so called because the powdery substance resembles Epsom salts, contain a cathinone, which is a stimulant chemically similar to amphetamines. They are frequently inhaled or snorted, and their effects mimic those of cocaine and methamphetamines, and unfortunately, come with a host of nasty side effects. Users report painful headaches, heart palpitations, and nausea. The drug has also been associated with paranoia, anxiety, psychotic behavior, violent outbursts, heart attacks, kidney failure, liver failure, suicide, and rapid dehydration. In 2012, there were 2,655 calls about exposures to bath salts to national poison control centers—in 2010, there were only 236.

K2 or spice is marketed as synthetic cannabis, and is sold in the form of dried herbs that are sprayed with various chemical compounds. The potent herbal mixture is then smoked. Effects are said to mimic marijuana use, but many users have reported extreme agitation, hallucinations, heart palpitations, excessive sweating, and catatonic states. In 2012, 5,202 calls about K2/spice were taken by American poison control centers, a number that is nearly double the rate of 2010 calls. Deaths of teenagers have been reported as a result of both types of synthetics, causing the FDA to take emergency action in 2011 to ban them.

They were subsequently made illegal in July 2012, when President Obama signed a bill that banned the sale of 31 synthetic compounds. Despite the fact that the drugs cannot be sold in stores or online, they are still readily available. Internet searches reveal wide availability of both substances through mail order services.

CRITICAL THINKING

Why are these synthetic drugs so dangerous for youth?

Sources: National Institute on Drug Abuse. 2012, December. "DrugFacts: Spice (Synthetic Marijuana)." Online. Available at: http://www.drugabuse.gov/publications/drugfacts/spice-synthetic-marijuana. Retrieved April 30, 2013.

National Institute on Drug Abuse. 2012, November. "DrugFacts: Synthetic Cathinones ("Bath Salts"). Online.

Retrieved April 30, 2013.

American Association of Poison Control Centers. http://www.aapcc.org/

---

reflect facts. Stereotypes of the "drug fiend" that engaged in bizarre, unpredictable, irrational sexual aggression and violence were popular in the early 20th century. However, the drug epidemic of the late 1960s and early 1970s forced new research and responsible efforts to describe the relationship between drugs and violent offenders accurately. Opiate and narcotic (heroin) users were seen as less violent than their counterparts since opium-derived products are strong central nervous system depressants and have a tendency to suppress aggressive impulses. Individuals who abused heroin were seen as much more rational in their choice of crime, usually forced into prostitution or engaged in property crimes such as larceny and burglary in order to obtain money for their habit.

Third, and most important, the drug street culture has dramatically changed. The first studies indicating this significant change started to appear in the mid-1970s, which focused on the new generation of drug users and the emergence of a more violent group of addicts.[24] The single drug user of the past (usually heroin users) were becoming a scarcity. Opiate addicts showed a greater tendency to be poly-drug abusers or individuals who would take any drug available and not exclusively the one of their choice.[25] Drug-using populations started to grow significantly, not only as opiate users, but also as emerging amphetamine, cocaine, alcohol, and hallucinogen abusers. The new generation was much more likely to combine their drug use, making it even more difficult to study the impact of one specific drug on behavior.

Coupled with these significant changes were other important factors. The age of first drug use and the subsequent age of addiction have significantly declined over the past 20 years. Since younger age is a factor that has been associated with a greater tendency toward aggression and violence, the increase in violent, drug-related crime may be partially due to the younger age of addicts.[26] Thus, juvenile drug users appear to be much more willing to use violence than their adult counterparts.

Then, too, younger drug users and traffickers appear to be much more group-oriented and peer influenced.[27] The last two decades have given rise to vast increases in juvenile gang activity and development, particularly in large urban cities. Much of the literature concerning juvenile gangs focuses on the development of a distribution network for drugs, particularly cocaine (and crack cocaine) which also emerged during this time period.[28] Refer to Chapter 13 for a discussion of juvenile gangs. Traditional gang values such as secured and marked territory, heightened feelings of toughness, gang rivalry, and individual gang member respect have become important elements of the drug delivery system and street subculture. Adding to this already volatile situation is the proliferation of a powerful arsenal of weaponry. As one Los Angeles gang officer put it, "The switchblades and Saturday night specials of *West Side Story* have been replaced by the Uzis and Mac-10s of the Crips and Bloods." This statement reflects the significant changes in not only the sheer number of guns available to gang members active in the drug trade, but also the new and significant firepower presented by automatic weapons.[29]

14.3 SELF-CHECK

1. What is a drug, and what are the common drugs of abuse?
2. What is the connection between drugs and violence?

CAREERS IN JUVENILE JUSTICE

Licensed Chemical Dependency Counselor

Licensed chemical dependency counselors (L.C.D.C.) provide counseling for individuals with alcohol and drug abuse problems. These trained counselors provide specialized services to individuals and families who are experiencing the effects of substance abuse. Counselors work in both in-patient and out-patient treatment settings and halfway houses. The work involves planning, coordinating, and implementing substance abuse counseling activities. Often programs must be coordinated with other departments, divisions, agencies, and community organizations to ensure that all possible resources are made available to clients with substance abuse problems.

In most job settings, responsibilities include providing substance abuse counseling, recovery skills training, and participating in educational groups in compliance with substance abuse treatment program standards, guidelines, and policies. Counselors interview, screen, and evaluate offenders as potential participants in the program. The job also requires careful record keeping including preparing and maintaining offender records, workload statistics, and other documentation, as well as preparing periodic reports. In some settings, counselors act as liaisons to participants of training programs, workshops, and seminars. A key responsibility is follow-up and aftercare plans for offenders before and after their release.

Educational requirements include graduation from an accredited senior high school or GED equivalent and licensed chemical dependency counselor program. Many programs are offered as either a two-year associate degree program or as a one-year certificate program. To become certified, students must pass a test.

Critical Thinking

What do you think is the most important qualification for a licensed chemical dependency counselor?

Fourth and finally, some researchers have noted that most incidents of drug-related violence occur in deteriorated communities characterized by the loss of informal and formal social control, internal struggle between large numbers of disenfranchised subcultures, and the absence of meaningful economic processes and political decision making.[30] Such communities can be found in the barrios, ghettos, and skid rows of most large, urban cities. Author Ansley Hamid contends that aggression and violence are unavoidable and are tacitly sanctioned to maintain social order in a society divided by race, ethnicity, gender, and class.[31] Today, more communities and larger segments of our population appear to be living in these conditions as the economic gap between the haves and the have-nots widens.

Indeed, the street culture of drug addiction has changed significantly over the past 20 years to one which is much more volatile and, hence, much more violent.

Most of the crack cocaine in the United States is controlled by gangs in major cities. *Why do you think this is the case?*

Juvenile Sex Offenders

Historically, sexual misconduct and sexual aggression by youths have been dismissed as experimentation and curiosity, and therefore have not been taken seriously by juvenile justice or mental health systems. This was especially true when boys perpetrated sexually unacceptable and aggressive acts. Aggression was seen as a normal by-product of sexual development into adulthood. However, what was not understood was that many offenders continue their illegal sexual behavior as adults and become more dangerous predators. Views on sexual aggression have changed significantly over the past 20 years. Sexual misconduct is no longer dismissed as inconsequential; it is now recognized as a very serious problem linked to serious patterns of sexual aggression and violence in adulthood.

Sexual offending by youths is thought to be a much larger problem than is reported. It is estimated that juvenile sex offenders comprise more than one-quarter (25.8 percent) of all sex offenders and more than one-third (35.6 percent) of sex offenders against juvenile victims.[32]

THE PROGRESSION OF AGGRESSIVE SEXUAL BEHAVIOR

Aggressive sexual behavior seems to progress from less serious sexual misconduct such as obscene phone calls, voyeurism, or stealing undergarments to more serious and troubling behavior such as non-contact sexual misconduct (e.g., exhibitionism). Sexual aggression and violence often appear later. This progression and linkage to juvenile sexual behavior has been the focus for scholars studying serial murders.[33] Some youths may be driven to commit such acts as a result of urges or impulses, while others may not. The former group is especially important to consider, since it is this group of offenders who are likely to continue their crimes through adulthood if not identified and treated effectively.

PARAPHILIA Juveniles who have a chronic interest in sexually aggressive and/or deviant fantasy may suffer from a series of **paraphilia**, or sexual compulsions linked to continued violence and aggression during adulthood.[34] Classified as a mental disorder by the American Psychiatric Association, paraphilia are recurrent and intense arousal fantasies, sexual urges, and behaviors that involve

paraphilia Almost exclusively common to males, paraphilia are erotic sexual conditions involving obsessive deviant or bizarre images or activities to achieve or maintain sexual arousal.

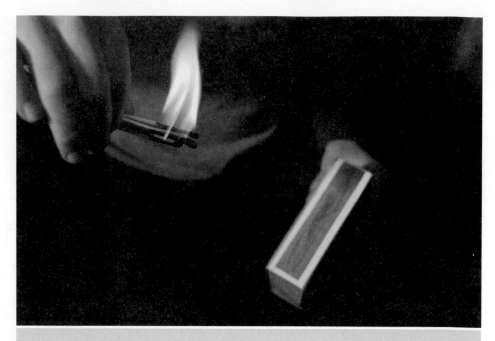

Pyromania is a well-known paraphilia among children and adolescents. *What harm could come from labeling a child with this type of mental disorder?*

objects, suffering, or humiliation either imposed on themselves or their sexual partners, animals, or children and other people who do not consent.[35] Often, psychologists, psychiatrists, and other professionals are hesitant to diagnose children and adolescents with such diseases for fear of stigmatizing or labeling the youth. (Recall from Chapter 5 that the labeling theory believes individuals who are given such a diagnosis are treated in a different and negative manner by teachers, friends, and family.) The juvenile may internalize the label, and then act in such a way as to express behavior characteristic of the condition. In other words, labeling youth sexually deviant or diagnosing a paraphilia may lead to a self-fulfilling behavior where the youth conforms to the label.

This presents a serious dilemma in the identification of juvenile sex offenders. Identifying a youth's sexual deviancy may create harmful consequences in terms of social stigma and self-fulfilling behavior. However, failing to diagnose such a condition may lead to ignoring a real problem, to lack of treatment, and to escalating aggressive behavior. The key to preventing such acts of sexual aggression among juveniles is to be able to identify problems early and find ways to treat them while minimizing potential unintended and harmful consequences that may arise from attaching labels.

OTHER CHARACTERISTICS OF JUVENILE SEXUAL OFFENDERS Not surprisingly, most juvenile sex offenders are male. Evidence suggests that adult sexual offending is rooted in juvenile sexual misconduct during childhood and adolescence. A study of adult rapists and child molesters found that dangerous sex offenders began committing sex crimes well before the age of 18.[36] Juvenile sexual offenders do not differ significantly from other youth with regard to demographic characteristics, ethnicity, or race. Factors which contribute to youthful sexual offending include drug- and fetal-alcohol-related syndromes, family dysfunction, and physical, emotional, and sexual abuse during childhood years.[37]

14.4 SELF-CHECK

1. What is paraphilia?
2. What factors may contribute to youthful sexual offending?

FOCUS ON POLICY

SEXTING: TEENAGE PITFALL OR SEX OFFENSE?

You can't go anywhere these days without seeing people glued to their cell phones. Text messaging is a major reason for the ubiquitous presence of cell phones among both adults and youth. But for youth, especially, text messaging is a must-have for social networking and communication. Juveniles plan outings, discuss schoolwork, gossip about others in their social circle, and also engage in conversations of a sexual nature. The passivity of the medium makes texting a perfect way for many teenagers to convey aspects of their sexuality, whether it's minor flirting or—in some cases—sending nude pictures of themselves to the person at the other end of the message. This photographic phenomenon is called "sexting," an amalgam of sex and texting. And although this behavior might be entirely consensual, it also technically violates statutes enacted to prevent the transmission of child pornography. More than one teenager has been caught in this situation—one that is not only embarrassing, but also potentially illegal.

For example, in Fairfax, Virginia, three high school students made cell phone videos of themselves engaging in sex with other juveniles and then shared the videos among themselves. They are now facing child pornography charges. Fairfax County prosecutors insist that the charges are fair, given the impact on the victims—particularly given that once the images have been sent, there is little control on how rapidly they are shared with other individuals, potentially spreading to large audiences or being posted on public websites.

However, many juvenile justice practitioners and law enforcement officials feel that this is a blatant misuse of laws intended to protect children from predators, not from their own consensual sexual transgressions. While juveniles would likely not face stiff sentences if they were convicted of such an offense, they would have to register as sex offenders after conviction, making college admissions, employment, and even housing a problem for years to come. Given that nearly 19 percent of teens surveyed recently by the National Campaign to Prevent Teen and Unplanned Pregnancy admitted to posting or sending nude or semi-nude photographs of themselves, if law enforcement agencies do decide to prosecute sexting cases, they could have their hands full, potentially diverting resources from more serious cases. As a result, North Dakota, Utah, Vermont, Florida, Pennsylvania, and Ohio have already passed legislation that reduces penalties for teenagers engaging in sexting. Fourteen other states are considering reducing penalties for minors so they are not punished under the same laws designed to punish child pornographers.

Sexting poses an interesting question for the juvenile justice system, one that should be addressed in policy in the coming years to define at what point the act should be a prosecutable offense. Perhaps merely sending self-taken photographs to someone should be more a parental concern than a law enforcement concern. However, unauthorized distribution of these portraits may indeed be crossing a legal line. Regardless, this touchy subject should be addressed in the home environment before it ever escalates to the point where police officials become involved in the sex lives of teenagers.

CRITICAL THINKING

Should child pornography laws encompass sexting incidents? Why or why not?

Sources: Brunker, Miles. "'Sexting' Surprise: Teens Face Child Porn Charges." MSNBC.com, January 15, 2009. Available: www.msnbc.com/id/28679588

Curtis, Brent. "16-Year-Old Boy Charged in Sexting Chase." *Rutland Herald*, June 5, 2009.

Juvenal, Justin. "Teen 'Sexting' Case Goes to Trial in Fairfax County." *New York Times, April 17, 2013*. Online. Available: http://articles.washingtonpost.com/2013-04-17/local/38616662_1_sexting-cases-videos. May 2, 2013.

Stone, Gigi. "'Sexting' Teens Can Go Too Far." ABC News, March 13, 2009. Available: www.abcnews.go.com/Technology/WorldNews/story?id=6456834&page=1

Chronic Juvenile Offenders

Most people who study criminal justice agree that a small proportion of delinquent youth is responsible for a large proportion of serious crimes such as burglary and robbery. These youths are generally referred to as *chronic juvenile offenders* because of their persistent or habitual involvement in delinquency. Chronic juvenile offenders begin their "criminal careers" at a relatively young age (10–12) and have persistent involvement in crime through adulthood. They tend *not* to "grow out" of crime in their youth.[38]

The terms *chronic delinquent* and *chronic juvenile offender* were not popularized until a famous delinquency study was conducted in Philadelphia by authors Marvin Wolfgang, Robert Figlio, and Terrence Sellin.[39] The trio studied the criminal careers of a birth **cohort** made up of boys born in 1945. They gathered personal background and school related data as well as police records about these 9,945 boys from before age 11 through age 18. Results showed that about one-third of the group (3,475) had been involved with the police at least once and about two-thirds (6,630) had no involvement with law enforcement. Among those delinquents having had significant involvement with the police, most boys (1,862 or 54 percent) were **recidivists**, meaning they had committed more than one offense in the past. Within this group of recidivists was a subgroup (627 or 6 percent) of *chronic offenders* who had committed at least four criminal offenses. Amazingly, this very small group of chronic offenders was responsible for more than half of the entire number of offenses that could be attributed to the total cohort. Their acts were also the most serious: they accounted for 71 percent of the homicides, 73 percent of the forcible rapes, 82 percent of the robberies, and 69 percent of the aggravated assaults.

More recent studies and a follow-up of the original cohort study indicated that boys classified as chronic offenders continued through adulthood in persistent involvement in crime. These results also support the general concept of a chronic juvenile offender phenomenon; a very small proportion of the total offender population is responsible for a large proportion of serious offenses reported to the police.[40]

CHARACTERISTICS OF CHRONIC JUVENILE OFFENDERS

Studies by Wolfgang and colleagues found that race is not a consistent factor in predicting chronic offenders. As with most juvenile crime, the offenders are most often male. One factor that may help to identify the chronic juvenile offender is performing poorly in school and becoming a school dropout.[41] Certainly, not all juveniles who do poorly in school or who drop out of school engage in delinquent behavior. Other factors correlated with both poor school performance and chronic juvenile offending were low I.Q., low educational attainment, and a history of family problems often involving some form of physical or sexual abuse.

"HACKERS AND CRACKERS"

The information age and the new millennium have produced a new and colorful form of criminality often associated with chronic juvenile offending. However, research shows that this new breed of criminal has little in common with their counterparts. **Hackers** or **crackers** are slang words to describe an entire subculture of juvenile delinquents engaged in attacking secure computer systems or various Internet sites. These are the offspring of *War Games, Ferris Bueller's Day Off, The Matrix, Antitrust,* and other hit movies that romanticize the merry pranksters as intelligent, fun-loving, young Robin Hoods battling the evil forces of the world. However, for the people whose businesses and lives depend on computers, the actions of these individuals are anything but fun little games or science fiction fantasies. The newspapers are filled with new intrusions to Internet and computer sites by such individuals. Usually, the damage is limited to vandalism of the site or insertion of a **computer virus** into the e-mail of an unsuspecting recipient. Such is the case of recent vandalism

cohort A group of individuals being observed over a long period of time under scientific research and analysis.

recidivist An individual who commits the same crime or returns to illegal activity *after* conviction and release from incarceration.

hackers/crackers Individuals who break into a secure computer or data system or vandalize an Internet site.

computer virus An encoded, rogue program secretly inserted into a normal software program or into a computer's operating system with the express purpose of vandalizing data.

FIGURE 14.3	The Hacker Subculture

Demographic profile of the juvenile hacker subculture based on interviews and empirical observations of more than 100 convicted hackers.

- White males
- 14 to 20 years of age
- From families of medium to high socioeconomic status
- Highly intelligent individuals, yet underachievers in school
- Self-descriptions include feelings of boredom and apathy
- Favorite activities include computer games and/or other games emphasizing a fantasy world (e.g., Dungeons and Dragons)
- Membership in a thrill-seeking subculture group of computer hackers, often taking on the name of fantasy world characters (e.g., Zod, Captain Zap, The Wizard)

Source: Adapted from a study by Robert Taylor, reported in Swanson, Charles R., Neil C. Chamelin, Leonard Territo, and Robert Taylor. *Criminal Investigation*, 9th ed., New York: McGraw-Hill, 2006, pp. 550–57. Also, see 10th ed., 2009, pp. 520–64.

on the FBI, Yahoo, and eBay websites or the intrusion into the nuclear weapons laboratories in Los Alamos, New Mexico.[42]

In the only known study based on actual interviews with over 100 convicted juvenile hackers, author Robert Taylor reports that they do not meet the common profile of their chronic juvenile offender counterparts.[43] (See Figure 14.3.) Even though these hackers maintain significant collaboration between each other and engage in elaborate, sophisticated, and ongoing criminal activity, few have ever been arrested. Most of them are relatively young, white males from middle- and upper-class environments. Their families are intact and, in fact, most have loving and caring parents. Generally, they range from 14 to 25 years of age. They are not socially integrated and tend to be loners, except when communicating by e-mail and over the Internet. There, they often lead make-believe lives involving highly involved, complex, and sophisticated networks complete with fantasy names and challenging missions. They tend not to associate with their peer groups or become actively involved in peer group behavior such as dating or participating in school activities. They take on the air of self-assurance only when they are with fellow hackers. They form a unique and secret subculture which places value on new intrusions into secure systems, developing a new virus, or "one-upping" the latest vandalism on the Internet. In most cases, their parents rarely suspect problems, as their children appear to be "model" young adults. As one investigator pointed out, "They [hackers] don't race cars, chase girls, drink beer, take drugs, or get into trouble." Although hackers are smart, they tend to be underachievers in school. They stay in their rooms, communicating with their friends in their own world—seemingly addicted to the computer. As one convicted teenager reported, "Hacking is like cocaine . . . it's a rush you can't forget."[44]

Violent Juvenile Offenders

Aside from those juveniles who can be categorized as chronic offenders, there is an even smaller group that can be classified as violent juvenile offenders. Violent offenses are those that produce physical harm, or the threat of harm, to victims. They are often called person offenses and include the **FBI Index Crimes** of homicide, assault, forcible rape, and robbery. Kidnapping and arson are often included in the list of violent offenses. Violent offenses do not always result in someone being physically injured. A threat of bodily injury is enough to classify as violence. Violent offenses are not always considered serious.

Common Internet Scams

According to the Internet Fraud Watch, these were the top 10 rip-offs on the Internet in 2004:

- *Web auctions:* Items bid for but never delivered by the sellers, value of items inflated, shills suspected of driving up bids, prices increased after highest bids accepted.
- *Internet services:* Charges for services that were supposedly free, payment for online and Internet services that were never provided or falsely represented.
- *General merchandise:* From toys to clothes, goods never delivered or not as advertised.
- *Computer equipment and software:* Sales of computer products that were never delivered or were misrepresented.
- *Pyramids and multilevel marketing:* Schemes in which profits were made only from recruiting others, not from sales of goods or services to the end users.
- *Business opportunities and franchises:* Empty promises of big profits with little or no work by investing in prepackaged businesses or franchise operations.
- *Work-at-home plans:* Materials and equipment sold with false promises of payment for piecework performed at home.
- *Easy credit cards:* False promises of credit cards to people with bad credit histories upon payment of up-front fees.
- *Prizes and sweepstakes:* Requests for up-front fees to claim winnings that were never awarded.
- *Book sales:* Genealogies, self-help improvement books, and other publications that were never delivered or were misrepresented.

FBI Index Crimes The Part I offenses in the *Uniform Crime Reports* developed each year by the Federal Bureau of Investigation are: (1) murder and nonnegligent manslaughter, (2) forcible rape, (3) robbery, (4) aggravated assault, (5) burglary, (6) larceny-theft, (7) motor vehicle theft, and (8) arson.

A simple assault, where the offender may place a victim in fear of harm but never actually inflict harm, is classified as a misdemeanor. In many states, a misdemeanor is considered a less serious crime than aggravated assault where an injury actually occurred. Crimes of homicide, aggravated assault, robbery, and forcible rape are considered serious violent crimes. Many youths who commit violent crimes start their offending early and eventually become chronic violent offenders.[45]

In 2011, juvenile offenders accounted for about 13 percent of all arrests for violent crimes. We have previously mentioned that arrest rates for violent crimes have decreased, but it is interesting to note that those declines are more substantial for juveniles than for adults. The percent change in violent crime arrests for adults between 2007 and 2011 was negative 7.7 percent; for juveniles that number was negative 11.5 percent. Property crime arrests did increase slightly for juveniles (2.2 percent), though at a slower rate than for adults (11.1 percent).[46]

Arrest data continues to show disproportionate arrests involving minorities for violent crime. Theoretically, these numbers coincide with urban areas where poverty, low education, poor health care access and high teen pregnancy rates also appear. Unfortunately, minorities are overrepresented in these areas as well. For property crimes, the trend of overrepresentation for minority youth could also be observed.

14.5 SELF-CHECK

1. Define the concept of "chronic juvenile offenders."
2. What is a hacker or cracker? Describe their subculture.

CAREERS IN JUVENILE JUSTICE

FBI Agent

Federal agents usually do not encounter many youth problems or juvenile justice issues. For the most part, juvenile justice is a local issue. Recently, however, juvenile offending in serious crimes has changed this picture. Juvenile criminals in computer crime (hackers and crackers), extremist groups (skinheads and various militia groups), and sophisticated street gangs (Crypts, Latin Kings) have drawn federal enforcement attention. The FBI is responsible for investigating crimes that cross state or national boundaries, are of an organized nature, or pose a significant threat to the security of the United States. For instance, a juvenile member of the Skinheads may threaten an individual because of his or her race, religion, or ethnicity. The FBI would be involved in this type of hate crime since it violates federal civil rights laws. In like manner, juvenile hackers who gain access into a NASA computer system containing secret and sensitive data would be investigated by the FBI Computer Crime Unit. For these reasons, agents often receive specific training in understanding the juvenile subculture and investigating juvenile offenders.

Federal agents also come into contact with juveniles as victims. Major transnational crimes such as organized prostitution and pornography rings which exploit children and violate specific U.S. federal statutes fall within the jurisdiction of the FBI. As technology continues to evolve in the transportation and communication industries by bringing our world closer together, cross-jurisdictional crime involving juveniles as both offenders and victims will continue to rise.

To become an FBI agent, a person must be a U.S. citizen, or a citizen of the Northern Mariana Islands and at least 23 years old. Excellent vision and hearing are both required. Candidates must possess a valid driver's license, and be in excellent physical condition with no defects which would interfere in firearm use, raids, or defensive tactics. All candidates must have received a four-year degree from a college or university accredited by one of the regional or national institutional associations recognized by the United States Secretary of Education.

Critical Thinking

As technology rapidly evolves, what new useful methods can federal agents adopt to understand and prevent juvenile crime better?

CHARACTERISTICS OF VIOLENT JUVENILE OFFENDERS

Data shows that most serious violent offenders are male and from a racial minority. In 2009, the racial composition of the U.S. juvenile population ages 10 to 17 was 77 percent white, 16 percent black, 5 percent Asian/Pacific Islander, and 1 percent American Indian (juveniles of Hispanic ethnicity are mostly included in the white racial category). Of all juvenile arrests for violent crimes that same year, 47 percent involved white youth, 51 percent involved black youth, 1 percent involved Asian youth, and 1 percent involved American Indian youth.[47] Furthermore, the Violent Crime Index arrest rate in 2010 for black juveniles was five times the rate for white youth, six times the rate for American Indian juveniles, and nearly 15 times the rate for Asian juveniles.[48] Fifty-eight percent of all juveniles arrested for murder in 2009 were African American, as well.[49]

Female juvenile arrest rates are also an interesting phenomenon. Law enforcement made 578,500 arrests of female juveniles in 2009. From 2000 through 2009, arrests of juvenile females did decrease, but less so than male arrests in several offense categories such as aggravated assault.

Violent juvenile offenders tend to have histories of substance abuse and mental health problems. Their school-related difficulties may include truancy and dropout. Just as serious offenders who commit crimes like burglary and motor vehicle theft, violent juvenile offenders also tend to start offending at young ages and many continue through adulthood.

In the mid-1990s, there was some worry that juvenile offenders were getting involved in violent crimes at younger ages. However, that trend seems to have reversed in recent years. It is true that juveniles under the age of 15 account for about 26 percent of violent crimes; however, this number remains relatively steady. Those 17 and older account for the majority of violent juvenile offenders.[50]

HATE CRIME

One of the most disturbing trends of the past decade has been the growing number of youths involved in **hate crime** incidents. These often include high-profile cases such as the dragging death of an African American man in Jasper, Texas, the fatal beating of a gay college student in Wyoming, the beating death of an Ethiopian student in Portland, Oregon, a shooting spree in Illinois and Indiana by an ex-college student, and the Columbine High School shooting in Colorado. Based in part on links to other social youth movements involving music and dress (skinheads, black cults), aggressive recruiting on college campuses, and the development of Internet Web pages designed to attract young people, extremist groups have seen an explosion in youth membership. According to one skinhead source, young people represent the future, "they are the front-line warriors in the battle for white supremacy."[51]

Extremist groups[52] can be separated into three distinct categories:

- **Traditional hate groups** These groups have a historical linkage with hate and white supremacy. They include various neo–Nazi groups, the New Order, The United Racist Party, the White People's Party, and the Ku Klux Klan. The group of particular importance to young people is the skinheads, composed of young men and women aged 15 to 20 years, generally centered in urban areas. They are often characterized as the "new storm troopers" donning black clothing and black boots, chains, piercings, tattoos, and, of course, a shaved head. Unfortunately, many young people are attracted to these groups, which offer formalized outlets through music, dress, and behavior to rebel against society.

hate crime A crime committed against an individual because of his or her race, color, religion, national origin, sexual orientation, gender, or disability.

- **The Christian Identity groups** These groups are composed of individuals expressing a racist North American theological movement based on a distorted interpretation of the Bible. Adherents of Christian Identity believe that white northern Europeans are the true Israelites descended from the "Lost Tribes of Israel," that Jews are imposters and the descendants of Satan, and people of color are an inferior sub-species of humans, commonly referred to as "mud people." Their rhetoric often foretells of a race war between blacks and whites wherein Identity followers are called to a holy war against the forces of darkness. They must take up the sword and prepare for the militant coming of Jesus. These groups include the Aryan Nations, the Posse Comitatus, the Church of Christ's Christians, and the World Church of the Creator. Considerable effort has been given to recruiting young members to the Christian Identity churches. Several incidents have involved recruiting and soliciting at local high schools and area malls in large cities across the United States.

- **The survivalist and militia groups** These paramilitary organizations call for "American patriots everywhere" to arm themselves. These groups gained notoriety in August 1992 when a tragic encounter occurred between federal agents and survivalist Randy Weaver in a remote part of northern Idaho, known as Ruby Ridge. Believing that the federal government has become involved in a conspiracy to enact martial law in the United States (taking away all guns and rights of Americans) and to turn the government over to a Jewish-controlled "New World Order—Zionist Occupied Government (ZOG)," these groups have banded together to form citizen militias. Fueled by other incidents such as the assault on the Branch Davidian compound in Waco, Texas, and the attacks of 9/11, the movement has swelled to over 200 separate militia groups operating in every state. Their anti-government conspiracy theories and references to a New World Order that is intent on taking away the rights of Americans played an important part in the life of Timothy McVeigh, who was convicted of the 1995 bombing of the Alfred P. Murrah Building in Oklahoma City, Oklahoma, that killed 167 people. These groups have colorful and patriotic names, such as the Michigan Militia, the Arizona Patriots, the Texas Brigade, and Militiamen of Montana (MOM). They often train for urban warfare wearing camouflage clothing, stockpiling food and ammunition, and expressing their belief as "Constitutionalists" or "Real Americans." Unfortunately, young people are often drawn to these groups for the sense of excitement and adventure. Their rhetoric often talks about comradery and family, as the group practices with automatic weapons and "plays army" in nearby forests and fields.

Young people drawn to the extremist movement in the United States are not just the sons and daughters of participants, but represent a vast number of juveniles seeking identity with a specific group or ideology. Some scholars argue that there is a psychological loss of faith in the institutions of society (family, school, church, government in general) to govern the social interaction

Myth / Fact

Myth	Fact
Militia groups are defenders of the U.S. Constitution.	Militia groups talk about the Constitution, but in reality they pick and choose what they like. They interpret the Second Amendment as meaning that all Americans should be able to own arms, including rocket-propelled grenades, heavy armament, and fully automatic weapons. Most militia groups reject all of the amendments to the Constitution after the first ten, particularly the Thirteenth Amendment, which ended slavery, and the Fourteenth Amendment, which guarantees equal protection under the law and effectively abolished discrimination against people of color.

14.6 SELF-CHECK

1. What are the characteristics of violent juvenile offenders?
2. Define hate crime. What are the three distinct categories of extremist groups in America?

Hate crime incidents appear to be increasing in America. *Why do you think teenagers often seek identity with right-wing groups?*

of people and provide meaning to life.[53] Joining an extremist group is similar to joining a gang. The feelings of acceptance and belonging are reinforced by peers, and the group is tightly bound by shared goals and perceived threats and conspiracies from the outside. The surge in juvenile involvement in these groups is a disturbing trend that must be addressed by not only the law enforcement and juvenile justice community, but by all of society—parents, families, schools, churches, and communities.

Juvenile Victimization and Exploitation

The victimization and exploitation of juveniles is a global problem that can be found in all cultures. Industrialized and developing nations alike experience the phenomenon, and worldwide efforts are being made to combat it. In the United States, law enforcement efforts to combat child exploitation have become more sophisticated with the advent of new technology and new information systems.[54] For the last year that statistics were available on juvenile victimization, the following key findings have emerged:[55]

- On average, juveniles were about twice as likely as adults to be victims of serious violent crimes between 1994 and 2010.
- In 2010, male and female juveniles were equally likely to experience serious violent crimes (like rape or sexual assault, robbery, and aggravated assault). In comparison, male juveniles were nearly twice as likely as female youth to experience these same crimes in 1994.
- Youths who lived in a home where the head of household was unmarried were 3.8 times more likely to be the victim of a violent crime than those who lived in a home where the head of household was married.
- Adult offenders are responsible for a majority of all crimes against juveniles, and family members make up the bulk of offenders against children.

These are sad and frustrating statistics, particularly those that reveal that children are much more likely to be victimized by those they trust. In fact, the greater potential for serious physical and sexual assault in juvenile victimization resides in the home, with an adult family member and a child age 4 or younger.

CHILD ABUSE AND NEGLECT

Neglect is a legal term used to define the criminal abandonment of a juvenile, usually by a family member, parent, or guardian who does not provide adequate supervision, a safe and secure environment, and boundary setting for a child. There are too many children in today's society who are left to raise themselves in a world where they do not know their father, and their mother works two jobs just to buy food and pay rent. Due to tough economic times, poverty rates among children in the United States are expected to increase dramatically.

Data reported by various state child protection agencies to the Department of Health and Human Services show that of the 681,000 known victims of child abuse and neglect, 78.5 percent were neglected, 17.6 percent were physically abused, and 9.1 percent were sexually abused.[56] These children came from all socioeconomic levels. In neglect cases, poverty level has less to do with the incident than *disorganization level*. In high levels of disorganization, there are no rules or moral guidance for children to develop an adequate emotional state which will govern their own decision making. Children are often neglected through inadequate nutrition, ignored physical or emotional problems, unattended health-care issues, and abandonment.

The second most common type of maltreatment is physical abuse. Oftentimes, these cases are discovered at school when teachers and coaches observe a variety of physical and behavioral indicators. (See Figure 14.5.) Their observations lead to investigations and subsequent help for the child or adolescent suffering at the hands of their parents.[57]

Although these indicators may be easy to identify, the causes of child abuse and neglect are not. Child abuse is a complex issue that many different theories try to explain. Some common contributors that increase the risk of children's becoming victims are parent substance abuse, economic stress, lack of

neglect Failure to protect or give care to a child. Types of neglect often involve failure to provide food and clothing, maintain a healthy and clean environment, and failure to supervise and control behavior.

| FIGURE 14.4 | The National Incident-Based Reporting System |

The U.S. Department of Justice is replacing its long-established Uniform Crime Report (UCR) system with a more comprehensive National Incident-Based Reporting System (NIBRS). While the UCR monitors have only a limited number of index crimes and, with the exception of homicides, gather only a few details on each crime event, the NIBRS system collects a wide range of information on victims, offenders, and circumstances for a greatly increased variety of offenses. Offenses tracked in NIBRS include violent crimes (e.g., homicide, assault, rape, robbery), property crimes (e.g., theft, arson, vandalism, fraud, embezzlement), and crimes against society (e.g., drug offenses, gambling, prostitution). Moreover, NIBRS collects information on multiple victims, multiple offenders, and multiple crimes that may be part of the same episode.

Under the new system, as with the old, local law enforcement personnel compile information on crimes coming to their attention, and this information is aggregated in turn at the state and national levels. For a crime to be counted in the system, it simply needs to be reported and investigated. It is not necessary that an incident be cleared or an arrest made, although unfounded reports are deleted from the record.

NIBRS holds great promise, but it is still far from a national system. Its implementation by the FBI began in 1988, and participation by states and local agencies is voluntary and incremental. In 2007, approximately 38 percent of the nation's law enforcement agencies participating in the UCR program submitted their data via NIBRS, and the crime data collected comprised approximately 25 percent of the data submitted to the FBI. The jurisdictions that reported crime data to the FBI via the NIBRS covered approximately 25 percent of the nation's population. The crime experiences of large urban areas are particularly underrepresented. The system, therefore, is not yet nationally representative nor do findings represent national trends or national statistics. Nevertheless, the system is assembling large amounts of crime information and providing a richness of detail about juvenile victimizations previously unavailable. The patterns and associations this data reveals are real and represent the experiences of a large number of youth. However, patterns may change as more jurisdictions join the system.

Source: Adapted from Finkelhor, David and Richard Ormrod. "Characteristics of Crimes against Juveniles," U.S. Department of Justice: OJJDP *Juvenile Justice Bulletin*, June 2000, p.3.

FIGURE 14.5	Child Maltreatment Victims by Age, 2011									
	MEDICAL NEGLECT		NEGLECT		PHYSICAL ABUSE		PSYCHOLOGICAL MALTREATMENT		SEXUAL ABUSE	
AGE	NUMBER	PERCENT	NUMBER	PERCENT	NUMBER	PERCENT	NUMBER	PERCENT	NUMBER	PERCENT
<1–2	5,212	34.6	159,753	30.1	28,565	24.0	12,946	21.3	1,650	2.7
3–5	2,313	15.3	110,335	20.8	19,394	16.3	11,767	19.3	8,585	14.0
6–8	2,046	13.6	86,282	16.2	19,644	16.5	10,787	17.7	9,978	16.2
9–11	1,820	12.1	68,212	12.8	16,779	14.1	9,782	16.1	11,347	18.5
12–14	1,965	13.0	58,603	11.0	18,207	15.3	8,976	14.8	16,178	26.3
15–17	1,695	11.2	46,660	8.8	15,579	13.1	6,377	10.5	13,411	21.8
Unborn, Unknown, and 18–21	23	0.2	1,568	0.3	657	0.6	204	0.3	323	0.5
Total	15,074		531,413		118,825		60,839		61,472	
Percent		100.0		100.0		100.0		100.0		100.0

Source: "Child Maltreatment 2011." Online. Available at: http://www.acf.hhs.gov/sites/default/files/cb/cm11.pdf#page=28 May 2, 2013.

parenting skills, and a fragmented family. A 1993 study by the U.S. Department of Health and Human Services found that children in alcohol-abusing families were nearly four times more likely to be abused and neglected overall, almost five times more likely to be physically neglected, and ten times more likely to be emotionally neglected than children in non-alcohol-abusing families. Estimates suggest that 50 to 80 percent of all child abuse cases, substantiated by child protective service agencies, involve some degree of substance abuse by the child's parents.[58]

The other most common type of child abuse is sexual in nature. There are approximately 100,000 cases of child abuse that are reported each year. Actual statistics on total cases are very controversial, but it is clear that the vast majority of juvenile sexual abuse cases go unreported. Quite interestingly, young juveniles (under the age of 12) are most likely to be sexually assaulted by persons under age 18, while older juveniles (ages 12–17) are most likely to be sexually assaulted by young adults ages 18–24. Obvious physical indicators of sexual abuse are venereal disease and pregnancy. Some behavioral indicators are nightmares, trouble sleeping, fear of the dark, bed-wetting, sexual activities with toys or other children, unusual sexual knowledge, and the child's refusal to talk about a "secret" that he or she has with an adult. See Figure 14.6.

FIGURE 14.6	Physical and Behavioral Indicators of Abuse
PHYSICAL INDICATORS	BEHAVIORAL INDICATORS
<ul><li>Unexplained bruises and welts</li><li>Unexplained burns</li><li>Unexplained fractures</li><li>Unexplained lacerations or abrasions</li><li>Head injuries</li><li>Human bite marks</li><li>Frequent injuries that are "accidental" or "unexplained"</li></ul>	<ul><li>Wary of adult contacts</li><li>Anger, aggression, hyperactivity (consistent)</li><li>Apprehensive when other children cry</li><li>Behavioral extremes</li><li>Withdrawn, introverted, extremely passive</li><li>Frightened of parents or unnaturally dependent</li><li>Frequently truant or late to school</li><li>Afraid to go home</li></ul>

NEW BEAT FOR LOCAL POLICE: THE INTERNET

Keene, N.H.—Real-life law and order has come to the electronic frontier, even in the nation's smaller communities. Police across the country are taking up an undercover tool: the Internet sting.

These frontier law officers generally are not software geeks. Many are old-fashioned gumshoes with well-thumbed copies of *Internet for Dummies*. They're looking for sexual predators who use the anonymity of electronic chat rooms and e-mail to find victims or trade kiddie porn.

James McLaughlin, a veteran of the force in Keene, N.H. (pop. 22,430), is one such cybercop. Before his wife brought home a secondhand computer last year, he says he knew next to nothing about the Internet. Now he surfs the electronic data stream almost daily, stopping at X-rated forums so raunchy that he expects his mouse to blush.

McLaughlin poses as a teenager to lure in those who might be looking for sex with youngsters. He uses the online anonymity that hides Internet stalkers to hunt the hunters.

"In less than a year I've busted more than 60 people," McLaughlin says. He has brought charges which include traveling across state lines to have sex with children and distributing child pornography.

"If one officer in Keene, N.H., can do that, you can imagine how big the problem is."

Such success has prompted the FBI to take up the technique. This year, the agency hired 60 employees with expertise in computers and budgeted $10 million to combat computer sex crimes.

Not everyone applauds the crusade. Civil liberties watchdogs question whether police patrolling websites go too far.

"Innocent people are being brought into activity they would not otherwise engage in but for the guile and imagination of the police," says New Hampshire lawyer Mark Sisti, who represents three men arrested by McLaughlin.

"We're paying tax dollars to have police officers and FBI agents masquerade as nubile teen-age girls," says Stanton McCandlish of the Electronic Frontier Foundation, a group that advocates Internet privacy.

Investigators say their critics are, at best, naïve. They point to chilling case files:

- After one conviction for molesting a child in his hometown of Framingham, Mass., janitor Michael Austin was watched closely; he could no longer go near a school or playground without attracting police attention. He began using a computer

CHILD PORNOGRAPHY

Various federal and state statutes typically define **child pornography** as any depiction of a minor (under 18) in a sexual act or in a sexual manner. This definition also commonly applies to drawings or sketches of children in nude or sexually oriented poses.[59] An important point in the discussion of child pornography and explicit materials is that under federal law, mere possession, even without knowledge or intent, still constitutes a crime.

While child pornography has been a problem in society since recorded history, the expansion of the Internet has created a new and much more universal method for distribution. Recent cases involving large, multinational rings of profiteers highlight this sad exploitation of the world's children (see Focus on Practice). Prior to the Internet, child pornography distribution was relegated to a dark and clandestine underground system using the mail and personal contact. Involvement in this network was high-risk, and participants were limited by personal knowledge and histories. Because of the impersonal and global nature of the Internet, it has now become the preferred pathway for trading and exchanging child pornography. The Internet provides an anonymous and much less risky environment in which to exchange this type of media.

The effects of child pornography are widely debated. No empirical evidence exists that can definitely show that child pornography causes child molestation. There are, however, some possible links. In a survey of 42,000 sex offenders, 42 percent reported the use of child pornography either immediately prior to, or during the commission of, the criminal act.[60] One study showed that between

child pornography Depiction of a minor (under 18) in a sexual act or in a sexual manner.

bulletin board to contact young boys by advertising items for sale. Two who met him to buy items were raped. Austin is in prison.

- When Sharon Lopatha of Maryland disappeared in 1996, police checked her home computer for clues. They learned she had posted messages in a forum devoted to sexual sadism. Her body was found in North Carolina, buried in the front yard of a man who browsed the same forum.

- On July 12, police in Holden, Mass., arrested a convicted sex offender from Michigan. They say he drove there to meet a 16-year-old girl with whom he had corresponded in an Internet chat room. The girl was running toward his pickup with a suitcase, police said, when they stopped her.

"This isn't a crime that's going to go away. As more and more people go online, the problem will grow," says Doug Rehman, a former state of Florida investigator who now teaches others how to combat computer vice.

Some police officers say patrolling the Internet is not always an efficient use of time. Others say police should focus instead on school programs promoting Internet safety.

"There are websites dedicated to hacking, cult recruitment and dangerous pranks," says Al Olsen, police chief in Warwick Township, Pa. "I tell parents,

'Don't think you can drop off your kids on the information highway without any worries.'"

In Keene, McLaughlin has helped federal agents bust a New York man who met with more than 20 teens he had contacted online.

In March, McLaughlin arrested a Norwegian man who drove to Keene believing he would meet a boy.

McLaughlin describes the more than 60 suspects he has helped bring in as men ages 13 to 60 from all walks of life.

"Almost half of them have kids of their own or jobs involving kids," he says. "We've arrested a dozen school teachers, a half-dozen ministers and priests, police officers, and a psychologist."

"A few weeks ago I was chatting online with a guy in Europe, and he told me he couldn't send me any pictures because I was in New Hampshire. He'd heard how we had busted a Norwegian guy," McLaughlin says. "That tells me we've sent a message to pedophiles on the Net: Stay away from New Hampshire kids."

CRITICAL THINKING

What other means of combatting cyberstalking can you think of?

Source: Larrabee, John, "New beat for local police: The Internet On-line stings collar sexual predators," *USA Today*, August 17, 1998, p. 8A. Reprinted with Permission.

---

77 and 87 percent of convicted child molesters used pornography to stimulate themselves, to lower the inhibitions of the child victim, or to teach the child to model the sexual activity.[61]

CHILD PREDATORS

While stalking was the high profile crime of the 1990s, the Internet now provides a new twist or variation on this problem of the new millennium—**cyberstalking**. Internet child predators begin their effort by visiting popular sites on the World Wide Web. Often, these sites are frequented by unsuspecting juveniles curious about dating, sexuality, and/or modeling. In some cases, adolescent boys and girls visiting adult sites have also become victims. Initial contact is made on the public Internet site and usually progresses to a one-on-one conversation between the potential victim and the child predator in an adjoining **chat room**. These private sites provide the ideal setting for meeting and exploiting the unsuspecting juvenile. Conversation usually starts out slowly, many times, with the predator posing as a juvenile. The topic of conversation then moves directly to sexually oriented content, preying on the juvenile's natural curiosity in this area. The predator will then seek out personal information from the juvenile, and try to set up a meeting with him or her in person. This meeting is often used as a first step in establishing a relationship with the juvenile and, if possible, a first-time sexual encounter.

In a similar manner, phony modeling agencies prey on adolescents attempting to "hit it big" in the movies or as models. After initial inquiry on the Internet, the juvenile (usually a young girl) is asked to meet for a photo session at

cyberstalking Using a computer via the Internet to harass or invade the privacy of another individual.

chat room Public or private sites on the Internet that allow one-on-one conversations between two individuals

a nearby hotel. The juvenile unsuspectingly meets the predator (who poses as a photographer), who then escorts the young person to a secluded room. The session quickly regresses to sexually oriented or nude photography, often involving the predator. Not only is the juvenile physically exploited, but the pictures are then distributed on the Internet as well. Social networking websites such as MySpace, Facebook, and Twitter have contributed greatly to fears of child exploitation. These sites allow users to post profiles and personal information about themselves. Child predators with access to personal details and photographs are able to strike up relationships with users, using a variety of ruses to lure their victims. MySpace found over 28,000 profiles belonging to predators in 2007, and since that time, both MySpace and Facebook, each popular sites among juveniles, have implemented a variety of tools to hinder predators from contacting juveniles. Both sites flag users exhibiting suspicious activity (such as 40-year-olds trying to friend 13-year-olds), and both allow privacy options that restrict unknown users from viewing profiles.

There is no way to know for sure the extent of this problem, but many law enforcement agencies, including the FBI, have set up special investigative units to combat this form of child exploitation. Officers and agents routinely surf the Net for potential sites and X-rated forums that attempt to attract young juveniles and adolescents.

CHILD PROSTITUTION

If prostitution is indeed the world's oldest profession, then child prostitution is certainly the world's greatest tragedy. In his book *The Prostitution of Women and Girls*, R. Barri Flowers recounts the shameful history of child prostitution throughout history.[62] Teenage prostitution is commonly called child prostitution, though the vast majority of minors involved in prostitution are in their teens.[63] The scope of the problem is huge, with an estimated half a million children under 16 involved in prostitution in the United States alone. That

Teenage prostitution is a growing problem in American cities. *What is the link between teenage prostitution and runaways?*

number doubles or triples when including 16- and 17-year-olds; and globally, the number approaches 5 million children under the age of 18 engaged in such activity. In one recent survey, child prostitution had increased in 37 percent of the cities in the United States.[64] This growth was attributed to a greater number of teenage runaways, and common links were found between these exploited children:

- A vast majority of the child prostitutes were runaways with alcohol and drug problems;
- Age varied most often between 13 and 17 years, though many were found to be much younger; and
- Prostitution and other sexually oriented business was primarily conducted in central business districts of cities, arcade game rooms, and bus/train stations.

Child prostitution involves both males and females. It is often a desperate struggle where the victim is trapped in an ugly world of violence and exploitation (refer to Focus on Practice, pages 416–417). According to the *Uniform Crime Report* data produced by the FBI, there are more arrests of male prostitutes than female in the under-18 category.[65] While this statistic is reflective of the extent of male child prostitution, it can also be partly attributed to differential arrest patterns by police. Most experts agree that the majority of teen prostitutes are female, with some estimating that females account for as many as two-thirds of the juvenile prostitutes in this country.[66]

Some juvenile prostitutes find themselves the victims of international organized crime rings. These operations traffic young girls and boys to distant places with the promise of employment and money. While most of these cases involve children from developing countries (e.g., Cambodia, India, Philippines, Romania), there are a growing number of cases that involve American children being trafficked to other countries. Within the United States, the problem is much more insidious, usually involving immigrant children from other countries (e.g., Mexico, Guatemala, Thailand, China) trafficked into the United States for prostitution. Many times, the children are used to service other members of the minority or ethnic community living within the United States. Worldwide, approximately 80 percent of trafficking victims are female, and 70 percent of those are trafficked for the commercial sex business. In the most egregious cases, these youths are kidnapped from their towns and villages and sold into all forms of forced labor and servitude, including prostitution, sweatshops, domestic labor, farming, and child armies. The **Victims of Trafficking and Violence Protection Act** was passed in 2000 to combat this growing international problem. The act defines human trafficking as trafficking in which a commercial sex act is induced by force, fraud, or coercion, or in which the person induced to perform such an act is a juvenile. While new, the act has been having an impact on slowing the numbers of youth being smuggled into the country for prostitution.

While significant enforcement efforts have focused on reducing the demand for child prostitution, the problem appears to continue and grow. Since most child prostitutes are runaways and the product of a dysfunctional family, efforts toward prevention could have a significant impact. Stiffer teenage curfew and loitering laws, more runaway shelters, tougher penalties for **pimps** and customers, and a concerted effort to prevent teenage runaways through counseling and direct family involvement are all recommended strategies aimed at reducing child prostitution.

JUVENILE JUSTICE ONLINE

Visit the *OJJDP Bulletin Online* that discusses the "Prostitution of Juveniles: Patterns from NIBRS," published in June 2004, at: **https://www.ncjrs.gov/ pdffiles1/ojjdp/203946.pdf** What are the patterns and trends observed in juvenile prostitution across the nation? Discuss how law enforcement agencies should respond to the prostitution of juveniles.

14.7 SELF-CHECK

1. What is the most common type of child abuse?
2. How has the Internet affected child pornography and child exploitation?
3. What are the common linkages found in child prostitution?

Victims of Trafficking and Protection Act of 2000 A law specifically designed to curb the illegal trafficking of human beings, especially juveniles into the United States for the purposes of forced labor and servitude, including prostitution.

pimp Middleman for the prostitute and her or his client. These individuals often force or compel others to work as prostitutes through intimidation and fear. The pimp takes a significant share of the money from a paying customer.

SUMMARY BY CHAPTER OBJECTIVES

1. Explain the difference between a rampage killing and a typical homicide

Rampage killings do not appear to be impulsive acts. Indeed, they are premeditated and highly staged or planned acts of violence. Many of the suspects openly express their violent intent before the event. There is often a precipitating factor, or "spark that sets off the tinder." The demographic profile of rampage killers is also significantly different from that of typical murderers: they are older, more likely to be white, better educated, and usually unemployed. Most rampage killers do not get away, but are often apprehended or commit suicide at the scene. Examples of juvenile-involved rampage killings involve the high-profile shootings at high schools in Littleton, Colorado (1999), and Jonesboro, Arkansas (1998).

2. Define paraphilia

Aggressive sexual behavior seems to progress from less serious sexual misconduct such as obscene phone calls, voyeurism, or stealing undergarments to much more serious behavior such as offensive touching and rape. This progression and linkage to juvenile sexual behavior have been the focus for scholars studying serial murder. Some youths may be "driven" to commit such acts as a result of urges or impulses. This group may likely continue their criminal (sexual) behavior into adulthood if not identified and treated effectively. Juveniles who have a chronic interest in sexually aggressive and/or deviant fantasy may suffer from a series of paraphilia, or erotic-sexual compulsions focusing on deviant and bizarre images or activities, and linked to continued violence and aggression during adulthood.

3. Define what drugs are and assess their impact on American youths

A drug can be defined as a chemical that interacts with the body and alters basic body functioning, usually through the central nervous cord and system. The drugs which are most commonly associated with abuse are generally classified as opiates, stimulants, depressants, hallucinogens, and marijuana. Drug use and American youth culture appear to be inseparable. Recent self-report surveys continue to document extensive drug use among adolescents. Abuse of alcohol remains consistently high, and the number of alcohol-related fatal accidents involving juveniles is staggering. Most alarming is the use of harder drugs among juvenile populations including heroin, cocaine, and methamphetamine. Drugs are often linked with juvenile violence, but it is a misconception that drug use causes violence and/or crime.

4. Explain the concept of a chronic juvenile offender

Chronic juvenile offenders engage in repeated acts of delinquency. They represent a very small proportion of delinquent youths but are responsible for a large proportion of crimes, especially serious and violent crimes. They are distinguished from other youth by their high rate of offending. Chronic juvenile offenders begin their "criminal careers" at a relatively young age (10–12 years) and have persistent involvement in crime through adulthood. They tend not to "grow out" of crime as they get older.

5. Describe the demographic profile of the juvenile hacker

Juvenile hackers tend to be white males, 14 to 20 years of age, from families of medium to high socioeconomic status. They are highly intelligent individuals, yet underachievers in school, probably because they are not challenged and feel bored by schools and other institutions. Their favorite activities focus on make-believe and fantasy games, where they assume colorful and magical identities often associated with the occult or science fiction. They seek new challenges and new thrills through their involvement in computer crime and hacking.

6. List the categories of hate groups and explain their attractiveness for juveniles

Extremist hate groups can be separated into three distinct categories. First, the *traditional hate groups* have historical linkages with hate and white supremacy. They include various neo–Nazi groups, the New Order, the United Racist Party, the White People's Party and the Ku Klux Klan. A second group can be broadly categorized as Christian Identity groups expressing a racist North American theological movement based on distorted interpretations of the Bible and the U.S. Constitution. These groups include the Aryan Nations, the Posse Comitatus, the Church of Christ's Christians, and the World Church of the Creator. The final category is composed of a variety of *survivalist* and *militia groups*. These groups believe that a conspiracy exists within the government to take over the United States and take away the rights of Americans. Young people are often drawn to these groups for a sense of identity and belonging. Others join for the excitement and adventure often associated with believing and fighting for a cause, even though that cause may be misguided and false.

7. Learn what the most common kind of child abuse is

The most common type of child abuse is sexual. Sadly, most of the time, the perpetrator is a parent, guardian, or other family member. Pregnancy and venereal disease are obvious physical indicators of abuse. However, oftentimes, these cases are discovered away from home, usually at school when teachers and coaches observe a variety of other physical indicators such as unexplained bruises, burns, fractures, cuts, and bites. Behavioral indicators are also commonly present such as a fear of adult contacts and of home; anger, aggression, introversion, and other behavioral extremes.

8. Describe the worlds of child prostitution and child exploitation

Teenage prostitution is commonly called child prostitution, even though the vast majority of minors involved in the activity are in their teens. In recent years, there has been a huge rise in child prostitution in the United States. A vast majority of child prostitutes are runaways with alcohol and drug problems, most often between the ages of 13 and 17 years. The actual prostitution or sexually oriented business is primarily conducted in central business districts of large cities, arcade game rooms, and bus/train stations. Child prostitution involves both males and females. Often these young people find themselves in a desperate struggle, where they are trapped in an ugly world of violence and exploitation.

KEY TERMS

rampage killings, p. 397
zero tolerance, p. 397
drugs, p. 399
synthetic marijuana, p. 400

paraphilia, p. 405
cohort, p. 408
recidivist, p. 408
hackers/crackers, p. 408
computer virus, p. 408

FBI Index Crimes, p. 409
hate crime, p. 411
neglect, p. 414
child pornography, p. 416
cyberstalking, p. 417

chat room, p. 417
Victims of Trafficking and Protection Act of 2000, p. 419
pimp, p. 419

REVIEW QUESTIONS

1. What is Generation X? Generation Y?
2. What does the term "Goth" mean and how does it relate to recent school violence?
3. How do rampage killers differ from typical murderers?
4. Describe the characteristics associated with mentally ill juvenile offenders.
5. Define the word "paraphilia."
6. What is the demographic profile of a juvenile sex offender?
7. What factors may help to identify chronic juvenile offenders?
8. What is a "hacker" or "cracker"? Describe their demographic profile.

9. What is the demographic profile of a serious juvenile offender?
10. Describe the three categories of extremist hate groups. Why are young people attracted to this movement?
11. What are the key findings regarding juvenile victimization in the United States?
12. What is the most common type of child abuse?
13. Define child pornography. What technological event has increased the distribution capability for child pornographers?
14. Describe the world of child prostitution. What are the common links between these exploited children?

HANDS-ON ACTIVITIES

1. Initiate Discussion With fellow students, family members, or friends, discuss the impact of violence in American culture. Do violent motion pictures, video games, television shows, and rock music encourage violence among juveniles? Is there a relationship between violence in American culture and recent school shootings?

2. Find Out More about At-Risk Youths and Delinquents Visit your local bus depot or train station, or drive by an adult bookstore at night. Do you see young juvenile adolescents milling around in the area? How do they look? What do you think the chances are that they are involved in drugs? Prostitution? Are runaways? Compare what you see with what you have read in this chapter about juvenile exploitation.

3. **Search the Internet for Potentially Dangerous Sites That Might Attract Young Women** Search the Internet for modeling agencies. How do they attract juvenile

models? How many of them do you think are legitimate? Discuss with your fellow students, family members, or friends how easy it is to become a potential victim to the sex trade. Discuss what can be done, if anything, to curtail such operations.

INTERNET ACTIVITIES

1. Access the National Institute for Drug Abuse website at **www.nida.nih.org** and the companion site focusing on juvenile drug taking at **www.clubdrugs.org**. Find intervention and prevention programs that focus on juvenile drug use. Notice that many of these programs address issues which are unique to juvenile drug users, such as inhalant abusers, date-rape drug awareness programs, the dangers of club drugs, and the like. Write a brief statement expressing your opinion as

to the effectiveness of such programs. How can your community take advantage of these programs?

2. **Do Internet Research** Search the Internet for various extremist groups and militias. Does your state have its own militia? Find several groups and discuss their basic principles. How do they appeal to juvenile members? Write a brief summary of hate on the World Wide Web.

CRITICAL THINKING EXERCISES

1. **Explore Survivalist Frame of Mind** Frank, Brent, Mike, Dave, and Bob are all juniors at Beaver High School in Helena, Montana. Last year Frank and Bob both tried out for the football team but were cut by Coach Davies, a retired NFL defensive tackle for the Denver Broncos. According to Bob, they didn't make the team because Coach Davies is African American and he favors only athletes that are African American. That's okay according to Bob, since he and his friends have started a new club called "The Pagans." They enjoy listening to "twisted" metal music and are really into the new Mad Max video games. Brent even plays in a band that uses red dye to simulate blood on stage when they "kill" the teachers from school in a theatrical event. They like to read about the occult, and Mike actually believes he is a warlock. Last week, Frank came back to the group with some neat literature on the Montana Grizzly Brigade, a survivalist outfit in the Bitter Root Mountains. They all plan to visit the leader this summer for a weekend retreat.

   a. Do you think that this group has a potential for conducting real violence at school? If so, why?
   b. Can the group's interest in non-mainstream culture, music, and theatrics cause violence? What potential problems can you see if the group actually visits the Montana Grizzly Brigade?
   c. What steps can you suggest that might help the individuals in this group, or do they even need

help? Under what conditions would you act in reporting these individuals to police or school authorities? Why?

2. **Help an At-Risk Young Woman** Jill is a very attractive 16-year-old with a great personality who does very well in school. Because she is your younger brother's girlfriend, the two of you have become fast friends. Recently, she appears to be depressed, especially since her mother remarried a few months ago. The other night, she confided in you that she was very unhappy at home and thinking about running away. When you ask her to confide in you, she just says that she doesn't like her new stepfather. She won't say why, but becomes terrified with the thought of being in the house alone with him. She says that she will probably take the bus to New York and try to find some modeling jobs to support herself . . . this weekend! She says she is aware of the potential threats and problems, but she is desperate and has to get away.

   a. What steps can you take, if any, to remedy this situation? Should you talk to your brother about this? How about her mother or stepfather?
   b. What agencies or professionals in your community might be available to assist you in addressing this situation with Jill?

14.1 Self-Check

1. Describe zero-tolerance programs.

Zero-tolerance programs were implemented primarily as a response to the public perception of violence in schools. Most of them were implemented after Columbine, and were designed to "get tough" on delinquency activities that occurred in schools. While the first zero-tolerance programs were aimed at preventing guns on campus, the concept quickly expanded to include expulsion or suspension of students for drug and alcohol use, fighting, swearing, disrupting class, disobedience, truancy, and many other forms of misbehavior.

2. What are the differences between rampage killings and typical murders? Give some examples of rampage killings involving juveniles.

Rampage killings, although they make up less than 1 percent of all homicides, still have certain characteristics that separate them from typical murders. Rampage killings are rarely impulsive, as typical murders can be, and are usually meticulously planned. Many of the suspects openly expressed violent viewpoints before the killings, and in most cases had threatened violence previously. In addition, there is often a precipitating event that sets off the rampage killing, and the killers usually commit suicide afterwards. More than half of rampage killers had a history or showed signs of mental health problems. Common examples of rampage killings are:

- Columbine High School in Littleton, Colorado (1999)
- Santana High School in Santee, California (2001)
- Jonesboro Middle School in Jonesboro, Arkansas (1998)

14.2 Self-Check

What types of family events may lead to emotional and behavioral problems among juveniles?

Witnessing domestic violence, being abused, being victimized through incest, and experiencing the death of a parent can lead to these problems. There are also the effects of the biochemical factors discussed in Chapter 4, including dietary influences, Fetal Alcohol Syndrome, and prenatal drug use.

14.3 Self-Check

1. What is a drug, and what are the common drugs of abuse?

A drug is any chemical that interacts with the body, altering normal body and mind functioning, usually through the central nervous system. The drugs that are most commonly associated with abuse are classified as opiates, stimulants, depressants, hallucinogens, and marijuana.

2. What is the connection between drugs and violence?

There are four main factors to remember when discussing the relationship between drugs and crime:

- General forms of drug use and delinquency in adolescence and adulthood are not causally related. In other words, drug use does not cause crime.
- There has been a historically erroneous misconception concerning the relationship between drugs and violence.
- The drug street culture has dramatically changed; people are no longer as likely to be loyal to a single drug. This shift made it much more difficult to study the effect of any particular drug on a person's behavior. In turn, it became more difficult to find a connection between drugs and violence.
- Most incidents of drug-related violence occur in deteriorated communities characterized by the loss of informal and formal social control, internal struggle between large numbers of disenfranchised subcultures, and the absence of meaningful economic processes and political decision making. Therefore, factors other than drug use are large factors in predicating violence.

14.4 Self-Check

1. What are paraphilia?

Paraphilia are erotic compulsions involving obsessive deviant images or activities to achieve or maintain sexual arousal. They can involve objects, people who do not consent, and the suffering or humiliation of the offender, the offender's partner, animals, or children.

2. What factors may contribute to youthful sexual offending?

Perhaps the most obvious factor is being sexually victimized as children. Other factors include prenatal drug and alcohol abuse, family dysfunction, and physical and emotional abuse.

14.5 Self-Check

1. Define the concept of "chronic juvenile offenders."

Chronic juvenile offenders are a small minority among juvenile offenders. They are responsible for a large proportion of juvenile crimes, including serious ones like robbery and burglary. They are labeled chronic juvenile offenders because of their persistent and habitual involvement in delinquency.

2. What is a hacker or cracker? Describe their subculture.

Hackers and crackers are a subculture of juvenile delinquents that engage in attacking secure computer systems or various Internet sites.

Their subculture values new ways of invading computer systems, developing a new virus, or "one-upping" the latest vandalism on the Internet with more elaborate examples of vandalism. One of the reasons that they are rarely caught is that they appear to be model teenagers (although they do tend to be underachievers in school). As one investigator pointed out, "They don't race cars, chase girls, drink beer, take drugs, or get into trouble."

14.6 Self-Check

1. What are the characteristics of violent juvenile offenders?

They are an even smaller minority of the total juvenile offender population than chronic juvenile offenders are. Their characteristics are as follows:

- Most are male, but the number of girls is on the rise: in 2003, girls were arrested for 29 percent of all juvenile violent crime.
- Most are from a racial minority; 48 percent of all juveniles arrested for murder in 2003 were African Americans.
- Violent juvenile offenders tend to have histories of substance abuse and mental health problems.
- School-related difficulties may include truancy and dropping out.
- They tend to start offending at young ages and many continue through adolescence.
- They appear to be getting younger: the arrest rate for youth under 15 years of age was higher than it was in 1980. However, violence still remains highest between the ages of 17 and 19.

2. Define hate crime. What are the three distinct categories of extremist groups in America?

Hate crime is a crime committed against an individual victim because of his or her race, color, gender, religion, national origin, sexual orientation, or disability. Right-wing hate groups can be separated into three distinct categories:

- *Traditional hate groups* that have historical linkages with hate mongering and white supremacy. They include various neo–Nazi groups and the Ku Klux Klan.
- *Christian Identity groups* that follow a racist North American theological movement based on distorted interpretations of the Bible and the U.S. Constitution. These groups include the Aryan Nations and the Posse Comitatus.
- A variety of *survivalist and militia groups* operating throughout the United States which believe that a conspiracy exists within the government to take over the United States and take away the rights of Americans. These groups have colorful and patriotic names such as the Michigan Militia, the Arizona Patriot, the Texas Brigade, and the Militiamen of Montana.

14.7 Self-Check

1. What is the most common type of child abuse?

Sadly, sexual abuse is the most common. There are approximately 100,000 cases of child abuse that are reported each year. Actual statistics on total cases are hotly debated, but it is clear that the vast majority of juvenile sexual abuse cases go unreported.

2. How has the Internet affected child pornography and child exploitation?

Prior to the Internet, child pornography distribution was an underground system using the mail and personal contacts, and involvement in this network was high-risk. In contrast, the Internet has created a universal method for distributing child pornography. It has now become the preferred pathway for trading and exchanging child pornography because it provides an anonymous and much less risky environment in which to exchange this type of media.

3. What are the common linkages found in child prostitution?

Most child prostitutes are runaways with drug and alcohol problems; their ages generally vary between 13 and 17, although many are much younger; and they tend to conduct their business in central business districts of cities, arcades, and bus/train stations.

FUTURE DIRECTIONS IN JUVENILE JUSTICE

Chapter Outline

Chapter Objectives

After completing this chapter, you should be able to:

1. Identify the current trend in the legislation and philosophy of juvenile justice.

2. Describe the BARJ model of juvenile justice.

3. Outline the arguments both for and against abolishing the juvenile justice system.

4. Identify the three major types of specialty courts used in juvenile justice.

5. Describe Project CRAFT and discuss its success as an intervention strategy.

6. Describe the parental liability movement in juvenile justice.

The Juvenile Court Will Change

In the 100 years since the first juvenile court was established in Cook County, Illinois, the juvenile justice system in the United States has changed dramatically. What does the future hold for juvenile justice? Some scholars and legal analysts have called for an abolition of the separate system of juvenile justice in the United States. Others advocate new theories and philosophies for the juvenile justice system. Finally, the debate over the form and function of the current juvenile justice system continues. Without a doubt, the juvenile justice system of today will likely change again in the next 100 years.

15.1 SELF-CHECK

What possible changes may occur to the juvenile justice system in the future?

Current Directions in Juvenile Justice

As juvenile crime rates rose in the 1980s and 1990s, there was pressure on juvenile justice personnel and politicians to rectify this growing problem in juvenile crime. Today's juvenile offenders are portrayed as more violent, less remorseful, and less receptive to treatment. In addition, the media began to focus on violent juvenile offenders who were getting off with a slap on the wrist when handled in the juvenile court. Problems in the juvenile justice system came under the spotlight of media attention as gangs rapidly grew in numbers and violent juvenile crime increased.

Recently, many legislatures in the United States have altered the fundamental purpose of the juvenile justice system.[1] Many of the changes reflect a desire to hold juveniles more accountable for their criminal acts and to introduce a level of punishment into juvenile justice. Traditionally, state statutes describing the purpose of juvenile justice contain language embracing rehabilitation, diversion, and protection in regard to juveniles within the juvenile justice system. Now, however, the statutes are being rewritten to include the words "punish," "hold accountable," and "protection of society." As discussed throughout this text, current policy in juvenile justice reflects a desire to hold juveniles more accountable for the crimes they commit.[2]

The direct results of toughening the laws on juvenile crime were the increased use of waiver to adult court, switching from the traditional indeterminate sentence to determinate sentencing (Chapters 2 and 11), and creating new laws as well as altering existing ones to hold juveniles more accountable and punish them for the crimes they commit. The **punitive model of juvenile justice** was embraced by many politicians running for office in the 1980s and 1990s, who were elected on "get tough on crime" platforms. These politicians followed through on election promises by enacting tougher legislation, particularly in the realm of juvenile justice. Juvenile justice was targeted due to the rising concern that a new generation of "superpredators" was gestating, a fear that has turned out to be unfounded.

However, the result of the emphasis on tougher juvenile justice policies lingered past the realization that a generation of hardened criminals would not materialize. Discretion of juvenile court judges remained curtailed, and juvenile corrections facilities were discovered to house unspeakable horrors of sexual assaults and other offenses. As a result, a backlash against a harsh and inflexible system of juvenile justice began with a model promulgated by the Office of Juvenile Justice and Delinquency Prevention. The **Balanced and Restorative Justice Model (BARJ)** was adopted in jurisdictions around the country and received a fair amount of academic attention. BARJ attempts to bridge traditional models of juvenile justice with the accountability aspects championed by

punitive model of juvenile justice Model of juvenile justice which holds that juveniles are just as responsible as adults for their criminal behavior.

Balanced and Restorative Justice (BARJ) A new philosophy of juvenile justice that advocates accountability, community safety, and youth development in combination with restorative justice between offenders, victims, and communities.

the punitive model. The goals and philosophies of BARJ have also received support in the legislative arena over the past decade and a half.

This shift occurred right at the beginning of what may prove to be a sea of change in juvenile justice. We have previously discussed in Chapter 12 that scandals in correctional institutions in the past decade have forced changes at all levels of the system: each of the players in the juvenile justice system is affected by the revelations of rampant sexual/abuse in juvenile facilities. It becomes a factor when deciding how to dispose of a case: what offenses really warrant years of potential abuse?

Other factors have lined up to influence our current juvenile justice system as well. The economic downturn that peaked in 2009 and continues to affect the United States as of this publication also influences how juvenile offenders are dealt with. Juveniles are expensive to detain, prosecute, and incarcerate, requiring mental health services, educational programs and security measures not required when dealing with adults. Get-tough states that frequently remanded juveniles to adult courts and correctional facilities are now changing course, faced with increased costs incurred by that tactic. In the past few years, at least four states have passed legislation that limits the ability to house juveniles in adult prisons and jails, and ten states have changed transfer laws so that juveniles are less likely to be transferred to the adult criminal justice system.[3]

Economic realities have also forced cutbacks at every level of the juvenile justice system. Grant programs at the federal level, such as Community Oriented Policing Services grants, fell victim to budgetary sequestration in early 2013, as did federal funding for substance abuse and mental health programs offered in state and local correctional facilities. The results of these budget cuts may not be fully realized for years, but it is a sure bet that juvenile justice will need to adapt to the decrease in available funds for programming.

Finally, a political shift has had an influence on juvenile justice. The Obama administration, in office as of this publication, has emphasized an approach to drug abuse and juvenile delinquency that is more rooted in public health than in punitive measures. This outlook is diametrically opposed to the "get tough" policies of the 1980s and 1990s, and it is beginning to shape the way police, courts, and corrections all deal with young offenders.

Myth	Fact
Youth offenders have a high rate of recidivism.	70 percent of arrested juveniles will not be arrested again. Source: Siegel, L., and B. C. Welsh. 2006. "*Juvenile Delinquency: Theory, Practice, and Law.*" Belmont, CA: Wadsworth Publishing Company.

ABOLISH THE JUVENILE JUSTICE SYSTEM?

Criticism of the utility of a separate juvenile system virtually coincided with its inception in the early 1900s in the United States. The operations and practices of the juvenile court have been "tinkered" with by politicians throughout its one-hundred-year history. However, the recent shift toward more punitive juvenile sentencing, increased waivers to adult court, and harsher correctional systems has led to a substantial increase in academic attention concerning the fundamental assumptions and philosophies of the juvenile justice system.[4] A reexamination of system operations leads some commentators to conclude that it is time to reinvent the system, while others conclude that it is time to abolish it. The impetus behind such arguments lies in criticisms of the fundamental mission of the juvenile court system and in its current operational status across the United States.

Changes in the juvenile justice system since the **procedural due process** revolution of the 1960s have led some philosophers to conclude that the current state of the system has outlived its usefulness. Those in favor of abolishing the juvenile court as a separate system argue that original foundations of

procedural due process The rights and process given to a person charged with a crime. Procedural due process is more formalized in the adult criminal justice system than in the juvenile justice system.

the juvenile system, specifically the focus on rehabilitation and treatment, have given way to ideologies of punishment and accountability that no longer justify a separate system.[5] A combination of events in the past 40 years has led to substantive changes in state legislation on juvenile justice; indeed, many states have rewritten the fundamental purpose of their juvenile justice systems. As violent crime rates rose sharply in the 1980s, especially among juvenile offenders, more attention toward punishment of the juvenile officer arose. Thus, recent changes in state juvenile justice legislation focus on community safety and protection resulting in the juvenile court's increasingly considering the punishment of juveniles in both sentencing and waiver decisions. In Texas, for example, juveniles accused of serious felonies can be sentenced to up to 40 years of incarceration by juvenile court.

Revised juvenile justice codes emphasize responsibility, accountability, and deterrence of juvenile offenders while still refusing to extend to them the full range of due process rights that adults have in criminal proceedings. This shift also reflects a change in the view of the juvenile by society as well as the courts that no longer practice the ideals of *parens patriae* or the state as parent. Abolitionists feel that juveniles are unduly penalized by the two-tiered system and feel they would benefit from a single unified system giving every offender equal due process rights as entitled by law. The Supreme Court decisions in *Kent* v. *United States*, *In re Gault*, and *In re Winship* afforded juveniles the basic due process rights adult offenders enjoy in the criminal system.[6] Nonetheless, there are important due process rights still not specifically guaranteed to juveniles, specifically the right to a jury trial. In addition, although one of the primary philosophical foundations of the juvenile court is that juveniles are less culpable than adults due to their age, many states still do not automatically require that an attorney be present when juveniles waive their rights. Indeed, recent research has found that juveniles are far less capable of understanding their rights or what a waiver of their rights means in subsequent proceedings against them.[7] Get-tough-on-crime laws allow juvenile court judges to hand out harsher sentences, thus narrowing the gap in sentencing between the juvenile and adult systems of justice.

Debate exists on both sides of this issue and is likely to increase as juvenile justice becomes more punitive nationwide. Some argue that the serious consequences now associated with juvenile justice require even more procedural formality than currently exists. Those who favor more procedural formality believe that if juveniles can receive punitive sentences, they should receive the same due process protections as adults, if not more. The arguments on both sides of the abolition debate are summarized in Figure 15.1.

Some people who argue for the abolition of the juvenile justice system limit their comments to the juvenile court process or legal aspects of the system. This view tends to dismiss the other components of the system which might also be affected if the system were abolished, especially correctional and community-based programs and intervention efforts. Most communities offer a multitude of public and private programs that specifically target juveniles. Many of these programs are very effective in serving juveniles, preventing delinquency, and protecting the community. Many of these programs never receive national attention because they are so localized. Typically, the only person(s) in a county or state with knowledge of the wide range of programs available are juvenile court personnel. Legal issues and due process are but a small aspect of the big picture of juvenile justice. Arguments to abolish the juvenile justice system based solely on these reasons are a bit short-sighted. The simple fact that there are so many programs available in many counties speaks volumes for retaining a separate system of juvenile justice.

15.2 SELF-CHECK

1. What are some of the suggested methods for "getting tough" on juvenile crime?
2. List some of the arguments for and against abolishing the juvenile justice system.

FIGURE 15.1	Arguments For and Against Abolishing the Juvenile Justice System

ARGUMENTS FOR ABOLITION

- The current state of the juvenile justice system does not reflect the original intentions of the founders. The system has become increasingly punitive and harsh.
- Children in juvenile court are denied basic due process rights. The move to a more punitive system has not been accompanied by an increase in the due process rights of children in juvenile court.
- The current juvenile justice system duplicates the adult system. Juveniles get all of the punishment and none of the protection of the adult system of justice.
- Increased use of determinate sentencing has led some juvenile courts to become more punitive than their adult counterparts.
- Juveniles are routinely not represented by counsel in proceedings where their liberty is at stake. The presence of counsel in juvenile court does not have a positive effect in many cases.
- The distinction between the juvenile and adult systems of justice has become blurred, thus eliminating the need for a separate system of justice.
- A unified, streamlined system of justice could take age into account as a mitigating factor and provide juveniles with increased due process rights.

ARGUMENTS AGAINST ABOLITION

- Juveniles are still less culpable than adults and deserve to be treated differently.
- The adult system of criminal justice is not equipped to deal with juveniles. The adult correctional system simply warehouses inmates with little if any rehabilitation potential.
- Juveniles have a greater rehabilitation potential than adults. They have lower rates of recidivism.
- The worst aspects of the adult system are not present in the juvenile system, specifically bail and the game-like adversarial system.
- The violent criminals that serve as the basis for arguments about abolishing the juvenile system make up less than 1 percent of the offenders processed by the system. Throwing away an entire system for less than 1 percent of the offenders is not logical.
- The juvenile justice system is still more benign than the adult criminal justice system, and this allows the juvenile system to individualize justice for most of the offenders it deals with.
- The range of placement options and other mechanisms available in juvenile court far overshadows those in the adult system.
- The juvenile justice system is the most successful system in American criminal justice. Most juveniles who are processed do not come back, and the system enjoys high rates of success in changing juveniles.

Balanced and Restorative Justice (BARJ) Model

The debate continues over the future of the juvenile justice system between proponents of a retributive, punitive philosophy and advocates of the traditional individual treatment and protection model. Both approaches have failed to satisfy the basic needs of individual crime victims, the community, and juvenile offenders.[8]

The Balanced and Restorative Justice Model is an alternative philosophy and a back-to-basics mission for juvenile justice. The new "balanced approach" supports a community's need to sanction crime, rehabilitate offenders, and ensure public safety. Toward these ends, it articulates three goals for juvenile justice that are depicted in Figure 15.2.

ACCOUNTABILITY. Crime is sanctioned most effectively when offenders take responsibility for their crimes and the harm caused to victims, when offenders make amends by restoring losses, and when communities and victims take active roles in the sanctioning process. The offender's primary obligation is to his or her victim, not to the state. Therefore, accountability is not equated with obeying a curfew, complying with drug screening, or writing an essay. Nor is it equated with punishment. It is easier to make offenders take their punishment than it is to make them take responsibility for their actions. The BARJ Model enables offenders to make amends to their victims and to the community.

COMPETENCY DEVELOPMENT. The most successful rehabilitation ensures that young offenders make measurable gains in educational, vocational, social, civil, and other competencies that enhance their function as productive adults. When competency is defined as the capacity to do something well that others value, the standards for achieving success are measured in the community. Competency development is not the mere absence of bad behavior. It should encourage adults and communities to involve young people in work and community service to help teach them community problem-solving, dispute resolution, and cognitive skills.

COMMUNITY SAFETY. Assuring public safety requires more than mere confinement. Communities cannot be kept safe solely by locking up offenders. Locked

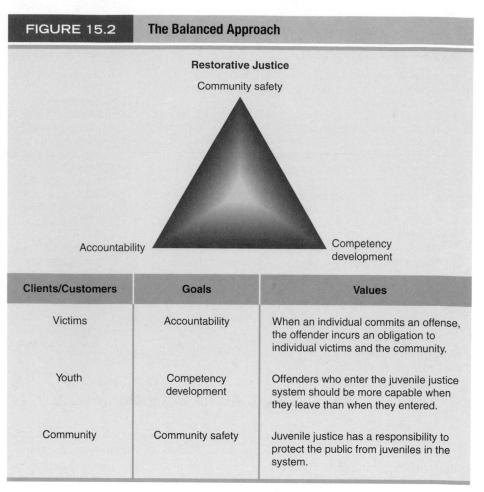

FIGURE 15.2   The Balanced Approach

Restorative Justice
Community safety

Accountability   Competency development

Clients/Customers	Goals	Values
Victims	Accountability	When an individual commits an offense, the offender incurs an obligation to individual victims and the community.
Youth	Competency development	Offenders who enter the juvenile justice system should be more capable when they leave than when they entered.
Community	Community safety	Juvenile justice has a responsibility to protect the public from juveniles in the system.

Source: Adapted from Malloney, D., D. Romig, and T. Armstrong. *Juvenile Procedure: The Balanced Approach.* Reno, NV: National Council of Juvenile and Family Court Judges, 1998.

facilities must be a part of any public safety strategy, but they are the least cost-effective component. A "balanced" strategy invests heavily in preventing and controlling crime. A problem-oriented focus ensures that the time of offenders who are under supervision in the community is structured around such activities as work, education, and community service. Adults, including parents, are assigned distinct roles in monitoring offenders. A balanced strategy cultivates new relationships with schools, employers, and other community groups to enhance the role of juvenile justice professionals as resources in prevention and positive youth development. Essentially, the BARJ model focuses on protecting the community through prevention, and through a process in which individual victims, the community, and offenders are *all* active participants. It is a healing, as well as a preventive-based, philosophy.

The principle behind BARJ is that justice is best served when victims, offenders, and communities receive equitable attention in the justice process. The needs of one client cannot be met unless the needs of other clients are addressed as well. Crime severs bonds between victims, offenders, and families. It breaks down the basics of security and trust on which community is built. Although offenders must take full responsibility for restoring mutual respect, the entire community must be involved to provide understanding and support. The BARJ Model is a vision for the future of juvenile justice that builds on current innovative practices and is based on core values inherent in all communities. It provides a framework for systemic reform and offers hope for preserving and revitalizing the juvenile justice system.[9] See Figure 15.3.

15.3 SELF-CHECK

What is the BARJ Model?

FIGURE 15.3	Focus on Practice: Restorative Justice Practice, Location, and Objectives

Restorative Justice intervention includes a wide array of programs and practices that may be applied at virtually any point in the juvenile justice process, or in the community.

OBJECTIVE/FOCUS	PRACTICE	LOCATION
Conflict resolution; prevention; peacemaking	Community mediation; alternative dispute resolution; school and neighborhood conferencing; victim awareness education; youth development	Schools; neighborhoods; churches; civic groups
Provide decision-making alternatives to formal court or other adversarial process for determining obligations for repairing harm	Victim-offender dialog; family group conferencing circles; reparation boards; other restorative conferencing	Police and community diversion; court diversion; dispositional/sentencing alternatives; post-dispositional planning; residential alternative discipline; conflict resolution; post-residential reentry
Victim and community input to court or formal decision making	Written or oral impact statement to court or other entity	Court; probation; residential
Provide reparative sanctions or obligation in response to crime or harmful behavior	Restitution; community service; service to victims; service for surrogate victims; payment to victim service funds	Diversion; court sanction; probation condition; residential program; post-incarceration
Offender treatment; rehabilitation; education	Victim impact panels; victim awareness education; Mothers Against Drunk Driving panels; community service learning project designed to build offender competency and strengthen relationships with law-abiding citizens	Probation; residential facilities; diversion program; jails
Victim services and support groups	Counseling; volunteer support groups; faith community groups	Multiple settings
Community building	Family support and discussion groups	Neighborhood and community

Source: Bazemore, Gordon, Jay G. Zaslaw, and Danielle Riester. "Behind the Walls and Beyond: Restorative Justice, Instrumental Communities, and Effective Residential Treatment." *Juvenile and Family Court Journal,* Winter 2005, pp. 53–73.

Future Directions in Juvenile Justice

What does the future hold for the juvenile justice system? As we have discussed previously in this chapter and throughout this text, there is unprecedented change afoot that will affect the way we intervene with youthful offenders. Economic uncertainties and political philosophies are influencing every aspect of the juvenile justice system. There are several trends and directions worth mentioning as a result.[10]

DECENTRALIZATION OF STATE JUVENILE JUSTICE SYSTEMS

Decentralization has already begun to occur in some states, with California leading the charge. The California Division of Juvenile Justice announced in 2011 that it would be phased out over a period of several years, as the juveniles housed in its facilities aged out or are released. The funds budgeted for the system in the coming years will then be distributed to each of the 58 counties in the state, eliminating a massive bureaucracy and shifting responsibility for rehabilitation and incarceration to the individual communities.[11] But beyond that, the move emphasizes that juveniles should be dealt with on a community level, receiving local services that could be targeted to high-needs offenders.

Without the seemingly boundless space in the state prison system to rely on, police and courts will be forced

Conditions during pregnancy are believed to contribute to early delinquent behavior. *What are some ways to ensure quality prenatal care?*

JUVENILE JUSTICE
ONLINE

What innovative Restorative Justice programs have been implemented in this country? Go to **www.restorativejustice.org** and look for links associated with programs in North America.

to examine options that minimize incarceration for nonviolent offenders. Communities will have to examine the costs and benefits of programming options and choose alternatives to expensive and dangerous institutions. The State of California will still monitor and provide best practices for juvenile corrections, but will largely be out of the business of imprisoning juveniles. Illinois, Ohio, Oregon, New York, and Pennsylvania are each examining versions of the California plan.[12]

Rather than focusing on punitive reactions to youth crime as in the past, valuable policies addressing quality of life issues have the potential to ameliorate conditions that contribute to crime and delinquency. These early intervention policies attempt to impact the social and living environment of the child (e.g., poverty, family, neighborhood setting, school environment). Indeed, recent research suggests the importance of intervention efforts before or shortly after birth. In their analysis of low birth weight and its relationship to early onset offending of minority youth in Philadelphia, authors Stephen Tibbetts and Alex Piquero found that individuals who were born at low birth weight and were from a low socioeconomic status were more likely to have an early onset of delinquent behavior.[13] Low birth weight is often associated with a number of other factors including lack of prenatal care for pregnant women, drugs and/or alcohol abuse by the mother, smoking during pregnancy, poor diet, low socioeconomic status, and low education attainment. Low birth weight can be prevented through direct and early intervention strategies aimed at providing quality prenatal care, home nursing visitation, and expectant mother education.

Evidence suggests that these types of efforts can be effective as delinquency "prevention" strategies.[14] With attention on these issues, policy debates are more likely to shift away from punitive, retributive juvenile justice legislation that emphasizes statutory waiver and detention. Instead, strategies can be assessed to reduce risks of delinquency and enhance parent-child relationships, increase emotional and/or cognitive development for children, improve educational outcomes, and decrease criminal activity. Greenwood reports that policymakers are beginning to recognize that wise investments in early prevention and intervention programs are not only effective ways of reducing crime, but are much more cost-effective in the long term.[15]

SPECIALTY COURTS

An important alternative to the formal juvenile court system is the implementation of a number of specialty courts designed to address youthful offending.[16] These courts target specific groups of offenders who have unique needs that can best be addressed by the agencies and organizations which have staff and treatment programs to serve the identified population.

TEEN COURTS Teen courts, also referred to as youth courts and peer courts, have been in existence since the early 1990s. By 1995, 25 states had opted to establish teen courts, and by 2005 there were more than 1,037 teen court programs operating in 48 states and the District of Columbia.[17] Only two states, Connecticut and New Jersey, do not have active teen courts. Most teen courts are dispositional in nature; that is, the youth are required to have admitted to the charges brought against them to be eligible for a teen court disposition. The most common teen court utilizes an adult judge with youth in the roles of attorneys, jurors, clerks, and other court personnel. Teen courts have rapidly developed across the country, even though significant research on the effectiveness of these systems has not been undertaken. While their overall effectiveness may be somewhat dubious, they do appear to require much more community involvement than traditional juvenile court processing.

DRUG COURTS Although drug courts are more widely used in the adult system, there are approximately 1,500 drug courts in the operational and planning phases for juveniles in the United States. Typically, the courts require the offenders to participate in drug treatment while being subject to strict monitoring. These courts offer great promise, not only as relevant approaches for dealing with the youthful drug offender, but also as an incentive to make critically important changes in court-order treatment programs.[18] In a 2001 study, Columbia University's National Center on Addiction and Substance Abuse (CASA) concluded that drug courts provide comprehensive and effective control of the drug-using offenders' criminality and drug usage while under the court's jurisdiction. Indeed, drug courts provide closer, more comprehensive supervision and much more frequent drug testing and monitoring during the program than other forms of community supervision. Average recidivism rates for those who complete the drug court program is between two and four times lower than for those who do not participate in a drug court program.[19] As authors Lisa Roberts and Peter Benekos state, "Juvenile drug courts seem to be an encouraging option for providing treatment while still ensuring accountability."[20]

GUN COURTS Drawing on the success of the drug courts, gun courts operate with a similar orientation. Typically, they service first-time, nonviolent offenders, and they require parental involvement and education. Unlike teen courts, drug and gun courts do not use peer jurors to determine disposition, involvement, or course of action. Instead they use a very structured program. A number of jurisdictions have established such diversion programs for youths involved with weapons offenses. These programs include a firearms education course and classroom presentations by experts or victims and/or their survivors who have been affected by firearm violence. These programs also provide social services for youths and their families. Established in 1995, the gun court program in Birmingham, Alabama, is an intense program with strict supervision guidelines and requires parental involvement in a seven-week workshop. Youth who admit their involvement in a gun violation are sent to a boot camp program for short-term incarceration and then placed on maximum supervision probation from 30 days to 6 months. While on probation, the youth are required to complete the Alabama Substance Abuse Program. Recidivism data indicates that gun court youth had a lower recidivism rate than pre–gun court youth; and they were less likely to return to the juvenile court on offenses related to gun charges.[21]

Minnesota also developed a gun program in Hennepin County. When a juvenile is adjudicated delinquent in the juvenile court for an offense involving a gun, he or she is ordered to be placed in a residential facility and referred to a work program. However, the disposition is held pending the youth's involvement in a special program. To successfully complete the Juvenile Gun Program, a youth must participate in a 40-hour educational program which is spread over 16 weeks. During the course of the program, the youths are given random drug tests. A positive drug test results in a referral for treatment and the formalization of a juvenile record. Preliminary research suggests that those youths who complete the program tend to have a somewhat lower rate of new charges than youths who do not complete the program. These new charges are more likely to be status offenses or misdemeanors (88 percent) rather than felonies (12 percent). By contrast, the majority of youth who did not complete the program tend to be referred subsequently for felonies (65 percent) rather than misdemeanors (35 percent).[22]

These specialized courts provide insightful examples into the alternative programs that can be offered to deal with youth who are involved in relatively minor property offenses (i.e., shoplifting and vandalism), drug offenses, and weapon violations. By targeting specific offenders and providing intensive treatment and sanctions, these programs appear to offer some success in preventing future offending.

Tools for the Future

Police agencies and juvenile courts are working together in an attempt to predict and influence the future. Special units within police departments (called Futures Research Units—FRUs) use environmental scanning and advance forecasting techniques to assess trends, counter-trends, shifting values, and other indicators within popular juvenile culture and evaluate how these changes will impact crime and the entire juvenile justice system.

INTERVENTION STRATEGIES

In addition to the utilization of specialty courts, there are a number of **intervention strategies** that target at-risk youths and provide them with a comprehensive array of programs and services. The most promising strategies to prevent youth from engaging in delinquency or to deter youth who have already been involved in some law-violating behavior are collaborative efforts that include the family, the school, and the community.

Intervention strategies that embrace a holistic treatment of juvenile offenders are becoming more popular, providing a comprehensive array of programs and services that address the reasons behind delinquency. These collaborative efforts between communities, families, schools, law enforcement, and justice agencies focus on creating a system of care for special-needs youth. Note that the language related to such programs removes more punitive references—youths are "special needs," not "delinquents" or "offenders." These interventions work to reverse long-term emotional problems and behavioral issues by habilitating and reintegrating troubled youth.[23]

Intervention programs seek to identify risk factors for recidivism among offenders, including the following:

- Past criminal history
- Family problems
- Disorganized community environment
- Criminal behavior among family members and peers
- Poor educational performance
- Substance abuse/dependency
- Abuse and neglect
- Poverty
- Chronic illness
- Mental illness
- Parenting as teenagers
- Homelessness

Intervention models for those juveniles identified to be at highest risk look to the juvenile justice system to maximize access to agencies that can address these issues and coordinate care between them. Culturally competent and community-based intervention programs require high levels of cooperation among organizations.

Unfortunately, the intervention model—while politically and socially popular—also flies in the face of current economic woes. Non-profit agencies and local governments have seen funding slashed in the past few years, and it does not appear that more monies will be forthcoming in the near future. Further, access to mental health care is difficult and extremely expensive to procure among the uninsured—which many juvenile delinquents are.

Some suggest that not focusing intensive intervention strategies on first-time offenders will help reduce costs. Seventy percent of juvenile offenders will not recidivate;[24] therefore focusing a holistic model of intervention on them may not be the best strategy. Identifying higher-risk offenders and only devoting concentrated programming to their needs may be more cost effective.[25] Striking a balance between high spending and holistic, nonpunitive models of juvenile justice will be tricky. The programs described in the paragraphs that follow are good examples of that balance.

COLLABORATIVE INTENSIVE COMMUNITY TREATMENT PROGRAM: CICTP As an alternative to residential incarceration, the CICTP attempts to offer a "managed care" approach to allocating resources for youthful offenders. Offenders are carefully and individually selected for the program on the basis of criteria for success (age, past record, school performance, nature of the offense, etc.). The program supports the principles of the Balanced and Restorative

intervention strategies Programs designed to target specific youth offenders, attempting to prevent youths from engaging in delinquency or deter youths who have already been involved in some law-violating behavior.

Justice Model previously described in this chapter. The CICTP emphasizes competency development, community service, and offender accountability. In their preliminary evaluation of CICTP, authors Maria Garase and Sherrie Sonnenberg found that the program significantly reduced juvenile incarceration by screening and selecting eligible youth for a comprehensive, community-based treatment strategy.[26] The CICTP is an example of a collaborative effort by treatment providers, school officials, juvenile court personnel, and youth workers to impact troubled youth without incarceration.

PROJECT CRAFT One of the most successful vocational training programs is sponsored by the Home Builders Institute. Project CRAFT (Community Restitution and Apprenticeship Focused Training Program) began in 1994 and has been adopted in North Dakota, Tennessee, Maryland, Florida, and Texas. Utilizing a holistic and comprehensive approach that incorporates career training, community service activities, and support services like social skills training and case management, this program demonstrates how a private business (the construction industry) can collaborate with the juvenile justice system to assist youth.[27] Project CRAFT represents a comprehensive approach to high-risk youth and juvenile offenders. In partnership with schools, court staff, drug and alcohol counselors and treatment programs, private organizations, mentors, local government agencies, and court judges, Project CRAFT demonstrates the importance of addressing youthful offenders through a cooperative and inclusive strategy. An independent evaluation of Project CRAFT reports that:

- It had a very high placement for its graduates in the home building industry.
- The recidivism rate for youth in the program (2003) was only 12 percent, which is significantly lower than the national average for a treatment program.
- The program was very successful in continuing to work with youthful offenders long after they had been placed in jobs, particularly those who were in residential facilities.[28]

Troubled youth work together to develop a new skill and trade valuable for their future. *How do you think holding a steady job impacts delinquency and crime?*

JUVENILE JUSTICE
ONLINE

Go to **www.lao.ca.gov/analysis 2012/ crim_justice/juvenile-justice-021512 .pdf** and examine the California Department of Juvenile Justice realignment document. Explore the reasons behind this realignment to local communities. Do you think this will be cost-effective? Will communities have the resources to deal with juvenile offenders on this level? Learn more about the plans for realignment, and think about how such a plan might look if it were instituted in your community.

Project CRAFT has successfully demonstrated that agencies and organizations can collaboratively intervene in the lives of troubled and delinquent youth.

FAMILY EMPOWERMENT Historically, family empowerment networks focused on providing services for children and young adults with physical and mental disabilities. The concept of providing family-oriented, person-centered support for integrating challenged people within the community and, hence, allowing each person to reflect on and improve the quality of his or her life was a natural philosophy to be applied to delinquent and at-risk youth. Family empowerment teams are relatively new, sprouting amid a variety of community-based programs mainly in urban settings. Family empowerment teams provide single points of contact in order to understand the increasingly complex juvenile justice system. They are confidential and often provide extensive training for all members within the family. Concentrating on at-risk youth, these teams provide basic necessities such as food and transportation, parenting skill development, job training and support, counseling and advocacy for the entire family, and access to other community services. Family empowerment has gained significant support, particularly in light of the faith-based movement in the United States. These teams are innovative and low-cost intervention strategies that have shown success through reduced recidivism rates and improved psychosocial interaction of youth within the family and community.[29]

COGNITIVE-BEHAVIORAL THERAPY Many juvenile justice programs that focus on rehabilitation have long had components related to cognitive behavioral therapy (CBT). However, cognitive behavioral therapy is increasingly becoming a buzzword in juvenile justice among policymakers and practitioners alike. Several empirical studies have shown that the psychology-based programs are successful in rehabilitating juvenile delinquents, even the notoriously difficult sex offender population.[30] Basically, CBT is a highly structured program that involves teaching youth about the relationships between thoughts, emotions, and behaviors. Then the rehabilitation process begins, helping to modify thinking patterns in a way that will help juveniles to identify the triggers to their bad behavior and eventually lead to better, more adaptive behavior in situations they find taxing. This type of treatment is generally short term and can include group sessions or individual "homework." Types of CBT include rational emotive behavior therapy,

CAREERS IN JUVENILE JUSTICE

Intervention Officer

Most juvenile justice agencies have intervention officers or counselors. These individuals assist troubled youth in finding appropriate programs for intervention. Many times, they are the experts in locating a focused treatment program or strategy for a specific individual. For instance, if an older youth has dropped out of high school and been apprehended on one or two minor drug charges, the intervention officer or counselor may recommend attending a specially designed job-skill enhancement program. In this manner, the youth receives specific attention to the problems that he or she may have (drug addiction), as well as developing valuable skills for future employment. Intervention officers often work closely with the juvenile court and are often

called upon to evaluate and make recommendations to treatment programs. Sometimes these officers monitor the progress of specific individuals in a program.

Officers usually have two-year associate degrees. They receive training and are often certified in youth counseling.

Critical Thinking

Suppose you are an intervention officer in a local juvenile justice agency. List available programs in your area and specific information that will allow you to determine the focus and philosophy of each program.

FOCUS ON PROGRAMS

PHOENIX CURFEW PROGRAM

An innovative program designed to deal with curfew violators was initiated in Phoenix, Arizona. The Phoenix Police Department began to enforce curfew violations more stringently. The Police Department processes curfew violators while recreation staff provides recreation programs and assists police officers when necessary. Juvenile curfew violators receive information on recreation opportunities and social service agencies. Parents or guardians are contacted and asked to pick up the youth. Instead of being charged with a curfew violation, first-time offenders can take a four-hour communication class for a fee. Officers simply have to pick up and transport the juvenile to a centralized processing facility where other officers are stationed to process the juvenile. This allows the officer to process the juvenile quickly and get back on the street. Once the juvenile is processed, the parents are called and required to come to the facility and pick up their child. Many parents are surprised that their child was even out of the house and express gratitude to the police officer upon arrival. The Phoenix Police Department credits the program for reducing juvenile crime and victimization in their city.

CRITICAL THINKING

What do you think the main strength of such a program is? Find out whether a similar program is available in your area.

rational behavior therapy, rational living therapy, cognitive therapy, cognitive restructuring, aggression replacement training and dialectic behavior therapy.

Cognitive restructuring appears to be the most utilized aspect of CBT in juvenile justice, and is focused on identifying patterns that lead to criminal thought. These can include:[31]

- Blaming others for criminal behavior
- Failing to understand the concept of injury to others
- Justifying, minimizing or rationalizing criminal behavior
- Assuming an attitude of ownership or entitlement to the property of others
- Using a self-serving sentimentality to excuse and avoid dealing with antisocial characteristics

CBT can be used throughout the juvenile justice experience, in educational programs, mental health programs, restorative justice programs, and probation and parole programs. The approach is considered by many professionals as a "common sense" approach, in contrast to many of the panaceas that appeal to our punitive inclinations, and is experiencing renewed popularity in research and practice models.

CURFEW AND TRUANCY PROGRAMS

Another area receiving increased attention in juvenile justice is the use of minor and status offenses to attempt to control juveniles in the community, particularly aggressive law enforcement of curfew and truancy. Preliminary evidence indicates that this strategy is effective in reducing some juvenile crimes and juvenile victimization in particular.[32] Many innovative programs have been initiated to deal with habitual truants and curfew violators. One such program moves beyond simply writing tickets or ignoring minor juvenile offenses and attempts to involve the parents of the juvenile. The Phoenix Program (see Focus on Programs) allows officers to take curfew violations seriously and attempt to keep juveniles off the streets and out of crime.

PARENTAL LIABILITY

To what extent should parents be held responsible for the actions of their delinquent children? In the past, parents were typically responsible for financial damages that their children caused. However, in a more controversial direction,

FOCUS ON POLICY

PARENTAL LIABILITY LAWS

Background

The Provenzinos said that their son's behavior took a turn for the worse when he started listening to different music and hanging with a bad crowd. Alex Provenzino was first arrested in May 1995 for three burglaries at his family's church in which Alex stole over $11,000 in cash and checks from a safe.

After confessing to the crime, Alex told his parents that it was a "stupid mistake" and that he would never do anything like that again. Police came back to the Provenzino house in June, after Alex attacked his father. Alex was kept in a detention facility for two days, but was eventually released. The parents had set several conditions for his release. Between the June arrest and September, Alex was once again taken into custody after being suspected of committing six more burglaries and growing and selling marijuana. The police searched for evidence and found more drugs, a stolen .25 caliber pistol, cash, and other stolen goods—some of them in plain sight in Alex's room.

Prosecutors contended that Anthony and Susan Provenzino had plenty of warning that their son Alex was breaking the law, but did nothing to try to control him. Defense attorney William Bufalino II portrayed the parents as victims of an angry, sometimes violent son who towered over his father and fended off all their attempts to control him. City attorney Robert Ihrie said the Provenzinos were not on trial for Alex's crimes, but for failing to either control his actions or seek outside help.

Charges

The Provenzinos were charged with violating a city ordinance requiring them to be responsible parents. The city contended that 16-year-old Alex Provenzino got into drugs and became a burglar because his parents did not keep a close eye on him. The charge against the Provenzinos was a misdemeanor.

Trial

In the first day of testimony, prosecution witnesses declared Alex to be a young man who repeatedly broke the law and openly defied his parents. But the question is whether Anthony and Susan Provenzino neglected their parental duties to discipline Alex, who they knew was smoking marijuana and drinking and who was the prime suspect in a series of burglaries at a local church. Alex testified that his parents did not know what he was doing.

Several prosecution witnesses testified that the Provenzinos indeed knew of Alex's behavior. Sgt. Jack McFadzen said that he warned Anthony Provenzino to take control of his home. Andrew Nowak, a friend of Alex's, testified about several instances when Alex's temper cowed his parents. "Who controlled the Provenzino household?" the prosecutor asked. "Alex did," Nowak answered.

Defense witnesses portrayed a different picture. Anthony Provenzino testified that he did all he could to control his son. He also stated that the justice system should share some of the responsibility for releasing his son and not sending him a message. The other Provenzino children testified that Alex did not control the household and their parents did hold them all accountable.

several cities and states in the 1990s began to revisit the idea of *criminally* prosecuting parents for their children's actions. Many earlier parental criminal liability laws were found to be unconstitutional by appellate courts. However, the new laws seek to attach criminal responsibility to parents for "failing to supervise" or "intervene" in the lives of their children. Several cities received national attention for passing so-called parental responsibility statutes, including Silverton, OR; Arlington Heights, IL; Roanoke, VA; and St. Clares Shores, MI. A parental liability case from St. Clares Shores drew national attention as Anthony and Susan Provenzino went on trial for failing to be responsible parents to their son Alex (refer to Focus on Policy).

Many new laws are also being adopted and tested which attempt to increase the accountability of both the juvenile and their parents. In many cases, the goal is to involve the parents in the child's treatment; some laws even seek to hold parents liable for their child's behavior. The concept of **parental liability** for a child's behavior is not new. Parents have long been subject to laws on contributing to the delinquency of a minor and providing dependent children with the necessities of life, including a suitable home environment. However, a movement to hold parents criminally liable for their children's actions has been a

parental liability The idea that parents should be held responsible to varying degrees for their children's behavior.

Verdict and Sentence

On May 9, 1996, the jury deliberated for 30 minutes before finding the Provenzinos guilty of violating the ordinance. The Provenzinos were each ordered to pay a $100 fine and $1,000 in court costs. But the judge threw out the portion of the ordinance allowing for civil restitution.

In the view of the Provenzinos' attorney, the verdict will have a chilling effect on parents struggling with rebellious kids. "In order to defend this type of lawsuit, parents will have to keep a diary any time they chastise or praise their child," said William Bufalino II, who plans to appeal.

Prosecutors were pleased with the verdict. "This was a vote in favor of the family and a vote in favor of parental responsibility," said Robert Ihrie, city attorney. Several jurors also commented on the case. One juror stated, "You already knew your son broke into a church. What else did you need to know?" "When they asked him to get counseling, he told them he wouldn't go," said another juror, who wouldn't give her name. "You don't ask your son to go. You tell him what he's going to do." The counseling issue proved crucial to the judge.

The night after Alex's parents were found guilty, they spoke to their son by phone. "He sounded very somber and quiet," said Susan Provenzino. "This is a tremendous amount of guilt for a 16-year-old to be feeling." The Provenzinos have high hopes for Alex's rehabilitation, but they will never understand their conviction. "Look, we're educated," said his father. "We have a good marriage. We don't have any substance abuse problems. We live a small hometown life. And we know in our hearts we did everything we could. This ordinance would have been much better served on a whole lot of other people rather than us."

Appeal

The appellate court found that the statute was *overboard*, reversed the conviction, and dismissed the charges against Anthony and Susan Provenzino.

Epilogue

Alex Provenzino was eventually released from custody, but he did not stay out of trouble for long. Alex is now facing charges of possessing LSD and driving without a license after he took the family car without permission. Anthony Provenzino said news that his son took the family car without permission hit him "straight out of the blue." Provenzino said his son's attitude had improved dramatically when he returned from a juvenile work center in February. Anthony Provenzino said the arrest was surprising because his son was helping out with chores at home and looking forward to starting a carpentry job.

If convicted, Alex Provenzino could face 90 days in jail on the traffic violation and could be returned to a state youth detention home for violating his juvenile probation. If he is found guilty on the drug charge, he could be sentenced to one year in jail.

CRITICAL THINKING

The example above clearly shows at least two very different views on parental responsibility. Where do you stand? Explain.

Source: Excerpted from Naylor, Janet, Mark Puls Marney, Rich Keenan, Jeffrey Savitskie, and Kevin Lynch. *The Detroit News;* and the *Criminal Defense Newsletter,* Vol. 20m, No. 11, August 1997.

---

relatively new development.[33] In the United States, at least 10 states and dozens of municipalities have enacted parental liability laws. California enacted a law that holds parents/legal guardians criminally liable when they have not exercised "reasonable care, supervision, protection and control over the minor child." Punishments range from fines to imprisonment for up to one year. As mentioned earlier, St. Clares Shores, Michigan, was the first municipality to adopt a parental responsibility ordinance which allows parents to be fined up to $100 for failing to control their children's actions or seek professional assistance.[34] These laws attempt to involve parents in the lives of their children by holding them civilly and/or criminally liable for their children's actions. Penalties for violation of these laws include increased participation by parents in juvenile proceedings; financial responsibility for restitution payments and court costs; financial responsibility for detention, treatment, and supervisory costs; participation in treatment, counseling, or other diversion programs; and criminal responsibility and possible jail time for parents found negligent in their supervision.[35]

15.4 SELF-CHECK

1. Describe three types of specialty courts. What are their advantages over traditional juvenile justice processes?

2. What is an intervention strategy? Can you describe one in detail?

3. Describe the concept of parental liability.

Final Thoughts

One recent trend that is likely to continue is the separation of juveniles who are deemed appropriate for juvenile court processing from those deemed inappropriate. In other words, legislatures and juvenile justice personnel are actively trying to exclude from the juvenile court repeat and violent offenders. The most common method is through waiver to criminal court; other mechanisms include the increased use of determinate sentencing. Related to this trend are the increased use and development of programs designed for early intervention.

Without much doubt, the programs and practices of juvenile justice continue to be much more innovative and successful when compared to the adult system. This fact alone serves as a powerful reason to keep a separate system of juvenile justice in place. Indeed, even with pressing economic conditions that forced some states (e.g., California) to de-centralize juvenile justice, it was not completely abolished. The range of programs and options available in juvenile justice far exceeds any available in the adult system. Future efforts are likely to attempt to involve more than just criminal justice personnel in the lives of juveniles. New theories that embrace public health prevention and early intervention models are receiving greater attention and support as is evidenced by the myriad of programs discussed in this chapter. Over the next 100 years of juvenile justice, we are likely to see the innovation, change, and debate continue over what to do with juveniles who violate the law. However, we still cling to the fundamental hope that juveniles are more amenable to treatment and intervention than adult criminals. If that belief erodes, we may well see the end of the juvenile justice system in the United States.

15.5 SELF-CHECK

What are some of the common trends that will characterize juvenile justice in the future?

1. Identify the current trend in the legislation and philosophy of juvenile justice

After years of a "get-tough" paradigm, juvenile justice is experiencing a major shift. Due to changing social climates and harsher economic times, the focus is shifting from more punitive measures to those that work on levels of prevention and intervention. State juvenile justice agencies are decentralizing in favor of community-based treatment options that de-emphasize incarceration for all but the most violent offenders.

2. Describe the BARJ Model of juvenile justice

The Balanced and Restorative Justice (BARJ) Model attempts to bridge the traditional model of juvenile justice with the accountability aspects of the punitive model. The balanced approach supports a community's need to sanction crime, rehabilitate offenders, and ensure public safety. Toward these ends, it articulates three goals for juvenile justice: (1) accountability, (2) competency development, and (3) community safety. The principle behind BARJ is that justice is best served when victims, offenders, and communities receive equitable attention in the justice system.

3. Outline the arguments both for and against abolishing the juvenile justice system

Arguments for the abolishment of the juvenile justice system are primarily procedural, suggesting that: (1) Distinction between the juvenile and adult systems are blurred and do not make sense; (2) Increased penalties available within the juvenile justice system require increased due process, often found in the adult system; (3) The juvenile justice system is ill equipped to handle seriously violent and habitual offenders who could be more easily handled in the adult system; and (4) Rehabilitation as a goal of criminal justice is not realistic and simply doesn't work. On the other hand, proponents who favor the juvenile justice system argue that: (1) Although the legal distinctions and processes in the juvenile court are closer now to the adult system, the informal and paternalistic nature of the juvenile court still remains; (2) In serious cases where a juvenile is charged with a violent crime, extra protections can be implemented if the case stays in the juvenile court; (3) Most of the cases handled by the juvenile justice system are not serious; (4) Juveniles are still less culpable than adults for their criminal behavior; (5) The juvenile court is in a unique position to refer juveniles to a wide range of services and programs designed specifically for juveniles; and (6) Most juveniles who come into contact with the juvenile justice system do not re-offend. Juvenile treatment programs are much more successful than adult rehabilitation programs.

4. Identify the three major types of specialty courts used in juvenile justice

Specialty courts are designed to target specific groups of offenders who have unique needs that can best be addressed by the agencies and organizations which have staff and treatment programs to serve the identified population. Three of the more successful specialty court programs in the country are: (1) teen courts, (2) drug courts, and (3) gun courts.

5. Describe Project CRAFT and discuss its success as an intervention strategy

Project CRAFT is a very successful vocational training program for juvenile offenders sponsored by the Home Builders Institute. Project CRAFT (Community Restitutions and Apprenticeship Focused Training) began in 1994 and has been implemented in several states. Project CRAFT emphasizes a comprehensive and holistic approach to treatment, focusing on partnerships between schools, juvenile justice staff, drug and alcohol counselors, private organizations, mentors, and juvenile court judges to build a cooperative and inclusive program for juvenile offenders. Project CRAFT has been very successful in that its graduates have a very high employment placement in the home building industry. Further, the recidivism rate for youth in the program is only 26 percent, which is significantly lower than the national average for treatment programs. Maybe most important, the program has been very successful in continuing to work with youthful offenders long after they have been placed in jobs, reinforcing positive behavior and reducing criminality.

6. Describe the parental liability movement in juvenile justice

The concept of parental liability is not new. Parents have long been subject to laws on contributing to the delinquency of a minor and providing dependent children with the necessities of life, including a suitable home environment. However, more recently, some cities and states have developed laws which attempt to involve parents in the lives of their children by holding them civilly and/or criminally liable for their children's actions. Penalties for violation of these laws include increased participation by parents in juvenile proceedings; financial responsibility for restitution payments and court costs; financial responsibility for detention, treatment, and supervisory costs; participation in treatment, counseling, or other diversion programs; and criminal responsibility including possible jail time for parents found negligent in their supervision.

KEY TERMS

punitive model of
juvenile justice, p. 428

Balanced and Restorative
Justice (BARJ), p. 428

procedural due process, p. 429
intervention strategies, p. 436

parental liability, p. 440

REVIEW QUESTIONS

1. How is the juvenile justice system changing from its "get-tough" philosophy?

2. What is BARJ?

3. What alternatives are available to the punitive model of juvenile justice?

4. Describe the important study by Tibbetts and Piquero concerning minority youth in Philadelphia.

5. Name three important specialty courts designed to be an alternative to the formal juvenile court system.

6. What is Project CRAFT? Has it been successful?

7. What is the Phoenix Program?

8. What is "parental liability"?

HANDS-ON ACTIVITIES

1. **Develop your own opinion about the future of juvenile justice** With fellow students, family members, or friends, discuss the merits of abolishing the juvenile justice system. Can the existing system handle serious, violent, and habitual juveniles adequately? Do we need the informal and paternalistic protections offered by the existing juvenile justice system? What impact would abolishing the juvenile justice system have on the entire criminal justice process?

2. **Find out what the rules governing juveniles are in your own community** Visit your local police department and juvenile probation office. Does your jurisdiction have a curfew law or is it used only as a condition for probation with troubled youth? What do you think the impact of having strongly enforced curfews may be on juvenile crime? Gang activity? Juvenile drug use? Teenage prostitution? Youth violence? Compare what your local jurisdiction enforces with what you have read in this chapter.

INTERNET ACTIVITIES

1. With a small group of friends, search the Internet for new and innovative juvenile treatment programs. Start your search at the site of the National Center for Juvenile Justice. What community-based programs do you think have merit for the future in lowering juvenile crime and assisting troubled youth? Write a brief summary of what you think are the "best" alternatives to juvenile incarceration.

2. Find your state's juvenile justice system online and determine which type of intervention strategies they employ. Why do you think your state uses this model? Is this model likely to change given some of the national trends in juvenile justice?

1. **Decide the best solution for a first-time offender** Jamie is a 14-year-old junior high school student in Dallas, Texas. She tries to maintain good grades, but usually is satisfied with a "C" average in most of her course work. She has no real plans for college and really doesn't know what she wants to do with her life. Her mom and dad are divorced and she lives with her mother and two brothers. Jamie has several girlfriends, but no steady boyfriends. She is not active in extracurricular school events, but does attend the nearby Baptist Church where she engages in various youth activities. Last week, Jamie and one of her girlfriends were arrested for shoplifting. They were caught placing two Britney Spears CDs in their purses. When questioned by store security, Jamie contended that this was her first time ever being in trouble, and that it was her girlfriend's idea to steal the CDs. She says she is sorry and that it will never happen again. During most of the interview with store security, Jamie and her friend were visibly shaken and crying. She has been referred to the local teen court where you serve as the judge.

   a. What do you think is the best punishment or treatment strategy for Jamie? Why?

   b. Should officials at her school and church be notified that she has been arrested for shoplifting? Why or why not?

   c. How do you think any sentence levied against Jamie will meet the basic principles of restorative justice?

   d. What should be the next steps of adjudication if Jamie is caught shoplifting again?

15.1 Self-Check

What possible changes may occur to the juvenile justice system in the future?

There is some speculation that the entire separate system for juveniles could be abolished in the United States, although it seems more likely that it will be decentralized in the manner that California has undertaken. New theories that embrace public health prevention and intervention models will supplant the more punitive paradigm, and economic woes will also shape the future of the system.

15.2 Self-Check

1. What are some of the suggested methods for "getting tough" on juvenile crime?

Some common methods, which reflect the punitive model of juvenile justice that has been popular for the last 20 years, are:

- The switch from indeterminate sentencing, which is the hallmark of the traditional juvenile justice system, to determinate sentencing.
- The creation of new laws and alteration of existing ones to hold juveniles more accountable and punish them for their crimes.
- New laws that criminalize gang membership.
- More severe penalties for chronic and violent offenders.
- Holding parents responsible for the crimes their children commit. This is also called parental liability.

2. List some of the arguments for and against abolishing the juvenile justice system.

There are a number of arguments *for* abolishing the juvenile justice system including:

- The current state of the juvenile justice system does not reflect the original intentions of the founders. The system has become increasingly punitive and harsh.
- Children in juvenile court are denied basic due process rights. The move to a more punitive system has not been accompanied by an increase in the due process rights of children in juvenile court.
- The current juvenile justice system duplicates the adult system. However, juveniles can receive significant punishment without being afforded many of the protections offered in the adult system of justice.
- Increasing use of determinate sentencing has led some juvenile courts to become more punitive than their adult counterparts.
- Juveniles are routinely not represented by counsel in proceedings where their liberty is at stake. The presence of counsel in juvenile court does not have a positive effect in many cases.
- The distinction between the juvenile and adult systems of justice has become blurred, thus eliminating the need for a separate system of justice.
- A unified, streamlined system of justice could take age into account as a mitigating factor and provide juveniles with increased due process rights.

There are also a number of arguments *against* abolishing the juvenile justice system. These include:

- Juveniles are still less culpable than adults and deserve to be treated differently.
- The adult system of criminal justice is not equipped to deal with juveniles. The adult correctional system simply warehouses inmates with little if any rehabilitation potential.
- Juveniles have a greater rehabilitation potential than adults. They have lower rates of recidivism.
- The worst aspects of the adult system are not present in the juvenile system, specifically bail and the game-like adversarial system.
- The violent criminals that serve as the basis for arguments about abolishing the juvenile system make up less than 1 percent of the offenders processed by the system. Throwing away an entire system for less than 1 percent of the offenders is not logical.
- The juvenile justice system is still more benign than the adult criminal justice system, and this allows for the juvenile system to individualize justice for most of the offenders it deals with.
- The range of placement options and other mechanisms available in juvenile court far overshadows those in the adult system.
- The juvenile justice system is the most successful system in American criminal justice. Most juveniles who are processed do not come back, and the system enjoys high rates of success in changing juveniles.

15.3 Self-Check

What is the BARJ Model?

The Balanced and Restorative Justice (BARJ) Model is an alternative philosophy and a back-to-basics mission for juvenile justice. The new "balanced approach" supports a community's need to sanction crime, rehabilitate offenders, and ensure public safety. BARJ articulates three goals for juvenile justice: accountability, competency development, and community safety.

15.4 Self-Check

1. Describe three types of specialty courts. What are their advantages over traditional juvenile justice processes?

The three types are teen courts, drug courts, and gun courts.

Their key advantage is that they target specific groups of offenders, each of which has unique needs that can best be addressed by the agencies and organizations that have staff and treatment programs to serve those specific needs.

2. What is an intervention strategy? Can you describe one in detail?

Intervention strategies are delinquency prevention strategies that target at-risk youth, and then provide them with a variety of programs and services. The most promising prevention strategies are collaborative efforts that include the juvenile's family, school, and community.

The following are examples of these programs:

Collaborative Intensive Community Treatment Program (CICTP) is an alternative to residential incarceration that attempts to offer a "managed care" approach to allocating resources for youthful offenders. Offenders are carefully and individually selected for the program on the basis of criteria for success (age, past record, school performance, nature of the offense, etc.). The program supports the principles of the BARJ model that were previously described in this chapter.

Project CRAFT is one of the most successful vocational training programs. Utilizing a holistic and comprehensive approach that incorporates career training, community service activities, and support services like social skills training and case management, this program demonstrates how private business (the construction industry) can collaborate with the juvenile justice system to assist youth. An independent evaluation of Project CRAFT reports that:

- It had a very high placement for its graduates in the home building industry.
- The recidivism rate for youth in the program was only 26 percent, which is significantly lower than the national average for treatment programs.
- The program was very successful in continuing to work with youthful offenders long after they had been placed in jobs, particularly with youth who were in residential facilities.

3. Describe the concept of parental liability.

Although past parental liability laws were found to be unconstitutional by appellate courts, new laws seek to attach criminal responsibility to parents for "failing to supervise" or "intervene" in the lives of their children. Several cities have received national attention for passing so-called parental responsibility statutes, including Silverton, OR; Arlington Heights, IL; Roanoke, VA; and St. Clares Shores, MI.

(Refer to the Focus on Policy box on pages 440–441, which offers an in-depth look at how the St. Clares Shores, MI, statutes applied in the case of a family that failed to take responsibility for their son Alex.)

15.5 Self-Check

What are some of the common trends that will characterize juvenile justice in the future?

Trends that will influence the future can include any of the following:

- The increased use and development of programs designed for early intervention.
- The use of programs and practices that are much more innovative and successful when compared to the adult system; this fact alone serves as a powerful reason to keep a separate system of juvenile justice in place.
- A range of programs and options available in juvenile justice that far exceeds any available in the adult system.
- Future efforts that are likely to attempt to involve more than just criminal justice personnel in the lives of juveniles.
- A community approach to juvenile justice that is receiving greater attention and support, as you can see by the myriad of programs discussed in this chapter.

ENDNOTES

Chapter 1

1. Platt, Anthony M., *The Child Savers: The Invention of Delinquency,* Chicago: University of Chicago Press, 1977.
2. Snyder, Howard N. and Melissa Sickmund, *Juvenile Offenders and Victims: 2006 National Report,* Pittsburgh, PA: National Center for Juvenile Justice, 2006.
3. Puzzanchera, Charles and Benjamin Adams, *Juvenile Arrests 2009,* Washington DC: Office of Juvenile Justice and Delinquency Prevention, 2011.
4. Knoll, Crystal and Melissa Sickmund, *Delinquency Cases in Juvenile Court, 2009,* Washington DC: Office of Juvenile Justice and Delinquency Prevention, 2012.
5. Ibid.
6. Ibid.
7. Snyder and Sickmund, 2006.
8. Knoll and Sickmund, 2012.
9. Ibid.
10. Ibid.
11. Ibid.
12. Ibid.

Chapter 2

1. Faust, Frederick L. and Paul J. Brantingham, *Juvenile Justice Philosophy: Readings, Cases and Comments,* St. Paul, MN: West Publishing, 1979.
2. Platt, Anthony, "The Child-Saving Movement and the Origins of the Juvenile Justice System," in *Juvenile Delinquency: Historical, Theoretical and Societal Reactions to Youth,* edited by P. M. Sharp & B. W. Hancock, Englewood Cliffs, NJ: Prentice Hall, 1969.
3. National Center for Juvenile Justice, *Desktop Guide to Good Juvenile Probation Practice,* Pittsburgh, PA: National Center for Juvenile Justice, 1991.
4. National Center for Juvenile Justice, *Desktop Guide to Good Juvenile Probation Practice,* Pittsburgh, PA: National Center for Juvenile Justice, 1996.
5. del Carmen, Rolando V., Wendy Hume, Elmer Polk, Frances Reddington, and Betsy Witt, *Texas Juvenile Law and Practice,* Huntsville, TX: College of Criminal Justice, Sam Houston State University Press, 1991; Aumann, F.R., "The Juvenile Court Movement in Ohio," *American Institute of Criminal Law* 22: 556–565, 1931, in Forst, Martin L., *The New Juvenile Justice,* Chicago, IL: Nelson Hall, 1995; Mack, Julian, "The Juvenile Court," *Harvard Law Review* 23: 104–126, 1909, in Forst, Martin L., *The New Juvenile Justice,* Chicago, IL: Nelson Hall, 1995.
6. Bernard, Thomas J., *The Cycle of Juvenile Justice,* New York: Oxford University Press, 1992; Ferdinand, Theodore N.,"History Overtakes the Juvenile Justice System," *Crime & Delinquency,* 37. 204–24, 1991.
7. Albanese, Jay, *Dealing With Delinquency: The Future of Juvenile Justice,* Chicago, IL: Nelson-Hall Publishers, 1993; Pisciotta, Alexander W., "Saving the Children: The Promise and Practice of *Parens Patriae,* 1838–98," *Crime & Delinquency* 28: 410–25, 1982; Platt, Anthony, "The Child-Saving Movement and the Origins of the Juvenile Justice System," in *Juvenile Delinquency: Historical, Theoretical and Societal Reactions to Youth,* edited by P. M. Sharp & B. W. Hancock, Englewood Cliffs, NJ: Prentice Hall, 1969.
8. Faust and Brantingham, 1979.
9. Platt, 1969.
10. National Center for Juvenile Justice, *Desktop Guide to Good Juvenile Probation Practice,* Pittsburgh, PA: National Center for Juvenile Justice, 1991; Mack, Julian, "The Juvenile Court," *Harvard Law Review* 23: 104–126, 1909, in Forst, Martin L., *The New Juvenile Justice,* Chicago, IL: Nelson Hall, 1995.
11. Platt, 1969.
12. Albanese, Jay, *Dealing With Delinquency: The Future of Juvenile Justice,* Chicago, IL: Nelson-Hall Publishers, 1993.
13. Schlossman, Steven L., *Love and the American Delinquent: The Theory and Practice of "Progressive" Juvenile Justice, 1825–1920,* Chicago, IL: University of Chicago Press, 1977.
14. Tappan, Paul W., "Treatment Without Trial." *Social Forces,* 1946.
15. Albanese, 1993.
16. Platt, Anthony M., *The Child Savers,* Chicago, IL: University of Chicago Press, 1969.
17. Krisberg, Barry, Ira M. Schwartz, Paul Litsky, and James Austin, "The Watershed of Juvenile Justice Reform," *Crime & Delinquency* 32: 5–38, 1986.
18. Fabelo, Tony, *A Framework for Examining Texas Policies on Children and Youth: Slowing Down the Crime Factory,* Bulletin from the Executive Director, January, no. 5, Austin, TX: Criminal Justice Policy Council, 1994; Hirschi, Travis and Michael Gottfredson, "Rethinking the Juvenile Justice System," *Crime & Delinquency,* 39: 262–71, 1993; Krisberg, Barry, Ira M. Schwartz, Paul Litsky, and James Austin, "The Watershed of Juvenile Justice Reform," *Crime & Delinquency,* 32: 5–38, 1986; Feld, Barry C. "Juvenile Court Legislative Reform and the Serious Young Offender: Dismantling the 'Rehabilitative Ideal'," *Minnesota Law Review,* 65: 1187–1239, 1980; Feld, Barry C., "Legislative Policies toward the Serious Juvenile Offender: On the Virtues of Automatic Adulthood," *Crime & Delinquency* 27: 497–521, 1981.

19. Hirschi, Travis and Michael Gottfredson, "Rethinking the Juvenile Justice System," *Crime & Delinquency* 39: 262–71, 1993; Krisberg, Barry, Ira M. Schwartz, Paul Litsky, and James Austin, "The Watershed of Juvenile Justice Reform," *Crime & Delinquency*, 32: 5–38, 1986; Bazemore, Gordon, "On Mission Statements and Reform in Juvenile Justice: The Case of the 'Balanced Approach'," *Federal Probation*, 56:3, 64–70, 1992.

20. Sharp, Paul M. and Barry W. Hancock, eds., *Juvenile Delinquency: Historical, Theoretical and Societal Reactions to Youth*, Englewood Cliffs, NJ: Prentice Hall, 1995.

21. Torbet, Patricia, Richard Gamble, Hunter Hurst IV, Imogene Montgomery, Linda Szymanski, and Douglas Thomas, *State Responses to Serious and Violent Juvenile Crime: Research Report*, Washington, D.C.: Office of Juvenile Justice and Delinquency Prevention, 1996; Sanborn, Joseph B., "Remnants of Parens Patriae in the Adjudicatory Hearing: Is a Fair Trial Possible in Juvenile Court," *Crime & Delinquency* 40: 599–615, 1994; Anderson, George M., "Punishing the Young: Juvenile Justice in the 1990s," *America* 166:7, February 29, 158–163, 1992; Gardner, M. R., "Punitive Juvenile Justice: Some Observations on a Recent Trend," *International Journal of Law and Psychiatry* 10, 129–151, 1987; Feld, Barry C., "Juvenile Court Legislative Reform and the Serious Young Offender: Dismantling the 'Rehabilitative Ideal'," *Minnesota Law Review* 65: 1187–1239, 1980; Feld, Barry C., "Legislative Policies toward the Serious Juvenile Offender: On the Virtues of Automatic Adulthood," *Crime & Delinquency* 27: 497–521, 1981.

22. Torbet, Patricia, Richard Gamble, Hunter Hurst IV, Imogene Montgomery, Linda Szymanski, and Douglas Thomas, *State Responses to Serious and Violent Juvenile Crime: Research Report*, Washington DC: Office of Juvenile Justice and Delinquency Prevention, 1996; Krisberg, Barry, Ira M. Schwartz, Paul Litsky, and James Austin, "The Watershed of Juvenile Justice Reform," *Crime & Delinquency* 32:1, 5–38, 1986.

23. Forst, Martin L., *The New Juvenile Justice*, Chicago, IL: Nelson Hall, 1995.

24. Fritsch, Eric J. and Craig Hemmens, "Juvenile Waiver in the United States 1979–1995: A Comparison and Analysis of State Waiver Statutes," *Juvenile and Family Court Journal* 46: 17–35, 1995.

25. Faust, Frederick L. and Paul J. Brantingham, *Juvenile Justice Philosophy: Readings, Cases and Comments*, St. Paul, MN: West Publishing, 1979.

26. Barry C. Feld, "Legislative Policies toward the Serious Juvenile Offender: On the Virtues of Automatic Adulthood," *Crime and Delinquency* 27, 1981, 497–521.

27. Bernard, Thomas J., *The Cycle of Juvenile Justice*, New York: Oxford University Press, 1992.

28. Ibid.

29. Ibid.

Chapter 3

1. Prothrom-Stith, Deborah, *Deadly Consequences*, New York: Harper Collins, 1991.

2. Wass, Hannelore, M. David Miller, and Carol Anne Redditt, "Adolescents and Destructive Themes in Rock Music: A Follow-Up," *Omega: The Journal of Death and Dying* 23(3), 199–206, 1991.

3. Puzzanchera, Charles and Melissa Sickmund, *Juvenile Court Statistics 2005*, Pittsburgh, PA: National Center for Juvenile Justice, 2008.

4. Truman, Jennifer and Michael Planty, 2012, *Criminal Victimization, 2011*, Washington, D.C.: Bureau of Justice Statistics. Online. Available at: http://bjs.gov/content/pub/pdf/cv11.pdf. Retrieved March 10, 2013.

5. Rennison, Carrie Marie, Angela Gover, Stacey J. Bosick, and Mary Dodge, 2011, "Reporting Violent Victimization to the Police: A Focus on Black, White, Asian and Hispanic Adolescent Victims," *The Open Family Studies Journal*. Online. Available at: http://benthamscience.com/open/tofamsj/articles/V004/SI0015TOFAMSJ/54TOFAMSJ.pdf. Retrieved April 19, 2013.

6. Finkelhor, David and Richard Ormrod, *Reporting Crimes Against Juveniles*, Washington, DC.: Office of Juvenile Justice and Delinquency Prevention, 2000.

7. *OJJDP Statistical Briefing Book*. Online. Available: http://www.ojjdp.gov/ojstatbb/victims/qa02607.asp?qaDate=20050531. Retrieved March 19, 2013.

8. *Criminal Victimization in the United States, 2008 Statistical Tables*, 2011. Online. Available at: http://bjs.gov/content/pub/pdf/cvus0805.pdf. Retrieved March 22, 2013.

9. See Bachman, Jerald G., Lloyd D. Johnston, and Patrick M. O'Malley, *The Monitoring the Future Project After Twenty-Seven Years: Design and Procedures*, 2011. Online. Available at: http://www.monitoringthefuture.org/pubs/occpapers/occ54.pdf. Retrieved April 26, 2013; Centers for Disease Control and Prevention, *2011 Youth Risk Behavior Survey (YRBS) Results*, 2012. Online. Available at: http://www.cdc.gov/features/YRBS/. Retrieved April 26, 2013; and Centers for Disease Control and Prevention, *Youth Risk Behavior Surveillance System (YRBSS) Website*, 2013. Online. Available at: http://www.cdc.gov/healthyyouth/yrbs/index.htm. Retrieved April 26, 2013.

10. Browning, Katharine, David Huizinga, Rolf Loeber, and Terence P. Thornberry, *Causes and Correlates of Delinquency Program, OJJDP Fact Sheet #100*, Washington, DC: OJJDP, 1999.

11. Ibid.

12. Hindelang, Michael J., Travis Hirschi, and Joseph G. Weis, *Measuring Delinquency*, Newbury Park, CA: Sage Publications, 1981.

13. Cernkovich, Steven A., Peggy C. Giordano, and Meredith D. Pugh, "Chronic Offenders: The Missing Cases in Self-Report Delinquency Research," *Journal of Criminal Law and Criminology*. 76(3), 705–732, 1985.

14. Ibid.

15. Browning, Katharine and David Huizinga, *Highlights of Findings from the Denver Youth Survey Series: OJJDP Fact Sheet #106*, Washington, DC: Office of Juvenile Justice and Delinquency Prevention, 1999.

16. Finkelhor, David and Annie Shattuck, 2012, *Characteristics of Crimes Against Juveniles*, Durham, NH: Crimes Against Children Research Center, University of New Hampshire. Online. Available at http://www.unh.edu/ccrc/pdf/CV26_Revised%20Characteristics%20of%20Crimes%20against%20Juveniles_5-2-12.pdf. Retrieved March 19, 2013.

17. Snyder, Howard N. and Melissa Sickmund, *Juvenile Offenders and Victims: 1999 National Report*, Washington, DC: Office of Juvenile Justice and Delinquency Prevention, 1999.

18. Snyder, Howard and Melissa Sickmund, 2006. *Juvenile Offenders and Victims: 2006 National Report*, Washington, DC: Office of Juvenile Justice and Delinquency Protections.

19. *OJJDP Statistical Briefing Book.* Online. Available: http://www.ojjdp.gov/ojstatbb/victims/qa02201.asp?qaDate=2010. Retrieved March 19, 2013.

20. *OJJDP Statistical Briefing Book.* Online. Available: http://www.ojjdp.gov/ojstatbb/victims/qa02202.asp?qaDate=2010. Retrieved March 19, 2013.

21. From "A Summary of a Profile of an At-Risk Youth," *Pathways: Fostering Spiritual Growth Among At-Risk Youth,* Boys Town, NE.

22. Huizinga, David, Rolf Loeber, and Terence P. Thornberry, *Urban Delinquency and Substance Abuse: Initial Findings,* Washington, DC: Office of Juvenile Justice and Delinquency Prevention, March 1994.

23. Several sources are used to develop the concepts of risk and protective factors, including: Browning, Katharine, David Huizinga, Rolf Loeber, and Terence P. Thornberry, *Causes and Correlates of Delinquency Program, OJJDP Fact Sheet #100,* Washington, DC: OJJDP, 1999; Hawkins, J. David, Todd. I. Herrenkohl, David P. Farrington, Devon Brewer, Richard F. Catalano, Tracy W. Harachi, and Lynn Cothern, *Predictors of Youth Violence,* Washington, DC: Office of Juvenile Justice and Delinquency Prevention, 2000; Jessor, Richard, "Risk Behavior in Adolescence: A Psychosocial Framework for Understanding and Action," in *Adolescents at Risk: Medical and Social Perspectives,* pp. 374–389, D. Rogers and E. Ginzburg, eds., Boulder, CO: Westview Press, 1992; Benson, P., *The Troubled Journey: A Portrait of 6th–12th Grade Youth.* Minneapolis: Search Institute, Thresher Square, Suite 120, 700 S. 3rd St., Minneapolis, MN 55415. (612) 376-8955, 1993; *Father Flanagan's Boys Home Boys Town,* Nebraska 68010 (402) 498–1111; *A Study of Prevention and Early Intervention Service in Virginia,* Virginia Department of Planning and Budget, Dec. 1992; Caliber Associates. *Community Prevention Grants Program Community Self-Evaluation Workbook,* Washington, DC: Office of Juvenile Justice and Delinquency Prevention, 1999; Browning, Katharine and Rolf Loeber, *Highlights of Findings From the Pittsburgh Youth Study Series: OJJDP Fact Sheet #95,* Washington, DC: Office of Juvenile Justice and Delinquency Prevention, 1999; Browning, Katharine, Terence P. Thornberry, and Pamela K. Porter, *Highlights of Findings From the Rochester Youth Development Study Series: OJJDP Fact Sheet #103,* Washington, DC: Office of Juvenile Justice and Delinquency Prevention, 1999; Browning, Katharine and David Huizinga, *Highlights of Findings From the Denver Youth Survey Series: OJJDP Fact Sheet #106,* Washington, DC: Office of Juvenile Justice and Delinquency Prevention, 1999.

24. Browning, Katharine and Rolf Loeber, *Highlights of Findings from the Pittsburgh Youth Study Series: OJJDP Fact Sheet #95,* Washington, DC: Office of Juvenile Justice and Delinquency Prevention, 1999.

25. Ibid.

26. Ibid.

27. Synder, H. *Juvenile Arrests 2006,* 2008. Washington, DC: Office of Juvenile Justice and Delinquency Prevention.

28. Chaiken, Marcia R., *Violent Neighborhoods-Violent Kids: What Could Be Done With Boys in DC,* Alexandria, VA: LINC, 1998.

29. Hawkins, J. David, Todd. I. Herrenkohl, David P. Farrington, Devon Brewer, Richard F. Catalano, Tracy W. Harachi, and Lynn Cothern, *Predictors of Youth Violence,* Washington, DC: Office of Juvenile Justice and Delinquency Prevention, 2000.

30. Loeber, Rolf and Magda Strouthhamer-Loeber, "Family Factors as Correlates of Juvenile Conduct Problems and Juvenile Delinquency," in *Crime and Justice: An Annual Review of Research,* Vol. 7. Chicago, IL: University of Chicago Press, 1986.

31. Ibid.

32. Ibid.

33. Wells, L. Edward and Joseph H. Rankin, "Families and Delinquency: A Meta-Analysis of the Impact of Broken Homes," *Social Problems* 38, 71–90, 1991.

34. Nye, F., *Family Relationships and Delinquent Behavior,* New York: John Wiley, 1958; Hindelang, Michael J., "Causes of Delinquency: A Partial Explication and Extension," *Social Problems* 20: 471–487, 1973; Hirschi, Travis, *Causes of Delinquency,* Berkeley, CA: University of California Press, 1969.

35. Johnson, Richard E., "Family Structure and Delinquency: General Patterns and Gender Differences," *Criminology* 24:1, 65–84, 1989.

36. Browning, Katharine and Rolf Loeber, *Highlights of Findings From the Pittsburgh Youth Study Series: OJJDP Fact Sheet #95,* Washington, DC: Office of Juvenile Justice and Delinquency Prevention, 1999.

37. Thornberry, Terence P., Carolyn A. Smith, Craig Rivera, David Huizinga, and Magda Stouthamer-Loeber, *Family Disruption and Delinquency,* Washington, DC: Office of Juvenile Justice and Delinquency Prevention, 1999.

38. Browning, Katharine, Terence P. Thornberry, and Pamela K. Porter, *Highlights of Findings From the Rochester Youth Development Study Series: OJJDP Fact Sheet #103,* Washington, DC: Office of Juvenile Justice and Delinquency Prevention, 1999.

39. Huizinga, David, Rolf Loeber, and Terence P. Thornberry, *Urban Delinquency and Substance Abuse: Initial Findings,* Washington, DC: Office of Juvenile Justice and Delinquency Prevention, March 1994.

40. Hawkins, J. David, Todd. I. Herrenkohl, David P. Farrington, Devon Brewer, Richard F. Catalano, Tracy W. Harachi, and Lynn Cothern, *Predictors of Youth Violence,* Washington, DC: Office of Juvenile Justice and Delinquency Prevention, 2000.

41. Ibid.

42. Weis, Joseph G., "Social Class and Crime," in *Positive Criminology* (pp. 71–90), Michael Gottfredson and Travis Hirschi, eds., Newbury Park, CA: Sage Publications, 1987.

43. Office of Juvenile Justice and Delinquency Prevention, *Report to Congress on Juvenile Violence Research,* Washington, DC, 1999.

44. Hawkins, J. David, Todd. I. Herrenkohl, David P. Farrington, Devon Brewer, Richard F. Catalano, Tracy W. Harachi, and Lynn Cothern, *Predictors of Youth Violence,* Washington, DC: Office of Juvenile Justice and Delinquency Prevention, 2000.

45. Ibid.

46. Huizinga, David, Rolf Loeber, and Terence P. Thornberry, *Urban Delinquency and Substance Abuse: Initial Findings,* Washington, DC: Office of Juvenile Justice and Delinquency Prevention, March 1994

47. Browning, Katharine, Terence P. Thornberry, and Pamela K. Porter, *Highlights of Findings From the Rochester Youth Development Study Series: OJJDP Fact Sheet #103,* Washington, DC: Office of Juvenile Justice and Delinquency Prevention, 1999.

48. Thornberry, Terence P., Melanie Moore, and R. L. Christenson, "The Effect of Dropping Out of High School on Subsequent Criminal Behavior," *Criminology* 23, 3–18, 1985.

49. Browning, Katharine and Rolf Loeber, *Highlights of Findings From the Pittsburgh Youth Study Series: OJJDP Fact Sheet #95*, Washington, DC: Office of Juvenile Justice and Delinquency Prevention, 1999.

50. Ibid.

51. *Juveniles and Drugs: Facts and Figures.* Office of National Drug Control Policy. Online. Available: http://www.whitehousedrugpolicy.gov/drugfact/juveniles/juvenile_drugs_ff.html. Retrieved May 10, 2009.

52. McLelland, G., L. Teplin, and K. Abram. *Detection and Prevalance of Substance Use Among Juvenile Detainees*, 2004, Washington, DC: Office of Juvenile Justice and Delinquency Prevention.

53. Inciardi, James A., "The Crack-Violence Connection Within a Population of Hard-Core Adolescent Offenders," in *Drugs and Violence: Causes, Correlates, and Consequences*, NIDA Research Monograph 103, 1990.

54. Ibid.

55. Huizinga, David, Rolf Loeber, and Terence P. Thornberry, *Urban Delinquency and Substance Abuse: Initial Findings*, Washington, DC: Office of Juvenile Justice and Delinquency Prevention, March 1994.

56. Browning, Katharine, Terence P. Thornberry, and Pamela K. Porter, *Highlights of Findings From the Rochester Youth Development Study Series: OJJDP Fact Sheet #103*, Washington, DC: Office of Juvenile Justice and Delinquency Prevention, 1999.

57. Huizinga, David, Rolf Loeber, and Terence P. Thornberry, *Urban Delinquency and Substance Abuse: Initial Findings*, Washington, DC: Office of Juvenile Justice and Delinquency Prevention, March 1994.

58. Browning, Katharine and Rolf Loeber, *Highlights of Findings From the Pittsburgh Youth Study Series: OJJDP Fact Sheet #95*, Washington, DC: Office of Juvenile Justice and Delinquency Prevention, 1999.

59. Browning, Katharine and David Huizinga, *Highlights of Findings From the Denver Youth Survey Series: OJJDP Fact Sheet #106*, Washington, DC: Office of Juvenile Justice and Delinquency Prevention, 1999.

60. Ibid.

61. Jessor, Richard, "Risk Behavior in Adolescence: A Psychosocial Framework for Understanding and Action," in *Adolescents at Risk: Medical and Social Perspectives*, pp. 374–389, D. Rogers and E. Ginzburg, eds., Boulder, CO: Westview Press, 1992.

62. Thornberry, Terence P., Evelyn H. Wei, Magda Stouthamer-Loeber, and Joyce Van Dyke, *Teenage Fatherhood and Delinquent Behavior*, Washington, DC: Office of Juvenile Justice and Delinquency Prevention, 2000.

Chapter 4

1. Beccaria, Cesare, *On Crimes and Punishments*, translated by Henry Paolucci, New York: Macmillan, 1963.

2. Ibid.

3. Siegel, Larry J., *Criminology: Theories, Patterns, and Typologies*, 4th ed., St. Paul, MN: West, 1992.

4. Martinson, Robert, "What Works? Questions and Answers About Prison Reform," *The Public Interest*, Vol. 35, 1974, pp. 22–54.

5. Cohen, Lawrence and Marcus Felson, "Social Change and Crime Rate Trends: A Routine Activities Approach," *American Sociological Review*, Vol. 44, 1979, pp. 588–608.

6. Ibid.

7. Ibid.

8. Kadish, Sanford H. and Monrad G. Paulsen, *Criminal Law and Its Processes*, Boston: Little, Brown, 1969, p. 85.

9. Walker, Samuel, *Sense and Nonsense About Crime and Drugs: A Policy Guide*, 4th ed., Belmont, CA: West/Wadsworth, 1998.

10. Ibid.

11. Ibid.

12. Paternoster, Raymond, "The Deterrent Effect of Perceived and Severity of Punishment: A Review of the Evidence and Issues," *Justice Quarterly*, Vol. 42, 1987, pp. 173–217.

13. Green, Donald, "Measures of Illegal Behavior in Individual- Level Deterrence Research," *Journal of Research in Crime and Delinquency*, Vol. 26, 1989, pp. 253–75.

14. Bureau of Justice Statistics, *Prisoners and Drugs*, Washington, DC: U.S. Government Printing Office, 1983.

15. Bernard, Thomas J, Jeffrey B. Snipes, and Alexander L. Gerould. *Vold's Theoretical Criminology*, 6th ed. New York: Oxford University Press, 2009.

16. Ferrero, Gina Lombroso, *Criminal Man According to the Classification of Cesare Lombroso*, New York: Putnam, 1911.

17. Ibid.

18. Sheldon, William, *Varieties of Delinquent Youth*, New York: Harper, 1949.

19. Ibid.

20. Ibid.

21. Christiansen, Karl O., "A Preliminary Study of Criminology Among Twins," in Sarnoff Mednick and Karl Christiansen (eds.), *Biosocial Bases of Criminal Behavior*, New York: Gardner Press, 1977.

22. Ibid.

23. Dalgard, Odd Steffen and Einar Kringler, "Criminal Behavior in Twins," in Leonard D. Savitz and Norman Johnston (eds.), *Crime in Society*, New York, Wiley: 1978.

24. Mednick, Sarnoff, W. F. Gabrielli, and B. Hutchings, "Genetic Influences in Criminal Convictions: Evidence from an Adoption Cohort," *Science*, Vol. 224, 1984, pp. 891–94.

25. Schoenthaler, Stephen and Walter Doraz, "Types of Offenses Which Can Be Reduced in an Institutional Setting Using Nutritional Intervention," *International Journal of Biosocial Research*, Vol. 4, 1983, pp. 74–84.

26. Roberts, Albert R. and Judith A. Waters, "The Coming Storm: Juvenile Violence and Justice System Responses," in Albert R. Roberts (ed.), *Juvenile Justice: Policies, Programs, and Services*, 2nd ed., Chicago: Nelson-Hall, 1998.

27. Ibid.

28. Ibid.

29. Maplin, D., "FAS and FAE: Prevention, Intervention, and the Counselor's Role," *The Counselor*, May-June, 1995, pp. 28–32.

30. Roberts and Waters, "The Coming Storm: Juvenile Violence and Justice System Responses."

31. Ibid.

32. Fishbein, Diana, "The Psychobiology of Female Aggression," *Criminal Justice and Behavior*, Vol. 19, 1992, pp. 99–126.

33. Bernard, Snipes, and Gerould, *Vold's Theoretical Criminology*.

34. Ibid.
35. Ibid.
36. Mednick, S. A., V. Pollock, J. Volavka, and W. F. Gabrielli, "Biology and Violence," in M.E. Wolfgang and N. A. Weiner (eds.), *Criminal Violence*, Beverly Hills: Sage, 1982.
37. Ibid., pp. 39–40.
38. Bernard, Snipes, and Gerould, *Vold's Theretical Criminology*.
39. Ibid.
40. Roberts and Waters, "The Coming Storm: Juvenile Violence and Justice System Responses."
41. Ibid.
42. Ibid.
43. Ibid.
44. *Diagnostic and Statistical Manual of Mental Disorders*, 4th ed. Washington, DC: American Psychiatric Association, 1994.
45. Aichhorn, August, *Wayward Youth*, New York: Viking Press, 1963.
46. Erikson, Erik, *Identity, Youth and Crisis*, New York, Norton, 1968.
47. Critelli, Joseph W., *Personal Growth and Effective Behavior: The Challenge of Everyday Life*, New York: Holt, Rinehart and Winston, 1987, pp. 67–69.
48. Kohlberg, Lawrence, *Stages in the Development of Moral Thought and Action*, New York: Holt, Rinehart and Winston, 1969.
49. Henggeler, Scott, *Delinquency in Adolescence*, Newbury Park, CA: Sage, 1989.
50. Glueck, Sheldon and Eleanor Glueck, *Unraveling Juvenile Delinquency*, New York: Commonwealth Fund, 1950.
51. *Diagnostic and Statistical Manual of Mental Disorders*, 4th ed., p. 645.
52. Ibid.
53. *Diagnostic and Statistical Manual of Mental Disorders*, 4th ed.
54. Ibid.
55. Vold, Bernard, and Snipes, *Theoretical Criminology*, p. 180.
56. Trasler, G., *The Explanation of Criminality*, London: Routledge and Kegan Paul, 1962.
57. Ibid.
58. Bandura, Albert and Richard H. Walters, *Social Learning and Personality Development*, New York: Holt, Rinehart and Winston, 1963.
59. Wood, Wendy, Frank Wong, and J. Gregory Chachere, "Effects of Media Violence on Viewers' Aggression in Unconstrained Social Interaction," *Psychological Bulletin*, Vol. 109, 1991, pp. 371–83.

Chapter 5

1. Shaw, Clifford R. and Henry D. McKay, *Juvenile Delinquency and Urban Areas*, Chicago: University of Chicago Press, 1942.
2. Burgess, Ernest W., "The Growth of the City," in Robert E. Park, Ernest W. Burgess, and Roderick D. McKenzie, *The City*, Chicago: University of Chicago Press, 1928.
3. Shaw and McKay, *Juvenile Delinquency and Urban Areas*.
4. Ibid.
5. Merton, Robert K., *Social Theory and Social Structure*, Glencoe, IL: The Free Press, 1968.
6. Ibid.
7. Agnew, Robert, "Foundation for a General Strain Theory of Crime and Delinquency," *Criminology* 1992, 30: 47–87.

8. Ibid.
9. Ibid.
10. Cohen, Albert K., *Delinquent Boys: The Culture of the Gang*, New York: The Free Press, 1955.
11. Ibid.
12. Ibid.
13. Ibid.
14. Ibid.
15. Ibid.
16. Ibid.
17. Cloward, Richard and Lloyd Ohlin, *Delinquency and Opportunity*, New York: Free Press, 1960.
18. Ibid.
19. Ibid.
20. Ibid.
21. Miller, Walter B., "Lower Class Culture as a Generating Milieu of Gang Delinquency," *Journal of Social Issues*, Vol. 14, 1958, pp. 5–19.
22. Ibid.
23. Sutherland, Edwin H. and Donald R. Cressey, *Criminology*, 10th ed. Philadelphia: J.B. Lippincott Co., 1978, pp. 77–83.
24. Burgess, Robert and Ronald Akers, "Differential Association—Reinforcement Theory of Criminal Behavior," *Social Problems*, Vol. 14, 1968, pp. 128–47.
25. Ibid.
26. Sykes, Gresham M. and David Matza, "Techniques of Neutralization: A Theory of Delinquency," *American Sociological Review*, Vol. 22, 1957, pp. 664–70.
27. Ibid.
28. Reckless, Walter C., "A Non-Causal Explanation: Containment Theory," *Excerpta Criminologica*, Vol. 1, 1962, pp. 131–34.
29. Hirschi, Travis, *Causes of Delinquency*, Berkeley, CA: University of California Press, 1969.
30. Gottfredson, Michael and Travis Hirschi, *A General Theory of Crime*, Stanford, CA: Stanford University Press, 1990.
31. Thornberry, Terence, "Toward an Interactional Theory of Delinquency," *Criminology* 1987, 25: 863–891.
32. Ibid.
33. Ibid.
34. Sampson, Robert and John Laub, *Crime in the Making: Pathways and Turning Points through Life*, Cambridge, MA: Harvard University Press, 1993.
35. Ibid.
36. Ibid.
37. Becker, Howard S., *Outsiders: Studies in the Sociology of Deviance*, New York: The Free Press, 1963, p. 9.
38. Lemert, Edwin M., *Social Pathology*, New York: McGraw-Hill, 1951.
39. Ibid.
40. Garfinkel, Harold, "Conditions of Successful Degradation Ceremonies," *American Journal of Sociology*, Vol. 61, 1965, pp. 420–24.
41. Hagan, John, *Structural Criminology*, New Brunswick, NJ: Rutgers University Press, 1989.
42. Ibid.
43. Colvin, Mark and John Pauly, "Toward an Integrated Structural-Marxist Theory of Delinquency Production," *American Journal of Sociology*, Vol. 89, 1983, pp. 513–51.

Chapter 6

1. Loeber, Rolf, David P. Farrington, and David Petechuk, *Child Delinquency: Early Intervention and Prevention*, Child Delinquency Bulletin Series—May 2003, Washington, DC: Office of Juvenile Justice and Delinquency Prevention, 2003.

2. Office of Juvenile Justice and Delinquency Prevention, *Employment and Training for Court-Involved Youth*, Washington, DC: Office of Juvenile Justice and Delinquency Prevention, 2000.

3. Muller, Janine and Sharon Mihalic, *Blueprints: A Violence Prevention Initiative*, OJJDP *Fact Sheet #110*, Washington, DC: Office for Juvenile Justice and Delinquency Prevention, 1999.

4. Source: www.ncjrs.org/html/ojjdp/ojjdpreport_11_2000/#4.

5. Source: www.colorado.edu/cspv/blueprints/query/Default.htm.

6. Ibid.

7. Wyrick, Phelan A., "Law Enforcement Referral of At-Risk Youth: The SHIELD Program," *Juvenile Justice Bulletin*, November, Washington, DC: OJJDP, 2000.

8. Harrell, Adele, Shannon Cavanaugh, and Sanjeev Sridharan, *Evaluation of the Children at Risk Program: Results 1 Year After the End of the Program*, National Institute of Justice Research in Brief. Washington, DC: National Institute of Justice, 1999.

9. McDonald, Lynn and Deborah Howard, *Families and Schools Together Series*, OJJDP *Fact Sheet #88*, Washington, DC: OJJDP, 1998.

10. Ibid.

11. Ibid.

12. Shelden, Randall G., "Detention Diversion Advocacy: An Evaluation," *Juvenile Justice Bulletin*, September 1999, Washington, DC: OJJDP, 1999.

13. Ibid.

14. Ibid.

15. Kurlychek, Megan, Patricia Torbet, and Melanie Bozynski, "Focus on Accountability: Best Practices for Juvenile Court and Probation," *JAIBG Bulletin*, August 1999, Washington, DC: Office of Juvenile Justice and Delinquency Prevention, 1999.

16. Shelden, Randall G., "Detention Diversion Advocacy: An Evaluation," *Juvenile Justice Bulletin*, September 1999, Washington, DC: OJJDP, 1999.

17. Ibid.

18. Wilson, James Q., "Strategic Opportunities for Delinquency Prevention," in *Families, Schools, and Delinquency Prevention*, pp. 291–311, James Q. Wilson and Glenn C. Loury, eds., Secaucus, NJ: Springer-Verlag Publishers, 1987.

19. Ibid.

20. Lovell, Phillip and Ashley Price, *Involving Youth in Civic Life*, YIA *Fact Sheet*, Washington, DC: OJJDP, 2000.

21. Ibid.

22. Pete, Shannon, *Hands Without Guns. Youth in Action*, Washington, DC: Office of Juvenile Justice and Delinquency Prevention, 2000.

23. Grossman, Jean Baldwin and Eileen M. Garry. *Mentoring—A Proven Delinquency Prevention Strategy*, Washington, DC: Office of Juvenile Justice and Delinquency Prevention, 1997.

24. Ibid.

25. Source: www.bbbsa.org and www.colorado.edu/cspv/blueprints/query/Default.htm

26. Source: www.bbbsa.org and www.colorado.edu/cspv/blueprints/query/Default.htm

27. Communities In Schools, Inc., *School-to-Work: Bridging Two Worlds, Facts You Can Use*, Volume: 2, Issue: 4, Dated: Summer 1998, Washington, DC: Office of Juvenile Justice and Delinquency Prevention, 1998.

28. Ibid.

29. Kracke, Kristen, *YES: Youth Environmental Service Initiative*, Washington, DC: OJJDP, 1996.

30. http://www.youthcourt.net

31. Butts, Jeffrey, Dean Hoffman, and Janeen Buck, *Teen Courts in the United States: A Profile of Current Programs*, OJJDP *Fact Sheet*, Washington, DC: Office of Juvenile Justice and Delinquency Prevention, 1999.

32. Butts, Jeffrey A., Janeen Buck, and Mark B. Coggeshall, *The Impact of Teen Courts on Young Offenders*, Washington, DC: OJJDP and the Urban Institute, 2002.

33. Butts, Jeffrey, Dean Hoffman, and Janeen Buck, *Teen Courts in the United States: A Profile of Current Programs*, OJJDP *Fact Sheet*, Washington, DC: Office of Juvenile Justice and Delinquency Prevention, 1999.

34. Butts, Jeffrey A. and Janeen Buck, "Teen Courts: A Focus on Research," *Juvenile Justice Bulletin*, October 2000, Washington, DC: Office of Juvenile Justice and Delinquency Prevention, 2000.

35. http://www.youthcourt.net/?page_id=24

36. Ibid.

37. Butts, Jeffrey, Dean Hoffman, and Janeen Buck, *Teen Courts in the United States: A Profile of Current Programs*, OJJDP *Fact Sheet*, Washington, DC: Office of Juvenile Justice and Delinquency Prevention, 1999.

38. Butts, Jeffrey A., Janeen Buck, and Mark B. Coggeshall, *The Impact of Teen Courts on Young Offenders*, Washington, DC: OJJDP and the Urban Institute, 2002.

39. Butts, Jeffrey A. and Janeen Buck, "Teen Courts: A Focus on Research," *Juvenile Justice Bulletin*, October 2000, Washington, DC: Office of Juvenile Justice and Delinquency Prevention, 2000.

40. Ibid.

41. Finkenauer, James, *Scared Straight and the Panacea Phenomenon*, Englewood Cliffs, NJ: Prentice Hall, 1981.

42. Garry, Eileen M., *A Compendium of Programs That Work for Youth*, OJJDP *Fact Sheet #121*, Washington, DC: Office of Juvenile Justice and Delinquency Prevention, 1999.

43. Ibid.

44. Montgomery, Imogene and Marilyn Landon, *What Works: Effective Delinquency Prevention and Treatment Programs Fact Sheet #20*, Washington, DC: Office of Juvenile Justice and Delinquency Prevention, 1992.

45. Greenwood, Peter W., *Costs and Benefits of Early Childhood Intervention*, OJJDP *Fact Sheet #94*, Washington, DC: Office of Juvenile Justice and Delinquency Prevention, 1999.

46. Ibid.

47. Ibid.

48. Greenwood, Peter W., Karyn E. Model, C. Peter Rydell, and James Chiesa, *Diverting Children from a Life of Crime: Measuring Costs and Benefit*, Santa Monica, CA: Rand Corporation, 1996.

Chapter 7

1. Puzzanchera, Charles. "Juvenile Arrests 2007." *Juvenile Justice Bulletin* April 2009. Washington, DC: Office of Juvenile Justice and Delinquency Prevention, 2009.

2. *Crime in the United States 2007*. Washington, DC: Federal Bureau of Investigation, 2008.

3. Keith, Bryant L., Jr., "The Juvenile Court Movement: Oklahoma as a Case Study," *Social Science Quarterly* 49, September 1968: 368–76.

4. Wilson, James Q. *Varieties of Police Behavior*. Cambridge, MA: Harvard University Press, 1968.

5. Werthman, C. and Irving Piliavin, "Gang Members and the Police," in D. Bordura (ed.), *The Police: Six Sociological Essays*, New York: John Wiley and Sons, 1974, pp. 72–94.

6. National Advisory Committee on Criminal Justice Standards and Goals, *Juvenile Justice and Delinquency Prevention: Report of the Task Force on Juvenile Justice and Delinquency Prevention*, Washington, DC: Law Enforcement Assistance Administration, U.S. Department of Justice, 1971–1974.

7. Caeti, Tory J., *Written Policy Directives: Juvenile Offenders*, Texas Law Enforcement Management and Administrative Statistics Program Bulletin, Huntsville, TX: Law Enforcement Management Institute of Texas, 1994.

8. Piliavin, Irving and Scott Briar, "Police Encounters with Juveniles," *American Journal of Sociology*, 1964, 70: 206–214; Merry Morash, "Establishment of a Juvenile Police Record: The Influence of Individual and Peer Group Characteristics," *Criminology*, 1984, 22: 97–111; Chicago Crime Commission, 1995; Guarino-Ghezzi, 1994; Klingler, David A., "Demeanor or Crime? Why 'Hostile' Citizens Are More Likely to Be Arrested." *Criminology*, 1994, 32: 475–493; Klingler, David A., "More on Demeanor and Arrest in Dade County," *Criminology*, 1996, 34: 61–82.

9. Mixdorf, Lloyd, "Pay Me Now, Or Pay Me Later," *Corrections Today*, 1989, 51: 106–110; Snyder, Howard, *Court Careers of Juvenile Offenders*. Pittsburgh, PA: National Center for Juvenile Justice, 1988; Snyder, Howard and Melissa Sickmund, *Juvenile Offenders and Victims: A Focus on Violence*, Washington, DC: Office of Juvenile Justice and Delinquency Prevention, 1995.

10. Ibid.

11. See Robert W. Taylor, Eric Fritsch, and Tory Caeti, "Core Challenges Facing Community Policing: The Emperor Still Has No Clothes," *ACJS Today*, XVII: 1, May/June 1998.

12. Ibid.

13. Fritsch, Eric J., Tory J. Caeti, and Robert W. Taylor, "Gang Suppression Through Saturation Patrol and Aggressive Curfew and Truancy Enforcement: A Quasi-Experimental Test of the Dallas Anti-Gang Initiative," *Crime and Delinquency*, 1999, 45: *1*.

14. Fox, James A. and Sanford A. Newman, *After-School Crime or After-School Programs: Tuning in to the Prime Time for Violent Juvenile Crime and Implications for National Policy*, A Report to the United States Attorney General from Fight Crime: Invest in Kids, 1999. www.fightcrime.org/CrimeReportF15.html.

15. Justice Based After-School Program. Office of Community Oriented Policing Services, USDOJ. Available online at http://www.cops.usdoj.gov/default.asp?Item=485. Retrieved May 19, 2009.

Chapter 8

1. Hemmens, Craig, Tory J. Cacti, Eric J. Fritsch, "Juvenile Justice Purpose Clauses: The Power of Words," *Criminal Justice Policy Review*, 8: No. 2–3 June/ September, 1997.

2. *Ex Parte Crouse* 4 Whart. 9 (Sup. Ct. Pa. 1839).

3. *Kent* v. *United States* 383 U.S. 541 1966.

4. The act stated: "If a child sixteen years of age or older is charged with an offense which would amount to a felony in the case of an adult, or any child charged with an offense which if committed by an adult is punishable by death or life imprisonment, the judge may, after full investigation, waive jurisdiction and order such child held for trial under the regular procedure of the court which would have jurisdiction of such offense if committed by an adult; or such other court may exercise the powers conferred upon the juvenile court in this subchapter in conducting and disposing of such cases." Ibid. p. 547.

5. Ibid. pp. 554–555.

6. Ibid. pp. 555–556.

7. 387 U.S. 1 1967.

8. Ibid. p. 27.

9. The Court stated, "Under traditional notions, one would assume that in a case like that of Gerald Gault, where the juvenile appears to have a home, a working mother and father, and an older brother, the Juvenile Court Judge would have made a careful inquiry and judgment as to the possibility that the boy could be disciplined and dealt with at home, despite his previous transgressions. Indeed, so far as appears in the record before us, except for some conversation with Gerald about his school work and his "wanting to go to . . . Grand Canyon with his father," the points to which the judge directed his attention were little different from those that would be involved in determining any charge of violation of a penal statute." Ibid. p. 28.

10. 397 U.S. 358 1970.

11. 403 U.S. 528 1971.

12. The Court stated, "If the formalities of the criminal adjudicative process are to be superimposed upon the juvenile court system, there is little need for its separate existence. Perhaps that ultimate disillusionment will come one day, but for the moment we are disinclined to give impetus to it." Ibid. p. 551.

13. 421 U.S. 519 1975.

14. *Harvard Law Review*. "Assessing the Scope of Minors' Fundamental Rights: Juvenile Curfews and the Constitution," *Harvard Law Review* 97, 1984, 1163 p. 1167.

15. Ibid. p. 1168.

16. Ibid. p. 1168.

17. Ibid. p. 1169.

18. Ibid. p. 1170.

19. 442 U.S. 707 1979.

20. Ibid. p. 724.

21. The Court stated, "The per se aspect of Miranda was based on the unique role the lawyer plays in the adversary system of criminal justice in this country. Whether it is a minor or an adult who stands accused, the lawyer is the one person to whom society as a whole looks as the protector of the legal rights of that person in his dealings with the police and the courts. For this reason, the Court fashioned in Miranda the rigid rule that an accused's request for an attorney is per se an invocation of his Fifth Amendment rights, requiring that all interrogation cease . . . Courts repeatedly must deal with these issues of waiver with regard to a broad variety of constitutional rights. There is no reason to assume that such courts—especially juvenile courts, with their special expertise in this area—will be unable to apply the totality-of-circumstances analysis so as to take into account those special concerns that are present when young persons, often with limited experience and education and with immature judgment, are involved. Where the age and experience of a juvenile indicate that his request for his probation officer or his parents is, in fact, an invocation of his right to remain silent, the totality approach will allow the court the necessary flexibility to take this into account in making a waiver determination. At the same time, that approach refrains

from imposing rigid restraints on police and courts in dealing with an experienced older juvenile with an extensive prior record who knowingly and intelligently waives his Fifth Amendment rights and voluntarily consents to interrogation." Ibid. pp. 724–725.

22. See e.g., Samuel M. Davis. *Rights of Juveniles: The Juvenile Justice System*, New York: Clark Boardman 1996. Davis cites numerous cases decided pre- and post-*Fare* v. *Michael C.* and concludes that most courts determine the effectiveness of a juvenile waiver of rights through an examination of the totality of circumstances. In *Woods* v. *Clusen*, 794 F.2d 293 7th Cir. 1986, the Seventh Circuit Court of Appeals held that a 16-year-old's confession was inadmissible. In examining the totality of circumstances the court noted that the juvenile had been taken from his home at 1:00 A.M., handcuffed, stripped, forced to wear institutional clothing but no shoes or socks, shown pictures of the crime scene, and was intimidated and interrogated by detectives for several hours. The court stated, "(T)here was little meaningful effort by the police in this case to uphold and respect the . . . constitutional principles and safeguards . . . the police tactics violated the Fourteenth Amendment's guarantee of fundamental fairness." In *United States* v. *Bernard S.* 795 F.2d 749 9th Cir. 1986, the Ninth Circuit Court of Appeals found that although the defendant in this case was 17 years old and had difficulty with English, the totality of circumstances justified inclusion of the juvenile's confession into evidence. Thus, the application of the totality of circumstances test in recent cases results in both affirmed and invalidated waivers. There is no per se rule in case law which affords juveniles protection; See, e.g., Holtz, "Miranda in a Juvenile Setting: A Child's Right to Silence," 78 *Journal of Criminal Law and Criminology* 534, 1987, 534–539.

23. Ferguson and Douglas, "A Study of Juvenile Waiver," *San Diego Law Review* 7, 1970, 39.

24. Ibid. p. 54.

25. *See generally*, Driver, "Confessions and the Social Psychology of Coercion," *Harvard Law Review* 82, 1968, 42; Note. 1972. The Admissibility of Juvenile Confessions: Is an Intelligent and Knowing Waiver of Constitutional Rights Possible Without Adult Guidance?, *University of Pittsburgh Law Review* 34: 321; Holtz, *supra* note 23 p. 534. Thomas Grisso, "Juveniles' Capacities to Waive Miranda Rights: An Empirical Analysis," *California Law Review* 68, 1980: 1134, 1142; Pomicter and Grisso, *Two-Year Study of Interrogation of Juveniles and Understanding of Miranda Warnings: Summary of Results*, St. Louis, MO: National Juvenile Law Center. Unpublished Manuscript, 1977.

26. Interrogation of Juveniles: An Empirical Study of Procedures, Safeguards, and Rights Waiver, *Law and Human Behavior* 1, 1980, 321.

27. Grisso, *supra* note 26.

28. See, e.g., *Com.* v. *A Juvenile* (No. 1), 449 N.E.2d 654 Mass. 1983.

29. Grisso & Pomicter, *supra* note 26, p. 339.

30. See, e.g., Barry Feld, "Criminalizing Juvenile Justice: Rules of Procedure for the Juvenile Court," *Minnesota Law Review* 69: 1984, 141–276; Martin Gardner, "Punitive Juvenile Justice: Some Observations on a Recent Trend," *International Journal of Law and Psychiatry* 10: 1987, 129; L. Williams, "Right to Counsel p. Detention Hearings," *West Virginia Law Review* 86: 1984, 618; Barry Feld, "*In Re Gault* Revisited: A Cross-State Comparison of the Right to Counsel in Juvenile Court," *Crime & Delinquency* 34: 1988, 393.

31. Clarke, S. and G. Koch, "Juvenile Court: Therapy or Crime Control, and Do Lawyers Make a Difference?," *Law & Society Review* 14, 1980, 263, 307.

32. 387 U.S. 1 1967, p. 42.

33. For example, two cases, *United States* v. *Wade* 388 U.S. 218, 1967, and *Gilbert* v. *California*, 388 U.S. 263, 1967, involved confrontation for identification purposes. Taken together, *Wade* and *Gilbert* established that such confrontation is a critical stage in criminal prosecution, thus entitling the juvenile the right of counsel.

34. *Kirby* v. *Illinois* 406 U.S. 682, 1972, specifically dealt with a pre-indictment line-up, and the Court found that a juvenile is not entitled to counsel at a pre-indictment line-up. More importantly, *Kirby* established that juveniles are entitled to a Sixth Amendment right to counsel only after adversarial proceedings have commenced against them. The "critical stage" analysis gave way to an analysis based on the formal commencement of criminal prosecution in *Kirby*. The analysis delineated in this case has been used as controlling in numerous recent cases. See, e.g., *Guenther* v. *Holmgreen*, 573 F.Supp. 599, 601, 1983; *U.S.* v. *Batista*, 834 F.2d. 1,3, 1987; *Barnes* v. *Henderson*, 142, 145, 1989; and *U.S.* v. *Garcia*, 780 F.Supp. 166, 170, 1991.

35. Feld, *supra* note 31 p. 222, 1993. Feld reports that in a sample of states surveyed, only between 37.5 and 52.7 percent of the juveniles charged with delinquent and status offenses were represented. In Minnesota, a majority of all juveniles are unrepresented: in 1984, 53.2 percent of juveniles appeared without counsel; in 1986, 54.7 percent of juveniles appeared without counsel; in 1988, 58.9 percent had no attorney; Clarke and Koch, *supra* note 32 p. 301–3, 1980, found that the juvenile defender project represents only 22.3 percent of the juveniles in Winston-Salem, North Carolina, and only 45.8 percent in Charlotte, North Carolina.

36. Dodge, Douglas C., *Due Process Advocacy, Fact Sheet #49*, January, Washington, DC: Office of Juvenile Justice and Delinquency Prevention, 1997.

37. Caeti, Tory J., Craig Hemmens, and Velmer Burton, "Juvenile Right to Counsel: A National Comparison of State Legal Codes," *American Journal of Criminal Law*, 23:3, Spring 1996.

38. Dodge, *supra* note 37.

39. The ABA completed a national survey and released a report on its findings in *A Call for Justice: An Assessment of Access to Counsel and Quality of Representation in Delinquency Proceedings*, 1995.

40. 469 U.S. 325, 1985.

41. *Acton* v. *Vernonia School District* 115 S. Ct. 2386 1995.

42. Shepherd, Robert E., Jr. and Anthony J. DeMarco, *Weapons in Schools and Zero Tolerance*, Chicago, IL: American Bar Association, 1996.

43. *Safford Unified School District* v. *Redding*, 557 U.S. 364 (2009).

44. *Haley* v. *State of Ohio*, 68 S. Ct. 302, 1948.

45. *Gallegos* v. *Colorado*, 370 U.S. 49, 1962.

46. National Criminal Justice Association, *Juvenile Justice Reform Initiatives in the States: 1994–1996*, Washington, DC: Office of Juvenile Justice and Delinquency Prevention, 1997.

47. 18 U.S.C. § 5038(d) and 5038(f) as amended by Pub. L. 103–322, September 13, 1994.

48. *Davis* v. *Alaska* 415 U.S. 308, 1974.

49. *Smith* v. *Daily Mail Publishing Co.* 443 U.S. 97, 1979.

50. *United States* v. *Three Juveniles* 61 F.3d 86 1st Cir., 1995.

51. National Criminal Justice Association, *supra* note 48.

52. U.S.C. § 5031 et seq.

53. National Criminal Justice Association, *supra* note 48.

54. Etten, Tamryn J. and Robert F. Petrone, "Sharing Data and Information in Juvenile Justice: Legal, Ethical, and Practical Considerations," *Juvenile and Family Court Journal*, 1994, 65–89.

55. Torbet et al., *supra* note 14.

56. Etten and Petrone, *supra* note 56.

57. Etten and Petrone, *supra* note 56, p. 48, Torbet et al., *supra* note 14 p. 53.

58. Torbet et al., *supra* note 14.

59. GA. Code Ann. § 15–11–28, Supp. 1996.

60. National Criminal Justice Association, *supra* note 48.

61. *Oklahoma Publishing Co.* v. *District Court*, 480 U.S. 308, 1977; *Smith* v. *Daily Mail Publishing Co.*, 443 U.S. 97, 1979.

62. National Criminal Justice Association, *supra* note 48.

63. Miller, Neal and Tom McEwen, "National Assessment of Criminal Court Use of Defendants' Juvenile Adjudication Records," Washington, DC: National Institute of Justice, 1996.

64. Ibid.

65. Ibid.

66. Miller, Neil, *Privacy and Juvenile Justice Records: A Mid-Decade Status Report*, Washington, DC: Bureau of Justice Statistics, 1997.

67. Alaska Sess. Laws, chap. 10, 1995.

68. Iowa Acts, chap. 191 amending § 14–17, 46, 1995.

69. Minn. Laws, chap. 259, Art. 1, § 57, 1995.

70. Tex. Gen. Laws, chap. 262, 1995.

71. Laney, Ronald, *Information Sharing and the Family Educational Rights and Privacy Act, Fact Sheet #39*, Washington, DC: Office of Juvenile Justice and Delinquency Prevention, 1996.

72. Ibid.

73. Miller and McEwen, *supra* note 66.

74. Miller, *supra* note 69.

75. Ibid.

76. Ibid.

77. 104 S. Ct. 2403, 1984.

78. Weiss, Lee A., "Supreme Court Review: Fourteenth Amendment—Due Process and the Preventive Detention of Juveniles: *Schall* v. *Martin*, 104 S. Ct. 2403 1984, *Journal of Criminal Law & Criminology* 75, 1984, 855–871.

79. Ibid.

80. Larsen, Korine L., "Comment: With Liberty and Juvenile Justice For All: Extending the Right to a Jury Trial to the Juvenile Courts," *William Mitchell Law Review*, 20, 1994, 836.

81. Ibid.

82. Puritz, Patricia and Mary Ann Scali, *Beyond the Walls: Improving Conditions of Confinement for Youth in Custody*, Washington, DC: Office of Juvenile Justice and Delinquency Prevention, 1998.

83. Swenson, Karen B., "*John L.* v. *Betty Adams*: Taking Bounds in the Right Direction for Incarcerated Juveniles," *Memphis State University Law Review* 24, 1994, 429.

84. Pattison, Brent, "Minority Youth in Juvenile Correctional Facilities: Cultural Differences and the Right to Treatment," *Law and Inequality* 16, 1998, 573.

85. Ibid.

86. Some courts found the right to treatment in the Eighth or Fourteenth Amendments of the U.S. Constitution. Other courts based the right to treatment on state juvenile court statutes. In these latter cases, the court examined the promise of rehabilitation in the statutes authorizing juvenile court jurisdiction over youthful offenders. Because the stated purpose of the statutes was to rehabilitate young offenders, the courts held states accountable for providing services to youths in confinement. In *Jackson* v. *Indiana*, the U.S. Supreme Court stated that "at the least, due process requires that the nature and duration of commitment bear some reasonable relation to the purpose for which the individual is committed." Because the stated purpose of confinement was rehabilitation or treatment, due process required that treatment be provided to confined juveniles. However, the Court in another case limited the right to treatment and declared that judges should defer to the professionals in charge of the facilities.

The Eighth Amendment basis for the right to treatment has also been limited in lower court decisions. In *Morales* v. *Truman*, a Texas district court explained that while the Eighth Amendment protects juveniles from abusive conditions, it does not necessarily include a right to a certain kind of treatment because treatment options are open to discretionary interpretation. While the *Morales* court recognized that the Eighth Amendment requires adequate food, shelter, clothing and medical care, it decided that the failure to provide these services only reached a constitutional violation when it was sufficiently dangerous and a result of a prison official's disregard of the prisoner's health and safety. In *Alexander S.* v. *Boyd* 876 F. Supp. 773, D.S.C. 1995, a federal appellate court ruled that under the Fourteenth Amendment, "a minimally adequate level of programming is required in order to provide juveniles with a reasonable opportunity to accomplish the purpose of their confinement, to protect the safety of the juveniles and the staff, and ensure the safety of the community once the juveniles are released." Furthermore, the court defined "minimally adequate training" to be services "designed to teach juveniles the basic principles that are essential to correcting their conduct." These generally recognized principles include: (1) taking responsibility for the consequences of their actions; (2) learning appropriate ways to respond to others (coping skills); (3) learning to manage their anger; and (4) developing a positive sense of accomplishment. See Pattison, *supra* note 94.

87. *Goss* v. *Lopez* 419 U.S. 565, 1975.

88. Shepherd and DeMarco, *supra* note 43.

89. Ibid.

90. Ibid. An example of these policies is a section of the Massachusetts "Education Reform Act," Chapter 71, 37H, enacted in 1993. One of the provisions of that act provides for the mandatory expulsion, after a hearing, of a student found in possession of a weapon or drugs at school, or during a school-sponsored or school-related event. The school principal is given discretion to utilize suspension, instead of expulsion, where the official determines that the student is not a threat to the safety, security, and welfare of the staff and other students. The enactment in Massachusetts has led to a number of expulsions, with principals rarely exercising their discretion to suspend, rather than expel, the students found in possession of the proscribed items.

91. Shepherd and DeMarco, *supra* note 43.

92. Torbet et al., *supra* note 14.

93. Ibid.

94. Ibid.

95. Ibid.

96. Ibid.

97. Ibid.

98. Author's personal observation while working in juvenile corrections in Colorado: Several juveniles in our custody had upwards of $20,000 owed in restitution. Generally, we were able to get them to pay off approximately $1,000 by the time they were released.

99. LeBoeuf, Donni, *Curfew: An Answer to Juvenile Delinquency and Victimization?* Washington, DC: Office of Juvenile Justice and Delinquency Prevention 1996. In 1975, the first federal case concerning the constitutionality of juvenile curfews was heard by the U.S. District Court for the Middle District of Pennsylvania. In *Bykofsky* v. *Borough of Middletown*, 401 F.Supp. 1242, 1975, the court upheld a juvenile curfew that was challenged on the grounds that it violated juveniles' First and Fourteenth Amendment rights and encroached upon parents' rights to raise their children, which is embodied in the Ninth Amendment and in the due process and equal protection clauses of the Fourteenth Amendment. In its opinion, the court found that the regulations on juveniles' Fourteenth Amendment due process rights were "constitutionally permissible." The court further declared that the curfew ordinance did not suppress or impermissibly regulate juveniles' right to freedom of speech or parents' rights to raise their children as they saw fit. The court stated, "The parents' constitutionally protected interest . . . which the ordinance infringes only minimally, is outweighed by the Borough's interest in protecting immature minors. . . ." Fourteen years later, in 1989, the juvenile curfew ordinance in the District of Columbia was challenged on the grounds that it violated First, Fourth, and Fifth Amendment rights. The U.S. District Court for the District of Columbia, in *Waters* v. *Barry*, 711 F.Supp. 1125, 1989, found the juvenile curfew law to be unconstitutional on the grounds that it violated the First and Fifth Amendment rights of juveniles in the District: "The right to walk the streets, or to meet publicly with one's friends for a noble purpose or for no purpose at all—and to do so whenever one pleases is an integral component of life in a free and ordered society." However, the court did not find that the curfew violated the Fourth Amendment rights of District juveniles: "So long as the officer could reasonably have believed that the individual looked 'young,' the search, seizure, or arrest would take place on the basis of probable cause and no Fourth Amendment violation would occur." Although the district court invalidated this particular curfew, in July 1995 the District of Columbia enacted another juvenile curfew ordinance modeled after one enacted in Dallas, Texas, that had survived constitutional scrutiny by the U.S. Court of Appeals for the Fifth Circuit in 1993.

100. Ruefle, William and Kenneth Mike Reynolds, "Curfews and Delinquency in Major American Cities," *Crime & Delinquency* 41, 1995, 347–363.

101. LeBoeuf, *supra* note 114.

102. *Qutb* v. *Strauss*. 11 F.3rd 488, 5th Cir., 1993.

103. Ibid.

104. Feld, Barry C., "The Right to Counsel in Juvenile Court: An Empirical Study of When Lawyers Appear and the Difference They Make," *Journal of Criminal Law and Criminology*, 79, 4, 1989, 1185–1346; Feld, Barry C., Criminalizing Juvenile Justice: Rules of Procedure for the Juvenile Court, *Minnesota Law Review*, 69, 1984, 141, 150–51.

105. Ainsworth, Janet E., "Re-imagining Childhood and Reconstructing the Legal Order: The Case for Abolishing the Juvenile Court," *North Carolina Law Review*, 69, 1991, 1083–1133.

Chapter 9

1. Knoll, Crystal and Melissa Sickmund, *Delinquency Cases in Juvenile Court, 2009*, Washington, DC.: Office of Juvenile Justice and Delinquency Prevention, 2012.

2. Ibid.

3. Ibid.

4. Charles Puzzanchera, Benjamin Adams, and Sarah Hockenberry, *Juvenile Court Statistics 2009*, Pittsburgh, PA: National Center for Juvenile Justice, May 2012.

5. Knoll and Sickmund, 2012.

6. Ibid.

7. Ibid.

8. 387 U.S. 1 1967.

9. Snyder, Howard N. and Melissa Sickmund, *Juvenile Offenders and Victims: 2006 National Report*, Pittsburgh, PA: National Center for Juvenile Justice, 2006.

10. Stahl, *Offenders in Juvenile Court, 1996* and Melissa Sickmund.

11. Puzzanchera, Charles, Benjamin Adams, and Sarah Hockenberry, *Juvenile Court Statistics 2009*, Pittsburgh, PA: National Center for Juvenile Justice, May 2012.

12. Knoll and Sickmund, 2012.

13. Rubin, H. Ted, "The Juvenile Court Landscape," in Albert R. Roberts (ed.), *Juvenile Justice: Policies, Programs, and Services*, 2nd ed., Chicago: Nelson-Hall, 1998.

14. 104 S. Ct. 2403 1984.

15. Knoll and Sickmund, 2012.

16. Ibid.

17. Ibid.

18. Ibid.

19. Ibid.

20. 387 U.S. 1 1967.

21. Feld, Barry, "*In re Gault* Revisited: Cross-State Comparison of the Right to Counsel in Juvenile Court," *Crime and Delinquency*, Vol. 34, 1988, pp. 393–424.

22. 397 U.S. 358 1970.

23. 403 U.S. 528 1971.

24. Trester, Harold B., *Supervision of the Offender*, Englewood Cliffs, NJ: Prentice Hall, 1981.

25. Rogers, Joseph W., "The Predisposition Report: Maintaining the Promise of Individualized Juvenile Justice," *Federal Probation*, Vol. 54, 1990, pp. 43–57.

Chapter 10

1. Bortner, M. A., *Inside a Juvenile Court*, New York: New York University Press, 1982; Barry C. Feld, "Juvenile Court Legislative Reform and the Serious Young Offender: Dismantling the Rehabilitative Ideal," *Minnesota Law Review*, Vol. 65, 1980, pp. 167–242.

2. Knoll, Crystal and Melissa Sickmund, *Delinquency Cases in Juvenile Court, 2009*, Washington DC.: Office of Juvenile Justice and Delinquency Prevention, 2012.

3. Stahl, Anne L., *Delinquency Cases in Juvenile Courts, 1999,* Washington, DC: Office of Juvenile Justice and Delinquency Prevention, 2004.

4. Knoll and Sickmund, 2012.

5. Ibid.

6. Hamparian, Donna M., Linda K. Estep, Susan M. Muntean, Ramon R. Priestino, Robert G. Swisher, Paul L. Wallace, and Joseph L White, *Major Issues in Juvenile Justice Information and Training: Youth in Adult Courts: Between Two Worlds,* Columbus, OH: Academy for Contemporary Problems, 1982.

7. Fagan, Jeffrey, "Social and Legal Policy Dimensions of Violent Juvenile Crime," *Criminal Justice and Behavior,* Vol. 17, 1990, pp. 93–133.

8. Feld, Barry C., "Bad Law Makes Hard Cases: Reflections on Teen-Aged Axe-Murderers, Judicial Activism, and Legislative Default," *Law and Inequality: A Journal of Theory and Practice,* Vol. 8, 1989, pp. 1–101.

9. *OJJDP Statistical Briefing Book.* Online. Available: http://www.ojjdp.gov/ojstatbb/structure_process/qa04115.asp?qaDate=2011

10. Torbet, Patricia, Richard Gable, Hunter Hurst IV, Imogene Montgomery, Linda Szymanski, and Douglas Thomas, *State Responses to Serious and Violent Juvenile Crime,* Washington, DC: Office of Juvenile Justice and Delinquency Prevention, 1996.

11. United States General Accounting Office, *Juvenile Justice: Juveniles Processed in Criminal Court and Case Dispositions,* Washington, DC: United States General Accounting Office, 1995.

12. Griffin, Patrick, *Trying and Sentencing Juveniles as Adults: An Analysis of State Transfer and Blended Sentencing Laws,* Pittsburgh, PA: National Center for Juvenile Justice, 2003.

13. Singer, Simon, "The Automatic Waiver of Juveniles and Substantive Justice," *Crime and Delinquency,* Vol. 39, 1993, pp. 253–61.

14. Feld, "Bad Law Makes Hard Cases: Reflections on Teen-Aged Axe-Murderers, Judicial Activism, and Legislative Default".

15. Champion, Dean J. and G. Larry Mays, *Transferring Juveniles to Criminal Courts: Trends and Implications for Criminal Justice.* New York: Praeger, 1991.

16. Grifffin, Torbet, and Szymanski, *Trying Juveniles as Adults in Criminal Court: An Analysis of State Transfer Provisions.*

17. Champion and Mays, *Transferring Juveniles to Criminal Courts: Trends and Implications for Criminal Justice.*

18. Bishop, Donna M., Charles E. Frazier, and John C. Henretta, "Prosecutorial Waiver: Case Study of a Questionable Reform," *Crime and Delinquency,* Vol. 35, 1989, pp. 179–201.

19. Fagan, "Social and Legal Policy Dimensions of Violent Juvenile Crime."

20. Fagan, Jeffrey and Elizabeth P. Deschenes, "Determinants of Judicial Waiver Decisions for Violent Juvenile Offenders," *Journal of Criminal Law and Criminology,* Vol. 81, 1990, pp. 314–47; Feld, "Bad Law Makes Hard Cases: Reflections on Teen-Aged Axe-Murderers, Judicial Activism, and Legislative Default."

21. Barnes, Carole and Randal Franz, "Questionably Adult: Determinants and Effects of the Juvenile Waiver Decision," *Justice Quarterly,* Vol. 6, 1989, pp. 117–35; Nimick, Ellen, Linda Szymanski, and Howard Snyder, *Juvenile Court Waiver: A Study of Juvenile Court Cases Transferred to Criminal Court,* Pittsburgh, PA: National Center for Juvenile Justice, 1986.

22. Knoll and Sickmund, 2012.

23. Dawson, Robert O., "An Empirical Study of *Kent* Style Juvenile Transfers to Criminal Court," *St. Mary's Law Journal,* Vol. 23, 1992, pp. 975–1054; Fagan, "Social and Legal Policy Dimensions of Violent Juvenile Crime"; Fisher, Wayne S., and Lori Teichman, "Juvenile Waivers to Adult Court: A Report to the New Jersey State Legislature," *Criminal Justice Quarterly,* Vol. 9, 1986, pp. 68–103.

24. Bortner, M. A., "Traditional Rhetoric, Organizational Realities: Remand of Juveniles to Adult Court," *Crime and Delinquency,* Vol. 32, 1986, pp. 53–73; Champion, Dean J., "Teenage Felons and Waiver Hearings: Some Recent Trends, 1980–1988," *Crime and Delinquency,* Vol. 35, 1989, pp. 577–85; Norman, Michael and L. Kay Gillespie, "Changing Horses: Utah's Shift in Adjudicating Serious Juvenile Offenders," *Journal of Contemporary Law,* Vol. 12, 1986, pp. 85–98.

25. Feld, Barry C., "The Juvenile Court Meets the Principle of the Offense: Legislative Changes in Juvenile Waiver Statutes," *Journal of Criminal Law and Criminology,* Vol. 78, 1987, pp. 471–533.

26. Dawson, "An Empirical Study of *Kent* Style Juvenile Transfers to Criminal Court"; Rudman, Cary, Eliot Hartstone, Jeffrey Fagan, and Melinda Moore, "Violent Youth in Adult Court: Process and Punishment," *Crime and Delinquency,* Vol. 32, 1986, pp. 75–96.

27. Maguire, Kathleen and Ann L. Pastore (eds.), *Sourcebook of Criminal Justice Statistics 1995,* Washington, DC: Bureau of Justice Statistics, 1996.

28. www.albany.edu/sourcebook/

29. Torbet, Gable, Hurst IV, Montgomery, Szymanski, and Thomas, *State Responses to Serious and Violent Juvenile Crime.*

30. United States General Accounting Office, *Juvenile Justice: Juveniles Processed in Criminal Court and Case Dispositions.*

31. Austin, James, Kelly Dedel Johnson, and Maria Gregoriov, *Juveniles in Adult Prisons and Jails: A National Assessment,* Washington, DC: Bureau of Justice Assistance, 2000.

32. *Roper* v. *Simmons,* 543 U.S., 2005.

33. Haas, Kenneth C., "Too Young to Die? The U.S. Supreme Court and the Juvenile Death Penalty," in Albert R. Roberts (ed.), *Juvenile Justice: Policies, Programs, and Services,* 2nd ed., Chicago: Nelson-Hall, 1998.

34. Adaptation and update of Victor Steib, *The Juvenile Death Penalty Today: Death Sentences and Executions for Juvenile Crimes.* Available online at www.law.onu.edu/faculty/streib/juvdeath.htm.

35. Sickmund, Melissa. *Juveniles in Corrections,* Washington, DC: Office of Juvenile Justice and Delinquency Prevention, 2004.

36. *Thompson* v. *Oklahoma,* 487 U.S. 815, 1988.

37. *Stanford* v. *Kentucky,* 492 U.S. 361, 1989.

38. *Wilkins* v. *Missouri,* 109 S. Ct. 2969, 1989.

39. www.internationaljusticeproject.org/juvInstruments.cfm.

40. *Roper* v. *Simmons,* 543 U.S., 2005.

Chapter 11

1. Knoll, Crystal and Melissa Sickmund, *Delinquency Cases in Juvenile Court, 2009,* Washington, DC: Office of Juvenile Justice and Delinquency Prevention, 2012.

2. Caeti, Tory, Craig Hemmens, Francis T. Cullen, and Velmer S. Burton, "Management of Juvenile Correctional Facilities," *Correctional Management Quarterly*, 2001.

3. Office of Juvenile Justice and Delinquency Prevention, *Employment and Training for Court-Involved Youth*, Washington, DC: Office of Juvenile Justice and Delinquency Prevention, 2000.

4. Sieh, Edward W., "From Augustus to the Progressives: A Study of Probation's Formative Years," *Federal-Probation*, 57, (3), pp. 67–72, 1993.

5. Torbet, Patricia M., "Juvenile Probation: The Workhorse of the Juvenile Justice System," *Juvenile Justice Bulletin*, March 1996, Washington, DC: Office of Juvenile Justice and Delinquency Prevention, 1996.

6. Snyder, H., *Court Careers of Juvenile Offenders*, Washington, DC: U.S. Department of Justice, Office of Justice Programs, Office of Juvenile Justice and Delinquency Prevention, 1988.

7. Torbet, Patricia M., "Juvenile Probation: The Workhorse of the Juvenile Justice System." *Juvenile Justice Bulletin*, March 1996, Washington, DC: Office of Juvenile Justice and Delinquency Prevention, 1996.

8. Ibid.

9. Office of Juvenile Justice and Delinquency Prevention, *Employment and Training for Court-Involved Youth*, Washington, DC: Office of Juvenile Justice and Delinquency Prevention, 2000.

10. *OJJDP Statistical Briefing Book*. Online. Available: http://www.ojjdp.gov/ojstatbb/structure_process/qa04203.asp?qaDate=2013.

11. Scahill, Meghan C., *Juvenile Delinquency Probation Caseload, 1988–1997*, Washington, DC: Office of Juvenile Justice and Delinquency Prevention, 2000.

12. Torbet, Patricia M., "Juvenile Probation: The Workhorse of the Juvenile Justice System," *Juvenile Justice Bulletin*, March 1996, Washington, DC: Office of Juvenile Justice and Delinquency Prevention, 1996.

13. Ibid.

14. Ibid.

15. Ibid.

16. Ibid.

17. Krisberg, Barry, Deborah Neuenfeldt, Richard Wiebush, and Orlando Rodriguez. *Juvenile Intensive Supervision: Planning Guide*, Washington, DC: National Council on Crime and Delinquency and Office of Juvenile Justice and Delinquency Prevention, 1994.

18. Ibid.

19. Ibid.

20. Ibid.

21. Ibid.

22. Ibid.

23. Kurlychek, Megan, Patricia Torbet, and Melanie Bozynski, "Focus on Accountability: Best Practices for Juvenile Court and Probation," *JAIBG Bulletin*, August 1999, Washington, DC: Office of Juvenile Justice and Delinquency Prevention, 1999.

24. Metzger, D., *School-Based Probation in Pennsylvania*. Philadelphia, PA: University of Pennsylvania, Center for Studies of Addiction, 1997.

25. Kurlychek, Megan, Patricia Torbet, and Melanie Bozynski, "Focus on Accountability: Best Practices for Juvenile Court and Probation," *JAIBG Bulletin*, August 1999. Washington, DC: Office of Juvenile Justice and Delinquency Prevention, 1999.

26. Ibid.

27. Personal correspondence with juvenile court judge.

28. Source: www.hsdyc.state.ut.us/dnrec.htm#dnrec

29. Krisberg, Barry, Deborah Neuenfeldt, Richard Wiebush, and Orlando Rodriguez, *Juvenile Intensive Supervision: Planning Guide*, Washington, DC: National Council on Crime and Delinquency and Office of Juvenile Justice and Delinquency Prevention, 1994.

30. Source: https://www.ncdps.gov/Index2.cfm?a=000003,002476, 002483,002517

31. Altschuler, David M., Troy L. Armstrong, and Doris Layton MacKenzie, "Reintegration, Supervised Release, and Intensive Aftercare," *Juvenile Justice Bulletin*, July 1999, Washington, DC: Office of Juvenile Justice and Delinquency Prevention, 1999.

32. Ibid.

33. Ashford, Jose B. and Craig Winston LeCroy, "Juvenile Parole Policy in the United States: Determinate versus Indeterminate Models," *Justice Quarterly*, 1993, 10: 2, 179–195.

34. Altschuler, David M. and Troy L. Armstrong, *Intensive Aftercare for High-Risk Juveniles: A Community Care Model*, Washington, DC: Office of Juvenile Justice and Delinquency Prevention, 1994.

35. Source: www.cdcr.ca.gov/Juvenile_Justice/

36. Source: www.cdcr.ca.gov/Juvenile_Justice/

37. Kurlychek, Megan, Patricia Torbet, and Melanie Bozynski, "Focus on Accountability: Best Practices for Juvenile Court and Probation," *JAIBG Bulletin*, August 1999, Washington, DC: Office of Juvenile Justice and Delinquency Prevention, 1999.

38. Ibid.

39. Ibid.

40. Jones, Michael A. and Barry Krisberg, *Images and Reality: Juvenile Crime, Youth Violence, and Public Policy*, San Francisco, CA: National Council on Crime and Delinquency, 1994.

Chapter 12

1. Davis, Antoinette, C. Tsukida, S. Marachionna, and B. Krisberg. "The Declining Number of Youth in Custody in the Juvenile Justice System." Oakland, CA: Nation Council for Crime and Delinquency: August 2008.

2. Sickmund, M., T. J. Sladky, W. Kang, and C. Puzzanchera, 2011, "Easy Access to the Census of Juveniles in Residential Placement." Online. Available: http://www.ojjdp.gov/ojstatbb/ezacjrp/ Retrieved May 3, 2013.

3. Ibid.

4. Ibid.

5. Sickmund, Melissa, T. J. Sladky, and Wei Kang. "Census of Juveniles in Residential Placement Databook." 2008. Online. Available: www.ojjdp.ncjrs.gov/ojstatbb/cjrp.

6. Hockenberry, Sarah, Melissa Sickmund, and Anthony Sladky, "Juvenile Residential Facility Census, 2008: Selected Findings," July 2011, *Juvenile Offenders and Victims:* National Report Series Bulletin. Office of Juvenile Justice and Delinquency Prevention. Online. Available at: https://www.ncjrs.gov/pdffiles1/ojjdp/231683.pdf. Retrieved April 13, 2013.

7. Sickmund, Melissa, *State Custody Rates, 1997*, Washington, DC: Office of Juvenile Justice and Delinquency Prevention, 2000.

8. Sickmund, M., T. J. Sladky, W. Kang, and C. Puzzanchera, 2011, "Easy Access to the Census of Juveniles in Residential Placement." Online. Available: http://www.ojjdp.gov/ojstatbb/ezacjrp/ Retrieved May 3, 2013.

9. Office of Juvenile Justice and Delinquency Prevention, *Employment and Training for Court-Involved Youth*, Washington, DC: Office of Juvenile Justice and Delinquency Prevention, 2000.

10. Ibid.

11. *OJJDP Statistical Briefing Book*. Online. Available: http://www.ojjdp.gov/ojstatbb/court/qa06301.asp?qaDate=2009. Retrieved April 23, 2013.

12. Ibid.

13. Avila, Jim and Allison Lynn. "Teen's Boot Camp Death Provokes Outrage." Available: http://abcnews.go.com/2020/Story?id=404909&page=1. Retrieved May 22, 2009.

14. MacKenzie, D. L. and C. Souryal, *Multisite Evaluation of Shock Incarceration*, Washington, DC: Office of Juvenile Justice and Delinquency Prevention, 2000.

15. Felker, Daniel D. and Blair B. Bourque, "The Development of Boot Camps in the Juvenile System: Implementation of Three Demonstration Programs," in *Correctional Boot Camps: A Tough Intermediate Sanction*, Chapter 9, Doris L. MacKenzie and Eugene E. Hebert, eds., Washington, DC: National Institute of Justice, 1996.

16. Ibid.

17. Ibid.

18. Ibid.

19. Beyer, Margaret, *Juvenile Boot Camps Don't Make Sense*, American Bar Association, 1996. Online, Available: www.abanet.org/crimjust/juvjus/cjbootcamp.html.

20. Office of Juvenile Justice and Delinquency Prevention, *Employment and Training for Court-Involved Youth*, Washington, DC: Office of Juvenile Justice and Delinquency Prevention, 2000.

21. Caeti, Tory J., Craig Hemmens, Francis T. Cullen, and Velmer S. Burton, "Management of Juvenile Correctional Facilities," *Correctional Management Quarterly*, 2001, 5: 3.

22. "Potential for Change: Public Attitudes and Policy Preferences for Juvenile Justice Systems Reform." Center for Children's Law and Policy. Online. Available: http://www.macfound.org/media/article_pdf/CCLPPOLLINGFINAL.PDF. Retrieved April 10, 013

23. Brooks, Carol Cramer and Carter White, *Curriculum for Training Educators of Youth in Confinement*, OJJDP Fact Sheet #05, Washington, DC: Office of Juvenile Justice and Delinquency Prevention, 2000.

24. Ibid.

25. Gemignani, Robert J., "Juvenile Correctional Education: A Time for Change," *Juvenile Justice Bulletin: Update on Research*, Washington, DC: Office of Juvenile Justice and Delinquency Prevention, 1994.

26. Brooks, Carol Cramer and Carter White, *Curriculum for Training Educators of Youth in Confinement*. OJJDP Fact Sheet #05, Washington, DC: Office of Juvenile Justice and Delinquency Prevention, 2000.

27. Texas Youth Commission. "CoNEXTions Treatment Program Overview." Available: www.tyc.state.tx.us/programs/treatment_program.html. Retrieved May 29, 2009.

28. Gemignani, Robert J., "Juvenile Correctional Education: A Time for Change." *Juvenile Justice Bulletin: Update on Research*, Washington, DC: Office of Juvenile Justice and Delinquency Prevention, 1994.

29. State of California Prison Industry Authority. "Free Venture Program (Youth)." Available: http://www.pia.ca.gov/Inmate_Development/JointVenture.html. Retrieved May 29, 2009.

30. Gemignani, Robert J., "Juvenile Correctional Education: A Time for Change," *Juvenile Justice Bulletin: Update on Research*, Washington, DC: Office of Juvenile Justice and Delinquency Prevention, 1994.

31. Ibid.

32. Texas Youth Commission. "Specialized Correctional Treatment." Available: www.tyc.state.tx.us/programs/special_treat.html.

33. Greenwood, Peter W., *A Summary of Correctional Programs for Chronic Juvenile Offenders: Characteristics of Three Exemplary Programs*, Santa Monica: CA: The Rand Corporation, 1988.

34. Ibid.

35. Caeti, Tory J., Craig Hemmens, Francis T. Cullen, and Velmer S. Burton, "Management of Juvenile Correctional Facilities," *Correctional Management Quarterly*, 2001, 5: 3.

36. Livesy, Sarah, Melissa Sickmund, and Anthony Sladky, "Juvenile Residential Facility Census, 2004: Selected Findings." Juvenile Offenders and Victims: National Report Series Bulletin. Washington, DC: Office of Juvenile Justice and Delinquency Prevention, January 2009.

37. Hayes, Lindsay. "Characteristics of Juvenile Suicide in Confinement." Juvenile Justice Bulletin. Washington, DC: Office of Juvenile Justice and Delinquency Prevention, February 2009.

38. Ibid.

39. Swanson, D. "Sex Abuse Reported at Youth Jail." *Dallas Morning News*, February 18, 2007.

40. Krisberg, Barry. "Breaking the Cycle of Abuse in Juvenile Facilities." Oakland, CA: National Council on Crime and Delinquincy. February 2009.

41. "Report on Sexual Victimization in Juvenile Correctional Facilities," October 2010, Review Panel on Prison Rape, U.S. Department of Justice. Online. Available: http://www.ojp.usdoj.gov/reviewpanel/pdfs/panel_report_101014.pdf. Retrieved April 29, 2013.

42. Porpotage, F.M., II, *Training of Staff in Juvenile Detention and Correctional Facilities*, OJJDP Fact Sheet #37, Washington, DC: Office of Juvenile Justice and Delinquency Prevention, 1996.

Chapter 13

1. Huff, C. Ronald, "Denial, Overreaction, and Misidentification: A Postscript on Public Policy," in C. Ronald Huff (ed.), *Gangs in America*, Newbury Park, CA: Sage, 1990; L.T. Winfree, K. Fuller, T. Vigil, and G.L. Mays, "The Definition and Measurement of 'Gang Status': Policy Implications for Juvenile Justice," *Juvenile and Family Court Journal*, Vol. 43, 1992, pp. 29–37.

2. Short, James. F., "New Wine in Old Bottles? Change and Continuity in American Gangs," in C. Ronald Huff (ed.), *Gangs in America*, Newbury Park, CA: Sage, 1990.

3. Klein, Malcolm W., *Street Gangs and Street Workers*, Englewood Cliffs, NJ: Prentice Hall, 1971.

4. Miller, Walter B., "Gangs, Groups, and Serious Youth Crime," in D. Shichor and D.H. Kelly (eds.), *Critical Issues in Juvenile Delinquency*, Lexington, MA: Lexington Books, 1980.

5. Morash, Merry, "Gangs, Groups, and Delinquency," *The British Journal of Criminology*, Vol. 23, 1983, pp. 309–331.

6. Ibid.

7. Jankowski, Martin, *Islands in the Street: Gangs and American Urban Society*, Berkeley, CA: University of California Press, 1991.

8. Cal. Penal Code § 186.22 (a).

9. Curry, G. David and Scott H. Decker, *Confronting Gangs: Crime and Community,* Los Angeles: Roxbury Publishing, 1998.

10. Ibid.

11. Ibid.

12. Ibid.

13. Vigil, James D., *Barrio Gangs* Austin, TX: University of Texas Press, 1988, p. 154.

14. Maxson, Cheryl L. and Malcolm W. Klein, "Street Gang Violence: Twice as Great, or Half as Great?," in C. Ronald Huff (ed.), *Gangs in America,* Newbury Park, CA: Sage, 1990.

15. Ibid.

16. Illinois 740ILCS 147/10 (3)

17. National Gang Center, *National Youth Gang Survey Analysis.* Retrieved July 23, 2013 from http://www.nationalgangcenter .gov/Survey-Analysis.

18. Ibid.

19. Egley, Arlen, Jr. and Aline K. Major. *Highlights of the 2002. National Youth GangSurvey.* Washington DC: Office of Juvenile Justice and Delinquency Prevention, 2004.

20. Ibid.

21. National Gang Center, 2013.

22. Ibid.

23. Huff, C. Ronald, "Youth Gangs and Public Policy," *Crime and Delinquency,* Vol. 35, 1989, pp. 524–537.

24. Ibid.

25. Ibid.

26. Maxson, Cheryl and Malcolm Klein, "Investigating Gang Structures," *Journal of Gang Research,* Vol. 3, 1995, pp. 33–42.

27. Ibid.

28. Ibid.

29. Ibid.

30. Ibid.

31. Knox, George, et al., *Gang Prevention and Intervention: Preliminary Results from the 1995 Project Gangprint National Needs Assessment Gang Research Task Force,* Chicago: National Gang Crime Research Center, 1995.

32. National Gang Center, 2013.

33. Hagedorn, John, People and Folks: *Gangs, Crime and the Underclass in a Rustbelt City,* Chicago: Lake View Press, 1988.

34. National Gang Center, 2013.

35. Conly, Catherine H., Patricia Kelly, Paul Mahanna, and Lynn Warner, *Street Gangs: Current Knowledge and Strategies,* Washington, DC: U.S. Department of Justice, 1993.

36. National Gang Center, 2013.

37. Bjerregaard, Beth and Carolyn Smith, "Gender Differences in Gang Participation, Delinquency, and Substance Use," in Malcolm W. Klein, Cheryl L. Maxson, and Jody Miller (eds.), *The Modern Gang Reader,* Los Angeles: Roxbury, 1995.

38. Ibid.

39. Knox, George W., James G. Houston, Edward D. Tromanhauser, Thomas F. McCurrie, and John L. Laskey, "Addressing and Testing the Gang Migration Issue: A Summary of Recent Findings," in J. Mitchell Miller and Jeffrey P. Rush (eds.), *Gangs: A Criminal Justice Approach,* Cincinnati, OH: Anderson, 1996.

40. Ibid.

41. National Gang Center, *National Youth Gang Survey Analysis.* Retrieved July 23, 2013 from http://www.national-gangcenter.gov/Survey-Analysis

42. Ibid.

43. Arlen Egley, Jr. and James C. Howell, *Highlights of the 2010 National Youth Gang Survey,* April 2012, Washington DC: Office of Juvenile Justice and Deliquency Prevention, p. 2.

44. Jackson, Robert K. and Wesley D. McBride, *Understanding Street Gangs,* Incline Village, NV: Copperhouse, 1996.

45. Ibid.

46. Ibid.

47. Ibid.

48. Bjerregaard and Smith, "Gender Differences in Gang Participation, Delinquency, and Substance Use."

49. Hagedorn, *People and Folks: Gangs, Crime and the Underclass in a Rustbelt City.*

50. Fagan, Jeffrey, "Social Processes of Delinquency and Drug Use Among Urban Gangs," in C. Ronald Huff (ed.), *Gangs in America,* Newbury Park, CA: Sage, 1990.

51. Office of Juvenile Justice and Delinquency Prevention, 2010, *Best Practices to Address Community Gang Problems: OJJDP's Comprehensive Gang Model, Second edition.* Washington, DC: Office of Juvenile Justice and Delinquency Prevention.

52. Spergel, Irving A. and G. David Curry, "The National Youth Gang Survey: A Research and Development Process," in Malcolm W. Klein, Cheryl L. Maxson, and Jody Miller (eds.), *The Modern Gang Reader,* Los Angeles: Roxbury, 1993.

53. Ibid.

54. Ibid.

55. Kent, Douglas R. and Peggy Smith, "The Tri-Agency Resource Gang Enforcement Team: A Selective Approach to Reduce Gang Crime," in Malcolm W. Klein, Cheryl L. Maxson, and Jody Miller (eds.), *The Modern Gang Reader,* Los Angeles: Roxbury, 1993; Robert P. Owens and Donna K. Wells, "One City's Response to Gangs," *Police Chief,* Vol. 58, 1993, pp. 25–27.

56. Fritsch, Eric J., Tory J. Caeti, and Robert W. Taylor, "Gang Suppression Through Saturation Patrol, Aggressive Curfew, and Truancy Enforcement: A Quasi-Experimental Test of the Dallas Anti-Gang Initiative," *Crime & Delinquency,* Vol. 45, 1999, pp.122–139.

57. Johnson, Claire, Barbara Webster, and Edward Connors, *Prosecuting Gangs: A National Assessment,* Washington, DC: U.S. Department of Justice, 1995.

58. Bonney, L. S., "The Prosecution of Sophisticated Urban Street Gangs: A Proper Application of RICO," *Catholic University Law Review,* Vol. 42, 1993, pp. 579–613.

59. Finley, M. D., "Anti-Gang Legislation: How Much Will It Take?," *Journal of Juvenile Law,* Vol. 14, 1993, pp. 47–62.

60. Bonney, "The Prosecution of Sophisticated Urban Street Gangs: A Proper Application of RICO."

61. Ibid.

62. Ibid.

63. Johnson, Webster, and Connors, *Prosecuting Gangs: A National Assessment.*

64. Ibid.

65. Boga, T. R., "Turf Wars: Street Gangs, Local Governments, and the Battle for Public Space," *Harvard Civil Rights–Civil Liberties Law Review,* Vol. 29, 1994, pp. 477–503.

66. Ibid, p. 477.

67. No. WEC 118860 [Cal. Sup. Ct. L.A. County Dec. 11, 1987], order granting preliminary injunction.

68. Boga, "Turf Wars: Street Gangs, Local Governments, and the Battle for Public Space."

69. Ibid.

70. Ibid.

71. Yoo, C. S., "The Constitutionality of Enjoining Criminal Street Gangs as Public Nuisances," *Northwestern University Law Review,* Vol. 89, 1994, pp. 212–267; Boga, "Turf

Wars: Street Gangs, Local Governments, and the Battle for Public Space."

72. Ind. Code Ann. § 35–45–9–3.

73. Ca. Penal Code § 186.22 (a); Mo. Ann. Stat. §578.423.

74. Destro, R. A., "Hostages in the 'Hood'," *Arizona Law Review*, Vol. 36, 1994, pp. 785–820.

75. Colo. Rev. Stat. Ann. 16–13–301; Colo. Rev. Stat. Ann. 16–13–303.

76. Spergel and Curry, "The National Youth Gang Survey: A Research and Development Process."

77. National Youth Gang Center (2007). *National Youth Gang Survey Analysis*. Retrieved April 24, 2009 from http://www.iir.com/nygc/nygsa

Chapter 14

1. "Crime in the United States, 2011," October 2012, Federal Bureau of Investigation. Online. Available at: http://www.fbi.gov/about-us/cjis/ucr/crime-in-the-u.s/2011/crime-in-the-u.s.-2011/offenses-known-to-law-enforcement/expanded-offense-data. April 24, 2013.

2. For further information on the concept, see Coupland, Douglas, *Generation X: Tales for an Accelerated Culture*, New York: St. Martin's Press, 1991.

3. Tapscott, Don, *Growing Up Digital: The Rise of the Net Generation*, New York: McGraw-Hill, 1998.

4. Buck, William R. and Tracy Rembert, "Just Doing It: Generation X Proves That Actions Speak Louder Than Words," *E. Magazine*, 8, Sept.–Oct. 1997, pp. 28–35.

5. School shootings have marked recent history in the United States since the late 1990s. Several of these incidents have been so tragic as to be known simply by the city in which they occurred. The first three incidents mentioned here represent some of the more infamous school shooting incidents: **Jonesboro, Arkansas** (March 24, 1998)—Two boys, Mitchel Johnson, age 13, and Andrew Golden, age 11, open fire from the woods on students conducting a fire drill at a middle school in Jonesboro, Arkansas. Four girls and a teacher are shot to death and 10 others wounded. **Columbine** (April 20, 1999)—Two heavily armed students, Eric Harris and Dillon Klebold, attack students at Columbine High School in Littleton, Colorado, with homemade bombs and automatic weapons. Fifteen students and teachers (including the suspects) are killed and another 25 wounded. **Red Lake, Minnesota** (March 21, 2005)—Jeff Weise, age 16, kills a teacher, a security guard, and five students before committing suicide at Red Lake High School. Weise also kills his grandfather and his grandfather's wife before arriving at the school. **Virginia Tech** (April 16, 2007)—On the campus of Virginia Tech University in Blacksburg, Virginia, Seung-Hui Cho kills 29 students and three faculty members and wounds another 30 before killing himself in the deadliest shooting incident in U.S history. **Sandy Hook** (December 14, 2012)—Adam Lanza, age 20, fatally shoots 20 children and six adult staff members at Sandy Hook Elementary School in Newtown, Connecticut, before committing suicide.

6. Cullen, Dave, "The Depressive and the Psychopath," April 20, 2004, Salon.com. Online. Available: http://www.slate.com/articles/news_and_politics/assessment/2004/04/the_depressive_and_the_psychopath.2.html. Retrieved April 24, 2013.

7. Peterson, Kavan, "Schools Rethink Post-Columbine Discipline," at www.stateline.org. Retrieved July 16, 2005, p. 2.

8. "Understanding School Violence Factsheet, 2012," Centers for Disease Control. Online. Available: http://www.cdc.gov/violenceprevention/pdf/schoolviolence_factsheet-a.pdf. Retrieved April 24, 2013.

9. Bjelopera, Jeroma, et al., "Public Mass Shootings in the United States: Selected Implications for Federal Public Health and Safety Policy," March 2013, Congressional Research Service. Online. Available at: http://journalistsresource.org/wp-content/uploads/2013/03/MassShootings_CongResServ.pdf. Retrieved April 26, 2013.

10. Cocozza, Joseph J., "Identifying the Needs of Juveniles with Co-Occurring Disorders," *Corrections Today*, 59, July 1997, pp. 146–149.

11. Berman-Graham, Sandra G. and Alytia A. Levendosky, "Traumatic Stress Symptoms in Children of Battered Women," *Journal of Interpersonal Violence*, 13, January 1998, pp. 25–38.

12. Moore, Solomon, "Mentally Ill Offenders Strain Juvenile System," August 9, 2009, *New York Times*. Online. Available at: http://www.nytimes.com/2009/08/10/us/10juvenile.html?pagewanted=all&_r=0 Retrieved April 26, 2013.

13. Hamid, Ansley, *Drugs in America: Sociology, Economics, and Politics*. Gaithersburg, MD: Aspen Publishers, 1998, p. 120.

14. There is an exhaustive list of reports and articles discussing the linkage between drug use and crime (and delinquency). See Johnson, Lloyd D., et al., "Drugs and Delinquency: A Search for Casual Connections," in *Longitudinal Research on Drug Use: Empirical Finds and Methodological Issues*, edited by Denise B. Kandel et al., Washington, D.C.: Hemisphere, 1978; Inciardi, James A., *The War on Drugs: Heroin, Cocaine, and Public Policy*, Palo Alto, CA: Mayfield, 1986; Huizinga, David, Rolf Loeber, and Terence Thornberry, *Urban Delinquency and Substance Abuse*, Washington, DC.: U.S. Department of Justice, 1991; Greenwood, Peter W., "Substance Abuse Problems among High Risk Youth and Potential Interventions," *Crime and Delinquency*, 38, October 1992; Harrison, Lana D., "The Drug-Crime Nexus in the USA," *Contemporary Drug Problems*, vol 19, 1992, pp. 203–245; Kaplan, Howard, ed., *Drugs, Crime, and Other Deviant Adaptations: Longitudinal Studies*, New York: Plenum Books, 1995; and Inciardi, James A. and Karen McElrath, eds., *The American Drug Scene*, 2nd ed., Los Angeles, CA: Roxbury Publishing, 1998.

15. "Results from the 2011 National Survey on Drug Use and Health: Summary of National Findings," U.S. Department of Health and Human Services. Online. Available at: http://www.whitehouse.gov/sites/default/files/ondcp/policy-and-research/nsduhresults2011.pdf. Retrieved April 26, 2013.

16. Ibid.

17. "Drug Facts: High School and Youth Trends," December 2012, National Institute on Drug Abuse. Online. Available at: http://www.drugabuse.gov/publications/drugfacts/high-school-youth-trends. Retrieved April 26, 2013.

18. "Results from the 2011 National Survey on Drug Use and Health," 2013.

19. "Traffic Safety Facts 2008: Young Drivers," National Highway Traffic Safety Administration, Washington, DC: 2009.

20. Goldstein, Paul J., "The Drugs/Violence Nexus: A Tripartite Conceptual Framework," *Journal of Drug Issues*, Fall 1985, pp. 493–506.

21. Ibid.

22. See Ball, John C., John W. Shaffer, and David N. Nurco, "The Day-to-Day Criminality of Heroin Addicts in Baltimore—A Study in the Continuity of Offense Rates," *Drug and Alcohol Dependence,* 12, 1983, pp. 119–142; Nurco, David N., John C. Ball, John W. Shaffer, and Thomas E. Hanlon, "The Criminality of Narcotic Addicts," *Journal of Nervous and Mental Disease* 173, 1985, p. 98.; and Johnson, Bruce D. , Paul J. Goldstein, Edward Preble, James Schmeidler, Douglas S. Lipton, Barry Spunt, and Thomas Miller, *Taking Care of Business: The Economics of Crime by Heroin Abusers,* Lexington, MA: Lexington Books, 1985.

23. Inciardi, op. cit., p.158.

24. Researchers probing the linkages between drugs, crime and violence are numerous. See footnote 2 and Inciardi, James A., " Heroin Use and Street Crime," *Crime and Delinquency,* 25, 1979, pp. 335–346; Nurco, D. C., J.W. Schaeffer, J.C. Ball, and T. W. Kinlock, "Trends in the Commission of Crime Among Narcotic Addicts Over Successive Period of Addiction," *Journal of Drug and Alcohol Abuse* 10, 1984, pp. 481–489; and J.J. Collins (ed.), *Drinking and Crime,* New York: Guilford Publishing, 1981.

25. White, Helen Raskin, "The Drug Use–Delinquency Connection in Adolescence," p. 240.

26. Ibid.

27. See Zahn, Margaret and Michael Bencivento, "Violent Death: A Comparison Between Drug Users and Non-Drug Users." *Addictive Diseases,* 1, 1974, pp. 283–296.

28. Inciardi, op. cit.

29. McBride, Duane C. and James A. Swartz, "Drugs and Violence in the Age of Crack Cocaine," in Ralph Weisheit, *Drugs, Crime and the Criminal Justice System.*

30. Hamid, Ansley, op. cit., p. 144.

31. Ibid.

32. Finkelhor, David, Richard Ormrod, and Mark Chaffin, "Juveniles Who Commit Sex Offenses Against Minors," *Juvenile Justice Bulletin,* December 2009, Office of Juvenile Justice and Delinquency Prevention. Online. Available at: https://www.ncjrs.gov/pdffiles1/ojjdp/227763.pdf

33. Many scholars have focused on juvenile sexual aggression and its linkage to serial homicide. See Hickey, Eric W., *Serial Murderers and Their Victims,* 2nd ed., Belmont, CA: Wadsworth Publishing Company, 1997.

34. See American Psychiatric Association, *Diagnostic Statistical Manual of Mental Disorders (DSM-IV),* 4th ed., Washington, DC: APA, 1994; Money, J. and J. Werlas, "Paraphiliac Sexuality and Child Abuse: The Parents," *Journal of Sexual and Marital Therapy,* 8, pp. 57–64; and Hickey, E. W., ibid.

35. American Psychiatric Association, *Diagnostic and Statistical Manual of Mental Disorders: DSM-IV,* 4th ed., Washington, DC: APA, 1994.

36. Groth, A. Nicholas, Robert E. Longo, and J. Bradley McFaddin, "Undetected Recidivism Among Rapist and Child Molesters," *Crime and Delinquency,* 28, March 1982, pp. 450–458.

37. Martin and Pruett, p. 280.

38. Barnett, Arnold, Alfred Blumstein, and David P. Farrington, "A Prospective Test of a Criminal Career Model." *Criminology,* 27, February 1989, pp. 373–388.

39. Wolfgang, Marvin E., Robert M. Figlio, and Thorsten Sellin, *Delinquency in a Birth Cohort,* Chicago, IL: University of Chicago Press, 1972.

40. See follow-up studies by Wolfgang, Marvin E., Terrence P. Thornberry, and Robert M. Figlio, *From Boy to Man, From Delinquency to Crime,* Chicago, IL: University of Chicago Press, 1987; Tracy, Paul M., Marvin E. Wolfgang, and Robert M. Figlio, *Delinquency in Two Birth Cohorts: Executive Summary,* Washington, DC: National Institute for Juvenile Justice and Delinquency Prevention, 1985; and Howell, James C., *Guide for Implementing the Comprehensive Strategy for Serious, Violent, And Chronic Juvenile Offenders,* Washington, DC: National Institute for Juvenile Justice and Delinquency Prevention, 1995.

41. Howell, ibid.

42. See "Playing Games," *Time,* August 22, 1993, p. 14.

43. See Taylor, Robert W., "Hacker, Phone Phreakers, and Virus Makers," Paper presented at the Second Annual Conference on Computer Viruses, London, England, June 1990 and reported in C.R. Swanson, N.C. Chamelin, and L. Territo, *Criminal Investigation,* 7th ed., New York: McGraw-Hill, 2000, Chapter 18, and 11th ed., 2012, Chapter 16.

44. Ibid, p. 528.

45. Howell, ibid.

46. "Crime in the United States, 2011," Table 34, October 2012, Federal Bureau of Investigation. Online. Available at: http://www.fbi.gov/about-us/cjis/ucr/crime-in-the-u.s/2011/crime-in-the-u.s.-2011/tables/table-34. Retrieved April 30, 2013.

47. Puzzanchera, Charles and Benjamin Adams, "Juvenile Arrests, 2009," *Juvenile Arrests and Victims: National Report Series Bulletin,* December 2011, Office of Juvenile Justice and Delinquency Prevention. Online. Available: http://www.ojjdp.gov/pubs/236477.pdf. Retrieved May 3, 2013.

48. *OJJDP Statistical Briefing Book.* Online. Available: http://www.ojjdp.gov/ojstatbb/crime/JAR_Display.asp?ID=qa05261 Retrieved April 30, 2013.

49. Puzzanchera and Adams, 2013.

50. Ibid.

51. An interview with leaders of the Texas Militia in Dallas, Texas (January 2012) reflecting much of the sentiments expressed by Tom Metzger, an infamous leader of the White Aryan Resistance (WAR).

52. For additional information on right-wing groups, refer to Jonathan White, *Terrorism: An Introduction,* Pacific Grove, CA: Brooks-Cole, 1991; H. L. Bushart, J. R. Craig, and M. Barnes, *Soldiers of God,* New York: Kensington Books, 1998; and John George and Laird Wilcox, *American Extremists: Militias, Supremacists, Klansmen, Communists, and Others,* Amherst, NY: Prometheus Brooks, 1996.

53. A number of scholars have attempted to bring meaning and reason to joining extremist groups in general. For a thorough discussion on this topic, see John George and Laird Wilcox, *American Extremists: Militias, Supremacists, Klansmen, Communists, and Others,* Amherst, NY: Prometheus Books, 1996, Chapter 3.

54. As the National Incident-Based Reporting System (NIBRS) continues to develop through the efforts of the Federal Bureau of Investigation, primary statistical data concerning juvenile victimization is being collected and analyzed. NIBRS will allow, for the first time, analysis of crime against children through a national reporting system.

55. U.S. Department of Justice, Office of Justice Programs, Evidence Integration: Children Exposed to Violence (CEV). Available online: www.crimesolutions.gov/ojpresearch.aspx?research_id=7. May 7, 2013.

56. "Child Maltreatment 2011". U.S. Department of Health and Human Services. Online. Available at: http://www.acf.hhs.gov/sites/default/files/cb/cm11.pdf#page=28. April 30, 2013.

57. For an excellent discussion of crimes against children, see Charles R. Swanson, Neil Chamelin, Leonard Territo, and Robert W. Taylor, *Criminal Investigation,* 7th ed., New York: McGraw-Hill, 2000, Chapter 12 and 11th ed., 2012, Chapter 11.

58. See www.state.ng.us/humanservices/capques2.html. Retrieved May 2, 2013.

59. Caeti, Tory J., "Child Pornography," in *The Encyclopedia of Criminology and Deviance,* New York: Taylor and Francis Publications, 2000.

60. See Levesque, Roger J.R., *Sexual Abuse of Children: A Human Rights Perspective,* Bloomington, IN: Indiana University Press, 1999.

61. Ibid.

62. Flowers, W. Barri, *The Prostitution of Women and Girls,* Jefferson, NC: McFarland and Company, 1998.

63. Ibid, p. 69.

64. See Meddis, Sam, "Teen Prostitution Rising, Study Says," *USA Today,* April 23, 1984, p 3A.

65. Federal Bureau of Investigation, *Uniform Crime Reports 2011,* Washington, DC: USGPO, 2012.

66. The landmark work of W. Barri Flowers in the area of female crime and criminality has been outstanding. See other works: W. Barri Flowers, *The Adolescent Criminal: An Examination of Today's Juvenile Offender,* Jefferson, NC: McFarland, 1990; W. Barri Flowers, *Female Crime, Criminals, and Cellmates: An Exploration of Female Criminality and Delinquency,* Jefferson, NC: McFarland, 1995; and W. Barri Flowers, *The Prostitution of Women and Girls,* Jefferson, NC: McFarland, 1998.

Chapter 15

1. Hemmens, Craig, Tory J. Caeti, Eric J. Fritsch. "Juvenile Justice Purpose Clauses: The Power of Words," *Criminal Justice Policy Review,* 8: no. 2–3, June/September, 1997.

2. Feld, Barry, *Bad Kids: Race and the Transformation of the Juvenile Court,* New York: Oxford Press, 1999.

3. "State Trends: Legislative Victories from 2005 to 2010, Removing Youth from the Adult Criminal Justice System." Campaign for Youth Justice, 2011: Available Online: http//www.campaignforyouthjustice.org/documents/CFYJ_State_Trends_Report.pdf. Retrieved May 19, 2013.

4. For a discussion on the abolition of the juvenile justice system, please see B. C. Field, "Abolish the Juvenile Court: Sentencing Policy When the Child Is a Criminal and the Criminal Is a Child," *Bad Kids,* New York: Oxford University Press, 1999, pp. 287–330; Eric J. Fritch, C. Hemmens, and Tory J. Caeti, "Violent Youth in Juvenile and Adult Court: An Assessment of Sentencing Strategies," *Law and Policy,* 1996, 18, pp. 115–136; R. O. Dawson, "The Future of Juvenile Justice: Is it Time to Abolish the System?" *Journal of Criminal Law and Criminology,* 1990, 81, pp. 136–155; and S. Wizner and M. F. Keller, "The Penal Model of Juvenile Jutice: Is Delinquency Court Jurisdiction Obsolete?" *New York University Law Review,* 1977, 52, pp. 1120–1135.

5. See Ainsworth, J. E., "Youth Justice in a Unified Court: Response to Critic of Juvenile Court Abolition," *Boston College Law Review,* 1995, 36, pp. 927–951; K. H. Federle, "The Abolition of the Juvenile Court: A Proposal for the Preservation of Children's Legal Rights," *Journal of Contemporary Law,* 1990, 16, pp. 23–51; and F. B. McCarthy, "Should Juvenile Delinquency Be Abolished?" *Crime and Delinquency,* 1977, 23, pp. 196–203.

6. See the landmark cases in the juvenile settings: *In re Gault* 387 U.S. 1 (1967); *In re Winship* 397 U.S. 358 (1970); and *Kent* v. *United States* 383 U.S. 541 (1966).

7. Cowden, V. I. and G. R. McKee, "Competency to Stand Trial in Juvenile Delinquency Proceedings: Cognitive Maturity and the Attorney-Client Relationship," *University of Louisville Journal of Family Law,* 1995, 33, pp. 629–660, and R. O. Dawson, op. cit.

8. Much of the material on BARJ has been adapted from material presented on the Office of Juvenile Justice and Delinquency Prevention website, and from D. Malloney, D. Romig and T Armstrong, *Juvenile Procedure: The Balanced Approach,* Reno, NV: National Council of Juvenile and Family Court Judges, 1998. In the first edition, this material was presented as a box item focusing on juvenile policy. For more information, refer to www.ojjdp.ncjrs.org

9. Ibid.

10. Much of the sections on *Prevention and Early Intervention, Specialty Courts,* and *Promising Strategies for Juvenile Intervention* was adapted with permission from Alida V. Merlo and Peter J. Benekos. February 2000, Paper presented at the Annual Meeting of the Western Society of Criminology in Kona, Hawaii.

11. Taylor, M. "The 2012-13 Budget: Completing Juvenile Justice Realignment." Legislative Analyst's Office, State of California. Available online: http://www.lao.ca.gov/analysis/2012/crim_justice/juvenile-justice-021512.pdf. Retrieved March 22, 2013.

12. Center on Juvenile and Criminal Justice. "Renewing Juvenile Justice: A Report to the Sierra Health Foundation." 2012. Online. Available at: www.sierrahealth.org/assets/pubs/shf_rjj_report_final.pdf. Retrieved May 28, 2013.

13. Tibbetts, Stephen G. and Alex R. Piquero, "The Influence of Gender, Low Birth Weight, and Disadvantage Enfionment in Predicting Early Onset Offending: A Test of Moffitt's Ineractional Hypothesis," *Criminology* 37: 4, November 1999, pp. 843–877.

14. Greenwood, Peter, *Costs and Benefits of Early Childhood Intervention,* Washington, DC: Office of Justice Programs, 1999.

15. Ibid., p. 137.

16. Butts, Jeffery A. and Adele V. Harrell. *Crime Policy Report: Delinquents or Criminals. Policy Options for Young Offenders,* Washington, DC: The Urban Institute, 1998.

17. See Goodwin, Tracy A., *A Guide for Implementing Teen Court Programs: Fact Sheet #45,* Washington, DC: Office of Justice Programs, August 1996; Minor, Kevin I., James B. Wells, Irina R. Soderstrom, Rachel Bingham, and Deborah Williamson, "Sentence Completion and Recidivism Among Juveniles Referred to Teen Courts," *Crime and Delinquency* 45: no 4, October 1999.

18. Inciardi, James A., Duane C. McBride, and James E. Rivers, *Drug Control and the Courts,* Thousand Oaks, CA: Sage Publications, 1996.

19. National Center on Addiction and Substance Abuse at Columbia University (CASA), *Crossing the Bridge: An Evaluation of Drug Treatment Alternatives to Prison (DTAP) Program,* New York: Columbia University, March 2003.

20. Roberts, Lisa M. and Peter J. Benekos, "Assessing the Feasibility of Drug Courts for Youthful Offenders," Paper

presented at the Annual Meeting of the American Society of Criminology, Toronto, Canada, November 1999, p. 6.

21. Much of the section on *Gun Courts* has been adapted from: Office of Juvenile Justice and Delinquency Programs. *Promising Strategies to Reduce Gun Violence.* Washington, DC: U.S. Department of Justice, February 1999.

22. Ibid.

23. "Renewing Juvenile Justice: A Report to the Sierra Health Foundation." Center on Juvenile and Criminal Justice. Available online: http://www.sierrahealth.org/assets/pubs/shf_rij_report_final.pdf. Retrieved May 28, 2013.

24. Siegel, L. and B.C. Welsh. *Juvenile Delinquency: Theory, Practice and Law*, Belmont, CA: Wadsworth Publishing, 2006.

25. "Renewing Juvenile Justice: A Report to the Sierra Health Foundation." Center on Juvenile and Criminal Justice. Available online: http://www.sierrahealth.org/assets/pubs/shf_rij_report_final.pdf. Retrieved May 28, 2013.

26. Garase, Maria and Sherrie L. Sonnenberg, "Community Alternatives to Juvenile Placement," Paper presented at the Annual Meeting of the American Society of Criminology, Toronto, Canada, November 1999.

27. Hamilton, Robin and Kay McKinney, *Job Training for Juveniles: Project CRAFT*, Washington, DC: Office of Juvenile Justice and Delinquency Prevention, August 1999.

28. Ibid.

29. See Dembo, Richard and Nathaniel J. Pallone, *Family Empowerment as an Intervention Strategy in Juvenile Delinquency*, New York: Haworth Press, 2002.

30. Roush, David. "Cognitive Behavioral Intervention with Serious and Violent Offenders: Some Historical Perspective." Federal Probation: December 2008 Newsletter. Available: www.uscourts.gov/fedprob/December_2008/BehavioralIntervention.html

31. Florida Department of Juvenile Justice. "Cognitive-Behavior Therapy: The Florida Model." Available: www.djj.state.fl.us/faith/Cognitive-Behavior_Therapy.html

32. Fritsch, Eric J., Tory J. Caeti, and Robert W. Taylor, "Gang Suppression Through Saturation Patrol and Aggressive Curfew and Truancy Enforcement: A Quasi-Experimental Test of the Dallas Anti-Gang Initiative," *Crime and Delinquency* 45: 1, 1999.

33. Geisand, Gilbert and Arnold Binder, "Sins of Their Children: Parental Responsibility for Juvenile Delinquency," *Notre Dame Journal of Law, Ethics, and Public Policy* 5, 1991; and Toni Weinstein, "Visiting the Sins of the Child on the Parent: The Legality of Criminal Parental Responsibility Statutes," *Southern California Law Review* 64: 863, 1991.

34. National Criminal Justice Association, *supra.*

35. Davidson, Howard, "No Consequences—Reexamining Parental Responsibility Laws," *Stanford Law and Policy Review.* 7: 23, 25, 1996.

GLOSSARY

Numbers in parenthesis indicate the chapters in which the terms are defined.

adjudication Decision by a juvenile court judge that a juvenile committed the delinquent act. (1)

adjudication hearing A hearing to determine whether there is evidence beyond a reasonable doubt to support the allegations against the juvenile. (9)

aftercare The monitoring and support of juveniles who have been released from custody or supervision by the juvenile court. (11)

aggregate data Data collected by agencies on how many crimes or dispositions they process. No individual-level data are collected, only summary statistics and counts. (3)

alternative sanctions A range of correctional sanctions that are designed to take the place of traditional ones such as probation or incarceration. (11)

arraignment A hearing held in juvenile court prior to the adjudication hearing in which the juvenile is made aware of their rights and is asked to enter a plea to the charges. (9)

assessment facilities Secure facilities responsible for orienting the juvenile to the correctional system in that particular state and to what the expectations are. In addition, these centers are responsible for conducting a multitude of testing and diagnosis of each juvenile committed to the juvenile correctional authority. (12)

assumptions Ideas and beliefs that serve as the foundation for theories, programs, and policies. In juvenile justice, these assumptions consist of what people believe about the causes of juvenile delinquency, what we should do about juvenile delinquency, and how the juvenile justice system should function. (2)

atavism Reversion to a primitive type. (4)

at-risk youth A youth that is in danger of becoming a delinquent. (3)

attention-deficit/hyperactivity disorder (ADHD) A learning disability characterized by inattention, hyperactivity, and impulsivity. (4)

Augustus, John The initiator of probation. (11)

automated case-level data Data collected by agencies at the individual case level. The data contains detail of the offenders, victim, disposition, and other relevant items. (3)

autonomic nervous system Controls the body's involuntary functions, such as blood pressure and heart rate. (4)

Balanced Juvenile Justice and Crime Prevention Act of 1996 A law passed by Congress that embraces the punitive and accountability assumptions advocated in the late 1970s and 1980s and continue into today. This act is reflective of the fundamental changes in assumptions about juveniles and juvenile justice. (2)

BARJ (Balanced and Restorative Justice) A new philosophy of juvenile justice that advocates accountability, community safety, and youth development in combination with restorative justice between offenders, victims, and communities. (15)

bifurcated This type of juvenile court exists when the adjudication and disposition hearings are held separately. (9)

biology and genetics A set of factors correlated with juvenile delinquency, focusing on heredity and chemistry. (3)

biosocial factors Interaction between biological and social factors that lead to delinquency. (4)

blended sentencing Involves the imposition of juvenile and/or adult correctional sanctions for serious and violent juvenile offenders who have been processed in either the juvenile or adult court. (10)

Blueprints Model Programs Ten model prevention and intervention programs that meet scientific standards of proven program effectiveness. The programs identified focus on a variety of prevention methods and target several different populations for interventions. (6)

Breed v. Jones Case in which U.S. Supreme Court ruled that juveniles are protected against double jeopardy by the U.S. Constitution. (8)

broken home A term used to describe a home that is plagued by a variety of serious problems, such as abuse or neglect; a correlate of juvenile delinquency. (3)

causal factor A factor that is said to cause another factor or outcome. (3)

chat room Chat rooms are public or private areas on the Internet that allow one-on-one conversations between two individuals. Most of the time, the two-party conversation is relatively secure from outside observation or monitoring. (14)

chattel The legal term for property. In the past, juveniles were viewed as property in the eyes of the law. (2)

child pornography Any depiction of a minor (under 18) in a sexual act or in a sexual manner. (14)

child savers The group of progressive reformers who, in the late 1800s and early 1900s, were responsible for the creation of the juvenile justice system in the United States. (2)

civil nature of juvenile proceedings The juvenile court was operated and proceeded similarly to a civil court. Proceedings were much less formalized and due process did not apply. (8)

classical conditioning A learning theory that states people learn by associating stimuli with certain responses. (4)

classification instruments Instruments that are used to determine which placements are most appropriate for a specific juvenile. (11)

cohort A group of individuals under scientific research and analysis. Most commonly used in the social sciences to describe a group of people being observed over a long period of time. (14)

collective gang A type of gang identified by Maxson and Klein that has a short history, limited size, and little defined territory. (13)

colors Clothing used by gang members to demonstrate their affiliation with a particular gang. (13)

commitment An order by a juvenile court judge putting the juvenile in the custody of a state juvenile correctional authority or specific juvenile correctional facility. (12)

community corrections Correctional programs and facilities located in the community the delinquent youth lives in. (11)

community-oriented policing (COP) A philosophical movement in policing designed to make the community a co-active partner with law enforcement. (7)

community organization A response to gangs which involves efforts to mobilize the community in an effort to deal with gangs. (13)

community service A sanction imposed requiring a juvenile offender to perform a predetermined number of hours of volunteer work in the community. (9, 11)

compressed gang A relatively new gang with less than 50 members around the same age. The gang does not have a defined territory. (13)

computer virus An encoded, rogue program secretly inserted into a normal software program or into a computer's operating system with the express purpose of vandalizing data. (14)

conceptual model A model designed to show the interrelations of several different components. (3)

concordance rate The similarity of delinquent behavior. (4)

conduct disorder A personality disorder that involves the commission of delinquent acts and little concern for the feelings and well-being of others. (4)

confidentiality laws Statutes that protect the identity and records of juvenile offenders in an attempt to avoid the stigmatization that comes with adjudication. (7)

confidentiality and sealing restrictions Laws that keep juvenile records confidential and prevent people from viewing the records. (3)

conflict gangs Gangs that develop in highly disorganized areas in which there are not adult criminal role models. (5)

conformity A mode of adaptation that involves acceptance of the cultural goal of economic success and acceptance of the institutionalized means to obtain it. (5)

correlates Variables that are related to each other are said to be correlated; correlates should not be interpreted to imply causation. (3)

criminal gangs Gangs in organized communities in which younger offenders can obtain the necessary knowledge and skills to be successful criminals from older offenders. (5)

criminal-exclusive blend A type of blended sentence in which the case is processed in adult court; and once convicted, the juvenile offender may receive a sentence in either the juvenile or adult correctional system. (10)

criminal-inclusive blend A type of blended sentence in which the case is processed in adult court; and once convicted, the juvenile offender may receive a sentence in both the juvenile and adult correctional systems. (10)

criminal justice system The system of agencies that is designed to manage adult offenders. (1)

cumulative effect The total result of combined risk factors, emphasizing that individual risk factors are not as important as the total effect. (3)

curfew A law which makes it a crime for a juvenile to be out in public after a certain hour or during certain times of the day. (7)

custody Essentially the same as arrest for adults. (7)

cyberstalking Using a computer via the Internet to harass or invade the privacy of another individual. (14)

D.A.R.E. (Drug Abuse Resistance Education) A controversial, school-based program designed to encourage youth to avoid drugs. (7, 12)

dark figure of crime The phrase used to describe the number of crimes committed but undiscovered or unreported. (3)

day treatment programs A type of community correctional facility where juvenile offenders report during the day for school, vocational, and other treatment programs. (11)

deferred adjudication In deferred adjudication, a youth agrees to follow certain probation conditions without going to court. There is generally no direct supervision by the probation department, and the probation is terminated within a short period of time, as long as the juvenile does not commit any new offenses. (11)

deinstitutionalization The idea of removing certain classes of juvenile offenders from incarceration because of the labeling effects and their placement in community-based corrections. The deinstitutionalization of status offenders was brought about under the JJDP Act of 1974. (5, 6)

deinstitutionalize The process of teaching the juvenile how to remain in the community. (11)

delinquency Any behavior that is prohibited by the juvenile law of a state. (1)

delinquency prevention A broad term used to identify a variety of programs designed to prevent juveniles from becoming delinquent in the first place. (6)

denial A defense mechanism that refers to blocking out part of external rather than internal reality. (4)

Denver Youth Survey, Pittsburgh Youth Study, and Rochester Youth Survey Three interrelated studies designed to assess the level of juvenile crime and the correlates of juvenile crime. (3)

detention center A facility designed for short-term secure confinement of the juvenile prior to court disposition or execution of a court order. (9)

detention hearing A hearing held in juvenile court during which the judge decides whether the current detention of the juvenile is justified and whether continued detention is warranted. (9)

determinate The juvenile is subject to aftercare supervision for a fixed period of time. (11)

determinate sentence Fixed length sentencing; the juvenile is sent to a facility for a fixed length of time. The time is served independent of any perceived progress or rehabilitation on the part of the juvenile. (2)

deterrence Arranging conditions in the law and corrections so that juveniles are aware of the risks and consequences involved in committing crimes. If the risks and consequences are greater than the rewards, juveniles will choose not to commit crime. (12)

differential association The theory that delinquency results from social interaction and learning. (5)

discretion The decision-making power police officers have in determining how to handle calls for service. The police have increased discretion in determining juvenile matters. (7)

discretionary judicial waiver A type of judicial waiver that involves the prosecutor's filing a petition with a juvenile court requesting that the juvenile court waive a juvenile to adult court. (10)

displacement A defense mechanism that uses a substitute person or object to gratify an impulse. (4)

disposition hearing A hearing held after a juvenile has been adjudicated to determine what sanction should be imposed on the juvenile. (9)

dispositional plans The plans that are imposed on juveniles adjudicated delinquent that outline their entire course of treatment. (11)

diversion A general term for a wide range of programs that keep juveniles who commit crimes out of the formal juvenile justice system. Diversion programs are in place to correct or prevent future and more serious problems from occurring and to prevent further involvement with the juvenile and criminal justice system. (1, 5, 9, 6)

dizygotic or fraternal twins Twins that develop from two eggs and two sperm. (4)

drug A chemical that interacts with the body and alters normal body and mind functioning. (14)

due process revolution Period of time during the 1960s and early 1970s when the U.S. Supreme Court made several rulings that created or applied additional due process protections to juvenile justice. (8)

early pre-delinquent intervention and prevention A range of programs designed to target children at risk of becoming delinquent based on the identification of early risk factors. (6)

ecological environment A set of factors correlated with juvenile delinquency, focusing on the community and neighborhood. (3)

ectomorph Body structure that is thin and frail. (4)

educational environment A set of factors correlated with juvenile delinquency, focusing on the juvenile's school, attitudes toward education, and academic behavior and performance. (3)

ego The part of one's personality that represents the identity of the individual and actual behavior. (4)

electronic monitoring Restricting a juvenile through the use of an electronic tracking device. (11)

endomorph Body structure that is soft, round, and fat. (4)

Ex Parte Crouse The first court case in the United States that declared the concept of *parens patriae* constitutional. (2)

expunging or sealing Allows for the erasure or destruction of juvenile records once a juvenile reaches the age of majority. (8)

family A set of factors correlated with juvenile delinquency, focusing on parents, siblings, extended family members, and the inner workings of the family itself. (3)

Fare v. Michael C. Case that established ground rules for determining whether a juvenile has knowingly and voluntarily waived his or her rights. (8)

FBI Index Crimes The Part I offenses in the *Uniform Crime Reports* developed each year by the Federal Bureau of Investigation are: 1. murder and non-negligent manslaughter, 2. forcible rape, 3. robbery, 4. aggravated assault, 5. burglary, 6. larceny-theft, 7. motor vehicle theft, and 8. arson, which was added in 1979. (14)

female auxiliary gang A female gang that is affiliated with a male gang and generally takes on a feminized version of the male gang's name. (13)

Fetal Alcohol Syndrome (FAS) A condition caused by the effect that alcohol has on a developing fetus. (4)

foster care The care and custody of children by families willing to take them into their homes. (11)

free will The ability to make a choice among various alternatives. (4)

funnel effect The phrase used to describe the way in which the number of cases processed through the juvenile justice system decreases at each successive step of the process. (3)

gang Any denotable group of adolescents working to unlawful or antisocial ends. (13)

gang member An individual who actively participates in the activities of a gang. (13)

gang migration The movement of gangs from large metropolitan areas such as Los Angeles and Chicago to other areas of the country. (13)

gang-related crime Acts of delinquency in which the offender or the victim is a gang member. (13)

Gang Resistance Education and Training (G.R.E.A.T.) A school-based prevention program that is designed to help students set goals for themselves, resist pressures, learn how to resolve conflicts without violence, and understand how gangs and youth violence impact the quality of their lives. (7, 13)

general deterrence Seeks to discourage would-be delinquents from committing delinquent acts because of the threat of punishment. (4)

general intent A level of intent that involves an act in which a prohibited result follows (e.g., death) in the absence of a desire for the particular result. (13)

Generation X A term most often used to describe youth born in the 1980s and 1990s, just entering adolescence. (14)

graffiti Public markings that are used by gang members to identify their existence, to mark their territory, to challenge rival gangs, and to remember deceased gang members. (13)

grassroots movement A movement that starts with the general public and not the political arena. (2)

group homes Homes for groups of juveniles who have been adjudicated delinquent similar to their institutional counterparts. (11)

hackers/crackers Individuals who break into a secure computer or data system or vandalize an Internet site. (14)

hand sign A method of communication used by gang members which identifies the user with a particular gang. (13)

hands-off approach The idea that day-to-day operations of the juvenile justice system should be left up to the professionals working in the system without court review or intervention. (8)

hate crime A crime committed against an individual victimized because of his or her race, color, religion, national origin, sexual orientation, gender, or disability. (14)

hedonistic The attempt to maximize pleasure and minimize pain. (4)

hedonistic gang A type of gang identified by Huff that is primarily involved in using drugs and getting high with little involvement in crime. (13)

hierarchy rule Rule used in collecting data for the *UCR* that states that only the most serious crime in any one criminal event will be counted. For example, if a person kidnaps, rapes, and then murders another person, the crime is counted as one murder. (3)

holistic approach A comprehensive approach targeting multiple aspects of a problem using multiple agencies and groups instead of a single intervention method. (6)

hormones Substances produced by the body that control such bodily functions as central nervous system functioning and reproduction. (4)

house arrest Confining juveniles to their homes when they are not at school or undergoing treatment. (11)

house of refuge Early institutions specifically designed for juveniles in the United States. These facilities would take in and care for dependent, neglected, and delinquent children. (2)

id The part of one's personality that is comprised of unconscious biological and psychological desires and instincts including sex and aggression. (4)

illegitimate opportunity structure Neighborhood structures as established criminal enterprises and criminal mentors that lead youths to become criminals. (5)

Illinois Juvenile Court Act of 1899 The law that established the first separate juvenile court in the United States. (2)

in loco parentis "In place of the parents." Legal philosophy that gives the state the right to act as parent when the child's parents or guardian fails to do so or cannot do so. (2)

In re Gault U.S. Supreme Court case in which it was ruled that a juvenile is entitled to the essentials of due process including right to notice of the charges, right to counsel, right to confront and cross-examine witnesses, and the right against self-incrimination including the right to remain silent. (8)

In re Winship U.S. Supreme Court case that decided the standard of proof in juvenile delinquency proceedings is proof beyond a reasonable doubt. (8)

incapacitation Taking a juvenile out of the community so that he or she is prevented from being able to commit crimes. (12)

incommunicado Holding a person charged with a crime without allowing him or her to communicate with anyone. (8)

indeterminate Term used when a juvenile delinquent is placed on aftercare either with a maximum time allowed or on the basis of treatment goals and objectives. (11)

index felonies The eight felonies that comprise the FBI's *Uniform Crime Report:* murder, rape, robbery, aggravated assault, burglary, larceny/theft, auto theft, and arson. (7)

informal probation (informal adjustment, deferred prosecution) A procedure by which a juvenile agrees to meet certain requirements in exchange for having the case dismissed. (1, 9)

innovation A mode of adaptation that involves acceptance of the cultural goal of economic success and the rejection of the institutionalized means to obtain it. (5)

institutional facilities Secure facilities including detention centers, orientation and diagnostic assessment centers, transfer facilities, boot camps, youth ranches and camps, institutions and state schools, and transitional facilities. (12)

instrumental gang A type of gang identified by Huff that is primarily involved in committing property crime and is actively involved in using drugs. (13)

intake The procedure by which juvenile court staff decide whether to process the case further in court, handle the case informally, or dismiss the case. The first step in formal adjudication where a determination is made concerning detention and subsequent formal action by the juvenile court. (1)

intake officer The person at a detention facility responsible for processing a juvenile into the facility. They often have the authority to refuse to take a juvenile into custody. (7)

Intensive Supervision Probation (ISP) A form of probation characterized by increased supervision and treatment. The caseload of officers is typically reduced so they can spend greater amounts of time with smaller numbers of riskier juveniles. (11)

interstitial area Area of a city characterized by high delinquency rates in which factories and commercial establishments exist along with private residences. (5)

intervention strategies Programs designed to target specific youth offenders, attempting to prevent youths from engaging in delinquency or deter youths who have already been involved in some law-violating behavior. (15)

involuntary servitude A practice where children were sold into service to a business person or wealthy person for service. In exchange for money, the parents would essentially give up all rights to the child. (2)

IQ Intelligence Quotient, a standard test score used for measuring intelligence. (3)

job training programs and apprenticeship programs Programs specifically designed to teach the juvenile a skill that is marketable in the real world. (11)

judicial waiver A type of wavier to adult court in which a juvenile court judge makes the decision to waive a juvenile to adult court. (10)

jurisdiction The authority granted by law to hear a case. (1, 9)

jurisdictional age limit The age limit beyond which a juvenile court no longer has jurisdiction over a juvenile offender, usually between ages 19 and 21. (10)

juvenile An individual who falls within a specified age range and is subject to the jurisdiction of the juvenile court. (1)

juvenile boot camp A secure correctional facility that emphasizes military-style discipline, physical training, and an extremely regimented schedule. (12)

juvenile-contiguous blend A type of blended sentence in which the case is processed in juvenile court; and, once the case is adjudicated, a judge can impose a sentence on the juvenile offender that can exceed the jurisdictional age limit of the juvenile correctional agency. (10)

juvenile court judge The individual who is primarily responsible for the operation of the juvenile court, including deciding guilt or innocence and disposition of cases. (9)

juvenile detention facilities Short-term secure units that house juveniles awaiting court hearings or adjudications. They are similar to adult jails in operation; however, while adult jails also house criminals under sentence, juvenile detention centers are rarely used for this purpose. (12)

juvenile-exclusive blend A type of blended sentence in which the case is processed in juvenile court; and, once the case is adjudicated, a juvenile offender may receive a sentence in either the juvenile or adult correctional system. (10)

juvenile-inclusive blend A type of blended sentence in which the case is processed in juvenile court; and, once the case is adjudicated, a juvenile offender may receive a sentence in both the juvenile and adult correctional system. (10)

juvenile justice administrative body An organization responsible for the administration and management of juvenile justice within a state. (12)

Juvenile Justice and Delinquency Prevention Act of 1974 (JJDP) The law that limits the discretion of the juvenile justice system in dealing with status offenders. JJDP introduces more uniformity and fairness in the system. (2)

juvenile justice system The system of agencies that is designed to handle juvenile offenders. (1)

juvenile probation department The agency in charge of monitoring all youths on probation within a jurisdiction. (11)

***Kent* criteria** The factors established by the United States Supreme Court in *Kent* v. *United States* that juvenile court judges should take into consideration when deciding whether or not to waive a juvenile to adult court. (10)

Kent* v. *United States U.S. Supreme Court case in which it was ruled that juveniles facing waiver to adult court are entitled to some basic due process rights. (8)

labeling theory A criminological theory that contends that juveniles who are labeled delinquent or criminal will eventually commit secondary delinquent acts to live up to the label. (5)

learning Habits and knowledge that develop as a result of the experiences of an individual in entering and adjusting to the environment. (4)

legislative waiver A type of waiver in which a juvenile is automatically sent to adult court because of the types of offense that were committed. (10)

lifestyle An organized pattern of behaviors, attitudes, and outcomes adopted by a person. (3)

logo A descriptive emblem used to identify a gang and may include a group of Roman numerals, the gang's initials, or a picture or a symbol such as a pitchfork, crown, or Playboy bunny. (13)

mandatory judicial waiver A type of judicial waiver in which a juvenile court judge must waive a juvenile to adult court if the juvenile court judge finds probable cause that the juvenile committed the offense. (10)

maximum age of juvenile court jurisdiction The upper-age limit for which the juvenile court may hear a case. (1)

McKeiver v. Pennsylvania U.S. Supreme Court case in which it was ruled that juveniles are not entitled to trial by jury in delinquency proceedings. (8)

mediation These programs attempt to bring together juvenile delinquents and their victims, hoping to mediate the situation between the parties. (11)

medical model The basic philosophy behind the creation of the juvenile court. The court was more of a hospital where juveniles went to be cured of their illness. (8)

mens rea Literally translated means "guilty mind." In the juvenile justice system it was traditionally assumed that juveniles could not form the same level of intent to commit a crime that adults could. (2)

mesomorph Body structure that is muscular, firm, and strong. (4)

middle-class measuring rods The standards and values used to evaluate youth in school. (5)

minimum age of juvenile court jurisdiction The lower age limit for which the juvenile court may hear a case. (1)

Miranda rights The right to remain silent, the right to an attorney, and the right to indigent appointment of an attorney. (8)

modeling A learning theory that states people learn by imitating the behavior of others. (4)

model policies Written policies composed by national organizations in an effort to standardize operating procedures at the local level. (7)

monozygotic or identical twins Twins that develop from one egg and one sperm. (4)

National Crime Victimization Survey (NCVS) A national survey of households on the subject of victimization, conducted by the Bureau of Justice Statistics. (3)

National Incident-Based Reporting System (NIBRS) The new data collection system implemented to collect individual-level data on offenders, victims, and the crime itself from police departments. The system collects detailed statistical data on victims and perpetrators as well as the incident itself. It is designed to address many of the problems with the *UCR*. (3)

negative reinforcement A punishment that is designed to decrease the behavior. (5)

neglect Neglect can be either passive or active, that is, with or without intent on the part of a parent or guardian to fail to protect or give care to a child. Types of neglect often involve failure to provide for food and clothing, failure to maintain a healthy and clean environment, and failure to supervise and control behavior. (14)

neotraditional gang A type of gang that is smaller and newer than the traditional gang (*see* traditional gang). (13)

net widening Using diversion and prevention programs to bring more juveniles under court control instead of as an alternative to formal processing. (6)

New Jersey v. T.L.O. The court decision that school officials only need reasonable ground, not probable cause, to search a student when they suspect that the search will turn up illegal evidence. (8)

norms Prescriptions for appropriate behavior. (5)

nuisance abatement A method to deal with gangs that defines their behavior as a public nuisance and forbids certain legal and illegal behaviors. (13)

Office of Juvenile Justice and Delinquency Prevention (OJJDP) A department created by Congress in 1974 to help communities and states prevent and control delinquency and improve their juvenile justice systems. A component of the U.S. Department of Justice, Office of Justice Programs, OJJDP is the primary federal agency responsible for addressing the issues of juvenile crime and delinquency and the problem of missing and exploited children. (3)

official records Statistics and data collected by law enforcement agencies, courts, and correctional institutions. (3)

"once an adult always an adult" law A type of legislative waiver that mandates that all offenses a juvenile commits after having been waived to adult court and convicted will also be handled in adult court. (10)

operant conditioning Learning theory that argues that behavior is controlled by the consequences of that behavior. (4, 5)

opportunities provision A response to gangs that involves efforts to deal with gangs through employment, job training, and education. (13)

organizational change and development A response to gangs that involves organizational adaptations that facilitate the application of gang control strategies. (13)

orphanages, workhouses, training schools, and apprenticeships An informal system of public and private institutions that were designed to take in wayward children and raise them so that they would become productive members of society. (2)

outcomes and opportunities The results of the particular lifestyle adopted by a person; low-risk lifestyles lead to different outcomes and opportunities than high-risk lifestyles. (3)

panacea A quick fix, a cure-all. In juvenile delinquency prevention, these types of programs are often very short-term, are not individualized, and offer nothing in the way of follow-up or aftercare services. (6)

paraphilia Almost exclusively common to males, paraphilia are erotic-sexual conditions involving obsessive deviant or bizarre images or activities to achieve or maintain sexual arousal. (14)

parens patriae A legal doctrine in which the state plays the role of the parent. (1)

parental liability The idea that parents should be held responsible to varying degrees for their children's behavior. (15)

Part I Offenses Also known as the index offenses. The counts of the most serious crimes in the *UCR* (felonies), including murder, rape, robbery, aggravated assault. (3)

Part II Offenses The less serious crimes counted in the *UCR*, mainly misdemeanors. See Figure 2.1 for a complete listing of the offenses. (3)

peers A person's classmates, friends, and associates. (3)

***per se* attorney laws** Laws that require a juvenile to have an attorney present during interrogation or other critical police proceeding. *Per se* means that a juvenile cannot waive this right. (7)

***per se* test** Something is required in all circumstances regardless of the facts of a case. (8)

personality A set of factors that are correlated with juvenile delinquency focusing on psychological makeup and attitudes. (3, 4)

petition A document that states the allegations against a juvenile and requests the juvenile court to adjudicate the juvenile. (9)

pimp A person (usually a male) that acts as the middleman for the prostitute and her client. These individuals often force or compel women to work as prostitutes through intimidation and fear. As a result, the pimp takes a significant share of the money from a paying customer. (14)

plea bargaining The process by which a juvenile pleads guilty in exchange for concessions made by the prosecutor. (9)

Police Athletic Leagues (PAL) A police program focusing on recreation and sports designed to reduce delinquency and increase youth's commitments to legitimate activities. (7)

police cadet programs A police program designed for older adolescents and college students that allows participants to perform some police tasks and learn about law enforcement. (7)

police explorer posts A police program for younger adolescents, often associated with boy scouting, designed to teach youths about policing. (7)

positive reinforcement A reward that is designed to increase the behavior being rewarded. (5)

predatory gang A type of gang identified by Huff that is actively involved in committing serious crimes, including violent crime and selling drugs. (13)

predisposition report Contains background information on the juvenile, a description of the circumstances surrounding the juvenile's delinquent acts, as well as a disposition recommendation from the probation officer. (9)

preponderance of the evidence Evidence which is of greater weight or more convincing than evidence that is offered in opposition to it. Sometimes referred to as more than 50 percent, more than half of the level of certainty. (8)

presentence investigations Reports prepared by the probation department overviewing a juvenile's case, social history, criminal history, and treatment needs. (11)

presumptive waiver A type of judical waiver in which the defense bears the burden of proof and must justify to the judge why the juvenile should not be waived. (10)

preventive detention The holding of a juvenile without bond or bail prior to his or her adjudication hearing because the juvenile is a security risk or threat to society. (8)

primary deviance Initial acts of delinquency that go undetected by parents, family, friends, and the juvenile justice system. (5)

private facilities Correctional institutions run by private corporations or private individuals. (12)

probation A disposition imposed by the court allowing the adjudication offender to remain in the community, with a parent or other guardian, as long as the offender abides by certain conditions. (1, 11)

probation agreement Outlines the general conditions of probation and any special conditions imposed, and explains the probation process. (11)

probation revocation The termination of an unsuccessful probation. The youth is typically sent to a secure placement as a result. (11)

problem-oriented policing (POP) A philosophical movement in policing that attempts to take the focus of the police away from responding to calls and crime problems in a reactive fashion. (7)

procedural due process The rights and process given to a person charged with a crime. Procedural due process is more formalized in the adult criminal justice system than in the juvenile justice system. (15)

procedural rights Those rights that govern or dictate the process by which a hearing or court action will proceed. (8)

professional period The era in law enforcement when the goal was to increase the professionalization of policing, thus removing it from political pressures. (7)

proof beyond a reasonable doubt The facts and evidence are entirely convincing and satisfy that the person committed the act beyond any reasonable doubt, sometimes equated with 95 percent certainty. (8)

Property Crime Index The property crimes included in the Part I offenses: burglary, motor vehicle theft, theft, and arson. (3)

prosecutorial waiver A type of waiver to adult court that occurs when there is concurrent jurisdiction between juvenile and adult courts and the prosecutor has the option of filing charges against the juvenile offender in either court. (10)

protective custody Taking a minor into police custody to protect him or her from possible harm. (7)

protective factors A range of variables that research has found to protect or insulate a juvenile from becoming a delinquent. (3)

punishment gap The discovery that juveniles waived to adult court for the first time are usually given the leniency accorded to first-time adult offenders. (10)

punitive model of juvenile justice The current model of juvenile justice which holds that juveniles are just as responsible as adults for their criminal behavior, and they should be held accountable and punished. (15)

Puritans A religious group in early America who essentially believed that through hard work, religion, and education a person could get closer to God. These ideals served as the foundation for the creation of early institutions of juvenile justice in the United States. (2)

Racketeer Influenced Corrupt Organization (RICO) Act A federal statute which is used to prosecute gang members who participate in an organized criminal enterprise. (13)

rampage killings Multiple-victim killings that are random in nature, characterized by violent and quick outbursts on the part of one or two suspects for seemingly no reason or motive. These do not include homicides that are domestic or connected to the commission of another crime, such as a robbery or gang-related "drive-by shooting" or serial murder. (14)

rationalization A defense mechanism by which one justifies one's behavior with socially acceptable reasons. (4)

reaction formation A defense mechanism which occurs when a forbidden impulse is replaced with its opposite. (4)

rebellion A mode of adaptation that involves rejection and substitution of the cultural goal of economic success and rejection and substitution of the institutionalized means to obtain it. (5)

recidivist An individual who commits the same crime or returns to illegal activity *after* conviction and release from incarceration. (14)

referees, commissioners, masters Individuals who hear cases in juvenile court and tend to pre-adjudication hearings. (9)

regression A defense mechanism that involves going back to a reaction pattern characteristic of a less-mature mode of adjustment. (4)

rehabilitation Using methods of treatment and counseling in an effort to reform juvenile offenders so that they will return to society in a constructive rather than a destructive way. (12)

repression A defense mechanism in which threatening impulses, wishes, and feelings are automatically kept from consciousness. (4)

restitution The payment of money or the rendering of restorative service or work to the victim of a crime, whether a person or a business. (11)

retreatism A mode of adaptation that involves the rejection of the cultural goal of economic success and the rejection of the institutionalized means to obtain it. (5)

retreatist gangs Gangs that retreat into drugs and alcohol use. (5)

retribution Punishing and paying juveniles back for the harm they caused society. (12)

risk factors A range of variables that research has found to be correlated with juvenile delinquency. (3)

ritualism A mode of adaptation that involves rejection of the cultural goal of economic success and acceptance of the institutionalized means to obtain it. (5)

Schall v. Martin Court case that decided juveniles can be held in preventative detention prior to adjudication. (8)

school-based probation A model where the probation officer works and is housed within the walls of the school. (11)

secondary deviance Continued delinquent behavior because the individual is now acting according to the delinquent label. (5)

segregated incarceration The practice of housing juveniles convicted in adult court in a separate prison facility for younger offenders, usually between the ages 18 and 25. (10)

self-control The ability to control one's own behavior. (5)

self-report surveys Generic term for survey research conducted using offenders or potential offenders. (3)

serious or habitual delinquents Juvenile delinquents who persist in delinquency. Research has shown that a small number of habitual delinquents commit a disproportionate amount of crime. (3)

shock probation A relatively unique correctional strategy that involves shocking the juveniles with a brief commitment to an institutional facility and then releasing them on probation. (11)

sight and sound separated The concept that juveniles should not be able to see or hear adult offenders when taken into police custody. (7)

social class The socio-economic level of a juvenile's family, typically sorted as underclass, lower class, middle class, upper-middle class, upper class, etc. (3)

social environment A set of factors correlated with juvenile delinquency, focusing on the juvenile's peers, social class, and activities and interests. (3)

social intervention A response to gangs that involves counseling and other direct attempts to change the values of youth in order to make gang involvement less likely. (13)

specialty gang A type of gang identified by Maxson and Klein that has a defined territory, a narrow age range of members, and is small in size. The gang is actively involved in serious criminal activity, including drug trafficking. (13)

specific deterrence A sanction imposed on adjudicated delinquents in order to prevent them from continuing to commit delinquent acts in the future. (4)

specific intent A level of intent that occurs when the circumstances of the offense demonstrate that the offender must have consciously desired the result. (13)

standard operating procedure (SOP) manual The compilation of policies and procedures for each law enforcement agency. (7)

state institutions and schools Self-contained facilities that provide a variety of services for juveniles, including rehabilitation, health, education, counseling, recreation, employment, and training. (12)

status degradation ceremony Term coined by Garfinkel to describe the labeling process. (5)

status frustration Occurs due to a person's inability to obtain the goal of middle-class status. (5)

status offenses Behaviors that are typically legal for adults but illegal for juveniles. Examples include curfew, loitering, truancy, and being a runaway. (1)

statutory exclusion A type of legislative waiver that excludes certain offenses, usually violent crimes, from the jurisdiction of the juvenile court. (10)

straight adult incarceration The practice of housing juveniles convicted in adult court in the general adult prison population. (10)

Street Terrorism Enforcement and Prevention (STEP) Acts A type of statute which uses a series of predicate crimes as the basis for sentence enhancements and provides for civil forfeiture of a gang's assets and the proceeds of its criminal activities. (13)

subculture A set of values, norms, and beliefs that differ from those of the dominant culture. (5)

substantive rights Those rights that protect an individual against arbitrary and unreasonable action, such as the Bill of Rights. (8)

superego The part of one's personality that represents the conscience and moral character of the individual. (4)

suppression A response to gangs that involves the use of the criminal justice system to reduce gang behavior through the use of formal social control, including arrest and incarceration. (13)

synthetic marijuana An herbal mixture laced with synthetically made cannabinoids similar to the active ingredient in marijuana, THC. (14)

theory A formalized idea or set of principles that attempts to define and explain a phenomenon. (4)

three-strikes laws Mandate that three felony convictions result in imprisonment. (8)

totality of circumstances The test used to determine if a juvenile's waiver of rights was knowing and voluntary. (8)

traditional agrarian values The ideas and beliefs shared by those who worked the land and espoused Puritan or Quaker values. The idea was that the city was a source of many juveniles' "evil ways," and the best way to change the children was to remove them from the city and place them in remote rural locations. (2)

traditional gang A type of gang identified by Maxson and Klein that has as many as several hundred members and has been in existence for over 20 years. The gang has a well-defined territory and has members that range in age from 10 to over 30. (13)

traditional or political period The era in law enforcement marked by political corruption and political control of policing. (7)

transfer or transitional facilities A temporary facility where juveniles are either awaiting transfer to another facility or awaiting release into the community. (12)

truancy An unexpected absence from school by a juvenile. Truancy is a status offense. (7)

Uniform Crime Reports (UCR) The statistical count of crime, compiled by the FBI using reports from law enforcement agencies across the country. The main categories of offenses are Part I and II crimes. (3)

Victim Impact Statements Questionnaires distributed to victims of crime where they report their financial losses, mental and physical injuries, and impact of the crime on their lives. (11)

victim restitution A sanction by which a juvenile offender pays the victim for the harm done due to the offense. (1)

victimization survey Generic term for survey research conducted using victims or potential victims of crime. (3)

victimless crime Crimes that are said to not have a victim because the victim is often a willing participant, for example, in crimes of prostitution and drug use. (3)

Victims of Trafficking and Protection Act of 2000 A new law specifically designed to curb the illegal trafficking of human beings, especially juveniles into the United States for the purpose of forced labor and servitude, including prostitution. (14)

Violent Crime Index The violent crimes included in the Part I offenses: murder, rape, robbery, and aggravated assault. (3)

waiver hearing A hearing held in juvenile court in which a prosecutor and defense attorney may present evidence on whether or not the juvenile should be waived to adult court. (10)

waiver to adult court The process through which a juvenile court relinquishes jurisdiction over a juvenile offender and the case is processed in adult court. (1, 10)

Walnut Street Jail The first jail in the United States that separated inmates and sought to reform their behavior rather than just punishing them. Opened in 1790 in Philadelphia, Pennsylvania, it was also the first correctional facility to separate women and children from adult male inmates. (2)

wannabe A young individual who wants to be a gang member and emulates the behavior of gang members. (13)

wilderness and adventure programs Programs that emphasize physical challenges, survival skills, and mental challenges through outdoor adventures and nature trips. (11)

youth ranches and camps Facilities that operate similarly to state institutions with one exception: the atmosphere is more like a year-round summer camp than a maximum security facility. There are typically dorms or cottages, a school, vocational programs, and industry. The one component that sets them apart from other secure facilities is a program centering on a type of farming, ranching, or adventure. (12)

zero tolerance Policies designed to attack individual drug users as well as drug traffickers; attaches severe penalties for possession of even small quantities of drugs. (14)

CREDITS

INDEX

TEXT AND FIGURE CREDITS

Pages 15–16, Figure 1.5: From Snyder, Howard N. and Sickmund, Melissa. (1999). *Juvenile Offenders and Victims: 1999 National Report.* Washington, DC: Office of Juvenile Justice and Delinquency Prevention, pp. 94–96. Copyright 1999 National Center for Juvenile Justice. Reprinted with permission.

Page 150, Figure 6.4: Olds, D. L., Hill, P. L., Mihalic, S. F., and O'Brien, R. A. (2001). *Blueprints for Violence Prevention* (Book 7). Boulder, CO: Center for the Study and Prevention of Violence, University of Colorado.

Page 162, Figure 6.6: National Association of Youth Courts, Facts and Stats: Typical Offenses Youth Courts will Accept. National Youth Court Database. Reprinted with permission of the National Association of Youth Courts.

Page 163, Figure 6.8: Butts, Jeffrey A. and Janeen Buck, "Teen Courts: A Focus on Research." *Juvenile Justice Bulletin,* October 2000. Washington, DC: Office of Juvenile Justice and Delinquency Prevention, Table 1 (p. 6); Urban Institute, 1998. National Survey of Youth Courts and Teen Courts; National Association of Youth Courts, Facts and Stats: Typical Offenses Youth Courts will Accept. National Youth Court Database.

Page 182, Figure 7.3 and Page 183, Figure 7.4: Adapted from Snyder, H. & Sickmund, M. (2006). *Juvenile Offenders and Victims: 2006 National Report,* Chapter 3. Washington, D.C.: Office of Juvenile Justice and Delinquency Prevention. Data Source: National Archive of Criminal Justice Data. *National Incident-Based Reporting System, 2008: Extract Files* [Computer file]. Ann Arbor, MI: Inter-university Consortium for Political and Social Research [distributor], 2010–08–13.

Page 197: David Weisburd, Nancy Morris, and Justin Ready. 2005. Risk-Focused Policing at Places: An Experimental Evaluation of the Communities that Care Program in Redlands, CA. Police Foundation final report to the Office of Juvenile Delinquency and Juvenile Justice (OJJDP), Grant Number 2000-JR-VX-0004, and the Office of Community Policing Services (COPS), Cooperative Agreement 2002-CK-WX-0306.

Page 218, Figure 8.2: From Caeti, Tory J., Craig Hemmens, and Velmer Burton, "Juvenile Right to Counsel: A National Comparison of State Legal Codes," *American Journal of Criminal Law 23* (3): Spring 1996. Reprinted by permission of the publisher.

Page 224, Figure 8.4: From Szymanski, L. (2008). Confidentiality of Juvenile Delinquency Hearings (2008 Update), *NCJJ Snapshot,* 13(5). Pittsburgh, PA: National Center for Juvenile Justice. © National Center for Juvenile Justice. Reprinted with permission.

Page 225, Figure 8.5: From Szymanski, L. (2004). Releasing Names of Juvenile Offenders to the Media/Public (2004 Update), *NCJJ Snapshot,* 9(4). Pittsburgh, PA: National Center for Juvenile Justice. © National Center for Juvenile Justice. Reprinted with permission.

Page 227, Figure 8.6: Szymanski, Linda "Megan's Law: Juvenile Sex Offender Registration (2009 Update)." *NCJJ Snapshot,* 14(7).

Pittsburgh, PA: National Center for Juvenile Justice. © National Center for Juvenile Justice. Reprinted with permission.

Page 228, Figure 8.7: Szymanski, Linda A. (2008). Juvenile Delinquents' Right to a Jury Trial, *NCJJ Snapshot,* 13(2). Pittsburgh, PA: National Center for Juvenile Justice. © National Center for Juvenile Justice. Reprinted with permission.

Pages 233–234: From Thomas J. Flygare, "*Ingraham v. Wright:* The Return of Old Jack Seaver," *Inequality in Education,* Number 23 (Cambridge, MA: September 1978). Reprinted by permission the Center for Law and Education, Boston, MA.

Page 246: The list of services is reprinted by permission of Community Service Programs, Inc., Santa Ana, CA. http://www.cspinc.org/juveniled.html

Page 278, Figure 10.4: Snyder, Howard N., and Melissa Sickmund. (1995). *Juvenile Offenders and Victims: A National Report.* Washington, DC: Office of Juvenile Justice and Delinquency Prevention, p. 157. Copyright 1995 National Center for Juvenile Justice. Reprinted with permission.

Page 279, Figure 10.5: From Table 2.48 in *Sourcebook of Criminal Justice Statistics 2003.* Washington, DC: Bureau of Justice Statistics. http://www.albany.edu/sourcebook/pdf/t248.pdf. Data provided by The Gallup Organization, Inc. Reprinted by permission of Gallup, Inc.

Page 281, Figure 10.6: Adapted from Torbet, Patricia et al. (1996). *State Responses to Serious and Violent Juvenile Crime.* Washington, DC: Office of Juvenile Justice and Delinquency Prevention, p. 13. © 1996 National Center for Juvenile Justice. Updates in Griffin, Patrick, "National Overviews." *State Juvenile Justice Profiles.* Pittsburgh, PA: National Center for Juvenile Justice, 2008. © National Center for Juvenile Justice. Reprinted with permission. OJJDP Statistical Briefing Book.

Page 285, Figure 10.7: Adaptation and update of Victor L. Streib, *The Juvenile Death Penalty Today: Death Sentences and Executions for Juvenile Crimes, January 1, 1973 – February 28, 2005* [issue #77]. Used by permission of the author.

Pages 304–305: Reprinted by permission of Wood County Juvenile Court, Judge David E. Woessner.

Page 317: From www.vq.com. Reprinted by permission of VisionQuest.

Page 347, Figure 12.7 and Page 353, Figure 12.8: From Caeti, Tory, J., Craig Hemmens, Francis T. Cullen, and Velmer S. Burton, "Management of Juvenile Correctional Facilities," *The Prison Journal,* December 2003 vol. 83 no. 4: 383–405. Copyright © 2003, Sage Publications. Reprinted with permission.

Pages 383–384 and Figure 13.4: From www.oxnardpd.org. Reprinted with permission of the Oxnard Police Department.

Page 433, Figure 15.3: From Gordon Bazemore, Jay G. Zaslaw, and Danielle Riester, "Behind the Walls and Beyond: Restorative Justice, Instrumental Communities, and Effective Residential Treatment," *Juvenile and Family Court Journal,* Winter 2005, pp. 53–73. Reprinted by permission of the publisher.